WITNESS OF A CENTURY

The Life and Times of
Prince Arthur Duke of Connaught
1850-1942

WITNESS
OF A CENTURY

The Life and Times of
Prince Arthur Duke of Connaught
1850-1942

Noble Frankland

SHEPHEARD-WALWYN

© Noble Frankland, 1993

First Published 1993 by
Shepheard-Walwyn (Publishers) Limited
26 Charing Cross Road (Suite 34)
London WC2H 0DH

British Library Cataloguing in Publication Data

Frankland, Noble
    Witness of a Century: The Life and Times of
    Prince Arthur Duke of Connaught
    I. Title
    941.08092

ISBN 0-85683-136-0

Typeset by Alacrity Phototypesetters
Banwell Castle, Weston-super-Mare, Avon
Printed in Great Britain by WBC Limited, Bridgend

Contents

Illustration Acknowledgements

RC: Royal Collection, St James's Palace, © Her Majesty The Queen. RA: Windsor Castle, Royal Archives, © 1992 Her Majesty The Queen. PAC: reproduced by permission of the Public Archives of Canada. NT: reproduced by permission of the National Trust (Hughenden Manor). Author: reproduced from a photograph in the author's possession. *Punch*: reproduced from *Punch* or *The London Charivari*. *Daily Express*: reproduced by permission of the *Daily Express*. IWM: reproduced by permission of the Trustees of the Imperial War Museum. The portrait of Prince Arthur by de László on the front cover is reproduced by permission of the Royal Society for the encouragement of Art, Manufactures and Commerce.

List of Illustrations

39. The Duke and Duchess of Connaught returning from South Africa, 1910. RA.

Between pages 300 and 301

40. Prince Arthur and his family dressed for the coronation of King George V, 1911. W. & D. Downey. RA.
41. Prince Arthur's arrival in Canada, 1911. RA.
42. Prince Arthur being sworn in as Governor-General of Canada, Quebec, 1911. PAC. (PA 66852)
43. The Duke and Duchess of Connaught driving away from the swearing-in ceremony, Quebec, 1911. *Canadian Pictorial*. PAC. (C 23914)
44. Mr Robert Borden and his Cabinet, 1911. *Canadian Pictorial*. PAC. (C 23913)
45. Sir Robert Borden. IWM. (MH 31413)
46. Prince Arthur, Robert Borden and Sam Hughes. S.J. Jarvis. PAC. (PA 25088)

Between pages 332 and 333

47. Princess Patricia and Lieutenant-Colonel A.H. Gault. IWM. (31414)
48. Prince Arthur at Rockcliffe, Ontario, 1915. A.M.G.B. PAC. (PA 99742)
49. Sir Sam Hughes arriving in France, 1916. IWM. (CO 651)
50. Sir Sam Hughes in France, 1916. IWM. (CO 657)
51. Sir Sam Hughes demonstrating martial skills in France, 1916. IWM. (CO 675)
52. Prince Arthur with American troops in France. RA.
53. Prince Arthur on the battlefield of Messines, 1917. RA.
54. Prince Arthur examining an experimental trench mortar, 1917. IWM. (Q 3902)

Between pages 364 and 365

55. Prince Arthur's arrival in India, 1921. RA.
56. Prince Arthur at a garden party in Delhi, 1921. RA.
57. Prince Arthur with Léonie Leslie and his family at Bagshot Park, 1935. RA.
58. Prince Arthur watching army manoeuvres, 1931. RA.
59. Farewell, Sandhurst, 1937. RA.

Preface

DURING THE ELEVEN years in which I have been engaged upon the preparation and writing of this book, friends and acquaintances have repeatedly asked me either or both of two questions: who was the Duke of Connaught and, or, was he of much interest? My answers lie in the pages which follow, but the questions have been an encouragement to me throughout my endeavour. They show how completely or, in the second case, how almost completely, a royal figure who, so relatively recently as three quarters of a century ago occupied the centre of the stage, has faded from memory. They, therefore, also show the room which exists for a biography of him. But room alone would not have been enough; there had to be interest too and of that there is, to my mind, a great sufficiency. Prince Arthur, as I have preferred to call the Duke of Connaught, except when it seems inappropriate, was, after all, a son of Queen Victoria; he was the last British Prince to command a major formation in battle and the first to fill the position of Governor-General of a self-governing Dominion. With the possible exception of his elder brother, Prince Alfred, Duke of Edinburgh, whose unreliablility, however, severely qualified the value of his undoubted abilities, Prince Arthur was the only British Prince descended from Queen Victoria who combined the functions of royalty with the conduct of a professional career which ascended to the highest rank. It is true that Prince Arthur might not have been promoted to the rank of Field-Marshal if he had not been a member of the Royal Family, but it is also true that his training and ability enabled him to discharge the duties which normally go with that rank in a perfectly competent manner. Indeed, as we shall see, his zeal and efficiency sometimes gave his military and political masters embarrassing surprises. Royal or not, the commander who more than held his own against the then rising star of the Army, General Redvers Buller, as Prince Arthur did in the principal military manoeuvres of 1898, was qualified to reach the highest rank.

In many aspects of his public service, Prince Arthur, alone among his eight brothers and sisters, fully realised the formidable objectives and ideals which had been set for their children by the Prince Consort and Queen Victoria. Though his more famous eldest brother proved, in the last nine years of his life, to be a brilliant and successful King, he had been less than a complete success for the first fifty-nine, as Prince of Wales; and though his eldest sister, Princess Victoria, who became the German Crown Princess and ultimately the Empress Frederick, was more intellectually gifted than Prince Arthur, she failed to adjust to German modes and the premature death of her husband put the attainments set for her completely beyond her reach. The other six children, endowed as they were with various talents and prominent as they were in their own days, were not, by comparison with Prince Arthur, important historical figures. Even in the routine of royal functions, Prince Arthur's role as a representative of the Sovereign included some remarkable and historic missions. For example, he represented his mother at the Coronation of the last Tsar of Russia in 1896, his brother at the first Indian Coronation Durbar in 1903, his nephew at the opening of the first parliament of the Union of South Africa in 1910 and again at the inauguration of the Indian constitutional reforms in 1920.

The interest of Prince Arthur's life is, however, by no means confined to his professional career and his public functions; his private life is also an absorbing subject for, though he was in no sense a libertine and, in fact, made a particularly happy marriage, he was an inveterate admirer of feminine beauty and an appreciator of feminine wisdom and wit, especially as exemplified in American women, who were freer than their British sisters from the constraints of court etiquette and European habits. He was also the most socially gregarious of men, with an international acquaintanceship which seemed to result in his knowing somebody almost wherever he travelled, which was nearly everywhere. Indeed, his charm, freedom from the spirit of vindictiveness and the degree of civility which he displayed, were among his most remarkable characteristics.

For the greatest part of its span, Prince Arthur's life lay at or near the centre of great historical events and developments and the study of it, therefore, sheds shafts of light on several aspects of the history of the period. The Battle of Tel-el-Kebir in 1882, at which Prince Arthur commanded the Brigade of Guards, was one of Wolseley's most brilliant victories and the impression of it formed on the field by Prince Arthur is of singular interest. The encounter has been much neglected by military historians, perhaps because the official history of it is one of the dullest and most clumsily written which it is possible to imagine in response to such a scintillating episode. Prince Arthur's seven years of service in India, as a divisional commander and then as Commander-in-Chief of the Bombay Army, afford unique insights, not only into the military organisation and challenges of the Indian Empire, but also the nature and style of its government and social systems. During the period of Arnold-Forster's and Haldane's army reforms, Prince Arthur held successive commands at home, followed by appointments as Inspector-General of the Forces and lastly as Commander-in-Chief in the Mediterranean; his experiences show more clearly than seems to have been recognised heretofore what the real purposes of these reforms were. Indeed, Prince Arthur's rather naïve assumption that they were designed to improve the efficiency and terms of service of the Army got him into serious military and political difficulties with the Army Council and the Government. Finally, his term of office as Governor-General of Canada from 1911 to 1916 reveals the premier Dominion at a critical stage of her development from adolescence to maturity.

The unpublished and original material which has been available for this study is satisfyingly massive. Prince Arthur's personal papers, preserved in the Royal Archives at Windsor Castle, amount to more than nine thousand items and elsewhere in this same gold mine of biographical and historical evidence there are thousands of other items directly concerning him. There is a large seam of highly important material in the Public Archives of Canada at Ottawa and another in the Public Record Office at Kew. In addition, I have found considerable pockets of further evidence in numerous other archives and libraries situated throughout the United Kingdom. In my section of acknowledgements, which follows these prefatory paragraphs, I have sought to make clear my huge indebtedness to these institutions, but my immediate purpose in mentioning them here is to indicate not only the historical importance of Prince Arthur's life, but also the impressive volume and quality of primary material which has been available for writing it.

All these considerations make it very strange, in my opinion, that no attempt has been made before now to produce an authoritative biography of Prince Arthur. Though there are some reasons for this, which are discussed in my final chapter, it still strikes me as surprising. In some ways too it has been unfortunate. Although a superficial, laudatory, and very inaccurate account of Prince Arthur's life appeared in 1929, he has had no real chronicler. In consequence, it has been easy for his actions and motives to be misunderstood and, in some notable cases, to be traduced by biographers and historians of the period, especially so by A. J. P. Taylor in his biography of Beaverbrook and by Dr R. G. Haycock in his of Sam Hughes, the Canadian Minister of Militia and Defence in the First World War. Nor has there been the means of assessing such speculations as have appeared, for example, in Anita Leslie's *Edwardians in Love* or the more startling assertions of Rhoda Doubleday in her *Atlantic Between*. My purpose has been, not to defend, but to reveal Prince Arthur, both in character and in historical context.

In pursuing these objects, I have sought to convey not only the facts but also the flavour of Prince Arthur's life and style. I have, therefore, wherever it has seemed appropriate, written in the manner of his usage and that of his contemporaries. Thus, I have preferred 'motor' to car, 'cheery' to cheerful, 'native' to ethnic and so on. And if occasionally my narrative seems to move in staccato leaps from point to point, that is intended, for it is a reflection of the way in which Prince Arthur's mind tended to work. In the case of place names and their spellings, I have also tried to avoid giving an anachronistic effect. The difficulty is that many places underwent changes during Prince Arthur's life; St Petersburg, for example, became Petrograd, then Leningrad and has since returned to St Petersburg. Elsewhere the problems are legion. 'Jeypore' has become Jaipur, 'Ulwur' Alwar, 'Assuan' Aswan and so on. I have followed the forms used by Prince Arthur as nearly as possible. In the case of the titles of Indian Princes, I have followed the styles officially set out by the India Office in 1875. In such matters there is, in my opinion, no classically satisfactory solution.

In acknowledging the help I have received from many sources, I must begin by expressing my gratitude to Her Majesty The Queen, by whose gracious permission I was afforded access to the large volume of material concerning Prince Arthur in the Royal Archives at Windsor Castle. I must express the debt of gratitude which I owe to the Royal Librarian and Deputy Keeper of the Archives, Mr Oliver Everett, and I cannot adequately thank the three successive Registrars, Miss Jane Langton, Miss Elizabeth Cuthbert and Lady de Bellaigue, who have been in charge of the Royal Archives while I worked on this book. They and all the members of their staff, especially the Deputy Registrar, Miss Pamela Clark, have been unstinting in the expert advice, splendid archival service and seemingly inexhaustible tolerance and hospitality, which they have extended to me throughout my 397 research visits to the Round Tower and, latterly, their temporary accommodation at Frogmore. I must also mention my special indebtedness to Lady de Bellaigue for her marvellously swift reading and adept translation of what seemed to me to be incomprehensible *Deutsche Schrift*, particularly that of Prince Frederick Charles of Prussia. Lady Millar's interest in my work has been greatly appreciated and it is, in particular, to her that I owe my introduction to the papers of Sir Henry Ponsonby, which are in the Royal Archives.

This biography would have been fatally lacking in authority had I not been able to tap the large quantity of relevant material in the Public Archives of Canada in Ottawa. The provision of microfilms of the finding aids enabled me to identify the appropriate call numbers and, through those, to obtain photocopies of the requisite documents. In addition, members of the staff most kindly took great trouble in drawing my attention to documents which, by the process of conventional searching, I might well have missed. In these connections I must especially and most warmly thank Mr Brian Murphy of the Public Life Archives Programme, Mr David Fraser of the Social/Cultural Archives Branch, and Mr Paul Marsden of the Military and International Affairs Records Unit. I am also very grateful to the Librarian of Rhodes House, Mr Alan Bell, and the Deputy Librarian, Mr Alan Lodge, for arranging with the Public Archives of Canada for the Canadian microfilms to be made available to me in the Rhodes House Reading Room four and a half miles from my home. In the same Reading Room, I availed myself of the fine collection of Canadian historical literature which is accommodated and so efficiently made available in the Rhodes House Library.

Among the many other institutions in which I have worked, I must make special mention of the Prince Consort's Library at Aldershot, where the Librarian, Mrs J.L. Sears, and the Assistant Librarian, Yvonne Clephan, were so helpful to me; the National Army Museum, where the then Director, my long-standing friend Mr William Reid, opened up some treasures from the excellent Archive; Mr Reid has also educated me in some military mysteries of the British Army; the Royal Commonwealth Society, whose Librarian, Miss T.A. Barringer, made my visits to Northumberland Avenue so profitable, and the National Library of Scotland, where the efficiency, courtesy, enthusiasm and pride of every grade of staff are models which one can but hope may one day be emulated in the British and Bodleian Libraries. In the latter, however, I

have encountered islands of excellence, notably in the Modern Manuscripts Reading Room. To Mr J.F. Russell of the Department of
Manuscripts in the National Library of Scotland I extend my most
appreciative thanks. I am very grateful to Mr A. Crookston of the
Wiltshire Record Office, whose careful preparations greatly accelerated
the progress of my work there. Finally, in this category of gratitude, I
must refer to the extremely efficient and courteous service which I have
invariably encountered in the Oxfordshire Central Library, through
whose good offices I was, incidentally, able to gain access to resources in
the British Library which otherwise seemed to be virtually inaccessible. I
must add, too, that I am very grateful to the authorities in the many other
Libraries and Archives in which I have worked, ranging in scope from the
India Office Library and Record Office to the Durham University
Archive. The National Register of Archives and its helpful and patient
staff provided many of the leads to these widely spread Archives.

I am very much indebted to Lord Downe, who kindly lent me the
letters which his grandmother, Cecilia Lady Downe, wrote to her
mother, Lady Sefton, while she was in attendance on the Duchess of
Connaught, and to Mr Hugo Vickers, who gave me access to the letters
written by Prince Arthur to Gladys Deacon, which are now in his
possession. My friend Mr Martin Goldman of East Hampton most kindly
and diligently traced the life of Rhoda Doubleday subsequent to the
period of her friendship with Prince Arthur and, in thanking him, I must
also mention Cathy Walsh of the East Hampton Library and other
'persistent seekers' at the Suffolk Cooperative Library and the Newark
Library in New Jersey.

In connection with my search for illustrations, I must especially thank
Miss Frances Dimond, the Curator of Photographs in the Royal Archives,
Roanne Mokhtar of the Reference Services in the Public Archives of
Canada and Mr M. Willis of the Department of Photographs in the
Imperial War Museum. Sir Oliver Millar, formerly the Surveyor of the
Queen's Pictures, kindly placed at my disposal his encyclopaedic know-
ledge and I am most grateful to Mr Charles Noble, the Assistant Surveyor
of the Queen's Pictures, for guiding me to the portraits of Prince Arthur
in the Royal Collection. I must also thank Mr Noble and the Hon. Mrs
Sandra de Laszlo for their help in directing me to the portrait of Prince
Arthur by de László, which is in the possession of the RSA, and Mrs S.
Bennett, the Library Administrator of that Society, for her ready help in
reproducing it.

It was a great encouragement to me when I first formed the intention of writing this biography that Prince Arthur's grandson, Captain Alexander Ramsay of Mar, so warmly welcomed the project. My initial impulse to write the book was also powerfully nourished by Léonie Leslie's grand-daughter, the late Anita Leslie, whose inimitable charm and insight were great sharpeners of one's wits. The open-handed hospitality of the then Warden of the Royal Army Chaplains' Department at Bagshot Park, the Reverend Brian Pugh, and the Secretary, Lieutenant-Colonel Ralph Nye, enabled me to gather in the feel of the house and grounds which were so dear to Prince Arthur. I am also most grateful to Her Majesty The Queen for giving me access to Balmoral Castle where the Resident Factor, Mr Martin Leslie, took much trouble in showing me all I wanted to see.

To my late wife, Diana, though she died before the work was much advanced, I owe a great part of the courage which it requires to embark upon such a project and to my present wife, Sarah, I am incalculably indebted. Her skills as an historian and archivist have marched with such as I possess myself almost throughout the years of the enterprise. Without her extraordinary gift for finding the way into archives, the scope of this book would have been much less and without her sense of literary style, many a bêtise would have survived. Such as do and such errors as there may be, are entirely my own responsibility.

Thames House   NOBLE FRANKLAND
Eynsham
Oxford

February 1993

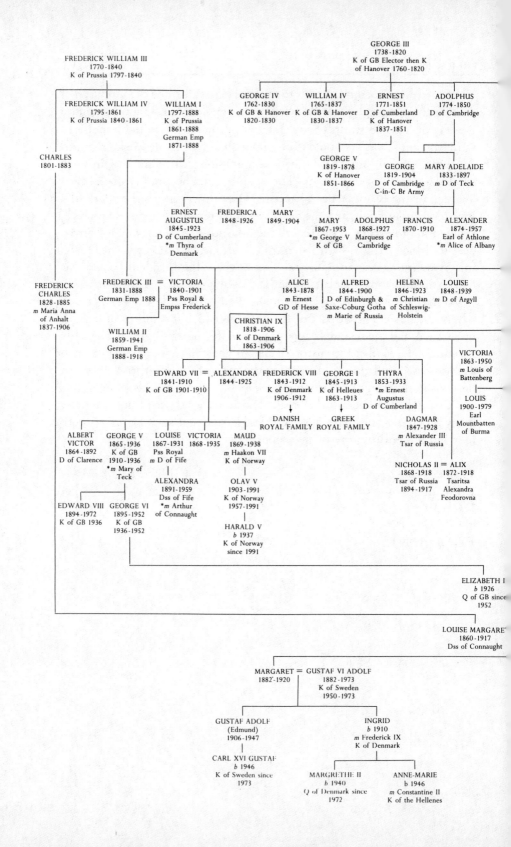

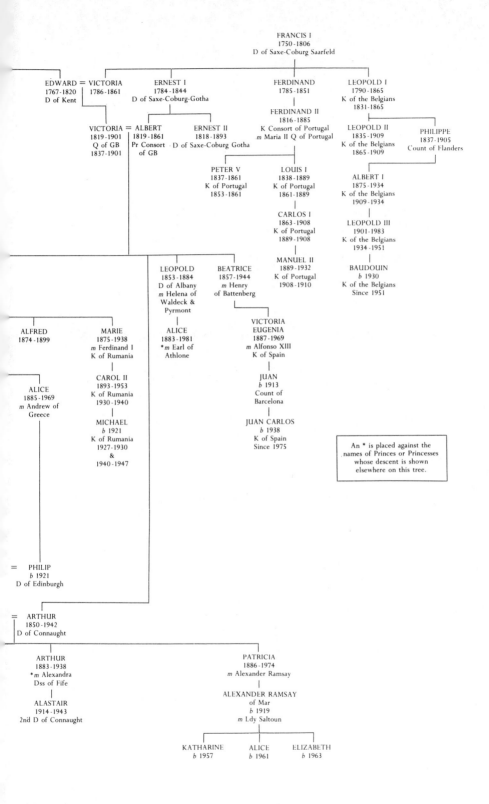

CHAPTER 1

Childhood 1850-1861

AT SEVENTEEN MINUTES after eight on the morning of 1st May 1850, a baby was born at Buckingham Palace. According to his mother, he was 'a fine large boy' who met her heart's desire, which she had cherished for five years. According to his father, the child 'glided into the light of day and was received by the sisters with *jubilates*.' The children of these parents were now as many as the days of the week, but, from what his father felt was well-bred courtesy, and notwithstanding that the day of his birth was Wednesday, the honour of being Sunday was conceded to the newcomer.[1]

This favoured newcomer was the third son and seventh child of Queen Victoria and Prince Albert. The other days of the week were Vicky, the Princess Royal and future Empress Frederick of Germany; Bertie, the Prince of Wales and future King Edward VII; Affie, later the Duke of Edinburgh and eventually the reigning Duke of Saxe-Coburg and Gotha; Alice, the future Grand Duchess of Hesse and mother of the last Tsaritsa of Russia; Lenchen, whose real name was Helena, and who became Princess Christian of Schleswig Holstein and Louise, later the Duchess of Argyll, and, of all these children, to become much the closest and most sympathetic to her new brother. Two more children were yet to come; Leopold, nearly three years later, who became the Duke of Albany, and Beatrice, who was born in 1857 and became her mother's acknowledged favourite child. Indeed, the Queen made no bones about such matters and precisely declared them. Though 'Sunday' was thus displaced in favour by his youngest sister, he was ever to retain the second position and, amongst his brothers, the first. Princess Beatrice, though eventually allowed to marry, was, however, to be required to remain about the Queen as a combination of daughter, private secretary and lady-in-waiting; the newcomer, despite many restrictions, was to be permitted to have a career and his birthday set the mould of it.

The new Prince's birthday was also the eighty-first birthday of the Duke of Wellington, who was selected as one of the Godfathers, and after whom he was given the name of Arthur. His other names were William, after another Godfather, Prince William of Prussia, later the first modern German Emperor, Patrick, because Ireland was enjoying a brief period of favour with the Queen, and Albert, because she intended all her sons and their male descendants to bear that name. The christening took place in the chapel of Buckingham Palace on the hot evening of 22nd June. The infant's names were announced to the Archbishop of Canterbury by Prince William of Prussia and everyone seemed to be well pleased. The Archbishop apparently declared him to be 'quite a Royal child,' which the Queen thought he had deduced from Prince Arthur's appearance.[2]

Certainly he grew rapidly in size and good looks. At four months, Lady Canning, who was in attendance on the Queen, saw him as a 'magnificent child' with the royal look which she had heard had been so pronounced in the Queen at the same age. Also, much to his mother's delight, he proved to be larger than the child of one her Keepers at Balmoral, though the two were of the same age.[3]

As the Queen and Prince Albert migrated regularly from there to Osborne to Windsor to Buckingham Palace to the Royal Yacht and elsewhere, Prince Arthur never had a home in the sense that most children do and he also frequently found himself separated from his parents. Among the consequences, was an early initiation into the art of correspondence and before he was six, it seems that he had mastered the knowledge that his letters must be punctual and that they must contain the correct expressions, such as of his determination to try to be wise so as to deserve the love of his dear parents.[4]

His father tended to respond in less formal terms. He liked to address his little son as a Colonel and, in September 1856, he sent him a hussar prisoner whom he had captured at Crathie near Balmoral. 'Do with him as you like,' he wrote, 'but take care that he does not bite you.' Whether this 'hussar' was a multi-coloured caterpillar or some other beast, the object was to foster the military spirit. The response seems always to have been favourable. Prince Arthur enjoyed playing his drum, at least until this was introduced as a form of punishment, and he gloried in his miniature Guards uniform. At Christmas 1855 he signed his card to his eldest sister 'Arthur Grenadier Guards.' This was the time of the Crimean War and, from the battlefield of Alma, Prince Arthur had received a medal taken from the body of a fallen Russian soldier. It was sent to him by the British Commander-in-Chief and came with 'Field Marshal Lord Raglan's humble duty.'[5]

Soon after the arrival of this Russian medal, the war was brought much nearer to Prince Arthur's realisation. Friday, 18th May 1855, was a day of great excitement. The Queen was to review and present medals to a large contingent of soldiers and sailors, several of them badly wounded, who had returned from the Crimea. The morning broke foggy but warm and already at breakfast time people were hurrying through Green Park betokening some great goings on. The Queen felt '*all* the agitation — all the *bustle* & all the very peculiar sensations which only great events occasion.' Prince Arthur drove out from Buckingham Palace with his aunt, Princess Feodore, and his sisters 'in a state of the greatest excitement as to all he was to see & do.' He watched his mother's arrival on the Horse Guards parade ground where the troops were drawn up in readiness for the presentation of medals by their Queen. She found the sight 'magnificent & overpowering.' It was also unique, for never before had medals been presented not only to officers, but also to Sergeants, Corporals and Privates and, as the Queen recorded, it was the first time that 'a simple Private touched the hand of his Sovereign.' She was proud of this tie but, despite her excitement and nervousness, she noticed that, on the balcony of the Horse Guards, 'Dear little Arthur was very conspicuous.' Later the men marched into the garden of Buckingham Palace where the Queen, Prince Albert and their children walked round talking to them. Some of the sailors ran to the lake and drank the 'horrid' water. Others strolled about with the soldiers, others sat on the benches and some lay down on the ground and smoked. How little, the Queen reflected, could these poor men from the field of Alma, the deadly charge of Balaclava, the fearful day of Inkerman or the crowded hospital at Scutari with their mangled limbs and wasted frames, have imagined that they would be sitting under the trees in the grounds of Buckingham Palace 'with the Queen and Prince & the Royal Family looking with pride & pleasure at them!' She prayed that her own sons might 'once be included amongst such noble devoted hearts.'[6]

So, at the age of five, Prince Arthur received a dramatic impression of the heroics and the horrors of war. He must also have absorbed something of the Queen's intensely personal feeling of connection with her army. In years to come these observations were to be guiding factors in his life. But now another fundamental influence was almost at hand. Among those who came home from the Crimean War, which at last was concluded in

March 1856, was Captain Howard Elphinstone of the Royal Engineers. His background was rather unusual in that he had been born in Russia in 1829 and partly educated in Germany before joining the British army. His family was old and distinguished, but his means were not great and he had to make his way in the world. In the Crimean War, he had lost an eye and won the Victoria Cross. In doing so, he had made the acquaintance of Lieutenant John Cowell, also of the Royal Engineers, and had served under Lieutenant-General Sir Harry Jones, who had formed a high opinion of him. Soon after these three officers had returned from the seat of war, Cowell was appointed by Prince Albert to manage the education of his second son, Prince Alfred. Sir Harry Jones was asked to recommend someone similar to do the same for Prince Arthur. The first proposal was Colonel Stanton, but he was either senior enough, brave enough or modest enough, to decline; the second choice was Elphinstone. Prince Albert thought that he would have liked to have seen a little more of the man personally before selecting him, but, nevertheless, he decided to do so without seeing him at all. This was the more surprising in that, while Prince Alfred's Governor was required at once, Prince Arthur's was not needed for another year.[7]

In these negotiations Cowell was the go-between and Elphinstone did not make a very good beginning. He found himself in a dilemma. He had hopes of rising in the military profession and, indeed, he had just been appointed to supervise the topographical department. He also wondered if the young Prince, whom he was being asked to manage, would take to him. He may have heard something of the difficulties which the Prince of Wales's tutors encountered and Cowell may have mentioned the rather hot-headed temper which Prince Alfred possessed. Perhaps, he may also have thought that a little hesitation would improve the terms of the offer which would be made to him. Cowell and Jones were only moderately tolerant of these doubts and it required but little effort on their parts to induce Elphinstone to accept the Prince Consort's offer. This was to take charge of Prince Arthur's education from the beginning of 1859 on the condition of a year's initial probation, at a salary £300, which was the same as Cowell received for coping with Prince Alfred.[8]

Meanwhile, Prince Arthur remained in the care of his Governess, Madame Rollande. She, who must have known a good deal about the behaviour of his elder brothers, was, perhaps, surprised to find him so amiable. He was usually in the best of spirits and, even in the company of the Queen and her guests at luncheon, was inclined to burst into song. But

the Queen, much as she loved and even indulged him, constantly sought
to subdue him to her own authority by imposing her framework upon the
habits of his life. For example, two letters from her 'darling little Pet'
gave great pleasure, as did 'everything that comes from our dear little love
whom we miss much.' All the same, the Queen was sorry that he had used
'the paper I gave you as I gave it on purpose to be kept as *views* of your
voyage & *first* long journey to be put in an album with the date which I
hope you will do.' Before his eighth birthday, she was considering whom
he should marry and, strangely enough, though she was later to be so
much opposed to the idea, she thought of one of the daughters of Prince
Frederick Charles of Prussia. In the fullness of time, Prince Arthur was,
indeed, to marry one such, though the particular one had not, at this date,
yet been born.[9]

Of more immediate import, were the Queen's views on Prince
Arthur's education. These were strongly held, somewhat vaguely and
even hysterically expressed, and markedly at variance with what the
Prince Consort thought and, by the appointment of Elphinstone, had
substantially arranged. The Queen dreaded the transition for the young
Prince from the care of a Governess and Nurse to that of a Tutor and
Valet, the more so because this was to happen when he would still be
three years younger than Prince Alfred was when it happened to him.
There was also another point which she felt she had to explain to the
Prince Consort; it was that to her, Arthur was 'dearer than any of the
others put together,' and that, after her husband, he was 'the *dearest* &
most precious object to *me* on Earth.' She believed that mistakes had been
made in the education of Bertie and Affie. Affie had been thrown in with
Bertie as a means of correcting his childish and disorderly behaviour, but
the result had been that both boys got worse. Fortunately, Arthur was still
too young to fall under the influence of either of these unruly elder
brothers and the Queen believed that he was without the 'absence' of
Alfred and the bad temper and stupidity of the Prince of Wales. All the
same she was apprehensive of what might happen when he was exposed to
the hazards of the world. She hoped, and, as far as the Prince Consort was
concerned, she was the supplicant, that Arthur might stay at home under
a tutor until he was twelve, which would be 1862. She was fearful that the
young Prince might be overworked and she recruited the opinion of one
of her doctors, Sir James Clark, to agree with her own that a little boy of
eight should not be expected to learn for long at a time. There would be
no difficulty in absorbing his leisure hours because he was so different

from his elder brothers and so good with other boys. She thought that he should not travel much until he was fourteen or fifteen. He should not join the Army until he was sixteen and a half or seventeen and, as he grew up, he should be kept away from London as much as possible. Thank God, she told the Prince Consort, 'we have 8 years before us till that terribly anxious time comes.'[10]

These views showed a marked divergence from, and even criticism of, the principles for the education of their sons which had been laid down, and hitherto practised, by the Prince Consort. They revealed the extent to which the Queen, despite her protestations to the contrary, had retained her independence of mind. They also showed how much more she cared for and believed in Prince Arthur's future than she did in that of the two elder boys. Elphinstone, no doubt, had some advance warning of this for the Queen had conveyed her views not only to the Prince Consort by the means he himself had taught her of a memorandum, but she had ensured too that Cowell, who was now, so to speak, Elphinstone's sponsor, should also see it.

When, however, Elphinstone came to Windsor Castle to be given his initial instructions, it was, of course, not the Queen, but the Prince Consort who received him. This was on 23rd October 1858. After lunching with the equerries, the distinctly nervous hero from the Crimea was brought into the Royal presence. The Prince Consort bowed graciously twice, gave Elphinstone his hand, exchanged a few remarks and then dried up. Elphinstone ventured a few objections to taking up his new work as soon as had been agreed, but the Prince seemed to be unimpressed by them and Elphinstone soon accepted that he would be ready to come by 14th January 1859. The Prince then discoursed a bit upon the education which his son was to be given. There was, he said, much to be learnt out of doors by being taught the birds, plants, botany, geology and even the formation and variety of pebbles. On some days, three hours of work would not be too much; on others, one would be. He thought that the defect of private education was the want of emulation, which would stir up a boy's energies, and he believed that the only remedy was the substitute of encouraging the thing to be done because it ought to be done. Elphinstone felt that he had a better alternative, which was an insistence upon the pupil obeying the will of the Governor. His courage, however, seems not to have run to the extent of actually expressing such an idea, or, indeed, any others.[11]

January 1859, therefore, saw the removal of Prince Arthur's care and education from female to male hands, or at least it did so to some extent. Madame Rollande gave way to Elphinstone and the Reverend W. R. Jolley, who, under Elphinstone's direction, became Prince Arthur's school-master. The Nurse gave way to a valet, Collins by name. Both the last two had been transferred from Prince Alfred and therefore, it can hardly be doubted, moved into rather quieter pastures. The arrival of all these men, however, by no means diminished the maternal influence nor the intensity and frequency of its intervention. Indeed, Elphinstone's regime was initiated with a torrent of instructions, hints and questions from the Queen. She meant to take Prince Arthur to the play; she hoped he had been good. As he had a cold he had better not go out unless it cleared up, and then not on wet grass. His rooms must be kept cool as it was very mild. He was to have holidays on the Queen's and Prince's birthdays and all the Royal children's, on the Queen's wedding anniversary, New Year's Day, Christmas Day and Good Friday, but, if a Royal child's birthday fell on a Sunday, there was to be no holiday, except for the child in question. Permission to play with his brothers and sisters would be an inducement to good behaviour. Eight to ten minutes was enough time for him to dress. As morning service would be a full and long one, he ought to go to evening service. His letter to the Prince Regent of Prussia was to go by Messenger. On Sundays he should wear a kilt with a thin waist coat and jacket and cotton stockings. In the afternoon, after his dinner was over, he could go out in his blouse if he liked. Could he come to Portsmouth to see the 32nd Regiment which had been at Lucknow? Could he come out this afternoon with the Queen and Princess Alice and, if so, would Major Elphinstone, for such he now was, also come and bring his sketch book with him?[12]

One day at Balmoral in September 1859, Elphinstone was summoned to the Queen's room. There she was sitting at a table writing her Journal. Was Prince Arthur improving? What was the cause of his naughtiness? The Queen admitted that he was inclined to deceive. The Prince Consort thought he ought to begin Latin. Elphinstone thought not; it would be hard to concentrate his attention and that would lead to further punish-ments; if these were persisted in, they would sour his nature and, if they were dropped, the boy would see who was master. One of the difficulties was that the parents did not see eye to eye about what was best for the boy. The Queen said that she had hated lessons; the Prince Consort had liked them above all else. Elphinstone felt insecure and incompetent. When dining with the Queen, he found himself feeling at one moment that his position was beneath him and then, at another, that he could not.

uphold it sufficiently. He observed that Cowell seemed to have solved his problems by a combination of self-confidence and politeness. He asked himself why he could not do the same.[13]

Prince Arthur too was beset by doubts, though of a somewhat different nature. When we rise again from the dead, are we clean and do we have our clothes? What did conceived by the Holy Ghost mean? How could the Queen be Head of the Church when she did not preach? He seemed to be most anxious to say his prayers when he was doing least well at arithmetic. Once, when he had been particularly idle at learning his poetry, Elphinstone suggested to Mr Jolley that he should be given a double ration. The little fellow turned sulky, kicked off his shoes and stamped. Elphinstone dealt him a good box on the ears, which caused Prince Arthur to cry out loudly. This at once produced the Queen, who took Elphinstone upstairs. She hoped this would not be a frequent occurrence; it was annoying to hear screams so often.[14]

In 1860, to meet the Prince Consort's wishes, Latin and German history were added to Prince Arthur's curriculum and, to meet those of the Queen, the plan that he should be more out of doors. She thought that too much learning and too little fresh air weakened and checked the growth of the brain. There was also another development. To meet the Prince Consort's view that emulation must be encouraged, it was decided that Prince Arthur should be provided with some companions of his own age. In the case of the Prince of Wales, the Queen recognised that this system had not worked very well. The Prince had bullied and even beaten the imported boys to the point at which at least some of their parents preferred to decline the honour. In Prince Arthur's case no such difficulties were expected. A beginning was made with the sons of a select few, most of them courtiers. Outings to the play became quite frequent and there were other excitements, such as, in March 1860, an inspection of the new liner *Great Eastern*. In October, there was a very enjoyable ceremony. This was the laying of the foundation stone of the miniature Albert Barracks in the Victoria Fort near the children's Swiss Cottage in the grounds of Osborne House by Prince Arthur's sister, Princess Helena. At this time, the Queen and Prince Albert were away in Coburg, an absence which at first had much upset Prince Arthur, but one which presently seems to have produced a pleasant and more than usually relaxed atmosphere at Osborne, especially, no doubt, for Elphinstone.[15]

Before leaving, the Prince Consort had arranged that Elphinstone and Jolley should take Prince Arthur on an incognito walking tour on the Isle of Wight. They rose each morning at seven and business began with Prince Arthur dictating a journal of the previous day to Jolley, who wrote it down verbatim for Prince Arthur to copy later. The eventual account was intended for the Prince Consort's perusal. The adventure began with a drive to within a mile of Colrock Bay. They walked along the beach collecting fossils and then lunched at the Needles Hotel. They went on to Freshwater Gate and spent the night in an hotel there. Next day, they drove by carriage, stopping at several places on the way, to the Blackgang Hotel, where they spent the last night of the expedition before returning to Osborne on the following day. Elphinstone claimed that nowhere was Prince Arthur recognised, a luxury to become much rarer in the future. He was well pleased with Prince Arthur's observation of, and interest in, what he was shown. This was a quality to become much more pronounced in the future.[16]

As Elphinstone, perhaps, began to feel a little more secure with the Queen and the Prince Consort, so he found more courage in expressing his own view of what would be best for Prince Arthur's education. He was afraid that the courtiers' sons were too much inclined to give way to their Royal companion and treat him with that reverence, which Elphinstone was sure was injurious. He should go down the hill to Eton and mix with some ordinary boys to rub off the eccentricities and softness of his character. If he met boys with bad manners, so much the better; it would correct a similar fault in Prince Arthur. Elphinstone thought that there was no danger of contagious disease because great care was taken at Eton. Nor did he think that the games, in which he hoped Prince Arthur would be allowed to join, would be hazardous. Only the big matches were violent and they could be avoided. As a start, a few boys should be summoned to Windsor Castle to form a nucleus around Prince Arthur so that he could advance upon Eton in company. Among those whom Elphinstone thought would do for this vulgarising process, were young Lascelles and, though he was a son of a member of the Queen's Household, Biddulph.[17]

Elphinstone's efforts to detach Prince Arthur a little from the Court and to bring on his maturity were now assisted by another event. On 16th March 1861, the Queen's mother, the Duchess of Kent, died. The Queen, who had previously had no intimate contact with death, took to a serious bout of mourning; it amounted to the hysterical and was accompanied by severe depression and bad headaches. She began to recognise that the constant perambulations of the Court, if followed by him, were unsettling for Prince Arthur. She conceded too that if his younger brother, Prince Leopold, who was delicate, could not be much of a companion to him, other boys should be found to fill the need. She even proposed that an establishment should be set up for Prince Arthur, perhaps in White Lodge, where he could live away from home for several months each year. The Queen's belief that what was best for the boy must come first had driven her to these ideas, but her nervous state may already have, as it certainly did later, made her less tolerant of young boys about her own house.[18]

In August, while the Queen and the Prince Consort were in Ireland, Elphinstone took Prince Arthur and Prince Leopold to Balmoral for a holiday. He had seldom seen Prince Arthur in such high spirits and Jolley was pleased to find when they got back to Windsor that he was attentive at his lessons and seemed to have forgotten little as a result of the holiday. Elphinstone thought that the prospect of being allowed to play with the boys at Eton had much to do with this. On 19th October, Prince Arthur wrote from Windsor to his parents, who had now returned to Balmoral, saying that they would hardly recognise the old part of the Castle so much had it been improved. He had been to Eton that morning and 'had such fun there in the game of football.' The next day he wrote again to report on a fishing expedition to Virginia Water with Mr Jolley and the Major. They had caught six pike and two eels. The Castle, he said, was in a very noisy state. The Queen wrote to him that Papa had got a stag and Bertie, who had since returned to Cambridge, two. She said she dreaded coming back to Windsor, which, without dearest Grandmama 'is *too* dreadful for me.'[19]

Alas, it was to be more dreadful than that. Within two months, after a short, unexpected and undiagnosed illness, the Prince Consort died. The date was 14th December 1861 and he had not reached his forty-third birthday. So, while still short of his twelfth birthday, Prince Arthur inherited, in Elphinstone, a substitute father and, in the Queen, a much modified mother.

CHAPTER 2

Tutelage 1862-1866

DESPITE THE TERRIBLE grief which beset the Queen and the awful gloom which pervaded the Court, her activity with regard to Prince Arthur's welfare was undiminished. In the course of 1862, Elphinstone received some forty letters from her, which, even for a correspondent of Queen Victoria's, was an ample ration. She laid it down to him that her object for the children was their success in life as good, moral and distinguished people. She wished her boys, and especially the younger ones, to be very intimate with her so that they could imbibe the right views and habits, by which, of course, she meant those of the Prince Consort, of which she was now the best judge, and her own. She was, however, constantly torn between the desirability of Prince Arthur being at home with her or away somewhere else with Elphinstone. Undoubtedly, she placed a heavy reliance upon Elphinstone, but she was by no means easily deceived as to reality. When Prince Arthur wrote to her at the end of March thanking her for allowing him to have some companions to stay at Osborne despite the fact that she was so sad, she wanted to know from Elphinstone if the letter was really Prince Arthur's own. Yes, it was, he told her; he had only spoken to Prince Arthur about his mother's kindness and her irreparable anguish and suggested that he should write to her.[1]

In May Prince Arthur went farther out into the world than he had yet been. He embarked with Elphinstone and, so that his regular lessons could continue, Jolley, in the Admiralty yacht *Vivid*. They cruised along the coast calling at Lyme Regis, Exmouth, Plymouth, Devonport, Penzance, Padstow and Bideford. Prince Arthur proved to be a good sailor, did his lessons well, admired the scenery and absorbed its historical connections, especially those provided by earlier visits from his parents. This progress created quite a stir and lengthy descriptions in the local newspapers. On one expedition, he visited the Bottalek copper mine not far from Land's End. According to Elphinstone, this produced a 'favourable sensation among the mining population.' According to the *Western Morning News*, which, Elphinstone warned the Queen, exaggerated in the usual manner of newspapers, the young Prince lunched in the open air from a white cloth spread on the green sward and then 'dashed on' to St Just, where the Volunteers had been under arms for some hours in readiness to receive the Queen's son with due honours. Prince Arthur bowed his respects and then went on to the mine where a splendid lunch had been prepared, which, if this was not an exaggeration, seems to have been the second of the day. Accompanied by Mr T. S. Bolitho, one of the principal managers of the mine, he then went down it to a depth of two hundred fathoms to see how the copper was got. On returning to the surface, or, as the miners called it, 'coming to grass,' he was reported to be a little fagged, having done enough for a strong man of middle age, but, apparently, he still showed 'his usual flow of spirits, and natural elasticity of manner.' To the *Western Morning News* reporter, Prince Arthur appeared to be 'simply a   neatly-dressed, cheerful, healthy-looking, round-faced, little boy of 12 years old, whose amiability of manner, gentlemanly bearing, and intelligent countenance would afford unmixed joy to the heart of any mother in the land.'[2]

However simple and cheerful Prince Arthur may have appeared, Elphinstone was uneasy at the amount of attention he had attracted. He was, therefore, pleased to find, when they went with the Queen to Germany in September, that no-one there paid much attention to him. Elphinstone hoped that the rough and tumble of a walking tour in the Harz Mountains would teach Prince Arthur to put up with unaccustomed discomforts and get over what, Elphinstone told the Queen, was a daintiness in food which, if not checked, would cause him misery when he became a soldier. One of the other advantages was that he would have to speak German. Prince Arthur did not respond as Elphinstone hoped and the Queen had to speak very seriously to him about the need for better behaviour. She told him that her impression of what he did was contrary to what he expressed and she held up to him the bad conduct of his eldest brother, the Prince of Wales, as an example of what not to do. She was more annoyed than she could say when, in spite of all this, Prince Arthur managed to be late for Church while staying with her at the sacred Rosenau, where the Prince Consort had been born. Perhaps his visit to old Baron Stockmar, the former mentor of the Queen and Prince Consort, was an adequate punishment.[3]

On returning from the Continent, Prince Arthur, with Elphinstone and

1. The First of May. *Winterhalter. The Duke of Wellington offers a casket to his Godson, Prince Arthur, on his first birthday. The painting gave rise to the legend that Prince Arthur would open the casket on his twenty-first birthday and read words of wisdom from Wellington. In fact, the casket was empty, having been picked up from the Queen's table by Prince Albert and put into Wellington's hands to give the picture a focus.*

2. *Queen Victoria and Prince Arthur at Osborne. 1850. Winterhalter*

3. *The Royal Family at Osborne, 26th May 1857. Left to right: Prince Alfred, Prince Albert, Princess Helena, Prince Arthur, Princess Alice, Queen Victoria with Princess Beatrice, the Princess Royal, Princess Louise, Prince Leopold, the Prince of Wales.*

4. *Prince Arthur in the uniform of the Scots Guards, 1853. Winterhalter.*

his dog, Max, moved into a separate establishment in the Ranger's House, Greenwich Park. A small secluded room served as his study and a large empty one as his playroom. The bedrooms were large and high. Prince Arthur's and Elphinstone's adjoined and the door between was always kept ajar. Fires were forbidden in the bedrooms and Elphinstone promised the Queen that every room was equipped with a thermometer and that in none would the temperature ever exceed sixty degrees. There was a large garden with ample space for games and exercise whenever the neighbourhood should be crowded or 'otherwise objectionable.' They would not go to the parish church because it was in the middle of the 'dirty town of Greenwich' but to St Mary's, which could be reached without leaving the Park. There would be no ill-feeling because both churches were under the same vicar. To his delight, Prince Arthur found that there were troops all over the place. Soon after his arrival, he wrote to the Queen that a 'divisian of troops marched out here consisting of the artillery the Buffs and the Marines with two waggons of the military train.' He went part of the way with them and later rode with Major, as he called Elphinstone, and Lord Sydney to what he described as 'Elthem the old palace of King John.' His handwriting had developed from its previous copperplate into an individual boyish style of his own. It was still a great deal more legible than it later became.[4]

Prince Arthur's studies under Mr Jolley, who was now also assisted by some of the professors from the Royal Military Academy, consisted of Latin, which, rather to the annoyance of the Queen, was the main subject, mathematics, French, German, English composition, ancient history, English history, geography, music and learning poetry, which he had to do in his spare time to induce the habit of learning quickly. He also did gymnastics. The Queen more or less gave in as regards the amount of Latin in the face of Elphinstone's citation of the Prince Consort's views on the subject, but she, in turn, cited the same authority as well as her own strongly held view about religious teaching. In the course of a conversation with Prince Arthur, and not as a complaint from him, she had learnt that Mr Jolley was giving him religious lessons on Sundays. She reminded Elphinstone that she had objected to this two years earlier and she now did so again. As Prince Arthur attended long services on Sundays, he should not also be subjected to these lessons; Elphinstone should set Prince Arthur's mind to religious subjects by bringing them into everyday life. During the week, one of the ancient history lessons could be given up for a religious one.[5]

When from time to time Prince Arthur came home, the Queen thought she saw a change in him. She feared that living alone in his own establishment was making him 'grand & bumptious.' Elphinstone admitted the danger, but observed that there was even greater danger from the deference shown to him by those about the Court when he was at home. At Greenwich, Elphinstone asserted, he walked about without being taken notice of and was frequently jostled by workmen. Even so, there does not seem to have been much jostling when Prince Arthur embarked upon his scientific education. This was on 4th February 1863 when he went to the Military Academy to hear a lecture there by Mr Bloxam, who had recently succeeded Professor Faraday. Upon his arrival, Prince Arthur was received by the Lieutenant-Governor of the Academy, General Sandham, who then presented to him various officers and the lecturer, who, the Queen was told, was much flattered by one of her sons coming to hear him speak. Prince Arthur then took his seat at the head of the forms on which the Cadets sat. That evening, Admiral Sir Montagu Stopford came to dine with Prince Arthur at Ranger's House. Say what he would, there was no way in which Elphinstone, nor, for that matter, the Queen, could get round the fact that Prince Arthur was a son of the Sovereign.[6]

A grand reminder of this fact, and some of its inconvenient attachments, came in March when Prince Arthur was whisked away from his educational environment in Greenwich to attend the wedding in St George's Chapel, Windsor of his eldest brother, the future King Edward VII, to Princess Alexandra, a daughter of the future King Christian IX of Denmark. Among the others present, was Prince Arthur's four year old nephew, Prince William of Prussia. This child amused himself by throwing an aunt's muff out of the carriage window, casting a stone across the floor of the chapel and, during the ceremony, biting the kilted Prince Arthur in the leg. As Kaiser Wilhelm II, this nephew was later to cause much more trouble. For the time being, however, this was, no doubt, useful training for Prince Arthur, who, in later years, prided himself on not showing his feelings in public.[7]

What the public wanted was, however, another thing; on the way up to Balmoral just after his thirteenth birthday and a tour of the Lake District, Prince Arthur strolled about in Penrith, before dining in the Crown Hotel, while awaiting the 8.27 train for Carlisle. He was dressed in a black cap, turned down collar, black jacket and grey trousers and he seemed to a disappointed local reporter to be 'nobbut like any other lal lad.' All the same, when he appeared on the platform to catch his train, he was loudly cheered. The train was late, but it seems that the Prince maintained a 'perfect composure' and a 'modest demeanour' in the face of glances from the fair sex which 'flared from the eyes.' On 3rd June 1863 Prince Arthur resumed his studies at the Ranger's House. Soon afterwards, Elphinstone wrote to the Queen that his hay fever was better. This seems to have marked the beginning of asthmatic troubles which were to be the cause of great inconvenience and a good deal of suffering to Prince Arthur for the rest of his life.[8]

Towards the end of July, Prince Arthur set forth on his first visit to Wales; it was full of enjoyment. There were garlands and flags, triumphal arches and royal salutes, cheering and singing, High Sheriffs and Mayors and also something of the special Welsh genius. At Beddgelert, welcoming salvoes were fired by the miners from hillocks above the town and in the evening crowds assembled in front of Prince Arthur's rooms and sang national airs until a late hour. Elphinstone thought that the effect was almost magical but what impressed Prince Arthur was that all the quarrymen were self-taught. He climbed Snowdon and Cader Idris, saw many of the castles, rowed on the Wye and wrote a Journal, which Elphinstone hoped, vainly as it turned out, would improve his handwriting. There were also moments of farce, such as when, he wrote to his sister Louise from The Goat at Beddgelert, he went to Lake Lyndor and, while building a pier, Mr Jolley 'and me rolled into the water.'[9]

Between these excitements and others, such as the sight of a flying column of 1,500 Marines, two troops of Horse Artillery, two batteries of Foot Artillery and one of the new forty pounder Armstrong guns, which advanced onto Dartford Common under Prince Arthur's eye and for his special gratification, it was difficult for him to settle to regular lessons and trial examinations. This led to some complaints from Elphinstone, but Christmas and the New Year of 1864 at Osborne were a great success. From there, on 6th January, the Queen wrote to Elphinstone that she could not say how pleased she was with 'our Darling Boy', who, she found, was '*quite* what a boy & a little P^{ce} sh^{ld} be. May God protect him keep him good & innocent!' Elphinstone, however, was not inclined to take chances with the Almighty and when Prince Arthur went skating on a pond at Blackheath, though it was only two and a half feet deep, was on private property and therefore had only a limited number of people on it, and had a Drill Sergeant in attendance, he, nevertheless, decided that he must himself remain constantly in sight of the proceedings.[10]

A risk of another sort arose when the Queen suddenly mentioned the possibility of Prince Arthur succeeding his Uncle, the Prince Consort's elder brother, as the reigning Duke of Saxe-Coburg and Gotha. Elphinstone, however, was well prepared for this. Indeed, as early as December 1861, he had adumbrated three principal objectives for Prince Arthur's education; first, that the Prince should become a 'thoroughly instructed & scientific soldier,' secondly, 'that he might perhaps have to succeed his brother at Coburg' and, thirdly, the 'distant chance' of his becoming the heir to the throne of England. He was, therefore, now able to assure the Queen that all along he had been ready to turn Prince Arthur into a German, whenever that should be required. His course of studies was suited to 'any eventuality' and his general character was being developed to exclude any 'bigoted anglican tendency.' Though nothing had been done to develop a love of Germany, nothing had been done to weaken it, and German was spoken on three days a week. Associates with antipathies to things foreign were avoided, and, though Prince Arthur had played with some such, he had never become intimate with them. A series of visits to Germany would perfect his knowledge of the language and, Elphinstone now suggested, these should culminate in a stay there of three or four months in 1866, when he could study German military history and especially the campaign of 1813. The Queen agreed.[11]

She was an internationalist and not at all in accord with what she described as the 'John Bullism' of her subjects, which was so amply revealed in the character and attitudes of her Prime Minister, Lord Palmerston. Alas for Europe, internationalism was fading and a particularly severe phase of violent nationalism was nigh. By 1866, when Elphinstone would have had Prince Arthur learning about the campaign of 1813 with a view to becoming an enlightened German sovereign Prince, his Godfather's Prussia, propelled by Bismarck, had launched a new campaign to smash Austria's remaining hold on Germany and had opened the way for a new German Empire. This was to make it a far less comfortable place for reigning Dukes and, eventually, for everyone else as well. Fortunately for Prince Arthur, his Uncle Ernest's health took a turn for the better and the prospect of a new Duke of Coburg being required receded. Prince Arthur had come into contention because his eldest brother, the Prince of Wales, and his newly born son, Prince Albert Victor, were in direct line of succession to the British crown and were, therefore, excluded from Coburg. The next heir was Prince Alfred, but he was ruled out by his pronounced antipathy to everything German, an antipathy which was unlikely to be diminished by the company he kept as a serving officer in the Royal Navy. The many ironies and eventually awful tragedies which grew from these situations were still largely concealed from sight, though not entirely from that of the Prince of Wales. He thought that his youngest brother, Leopold, should be made the heir to Coburg so that his next two brothers, Alfred and Arthur, could be left free to follow their careers in the Navy and the Army. Clearly, the future King looked to the advantage to the Crown of the two Princes being placed high in each of the Services. The Queen was very annoyed. The sickly Leopold, even if he lived, would not do for Coburg, which needed a man with the health and strength to be active in all that was of importance, such as military affairs and sport.[12]

The next step was for Prince Arthur to learn to appreciate Germany in general, Coburg in particular and, above all, the Rosenau itself. On 24th June 1864, he crossed with Elphinstone and Jolley to Ostende in H.M.S. *Vivid*, and then went on to Brussels where he dined with the King. On 28th June, he reached Coblenz, where he was greeted by the Queen of Prussia. She was kind enough to say that the war between Prussia, of which Prince Arthur's sister was the Crown Princess, and Denmark, of which his sister-in-law's father was the King, was 'unfortunate.' He went on to Würzburg and so to Coburg and the Rosenau.[13]

Uncle Ernest was away in the Tyrol, but Aunt Alexandrine, the Duchess of Coburg, was there to greet him. She had got together a group of nineteen boys with whom Prince Arthur might play and the Duke presently returned to say that he hoped his nephew would enjoy his visit. According to Elphinstone's letters to the Queen, he certainly was doing so. Though the weather was not very good and they had to have fires in the Rosenau, he told her that Prince Arthur's recollections of it would probably be among the most pleasant of all his life. He was apparently spending his time fishing, catching butterflies, feeding young pheasants, seeing wild boar fed, mixing with haymakers, dining out of doors under the trees and playing with suitable companions. Jolley, however, was in bed with a chill. The Queen doubted the wisdom of having fires in the Rosenau which, she thought, would catch alight and burn down very easily. This seems to have upset Elphinstone. He wrote to Sir Charles Phipps, the Keeper of the Queen's Privy Purse, with a revised view of the visit. He now said that Prince Arthur had been at the Rosenau for a fortnight and that it had rained steadily on every day except two. He said that he had made the best of it in his letters to the Queen because he knew that she liked the place extremely, but, for Phipps's eyes, he now wrote that the place was unhealthy and that he was beginning to be alarmed by the damp exhalations from the thickly wooded and watery valley. This, he thought, had caused an outbreak of scarlet fever and other illnesses in several of the villages. It had also laid out Prince Arthur's cook, his valet and Jolley. Hailstones the size of musket balls had scattered the children who had tried to assemble for the annual Coburg festival and the interruption of the American trade, due to the civil war between the States, had caused widespread poverty. Unfortunately, the Keeper of the Privy Purse was away when this letter arrived and it was opened by the Queen's Private Secretary, General Grey. He, for whatever reason, simply handed it to the Queen. She wrote to Elphinstone that she was sorry that the weather had spoilt the visit for the grown-ups, who, no doubt, needed to be acclimatised. As children, the Prince Consort and his brother had lived at the Rosenau from May to October. Her doctor Jenner had declared the situation, the air and the soil wholesome and, in any case, Elphinstone ought to know that Prince Arthur had already had scarlet fever. She said she did not believe in the effects of climate on healthy people and, as Elphinstone had told her that Prince Arthur was enjoying everything so much, their stay should be prolonged by an extra four days. Elphinstone changed his line and told the Queen that Prince Arthur was enjoying himself, that the illness was due not to the locality, but to the weather, which might have been as bad or worse in England. Jolley would have been all right if he had not been ill before they arrived. Nevertheless, when, after serving the extra sentence of four days, Prince Arthur and Elphinstone left for Switzerland, it may be doubted if the former's enthusiasm to become the Duke of Coburg had been much increased.[14]

'You can not imagine how delighted I am with Switzerland,' Prince Arthur wrote to the Queen from the Hotel du Belvédère at Interlaken on 1st August. He thought it was 'the most lovely country of the world.' He climbed the mountains, including Mont Blanc, absorbed the beauty of the profusion of wild flowers and wrote the Queen dramatic letters about the grandeur of the scenery. One of her courtiers thought that 'Your Majesty smiled a little perhaps at Prince Arthur's description of "mighty Phoebus rising up of a sudden",' but he thought there was nothing wrong in the application of what had been learnt in class. Mr Jolley, ill himself and worried by the worse illness of his son, could no longer stand the pace and the Queen sent out Colonel Seymour to relieve him. In doing so, she announced to Elphinstone that, though he might have 'a little peculiarity of manner,' he was 'thoroughly refined in feeling & tone' and had travelled with the Prince Consort. The Colonel told Prince Arthur not to stoop, to hold himself upright and to take a small quantity of beer every day. Elphinstone, who noticed that Colonel Seymour was anxious to cure many little defects in Prince Arthur's manners, assured the Queen that what he could not cure, a stranger certainly could not.[15]

Whatever these little defects may have been, they seem not to have been apparent to Lady Eastlake, who was staying in the Hotel Beaurivage at Ouchy near Lausanne. When she came down to dinner one evening, she found two gentlemen and a boy at the foot of the stairs. Colonel Seymour presented her to the little Prince, who entered into conversation with her 'about the rain and the drought.' He struck her as being very like his mother 'with beautiful teeth and a winning smile.' She was 'tickled' that a boy should address her so boldly and look up at her with such a 'self-possessed kind of condescension,' as if reversing the usual order of things. He then said all that was kind and proper to Sir Charles Eastlake, not forgetting that he had been ill and saying to him, 'you don't look so well as I could wish.'[16]

Elphinstone's sense of outrage about some untruths which Prince Arthur had told and Colonel Seymour's scarcely less pronounced annoyance at his bad deportment seem not to have bothered the Queen much. When she saw him again at Balmoral in October, she found him 'as childlike ("kindlich") as ever but not near so childish.' She was able to talk openly and seriously to him and she was much pleased with his response. He had been out deer stalking with Grant, who was 'very plain spoken, so honest & *wise* & keeps fancy people in g^t order.' Grant had praised Prince Arthur's patience to the Queen and she had decided to keep him at Balmoral until 1st November. She told Elphinstone that he would then be willing to resume his lessons from Mr Jolley at the Ranger's House. Christmas and the New Year at Osborne were slightly less satisfactory. Prince Arthur had developed the habit of saying 'What' almost before a person had finished their sentence. The Prince of Wales had once had the same fault and Prince Leopold was developing it. The Queen thought that this was not only uncivil, but reminiscent of the old Royal Family. She did not wish her sons to resemble her Uncles and, especially, she did not wish Prince Arthur to resemble the Prince of Wales. She was also worried about Prince Arthur's handwriting and feared that it would become as bad as that of his elder brothers.

Elphinstone admitted that it was not what might be desired, but he said that Prince Arthur had physical difficulty in holding a pen firmly.[17]

Broader matters than these had, however, been settled at Osborne and, on 1st March 1865, Prince Arthur left for Marseilles, where he was to join the Admiralty yacht *Enchantress* for his first cruise in the Mediterranean. On the way he stopped in Paris and went to call on the Emperor Napoleon III at the Tuileries. Elphinstone told the Queen that there was a most interesting conversation, which lasted for more than half an hour. Prince Arthur's manner and ingenuousness were all that could be desired and it seemed that, if he had rehearsed his part many hundreds of times beforehand, he could not have done it better. There may have been a little of Elphinstone's improvisation in this because, as the British Ambassador, Lord Cowley, wrote to the Dean of Windsor, he had somehow missed his way in the Tuilleries and was not present at the Imperial audience. Lord Cowley was and, according to his account, the Emperor had questioned Prince Arthur about his brothers and sisters, his former travels and matters of that sort. He too was pleased with Prince Arthur, and told the Dean that 'a more charming boy, if I may speak so unreservedly of a Prince, I never came across.' Prince Arthur's own impression of the event seems to have been confined to the observation that the Emperor had grown fat but that the Empress was as pretty as ever.[18]

Sailing from Marseilles on 4th March, Prince Arthur was soon confronted with the combination of formality, education, social obligation and amusement with which he was to become more and more familiar. In Naples, the local British naval commander, Admiral Yelverton, came on board to pay his respects, an invitation came from Prince Umberto of Piedmont to dine at the Palace, and, though this was declined, Prince Arthur called upon him to express his gratitude. He was shown the antiquities from Pompeii and Herculaneum at the Museum by its director, Signor Fiorelli. He lunched at the Hotel Washington with his mother's half sister, Aunt Feodore, Princess Hohenlohe, and then went to see the amphitheatre and temple of Seraphis. That night, he dined with Admiral Yelverton on board his flagship, H.M.S. *Revenge*. Next day he was shown the excavations at Pompeii by Signor Fiorelli, who had superintended them. He noted that there was said to be another twenty years of work ahead. What had been revealed impressed him very much, especially the wall paintings, bath houses, cooking ovens and the mummified bodies with their looks of agony in which they had died. *Enchantress* then steamed out of the Bay of Naples and into a strong gale. After formalities

with Italian authorities at Syracuse and more rough weather, Prince
Arthur arrived off Tunis. Here, though *Enchantress* showed no flag to mark
his presence on board, Prince Arthur was received with a twenty-one gun
salute, visits from the Captains of the English, French and Italian men of
war there, the Tunisian Admiral of the Port, the 'General-in-Chief' and
Mr Richard Wood, the British Consul. Prince Arthur came ashore in the
Bey's barge and, escorted by a Squadron of Spahis, drove in the Bey's
carriage to the Palace of Dakril-Bey, from where he went to see Carthage.
In the evening he entertained the naval Captains to dinner on board
Enchantress. Next morning he drove off towards Tunis; there was no
formed road, the carriage got bogged down several times and the journey
of six miles took two and a half hours. When he got to Tunis, he was
received at the Town Palace by the Bey's brother and offered a sumptuous
lunch. It was too early in the day and, though he sat down out of courtesy,
Prince Arthur did not eat it. He then drove to the Bardo Palace and was
received by Princes and Ministers before being conducted to the grand
staircase where he was received by the Bey, who led him to the audience
chamber. The Bey, who showed himself to be most cordial and affectionate, presented Prince Arthur with the Husseinite Family Order. Then,
contrary to custom, they visited the Bey's harem. These attentions were
not wholly disinterested; the Bey's greatest ambition, it was said, was to
add a British Order to the many he had received from other European
Sovereigns. This was duly attended to and the Bey was sent the G.C.B.[19]

As *Enchantress* headed for Malta, the weather stayed bad, the worst for
twenty years, Elphinstone told the Queen. When they got there, the
defensive system of the Island was explained to Prince Arthur and then
demonstrated by a mock battle between attacking warships and defending
forts. According to the Governor and Commander-in-Chief, Sir Henry
Storkes, the warships succeeded in gaining their objectives without any
being sunk; according to Elphinstone, the superiority of the forts over the
ships was 'most manifest' and the latter would have been sunk within easy
range. The lesson for Prince Arthur was, therefore, somewhat obscure.
The next area of exploration was the Holy Land, where, while studying
the relevant passages of the scriptures, Prince Arthur visited many of the
scenes described in them and was even able to ascend the Mount of
Olives. A few days later, surrounded by ships of every mercantile nation,
Enchantress lay off Smyrna and Prince Arthur made an expedition to
Ephesus. The situation here, as in Malta, was also obscure. The location
of the Temple of Diana was still undiscovered, but the remains of the

town were being excavated for the British Museum by Mr Wood and Mr Hyde Clarke. The theatre was the largest Prince Arthur had yet seen, but it was overgrown with grass and shrubs. *Enchantress* went up the Dardanelles far enough for Prince Arthur to see some of the lines which had been constructed by the British and French in the Crimean War and, on the way back, he rode overland to see the excavations at Troy. Heading west, the yacht again ran into rough weather, but she was able to put in at Lemnos, Thasos, Cavallo, Philippi, Aganthus and so to reach the Athos peninsula. Here Prince Arthur visited several of the monasteries where he was received with 'marked attention & reverence.' *Enchantress* then set course for the Adriatic, calling at Syra, Santorini and Corfu, where Prince Arthur regretted the passing of British rule. The cruise ended opposite St Mark's in Venice. From there, Prince Arthur hurried across Europe, dining with the Tsar and Tsaritsa of Russia on the way, and reaching Balmoral in time for the Queen's birthday on 24th May, which she had ordered him to do.[20]

During the expedition, Prince Arthur had gained much experience of ceremonial requirements, some of them in very unfamiliar style, he had shown himself to be a good sailor in what, for most of the time, had been rough conditions. He had appeared to be adaptable, cheerful and energetic. A young officer of H.M.S. *Magicienne*, one of the escorting vessels, who saw many of the goings on, told his father that, for a boy of fifteen, Prince Arthur was a 'most astonishing little fellow.' He went sight seeing day after day, riding forty miles one day and lending a hand at pitching tents on another. He seemed always to be happy, never tired and ever willing to talk to any and everyone in a most natural and unaffected style. Another characteristic which became clearly apparent, was Prince Arthur's interest in and ability to recall the details of people's appearance and dress. At the Russian monastery on Mount Athos, he was struck by the *Agounmenos*, whom he described to the Queen as an old man with a long white beard reaching nearly down to his waist, rather short, and dressed in a long black robe coming down to his ankles, black stockings and slippers and a high black cap with a loose black veil which hung over his shoulders. He had also taken a big step forward in his knowledge of the sights of the world, which, in time, was to become vast. The Queen was well pleased and, having obtained Palmerston's permission, she sent Elphinstone the C.B. with, however, the possibly rather less than thrilling news that at the same time she had given Cowell the K.C.B.[21]

The Queen also decided that Prince Arthur would now undertake his first formal public engagement. This was the unveiling of a statue of his father at Tenby and it would involve making a speech. As the date of the ceremony drew near, an increased awareness of Prince Arthur's approaching manhood beset the Queen. She owned to Elphinstone that she trembled at the thought of her younger sons growing up; it seemed that she had almost given up caring about her elder ones. She wished that Prince Arthur could be kept '*as long* as we can *innocent* & childlike,' but she, nevertheless, took a realistic and helpful attitude to the ceremony. She scrapped the formal and stately terms of his speech, which had been drafted by Sir Charles Phipps, and substituted a new version of her own, which everyone, including especially Phipps, agreed was far more appropriate to a boy of fifteen; she told Prince Arthur that he must speak distinctly and not between his teeth as, she said, he was inclined to do. Prince Arthur left London resolved to do his best, but with a sick headache, a trouble which was often to bother him all his life. At a halt on the way, Sir Charles Phipps, who was in attendance, overheard a young lady 'remonstrating "Oh ! Mama I can't" but however she did with much grace, present a bouquet to H.R.H.' At Pembroke Dock, and the next day, at Tenby, there were guards of honour, royal salutes, cheering crowds, triumphal arches, garlands, speeches, a grand dinner and a dance. He was kind and affable to all, the little girls who presented the bouquets, the Members of Parliament, the local magnates, the Mayors and other big-wigs, yet he never seemed to be without 'the diffidence that becomes his age.' He looked pleased and his 'handsome face' produced a favourable impression on the crowds.[22]

The Queen also took an active, though not altogether so helpful a part in Prince Arthur's preparation for confirmation. She did not want this left unaided to the orthodox Church of England Mr Jolley; she wanted Elphinstone to read a book of religious instruction with Prince Arthur, which, at the corresponding stage, the Prince Consort had read with Princess Helena. The work was by Bretschneider and the Queen thought that it should be read in the original German. Elphinstone at first readily agreed, though he said that half an hour a day of it would be enough. When he saw the book, he said he would translate it into language suitable for a boy; when he began to study it, he found it incomprehensible and said that he would convey the general sense of it to Prince Arthur. Even so, he stressed to the Queen how valuable the book was and how interesting Prince Arthur found it. He seemed rather confused about Prince Arthur's reaction to these preparations. Within a period of sixteen days, he told the Queen that Prince Arthur had a better knowledge of religious truths than most boys of his age and then that his lack of interest in his preparation for confirmation was 'unfortunate.' Within another seventeen days, he reported that Prince Arthur understood and appreciated all that was involved in confirmation. Some of the gaps, if there were any, were filled in by Prince Arthur's Godfather and his mother. The King of Prussia told him that everyone failed, but what mattered was how seriously we erred and the remorse and wish to improve which followed. The Queen told him that, though he would not be his own master for another five years, he would 'in a religious point of view' be '*now* responsible to God.' He must seek help to resist the temptations to which he would be exposed by his age and position; he should ever be honest, truthful, courageous and loving to all and he was to follow 'the unflinching sense of duty' of another Godfather, the Duke of Wellington. Prince Arthur was confirmed by the Archbishop of Canterbury in Whippingham Church, near Osborne, on 26th April 1866.[23]

Plans now proceeded for his entry to the Royal Military Academy at Woolwich, subject to passing the necessary examinations. At the end of the year, Lieutenant Pickard, who had won the Victoria Cross in New Zealand, was selected to accompany him as a kind of mixture between a mentor and an equerry. Rooms at Woolwich were prepared for them and consideration was given to the means by which Prince Arthur might be insulated from the influence of the wrong kind of Cadets. The Queen dreaded him becoming harsh and stuck up; she distrusted the regular type of young officer and thought that notions of so-called manliness being forced on the Prince of Wales had destroyed his qualities of affection.[24]

So, with these broadening and yet circumscribed prospects, Prince Arthur came to the end of his tutelage and the approach of his military training. Elphinstone had undoubtedly done much for Prince Arthur, especially by encouraging and organising the habits of learning and observing, as well as by setting standards of taste and appreciation. In one respect, however, through lack of qualification on his own part, Elphinstone had failed. Prince Arthur had not received that training of the mind which is required for systematic analysis and the logical development of thought. His ideas tumbled out in staccato style and often appeared as non sequiturs. In years to come this was to be a handicap, though it was not an unusual one for there were many in higher positions than Prince Arthur was ever to occupy who suffered from the same defect.

CHAPTER 3

Military and Imperial Training 1867-1870

ON THE MORNING OF Friday 4th January 1867, Prince Arthur went up from Ranger's House to Buckingham Palace; it was freezing cold and snow lay about in the streets. Having thawed out in the Palace, he left at 10.30 for Great George Street where, in the Board Room of the Council for Military Education, he began a week of examinations for entrance to the Royal Military Academy at Woolwich. During the week, letters and telegrams flew prolifically between the Queen at Osborne and Elphinstone in Buckingham Palace. The Queen thought that, if Prince Arthur passed well, she might give him the Garter but, on second thoughts, she agreed with Elphinstone that it would be better to await his seventeenth birthday. She wanted Elphinstone to warn him against talking and laughing so much and so loud when with her as this was very trying. She was much concerned to keep him away from his elder brother, Prince Alfred, who, she feared, would give him 'foolish & mischievous advice.' On 11th January, Elphinstone telegraphed to the Queen that the exams were over and that, though the full results were not yet known, he already knew enough to be able to congratulate Her Majesty most sincerely. For the other would-be entrants to Woolwich, the examination was competitive; on this occasion, there were about 130 boys trying for the forty available places. Prince Arthur, however, did not join in this competition; though his papers were of the same standard, they were not the same papers as the others took and he was required, not to win, but only to qualify for a place.[1]

When, therefore, Prince Arthur arrived at the Academy on 11th February, he did not come in the role of an ordinary Cadet. He signed the usual papers, met the professors and masters and then had tea with the

Governor, General Sandham. On the next day he was installed as a Cadet in Her Majesty's Army and became bound by the articles of war. It had been arranged that he would muster at the head of the role, but fall in on parade according to size. Though he was two years and five months younger than the oldest of the other entrants and four months younger than the youngest, only seven of them were shorter, and three lighter than he. His height was 5' 5$\frac{7}{10}$" and his weight 8 stone 1 lb. 'You will be pleased to hear,' he wrote to the Queen within a few days, 'that I like being at the Academy very much.' He found the work interesting and the life agreeable. For a Cadet, he had already done an unusual thing; he had driven up to London in his pony cart and called upon the Commander-in-Chief, the Duke of Cambridge. Uncle George, however, was so busy that he had only seen him for a few minutes. He continued to live at Ranger's House where, in the evenings, Mr Jolley gave him lessons and whence he often went up to London for concerts or other cultural treats and sometimes to attend Courts.[2]

Prince Arthur spent his seventeenth birthday with the Queen at Windsor but returned to Woolwich in the evening to attend a ball given by General Warde. He was received at it with the national anthem and he opened the dancing with Mrs Warde. He stayed until one o'clock and danced about thirteen times with the daughters of four Generals, two Colonels and a naval Commodore. Soon after, he went to another ball, this time in the Woolwich Mess. The proceedings began at ten, Prince Arthur danced nearly every dance and was disinclined to leave at 2.30, which was the time set by Elphinstone. Then, on 7th June, he was able to cut a new figure at a third ball. He appeared again in his Cadet's uniform, but now, for the first time, it was decorated with his birthday present, the star and riband of the Order of the Garter. Elphinstone thought that this set off the uniform very well and he told the Queen that the Prince had looked particularly nice. Apparently there were many instances of his picking up cards and handkerchiefs 'accidentally dropt by some lady near him.' Another late night was provided by a dinner party at Marlborough House given by the Prince of Wales, after which they went to a concert. He thought that the Princess of Wales was looking very well, despite the fact that she had to be wheeled into the dining room in a bed, and he also reported that his sister, Alice, was looking very well; Elphinstone thought that she looked pale and weary.[3]

The time which the Queen had so much dreaded had now come, or at least was getting very near. Indeed, she was most anxious about what

Prince Arthur might notice and what he knew. When his sister, Helena, was expecting her first baby in the Spring of 1867, the Queen found it necessary to tell Elphinstone to drop him a hint not to ask questions and not to make remarks. More than a year later and after his eighteenth birthday, she still wondered if Prince Arthur's eyes were opened to matters which she knew were often known to much younger boys. While she preferred that his eyes should remain closed for as long as possible, she recognised the danger, in that case, of them being opened by unhallowed lips and coarse jokes. The Prince Consort had left some suitable instructions to which Elphinstone could have recourse in case of need.[4]

Meanwhile, Prince Arthur's military education was proceeding with effects which were more easily discernible. In June 1867, he went to Paris and, having been to see the Exhibition there, he attended a review of the Garde Impériale at the Tuileries. Wearing his Cadet's uniform embellished with the Garter, he rode down the line of three thousand Infantry and eighteen hundred Cavalry. He was invited to join the Emperor Napoleon in his Camp at Chalons, the 'Aldershot' of France, for the army manoeuvres and the great Imperial Review, which would precede them. Some 28,000 Infantry, 2,500 Cavalry, seven hundred Engineers and ninety-six guns were involved. Prince Arthur was supposed to be incognito, but he was everywhere recognised, possibly because he had been received at the station by the commanding General's A.D.C., escorted to his pavilion by a detachment of Cavalry and then received by the General and his entire staff 'en grande tenue.' Nonetheless, he began to make his own observations, which, of course, was the point of attending other people's manoeuvres. He was interested in the French breech-loading guns, and he told the Queen that he saw an officer with one of these get off fourteen shots in one minute and that ten of them hit the target. He thought their artillery was not as good as ours and that their manner of grooming horses and cleaning harness was definitely inferior to the British. He had some conversation with a General who had just returned from Mexico where French bayonets had failed to save the unfortunate Emperor Maximillian from the firing squad.[5]

During his visit to France, Prince Arthur had suffered a good deal from hay fever but otherwise had been in his usual robust health. In early October, however, after a very cold railway journey back from Balmoral, he became seriously ill, his temperature soared, his pulse rate rose to 108 and his mind began to wander. Though in a form modified by vaccination, he had contracted smallpox. Several doctors came and, despite the Queen's strong objection, a nurse too. To reassure the Queen, Elphinstone arranged that the nurse should be in an adjoining room with her door shut; the door between Elphinstone's and the sick room was always open so the nurse could not get at the patient without his knowledge. The treatment included dressing the spots with collodion, soup twice a day, meat and two glasses of claret once a day, desultory conversation with Elphinstone while the latter sat in the room writing letters, the reading aloud by Pickard of Shakespeare from an expunged edition and of Schiller in a German edition by Elphinstone. It was very successful and, within a few days, Prince Arthur was well on the way to recovery and enjoying the *Illustrated London News*, of which he was very fond.[6]

After recuperating in Dover, Prince Arthur returned to his military education at Woolwich; it continued to be a good deal wider than that on offer to the other Cadets. On 26th November, he entertained the Lieutenant-Governor of the Academy and the Astronomer Royal to dinner at Ranger's House and the next day, wearing full dress Cadet's uniform, he opened the new recreation rooms for artillerymen. He was received by General Warde, who conducted him to a gallery crowded with officers and their families; the national anthem was played and then a specially composed 'Prince Arthur Gallop.' General Warde made a lengthy speech and Prince Arthur said three or four appropriate sentences to the men. Such displays of maturity failed, however, to save him from the Queen's reproof. She told Elphinstone to tell him that she was sorry he had taken up smoking without first mentioning it to her. She would not have objected to it in moderation, especially when out in the cold at Balmoral. She did not wish him to follow the examples of the Prince of Wales and Prince Alfred, who stayed up late at night smoking, nor did she wish him to do it much indoors. She wished he would be more open with her; she would always be sympathetic to his wishes and if she did not grant them, it would only be because they were not for his own good.[7]

The Queen may have granted too much, or so at least *The Times* thought, in allowing Prince Arthur to stay at Knowsley and, from there, to go about in public with Lord Derby. He was the Prime Minister and it might seem that the Queen's son was showing a bias towards the Conservative Party. Prince Arthur, who was greatly impressed by the fine buildings in Liverpool and by the docks, did not seem to agree. He told the Queen that he had been much cheered and that the people seemed pleased to see him and his sister and brother-in-law, Princess Helena and

Prince Christian, who had gone with him. He had also had the benefit of shooting in company with such well known exponents of the art as Lord Wharncliffe, Lord Courtnay, Mr de Grey and Major Cathcart. At Woolwich, Prince Arthur was given the duties of a Sergeant on parade to accustom him to delivering the words of command in a clear voice. On 21st February 1868, he received a visit from Prince and Princess Christian. He took them round with two Generals 'in attendance.' Nowadays he took lunch in his own private room which, Elphinstone told the Queen, had the advantage that he could have a glass of wine. When lunching with the Cadets he had always partaken of the beer which they drank so as not to mark himself out.[8]

The subjects he studied included the theory of the construction of field works, siege operations, pontooning and bridge construction, escalading, mining operations, the firing of fougasses, signalling and telegraphy and the firing of submarine mines and torpedoes by electricity. He went to stay in the Royal Hotel at Southend whence, usually driving himself in a phaeton, he went to Shoeburyness for practical instruction in firing large and small guns. One night the 'little village' of Southend was brilliantly illuminated in Prince Arthur's honour. There was a fireworks display and two or three thousand people appeared outside the hotel and cheered Prince Arthur when he came onto the balcony. Then, in June 1868, his course came to an end and he had to face a public oral examination in fortification, artillery and surveying. He did well and was passed for a commission in the Royal Engineers. On 23rd June, he arrived at the Brompton Barracks in Chatham to begin his training as an officer in the Regiment. He was met by the Garrison Commander, a guard of honour and a Royal Salute before getting down to the routine work, which was not very demanding. Nothing was required after 3.0 p.m., which left plenty of time for rowing and sailing with young fellow officers and Elphinstone to supervise.[9]

Presently, there was the excitement of welcoming back to Chatham the 10th Company of the Regiment from its service in the remarkable and successful Abyssinian Campaign. Prince Arthur met them at Rochester and then rode through the town at their head. Seventy-five of the men, waited on by their N.C.Os, sat down to a banquet in the Brompton Barracks and Prince Arthur walked round the tables talking to the bronzed soldiers. That night there was a grand dinner in honour of the victorious commander, General Lord Napier, who sat on the right hand of the Commander-in-Chief, the Duke of Cambridge; Prince Arthur sat on his left hand. In his speech, the Duke referred to one, who by his birth was among the highest in the realm, and yet was now taking the position of the junior Subaltern in the Regiment, and to the other, who by his own worth had shown what rewards were open to all.[10]

Soon after this, the junior Subaltern was given the duty of throwing a bridge across a ditch so that an advancing column could cross it. The first troops to do so were lead by an officer at the charge, probably, Elphinstone later concluded, with the intention of making a smart impression on Prince Arthur. They got across all right but then there was a check ahead and, despite Prince Arthur's attempts to warn the very peppery officer in charge of these troops, the bridge became congested with men marking time at the double; the bridge collapsed, one man was killed and fourteen were wounded. Prince Arthur was not blamed for the disaster since his bridge had not been intended for such stress.[11]

Whosoever's may have been the exact responsibility for the collapse of Prince Arthur's bridge, his posting to the Royal Artillery owed nothing to it. That move was in accordance with a preconceived plan. Prince Arthur was to be given a wide experience of the Army. He was not intended for any particular Corps or Regiment; the plan was to train him to become a judicious Commander-in-Chief and, in the meantime, to make use of him for the discharge of public Royal functions, which, since the Prince Consort's death, the Queen had largely given up. One such of particular interest was Prince Arthur's visit to Middlesborough in August 1868 to open the Albert Park. It had been donated to the town by its first Mayor, Mr H. W. F. Bolckow. Born a German, this man had first come to England at the age of twenty-one in 1827 and first to Middlesborough in 1841, when the town had a population of six or seven thousand. He had formed the partnership of Bolckow and Vaughan, a firm which bought raw material and worked it up into bars, rails and castings. In 1848, they began to mine their own material at Skinningrove and, by the time Prince Arthur came upon the scene, they employed some 8,000 men who mined 750,000 tons of ore and made up 300,000 tons of pig and manufactured iron per annum. Bolckow, it was said, always favoured councils of conciliation in trade disputes. He was now able to entertain Prince Arthur in grand style at his newly built home, Marten Hall, some three miles from the town. It was in the French style and, according to Elphinstone, resembled the Tuileries. Wealth was everywhere visible, there was much gilding and numerous valuable pictures; Bolckow had determined to spend £6,000 to £8,000 on the entertainment of the first Royal visitor to

Middlesborough since 1838. On that occasion, Prince Arthur's great uncle, the Duke of Sussex, had been entertained in a small dining room; now the great nephew sat down with four hundred others in Middlesborough's huge banqueting hall. In the interval, the population had quadrupled.[12]

On 2nd November 1868, Prince Arthur joined the Gunners at Woolwich. Elphinstone told the Queen that he looked well in his new uniform, mounted on his new charger and serving in a Battery which was one of the smartest in the Army. He began to learn how to manoeuvre a Battery in the field and he took his turn as Orderly Officer. His commanding officer was General Warde, whom he knew well from his Cadet days. There were plenty of amusements, including an endless series of balls, and Prince Arthur took piano lessons with Mr Gardner every evening. On 9th February 1869, Prince Arthur gave his first ball; it was at Ranger's House. The Queen wrote to him wishing that she could '(unseen) see *you* doing the honours.' The dancing was kept up till past 4.0 a.m. but, Elphinstone told the Queen, care was taken to have only quiet, humorous and pretty figures, such as one in which the ladies stood behind a curtain holding out crackers; these were then seized by the gentlemen and the curtain fell to show who would dance with whom.[13]

The Queen's authorisation of this ball was soon followed by a much bolder one. She decided that Prince Arthur should visit Ireland and then go to Canada for an extended term of service. As she well knew, this involved some risk. Her Private Secretary, General Grey, told her that the Irish peasant was engaged in a war against the system and felt as much entitled to take a life as in any other war. The Home Secretary, Mr H. A. Bruce, warned the Queen that agrarian outrages continued. He thought, however, that the Fenians, who had lately been much in the news, were now turning their attention to English towns with large Irish populations. There were also the Hibernians, but these, apparently, were mainly occupied with fighting the Fenians. The latter were also active in America but Mr Bruce thought, incorrectly as it turned out, that they lacked the funds to carry out an invasion of Canada. The Queen settled these difficulties by telling Elphinstone that no risks should be run by sea or on land.[14]

On the morning of 5th April 1869, H.M.S. *Vivid*, with Prince Arthur on board, raised the Royal Standard in Kingstown Harbour. All the ships there responded and the *Royal George* fired a salute. At noon the Viceroy of Ireland, Lord Spencer, came on board to welcome Prince Arthur and they then disembarked. A second salute from the *Royal George* was taken up ashore by the Horse Artillery. There was a Guard of Honour and a crowd of thousands of people. On his arrival by train in Dublin, Prince Arthur was welcomed by the Lord Mayor and Aldermen. He replied in a clear and audible voice. At Viceregal Lodge, Lady Spencer awaited him at the door. In the afternoon, he rode out with Lord and Lady Spencer. Throughout the day he wore plain clothes distinguished only by the star of the Order of St Patrick. He was charmed by the warmth of his reception by the people and Elphinstone told the Queen that the Spencers, who had spared neither trouble nor expense, had selected their house party so that there was plenty of fun without any approach to anything fast. These other guests were Lord and Lady de Vesci, Lord and Lady Charles Bruce, Lord Suffield, Mr Whyte Melville, the novelist, Mr E.Ross, the famous rifle shot, Mr Horace Seymour, Colonel Henry Wellesley and Mrs John Leslie. The last was, perhaps, the least known, but in later years she was to become the mother-in-law of another Mrs John Leslie, née Léonie Jerome of New York, one of the great influences upon Prince Arthur's later life.[15]

Outside Dublin, Prince Arthur's reception varied, or at least was variously reported. When he drove from Dundrum to Count Jarnac's castle of Thomastown, people ran for miles beside the carriage; at Cashel the town was full to suffocation due to Prince Arthur's presence and the races. The address in the market place, however, was never finished because the speaker was overcome with emotion. Such enmity as existed was aimed at the British party, Elphinstone told the Queen, and not at her or her family to whom there was strong loyalty. Sir Charles Napier, reporting, not to the Queen, but to the Home Secretary, took a rather different line. After travelling with Prince Arthur from Fermoy to Killarney, he found that the reception had been 'cordial' but 'not enthusiastic.' He thought that people who had recently had Fenian sentiments on their lips found it hard to change to expressions of loyalty. He believed that the danger of Prince Arthur being shot was no greater than in England and that harm had been done by the precautions taken to safeguard him. He thought that if the Prince went about freely and trustfully, 'his prepossessing manner would do a great deal to dissipate the remains of Fenianism and bring back a better tone.' Elphinstone was relieved when it was time to travel north. As they went, he noticed how the faces and the language became more and more Scotch; the wild Irish yell of the south was replaced by the more sober and more demonstrative welcome of the north. In Londonderry, Prince Arthur was received with immense cheering. Even so, within a few hours, there was fighting in the streets between rival religious groups. Someone fired a shot and, apparently without any order being given, the police opened fire. Two men were killed, another critically wounded and several badly hurt. Most of the damage was done by police bullets, but some of their men were injured by stones thrown at them by the demonstrators. It seemed that Prince Arthur's presence in the town had brought matters to a head.[16]

Two more Irish excitements were in store; at Portrush there was enthusiastic cheering from a large crowd but suddenly a rocket flew through it and then another crashed into Prince Arthur's hotel nearly setting the room alight. This, however, was judged to be no more than Irish good heartedness. In Belfast, Elphinstone permitted a carriage drive to take place only after he had been assured by two detectives, whom he had sent ahead, and the Mayor and Magistrate that this would be safe. Prince Arthur's reception was almost overwhelming and compared, in Elphinstone's opinion, with the enthusiasm which had greeted the Princess of Wales on her first appearance in London. For fear of inflaming opinion, however, there were no speeches beyond a brief response by Prince Arthur to the proposal of the Queen's health at a lunch in the Town Hall. There was an easier atmosphere on the Isle of Man, where he called on the way home. A reporter from *Mona's Herald and Fargher's Isle of Man Advertiser* judged him to resemble very much the Prince of Wales as he had been five or six years ago, 'with the difference that Prince Arthur has a far more pleasing expression on his face.'[17]

On 31st July 1869, the Commander-in-Chief came to Woolwich to see the Artillery manoeuvres. Prince Arthur was in command of his Battery for the last time and the Duke of Cambridge thought that he acquitted himself most creditably. That evening, in his honour, there was a grand farewell dinner in the Mess. The Duke of Cambridge gave his health and nothing, he later told the Queen, could have been more gratifying than the manner in which Prince Arthur replied. He spoke 'feelingly & well, & without the slightest nervousness or hesitation.' Elphinstone thought that it was 'altogether the most successful thing he has yet done.' Prince Arthur's accomplished performance took both the Commander-in-Chief and the Secretary for War, Mr Cardwell, by surprise. Whether or not his next move would be so successful or, indeed, if it was advisable at all, was quite another question.[18]

About the plans for going to Ireland and to Canada, there was

something of the frying pan and the fire. The Governor-General of
Canada, Sir John Young, reported to the Colonial Secretary, Lord
Granville, that, as Fenian hopes of an invasion of Canada from the United
States faded, so the chances of them turning to assassination increased.
They were very active in Montreal, where it was planned that Prince
Arthur would stay. It would be impossible to ensure Prince Arthur's
safety, especially if he kept late hours in places off the beaten track. He
firmly advised against a Royal visit. On the other hand, the British
Minister in Washington, Mr Thornton, advised the Foreign Secretary,
Lord Clarendon, that there would be little danger. It might be worth
employing an American detective to look out for any Fenian moves from
the United States, but he doubted it because anything discovered would,
in those circumstances, have to be reported to the American government
and the cost of such a detective would be high. On these opinions, the
responsible Ministers, Granville and Clarendon and Mr Gladstone, who
was the Prime Minister, had to decide what advice to give the Queen.
They agreed that the Fenians based in America would be a serious threat
to Prince Arthur's life if he went to Canada and they advised the Queen
that he should not do so. Gladstone specially confirmed that he endorsed
this opinion and Clarendon stressed that he did not share Mr Thornton's
lack of anxiety. The Queen was not impressed; she sent Elphinstone to
London to get the advice changed.[19]

This led the Prime Minister to shift his ground a little. He now
proposed to the Queen that they should consider 'how best to arrange a
departure from the present plan in such a way as not to excite speculation,
and give rise to constructions which might indicate indeed but in
indicating grossly exaggerate, the true cause.' He 'humbly' suggested that
Prince Arthur should proceed to Canada, apparently as arranged, but
that, before he joined his Regiment in Montreal, he should be recalled to
Europe. This would have to be for some 'suitable and adequate purpose'
sufficient to 'satisfy the public mind,' such as to attend the opening of the
Suez Canal. Elphinstone told the Queen that this was a good idea, but she
was still not impressed. She wondered if the danger was really so great;
she did not wish carefully laid plans for Prince Arthur's military training
to be disrupted, especially by such a silly idea as sending him to the
opening of the Suez Canal. That would be of no use to his professional
training and a young Prince, she said, 'should be made to work hard, and
not to be always representing at great ceremonies.' Prince Arthur was to
be kept employed and not allowed to idle at home, where he would be

exposed to the many temptations which beset all young men, 'but Princes more than any others.'[20]

This appears to have crushed Gladstone, but, if he had revealed his prolix style and the devious nature of his mind, the Queen now reacted with the inconsistency of hers. Nothing of a foolhardy nature was to be undertaken, Elphinstone was enjoined, and dear Arthur 'must not over exert himself for he looked very thin & not very strong tho' quite healthy.' Elphinstone duly promised that he would venture only on the safest ground so as to bring Prince Arthur back from Canada increased in stature, health and wisdom, but unaltered in innocence and pureness of heart.[21]

On 22nd August 1869, after a voyage of eight days from Liverpool, Prince Arthur arrived at Halifax; it was a Sunday so he paused until the next day. He then landed under a Royal Salute and rode into the town on horseback to the accompaniment of loud cheering. He thought the town, situated so near the sea and with plenty of woodland, a very nice place. The streets, however, were small and badly paved. Rails ran down their centres and cars were dragged along these at a very rapid pace to the extreme danger of other carriages and horses. For the next eight weeks his life was a whirl of receptions, drives, military reviews, balls, shooting expeditions and tours. Among the many places he visited were Prince Edward Island, Pictou, Shediac, Saint John, Fredericton, Woodstock, Grand Falls, Quebec, Petrolia, London, Niagara Falls and, across the border, Buffalo, then, back in Canada, Paris, Brantford, Hamilton, Toronto and Ottawa. Towards the end of October, he came to rest in Montreal where he joined his new Regiment, the 1st Battalion, the Rifle Brigade, and resumed a more normal life. During these weeks, Prince Arthur had lived and travelled sometimes in the greatest luxury and grandeur and at others in much harsher and more primitive ways. In Quebec, he stayed at Spencer Wood, a charming residence with a perfect cuisine. Nearby, on the St Lawrence, a steamer lay in readiness to take him where he pleased. On the last leg of his journey to this idyllic place, it had, however, taken him four days to cover 253 miles and nine or ten horses a day were needed to drive along the seemingly endless country roads. On hunting expeditions, the going was even rougher and, forging out from Hopewell in pursuit of moose, he went by bullock drawn sledge and, at night, slept under canvass.[22]

The newness and excitement of these Canadian experiences drew Prince Arthur out of the stereotype which had previously governed his letters to the Queen. At first the old style remained; his reception at Halifax had been most gratifying and nothing could have been more loyal or enthusiastic, but he went on to note that the harbour was large enough to contain the entire British Fleet. In Fredericton, he had scarcely 'jumped' into his carriage before he was bombarded with nosegays; he hardly dared to look up for fear of getting a black eye. The swirling waters of the mighty river Saint John seemed as though they would wash all before them. Quebec was like a Norman town, except for the tin roofs and the St Lawrence, still four or five miles wide though four hundred miles from the sea, was magnificent in size and beauty beyond what he had expected. Niagara Falls were 'the grandest & finest that one can possibly imagine.' The amount of timber floated down the Canadian rivers was 'something fabulous' and, he thought it would be almost absurd to paint the scarlet, yellow and orange of the trees around Montreal, as one would be accused of exaggeration. Above all, he was enchanted with the Canadians themselves. The more he was in Canada, he told the Queen, 'the more I like & admire the people,' whom he found to be 'fine, honest, free-thinking but loyal.' He was delighted by the pride they took in abhorring the idea of being annexed to the United States and he was sure that, if there was an American or a Fenian invasion, Canada would rise against it to a man.[23]

Such a possibility could not be ruled out. Relations between the United States and Canada were uneasy. Substantial opinion in the former favoured annexation of the latter, and many believed that this was inevitable if Canada's resources were to be developed and her commercial prosperity secured. These ideas did not, however, necessarily imply American hostility to Prince Arthur. For example, a report in the *New York Herald*, which assumed the desirability of American annexation, also made polite references to the Prince, whom it described as unassuming, courteous, intelligent and manly. Numerous letters arrived from Chicago, New York and the far West inviting Prince Arthur to visit the United States, with the result that Mr Gladstone and Lord Granville once more had to consider his movements, this time from a diplomatic point of view. The Queen was duly told that her government desired the visit and, on 6th October, she authorised it. Some days earlier Prince Arthur, with the Governor-General, had already made a brief excursion into the United States in response to an invitation from the Colonel commanding the troops at Buffalo. He spent four or five hours there driving round the town, which was the railway link between California and New York and

Canada; it was also thought to be a main Fenian base and it was from here that their invasion of Canada in 1867 had been launched. In going there, Prince Arthur had ignored reports that the Fenians would seize him as a hostage for the granting of an Irish Republic. His guide for the occasion was former President Millard Fillmore, who had been inaugurated in 1850 after the death in office of President Taylor.[24]

The second visit was to be altogether a more extensive and important affair. At about noon on 21st January 1870 Prince Arthur arrived by train in New York and was met by a large crowd which, so Elphinstone told the Queen, maintained perfect order. According to a press reporter, it and the police made a disgraceful rush which engulfed the Prince and endangered his life. There was, this reporter added, no welcome; only a few straggling cheers and a vulgar curiosity. The British Minister, Mr Thornton, took Prince Arthur to a hotel on Fifth Avenue, where his rooms were decorated with pictures of Queen Victoria and Prince Albert and a bust of Richard Cobden. After lunch, Prince Arthur walked in Central Park and down Broadway; the streets were crowded and the people seemed to recognise him. He was much impressed by the commercial bustle of the place but not by the architecture, which he thought was decidedly inferior to that of Montreal. In the evening he visited Wallack's Theater and the next morning left for Washington in a drawing-room car on the train. There he stayed with Mr Thornton at the British Legation. Washington, he wrote to the Queen, was a long straggling town of 150,000 people with appallingly badly paved streets and a deserted look. There were few good private houses and most people seemed to live in the numerous hotels. The White House reminded him of Frogmore and he admired the Grecian Capitol building. On 24th January, Prince Arthur went to the White House to call on the President, General Grant, and his wife. This and the two further meetings which followed were not very lively occasions, nor were they entirely cordial.[25]

Two nights later, the President entertained Prince Arthur to dinner to meet the Secretary of State and a number of Senators and Represent-atives, but not, Thornton thought, the most important ones. Mrs Grant did her best to make the affair pleasant, but the President seemed rather cold and distant. This was apparently due to a mixture of shyness, ignorance of the usages of society and the feeling that politeness to the Prince would lower his dignity and that of America. In Elphinstone's opinion, the ruling party was influenced by the mob and especially the Irish. If this was so, it did not apply to the Secretary of State, Mr Fish, or to the distinguished General Sherman, both of whom, when they gave dinners for Prince Arthur, were most cordial and, in the General's case, most amusing as well. To Prince Arthur, the Americans seemed to be rough and vulgar and, as he put it to the Queen, to have a total absence of manners and modesty, but he thought they were good and kind at heart, took trouble to please and had no thought of expense. He told his sister, Louise, that most of the young ladies were very pretty, extremely well dressed and great fun. He said they came out with no end of queer Yankee expressions which he was learning so that he could fire them off when he got home. Nearly sixty years later he was still to remember how he had lost his heart and divided it between Miss Wordsworth and Miss Lou King, both of whom, he recalled, were very handsome and charming.[26]

This, however, was less than the whole picture. Mr Thornton and Elphinstone were inundated with menacing letters and intelligence of assassination and abduction plots. In New York, six men, two of them apparently armed, had appeared outside Mr Stoughton's house which Prince Arthur was due to leave at 10.0 after dining there. He had, however, left twenty minutes early and the would-be kidnappers or assassins, having missed their prey, retired to the local Fenian Club. News of some of these plots fell into Prince Arthur's own hands but, according to Thornton, he did not seem to care about them. Mr Gladstone professed himself to be shocked by the President's coolness to Prince Arthur, but 'As Your Majesty will remember in Tennyson's Guinever,' he told her, 'scorn was allowed as part of his defect.' As to the six Fenians in New York, he explained to the Queen that their action was probably inspired by desperation following the favourable reception in Ireland of his Government's Land Bill.[27]

The Fenians apart, it may well be that neither the President nor his countrymen intended any real discourtesy to Prince Arthur and he certainly showed no sign of taking their reception of him in any way other than gratefully. He was warmly welcomed in Boston and, before he returned to Canada, he received a message from the President's A.D.C. conceding that, for a Prince to win golden opinions in a Republican country, was a difficult task. He hoped, however, that Prince Arthur had understood that, despite the omission of many of the forms to which he was used, his reception was meant to be a welcome to the son of a Sovereign who was universally esteemed in America. Prince Arthur also received a farewell letter from General Sherman, who expressed the hope that the Prince would become a constant link between two great nations committed to 'the high duty of spreading their peculiar civilisation to the whole world.' Late on the night of 7th February 1870, Prince Arthur arrived back in Montreal, where, according to Elphinstone, he was once more in a climate and among people that he liked.[28]

A few days later he went to Ottawa to attend the opening of Parliament, the first member of the Royal Family to do so. The Canadians made the most of the event and there were several glittering occasions. Prince Arthur stayed with the Governor-General and Lady Young at Rideau Hall. One night there were charades in which he took part before an audience of about a hundred Ministers, Senators, Representatives and officers of the garrison and their families. 'I may say,' he told the Queen, 'I knew everyone of them.' A Parliamentary ball was given in his honour, to which two thousand people came and danced on the specially boarded floor of the Senate Chamber. Nothing on such a scale had been attempted in Canada before; Prince Arthur thought it a beautiful sight and, despite the fact that he had nothing but duty dances with the wives and daughters of Senators and Representatives, a great success. He attended several debates in Parliament and his comments on how they compared with those he had heard in the American Congress went down well with his Canadian friends. There was a grand masquerade on the skating rink to which fifteen hundred people came. The scene was brilliantly lit by gas; almost all the ladies were beautiful skaters and Prince Arthur remained several hours watching the pretty sight of them on the ice. In later years, he would often recall of mature Canadian ladies of his acquaintance that he had first met them as girls in '69 or '70. In the meantime, however, he told his sister, Louise, that due to following her advice so closely, he had become something of a woman hater.[29]

Lent was scrupulously observed in Canada; all the balls and other festivities ceased. Among the advantages of this for Prince Arthur was the time it afforded him, when he got back to his house, Rose Mount, in Montreal, to work for his promotion to Captain examinations. This was quite a change, for his duties with the Rifle Brigade, though constant, had been nothing like as demanding as those which he undertook as a personification of the Crown. For the latter task, he was ideally suited by his courtesy and tact, his good looks and dignity, his wish to do right and his love of novelty. The Canadian experience, by enlarging his horizons and increasing his self-confidence, marked a decisive step forward in his Imperial training. The Queen was highly delighted. From all sides she heard the most gratifying accounts of her child's conduct and success. She had 'never felt so proud of any of her children.' The Prince of Wales, once more, was causing serious anxiety. He had been, from what the Queen described as imprudence and thoughtlessness, dragged in the dirt by getting mixed up in what she said was the most disgusting and scandalous trial on record. This was the Mordaunt divorce case, in which the heir to the throne was cited as a co-respondent. The Queen hoped that Prince Arthur could be prevented from reading the details in the press, but she also wanted Elphinstone to warn him of the danger to the future of the monarchy which was caused by his brother's imprudence.[30]

On 15th May, Prince Arthur wrote to the Queen for her birthday on 24th but, when it came to the day itself, he forgot to send a telegram. He later explained that this oversight was due to the 'excitement & confusion' caused by the Fenian invasion. He went as one of Lord Alexander Russell's A.D.Cs. to the headquarters at Saint John near the frontier. He told the Queen that, after fighting all day on 25th May, the Fenians had fled the field leaving behind arms, ammunition, accoutrements, five dead and twenty wounded. He said he had taken no part in the battle himself. Perhaps, however, he understated the case a little for, in later years, he was to recall how he had difficulty in preventing his men from opening fire while the Fenians were still on American territory; as soon as they crossed into Canada, he remembered, 'we opened fire and they rapidly broke up.' Canada easily survived the Fenian threat; whether or not she could survive the greater one of American annexation and, if she could, the rivalry between the Catholic French and the Protestant British within her own boundaries, remained to be seen. Prince Arthur was an optimist about these matters and was always in the future to be a believer in and advocate of Canadian national development. Canada was a great country, he wrote in a farewell letter to the Prime Minister, Sir John Macdonald, and he felt sure that in time it would become one of the most powerful countries in the world. He said that in Canada he had spent the pleasantest and most interesting time he might ever experience. On 8th July 1870, amid talk that he would one day return as Governor-General of the Dominion, Prince Arthur took his leave and sailed for England from Quebec in H.M.S. Crocodile. The Governor-General told Lord Granville that the Prince had visited nearly all the important towns in all the Provinces and that he had everywhere shown an unfailing courtesy and ready acquiescence in whatever was needed to meet the wishes of the people.[31]

In Europe people were being much less accommodating and, as soon as he landed in England, Prince Arthur heard from the Queen that there was the danger of a war between France and Prussia.[32]

CHAPTER 4

Lessons in Courtship
1870-1877

THE OUTBREAK OF THE Franco-Prussian War, this '*frightful* war,' as the Queen described it, further increased her belief in the 'utter uselessness' of inter-marrying with foreign Princes or Princesses and she was, therefore, moved to consent to a marriage between her daughter, Princess Louise, and a subject, the Marquess of Lorne, who was the son and heir of the Duke of Argyll. She did this in the face of opposition from the Prince of Wales and the Duke of Cambridge, who thought that, for the Queen's daughter to marry a commoner, was lowering to the Crown. The Queen told Elphinstone to warn Prince Arthur against any such silly ideas. She duly found him 'very helpful & most dear & kind & a g^t comfort.' The Duke of Cambridge was also in need of comfort, but for a different reason. When Prince Arthur went to see him on 26th July 1870, he found him disheartened by the war, which had led the Government to tell him to put the Army into an efficient state, but not to grant any extra money with which to do it. On the following day, Prince Arthur found the head of that Government, Mr Gladstone, very much grieved about the war. He told the Queen he had seldom seen a man take anything more to heart.[1]

These reactions reflected issues which were, or would become, central to Prince Arthur's life. The Queen was about to take up the question of whom he should marry; Mr Cardwell, the Secretary for War, was about to introduce a reform of the Army in which Prince Arthur's career was designed to be, and Mr Gladstone was bemoaning an explosion of nationalism, which foretold the destruction of the international society into which Prince Arthur had been born. Another difficulty was that the Queen was entering the lowest ebb of her life and reign, in which she became more than ever querulous, interfering, inconsistent, nervous and, a year later, seriously ill. Of her sons, this, perhaps, bore the hardest upon Prince Arthur, because she loved him the most and expected from him the best, and because he was still tolerant and indeterminate. As his twenty-first birthday approached and passed, the Queen, almost unceasingly, lectured him upon the need for duty to go before pleasure, the importance of remaining simple and kind, making no distinctions against lower people, staying away from the houses of any but the reputable, avoiding the style and manners of young army officers, refraining from advising her to appear more often in public, parting his hair in a different way, going to Ascot, if he insisted on going at all, only on Tuesdays and Thursdays, the days on which King William IV and Queen Adelaide had gone, not going to Catholic weddings unless friends or relations were involved, declining invitations to parties in Rome, not going to Naples and not saying the weather was bad when Elphinstone said it was good.[2]

These matters, however, were as nothing compared to the Queen's preoccupation with the choice of Prince Arthur's wife. For the most part, she forgot about the suitability of marriage with a commoner and produced a succession of lists of the unmarried Princesses of Europe between two years older and up to ten years younger than Prince Arthur. She flitted from one to another with surprising inconstancy depending upon the latest intelligence received from the network of her relations and, often enough, her own changing whims. In the pursuit of the object, she despatched Prince Arthur and Elphinstone on a series of tours of inspection throughout Europe which continued for seven years. From time to time, she reverted to the theme of a common marriage; 'a young lady of the Nobility,' if she was well brought up and had 'a good fortune,' would be 'perfectly possible & allowable.' She would be better than an unsuitable Princess with no money. On the other hand, a suitable Princess did not absolutely have to be rich. After all, 'if Arthur will *save & be prudent & not go flying about but live quietly*,' a poor Princess and he could get on very well on his £25,000 a year. One of the reasons for the rather protracted nature of the campaign, it struck the Queen's Private Secretary, was that Prince Arthur was keener on his duties as a Captain in the Rifle Brigade than on seeking a wife.[3]

There were also other possible reasons for which Prince Arthur was in less of a hurry than the Queen. In July 1871, he gave what Elphinstone described as a small dance at Ranger's House. A hundred and seventy people came to it, among them, the Turkish Ambassador and the

Mesdemoiselles Musurus, three Dukes with their Duchesses and daughters, five Marquesses, some with their Marchionesses and daughters, seven Earls, some also with their Countesses and daughters, and numerous other grand people, including Lord Randolph Churchill. Dancing began at 10.30 and the evening was notable for the fact that at about a quarter to twelve the tent caught fire and was entirely destroyed, whereupon dancing was resumed in Ranger's House proper. What struck the Queen's eye, however, was the name of Lady Rosamund Spencer-Churchill among the guests. Everyone talked of Prince Arthur's attentions to her, she warned Elphinstone, and he really ought to be 'more than usually careful.' He had been, Elphinstone assured her; when everyone had expected Prince Arthur to invite the Churchill lady for the cotillion, he had instead, apparently without giving any offence, asked a Miss Wordsworth, who, we have noticed, was one of the two American ladies who had captivated him while he was in New York. This was a straw in the wind which the Queen, or for that matter Elphinstone, may not have detected. Nor, probably, did either of them particularly notice the presence of Lady Listowel and, if Prince Arthur also did not on this occasion, he was soon to make amends for that.[4]

On 15th January 1872, Prince Arthur, accompanied by Elphinstone, left for Berlin to inspect Princesses of the Queen's selection. Elphinstone carried a detailed brief. The list was substantial; it included Princess Mary, a daughter of Prince Frederick Charles of Prussia, who was distinguished as a successful General in the recent Franco-Prussian War. The young lady was highly recommended by two of the Queen's daughters, the Crown Princess of Prussia and Princess Alice of Hesse. She was said to be about 16½ and to have had an unhappy childhood but to be well brought up, domestic and amiable. The Queen was doubtful as she thought that a marriage with a daughter of Prince Frederick Charles would be unpopular; he had an appalling reputation. If, however, she proved to be very nice and simple, that could be got over. Then there was a daughter of the Duke of Saxe-Altenburg, who was said to very nice, and a daughter of the Grand Duke of Mecklenburg-Schwerin, who was said to be very pretty but also a coquette who had thrown over a Russian Grand Duke after being engaged to him. She was not to be thought of. There was a very pretty and well brought up daughter of Duke George of Mecklenburg-Strelitz, whose mother was a cousin of the Tsar of Russia and was recommended by another of the Queen's daughters, Princess Helena. She, however, was only about 14½. Finally, there was Princess Thyra of

5. *Prince Arthur and Major Howard Elphinstone, 1860.*

6. *Prince Arthur's tutor, the Reverend W. R. Jolley, c1860.*

7. *Prince Arthur, May 1865.*

8. *Tobogganning at Rideau Hall, February 1870. Prince Arthur is in the centre rear holding a sledge.*

9. *Prince Arthur (4th from right) being entertained by Hugh Allan at Belmere near Lake Memphremagog, P.Q., 1870.*

Denmark, a younger sister of the Princess of Wales though, according to the Queen, excepting her eyes and fine figure, not nearly as pretty. She was said to have been romantically attached to Prince Arthur, since they met as children in 1863. They had not seen each other since. The brief was not quite straight forward; Prince Alfred was bidding for the Grand Duchess Marie, the daughter of the Tsar, and if that fell through, as from time to time it seemed it would, then any of the names on Prince Arthur's list might be required for Prince Alfred. Elphinstone, however, was told not to bother Prince Arthur with the problems as they might alarm him. Another difficulty was that Princess Thyra would not be on view as she was not in Germany but in Athens. In Berlin, Elphinstone was to rely upon the Crown Princess to guide her brother as to the civilities required.[5]

The expedition got off to rather a bad start; Prince Arthur's train arrived in Berlin two and a half hours late, having collided with another near Hanover. He was, nonetheless, met at the station by his brother-in-law, the Crown Prince, and later received by the Emperor, who invested him with the Order of the Black Eagle. Instead of inspecting Princesses, however, he called on Moltke and Bismarck and generally began to enjoy the military life of the German capital. Elphinstone, as he thought he had been directed by the Queen, began to plot with the Crown Princess. She invited Princess Mary and several other girls to tea at the *Neues Palais* where Prince Arthur was staying with her. She also happened to wish Elphinstone to see some paintings which chanced to be in the room in which the tea party would be. Thus, Elphinstone was able to report to the Queen. Princess Mary looked younger than her age, she was good looking but not handsome; her perfect German face conveyed a character which was simple, good and true. She had a straight well cut nose, pretty soft eyes and she was intelligent and thoughtful but small. If she was less shy, she might make an impression on Prince Arthur. Evidently, she did not; he made no mention of her. Elphinstone and the Crown Princess pressed on with a plan for a dance to which every Princess who could be got would be asked. Prince Arthur again remained silent on the subject of them and commented only that the Empress Augusta would talk to everyone so much before the ball was opened that one got quite tired before the dancing began. He was interested in visiting the Spandau works where the production of guns and small arms had been so much expanded that it was now a rival of Woolwich.[6]

Prince Arthur's course proved to be more prudent than Elphinstone's, for the Queen suddenly decided against the Princesses on view and in favour of the one who was not, Princess Thyra. She also told Elphinstone to keep the Crown Princess out of the explorations as she had a mania for match making. Elphinstone fell quickly into the new line; he told the Queen he had not really consulted the Crown Princess at all and that, as far as Princess Mary was concerned, he had taken great care to ensure that no conclusions could be drawn. He need not have protested so much, for, no sooner had he done so, than the Queen changed her mind again. Two photographs of Princess Mary now convinced her that she had a nice face and she no longer objected to the match. Moreover, one daughter was substituted for another as the enemy within, against whom Elphinstone was to be on guard. The next inspections were to be in Darmstadt, where Princess Alice would preside. Elphinstone was warned that her '*principles* of *mischief* & *intrigue*' were most sad as well as her 'want of forthrightness.' Also her 'greediness for money,' was 'terrible.' The dances in Darmstadt seemed no more decisive than those in Berlin and, on 15th February, Prince Arthur arrived back in Dover with his hand still uncommitted. All the same, Elphinstone thought he had been 'quite a sensation' in society and, by his charming manners, had improved what he rather oddly described as the '*entente cordiale*' between England and Germany.[7]

The Queen was, therefore, rather surprised when Prince Arthur arrived at Osborne and burst out about Thyra. The Queen observed that she was not handsome, but Prince Arthur said he already knew this. The Queen pointed out that, like the Prince of Wales's marriage to her elder sister, this would be another anti-German alliance. Prince Arthur thought that the Prusso-Danish War of 1864 had now been got over and the Queen conceded that this might be so. She then said that the King and Queen of Denmark did not wish their daughter to marry for another two years, to which Prince Arthur replied that this would suit him very well as he did not wish to marry at once. The Queen found it romantic that Princess Thyra had treasured a bit of Prince Arthur's handwriting since her last meeting with him in 1863, a fact which she had been told by the Princess of Wales. She gave her consent to the marriage and, a few days later, wrote to the Queen of Denmark to make a provisional booking. She said that Arthur had expressed a wish to see dear Thyra again and not without further intentions. She said he was steady and a good boy and she herself could not wish for a dearer daughter-in-law than one who looked like Alix. This apparently clear declaration was made still clearer by the accompanying hint from the Princess of Wales to her mother that other suitors should now be turned away.[8]

Three months later, at the end of June, when Princess Thyra was on the way to recovery from an illness which had caused her to lose her hair and become as thin as a rake, The Queen of Denmark wrote to say that Prince Arthur's visit would have to be postponed for a little longer until her daughter was looking better. If, when the time came, they met in love, then, the Queen of Denmark said, in God's name they would be free. This, however, was no longer at all what Queen Victoria wanted to hear. She agreed that the children must have a free choice, but she now asked the Queen of Denmark if, after mature consideration, she would not find it undesirable to see a second daughter established in England. This observation was apparently as clear as the earlier declaration and, indeed, the Queen was now investigating other Princesses again, this time on the advice of the German Empress Augusta. Among the recommendations from her were the two elder daughters of Prince Frederick Charles, one of whom had already been inspected. The youngest of these daughters, Princess Louise Margaret, was not mentioned, perhaps because she was as yet only twelve. At about the same time, the Queen was shown a photograph of Princess Hélène of Mecklenburg-Strelitz. Though still not yet sixteen, she was an interesting candidate because, so Elphinstone said, Prince Arthur thought that from a photograph she looked decidedly pretty and the Queen had heard that one day she would be very rich.[9]

Further tours of inspection were needed and, in January 1873, Prince Arthur once more set out for Germany. In so far as his letters to the Queen dealt with young ladies, they were, however, confined to his newest nieces. His sister Vicky's latest baby, Margarete, was now nine months old and, Prince Arthur thought, a nice good tempered child, very different from her nearest sister, Sophie, the future Queen of the Hellenes, who, apparently, was looking iller and crosser than ever. His sister Alice's newest baby was Alicky, the future last Tsaritsa of Russia. She was nearly eight months old and seemed to Prince Arthur to be a splendid child, very like her elder sister Ella, and very good tempered. By the time he wrote this, he had, however, already arrived in Rome where amusement rather than marriage seemed to be the order of the day. The visit began with some diplomatic work, audiences of the King and the Pope. The two were not on good terms because the bulk of the latter's territories had been absorbed into the former's new Kingdom. Prince Arthur seems, nevertheless, to have made an agreeable impression upon both and, though the King complained about the Pope, Pius IX was most affable and kept Prince Arthur longer than any of his previous royal visitors. Thereafter, Prince Arthur was lionised by the élite of Roman society and enchanted by the treasures of Rome, especially the picture galleries. In one, belonging to Prince Doria, he told the Queen that he had seen 800 pictures, 'nearly all by the greatest masters.' He was astounded by the beauty and magnitude of the interiors of the churches. He found Princess Umberto, the wife of the heir to the throne, 'gay & so natural' and it was a 'charm to talk to her.' All the ladies and gentlemen of Rome were 'most polished & agreeable.'[10]

The Queen was annoyed. The number of royal activities needed to be checked to prevent them from becoming too common. There could not be too much reserve shown to people in society and there were dangers in familiarity. Elphinstone tried to explain. *The Times* exaggerated; their correspondent was a 'most officious disagreeable man.' Even so, Sir Henry Ponsonby heard that Elphinstone had had some difficulties. It seemed that he had thought that Prince Arthur was going too far with a daughter of the Duchess of San Arpino and, to cut him out, had himself tried to make love to her. When, however, he extended his arm to the young lady she ignored him. Her mother, or it might have been her father, asked her why she did not take the gentleman's arm; she said she saw no gentleman. The Queen's Private Secretary, though in confidence to his wife, often liked to laugh a little at Elphinstone and sometimes at Prince Arthur too.[11]

The Emperor of Austria provided the next opportunity for Prince Arthur to look over the field by including him in the huge concourse of royalty which he invited to the opening of a great international exhibition in Vienna on 1st May 1873. To allay the Queen's anxieties about flirtations, Elphinstone managed to get a certain lady from Rome excluded from the Court Ball. The Queen, all the same, told Prince Arthur not to keep 'those foolish late hours wh you kept at Rome.' She also reminded him that he would have to go to Copenhagen without too much more delay to do something about Thyra. Prince Arthur told her that, at the Exhibition, England was far ahead in china, porcelain and furniture. He thought the Austrian and Hungarian jewelry and leather wonderfully good; France had little or nothing to show and he did not admire the German things. Russia had very good silks and gold and silver work, but their prices were ridiculously high. He said that he admired the Empress immensely but found her painfully shy. He was rather off-hand about Copenhagen, saying that Princess Thyra's brother, the Crown Prince of Denmark, who was with him in Vienna, thought that a visit in July would be soon enough. Meanwhile, the same Crown Prince, on getting back to Copenhagen himself, gave his mother such a good account of Prince Arthur that she began to look forward to the delayed visit with a mixture of apprehension and joy.[12]

This rather alarmed the Queen, who at once began to think of other Princesses. However, if Arthur was to marry Thyra, he would have to give up the Marlborough House and Sandringham ways of going on and stay quietly at home. His wife, before becoming a companion to her sister, the Princess of Wales, would have to look to how she could be useful to the Queen. By the end of June, the Queen had quite come round again to Thyra. Her other sister, Minnie, the wife of the Russian Tsarevitch, had been in England and the Queen was touched by how well she got on with her sister, the Princess of Wales. No such harmony seemed to bind her own children and she now thought that Thyra would be a peaceable element in the family. An opportunity for Prince Arthur to visit Copenhagen, without seeming to go there too deliberately, would be provided by the forthcoming coronation of the King of Sweden as King of Norway, which was to take place in Trondheim. So Prince Arthur duly attended this great occasion on 18th July 1873. He walked in the procession behind the King and immediately behind the banner of the realm. The officers 'had as much as they could do' to keep the flag up. It got caught in several trees and the end of the staff, as Prince Arthur described it to the Queen, 'kept running into my stomach.'[13]

This procession, for Prince Arthur, was, of course, really only the route to Copenhagen, but before he had even left Trondheim, the papers began to say that he was going to ask for Princess Thyra's hand. The Queen thought this very annoying and, in telegraphing to warn Elphinstone, she added that the Foreign Secretary, Lord Granville, preferred the idea of the 'rich handsome young Princess', who, in plain language, was Princess Hélène of Mecklenburg-Strelitz. Elphinstone, however, telegraphed back that they 'must await result of Copenhagen visit before looking elsewhere.' Indeed, the moment of truth was now at hand.[14]

At Friedensborg, Prince Arthur was heartily welcomed by the King and Queen of Denmark and other members of the Royal Family, including Princess Thyra. He found the Castle surrounded with the most splendid beech and lime trees, the latter making the air quite delicious with their blossom. From the Castle, the ground sloped down to a pretty lake, which

Prince Arthur thought was about the size of Virginia Water. The weather was delightful and the King and Queen were all kindness to their visitor. Elphinstone was delighted with Princess Thyra, who, he told the Queen, was far taller and more strongly built than her sisters, but very graceful in figure. Alas, she was not as pretty as Prince Arthur had expected and all he could say was that she was very nice. The disappointment, Elphinstone thought, was that he had expected her to look like the Princess of Wales and thus to be an ideal beauty. After much consultation but, it seems without any encouragement from Prince Arthur, the Queen decided to tell the Queen of Denmark that Arthur was favourably impressed and would like to see Thyra again. This was too little and too late for the Queen of Denmark, who was slow to reply and rather cool when she did so. The disadvantages of the Danish match again struck the Queen and Princess Thyra's chances of marrying Prince Arthur began to evaporate. By the end of the year the Queen was glad to be out of it. The Princess of Wales had fallen from favour; she and her sister, Minnie, had arranged for Captain Oliver Montagu to be invited to the marriage of Prince Alfred in St Petersburg, despite the fact that the Prince of Wales disliked him. This was not, the Queen thought, due to a wrong motive, but it showed a grievous want of dignity and knowledge of the world. It pointed to the great 'inadvisability of having another sister married to Arthur.' The fault of Alix and Minnie had apparently once been that of the mother too, and the Queen told Elphinstone that the Queen of Denmark 'used to have a vy familiar flirty way with men.' Oliver Montagu was subsequently to be cast apropos the Princess of Wales as Dante to Beatrice.[15]

Prince Alfred's marriage involved another great concourse of European royalty. It gave Prince Arthur an opportunity of seeing the splendours of St Petersburg and Moscow, of gaining some first hand knowledge of the Russian army and of meeting the rich Princess Hélène. As she was not yet confirmed, she did not appear at the great ceremonies and may hardly have realised why meetings with Prince Arthur were contrived. Nor, indeed, was Prince Arthur much the wiser because the Queen and Elphinstone, forewarned by the unfortunate publicity which had accompanied the abortive affair of Princess Thyra, had decided that everything was to be kept very confidential, so much so, that they scarcely mentioned the possibilities to Prince Arthur. While, however, the Queen continued to consider them and a large and changing list of alternatives, Prince Arthur became rather less cooperative. In fact, he made it so clear that he did not wish to marry just at present that Elphinstone felt bound to advise the Queen to postpone further tours of inspection until the summer of 1875. As an alternative to long railway journeys in the pursuit of German Princesses, he thought that it might be interesting for Prince Arthur to visit Egypt.[16]

Meanwhile, in preparation for Prince Arthur's marriage, the finding of the right Princess was not the only matter to be considered. There were also the questions of an income, a residence and a title. As to his income, the Queen's hope that the Parliamentary discussion of the annuity to be granted at his twenty-first birthday could be kept above politics, was, of course, forlorn. The occasion provided a minor field day for radical and republican feeling, which, in 1871, was far from dormant. The motion for £15,000 a year was carried by 276 to eleven votes, but that to reduce it to £10,000 was defeated only by 289 to 51. Upon Prince Arthur's marriage, there would be a proposal for an increase to £25,000 a year and the Queen wondered if this could not be settled at the time of the initial grant so as to avoid further controversy. Mr Gladstone, however, felt that it might not be expedient to raise such a measure 'while Your Majesty was at a distance,' or, in other words, at Balmoral or Osborne and, therefore, providing fuel for the radical and republican cause by not being seen to carry out her functions in the capital. The Queen's habits were not to be changed by such innuendoes and Prince Arthur's married income would, therefore, have to be subject to a further vote in the House of Commons when the time came. Even so, the Queen took pains to warn Prince Arthur against association with the Conservative opposition to Mr Gladstone's Liberal Government which, at the time, was engaged in pressing through army reforms. She deplored the fact that both her elder sons were considered to be illiberal and she thought the Duke of Cambridge and Prince Edward of Saxe-Weimar, who was a General in the British army, were very indiscreet in criticising Mr Gladstone. Prince Arthur was enjoined to remember the Prince Consort's maxim that the people should be conservative and the Princes liberal.[17]

When he was twenty-one, Prince Arthur began to wish to be made a Duke. According to Elphinstone, the title he fancied was York, but if an Irish one was desirable, there was Connaught. The Queen was unenthusiastic; she had always been against these titles for Princes, peerages brought them undesirably into politics and for a Prince of the Royal Blood to call himself a Duke was 'rather lowering.' She said she would not absolutely refuse, but she hoped the matter could be put off for four or five years. York, she said, he could not have, as that was reserved for the second son, though, in the case of hers, she had made him Duke of Edinburgh. She did not like the idea of Connaught because Ireland was a 'disaffected & unreliable country.' Within three years, however, the matter came up again and the Queen now wondered if, instead of making Prince Arthur Duke of something, she might not make him Prince of it. Disraeli, who had now displaced Gladstone as Prime Minister, thought that perhaps she could. He feared there might be an awkwardness about the Duke of Edinburgh, but he might also be made Prince of something, and Prince Leopold should not be forgotten. Suitable titles might be found from the most considerable Colonies and he suggested that Prince Arthur might be created Prince of Australia; that, he said, would be a 'symbol of Yr Majesty's power.' To judge of these matters, the advice of two experts, Ulster King of Arms, Sir John Burke, and Garter King of Arms, Sir Albert Woods, was called in. Ulster saw no difficulty; Richard II had created the title of Marquess, Henry VI that of Viscount and Queen Victoria could add that of Prince, which would confer a peerage and therefore a seat in the House of Lords. In any case The Prince of Wales was a peer as such. The other expert, Garter, took substantially the opposite view; the Queen could confer the title of Prince or any other title, but, unless it was enumerated in the peerage, it would not confer a seat in the House of Lords. She had granted Azamlah of the Carnatic the title of Ameer-i-Arcot or Prince of Arcot, but that had not made him a peer. The Lord Chancellor weighed in with other ideas and the Queen's Private Secretary, Ponsonby, seeing that difficulties might be involved, advised the Queen to drop the plan, which she did. On 18th May 1874, using the salutation 'Dearest' rather than her usual 'Darling', she wrote to Prince Arthur that she had 'according to your earnest wish (certainly *not mine* nor would it have been dear Papa's) given directions that you should be created Duke of Connaught & Strathearn & Earl of Sussex'. She added that she would wish him in her House to continue to be called by 'your far more distinguished name of Prince Arthur' and that he was to note that becoming a peer would be no excuse for constantly running up to London, which, she said was bad for his health and his professional duties.[18]

As a residence for Prince Arthur, the Queen had for some time had in mind the house at Bagshot which, until his death, had been occupied by her doctor, Sir James Clark. As this was Crown property like Windsor Castle or Buckingham Palace, and not in the Queen's personal possession like Osborne or Balmoral, the plans for its development had to be agreed with a Government department, that of Woods and Forests. This resulted in a series of bureaucratic delays, misleading estimates and, eventually, the decision that the house was beyond economic repair and that it would have to be pulled down and a new one built. The question then arose as to the proportion of the cost to be born by the Treasury and, what with one thing and another, nothing happened on the ground for several years. While Prince Arthur's courtship remained theoretical this did not greatly matter, but when it became serious a new urgency arose. On 12th June 1876, Mr Menzies, the Surveyor from the Department of Woods and Forests, the architect, Mr Ferrey, and Sir Howard Elphinstone met the contractor at Bagshot for the 'cutting' of the site of the new house. Precisely who decided what is somewhat obscure. The Queen had a poor opinion of Mr Menzies and of his department which, she said, was slower, paid more for its workmen and were 'more disagreeable than any people in the world.' Elphinstone assured her that he would endeavour to take the design and the building of the house into his own hands. So began the home of the Duke of Connaught, the last swallow of a royal summer of building — Osborne, Balmoral, Sandringham, Bagshot Park.[19]

The reason for the urgency at Bagshot was Princess Mary, the younger daughter of the blind King George V of Hanover, who had been deprived of his territory and a good deal of his money by Bismarck and therefore, in title, by Prince Arthur's Godfather, the German Emperor. This resulted from Hanover having taken the losing side in the war of 1866 between Prussia and Austria. Another twist was that if England had been subject to the same salic law which had governed Hanover, this King would have been King George V of Great Britain and Ireland and Queen Victoria would not have acceded. His daughter, among all the Princesses whom Prince Arthur was told to look at, struck him as preferable to any and, though he may have taken a little time to make up his mind, he did decide that it was she whom he wished to marry. There was also the irony that this courtship, Prince Arthur's first real one, began in a routine manner as he returned from his expedition to Egypt, which had been planned as a holiday from Princess hunting.[20]

Prince Arthur had begun his journey to Egypt on 9th January 1875. From Cairo he went by special train to Siout, from where he rode on a donkey to board the Viceroy's steamer on the Nile. This extremely comfortable boat was staffed by the Viceroy's servants and cooks, all of whom were French. As they steamed to Tabah, they saw a profusion of birds, including geese, duck, flamingoes, cranes, herons and eagles. From

Girgah, Prince Arthur rode out on a donkey with an escort of Sheiks, by which he meant heads of villages, mounted on grand Arab horses. They went for twelve miles through cultivated bean, Indian corn and wheat fields to the temples of Abydos, which, Prince Arthur told the Queen, were 3,200 years old and very fine with their massive pillars and hieroglyphics. The effect was enhanced by the handsome dress of the Sheiks and a demonstration of horsemanship which they put on. On 30th January Prince Arthur came to Luxor and the next day, accompanied by Mariette Bey, a Frenchman who had superintended the excavations during the previous fifteen years, he visited the fifteen temples of Karnac. He wrote to the Queen that it was 'the most interesting day I have ever spent.' The hall of one of them, in which he lunched, could have contained the whole of Notre Dame. He thought that the magnificence of these temples was 'simply stupendous' and he found it hard to imagine any man 'having a large enough mind to conceive so grand a design.' He was concerned to see how the temple at Luxor had been damaged by people building houses on top of it. He felt there was something 'rather sentimental & nice' about the doctrine of the second life which was enshrined in the tombs of the Kings, which he visited on 3rd February, but he found an Arab dinner, at which one had to tear the meat off and eat it with the fingers, rather an awkward business. At Assuan, he looked at the Indian and Ethiopian work in the bazaars and the granite quarries from which the temples had been built and, for the first time, he mentioned the flies; there was a plague of them.[21]

This was as far as the Viceroy's steamer could go, but the expedition went on in sailing boats, or *diabeeahs*, which were hauled up the cataracts by three or four hundred Nubians in the same way as described by Herodotus two thousand three hundred years earlier, so Elphinstone told the Queen. The air was full of sand and the temperature varied from ninety-six degrees in the shade to sixty-three, but Prince Arthur was in perfect health. He visited the temples of Abu Simbel by moonlight and found them illuminated by magnesium wire lighting, which, here and elsewhere, produced a fairy-like scene. On the way back to Assuan, Prince Arthur shot two crocodiles, which Elphinstone thought was as well, because he had been getting downhearted about earlier failures to do so. His *diabeeah* tore down the boiling caldron of the cataracts at nearly thirty miles an hour and then subsided into the still waters below. They landed at Kroda where Prince Arthur visited a sugar manufactory which belonged to the Viceroy. Four thousand men were employed at it, half of them by day and the other half by night and it took twenty-four hours to convert the raw cane into shipped sugar. Prince Arthur told the Queen that he reckoned that the Viceroy cleared between £60,000 and £100,000 per annum in the process. Another curiosity was the tombs at Beni Hassan, which Prince Arthur said were five thousand years old and, he believed, the oldest works in Egypt. In Cairo, he called on the Viceroy and then travelled to Suez from where he sailed to Tor and joined a large tented camp. With the aid of 160 camels, numerous horses and ten donkeys, it moved overland for three days until the foot of Mount Sinai was reached. Here the bells of a Convent rang out in greeting and Prince Arthur was received with an address of welcome as the first British Prince to visit the sacred place. Thereafter, he wandered for six days in the wilderness.[22]

On the way home across France, Prince Arthur stopped in Paris and called on King George V of Hanover. This, at the least, might have been taken as a normal courtesy, and, at the most, the opening gambit in a further routine inspection of Princesses; Princess Mary, indeed, had all along been on the Queen's list of candidates. There was, however, an immediate difference. Prince Arthur admitted to Elphinstone, though not yet to the Queen, that this Princess was preferable to anyone he had yet seen. Moreover, this impression must have been more apparent than he, perhaps, realised; rumour of it spread quickly and far. The Queen had to warn Elphinstone of how careful Prince Arthur would have to be; much harm could be done by a single word. It was a complicated position; The Prince of Wales was in the Danish camp on the side of his sister-in-law, Princess Thyra. His elder sister, Vicky, was in the Prussian, on the side of one of Prince Frederick Charles's daughters. Her mother-in-law, the German Empress Augusta, was against both these options and was the advocate of some relations of the Queen of Sweden. The Queen of the Belgians was in favour of, or at least sympathetic to, the Hanoverian match. The Queen herself was anxious to obtain as much intelligence as possible, but not to be too much influenced by those who supplied it; to reach the right decision from the point of view of obtaining a daughter-in-law who would be agreeable to herself and a wife to make Prince Arthur happy and domesticated; to reach the single right decision, but not to offend too many advocates of the alternatives. She and Elphinstone decided that Prince Arthur's attendance at the German autumn man-oeuvres and a royal wedding in Vienna would be used to visit various Princesses, including Princess Mary of Hanover.[23]

Matters got off to an unfortunate start when it appeared that the Austrian wedding was going to clash with the most important days of the German manoeuvres. It seemed that the Germans would be much offended if Prince Arthur failed to turn up to take advantage of the expensive arrangements they had made for him and both he and Elphinstone suggested that the Austrian wedding should be given up. The Queen thought otherwise, and told Elphinstone that civility and con-ciliatory behaviour towards the Prussians was one thing and flattering their overbearingness quite another. She obtained the necessary con-cession through the German Empress and Prince Arthur went both to Berlin and Vienna. Then there were more difficulties; at midday on 5th September, Prince Arthur left Berlin for Walsrode near Hanover to inspect the Prussian cavalry stationed there. He went by train to Hanover, where he was met by Prince Albrecht of Prussia, who commanded the military district. For the next two days they watched the cavalry movements at Walsrode. Prince Arthur was much interested as he was shown a new system of cavalry drill, but the Queen thought it a great mistake that Prince Arthur should have been under Prussian auspices in territory annexed by Prussia from the King of Hanover. At last, both the German manoeuvres and the Austrian wedding were over and Prince Arthur, having seen some and missed other Princesses, arrived at Gmunden, where the King of Hanover kept what remained of his Court.[24]

The King and the elder daughter, Princess Frederica, known as Lily, were away, but the Queen, Princess Mary and her brother, Crown Prince Ernest, were there. Prince Arthur wrote to his mother that the Queen was most kind and that 'Mary is quite charming, so handsome so unaffected & so unselfish, I feel quite sure you would like her.' This was wholly different from anything he had previously written on such a matter and, though Elphinstone's report was in his usual terms about handsome faces, graceful figures, gentleness, refinement and so on, he did add one new point, which was very revealing; he said that Princess Mary's features reminded one of those of Prince Arthur's sister, Princess Louise. Nor was this just another of Elphinstone's flights of tactful fancy; Prince Leopold soon after remarked upon the same resemblance. Lamentable weather favoured the romance by confining the couple to the drawing-room for most of the time and Elphinstone soon assured the Queen that the visit to Gmunden was a great success and would most probably lead to 'decided results.' Prince Arthur wrote that he was looking forward to seeing his mother as he had a great deal to tell her. This would be unlikely to be all about the German manoeuvres and the Austrian wedding.[25]

Decided results, however, did not follow and, instead, a great question mark appeared beside the whole prospect. What could be the cause? In May 1876, Prince Arthur dined and lunched several times with the King and Queen of Hanover and their family in Paris. There appeared to be some obstacle, which Elphinstone thought arose from the King wishing to be told that Queen Victoria would receive him if he came to England. When, however, she said she would, the difficulty still seemed to remain. Prince Arthur said that he was never given an opportunity of saying anything to Princess Mary. He thought he might have a better chance when she came with her parents to London. Elphinstone feared for a moment that Prince Arthur's attention might stray elsewhere. One night he dined at the duc de Montpensier's. He sat next to Princess Christina, on whose other side was Elphinstone, who told the Queen that she was decidedly pretty with large Spanish-looking eyes. He said that she made herself most agreeable and that Prince Arthur and she were much amused with each other's conversation. Just opposite, sat Princess Mary, who spoke not a word. Elphinstone soon regained his confidence and assured the Queen that Prince Arthur preferred the quiet retiring manners of the Hanoverian Princess, but when the Hanovers came to London at the end of May, things progressed no better. The Queen of Hanover went so far as to tell the Queen that, while another visit to Gmunden by Prince Arthur would be welcomed, she did not believe that his wishes had any chance of fulfilment.[26]

This bombshell grieved the Queen; she could not understand it at all. Elphinstone should now, she told him, be 'a little indiscreet' with members of the Hanoverian Household, and especially the Countess Bremer, who had brought the Princesses up and was now with the family in London. This, she hoped might bring out the truth. While Elphinstone knocked at the back, the Queen tried the front door; she wrote to the Queen of Hanover to ask if there was any insuperable objection to the match. The Queen of Hanover simply said that Princess Mary did not reciprocate Prince Arthur's feelings for her and that her parents would allow her the decision. This seemed incredible; further enquiries must be made, but all that Elphinstone could extract from Countess Bremer was that Princess Mary would not marry until she was sure that she liked the man and that their characters were suited. It then emerged from brother Ernest that Mary had had a little affair a few years ago with a man who could not marry; a matter which would be cured by a little more time. Elphinstone discovered that the King of Hanover had intended to give his daughters £100,000 each on marriage, but, since the Prussians had raided his coffers, he could only afford £15,000. He wondered if the German Emperor could now be persuaded to give back the £100,000 to Princess Mary on her marriage to his Godson, and so, presumably, restore some of the King's honour. The Queen thought there was little chance of that and declared that Prince Arthur would never stoop to beg Bismarck for anything. All the same, she did not object to stooping far enough to find out from Lord Odo Russell, the British Ambassador in Berlin, if the idea had any chance of success. Elphinstone decided, however, that there was no need for any stooping as Prince Arthur had now been invited to Gmunden, which he would not have been if Princess Mary intended to refuse him. When the Hanovers left London in the middle of June, Prince Arthur, who had been very depressed by his lack of success, had recovered enough to think that, as the whole of her family was on his side, it would have 'a certain weight with Mary.' Ponsonby thought not; he told his wife that Princess Mary thought Prince Arthur a fool and pined for some more decided man. Countess Bremer took a third view; she thought that if Princess Mary had remained another fortnight in London, the whole thing would have been settled.[27]

It seems that none of these views were near the mark, but before the denouement, there was one more episode. In the first days of 1877, Prince Arthur went once more to Paris, this time in the hope of having it out with the King. In consequence, it emerged that what was wanted was a guarantee that if Princess Mary married him, she would never have to meet Prince Arthur's Uncle, the Duke of Coburg, or his brother-in-law, the German Crown Prince, who had both taken the field against Austria (and Hanover) in the war of 1866. A somewhat Gilbertian solution was found to this rather awkward demand which, in essence, amounted to a scaling down of never to hardly ever, and the King then agreed to write to his daughter to ask her if she wished to marry Prince Arthur. At last, after further delay and continued speculation, Princess Mary's reply came. It said in the midst of much diplomatic verbiage that, as she could not love Arthur, so she could not marry him. The Queen hoped that a feeling of proper indignation and self-respect would prevent Prince Arthur from being downcast. As to the Hanoverian family, she declared, 'really they are too stupid,' and she remained convinced that there was '*some thing* at the bottom w^h we *dont know*.' Her Cousin, the Duchess of Teck, was yet more outraged; why, she asked, did not Arthur take to Lily instead of that 'selfish idiot?' Prince Arthur's reaction was quite different. 'Poor Mary,' he wrote to the Queen, 'she is so conscientious that I have no doubt she has passed a very anxious time quite as much as I.' The Queen was not to be influenced; why cannot 'the foolish girl return Arthur's love,' she wrote to Elphinstone. On the English side and, to a considerable extent, on the Hanoverian too, Prince Arthur seems to have been the only one prepared to concede that Princess Mary should be allowed feelings of her own. Nonetheless, it was a sad ending to what he described as his first attempt at matrimony. The other loser in what to all the others was virtually a game of chess, was Princess Thyra, who certainly wished to marry Prince Arthur as much as he wished to marry Princess Mary. While, however, the latter knew his feelings for her, it was only several years later that he learnt of Princess Thyra's for him.[28]

Princess Mary died at Gmunden in 1904 at the age of fifty-four; she was unmarried. Princess Thyra married Crown Prince Ernest of Hanover in 1878. He inherited the English title of Duke of Cumberland from his father, but, as a German Prince, was deprived of it after the First World War. She died at Gmunden in 1933 at the age of seventy-nine.

CHAPTER 5

A Real Bed of
Orange Flowers 1877-1879

THE HANOVERIAN DEBACLE, with its intricate tangle of diplomatic and emotional involvements, had absorbed much of Prince Arthur's energy but, both before that time and throughout it, he had also made decided progress in his military career. As a Captain in the Rifle Brigade, he learned, to the extent that they could be taught by simulated battles, some of the lessons of handling troops in the field and, during a quieter spell of duty in Dover, of managing them in barracks. On manoeuvres in the autumn of 1872, as a Brigade Major, he began to understand staff work and, in April 1874, his experience was further widened when he left the Rifle Brigade and joined the 7th Hussars to face the challenge of mastering the art of cavalry drill. In October 1875, he was posted as a Major to serve on the staff of the Adjutant-General in Gibraltar and, a year later, he was promoted Lieutenant-Colonel and given the command of the 1st Battalion, the Rifle Brigade, which was stationed in Dublin.[1]

No young officer had been more favoured in the matter of promotion, none by this stage had been given such a wide experience of different kinds of work in the Army nor, indeed, of observing that of foreign armies, and no other Lieutenant-Colonel had such a good chance as Prince Arthur of reaching the highest rank. On the other hand, no other young officer was under such close surveillance by his superiors, from the Sovereign downwards, as was Prince Arthur and on none did the impact of praise or criticism, whether justified or not, bear more severely than upon him.

Opinions as to his soldierly value differed widely; Prince Alfred's former Governor, Sir John Cowell, apparently thought that Prince Arthur had no real enthusiasm for his profession and liked only the glitter, the show and the dress. General Parke, under whom he served as Brigade Major, was impressed and clearly surprised by his anxiety to acquire a thorough knowledge of all the details of the military profession which, he thought, was at least the equal of that shown by the very few young men who really made the Army their calling in life. Ponsonby noticed at Balmoral in 1877 how Prince Arthur busied himself with military maps of the Russo-Turkish War and the way he ran round them reminded him of the Prince Consort; he thought, however, that most of the information had been got up by the Equerry, Major Pickard. The Queen feared that the distance which was necessary between officers and men was giving Prince Arthur a 'stiffness & a *distance* of manner, & a tendency to that snobbish style of a *young officer* w^h she much regrets.' General McMahon, who inspected Prince Arthur's cavalry troop in September 1874, was pleased with its superior style and thought that the Prince had shown much aptitude in adapting so quickly to the cavalry drill. The Adjutant-General in Gibraltar had difficulty in understanding that Prince Arthur had come out to serve as a Major on his staff and not to interfere with anyone. It was fortunate for Prince Arthur's reputation that it was his own actions, rather than the continued clash of such opinions, which ultimately provided the verdict upon him as a soldier.[2]

If, however, his lessons in courtship had not unduly disturbed the progress of his military career, they had certainly not encouraged Prince Arthur to plan for an early marriage. The Queen, on the other hand, had scarcely received news of Princess Mary's refusal before she began to plan the next phase of the campaign. On looking through her *Almanach de Gotha*, she found that there were still a number of Princesses in hand, but she also turned her mind to people in England. There was a daughter of the Duke of Westminster and two very nice ones of the Duke of Bedford. In both cases there was money. 'Nothing,' the Queen declared, 'but a good fortune & good looks & education w^{ld} of course counterbalance the difficulties of position'. There was a young lady to whom her grandfather, Lord Maynard, had left £80,000 to £90,000 a year; she was sixteen, but the Queen mentioned her because a fortune was nowhere else to be found outside Russia or, in some cases, in Prussia. After the difficulties of negotiating Prince Alfred's marriage to the Tsar's daughter, the Queen did not wish for another Russian connection and her friend, the Empress Augusta, had strongly advised against the daughters of the Prussian Prince Frederick Charles. Elphinstone thought there would be no harm in looking into candidates, including the grand-daughter of the late Lord

Maynard, but he foresaw a difficulty; Prince Arthur's tastes and feelings would also have to be consulted and he feared that he might not wish to discuss such matters at the moment. Prince Arthur himself told the Queen that he did not think there was need for 'much hurry'. This was, perhaps, fortunate. The Maynard grand-daughter later became well-known as Daisy Brooke, 'Babbling Brooke' and, in turn, the Countess of Warwick.[3]

When in Ireland, as at this time he was, Prince Arthur was often the guest of Lord and Lady Listowel at Convamore in County Cork. He had written to the Queen from there in February 1877 saying that the air was fine and bright and that he had enjoyed visiting Blarney Castle, which contained the famous Blarney Stone. Anyone who kissed it, he told the Queen, was supposed to get exactly what he wanted. It seems that he must have done so for he soon fell very much in love with his pretty hostess, Lady Listowel. A year or so older than Prince Arthur, safely married and already the mother of a suitable batch of children, she was an ideal friend whose response to his admiration was a great solace and, no doubt, an education as well, to Prince Arthur. Certainly there was no need to hurry on with the Queen's marriage plans.[4]

His eldest sister, the German Crown Princess, however, thought otherwise and, having failed with the elder two of Prince Frederick Charles's daughters, she was now the firm advocate of the youngest, Princess Louise Margaret, who was seventeen. The Queen was very doubtful; she objected to her daughter's interference, she believed that Prince Frederick Charles was unpopular and she expected that, as soon as the Emperor died, he and his wife would be divorced. Elphinstone was quite confident. Prince Arthur, he told the Queen, had taken a decided dislike to the eldest daughter and, judging from the appearance of the third one, he had 'no fears whatever of Pr: Arthur falling in love with her. Your Majesty may therefore rest perfectly reassured on this point,' he wrote. The Queen, nonetheless, presumably with a view to getting her crossed off the list, decided that it would be as well to inspect the girl, and Prince Arthur was given his marching orders for Berlin in January 1878. Before leaving London, he wrote a reassuring letter to the Queen. 'You need not fear as regards my being talked into an engagement with Prince Charles's daughter,' he told her. 'I have no wish to be married at present & I quite agree with you that a Prussian Princess would be unadvisable.'[5]

Three days later, Prince Arthur met the 'unadvisable' Princess at dinner in Berlin and wrote straight off to the Queen, 'I must say I thought her rather pretty.' After another four days, he wrote to the 'rather pretty' Princess, 'My dear Cousin, I take the great liberty of sending you my photograph direct as the surest way of its reaching you. Hoping that you are not very tired from the ball,' he remained, 'your very affec^{te} Arthur.' Two days later, they privately and mutually understood that they were engaged to be married. Poor Elphinstone soon rallied. 'The young lady,' he told the Queen, 'must have something pleasing in her character or manner, else this would not have happened.' He was already sure that the Princess would be 'a most dutiful daughter-in-law.' It now only remained to settle the formalities.[6]

The Queen thought that the time when international differences could be harmonised by dynastic marriages had passed. She observed that Prince Alfred's marriage to the Russian Grand Duchess Marie produced only a painful position while Russia and Britain hovered on the brink of war. She thought that the bitter feelings in England against Prussia in the three wars of 1864, 1866 and 1870 had not been diminished by the fact that her daughter was married to the Crown Prince of Prussia. This did not, however, mean that the love match now proposed between Prince Arthur and Princess Louise Margaret could be dealt with other than through dynastic formalities. Nor were they a simple matter; the Princess's parents were not only at loggerheads with each other but both, and not without reason, were considered to be difficult. The German Emperor, with whom the Queen would need to make the alliance, was kindly enough and was, of course, Prince Arthur's Godfather, but he and the Empress were not unduly attached to each other and, to a considerable extent, led separate lives. The Queen's son-in law, the Crown Prince Frederick, was not close to his father and her daughter's relationship with her mother-in-law, the Empress, was very uneasy. The Empress and the Queen, however, were friends and it was largely between them that the negotiations took place. Another difficulty was that, by negotiations, the Queen meant little more than Prussian acceptance of her conditions.[7]

These conditions were quite stiff; the marriage must be in England, and not, as Prince Alfred's had been, in the bride's country. She was the only daughter of Russia's sovereign; Princess Louise Margaret was only the grand-daughter of the German Emperor's brother. The Queen could not possibly travel to Berlin; the fatigue would be far too great. The Queen restricted the number of Prussian relations coming over for the marriage and also the size of their entourages; she had not much room, she said, in which to put people up. Before the marriage took place,

Princess Louise Margaret was to come to stay with the Queen for ten days or a fortnight and, though her father might bring her and take her home again, she was to do so alone. It was not necessary for the Princess to be guaranteed a residence in the event of her being left a widow; it was the English custom to provide grace and favour apartments in such an event and there was no need to have anything in writing about it. At an only slightly lower level of negotiation, the Queen also made a number of stipulations about the clothes in which Princess Louise Margaret would arrive for her preliminary visit and, later, her marriage. She also had pronounced views upon where the honeymoon would be spent and what social round the couple would undertake when they returned from it.[8]

The Prussians were remarkably tolerant and, though they occasionally tried a counter-suggestion, they ultimately conceded virtually everything. Even the supposedly objectionable Prince Frederick Charles proved to be very accommodating. When the Queen postponed the marriage from its original date of 10th February, her own wedding day, to 13th March, because of the death of her daughter, Alice, he at first objected because that was in Lent. When the Queen persisted, he had a talk with his priest and found that he could overcome his scruples. When difficulties arose about Prince Arthur coming to Germany to make a formal proposal of marriage in person, Prince Frederick Charles accepted that a letter would do. Most accommodating of all, however, or at least apparently so, were Prince Arthur and Princess Louise Margaret.[9]

Prince Arthur tended to accept the Queen's attitudes as though they were the weather. He was deeply concerned that she should take favourably to his chosen Princess and immensely relieved when she did so. At times he was irritated by her interferences but his love and respect for her led him to accept nearly all of them uncomplainingly. 'Mama,' he explained to his future wife, 'will always look at everything in her own light & will not allow anybody else to have *any views* of their own.' That was something they would have to put up with but, he said, she was 'true to the backbone & she has ever shown me the greatest affection & kindness.' The formidable Queen, as far as Prince Arthur was concerned, was also, more often than not, the doting mother and this feeling was at once extended to Princess Louise Margaret. The nervous Princess initially addressed her letters to 'Her Majesty The Queen of Great Britain & Ireland Empress of India,' began with 'Madame' and punctuated the contents with Majesties. The Queen responded with the injunction, never call me Madam or Majesty, but always Mama and the hope that, when she came to stay, 'you wont find *us* at all *alarming.*' But even the Queen's unalarming side, her love of simplicity, had its awkward aspect. Her antipathy to grand ideas, which she tended to believe Russians and Prussians possessed, was, Prince Arthur explained, '*one* of those ridiculous hobbies (manias) of Mama's in fact,' he said, 'it is her *chief* hobby & it all refers to one person Brown.' Indeed, being polite to servants, particularly so if they were Highlanders and, most of all, if they were John Brown, even if they were rude, was a prerequisite to Queen Victoria's favour and one which occasionally taxed even Prince Arthur's patience.[10]

Much of the content of Prince Arthur's constant stream of letters to the Princess was designed to prepare her for life as the daughter-in-law of the Queen and some of it to improve her already very good, but not yet impeccable, English. She was not to write 'nay bor' when she meant neighbour, she must not call the English Channel a 'canal' and his photograph would be in plain clothes, not plain 'dress.' The main message, however, was the depth of his love for her and how it, though by strangely gradual steps, led to the consignment of Lady Listowel to the scrap heap. He was sorry to hear from Louischen, as Princess Louise Margaret was known in her family, that her evenings at home were dull; he hoped that would be different when next he was able to visit her in Germany but he did not know what a bridegroom was allowed of a Prussian Princess. He hoped he was expected to see a good deal of her. After that visit in June 1878, she became 'My own darling' and his meaning became more overt. Though he said he tried not to show it in public, his whole life and feelings were centred in her and everything seemed tame without her. Luckily he had 'your dear self to think about,' but he told her that all his thoughts were 'not good in fact some of them were naughty.' He began to wonder when the 'infernal thing' would be coming on again and then to calculate how it might or might not coincide with their marriage date. He told her of his talks with the Queen's doctor, Sir William Jenner, about such matters and of his anxiety to learn all that a husband ought to know, not only for himself, but also so that he could instruct his wife. Married sisters were a useful source of information. Lenchen had expressed doubts about Louischen's prospective maid, Pauline, due to her youthfulness and, though Prince Arthur thought it would be wrong to throw her over, he supposed that it would be necessary to have a second maid aged about 28, who had been with a married lady. His sister Louise had warned him of the same thing; apparently she knew of several ladies who had completely ruined their health from want of knowledge and care in the first few months of marriage. Prince Arthur told Louischen that she was more sensible and careful than most girls, but he assured her that he himself intended to become 'acquainted with what ought to be done under different circumstances.' Meanwhile, on the recommendation of Lady Downe, he appointed her maid's sister to the key post. She was said to be very pretty, nicely mannered, a hard worker, a good nurse and fluent in English and German. She had been six years with a married lady and, as her salary had been £27 a year, £30 would be promotion. The only problem was that Mama would not be pleased at his choosing a maid without asking her, but Prince Arthur decided that this could not be helped; after all the treasure was not going to be Mama's maid and Mama was not going to pay her.[11]

The intimacy of Prince Arthur's letters was fully, perhaps more than fully, reciprocated by Princess Louise Margaret. Though he said he was not shocked because he knew how right minded she was on such things, he felt all the same that she had confided more in him than most girls would in a man, even one they were about to marry. As he read the letters over again one evening in his rooms at Buckingham Palace, he tore several of them up. It seemed unkind, he told her, but they were so private that he would have been sorry if they had ever come under anyone else's eyes. Fortunately, this was not an action reciprocated by the Princess. Prince Arthur, however, preferred to convey his most intimate thoughts by word of mouth. So well, indeed, had the courtship gone during his visits to Germany, that the Queen began to be rather worried about them being so much together and then concerned that Prince Arthur might be carried away by his marriage prospects. On getting a letter from him in Berlin saying that he would never have believed it possible to be so happy in this world, she induced him to recognise that married life would not be a bed of roses. Princess Louise Margaret's grandfather, Prince Charles, wanted to know how far they went; she told him what Prince Arthur said was rather a 'crammer' about their not kissing, but they justified the falsehood on the ground that it was none of Prince Charles's business. In any case, this grandfather was an unreliable quantity and Prince Arthur became concerned that Louischen should pay him no more private visits in case he took advantage of her again, which, apparently he had once done when they were about to go out hunting. Prince Arthur had been alerted to this sort of conduct by his sister Louise, who told him that the Grand Duke of Mecklenburg, Mecklenburg-Strelitz it seems, who was the same age as Princess Louise's father would have been, had tried it on with her in her own house in Kensington Palace. Apparently, Prince Arthur passed on to Princess Louise Margaret, the Grand Duke had said to his sister that he had heard that she was very handsome and then 'began kissing her violently & feeling her all over.' He now feared that Prince Charles was up to same sort to thing and he was very uneasy about Louischen taking a railway journey with him. The worst that transpired, however, was that she got a headache from the smoke of her grandfather's indifferent cigars. Prince Arthur concluded that she must have given him a sleeping draft.[12]

Princess Louise Margaret heard regularly about Lady Listowel from Prince Arthur. He told her how he had encountered her sitting opposite him at dinner looking very pretty, her hair done quite plain and displaying only two bands of diamonds. When he lunched with her she asked him to return the ring she had given him because Princess Louise Margaret would taunt him for wearing it. He said he had declined because 'you knew all about it' and he did not wish to give up a memento of an intimate friend 'who did me so much good.' He wrote to Louischen that he had no secrets from her and told her everything which happened and was happening. Then in July 1878, he went to say goodbye to Lady Listowel and was sorry he would not see her again for many months. She was soon back in the picture writing to upbraid Prince Arthur for not writing to her. How 'exigent ladies are,' he declared to Louischen. A night or so later he found himself sitting next to her at dinner when she again asked him to return the ring. A month later, he paid her a visit and found her looking so nice and pretty. The other people there soon left and she told him that if ever he had cared for her he would give her back the ring. After half an hour, he gave in and did so. He wrote to Louischen that it was not unreasonable of her to long after him; he did after her and, though he had once deeply loved Lady Listowel and had been nervous of meeting her again, his love for Louischen had stood the test; Lady Listowel was now as nothing compared to her, but if she could have seen how pretty Lady Listowel had looked on Sunday she would have realised what a victory she had gained. Prince Arthur was in quite a state, he dreamt that he was being married in St Peter's but had forgotten the ring.[13]

As 1878 went out, he was in low spirits; his sister Alice had died and, as a result, his marriage date had been postponed, his favourite sister Louise had gone to Canada with her husband, Lord Lorne, who had been appointed Governor-General and she seemed to be unhappy there, but then, as Prince Arthur told Louischen, she did not love Lorne as she ought to and never had done. The Queen and Vicky seemed to be thoroughly across each other; the latter's 'violently high & low spirits' tended to 'fidget Mama', who was seldom at ease with her clever daughter. The Prince of Wales had suspected Louischen of repeating the story that the Duchess of Manchester was his mistress and that he had several children by her. The Queen thought that Prince Arthur was altogether not well and, she told Elphinstone, he looked green and yellow. There were difficulties about the Germans coming over for the marriage; the Foreign Secretary, Lord Salisbury, and the Commissioner of Police, Sir William Henderson, said they could not answer for the lives even of the Crown Prince and Princess. Many German socialists had fled Bismarck's Germany for England. It was also rather awkward that Prince Henry of the Netherlands, having only just married one of Princess Louise Margaret's sisters, proceeded to die without making any proper financial provision for her.[14]

Prince Arthur had been rather poorly for some time. He was said to be suffering from slow circulation with the result that his feet were always cold and his head hot, which caused headaches. The treatment was to have the legs rubbed to take the heat from the head to the feet and so to cure the headaches. He continued to suffer from hay fever or asthma. One particularly bad attack caused him to consult the Surgeon-Major of the Rifle Brigade at the Curragh. His eyes, nostrils and throat were badly affected and he began to have 'quite distressing' difficulty in breathing. Surgeon-Major Ramsay began by sponging the throat and tonsils with a weak solution of nitrate of silver, which was followed by steam inhalations, hot water, alum and carbolic acid gargles. Belladonna and hyoscyannus were taken at bed time, but this proved ineffective so quinine was added. This caused headaches and was stopped. Sulphuric and other compounds and tinctures of camphor and nitrate of potash produced only temporary relief. When the attacks got worse, Major Ramsay ordered draughts of chloroform, tincture of lobelia and nitrate of potash, recommended the patient to smoke Datura cigars and to inhale burning paper soaked in nitrate of potash. He also advised that he should go to sea for a time. The last treatment was very successful. Princess Louise Margaret suffered from a more constant but apparently less serious range of complaints about which Prince Arthur, who was much interested in doctoring, was always eager to advise. He was afraid she took too much opening medicine and he advised a good mild tonic, such as lux romica powders twice a day after meals; they were strengthening and slightly aperient.[15]

Medical fashions change as fast as almost any, but Royal social behaviour tends to be more enduring and Prince Arthur's advice to Princess Louise Margaret had more permanent value when the subject was how she should behave at her first major appearance at the Prussian Court. It was a very stiff Court, the Empress, who had no great opinion of the Princess, expected little of her and the seventeen year old victim, who had as yet seen so little of the world, was full of apprehension. Prince Arthur told her she must try not to be shy, to face it bravely and show the Empress how wrong she was. She must think beforehand of something suitable to say to each of the diplomats. To the French, she could say she looked forward to seeing Paris, to the Turk, congratulations on the peace treaty with the Russians and to the Russian, the same. To the Austrian, she could ask after the Empress and enquire if she really was coming to hunt in Ireland, of the Italian, she could ask after the King and Queen and say she was looking forward to seeing Sicily. Her late poor brother-in-law, Henry, could be mentioned to the Dutch and to the Portugese she could say how much she looked forward to meeting the King and Queen on her marriage tour. To the Belgian, she could say how pleased she was that the King and Queen were coming to her wedding and to the Spaniard, how much she looked forward to seeing the Alhambra and Grenada. He also ventured to hope that she would not wear the Prussian crown jewels at their wedding as the Prussian habit of covering the bride with jewels was 'hideous & vulgar.' He thanked her for sending him a bangle, but said he would wear it on his forearm as he did not like to see men wearing bracelets, a view which he seems to have revised when he suddenly noticed, much to his surprise, that the Prince of Wales wore one. He coached her too in sitting for portraits. She was at first angry and cross about being painted by Angeli and Prince Arthur had to tell her that the picture was for him and not for her. He took Angeli's side in wishing to include her neck and shoulders, which she had not wished, and added that if he had been painting the picture himself, he would like to have put in even more than that. The result, he later told the Queen, was lovely, 'so like & yet so pretty & natural,' in a low gown of creamy colour with her hair quite plain and a thin gold chain round her neck with a ruby and diamond star left to her by her grandmother. He wondered if she intended to have her ears pierced; most people in England, he told her, wore ear rings, but he said that ear-piercing was a remains of barbarism.[16]

At last, the rumours of war having died down, the German Emperor, if only just, having escaped assassination, the mourning for Princess Alice of

Hesse having abated sufficiently and the problems of Prince Frederick Charles's entourage having been settled, the way to the marriage ceremony was clear, or almost so. One of Prince Arthur's supporters was to be the Prince of Wales but he did not know if the other was supposed to be unmarried or not. If not, he would invite Affie, but, if so, Willie, the same who had bitten him at the Prince of Wales's wedding almost exactly sixteen years ago. Bagshot Park was still behind schedule and Elphinstone could but hope that enough would have been completed by October to make it possible for the Duke and Duchess to begin to live there in a quiet way. Prince Frederick Charles began to be difficult; he wished to embark in the Royal Yacht at Flushing at a time when there would not be enough water there to bring her alongside. Princess Louise Margaret would have to be careful that the Queen did not realise that the tippet she was giving her for the going away drive was unwanted. Prince Arthur, in advising her to keep quiet about this, assured her that the tippet would be a good one and would come in useful sometime. At least, however, Princess Louise Margaret had come well through the ordeal of her appearance at the Prussian Court. The British Ambassador observed that, only slightly trembling in voice, she had said something appropriate to everybody and had addressed the diplomats in perfect English, French and Italian. Lord Odo Russell had never seen her looking better. Nevertheless, she was feeling unwell. Having discovered that this was not due to the 'infernal thing,' Prince Arthur thought she might be cured by taking more nourishment.[17]

13th March 1879, the day of the wedding, was favoured throughout by weather which was bright, sunny and cool. Special trains left London at hourly intervals bringing the great and the good to attend the ceremony in St George's Chapel, Windsor. While Prince Arthur and Princess Louise Margaret strolled in the gardens of the Castle, the Archbishop of Canterbury, the Bishops of London, Winchester, Oxford and Worcester and the Dean and Canons of Windsor assembled in the Deanery before taking their places within the altar rails of St George's Chapel. At a quarter to twelve, the Queen's royal guests began to leave the state entrance to the Castle in a carriage procession to the West door of St George's. The first five carriages conveyed the suites and then, in the sixth, came the Maharaja and Maharenee Duleep Singh, the Duke of Teck and Prince Edward of Saxe-Weimar. The slightly higher grandees of Saxe-Coburg and Gotha, Leiningen and Schleswig-Holstein followed. In the ninth carriage came Prince William of Prussia, the Queen's grandson,

who was destined to become the last German Emperor, Wilhelm II; her
Cousin, the Commander-in-Chief of her army, the Duke of Cambridge
and her daughter-in-law, the Tsar of Russia's daughter, the Duchess of
Edinburgh. Then, after the bride's mother and young brother Prince
Frederick Leopold, there came the Princess of Wales, her younger son
the future King George V, and his three sisters. The twelfth carriage
brought the Queen's eldest daughter, the German Crown Princess, and
the King and Queen of the Belgians. At twelve noon, accompanied by her
youngest child, Princess Beatrice, and her grandson, Prince Albert
Victor, the apparent future King, the Queen drove off from the state
entrance attended by an escort of the Royal Horse Guards and preceded
by two carriages of attendants. As the Queen moved up the Chapel,
Mendelsohn's March from *Athalie* was played and it was seen that she was
wearing a dress and train of black silk with a border of black terry velvet
embroidered in black silk, a veil of white tulle surmounted by a diadem of
diamonds, a necklace and ear rings and the Koh-i-noor diamond in the
form of a broach with a diamond pendant attached, which contained a
miniature of her dead daughter, Princess Alice. She displayed the riband
and star of the Garter and she also wore the Order of Victoria and Albert,
those of the Crown of India, Louise of Prussia and the family Order of
Saxe-Coburg and Gotha. She had not appeared in public at the Prince of
Wales's marriage and, at that of her second son the Duke of Edinburgh in
Russia, she had not been present. At a quarter past noon, Prince Arthur,
in the uniform of the Rifle Brigade, and supported by the Prince of Wales
and the Duke of Edinburgh, arrived at the West door. As they moved up
the Chapel, the March *Albert Edward* by Sir George Elvey was played. At
half past twelve, the bride arrived on Prince Frederick Charles's arm with
the German Crown Prince on her other side. Her dress, contrary to the
Prussian tradition, was not of *drap d'argent*, nor was it covered with
jewels; it was of white satin adorned with three wide *Duchesse-lace*
flounces. The cut away bodice was similarly trimmed and the train of
white satin was decorated with the same broad lace. The veil was
rectangular and of lace similar to that used to trim the dress. Though
German in production, the result was English in effect. None of this,
however, would have come as a surprise to the bridegroom or the others
there, because the whole of the Princess's trousseau down to her high
leather boots, foot muffs, combs, brushes, sponges, soaps, perfumes,
corsets and garters, and including the wedding dress itself, had earlier
been placed on public exhibition in Berlin and described in detail in the

press. As the bride entered, Handel's *Occasional Overture* was played. The Archbishop of Canterbury conducted the marriage service and the Duke and Duchess of Connaught then sat down to a royal luncheon party in the dining room of the Castle while the other guests were entertained to a buffet lunch in St George's Hall.[18]

That evening, after the couple had left to start their honeymoon at Claremont, the Queen, addressing them as 'Darling Children,' confessed to how sad and flat it seemed now that they had gone, but she was thankful to think of them 'quiet & alone after these days of trouble & anxiety & excitement.' The marriage had been a 'beautiful sight' and, to the Queen, a 'g^t comfort & satisfaction.' Louischen had looked 'the picture of a young bride, so sweet & gentle & graceful & the dress so beautiful & simple.' She scarcely felt it necessary to tell them never to forget the solemn words which had been spoken, but she wished 'just to say that to be thoroughly happy *both must* give way to one another, both accommodate oneself to one another.' She said she was not jealous of Louischen now being Arthur's first object for she knew that Louischen did not wish to wean Arthur away from his mother. They would sleep that night, she concluded, in 'a real bed of orange flowers.'[19]

CHAPTER 6

Marriage 1879-1882

ON 16TH MARCH, Prince and Princess Frederick Charles, for once in a way doing something together, came down to visit their daughter at Claremont. Prince Arthur told the Queen that Louischen had been dreading it and was sure that her Papa would be in a bad humour. On the next day, the Queen came and 'her very dutiful & affect: daughter' then wrote how sorry she was that the visit had been so short. On 26th March, the marriage tour began, and, after a rough crossing to Calais, the Duke and Duchess of Connaught arrived at the Hotel Bristol in Paris, where they had very comfortable apartments on the second floor with a sitting room overlooking the Place Vendome. They had delightful hot baths, which the Duchess said were peculiar to Paris, and then a slight breakfast. The journey did not, however, immediately obviate parental propinquity; the next event was the arrival of Princess Beatrice at the Hotel, after which they all drove to the British Embassy to have lunch with the Queen, who was on her way to Italy. Later the duc de Nemours and his two daughters called on them. Ultimately, they strolled out to shop before dining alone with Captain and Mrs Egerton, who were travelling with them in attendance. They stayed two more days in Paris sight-seeing, shopping and discharging formal duties, including an exchange of visits with the President of the French Republic, M. Grévy. They then travelled to Bordeaux, where they were joined by Sir Howard and Lady Elphinstone, and embarked in the Royal Yacht *Osborne*.[1]

The Atlantic swell was anything but pleasant and the next morning the Duchess found it difficult to dress. The stewardess, Mrs Prince, and Prince Arthur had to help; her maid had succumbed. After another night at sea, they came to Lisbon. The King of Portugal appeared in a wonderful galley rowed by eighty men in red shirts and jockey caps covered in gold. He came on board *Osborne* for half an hour and settled the day's arrangements. After lunch, the Duke and Duchess and their party disembarked at the Arsenal; the ladies wore coronets and long dresses and the gentlemen, full dress uniform. It was rather a rough drive up to the palace of Ajuda, where they were received by the King and Queen. He had struck the Duchess as short and fat and not very imposing, but the Queen's appearance was 'rather startling.' She was tall with a commanding look, a mass of red hair brushed up into the air and a decided moustache. Her two sons were tall nice looking boys but, the Duchess thought, very 'effeminet' with their hair brushed up the same as the Queen's. After paying some visits and seeing some sights, they returned to dine with the King and Queen. Prince Arthur thought that the latter improved on acquaintance and was really very nice. He agreed with the Duchess, however, that the two Princes looked more like girls than boys. King Louis made himself very agreeable; he was engaged upon the translation of Shakespeare's works into Portugese and played the violin and violincello, but the dinner was too long and the dishes, which were mainly chicken, rather cold. On the following evening, the Queen was unwell but the Duke and Duchess entertained the King in the *Osborne*. When he had gone, the honeymooners jumped into a steam launch to see the effect of their illuminated yacht from the outside.

Osborne cruised on to Cadiz from where the Duke and Duchess made their way to Seville for a stay of a few days in the Hotel of the *Quatras Nationes*. In the Cathedral, they saw the Murillo of Saint Anthony worshipping Christ. The head of Saint Anthony had been cut out and stolen, but it had been recovered in New York and was now back in place. One night in their hotel they were sung to sleep by people under their windows to the accompaniment of guitars and clapping hands. The morning, however, brought them the less romantic eventuality of what they thought was an excessive bill, and, though they had both enormously enjoyed Spain, they were quite glad to get back on board *Osborne* to sail on to Gibraltar. There they were received by the Governor, Lord Napier, presented with an address to which Prince Arthur replied and pelted with flowers on their drive to the Convent. There was a field day, rather spoilt by bad weather, but the tremendous noise of the heavy batteries and the roll of musketry produced a splendid effect. Prince Arthur addressed the assembled troops and the Governor was entertained to dinner in the *Osborne*. On another day, the Duke and Duchess went by steam launch to the North Front where they were mounted. Accompanied by Lord Napier, they rode across the neutral ground and into the Spanish lines, which only the Governor had the right to do. He then departed but, with some of his staff and the Elphinstones, they rode on up the Carthasian hills to the first Venta where they joined a meet of hounds. There were a hundred ladies and gentlemen mounted and ready to go, which made a pretty sight. They trotted for a short distance and then the hounds found a fox and away they all went. After following for three miles, the Duchess was beginning to fall behind, so she stopped and had lunch and then a lovely ride back to Gibraltar with Lady Elphinstone. Prince Arthur rode on and returned to say that they had run for one and a half hours and killed the fox. It was one of the best runs he had ever known. Before leaving Gibraltar, the Duke and Duchess toured the military hospital where they found it sad to see how pulled down many of the 42nd Highlanders were with 'Cyprus fever.'

After calls at Algiers and Palermo, *Osborne* steamed into the harbour at Malta where they found twenty-two warships of the Mediterranean and Channel Fleets all dressed overall with their yards manned. As *Osborne* passed slowly through them, the great ships stood out against a blue sky, the bands played on board and the water was covered with small boats. The effect was splendid. The Commanders-in-Chief of the Mediterranean and Channel Fleets, Admiral Sir G.Hornby and Admiral Lord John Hay, two other Admirals and the Captains of all the ships came on board to pay their respects, as did the Governor of Malta, General Sir Arthur Borton, and the German Consul. Lieutenant Prince Louis of Battenberg reported for duty aboard the Royal Yacht. The Duke and Duchess had a very cordial reception as they drove with the Governor to the Palace where, in the throne room, Prince Arthur received an address. They were then shown to some very comfortable apartments, but they used these only in the day time as they preferred to sleep aboard *Osborne*, which that night, after lunch and dinner parties and a reception for six hundred, they did not do until past midnight. As they returned to *Osborne*, the ironclads *Monarch*, *Minator* and *Agincourt* showed their electric lights with beautiful effect. The men stood out on the yards like ghosts against a now dark blue sky. Next day, Prince Arthur reviewed the troops. In the afternoon they went with Louis Battenberg and Lord John Hay to the races. They dined with the Governor and then went to the opera for the first act of *Norma* and a cantata specially composed for the occasion by the Governor's wife, Lady Borton. They again returned to the yacht at midnight, this time to the accompaniment of a revolving electric light which illuminated the whole harbour. On 26th April, they visited the flagships of the two fleets, *Monarch* and *Minator*. The Duchess fired some guns and launched torpedoes which sent columns of water a hundred feet into the air. She found that she could stand the noise of the guns better on board than when alongside. *Osborne* sailed late that night. The illuminations were better than ever; all the ships were lit up and as the royal couple were sent off with cheer after cheer, the national anthem rang out into a clear night. The brilliance of the farewell dazzled the Captain of *Osborne* and he found it difficult to see where he was going.

The next excitement was the island of Rhodes where Prince Arthur paid a call on the Turkish Governor, Abdul Kerim Pasha, while the Duchess visited his harem. She was terribly disappointed to find that he only had two wives and that only one of them was on show. The wife of another Pasha, a Hungarian who spoke indifferent German, acted as interpreter. The meeting took place in a whitewashed room with plaid curtains and furnished with low divans and a few European chairs. The inmates were dressed in what the Duchess described as muslin dressing gowns with an attempt at Parisian fashion. Coffee was served in hideous European cups by negro women servants. The Duke and Duchess then went to the Fort built by the Knights of St John and heard how the Church there had been blown up twenty years earlier by the explosion of a powder magazine. They saw a group of prisoners, some with heavy manacles, several of whom, they were told, were murderers. They went on to the former hospital, which was now a barracks and here they were much impressed with the soldier-like appearance of the Turkish troops. While crowds of people pressed round them, they walked in the town and looked at a bazaar. Evidently, it was not a very impressive one to the eye of a connoisseur. Elphinstone wrote to the Queen that it was small and unsatisfactory but had given pleasure to the Duchess as it was the first of its kind she had ever seen. There followed a glorious moonlit night and a piano was brought up onto *Osborne*'s deck. Prince Arthur, Prince Louis and Captain Egerton played it while, the Duchess recorded, 'we others' drew and read.

There was a different sort of interlude on the Island of Samos, where the party landed in varied attire. The gentlemen engaged in fishing with a seam net, Sir Howard Elphinstone and the ladies sketched the local inhabitants, who came down to watch the proceedings, and the sailors swam about in the sea. There was another delicious evening on deck in the moonlight after dinner. Formality returned with their arrival at Smyrna, where they beheld the striking old castle and splendid cypress trees. All around were French, Turkish and Austrian men of war. The British Consul came on board and with him came the German Consul, to whom the

10. *Prince Arthur, 1877. Angeli. Queen Victoria thought this was an excellent likeness.*

11. *Princess Louise Margaret of Prussia, 1878.*

12. *The Duchess of Connaught in her wedding dress, 13th March 1879.*

13. *Prince Arthur's arrival at Government House, Calcutta, 3rd December 1883.*

14. *The Duke and Duchess of Connaught in India, c1883.*

Duchess felt inclined to present a pair of scissors with which to trim his hair and beard. Prince Arthur called on the Governor, who had also been on board to welcome the royal visitors, and then they drove about in the town amidst a crowd which threw bouquets into their carriage. The bazaars seem to have been the main focus of interest but, according to Elphinstone, they were almost devoid of Turkish things and full of stuff produced in Manchester. It was Prince Arthur's birthday; his health was proposed at dinner on board *Osborne* by Prince Louis of Battenberg and afterwards they went ashore again to attend a concert in aid of the sufferers from the Hungarian inundations. Preceded to their box by the Austrian Consul-General and other gentlemen carrying lighted candles, the Duke and Duchess were greeted with the British and then the Hungarian national anthems. It was a pretty little theatre with a well dressed audience and many pretty faces. Next day, they went to Ephesus by train and, mounted on donkeys, rode round the ruins. Prince Arthur thought them less worth seeing than they had been when he was there in 1865; the Turks, he said, had taken many of the stones to build houses and trees and grass had invaded the surviving remains.

At 3.0 p.m. on 3rd May, *Osborne* sailed into the Piraeus and was saluted by four British men of war, the Russian and French flagships and three Greek men of war. As the harbour was small, it made a tremendous noise. *Osborne* anchored between the French and Russian ships and it was not long before the King of the Hellenes arrived on board in naval uniform wearing the star and riband of the Garter. This produced another blast from the saluting guns. The King, the Duchess noted, was small and thin with a long neck and a very pleasant expression. He reminded her very much of Alix, the Princess of Wales, whose brother he was. The Duke and Duchess disembarked with the King and went by special train to Athens. From their rooms in the palace they had a beautiful view of the Acropolis, the city and the sea. They were left to themselves until 7.30 when the King reappeared, presented Prince Arthur with his Order, and took them down to dinner. It was a very good one but Mrs Egerton was unable to appear at it because her box had been left on the *Osborne*. The Queen of the Hellenes was away in the Crimea, but the King encouraged his guests to live *en famille* and this they much enjoyed. At the Acropolis everything was explained to them by Dr Lüders, the tutor to the King's sons. There were some formal events as well. After a gala dinner one evening there was a Circle attended by the whole diplomatic corps at which the Duke and Duchess stood and talked to the guests for nearly two hours and, on 5th May, there was a Te Deum in the Cathedral to mark the King's fête day. The singing, however, was indifferent and the service was over in twenty minutes.

On returning to the Piraeus they visited H.M.S. *Temeraire*, one of Britain's most powerful vessels. This great turret ship was armed with twenty-five ton guns and the whole broadside could be fired by a central battery. She had only two masts and was painted grey, a portent of harsher times ahead. Prince Arthur also visited the French and Russian ships and, as she sat in the after cabin of the *Osborne* while they fired salutes, the Duchess thought her head would split. Escorted by *Temeraire*, they sailed to New Corinth from where they rode on donkeys and ponies up the two thousand feet or so to see the ruins. Amidst these they sat down to a picnic lunch, looking down as they ate to Kalamaki Bay on one side and the Gulf of Corinth on the other. The Duchess marvelled at how all that stone had been carried up such a height such a long time ago. She also enjoyed the Greek lunch, which she thought had been sent up by the King but which, according to Elphinstone, was a gift of the Municipality. It consisted of pilaff rice and pieces of meat in a sauce, roast lamb, which was killed and roasted on the spot, very good salads and a kind of pastry with honey in it. This was washed down with Greek wine which, however, proved to be sour and had to be watered. Having got out to sea again, Prince Arthur transferred to *Temeraire* to observe her firing at a range of 800 yards and launching a torpedo at a range of 250 yards which hit the anchor of the target ship. He then watched her clear for action, which involved the lowering of the masts. This was done, according to Elphinstone, with 'great alacrity' and, according to the Duchess, in seven minutes.

At Nepaulia, which they were told was the place from where the Argonauts were supposed to have started for the Trojan War, Prince Arthur left the Duchess on board *Osborne* to rest while he walked up a thousand steps to see the Castle of Palmedes. Later, while they dined on board the *Osborne*, *Temeraire* illuminated the town and the Fort with her electric light. One of the guests that evening was Captain FitzJames, the commander of the French gunboat *Bouvet*, which was also lying off Nepaulia. He proved to be both agreeable and picturesque and he accompanied the royal party next morning when they drove off in several carriages to Mycenae. It was a hot sultry day and the journey across the fertile plain of Argos seemed rather long but the scene was enlivened by Captain FitzJames, who the Duchess concluded must have been a Stuart. He appeared 'beautifully got up in knicker bockers & white canvas gaiters & a large patterned jacket & a white puggery round his straw hat.' At every village he jumped out and bought flowers which he presented to Lady Elphinstone. They were nearly roasted as they walked up to the stone mausoleum and then on to the Lion Gate at Mycenae, but Elphinstone at least, thought they had seen the tomb of Agamemnon which, he told the Queen, had recently been excavated by 'Dr Schilliemann.'

Cold and showery weather met them at Corfu and, though there were still many traces of the English occupation, Prince Arthur did not think the place was prospering under the Greeks; it seemed to be in sad decay. As they approached Cattaro, the Duchess was struck by the Montenegrin landscape, which she thought was the most picturesque they had seen. Prince Arthur's eye was taken by the Montenegrins themselves, whom he described to the Queen as wild curious looking men in very picturesque costumes and each armed with two pistols and three or four knives or daggers. From Spalato which, Prince Arthur told the Queen, had been built from the stone of Diocletian's enormous palace, they went to Salona, where there were more picturesque costumes to admire; the people wore long pigtails and grass sandals. Prince Arthur thought the men were fine looking, but much less wild than the Montenegrins. On 17th May, they came to Pola, the Portsmouth of the Austrian Empire. They were welcomed by Admiral de Barry, said to be a natural son of Lord Byron, and a Guard of Honour found by the 43rd Hungarian Regiment. Prince Arthur inspected the dockyard off which lay numerous ironclads out of commission. The Duchess was amused to notice that the visitors' book in the Naval Club contained some caricatures of Sandro Battenberg and his acceptance of the Bulgarian throne. Louis Battenberg may well have been less amused for he was the brother of this ill-starred ruler.

At 9.30 on the morning of 18th May, *Osborne* was off the entrance to Venice and for the next two hours the Duke and Duchess were on the bridge to watch the scene unfold as they moved to a mooring off the public gardens half a mile below St Mark's. Though chilly, it was a beautiful morning and the buildings were marvellously reflected in the glistening water as they moved along at half speed between the rows of piles, which Prince Arthur thought looked like bundles of black asparagus. When they tied up quantities of letters were brought aboard and the Duke and Duchess made it their first task to write theirs. At 3.15 they disembarked and walked into St Mark's Square. After dinner they had coffee at the Piazza and listened to the band. Next day they wandered around in a gondola seeing the sights of the place; they found the Church of St Lorenzo shut so they went to the Doge's Palace instead, they went up the

Campanile, admired sketches by Raphael and Michelangelo, which they saw at the *Accademia di Belle Arti*, and bought English newspapers. In the evening they returned to *Osborne* to dine and sleep and so they continued until 23rd May when they felt very low because the time had come to leave what seemed like home, the Yacht *Osborne*. Accompanied by Louis Battenberg, they cast off at 8.30 in the morning and went round by the bows to see the men who were all drawn up there. At 9.15 they left Venice in a very crowded train on which Prince Arthur found many old acquaintances. At 7.40 that evening, very tired and covered in dust, they arrived in Turin. After dinner they sat out on the balcony of their hotel listening to the music coming from a nearby *Café Chantant*. They left next morning for the twenty-one hour journey to Paris, where they moved into the same rooms they had occupied on the way out in the Hotel Bristol.

In Paris they found people dressed up to the eyes on their way out to the races at Chantilly, they walked in the Bois de Boulogne, watched children and adults riding elephants and camels in the *Jardin d'Acclimatisation* and, the next morning, went shopping. Prince Arthur exchanged visits with the President of the Republic and with Mrs Wodehouse, an old friend from his Canadian days, whom the Duchess found very clever and agreeable. They dined in a small room at a café and greatly enjoyed *Petite Mademoiselle* at the *Théatre de la Renaissance*. In their last two days, the Duchess had several seances with Madame Fromont, the dressmaker recommended to her by Lady Odo Russell, and also with Madame Corbay. She went with Prince Arthur to Versailles and to the Theatre of Varieties to see *La Vie Parisienne*, which proved to be 'very vulgar.' On the evening of 29th May, with much regret, they left Paris and arrived in their rooms at Buckingham Palace early the next morning.[2]

The marriage tour was over. Though pleasure had never been far separated from duty, it had been a great success and, for the Duchess, who had previously been hardly anywhere, an eye-opener. Prince Arthur, who knew everybody and had been all over the place, must have seemed a very sophisticated companion, but he, after all, was twenty-nine and she not yet nineteen.

While the finishing touches were applied to Bagshot Park, the Duke and Duchess took up residence in the Royal Pavilion at Aldershot and it was not until 29th December 1879 that they were at last able to move into their own home. Being the mistress of a household seems rapidly to have developed the Duchess's self-confidence and, even before the move to Bagshot, the Queen's hackles were up. The trigger was the age of the

Duchess's dresser which, in the Queen's opinion, was much too young. It was not 'respectable or proper for a young married Pcess of 19 to have no elderly person about her & to think that she knows everything.' She needed a dresser of thirty-five or thirty-six and not a fashionable lady's maid of the 'most pernicious kind.' The Queen began to fear that the Duchess was a very self-willed young girl and that, if Arthur was not firm, she would be the 'complete master over him.' The Queen, however, made these observations neither to the Duchess, nor even to Prince Arthur, but to Elphinstone. He, no doubt, had already recognised that beneath the shy and even deferential exterior, there lay in the Duchess a core of firm character and, at least by comparison with Prince Arthur, of considerable ambition. No doubt too, he found a diplomatic way of dropping a hint and at Christmas time the Duchess wrote to the Queen saying she would never forget how much she owed to her in what had been the happiest year of her life. She said that it made her tremble all over to think that Arthur was hers and she described him as 'kindness, thoughtfulness & everything good you can think of' and, in addition to that, devoted to his mother, 'a perfect husband & a perfect son.'[3]

The Commander-in-Chief thought that Prince Arthur should now take command of a Brigade, which would mean his promotion from Lieutenant-Colonel to Major-General, but the Prince thought otherwise. He told the Queen that so far he had worked his way up through every grade from Lieutenant to Lieutenant-Colonel and that he did not wish to skip the rank of Colonel. If he was considered fit for promotion, he would wish it to be to that rank and not to Major-General. He suggested that he might be given the opportunity to gain experience as a Colonel on the staff before coming to the command of a Brigade. He added, however, that, if this was not wished, he would give in. It was not, and, on 29th May 1880, he was promoted through the rank of Colonel to that of Major-General and then, on 6th September, given the command of a Brigade at Aldershot. 'I feel that I am very young for a Gen[l]'s command,' he wrote to the Queen, 'but I will do my utmost to prove worthy of so high an honor.' There was an immediate opportunity for some first hand study of the art of generalship, for, at the time of this appointment, Prince Arthur, with the Duchess, was in Germany for the autumn manoeuvres.[4]

As was not unusual, these operations were the occasion of a great concourse of grandees. Among the Emperor's other guests were the Grand Duke of Hesse, the Grand Duke and Duchess of Mecklenburg-Schwerin, Crown Prince Rudolph of Austria, the King and Queen of the Hellenes and a great number of foreign officers, among them, the Duke of Cambridge and Sir Garnet Wolseley, a brilliant General whose radical ambition and direct approach to military questions had evoked much hostility. Elphinstone told the Queen that it was fortunate the Duke of Cambridge had come as this would prevent Wolseley being taken as the chief representative of the British army. Prince Arthur was relieved to find that no one seemed to regard Wolseley as a hero, but he got the impression that he had been running things down, probably in opposition to Uncle George. He said little of the manoeuvres themselves, he was usually reluctant to bore the Queen with military matters, but he commented freely upon the personalities. Crown Prince Rudolph was not looking as ugly as his last photograph had suggested, the Queen of the Hellenes was looking handsome but had grown immensely stout, his father-in-law, Prince Frederick Charles, had become very fat and red in the face and he could not say that his arrival had been a 'source of unmixed pleasure' as he had not made himself agreeable and had been especially nasty to Louischen. This was apparently because she was now ranked above her two elder sisters. Bismarck and Moltke both spoke to him of larger matters. They said that in Germany there was now much suspicion and even fear of Russia. With a splendid harvest gathered in, it seemed that Russia would be in a position to make war. Prince Arthur gathered the impression that German opinion was in favour of the British remaining in Candahar, whither General Roberts had just marched.[5]

Prince Arthur had not been long back in England when he was given an opportunity to test his own powers of generalship. On 14th October, under the eye of the Commander-in-Chief, he commanded his Brigade for the first time in a divisional exercise carried out in the Long Valley at Aldershot. Elphinstone thought that he had done well, but Prince Arthur was by no means satisfied. He judged one element of his force, the 4th Hussars, to be badly commanded and he found that another, the 42nd Highlanders, was seriously under strength. Sometimes, however, there were touches of lighter relief. At the Volunteer manoeuvres near Brighton in April 1881, Prince Arthur rode out to the battlefield at Falmer in company with several Generals, the Colonels commanding the brigades, the artillery staff, the umpires and the French military attaché in what he described to the Duchess as that hideous bright blue uniform with red pantaloons. As they surveyed the ground and planned the battle, Prince

Arthur's horse behaved well, but a fellow officer, who had hired one from an Aldershot dealer, was less fortunate; his ran away twice and the second time took him round the race course before disappearing over the cliffs. Such were the foundations upon which Major-General the Duke of Connaught would shortly have to improvise and stake his reputation in the field of real battle.[6]

Meanwhile, Bagshot Park, so convenient for Aldershot, seemed to be nearing completion as a royal country house on a smaller scale than, but somewhat in the style of, Sandringham. When Queen Victoria came to see it in March 1880, she pronounced it very comfortable, though she thought that, with the exception of the dining and drawing rooms, it was all too dark because the windows were too small and the furniture not bright enough. She understood, however, that this was nowadays the fashion. Her more up to date daughter, the German Crown Princess, found the house 'as pretty as it is comfortable' and the taste of the arrangements pleased her very much; staying there had been like a pleasant dream. The Crown Princess's unpredictable son, Prince William, spoke admiringly of the place after taking his fiancée to lunch there. Prince Arthur was pleased. He thought his party for Ascot, which included Lord and Lady Listowel, had been a success and he told the Queen that the grounds had been in great beauty. Whether the interior was too dark or not, there was some light entertainment at Bagshot as, for example, on one evening in December 1880 when Prince Leopold's Equerry, Alec Yorke, amused the party there, including the German Ambassador, Count Münster, by preaching a parody of a sermon with the text 'Old Mother Hubbard, she went to the Cupboard.' The Prime Minister, Lord Beaconsfield, addressing his hostess as 'Madam & dear Princess,' accepted an invitation, and though by now a weary soul, seemed to be in good spirits and insisted on walking to and from Church. Even Prince Frederick Charles seemed to approve, though whenever he tried to remember the name of the house, he could only think of Bangok, which he knew was wrong.[7]

The new year of 1882 came in amidst much expectation; the Duchess was about to produce her first child. At Osborne, the Queen wished she was at Bagshot, but she was afraid of the uncertainty and, not being very well herself or, as on second thoughts she put it, not very strong, she felt that she had better stay on the Isle of Wight. Anyhow, Louischen was at a particularly good age, the same as her own when her first child had been

born, and, being slight and long, was sure to suffer less. Prince Arthur was
to remember that when the birth was imminent, he was to summon the
Home Secretary who should be put in an adjacent room where the child
could be brought for his inspection as soon as possible. A few more days
passed and the Queen feared that this long *attente* would be distressing to
Louischen. What could be the cause of 'this *mistake?*' She said that
Alfred's birth had been late and that instead of walking, or rather
wallowing about as she had been a great size, the Doctor had told her to sit
down. The child's head had got too far forward. So she lay down a good
deal and in twenty-four hours it came on. At last, at 10.15 on the morning
of 15th January, Prince Arthur telegraphed 'Have sent for Doctors, all
satisfactory.' The message reached the Queen at Osborne twelve minutes
later. At ten past five in the afternoon, he telegraphed again, 'Louischen
safely confined of a Daughter at ten minutes past three. Both doing well,
fine healthy child.' This took thirteen minutes to reach the Queen. At
10.35 that night, Dr Playfair telegraphed 'Her Royal Highness has passed
most comfortable afternoon and is as well as could be wished.' This took
fifteen minutes to travel. The Queen hoped that Prince Arthur would not
be disappointed at the child not being a son and she was afraid that
Louischen would be. For her own part, she had been sure it would be a
daughter.[8]

It all seemed to be plain sailing. The Liberal Home Secretary, Sir
William Harcourt, whom Prince Arthur had not forgotten to send for,
judged the child to be 'charming' and 'as healthy as possible.' He hoped he
might be forgiven for venturing to observe to the Queen that it was one of
the fortunate circumstances of her life and reign that whereas, of the four
previous Queens regnant of England, none had left any descendants, 'Your
Majesty counts more grand children than any King of England has ever
numbered.' He hoped that she would live to see the 'illustrious roll'
inscribed with many more names to inherit the loyalty of a grateful people.
The real truth, however, as in so many other cases, was not that which had
immediately been laid at the Queen's feet. In fact, the Duchess's pains had
come on at four in the morning. At 6.30 Prince Arthur sent for the nurse,
Mrs Taylor. The Duchess sat up until a quarter to ten when she could bear
the pain no longer and went to bed. Dr Laking arrived by special train at
11.0 and at mid day, when the pains became very severe, he gave some
ether. At 12.15 he thought the birth was imminent but instead there was
no progress and at 3.0 Dr Playfair advised Prince Arthur that instruments
should be used and then applied forceps. Prince Arthur had sat with the

Duchess until 2.0 when, feeling very upset at seeing her suffer so much, he retired to the next room, returning to her whenever there was a lull. When at last the birth was over and he collected his thoughts, it made him shudder to think of the ordeal Louischen had been through. The Queen was grieved to hear all this, though she said she had never doubted that Arthur would suffer greatly at 'what at best is a vy dreadful affair & vy painful to witness.' She began to wish that she had been there to help and now announced that she would come to see the child on 19th January. This would have to be without her usual companion, Princess Beatrice, who would be 'rather out of place' when there would be so much to tell that she ought not to hear.[9]

Alas, on 19th January there were two set backs; the Queen's visit had to be postponed because of fog and the Duchess had to give up feeding her baby, which she had set her heart on. Though she had plenty of milk, there was nothing, as Prince Arthur put it to the Queen, for the child to 'catch hold of' to suck. A wet nurse had to be sought. The German Crown Princess wrote to say how sorry she was that Louischen had to go through such a fight. She could sympathise, she said, because she had suffered so much more herself. The weather was better on 21st January and, accompanied by Lady Ely, Sir Henry Ponsonby and General Du Plat, the Queen crossed from the Isle of Wight in the yacht *Alberta* and went by special train to Bagshot station where Prince Arthur met her. She was happy and thankful to find everything going so well at Bagshot Park and it touched her more than she could express to see Prince Arthur bring in his dear little one himself. Over lunch, the talk was of the arrangements for the christening. The Queen hoped that Prince Arthur would see to it that the poor wet nurse's child was well cared for; they often got neglected and died, which, she said was shocking. On 28th January, the Duchess wrote the Queen a note in pencil saying that her doctors were astonished at how well she was doing after her terrible hours of suffering, but three days later they were concerned to note that she had some neuralgic pain and, on 31st January, Dr Laking found her pulse rather high. On 1st February, Prince Arthur described her as 'very poorly.' The neuralgic pain was in the back of the leg.[10]

The Queen wondered if Louischen was getting enough fresh air, which gave strength and, she said, 'makes blood.' Dr Playfair could find no symptom to account for the pain in the left leg but he decided that it was caused by the drains. Prince Arthur summoned a sanitary expert who found that the connections were not as good as they should be in a new house and Dr Playfair then advised that his patient should be got out of the place at once. The Queen was sorry for Prince Arthur's 'g^t trouble & anxiety,' but she told him that 'while poor old Mama lives you can *ever* turn to her for help in *any* trouble' and she promised him that 'a loving mother is one's *best friend*.' She gave instructions for rooms to be prepared at Windsor and she hoped that the move would soon put Louischen right. She was very angry with those who had neglected the drains, 'this *first* thing in building a House.' She now told Prince Arthur that she had noticed a smell in his dressing room where the baby was, but had not liked to say anything about it. Elphinstone was not a keen subscriber to the drain theory. The system, he told the Queen, had been thoroughly looked into only six weeks before and reported as perfect by an expert on the subject, namely, Messrs Verity, 'under whose superintendance everything had been constructed.' True, there had been a smell in the small waiting room but this was probably accounted for by a dead mouse or rat under the floor boards. Anyhow, the affected place was a long way from the Duchess and it was one of those accidents 'which it would have been impossible to foresee or guard against.' In other words, no one was to blame, and, if they were, they were Messrs Verity and not Sir Howard Elphinstone. The Queen was not convinced. She told Prince Arthur it was 'bad & shameful ab^t the drains' and that they should now be looked into by the very best man. She observed that Sir Howard seemed 'rather offended & hurt ab^t it' but she thought that he ought to have looked more into it himself.[11]

On Sunday 5th February, the Queen's chief doctor, Sir William Jenner, came to meet Dr Playfair at Bagshot Park. Sir William was very much concerned about the swelling in the upper part of the Duchess's left thigh. He reported to the Queen that the pain was in the region of the great vein. There were no symptoms of typhoid, but some cases of that did begin 'anomalously.' It seems that he thought the leg should be kept still but, as the air was very bad in the house, he fell in with Dr Playfair's view that the Duchess should leave it. She too was very anxious to go as she had heard so much about the drains in the last few days. So Dr Playfair gathered her into his arms, carried her to a carriage and drove with her to Windsor. Prince Arthur and Sir William Jenner followed in a second vehicle. The Queen wondered how Dr Playfair, who was a small man, had managed to carry the Duchess. She supposed he must be very strong and declared to Prince Arthur that a 'man's arms are always so much better than 2 womens!' Prince Arthur found it very strange being at Windsor without the Queen but he prayed that God would grant that it should be a turning point for

Louischen. It was not, however, until a week later that he could thank God 'who has spared me my darling little wife.'[12]

Meanwhile, Elphinstone had given up or forgotten the theory of the dead mouse or rat. He told the Queen that the cause of the bad smell had been discovered, though unfortunately not in time to make it unnecessary to remove the Duchess. He said that it was very satisfactory to find that the matter could easily be put right. A workman making a new door in the waiting room had cut through a drain pipe. This was the more unpardonable as the job had been supervised by the Clerk of the Works, whose negligence, Elphinstone told the Queen, had been 'most criminal.' No harm could have been done, however, as the source of the trouble was far removed from where the Duchess had been. This explanation too was to have a short life. Reports began to appear in the press and at the beginning of March the *Morning Post* informed its readers that the delayed convalescence of the Duchess was due to 'obstruction of the veins of the lower limb, giving rise to the well known oedematus swelling.' This was said to be traceable to a form of blood poisoning arising from the 'depressing influence of sewer gas.' Believing that the details of the unfortunate experience might be of value to medical science, Prince Arthur encouraged Dr Playfair to publish a note in the *British Medical Journal*. Writing in his capacity of Professor of obstetric medicine at King's College, London and Physician for diseases of women and children at King's College Hospital, he stated that the defects in the sanitary system at Bagshot Park were believed to have 'led directly' to the Duchess of Connaught's 'late serious illness.' He observed that the house was an entirely new construction which had been built at a cost of between £30,000 and £40,000. The sanitary system, as, he asserted, had been pointed out by Sir Howard Elphinstone at the time of its construction, was defective. Much of the work was carelessly carried out and it was astonishing that the consequences had not been worse. Offensive smells had long been perceived and were a common topic of conversation. Inmates of the house had suffered sore throats, diarrhoea, feelings of heaviness and malaise. The bath and sink drains ran under the house and were directly connected with land drains and the soil pipes. Many of them leaked and one discharged into the basement. There was a disagreeable smell in all the closets and smoke tests had shown that the bad smells and foul air passed into the saloon, study, writing room, vestibule, the Duchess's bedroom and the Duke's dressing room. The effect of such a state of affairs upon the puerperal condition needed more study but Dr Playfair gave the warning that exposure to sewage gas might cause puerperal septicaemia. He did not venture to explain why, if he had known about them from the outset, Elphinstone did nothing about these glaring defects in the drainage system; nor did he deal with the theories of the dead mouse or rat nor of the workman putting the new door into the waiting room.[13]

The Duchess, who never recovered from whatever was the cause of trouble in her leg, was well enough to be churched on 8th March and to attend the christening of her daughter at Windsor on 11th. The child, who was later to be the Crown Princess of Sweden, was given the names of Margaret Victoria Augusta Charlotte Norah. In the family, she became known as Daisy. While the drains at Bagshot were dealt with, the Duke and Duchess of Connaught decamped in search of better health to Biarritz. Prince Arthur was disappointed by the bad weather, the backward vegetation and the hideous country round about. The Duchess, however, was able to start a course of salt douches and baths for her leg. There were some amusing expeditions. On one to Cambo, they were joined by Princess Frederica of Hanover, sister of the one Prince Arthur had tried to marry, Lord and Lady Strathmore, and, among others, Sir Thomas Knox and his daughter. The last two were rather unusual; Sir Thomas had married a Siamese and his daughter had done the same. This repeat performance displeased the King of Siam, who had the Knox daughter's husband beheaded and, in exchange, sent her a yearly present of a chest of tea. When they got back to England, Prince Arthur resumed duty at Aldershot and, until 4th June when they were at last able to return to Bagshot Park, they lived in the North Camp. It was then Prince Arthur's turn to be ill; he was assailed by hay fever and had bad neuralgia in the head and jaw. Dr Laking diagnosed this as rheumatic gout but he feared to inject morphia because in cases of gout that was liable to bring on congestion of the liver. He prescribed complete rest and a change of air. Meanwhile, he applied a blister behind Prince Arthur's ear.[14]

The Duke of Edinburgh, with his flag in H.M.S. *Hercules,* happened to be about to take a Squadron to Gibraltar and he offered to take Prince Arthur with him. Sir William Jenner and Dr Laking thought this would be desirable so Prince Arthur got on board and put to sea. As usual, he took the greatest interest in the ships. *Hercules* was the newest in the Squadron and, with her eight large muzzle-loading guns, the most heavily armed. The largest was *Warrior,* which Prince Arthur had good opportunity to observe as she was the next ship to *Hercules* while several changes of formation were executed. Her engines, however, gave trouble and caused the whole Squadron to stop for half an hour during the night. Interesting exercises in fog signalling, firing and flag and siren drills were carried out and sails were set but Prince Arthur's enjoyment of all this was much impaired by headaches and toothache. Things were no better at Bagshot Park; the Duchess also had neuralgia and was suffering from stomach gripes.[15]

Despite his own sufferings and anxiety about those of the Duchess, another matter was now coming to the front of Prince Arthur's mind; he was 'dying to be employed in Egypt.' The opportunity arose from an armed rising against the Khedive's government led by the Minister of War, Arabi Pasha. The question in Prince Arthur's mind was whether British troops would be sent to put the rebellion down; that in the Queen's was whether Prince Arthur was medically fit for service in the field. On 27th June 1882, the Duke of Edinburgh's Squadron entered the Gibraltar Straights and on that day, for the Queen's consideration, he called for a medical report on his brother. Fleet-Surgeon R. C. P. Lawrenson detected signs of 'amelioration' in the course of Prince Arthur's illness, but he expressed some doubt as to whether he would be fit to take part in the manoeuvres at Aldershot in July. When pressed by Prince Alfred to be more specific, he added that the headaches might be due to taking quinine, or perhaps to dental irritation. Prince Arthur told him that he intended to return to his military duty on 4th July and Dr Lawrenson felt unable to find strong reason against his doing that. He thought his patient might become depressed if he was prevented from taking part in the manoeuvres, but he said he should rest as much as possible until then. So, on 4th July, having improved somewhat in the heat of Gibraltar, Prince Arthur left for Madrid, where he was entertained to lunch by the King. The next morning he left for Paris, where he had made an appointment to see Mr Evans, the dentist, and to meet the Duchess. The Queen was much perturbed as she was sure there was nothing the matter 'with your beautiful teeth' and, in any case, there were better dentists in England. She warned him strongly not to have the tooth pulled out as that would loosen all the others. As to his fitness to go on active service, she laid it down that he was to submit to a medical board. 'You must & are to do this,' she added when Prince Arthur began to cavil. She was also distressed about Louischen's 'state', which she said, should have been avoided and was too soon. Prince Arthur agreed to see the doctors and the Duchess explained that she too was put out by her state and wished it could have been put off for at least another year.[16]

The crucial medical examination, which had the making or the marring of Prince Arthur's military prospects, took place at Buckingham Palace on 12th July. Sir William Jenner, Dr Laking, Dr Wilks and Dr Scott found 'that no medical opinion adverse to His Royal Highness's going on active service could be expressed,' but they recommended that he should delay his departure to Egypt for three weeks or a month. Prince Arthur said that he was never upset in health by heat and that he would have to go when and where the troops he was to command were sent. The Commander-in-Chief now proposed that Prince Arthur should command the Brigade of Guards in the expeditionary force which was to go to Egypt under the command of Sir Garnet Wolseley. This brought tears to the Queen's eyes, but she gave her approval. In the first instance, she understood, the expedition would go to Malta and there was still the hope in her mind that there might be no fighting. She thought that Louischen should not live alone at Bagshot Park and she offered to put her up in Osborne Cottage, which she said would be very comfortable and where she could have anyone she liked to stay. The Queen promised Prince Arthur that she would do her best to soothe and comfort his wife. He was touched. 'The parting from you & my beloved little wife,' he wrote, 'is a thing I dread to think of & try to keep out of my head.'[17]

The prospect of action in the field, which now lay before Prince Arthur, promised to redeem the disappointment of the year before, when his old regiment, the 7th Hussars, had been sent overseas on active service. Then, he could only wish his former comrades good fortune and express to them his regret that he was not still with them to share their opportunity to prove that they were still the 7th of the Peninsula and India. Now, his own opportunity was nearly at hand. Then, he had been so much identified with the fortunes of his old regiment that he had wondered how they would carry their new Martini Henry rifles without impairing their freedom in the saddle and he had been anxious lest the regulation saddle might be too large for the small Hungarian horses and cause sores on their backs. Now, he would be responsible for the solution of such problems and the broader issues at the brigade, as opposed to the regimental, level.[18]

On 29th July 1882, Prince Arthur took leave of the Queen at Osborne and left for London with the Duchess. 'I felt as tho' my heart was torn in two when I parted with you this morg,' the Queen wrote to him. 'From your birth, excepting Baby (Beatrice),' she told him, 'you have been the dearest most loved of my children & this Expedition, the possibility of w^h somehow never entered my mind — has been a great shock & yet when the

Drs said you were well enough to go, I w ^{ld} not oppose it in any way — tho'
my heart sank within me!' Prince Arthur telegraphed his thanks and then,
accompanied by the Duchess, the Prince and Princess of Wales and their
children, the Duke of Edinburgh and the Duke of Cambridge, he went
down the Speaker's steps at Westminster and boarded a steam launch for
Woolwich. There, lying in the Albert Docks, was the P & O liner *Orient*, a
magnificent ship of five thousand tons. As the Royal party approached
there was tremendous cheering from the troops already on board and from
the crowds of onlookers. The Princes and Princesses went aboard and at
1.0 p.m. *Orient* sailed. About a mile downstream, those who had come to
bid Prince Arthur farewell disembarked. His heart sank as he watched
Louischen going off the ship. 'God bless you sweetest of wives,' he wrote
to her, '& help you to bear up bravely as becomes a soldier's wife.' As
Orient slipped down the river towards the yet unknown, there was a cheer
for her from every ship and every pier.[19]

CHAPTER 7

The Battle of
Tel-el-Kebir 1882

SAILING OFF TO WAR was an exhilarating experience. The men shook down wonderfully and, to Prince Arthur, they seemed splendid and up to anything. He thought that Louischen would not recognise the officers as the dandies of the Park and the clubs. They now looked dreadful ruffians and many of them, as he was too, were allowing their beards to grow. Prince Arthur was proud of his command and anxious to show devotion to his profession which, from his childhood, he wrote to the Queen, he had been taught to love and respect. After talking to his divisional commander, General Willis, about plans for the possibility of the landing being at Ismailia, he was filled with feelings of respect and confidence. He was delighted to take communion with his comrades when they were all in the same boat and on the edge of battle. Even so, the parting from wife and mother was painful and unsettling. Prince Arthur had hoped for a last contact as *Orient* steamed past the coast off Osborne, but the Captain would not take the ship through the Needles at night and he missed it. Instead, he walked about on deck and then turned in early and laid his head on the pillow, which Louischen had given him, under a photograph of her, which he had nailed to his bed. Though he was tired, his nerves were upset and he slept badly.[1]

Orient was a monstrous fast ship; it took her only twenty-seven hours to cross the Bay of Biscay. Her steam refrigerator held a hundred and twenty tons of frozen meat in place of the live stock of bygone days and Prince Arthur found it very good, if rather tough. While the present pointed in such ways to the future, the past also bore upon it. When the wind was right, *Orient* would still set her sails and when she cleared Biscay and came into fog she was soon lost and nearly aground. Also, as in the past, news was scarce at sea. *Orient* had been ordered to Malta, where Prince Arthur reckoned they would get orders for a landing at Ismailia or Alexandria; the former he hoped, but none on board knew. In the meantime they also knew nothing of what was happening in Egypt or that their Commander-in-Chief was still in England, feeling unwell. He had thought of speeding up his arrival at the seat of war by travelling as far as possible overland, but he was told not to do this as he needed the full sea voyage in which to recuperate. Prince Arthur also was learning the familiar military anxiety of being under strength. He had on board with him the 1st Battalion of the Scots Guards and he could only hope that the other two would be following not too far behind. He had hoped to muster two thousand in his Brigade, but he now foresaw that he would be lucky to find 1,600 and this force would soon dwindle through casualties and sickness. Meanwhile, the potential candidates danced to pipes on deck while Dr Lane, the Surgeon-Major of the Scots Guards, instructed Prince Arthur and the other officers in the application of tourniquets, splints and slings and the skill of carrying a wounded man.[2]

On 4th August *Orient* touched at Gibraltar. As she ran up to the new mole the flags of the divisional and brigade Generals were shown and a notice that the Scots Guards were on board was displayed. Intending heroes are, however, not always received as such and, as the ship lacked a bill of health, no one came on board to welcome the troops and wish them well. *Orient* soon sailed again without ado. Prince Arthur had probably never been in and out of port with such expedition. At 2.30 on the afternoon of 7th August they came within sight of Malta and about two hours later *Orient* was made fast alongside a Spanish man of war in harbour. At once, orders to sail for Alexandria were received from the War Office but, as Prince Arthur was to see again in later years, relations between the two Services did not make life easy. Sailing orders, it transpired, were a matter, not for the War Office, but the Admiralty and it took several hours to settle the formality. This gave Prince Arthur a chance to go ashore to see the Governor. He heard that Valletta had been full of refugees from Egypt and that it was costing £200 a day to support them. *Orient* was already amidst the consequences of Arabi Pasha's rising.[3]

At one in the morning on 8th August, *Orient* slipped her buoy and crept slowly out of Malta's Grand Harbour. Next afternoon her sails were set and she sped along at fourteen knots, which was kept up all night as well. On the morning of 10th August, Alexandria came in sight. The harbour

proved to be full of men of war and the forts presented a most curious
sight; a naval bombardment had smashed them about on all sides and
there were three shell holes in the lighthouse. When later he came to
inspect this damage closely, Prince Arthur realised that he had never seen
such destruction. Some of the guns were entirely dismounted and others
were tilted up with their magazines knocked to atoms. This, however,
had not brought Arabi Pasha to bay; he and his troops had moved inland.[4]

Prince Arthur went ashore to call on the Khedive. They sat on divans
smoking chibouks and drinking coffee. From what the Khedive said, it
seemed that Arabi's positions were strong and that he was well supported
by artillery. It was clear that it would not be easy to get rid of him. Prince
Arthur found the Khedive most affable but he observed that he had grown
much fatter since he had last seen him. Twice Prince Arthur went aboard
H.M.S. *Helicon* to attend Councils of War with Admiral Seymour,
commanding the Squadron at Alexandria, Admiral Hoskins, commanding
the naval forces in the Suez Canal, General Adye, Wolseley's Chief of
Staff, his own divisional General, Willis, General Earle, commanding the
lines of communication and General Alison, commanding the troops
ashore in Alexandria. At nine minutes past three on 12th August, Prince
Arthur telegraphed from Alexandria to the Queen that he was disembarking the Brigade of Guards and would form up opposite the enemy. At
about the same time the Queen telegraphed to Sir John McNeill, who was
with Prince Arthur, that she had heard that there was much bad feeling
among the Egyptian population and that she trusted that Prince Arthur
would not 'go about' on shore. What McNeill did with this instruction,
history seems not to record.[5]

Within twenty-four hours, Prince Arthur had moved the whole of his
Brigade up to Ramleh and established his Headquarters in a deserted girls'
school three hundred yards from his men, half a mile from the sea and a
mile and a half from the enemy, who were clearly visible at their earth
works. Prince Arthur saw Ramleh as the Brighton of Egypt; it consisted of
villas and gardens and had a perfect climate. Arabi, however, had reduced
it to a dead town and left it empty and looted. The streets were littered
with smashed furniture and the dust was awful. The three hundred young
ladies, who had lived in Prince Arthur's H.Q., had left in such a hurry that
their slippers were still there. Prince Arthur was in the saddle from
morning to night and for much of the nights as well. He was preparing to
repel an attack and also, if so ordered, to advance against the enemy
positions. On his first night ashore he had found it heavy going labouring

through the sand as he walked round his outposts and, within a few hours of that, he was woken by his Orderly with the news that firing had broken out and that his inlying picket was reinforcing the outlying one. Prince Arthur pulled on some clothes and rode straight out to the scene to find that the enemy cavalry had come up against his outposts but had quickly withdrawn. Two hours later, at 6.0 on the morning of 13th August, Prince Arthur despatched a small force of mounted infantry to reconnoitre Arabi's main position. The officer in command brought back a sketch of it, which he had taken from a vantage point. It showed that the position was already very strong and swarms of working parties had been seen strengthening it still further with massive earthworks. Prince Arthur learnt more from a deserter, who came over to his lines. Conversely, he had a French newspaper reporter arrested after he had tried to go over to Arabi's position.[6]

Until the Commander-in-Chief arrived it was impossible to say if the campaign would be fought from this position or some other, but, whatever was decided, would be fraught with difficulties. It seemed that Arabi had control of the railway system, which had been constructed with strategic considerations in mind. He also had control of the water levels and this was already causing problems in the Suez Canal. His defensive positions were very strong and his military strength seemed to be formidable. Any serious reverse to British arms might well lead to a massacre in Cairo and a sustained campaign in the interior of Egypt would be likely to alienate the heart of the Egyptian population and produce yet wider support for Arabi.[7]

On 16th August, Sir Garnet Wolseley, the Commander-in-Chief, arrived and rode round some of the positions at Ramleh with Prince Arthur, who, he noted, was 'burnt as brown as a saddle.' Next day, at a Council of War, Prince Arthur was ordered to strike his tents that afternoon and re-embark his Brigade; the battle was not to be at Ramleh. It was given out that it would be at Aboukir, but Prince Arthur suspected, or possibly knew, that the real move would be to Ismailia. As the troopships and their naval escorts prepared to sail from Alexandria, they did not omit to dress overall in honour of the birthday of the Emperor of Austria.[8]

It was a pretty sight, Prince Arthur wrote to the Queen, watching the armada forming up and then sailing with it from Alexandria. They did, indeed, proceed to Aboukir, the historic Bay, he reminded her, where the English army had landed in 1801 and where Nelson had destroyed the

French fleet. This time, no such events followed and the armada was ordered directly to the Suez Canal. So far, Prince Arthur thought, so good. His Brigade had exchanged its first shots with the enemy and it had learned much from its short time in Ramleh. He now hoped that it would have fought a successful engagement before the Queen received his letter, which he wrote on 19th August.[9]

This certainly seemed to be possible when *Orient*, with Prince Arthur on board, reached Port Said at 9.0 on the morning of 20th August but the risk of the engagement being a defeat, or of some other disaster, was now very real. De Lesseps had withdrawn all the Suez Canal pilots in protest against the entry of British troopships. The canal offices and the postal and telegraph services were under his hostile control and the Governor of Ismailia had adhered to Arabi's cause. Despite the serious risks, *Orient*, nevertheless, entered the canal and as she did so reports came that fighting had broken out in Ismailia. *Orient* had penetrated no more than three miles when she found her way blocked by the *Catalonia*, carrying the 50th, which had gone aground and there she was forced to spend the night. Prince Arthur found consolation in the coolness of the evening and the sight of the lagoons covered with lovely flamingoes. He slept well, disturbed only by the impact of a launch which collided with *Orient* in the night. His, after all, was not the responsibility for entering the Canal.[10]

Next morning a tug came up from Port Said and, with its help, *Orient* managed to squeeze past the stranded *Catalonia* and proceed on her way. As fighting in Ismailia continued, Prince Arthur was ordered to prepare to disembark his men as light as possible. For his own part, he decided to take only his camp bed, a change of flannels and a small tent. He was looking forward to getting off the ship in which the smell of men and horses had become anything but pleasant. He was also enjoying the thought of the Duchess singing with Tosti. She had such a nice voice, he wrote to her, which only needed practice.[11]

At 4.0 a.m. on 22nd August, Prince Arthur began to disembark his men at Ismailia. Temporarily reinforced by some Marines, they bivouacked that evening under an avenue of trees along the Sweet Water Canal. Prince Arthur set up his H.Q. on the ground floor of the Khedive's palace, where the rooms were fine but without any furniture. There was no fighting in the immediate vicinity. Next morning at 5.30 he rode out across the desert with McNeill for three miles to Nefisch, which was the junction of the Ismailia to Cairo railway line. They found that the enemy camp and the railway station had been smashed up by a naval bombardment. There was now no sign of the enemy and, though there were reports of fighting on the Suez, or left, side of his position, Prince Arthur heard no sound of firing all day. In his preparations for an advance, he was hindered by the lack of transport and he was handicapped by not being able to requisition accommodation and other necessities as they were not at war with the Egyptian people, only with those who had risen with Arabi. His first idea was that it would take him three days to get his Brigade ready to move, but, in the event, he was given not much more than twenty-four hours.[12]

At about 10.15 next morning, Prince Arthur was told that a reconnaissance force of the Household Cavalry and some mounted infantry, which was supported by two guns of the Royal Horse Artillery, had run into a much larger group of the enemy, amounting to some 9,000 men. A general engagement was developing and Prince Arthur was ordered to march his Brigade to reinforce his outnumbered comrades as soon as possible. This was very awkward; half the Brigade of Guards and all their transports were out on fatigue duties and the rest of the men had just drawn their rations which, at this moment, were half cooked. The best Prince Arthur could do was to call in his fatigue parties, push on with the meals and order a parade for 1.0 p.m. At 1.15 the Brigade marched off in the worst heat of the day. When they cleared the town they came straight into the desert where the sun blazed down on the sand. Many of the men had been on fatigues since 4.30 that morning and others had been out on picket duty all night. Now they were marching in full sun immediately after eating a meal. The route was soon littered with men lying in the sand groaning and vomiting. Prince Arthur thought it a terrible ordeal for his Brigade, but orders were orders and he resolved that if even half his men fell out, march he would to the relief of the beleaguered Household Cavalry. Presently they came within sound of firing and Lord Melgund, who had been second in command of the mounted infantry component, came up severely wounded in the hand. He was soon followed by the Commanding Officer, Captain Parr, who had been badly wounded in the leg. As he had lost a lot of blood, Prince Arthur gave him wine and water. It was evident that the engagement had been going on all day and that the British were suffering heavy casualties. At this juncture, Prince Arthur was ordered to halt to enable the 7th and 4th Dragoon Guards to march ahead of him along the railway line, on which he then resumed his march. As he came nearer the scene of action, Prince Arthur came upon Sir Garnet Wolseley, who told him that he now regretted that he had not ordered up the Brigade of Guards earlier in the morning. As it was, it was not until 6.15 in the evening that the Brigade of Guards came onto the field of battle. They did so in open order as shells were still bursting, but the firing quickly died down and the night came on pretty fast. Prince Arthur's Brigade had missed the action at Tel-el-Maskhuta.[13]

General Willis now appeared and ordered Prince Arthur to occupy the ground on the right flank and to cover his position with outposts. Having given his orders, Prince Arthur then rode round the placings and found that they accorded with Willis's intentions. He then rode back to his Brigade post in the rear of his centre and lay down on a small mound of sand. It was 8.30 and he had just begun to eat some biscuit when he was summoned by General Willis and told to shift the whole of his position to cover a gap on his left which had been opened by the posting of a regiment elsewhere. Though his men were asleep and it was pitch dark, the new positions were occupied within an hour and a half and when Prince Arthur rode round to satisfy himself that they were correct, the men were already asleep again. It was half past eleven when he got back to his own position for the night. He took a little wine, but there was nothing to eat except some biscuit. His baggage animals had not yet come up. Prince Arthur lay down beside his horse and, despite it now being very cold, managed to snooze a little.[14]

This was not for long; at 3.30 next morning, Prince Arthur buckled on his sword, ate a morsel of biscuit, took a little whisky and water and rode off to report to General Willis. He was told to stand the Brigade of Guards to arms and then to advance to attack the enemy. After several hours marching in the face of artillery fire, it became apparent that the enemy was withdrawing and when Prince Arthur's men came to the main enemy positions at Camp Maskhuta, they found them deserted. The ground was littered with the bodies of Arabi's soldiers and with dead horses and camels. The canal had been drained and the railway blocked by an enormous bank of earth. Clouds of sand, a plague of flies and temperatures of up to 102° in the shade, and 'anything you like' in the sun, made Camp Maskhuta a most unpleasant place.[15]

Prince Arthur lingered in Camp Maskhuta from 26th August until 5th September. He had precious little food and dare not drink wine in such a climate. As to comforts, he had little more than the clothes in which he stood; he recognised that campaigning was 'pretty rough work.' One false alarm followed another and there were some hard and fruitless marches. To Prince Arthur it seemed unfair that while other elements of Wolseley's expeditionary force had been engaged in hard fighting, his own Brigade had not. This pause in the proceedings was due to Wolseley's determination not to advance upon Arabi's position at Tel-el-Kebir until he had ten days supplies at the front. This was because he aimed to smash Arabi there and then push on at once to deny him the chance of rallying such forces as might escape. In writing on 3rd September to tell the Queen this, Wolseley added that the Duke of Connaught had begged him to allow his Brigade a prominent part in the attack when it came. Wolseley told the Queen, however, that his plan was to keep the Guards Brigade in reserve as much as possible.[16]

The interlude gave the opportunity for some leave and, on 5th September, Prince Arthur left the stinking conditions of Camp Maskhuta for the comparative luxury of Ismailia and the troopship *Orient*. He travelled back by train, lying in a goods truck on his bag, which contained his fatigue hat, stockings, sponge, nail brush, tooth brush and pyjamas. Among the officers going on leave with him were Major Lane, who, on an earlier occasion, had saved him from drowning when they were swimming together off the French coast, and Sir William Gordon-Cumming, who, on a later one, was to cause embarrassment by supposedly cheating at cards in the presence of the Prince of Wales at Tranby Croft. In Ismailia, Prince Arthur went to see Wolseley, who gave him lemonade and a cigarette and told him that his Brigade would soon be ordered up to Kassassin and that thereafter there would be a hard battle near Tel-el-Kebir. Arabi was now very strongly entrenched there and he was said to be supported by heavy guns. A hospital had been established in the Khedive's palace and Prince Arthur went there to see the inmates. Three of them had been very badly wounded and one, whose shoulder had been shattered, was in agonies and Prince Arthur detected death in his countenance. Elsewhere, he came upon a bivouac of the 87th Fusiliers whose band were playing as though, it struck Prince Arthur, they were still in England. He went to see his charger *Claremont*, which had fallen sick, and he called on the Admiral on board H.M.S. *Helicon*. He then retired on board *Orient* where he enjoyed a delicious salt bath and then the luxury of a good dinner and iced champagne. He was up next morning at 6.0 and, before returning to Maskhuta, he visited his valet, Harnach, who was on the sick list, and then went aboard the hospital ship *Carthage* to see the wounded who were being sent home. When he got back to Maskhuta, he found the camp full of flies and almost unbearable. Two days later, he was told that he was to move his Brigade up to Kassassin on 10th

September and that all available forces were to be there by 12th. The battle would not now be long delayed.[17]

Prince Arthur and all the other Generals were ordered to meet Sir Garnet Wolseley at 4.0 a.m. on 12th September. They assembled at the main picket of the camp at Kassassin and then, with an escort of a troop of Indian cavalry, Wolseley rode out with them for two miles in the direction of Arabi's position at Tel-el-Kebir. They dismounted and Wolseley told them that they would advance to the attack that night. The danger of moving into action in the dark was that direction might be lost and the concentrations required at the decisive points might not materialise. The advantage was that, if the right positions could be reached at the right times, the attack at dawn might take the enemy by surprise so that he might be destroyed before he could withdraw. Even if the enemy did observe the advance, he would not be able to bring his heavy guns into effective action until it was light. The aim, in short, was to bring off a frontal attack along the enemy's whole line and, in the course of it, to turn both his flanks. Prince Arthur thought it was a 'plucky thing' to undertake and he wrote to the Duchess that if it succeeded, the enemy might be smashed in this one battle; if it did not, the advance to Cairo would be a tedious business. His hope was that he would command his Brigade well.[18]

Prince Arthur struck his camp at Kassassin at 6.20 in the evening of 12th September and formed up his Brigade on the ridge above the camp at 7. He then waited while the artillery formed on his left and the 2nd Brigade in his front. His role was to march in support of the 2nd Brigade. He formed his force into half battalion columns and arranged files of the Scots Guards to maintain contact in the darkness with the artillery and the 2nd Brigade. At thirty minutes after midnight, he gave the order to advance, keeping direction by observing a star. The night was very dark and, after the heat of the day, it felt disagreeably cold. There was an unpleasant smell and the bodies of those who had fallen in the earlier fights lay all over the place. The going was difficult and the artillery kept poor direction, constantly taking the ground over which Prince Arthur's left should have been advancing. The 2nd Brigade veered now one side and then the other of the right direction. If these three elements, the two brigades and the artillery, should lose touch or become confused, Wolseley's plan might fail. To maintain the element of surprise, words of command were supposed to be kept to a minimum and smoking was forbidden. In the stillness of the night, however, Prince Arthur could constantly hear the voice of Colonel Gregorie, who was commanding the 2nd Royal Irish in the 2nd Brigade, and it proved difficult to enforce the no smoking rule. As dawn began to break, Prince Arthur realised that the artillery had veered off from the direction of the 2nd Brigade, but he decided to stay with the latter even at the cost of losing touch with the artillery because he knew that his vital role was to support the 2nd Brigade. 'At 4.55,' Prince Arthur later wrote to the Duchess, 'out boomed a gun in our front followed by three others and then a smart rattle of musketry.' The enemy had spotted the impending attack. The cavalry vedettes came 'tearing in' and Prince Arthur called back his advanced files, which had successfully kept contact with the 2nd Brigade. Soon after, there were 'shells whizzing over our heads.' Prince Arthur could now see the flashes of the enemy artillery and rifle fire. As his Brigade continued its advance, the enemy fire became incessant, wreaths of smoke rolled along his entrenchments and bullets whizzed through the air. In the absence of orders, Prince Arthur formed his Brigade into loose order for attack, but, though several of his men had now been hit, he continued to hold his fire.[19]

The air had filled with smoke and the din of guns and rifles combined with the roar of shells and the 'pinging' of bullets. General Willis now ordered Prince Arthur to swing to the right in preparation for turning the enemy flank. As he moved to execute this manoeuvre, Prince Arthur saw that his bugler had been hit in the leg. Almost at once, he and his men heard the sound of cheering on both flanks. This told them that the enemy position had been captured and when the Guards Brigade advanced, they found it abandoned; the enemy was clearly in precipitate flight. There were many dead of the 2nd Brigade and the enemy dead lay thick on the ground in much greater numbers. While giving a wounded man of the 84th a drink from his water bottle, Prince Arthur saw several of his men doing the same for wounded Egyptians. Having passed through the enemy entrenchments, Prince Arthur came to the edge of the high ground which commanded the canal and the railway in its rear. There he beheld Arabi's camp, into which British troops were now pouring, shouting and cheering. On the far side of the canal, the enemy was to be seen 'flying as fast as their legs, camels, horses, donkeys & mules would carry them.' Some tried to get away in a train, but before they could get it started, they were surrounded and captured by the cavalry. Prince Arthur halted his Brigade on this vantage point and then he went on ahead through a mass of troops and the wreckage of battle to report himself and offer his congratulations to Sir Garnet Wolseley, whom he saw on the canal bridge.[20]

Prince Arthur reckoned that Wolseley deserved the greatest credit and he thought that a more complete defeat of the enemy could not be imagined. The amount of stuff captured was not to be described, he wrote to the Duchess. Rifles, ammunition, accoutrements, clothing, musical instruments and flags lay on all sides and there were some magnificent tents, especially Arabi's, in which Prince Arthur picked up the nationalist leader's visiting card. With a force, which Prince Arthur estimated at 11,000 infantry, 3,000 cavalry, sixty guns and odds and ends including the Naval Brigade, an Army Hospital Corps and the Engineers, Wolseley had won a brilliant victory against an enemy, which Sir John McNeill numbered at 30,000. 'Even in Germany,' Prince Arthur thought, 'they will have to own that seldom if ever has such an advance been carried out in the dark with such success.' The British attack had been from a lower position in the open and, though the Egyptian rifle fire had been rather wild, Arabi had had the advantage of defending a high position from behind a parapet. The importance of the night march was yet further emphasised in Prince Arthur's mind when he saw that Arabi had seventy heavy guns in position and that these were splendidly served. His entrenchments extended over five miles and there were five large forts, each with several guns in it, and numerous smaller ones.[21]

The horrors of war were also borne in on Prince Arthur as he looked over the scene of battle. Though the losses to his own Brigade of two N.C.Os and two officers killed and about thirty or forty N.C.Os and men wounded, were not heavy, there had been considerable carnage elsewhere. There was an awful smell due to 'everything that is nasty' and hundreds of the dead and the dying lay about. Of the British, Prince Arthur counted ten of the 74th. Two of their officers, a Major and a Subaltern, lay in a ditch with five of their men, all with their faces to the enemy and their bayonets fixed. Piteous shouts came from wounded Egyptians and Prince Arthur wished he had water to give them. Ditches were chock full of the bodies of Arabi's soldiers. He told the Duchess that it was a terrible sight which he would never forget, but he found it curious how war blinded the feelings. What in ordinary times would have horrified him, he now found did not have much effect. Indeed, on the evening after the battle, he had a light dinner under an Arab awning while the combined drums and fifes played regimental marches, *See the Conquering Hero Comes* and *God Save the Queen*. Prince Arthur found the cheering which then broke out most affecting. Dosed with quinine against the risk of infection, he slept tolerably well, but not before he had said a fervent prayer of thanks to God for having been so merciful to him that day.[22]

In the hour of his victory, Wolseley had telegraphed to the Queen that his attack had begun at 5 a.m. and that by 7 he was in possession of the whole enemy camp and quantities of their supplies. The enemy had been completely routed with heavy losses. He regretted that his own force had suffered severe losses. He reported that the Duke of Connaught was well and that he had 'behaved admirably leading his Brigade to the attack.' This news triggered a bonfire on the top of Craig Gowan, one of the heights above Balmoral Castle, where the Queen's anxiety gave way to thanksgiving and rejoicing. She asked God to bless her 'darling child who I am so proud of!' Next day, Wolseley enlarged upon his telegram by writing to the Queen that he had heard on all sides of the cool courage which the Duke of Connaught had displayed under fire and he admitted that it had been a great relief to him to find that the Duke was unhit and well and cheery when he first saw him after the battle. He told the Queen that he was a 'first rate Brigadier general,' and that he took 'more care of his men and is more active in the discharge of his duties than any of the generals now with me.' He wrote that his next move with the Duke of Connaught and the Brigade of Guards would be directly into Cairo. He had already despatched a cavalry force there in the hope of seizing the capital at a stroke.[23]

Wolseley was, indeed, more than relieved that he had escaped the fate of being in command of an attack in which the Duke of Connaught had been killed and he admitted to the Duke of Cambridge the anxiety he had felt 'when the roar of musketry went rolling over to my right, where the Guards were,' and how the horrible thought 'that he might be killed came upon me.' He added that should it ever be his good fortune to command troops in the field again, he would always wish to have the Duke of Connaught with him and he said that in his blunt way, he thought this was the greatest praise he could bestow on anyone. One of the officers of the Brigade of Guards, who was near Prince Arthur during the action, recorded that as shells pitched near him, the Duke of Connaught had 'sat on his horse on a bit of rising ground as cooly as possible & I did not see him even attempt to move or duck his head although some shells must have passed precious close to him.' Sir John McNeill, himself an old campaigner who had won the V.C., said that the Duke of Connaught's behaviour had been beyond all praise and that he had remained 'perfectly cool' with 'his head all there.' He said that in the half hour during which the Brigade of Guards was a target of Arabi's guns, he had himself never before experienced such heavy fire. These estimates of Prince Arthur's conduct on the field of action, made by some who were there, were later, as we shall see, to be contradicted by some others who were not.[24]

On the morrow of the victory at Tel-el-Kebir, however, neither Wolseley nor Prince Arthur were resting on their laurels; they were in the greatest possible hurry to get to Cairo. After a number of hitches, they started out at 4.45 in the afternoon of 14th September. They went together, travelling by train in a worn out first class carriage which had lost its cushions. They soon changed to another train, which had come from Kassassin with the Commander-in-Chief's baggage on board and several of his staff. In addition to that, there was room only for one Company of the Scots Guards and Sir Garnet Wolseley's guard, which was found by the Royal Marines. Thus equipped, they resumed their journey to Cairo. On the way to Zagazig, they saw no end of British troops on the march and they passed through pickets of Blue Jackets and Indians. The Egyptian population was out in every direction and Prince Arthur thought they did not seem to know what to make of the swarthy Indian warriors who shared their religion but not their language. There were plenty of them about for only a few hours earlier General Macpherson, who commanded the Indian contingent, had seized Zagazig by a brilliant and bold stroke. He had then established his H.Q. in a waiting room on the station and there Wolseley and Prince Arthur now joined him for dinner. They then sought another waiting room to serve as a bedroom and there the Prince and the Commander-in-Chief lay down to sleep. Prince Arthur's feet almost touched Sir Garnet's head and Colonel Methuen's nearly did the same to his. Sandflies and mosquitoes made it an uncomfortable night and an unpleasant headache next morning proclaimed that General Macpherson's dinner had not agreed with Prince Arthur's stomach. Even so, he was on the platform at 3.30 a.m. to meet a train bringing in more Scots Guards. They were very surprised to find their General there. Rumours of fighting also arrived and it was said that Arabi had escaped in a railway engine. In a damp and foggy dawn Wolseley and Prince Arthur pushed on to Banka. Here they found a deputation of Egyptian notables from Cairo, which gave them the exciting news that the cavalry, despatched immediately after the victory at Tel-el-Kebir, had seized the Citadel in Cairo and that, on the previous evening, they had captured Arabi. Perhaps with more confidence than they can have felt when they started this extraordinary journey, Wolseley and Prince Arthur again pushed on for Cairo.[25]

When they got there they found a great crowd on the platform and, after making the best enquiries they could, they decided to march the Scots Guards into the Citadel. Prince Arthur drove there in a carriage through a great crowd of onlookers. The people seemed to be friendly, but Prince Arthur well knew that there were many fanatics about who hated the sight of the British. When he had formally taken possession of the Citadel, Prince Arthur retired to the house of Sir Edward Malet, the British Minister, but for food, he had to resort to the only functioning hotel, the Royal. He was nearly famished but so were the other officers and correspondents who thronged it and there was not enough to go round. By evening on 18th September the whole of Prince Arthur's Brigade had arrived in Cairo. The victory at Tel-el-Kebir had been fully exploited, Arabi Pasha was a prisoner of Prince Arthur's and the revolt was over. It had all been achieved in the nick of time. A delay of another six hours in entering Cairo, Prince Arthur wrote to the Prince of Wales, would probably have seen the place in flames, the Christians and the Jews murdered and Arabi fled into Upper Egypt. All praise, he said, was due to Sir Garnet Wolseley for the elaborate and careful plans he had made; the cavalry's seizure of the Citadel had been a tremendous march. He was not, however, much impressed by the Egyptian notables who fawned on him and protested their gratitude to the Queen and the English nation for having saved Cairo. Arabi, on the other hand, though crest-fallen, struck him as being a dignified figure. Tall and rather stout with a dark complexion and close cut beard, he greeted Prince Arthur with a salute, but then hung his head. Prince Arthur allowed him a servant and his own food, but he was allowed to see no one without the written consent of Sir Garnet Wolseley. It was, no doubt, the knowledge of what Arabi had done and the sight of the notables who now denounced him, which convinced Prince Arthur that the Egyptians were unfit to govern themselves.[26]

Now that the military expedition had achieved its purpose, Prince Arthur would have liked to have come home, but the Queen thought otherwise. Influenced, perhaps, by the bad effect of the Duke of Cambridge's sudden and early departure from the Crimea a generation earlier, she thought that Prince Arthur and the Guards should be, not the first, but the last to leave. He was to continue to command his Brigade, which would stay in Egypt for the time being, and, in addition, he was appointed Governor of Cairo with discretion to do what he thought best.[27]

At the Khedive's invitation, Prince Arthur moved into one of his palaces, Kasr el Nouszah, but he told the Queen that this sudden plunging into comfort and luxury was by no means entirely welcome. Living there was a nuisance and an expense because other people's carriages and servants got tacked onto him. In the Army there was more sickness among the officers and men than there had been during the campaign; they now had too much to eat and drink, Prince Arthur thought, and not enough to do. He had not much to do himself, a thing which he never enjoyed. Nor was he much impressed by the Khedive's re-entry into Cairo on 25th September. Prince Arthur, accompanied by Sir Garnet Wolseley and Sir Edward Malet, drove with the Khedive through crowds which were more enthusiastic that he had expected, but nothing rang true to his ear. He was sure that the upper and middle classes in Egypt were 'most despicable' and the ordinary people needed a strong hand if they were not to become the the tool of any scoundrel. He thought that Egypt for the Egyptians meant chaos and that if the British were not paramount, some other power would be.[28]

In contrast to this view of the Egyptians, Prince Arthur had developed a great admiration for the Indians, who had played such an important part in the campaign, and he now set about trying to obtain recognition of them by their sovereign. He told the Queen that two Native officers, one N.C.O. and one Private from each of the Indian regiments which had served in Egypt had been invited to England. He was afraid that she might be up in Balmoral but he knew that she would want to see the Brigade of Guards when it got home. He suggested, therefore, that when she did this on Horse Guards Parade, all the Indians should be invited and given specially prominent positions. He hoped she would see them again at Windsor and that she would then personally present them with their campaign medals. Thus, he began to introduce to the Queen his idea that Indians were very special people; it was one which eventually took a rather greater hold than he had expected.[29]

If he feared that the Queen might not pay enough attention to the Indians, he was also concerned that she might devote too much to him. At first he was afraid that, in her love and goodness, she was making a hero of him. He told the Duchess to try to curb her enthusiasm as he did so hate being made a fuss of and had 'done nothing so very wonderful beyond not running away when I was fired at.' He was then fearful that she would confer some honour on him higher than he deserved and, worse still, higher than that given to others who had done the same as himself. The Queen, indeed, did wish Prince Arthur to be made a G.C.B. but, fortunately for him, the Secretary of State for War, Mr Childers, deprecated the idea and said that he did not think that the Duke of Connaught would wish for anything higher than what was given to the others who had commanded brigades. He pointed out to Ponsonby that there had been some soreness about the Duke being selected to command the Guards Brigade, which evidently some others had their eyes on, and he did not wish any question about honours to be added to that. The Queen gave in and when he heard that he was to get, not the first, but the third class of the Order, the C.B., Prince Arthur was heartily relieved. The German Emperor was not concerned with such niceties; he conferred the *Pour Le Mérite* upon his Godson.[30]

On 19th October, Prince Arthur saw Wolseley off on his way home and found that he was now the last of the Generals of the expeditionary force left in Egypt. He had come to loathe the comfortable palace in which he was living and he feared that his men in the Brigade of Guards would blame him for the delay in their return home. At last, however, their release came, and on 6th November Prince Arthur arrived in drizzling rain at Dover. He came up to London with the Duchess and the Duke of Edinburgh, who came to meet him, by special train and was greeted by the Duke of Cambridge at Charing Cross. Despite a deluge of rain, he was immensely cheered by a great crowd. On stepping ashore in England, he had been handed a letter from the Queen, in which she welcomed him home 'crowned with success & such well earned praise.' She also laid much stress upon how improper it would be for him to go to stay with Bertie at Sandringham before coming to see her; nor did she wish him to go to public dinners and other such celebrations. Prince Arthur duly abandoned his visit to Sandringham and declined an invitation to dine with Mr Gladstone on 8th November. He did, however, manage to avoid the trek up to Balmoral and the Queen agreed to defer their reunion until she came to Windsor on the ground that it might be dangerous for Prince Arthur to be exposed to the cold of Scotland so soon after coming from Egypt.[31]

On 18th November the Queen came up to London to review her troops returned from the Egyptian campaign. Her heart was in her mouth as she watched Arthur ride past at the head of the troops he had commanded in action. He looked so like his dear father, 'who would have been as proud of you as I am,' she wrote. Some thought that the Queen had done all she could to spoil the occasion, even to the extent that the Crown Princess of Prussia, who had come all the way from Berlin to see it, had been reduced to tears. Prince Arthur, however, wished only to congratulate the Queen on the success of the day and the immense enthusiasm of the people. For his own part, he told her, it would ever be his pride to take the deepest interest in those brave men with whom he had served in Egypt. After these excitements and an investiture at Windsor, Prince Arthur was able to escape to Bagshot where he had a tremendous reception from the local people. When he arrived, the village streets were lined with Volunteers, including some from Wellington College, who were making their first appearance. There were triumphal arches, a line of fir trees and flags. The inhabitants presented an address to Prince Arthur.[32]

The trumpets of war are not always sounded in harmony. Before the year was out, Sir Edward Hamley, who had commanded the Second Division, published an article which rather took the Queen by surprise. She sent it to Prince Arthur, who told her that he found nothing very new in it. It showed that the losses of the Highland Brigade had been the heaviest, but that was already well known; it 'cleverly' tried to show that the whole position at Tel-el-Kebir had been taken by the Second Division and that the First, in which Prince Arthur's Brigade had been, had not arrived until half an hour later and had, therefore, been unable to do anything. Prince Arthur told the Queen that this was not a fair appraisal. Though Hamley had pierced the enemy's centre, his left was still very strongly held and had not the First Division come up at that time, Hamley might have been outflanked and taken in the rear. 'If the object of Gen[l] Hamley's pamphlet were to blow his own trumpet,' he concluded, 'no one can deny that he has succeeded.'[33]

Wolseley had contrived a brilliant victory at Tel-el-Kebir and, through a rapid and audacious follow up to Cairo, had, at a single stroke, achieved the political object of extinguishing Arabi Pasha's rising. Prince Arthur, though not in the van of the attack, had shown admirable steadiness under fire and had commanded the Brigade of Guards entirely to the satisfaction of the Commander-in-Chief. None could now say with justice that his soldiering was only for the show of uniforms and glitter of parades; he had experienced the privations and the hazards of campaigning and he had proved himself to be an efficient General at the brigade level. He was still only thirty-two.

15. *The arrival of the Amir of Afghanistan in the Viceroy's camp at Rawalpindi, April 1885.*

16. *The Viceroy's camp at Rawalpindi, April 1885. Prince Arthur is seated centre to the right of the tent pole, the Duchess on the left, the Viceroy, Lord Dufferin, centre to the left of the tent pole, Lady Dufferin is next to Prince Arthur and Sir Frederick Roberts is seated third from the right.*

17. *The Duke and Duchess of Connaught and their children (left to right: Princess Patricia, young Prince Arthur, Princess Margaret) with Queen Victoria. Behind are Princess Beatrice and Prince Henry of Battenberg, 1886.*

18. *The Duke and Duchess of Connaught with their children in India, c1888.*

CHAPTER 8

Divisional Command in India 1883-1885

AT A GREAT PARADE IN Cairo while he was still Governor of that city, Prince Arthur had thought that the 72nd Highlanders looked the best of the troops. They were magnificent men, beautifully turned out and each man, he noticed, wore two medals. They had been through the Afghan War and had taken part in the march from Kabul to Candahar. Earlier, during the campaign against Arabi Pasha, he had been much impressed by the swarthy warriors from India who had come to reinforce Wolseley's army and he had taken special steps to secure proper recognition of their services by the Queen Empress. Now he was hoping that his own next military appointment would be to a command in India, but it remained to be seen if the Queen would agree to this and, if she did, whether or not the War Office and the India Office would concur in a suitable vacancy being offered to him. Even if all this was resolved, the question would still remain as to how far Prince Arthur would go out as an ordinary Major-General and how far as the son of the Queen Empress.[1]

Meanwhile, the birth of their second baby was nearly due and, as it seemed unwise to risk another confinement at Bagshot, Prince Arthur and the Duchess moved into Windsor Castle in the middle of December 1882. The Queen half thought of staying there herself but then decided that this would upset Christmas for too many people and went to Osborne as usual. This meant that she would get the news of the event by telegraph and she was anxious that it should be conveyed in a proper form. To say 'confined of,' she told Prince Arthur, was 'really absurd.' The correct official phrase, she told him, was 'delivered of' or 'gave birth to' and that anyone should think that this last alternative was indelicate was also absurd. In private, she further explained, one could say 'confined with' or 'got a son.' In due course Prince Arthur was to find that he had to amend the doctor's bulletin to make it conform to the Queen's rubric but then the Queen seemed to forget her own rules and when she came to write out the announcement of the birth of Prince Arthur's son in the Court Circular she stumbled considerably over the words 'confined' and 'delivered.'[2]

On 13th January 1883 the Duchess was 'safely delivered of a Prince.' The baby's father had gone that morning to Woolwich to unveil a statue of the Prince Imperial but a telegram brought him back in haste to Windsor where he found Louischen looking rosy and radiant. She told him that the birth had been easy and that she had only had one or two sharp pains. In fact, things had not gone quite as well as that. At the onset of bad pains, Dr Laking had given her ether and as the birth approached, Lady Adela Larking, who was a lady-in-waiting and not a nurse, gave her more. After eight further bad pains, the boy was born. Forty-five minutes later the father and Dr Playfair arrived. The mother and the infant made excellent progress, which was a great improvement on last time. Even so, the Queen demanded caution. 'There must be *no No 3* for some *good long time*,' she commanded Prince Arthur. There was no disagreement that the child should be called Arthur, but the Queen made difficulties about the inclusion of Patrick among his other names, because Ireland, she said, had behaved so dreadfully. She gave in, however, when Prince Arthur told her that Patrick was the name of a Scotch saint and one which she and his Papa had given to him.[3]

Within little more than a month the parents left the children with the Queen in the care of their nurse, Mrs Chapman, and set off for a holiday on the French Riviera. Just before they left, Prince Arthur went to see the Indian exhibition which was being set up in South Kensington. He particularly noticed some beautiful pieces of Indian wood carving. When they arrived at the Hotel Bellvue in Mentone dark was falling and they found their rooms rather cold, but next morning they woke to bright sunshine and saw that the sky and the sea were deep blue. Their rooms opened onto a balcony from which steps led down to a terrace covered with orange trees. Later, as they drove through Nice and Cannes, they saw lovely gardens and smelt the delicious scent of orange blossom. They were not much troubled by ceremony for they were travelling incognito as the Earl and Countess of Sussex. The sight of the Indian carving at South Kensington and the oasis of the Riviera made permanent impressions, the first leading to important achievements of interior decoration

at Bagshot Park and Osborne and the second, in the fullness of time, to a
holiday home of great charm for Prince Arthur in his older age.[4]

After a stay in Florence, Prince Arthur and the Duchess went to Berlin
to join in the celebration of the Emperor's eighty-sixth birthday.
Relations abounded and one or other of the family was constantly in
Prince Arthur's rooms which, he told the Queen, made it hard for him to
write letters. The Queen, however, who was incapacitated by a fall on the
stairs, wrote to him that 'dear faithful Brown' had got 'erysipelas in the
head w^h is always alarming, or at least serious & is a great distress &
inconvenience to me.' She added that 'so devoted, true, honest & faithful
a servant & friend does not exist!' Indeed, he soon did not, for within an
hour of Sir William Jenner having reassured the Queen that he was getting
better, John Brown died and the Queen was overwhelmed with grief.
After such a loss she began to feel that she did not wish Prince Arthur to
go to India. By the beginning of June, however, he had overcome this new
obstacle and he had also sufficiently neutralised the familiar objections
which are raised whenever a member of the Royal Family is nominated for
an important appointment. It was now agreed that his name was to be
submitted for the command of the Division at Meerut in the Bengal Army
and he was accordingly so gazetted on 15th August 1883.[5]

The announcement was well received by the *Daily Telegraph* in which it
was observed that Meerut was an important command as in its area there
was, on the one hand, Delhi and, on the other, the Punjab. The public, it
was averred, liked to see their Princes at work and the native army would
be proud to serve under the Empress's son. Things, of course, were not as
simple as that. This was the first time that a Royal Duke had been
appointed to a command in India and it seemed likely that he might be
inundated by the attentions of Rajas and native Princes. The Queen came
to believe that a political officer should be included in Prince Arthur's
staff but the Secretary of State for India, Lord Kimberley, thought not. He
said that it was not a question of a Royal Prince visiting India; it was
simply one of a General going out to command a division. The Viceroy,
Lord Ripon, was more realistic in his expectation that Prince Arthur
would be welcomed in India as the Empress's son or, in other words, not
simply as an ordinary divisional commander. The idea of a political
officer was dropped; Lord Kimberley could not see who would pay him,
but Lord Ripon assured the Queen that he himself would provide Prince
Arthur with any political advice he might need. Indeed, he felt this could
not be provided by a 'lower functionary' than himself when dealings with

the great Princes of India or the Amir of Afghanistan were concerned. On the brink of his Indian adventure, Prince Arthur, no doubt, had a reasonably clear idea of what his duties would be as a divisional commander, but he can hardly have had much of a picture of what might be required of him as a Prince in the role of a diplomat or, even though there was a Viceroy, as a representative of the Crown. This last consideration also rather worried Lord Ripon.[6]

Before setting forth to test these problematical issues, Prince Arthur took the opportunity of attending the German manoeuvres of September 1883. They were on a very large scale and he was deeply impressed by the discipline and physique of the troops and also by that of the Emperor who, despite the fog and rain and his eighty-six years, was on horseback all day without a cloak. The infantry showed a wonderful power of marching and, of 24,000 men involved, Prince Arthur saw only one who fell out. Our men, he told the Queen, could not have matched that. He watched a Hessian regiment trying out a new repeating rifle and described its fire as 'something terrible.' Though the horses were not much to look at, he thought the cavalry drill was the best he had ever seen. He was less impressed by the artillery and, however good their guns might be, they were slow in taking up and changing their positions. Of course the capacity of the armies in India, which Prince Arthur was about to join, could not be compared to that of the German army nor, indeed, to those of any of the major European armies. Even so, the disparity between India and Russia in military terms was soon to become a big factor in Prince Arthur's calculations and those of his immediate superiors in India.[7]

At the outset of his Indian career, the Queen imposed two penalties on Prince Arthur and the Duchess. She insisted that the doctor who was to go with them was to be Dr Scott, who did not suit them at all, but who did suit the Queen as he could be relied upon to write regular and informative letters to her about their doings. She also forbad them to take their children with them and, instead, took them over herself. There is no need to suspect the Queen of anything but the best motives in keeping the children at home, but it was, nonetheless, a bitter blow to the parents and it deprived them of contact with Daisy and Little Arthur at vital stages of their development and charged them with determination to avoid the same result with their yet to be conceived third child, Patsy, in years to come.[8]

On 27th October 1883, Prince Arthur and the Duchess parted from the Queen and their children at Balmoral. On 29th Prince Arthur was out shooting with the Prince of Wales at Windsor and that evening he took the Duchess to the theatre in London. The Queen was rather offended as Prince Arthur had said that he had to leave Balmoral because there were many things he had to do in London before sailing for India. On 2nd November a stream of telegrams proceeded from London and Dover to Balmoral keeping the Queen minutely informed of the departure for India and assuring her that all precautions were being taken against the danger of explosions. Rumours that Prince Arthur's train would be blown up had reached the public and some thought that these had increased the size of the crowd which converged on Charing Cross to see him off on the evening of that day. However that may have been, the mass of people was so great that it extended all the way back to the National Gallery and this crowd, the *Standard* reporter thought, was the best protection which the royal couple could have. At Charing Cross the platform was carpeted with scarlet and there was a guard of honour found by the Scots Guards, of which Prince Arthur had recently been appointed Colonel. Among those who arrived early to see him off were Lord Wolseley, Prince Louis of Battenberg, the Duke of Westminster, Princess Frederica of Hanover, her husband Baron Alphonse von Pawel-Rammingen, the Duke of Cambridge and Sir Dighton Probyn. The Prince and Princess of Wales arrived to loud cheers and they were followed by Princess Christian, the Duke and Duchess of Edinburgh and the Duke and Duchess of Albany. Finally, the Duke and Duchess of Connaught appeared. Prince Arthur was kissed on the cheek by the Prince of Wales and on both cheeks by the Princess, the national anthem was played and the train steamed off. The chance of explosions was, of course, not the only hazard; as a journalist remarked at the time, every man who took service in the army in India 'whatever may be his rank or functions, knows that he must be ever ready to deal with unknown contingencies.' The Russians seemed to be looking towards the North-West Frontier and only twenty-six years had passed since the Indian Mutiny.[9]

Others around Prince Arthur at this moment of departure saw different points of emphasis. Lady Downe, travelling as lady-in-waiting to the Duchess, carried with her the impression of the great crowd at the station, the many goodbyes and then moving off into darkness from 'such a whirl of light and away from so many friends.' Princess Christian, who had driven from Buckingham Palace to Charing Cross with Prince Arthur and the Duchess, was struck by the sadness of the scene; the music, the soldiers and the cheering seemed to her to make it the more so.

Louischen, poor dear, she wrote to the Queen, was dreadfully upset at having to leave her children, but wonderfully brave. The Prince of Wales too was struck by the penalty which Louischen had to pay. Dear Arthur, he told the Queen, had born up manfully when taking leave of his many relations and friends. He acknowledged him as a kind and affectionate brother, who was always open and straightforward. The speeches he had made on the eve of his departure had been full of modesty and tact.[10]

Prince Arthur and the Duchess crossed from Dover to Calais in an hour and twenty minutes and went on by train to Bologna, where they changed into a very comfortable pullman car on a larger train. Lady Downe was much impressed by the luxury of the train and wrote to her mother that they were all special carriages 'for our royalties & so smart.' Even so, she already felt on easy terms with them, especially as the Duke had taken 'the earliest opportunity of observing me in bed.' In the small hours of the morning of 5th November they came to Brindisi and boarded the P & O steamship *Cathay*, their way being illuminated by men carrying torches. They sailed at 6.20 a.m. after the Duchess had gone to bed. Prince Arthur remained on deck until the pilot was dropped. As he always did on board ship, Prince Arthur was soon busy looking up old friends and making new acquaintances. This time he was particularly looking out for those he might see again in India. At Port Said he took the Duchess on board H.M.S. *Iris* in the evening when they enjoyed coffee and cigarettes in what seemed the quiet of a warship after the bustle and noise of *Cathay*. *Iris* illuminated the town with her searchlights and, as it was a glorious night, they went ashore with Sir Evelyn Baring, the Agent and Consul-General in Egypt. It was a great change to step into an eastern town with its variety of local costumes mixed with the uniforms of the Blue Jackets and the Gordon Highlanders. They strolled in the streets and visited some of the cafés listening in one to an Austrian female string band. Prince Arthur came across his former Maltese servant, Salvo Pace, who had accompanied him in the campaign of the year before.[11]

Next morning *Cathay* entered the Suez Canal and, as they approached Ismailia, Prince Arthur pointed out to the Duchess from the bridge the place where he had landed his Brigade before the Battle of Tel-el-Kebir. The little town now looked so pretty, surrounded as it was with brilliant vegetation. On 15th November they approached Aden, bleak and without vegetation, standing out grandly like Gibraltar. A salute was fired and *Cathay* was quickly surrounded by boats and canoes manned by wild looking Somali boys, jet black and naked save for loin cloths and some with their hair dyed yellow. The shore, crowded with natives, looked like a giant ant-hill. The Resident, General Blair V.C., came on board to welcome them and they then went ashore for an official reception at which the head Parsee, Mr Cowasjee Dinshaw, read an address to which Prince Arthur replied. The Parsee ladies struck the Duchess as being ugly and fat but they were dressed in lovely coloured silks and, at a distance, groups of them looked like bouquets of flowers. With the Resident and Mrs Blair, they were then driven into the town of Aden by a coachman wearing a green and red coat, a gold coloured shirt and a turban. There was an escort of strikingly smart native cavalry turned out in white linen uniform with black knee boots and turbans. Along the six mile route they were greeted by a huge crowd of Arabs, Parsees, Nubians, Indians, Abyssinians, Somalis, Jews and others. Many of the Arabs were mounted on camels and the dress worn by this cosmopolitan throng varied from the very gorgeous coloured to little or nothing. In the town, which was small and consisted mainly of a single square, the Arab women issued a curious rattling of their tongues in greeting and the royal visitors were shown the famous tanks set into extinct volcano craters, which were said to be the work of Solomon. After lunching at the Residency they returned to *Cathay* and re-embarked under a salute. They sailed in the light of a lovely sunset.[12]

After five more days at sea, Prince Arthur woke the Duchess early on 21st November. There was a nice breeze and it was a glorious morning; the brilliant colouring of the sunrise surpassed anything she had ever seen before. At 11 a.m. they sighted India and at noon they were twenty-four miles from Bombay. They had a last lesson in Hindustani, at which they had been working throughout the voyage, and then busied themselves with packing. After lunch Prince Arthur changed into the full dress uniform of a Major-General and the Duchess put on a light blue dress and a gold and white bonnet. They then went up onto the bridge to watch the entry into Bombay harbour. They were astonished by the spectacle; the green hills, looking like peas, had castellated peaks of delicate pink and the mass of picturesque native boats made a splendid scene. A naval salute of thirty-one guns was fired as *Cathay* dropped anchor off shore. The Admiral came on board and was followed by the Secretary of the Bombay Government and the Military Secretary to the Governor of Bombay. *Cathay's* passengers disembarked but Prince Arthur and the Duchess had to wait in growing heat until 4 p.m., which was the hour which had been set for their landing. At last the time arrived and they put off in the steam launch *Bee* and headed for the landing place where a huge crowd awaited them. The mass of red turbans and white costumes made a brilliant effect. They stepped ashore into a shamiana, which was lined in red and white and decorated with garlands and palm leaves, and were received by the Governor of Bombay, Sir James Fergusson, the Commander-in-Chief of the Bombay Army, General Hardinge, and several of the leading inhabitants. Indian children sang the national anthem in their own tongue, Gujerati, which was the first time this had been done in public. Mr Raghunath Nanayen Khote read an address to which Prince Arthur replied and Mrs Cowasjee Jehanjir placed a garland round Prince Arthur's neck and presented a bouquet to the Duchess. Prince Arthur and the Duchess then got into an open barouche drawn by four horses and drove forth escorted by the Governor's Bodyguard made up of Maharattas in 16th Lancer uniform with small black turbans. As they emerged from the dockyard they were met by a striking and wonderful scene. There was not the pomp and ceremony which had attended the earlier arrivals of the Prince of Wales and then the Duke of Edinburgh, but the reception was hearty and spontaneous and nothing like it had ever been seen before in India. The Duchess was the first European Princess to come to India and Prince Arthur hoped that her arrival would herald a new era for the poor downtrodden women of India; indeed, one of the first things he was to do in Bombay was to lay the foundation stone of a women's hospital which was to be managed by women doctors and at which women were to be trained as nurses and doctors. Driving through crowds of people in their brilliantly coloured costumes and turbans, the women in bright and gorgeous dresses, to the sound of deafening cheers, it took Prince Arthur and the Duchess an hour and a half to reach Government House. To Lady Downe, following behind, the mass of people was so solid that it gave the town the appearance of a single human body and it provided a sight which she told her mother she could not previously have imagined. In the evening the scene was lit by a fireworks display. The Duke and Duchess, she said, thoroughly enjoyed it all. Lord Kimberley had completely misread the meaning of royalty in thinking that Prince Arthur could go to India like any other divisional commander.[13]

On the evening of 24th November Prince Arthur and the Duchess set out on the long railway journey from Bombay to Meerut. There was much ceremony on the way. At Ahmedabad, where they changed to the narrow gauge Rajputana line, they breakfasted at the station to the accompaniment of the band of the 30th Bombay Native Infantry, who played under a German band master. A native merchant read an address and some native ladies, one of whom had never previously been out in public, were presented to the Duchess. As they travelled on in the very comfortable carriages of the Viceroy's train to Palanpur, their eyes were riveted to the windows by the sight of wild peacocks, monkeys and dark green storks. At Palanpur, the Maharaja received Prince Arthur in durbar, using the waiting room of the station, which belonged to him, for the purpose. Further up the line at Ulwur, where they arrived on the morning of 26th November, they were again met by the local Maharaja, who had just completed a private station there. He proved to be young, good looking and handsomely dressed with splendid pearls and emeralds round his neck and he spoke quite good English. Outside the station Prince Arthur was shown some of the Maharaja's troops, who wore cast off English uniforms and carried old-fashioned weapons. The cavalry horses, which the Maharaja had bred himself, looked useful. Among the dignitaries and natives who met them in Delhi were some descendants of the old Emperors of Delhi. They changed back to the broad gauge railway and reached Meerut at 4 o'clock that evening.[14]

On 27th November Prince Arthur took over the command of the Division at Meerut and, having seen his predecessor, Sir Robert Bright, off to England, he at once set about sizing up the troops who were now his responsibility. He was by no means wholly favourably impressed. Several of the regiments were under strength and the Native infantry, though soldierlike men, were badly clothed. Their corpulent English officers did not impress Prince Arthur at all well and the divisional staff seemed to need a good deal of waking up. He thought that British officers in India tended to get very lax and he decided that some new blood was needed. Among others, he may have had in mind Colonel Hancock, whom he had entertained to dinner on his first night in Meerut. He was known as 'Aunt Jane.'[15]

Hardly had Prince Arthur begun to weigh such matters than he was required to turn his attention to quite a different level of affairs. Three days after their arrival in Meerut, he and the Duchess embarked on another long railway expedition, this time to Calcutta, to be received by the Viceroy, Lord Ripon. 'These royal journeys,' Cecilia Downe wrote to her mother, 'are very unlike the general mode of conveyance.' She found herself with her husband, Lord Downe, who was travelling as Prince Arthur's A.D.C., in a saloon to themselves. They had two sofas, three arm chairs and there was a washing room and a balcony. Prince Arthur and the

Duchess had similar accommodation and the only bore was the constant changing and donning of uniform for the receptions which occurred at most of the stopping places. The Duke, she told her mother, was such a pleasant master and they all got on very well, except, perhaps, Dr Scott, who, she said, gave genuine '& other potions' from time to time. After three nights on the train, they arrived in Calcutta, the capital of the Indian Empire. The city had turned out in force to watch Prince Arthur and the Duchess drive from the station to Government House, which they did with a magnificent escort of the Governor-General's Cavalry Guard carrying lances and dressed in long scarlet shirts with yellow braid, high boots and turbans. As they walked up the steps leading to the Marble Hall and the Throne Room, the Viceroy came down a little way to receive them. It was a case of the Queen Empress's son deferring to the Queen Empress's representative and of the latter condescending a little. To either side, the steps were crowded with Government officials, members of the Municipality, leading inhabitants, English and native, and the representatives of Siam and Nepal. All were in full dress.[16]

The principal reason for this visit to Calcutta was to attend the opening by Lord Ripon of the Indian Exhibition. At 4 o'clock on 4th December Prince Arthur and Lord Ripon and the Duchess and Lady Ripon were due to drive off to the Museum for this ceremony. Their departure was delayed by torrents of rain but at last the state procession got under way. The proceedings began with a cantata specially composed for the occasion, which, to the royal ears, sounded very ugly. Three times during intervals in it, the national anthem was struck up and three times Prince Arthur and the Duchess rose, hoping that this was the end of the beginning, but, until the third time, it was not. A report was then read; it was very long. Lord Ripon then rose to declare the exhibition open; he made a very long speech. As he finished, electric illuminations were supposed to come on, but they did not and the company was plunged into darkness. The rain poured down into the court where the ceremony was being held and the people were soaked. Prince Arthur and the Duchess groped their way from the dais to the exhibition. Prince Arthur seems to have viewed these hitches with less than his usual sympathy. He did not find Lord Ripon good company and the Duchess wrote to the Queen that the Viceroy was 'stiffer & more pompous & particular about etiquette' than anyone she had ever seen. From someone who had been brought up in the Prussian Court this was a rather damning reference.[17]

Though this visit to Calcutta gave Prince Arthur the opportunity of meeting the Maharajas of Jeypore, Bhurtpore and Cooch Behar, two Nepalese Princes and many other dignitaries, he, nonetheless, found Calcutta a disappointing place, which, despite some fine buildings, was full of squalid houses and narrow streets and he was especially concerned about the evidence he found of the bad treatment of women. He visited Bethune College for native girls and found the pupils 'dreadfully awed,' so much so that they hung their heads and dared not look up. He heard that it had been difficult to persuade parents to allow their girls to come to the college, so great was the native prejudice against the education of women. One exception to the disappointments of the capital and the uneasy relationship with the Viceroy was, however, the exhibition. Prince Arthur and the Duchess found their way back to it in less formal and more agreeable circumstances than had attended the opening ceremony. There they met the Head of the School of Art at Lahore, Mr Kipling. He exerted an immediate impression upon them and was, over many years to come, to cultivate their spontaneous interest in Indian art, and especially wood carving.[18]

On the way back to Meerut, Prince Arthur and the Duchess paused in Benares where they visited the temple, which was famous for its well of knowledge; it was their first sight of pure Hindu architecture and they found it grand and imposing. They were, however, quite relieved to make their withdrawal as there were several sacred bulls running loose in the vicinity. They steamed down the Ganges and saw the bodies of the dead being burnt near the river's edge. They learned that those who could not pay for such a ceremony simply had their bodies cast into the river, which made it rather poisonous. They came ashore at the old fort in Ramnagar, which was the residence of the Maharaja, and were received by his son and numerous Sirdars. They scrambled up onto a gorgeously caparisoned elephant and took their seats on a handsome howdah of gold and silver. The Maharaja, who was old and quite blind, now appeared with his grandson of about six or seven. They were carried in a silver palanquin over which a large gold umbrella was extended. Roundabout, the Maharaja's troops were drawn up in strange array. Some wore chain armour, others leopard skin coats and yet others wore French cavalry helmets and cuirasses. They carried muskets, matchlocks, halberds and even bows and arrows. Fancying themselves in the Middle Ages, Prince Arthur and the Duchess rode up to the entrance of the Fort, where they were met by a very ferocious looking tiger in a not very strong looking cage. They dismounted and passed through two courtyards crammed with spectators to steps which led up to the durbar hall. The old Maharaja gave the Duchess his arm and she guided him to seats in the hall under a silver and velvet embroidered canopy. Actors appeared in barbaric costume and, after an exchange of courtesies, Prince Arthur and the Duchess returned to their launch on the Ganges. This was their first experience of a traditional reception by a native Prince. They were much impressed.[19]

In Lucknow they saw a different and more recent aspect of India's history, for here they went up a tower from which the positions taken up during the siege and relief of the place during the Mutiny could be seen and explained to them. They saw the room where Sir Henry Lawrence had been killed and some others underground where European women and children had sought shelter during many anxious months. Prince Arthur visited the lines of the 10th Hussars and, in yet another contrast, met some of the descendants of the King of Oudh. On 15th December they got back to Meerut and Prince Arthur resumed the command of his Division. It was so cold that he had to wear an overcoat while dressing and it was not long before everyone caught chills.[20]

On 11th January 1884 Prince Arthur's cold and loss of voice were bad enough to keep him indoors; the Duchess had to go to the 18th Royal Irish ball without him in Lord Downe's company instead. This left Prince Arthur free to write a report on his Division to the Duke of Cambridge. In an attempt to improve the operational efficiency of his Division, he had begun to brigade them and he had carried out one exercise in which the whole of his force of over 5,000 men had been involved. The assumption had been that an enemy force with six guns, three squadrons of cavalry and 4,000 infantry was advancing on Meerut. The defending force was to attack at once before the enemy could entrench. On the whole, Prince Arthur was quite pleased with the results but he also found numerous defects. The artillery had been ineffective and the infantry fire had been very variable. The 3rd Gurkas and the Royal Irish had shot well but the 5th (Liverpool) Fusiliers had been poor. Though some of the Native regiments had lost direction, the brigading had been more or less successful and Prince Arthur believed that field firing on such a large scale had not previously been carried out in any exercise in India. He thought well of the Native troops, but very badly of their British officers and also of the divisional staff officers. The latter, he said, had become very 'Indian,' by which he meant punctilious in manner and slovenly in action. He told the Duke of Cambridge that they avoided exerting themselves and each had two or three native Indian writers who did all the work. He added in a letter to the Queen that he had been especially pleased with the way in which the Native officers of the Bengal cavalry had handled their men and that he thought that the manoeuvres around Meerut had given a more real impression of warfare than anything other than action in the field.[21]

Prince Arthur followed up these experiments with a vigorous series of field days and inspections. On the principle of grouping his regiments into larger formations, he adopted a plan of telling off two of his senior Colonels in turn to command opposing forces in exercises in which he acted as the umpire. This gave the Colonels experience of commanding at brigade level and it gave Prince Arthur some opportunity of assessing their capabilities in the field. Even while he was in the midst of these energetic measures designed to bring about greater operational efficiency, Prince Arthur was already beginning to have doubts about how far they would be likely to achieve any worthwhile results. He was hoping eventually to be promoted to a higher command in India and, in particular, to that of the Bombay Army, but this was a prospect which, it now seemed, was unlikely to arise before 1886. Prince Arthur felt that he would have been quite content to carry on as a divisional commander until then, provided his work at the divisional level remained challenging enough to enable him to go on learning. He was now beginning to doubt this and he feared that the expectation of him in the Meerut command was only that he should vegetate.[22]

The Duke of Cambridge's response to his ideas can only have nourished such apprehensions. Uncle George quite understood why Arthur found some things unsatisfactory in India but he told him that he must 'make allowances for old local prejudices.' There was the Indian climate to take into account and the feeling of debility which it engendered. The Native army in India had to be a local one and so, through remaining with it, the European officers were bound to become slack. As to a higher command, the Duke of Cambridge hoped that one day, perhaps, Prince Arthur would get the Bombay Army, but in the meantime, he said, he was pressing General Hardinge to stay on as C-in-C of the Bombay Army, or, in other words, that he did not wish Prince Arthur to succeed him there, at least for the time being. The young Duke of Connaught may, perhaps, have tended to get bored too quickly with work which was not exciting and, as a very youthful Major-General, he may have expected reforms and results to be achieved more readily than was realistic. If so, there was at least no danger of the old Duke of Cambridge being lured into anything precipitate. The result was that

Prince Arthur, conservative as he was by nature, was being drawn away
from the side of reaction, which was represented by Uncle George, and
towards that of reform and advance, which was represented by Lord
Wolseley.[23]

The beginning of February marked the end of the 'campaigning' season
at Meerut and, on 7th, Prince Arthur and the Duchess left for Agra, where
they moved into the Lieutenant-Governor's Camp, which had been put
up in the shape of a long street with reception and dining rooms at the
end. Sir Alfred Lyall, who was the Lieutenant-Governor of the North-
West Province, in which Agra was situated, provided his royal visitors
with two sitting, a sleeping, two dressing and two bathroom tents, all of
which were provided with fireplaces, for, though the temperature by day
was up to 105°, it was cold at night. The Duchess's two maids were
provided with a large tent containing two bedrooms and a sitting room.
Prince Arthur noted that Louischen was much taken with the novelty of
living in tents.   Sir Alfred Lyall, though he appeared to be ill and
exhausted, gave large dinner parties every night and the Connaughts
found him to be a clever and amiable host. Prince Arthur went out on
several military inspections and one afternoon he and the Duchess went
to see the Taj Mahal. The fountains were all flowing in their honour and
the sight of the snow white tomb and its lovely gardens from the high
entrance gate struck Prince Arthur as fairy-like. The well-kept gardens
were full of bougainvillaea, orange coloured begonias, masses of roses,
flowering shrubs and trees punctuated by patches of green grass. The
proportion of the dome with its four beautifully tapered minarets and the
splendid position overlooking the Jumna were most striking. At that time
the Jumna flowed broadly between the Taj and the Fort reaching up to the
outer walls of the latter, for this was before the volume of the river had
been reduced by the diversion of much of its content for the benefit of
Delhi. The screen surrounding the tomb with its astonishing scrolls on
panels recalled Florentine work but was more delicately and artistically
executed, each small flower, for example, being made of six or seven
different coloured stones all set in beautiful harmony. Prince Arthur went
up one of the minarets from which he surveyed the splendid view. He and
the Duchess then lingered until dark revelling in the charm and beauty of
the place. For the pureness of its colour and the simplicity of it
architecture, the Taj, Prince Arthur wrote to the Queen, was worth a visit
to India. It looked to him as if it had been built yesterday.[24]

There were also other entertainments. One evening Prince Arthur and the Duchess went to a ball in Metcalfe Hall. They danced the first quadrille with the Lyalls but the Duchess then persuaded the Maharaja of Dholepur to dance the Lancers with her. He had never done such a thing before and though rather shy at first, he was, in the end, very much amused. Supper was served in an enormous tent which had originally been made for the Viceroy's use. It was said to be the largest tent in the world. The Connaughts left the party at 3 a.m. but Prince Arthur was up early again to inspect the field battery of the 3rd Brigade later that morning. In the evening they returned to the Taj to see it by moonlight. The interior was lit for their benefit by magnesium flares and the whole effect surpassed their expectations.[25]

Further delights awaited them at Fatipur Sikri to which they drove over watered roads. They entered the old city through an archway which bore an inscription in Arabic to the effect that this 'world is a bridge over which we must pass but not dwell.' They went on up the hill to a little gem of a palace in pure Hindu style and decorated within and without in carved red sandstone, which the Maharaja had put at their disposal. As to the town, they could only think that one building was finer than another. They watched young men and boys jumping eighty feet into a well full of stagnant green water, which gave the Duchess a shock of horror and they saw a ram fight which the Maharaja had laid on for their entertainment. The thud of heads gave the Duchess a headache, but the Maharaja enjoyed it immensely. Prince Arthur continued with his office work and military inspections in the mornings and went sightseeing with the Duchess on most of the afternoons, including, on one, a visit to Secundra to see the tomb of Akbar. Here, they were told, the Kohinoor diamond had been found.[26]

After staying a few days in Muttra, Prince Arthur and the Duchess drove out, again passing over watered roads, to the summer residence of the Maharaja of Bhurtpore at Deeg. They were taken to an arena to watch an elephant fight. As the animals grappled with each other the sound of their tusks shattering was all too apparent and in one encounter thirty feet of the coping of a stone wall was knocked off. The elephants had been drugged for several days before the fight and the unfortunate animals were urged on by spears and mallet blows but in the end they gave up and refused to fight any more. Prince Arthur and the Duchess were then not sorry to leave this barbaric display. They dined in the palace, but, for reasons of his religion, the Maharaja did not appear until the dessert arrived. The Queen's health was then given and Prince Arthur proposed the Maharaja's. Probably he was not very optimistic about it for he later wrote to the Queen that, though the Maharaja was only a year older than himself, he looked fifty and was very fat. Prince Arthur heard that he had an income of £700,000 a year. He was, however, an unattractive character with a gruff and abrupt manner.[27]

The Maharaja, technically the Maharao, of Ulwur made a very different impression. Prince Arthur thought him a nice young man, very keen on sport and fond of European society. This Maharaja had invited Prince Arthur and the Duchess to his camp at Siriska for tiger shooting. He met them at Ulwur station and presented his prime minister, or Divan, and the Political Agent, Colonel Peacock. They all got into a large charabanc, which was drawn by four horses and was complete with postillions. On the way, they changed to old fashioned *calèches*, which rode very high on C springs and finally they mounted elephants and rode into the camp. It was a lovely spot surrounded by green fields and palm trees. There was a guard of honour made up of the Maharaja's cadettes, in which all his servants were enrolled. They wore red uniforms and were commanded by a very smart native officer. Prince Arthur and the Duchess were given two nicely arranged tents, each containing a bedroom, sitting room and bathroom. After lunch, the Maharaja proposed an elephant ride from which they came back after dark to find the camp prettily illuminated by fires. The Maharaja took the Duchess in to dinner but, as he was Hindu, he did not partake of the food. He left in the middle of the meal to have his own and then returned. At noon next day the news of tigers was good and the party set out on elephants, Prince Arthur and the Duchess sharing one, the Downes another and the Maharaja a third with the Peacocks. All were in a state of excitement. While oranges and sandwiches were taken, Colonel Peacock went ahead to reconnoitre. He returned and told the party to advance which they did with bated breath. The beaters began to make their noise and there was soon a terrific roar and the Duchess was the first to see a tiger plunge out of the jungle, his tail held high as he charged the elephants. Prince Arthur had the first shot and wounded him but the tiger then jumped at the head of one of the beating elephants and everyone opened fire in what seemed to the Duchess to be rather a wild manner. There was shouting and the excitement rose to the highest pitch. At last, Prince Arthur got the opportunity of giving the tiger the *coup de grace*. He proved to be 104" nose to tail. In the village of Siriska, through which they passed on the way back to the Camp, the women had broken into a song of praise to the tiger, a great and dangerous enemy; this was a

Rajputana custom. Tiger shooting, Prince Arthur wrote to Elphinstone a few days later, was 'undoubtedly the most exciting sport in the world.'[28]

When the camp broke up, Prince Arthur and the Duchess went to stay with the Peacocks in Ulwur. On the first evening the Maharaja came to fetch them to dine in his summer palace. The only other guest was a missionary clergyman. On the next evening he entertained them to dinner in his city palace. When they arrived they found a wonderful gilt chariot awaiting them. In this they were drawn round a courtyard by four elephants. They then walked up a passage lined by men in chain armour with enormous halberds until they came to another courtyard lit by brilliant illuminations with a fountain playing in its centre. Beyond, the hills could be seen in the light of a brilliant moon. Troops in red tunics, white knickerbockers and white puggarees presented arms. The national anthem was played and they proceeded upstairs to a terrace and then to the durbar hall. Off this there was a pretty open room in which they dined. This time, in addition to the Peacocks, the other guests were the local clergyman and three young clergymen from the Cambridge mission in Delhi. The meal had been prepared by the Peacocks' cook, who had been sent ahead for the purpose. Prince Arthur was then taken to the roof top to see the illumination of the city and the Duchess and the other ladies were taken up more stairs to call on the Maharinis. On the way they passed through narrow passages where the air was stuffy and smelly. Suddenly they emerged into a well lit large tawdry room where two of the Maharaja's wives and their attendants were waiting. The favourite wife was 'on leave' visiting her family for six months and the fourth wife was absent ill, though Mrs Peacock told the Duchess that, in truth, the Maharaja had told her not to appear as she was not high enough. Though a lady by birth, she was not a King's daughter. This left two wives on parade. Mrs Peacock told the Duchess that it would have taken them two hours to dress and bejewel themselves for such an occasion. They had been ready and waiting for some eight hours as the Maharaja had not troubled to tell them when the Duchess would arrive. It was not proper for them to show their faces while the Maharaja was present, so the Duchess, who wished to see them, asked him to withdraw so that they might unveil. She then looked over their sleeping quarters, which proved to be untidy, badly lit and not too clean. The only access to fresh air which these ladies had was from a flat roof. Otherwise, they never went out.[29]

A further contrast was provided by the Maharaja of Jeypore. He too was quite young, but very stout and unhealthy looking and, though he had a fine shaped face, it was devoid of expression. He was as native and uneducated as possible and had no sense of how to treat ladies. He was said to have fallen under the influence of an intriguing prime minister, Bengal Babu, who apparently hated the British. Nevertheless, a magnificent entry into Jeypore was arranged for Prince Arthur, who rode into the town of 130,000 inhabitants on a magnificently decked elephant in a procession of no less than thirty of these grand animals. Next to his reception in Bombay when he first arrived, he wrote to the Queen, it was the most impressive ceremony he had seen in India. The tiger shooting was not as well organised as that provided by Ulwur and more than five thousand beaters produced more confusion than tigers.[30]

As he proceeded from one military inspection to another, Prince Arthur became more and more concerned about the chronic immobility of the Bengal Army. The Sappers had no organised railway company and their strength in relation to the number of regiments was wholly inadequate. He thought that Russian moves in the direction of Afghanistan necessitated urgent action to correct these defects and the first thing he wanted done was the construction of a railway to Quetta so that supplies and troops could be moved there quickly in the event of need. He also thought that there was scope in India for recruiting an army for service in Egypt. He thought that volunteers of good quality would come forward attracted by good pay and the prospect of a pension. They would stand the climate well and could make a useful contribution to the establishment of stability under British influence.[31]

While Prince Arthur grappled with the problem of the correct military response to the Russian threat to the North-West Frontier of India and that of the instability of the British position in Egypt and the Sudan, the Queen went to Darmstadt for the wedding of her granddaughter, Princess Victoria of Hesse, to Prince Louis of Battenberg. There she found herself preoccupied with thoughts of the death of her daughter, Princess Alice, the bride's mother, of John Brown and, most recently, of her youngest son, Prince Leopold. She began to hope that Prince Arthur would not get the Bombay command and that he would soon come home from India. Leopold had in some aspects acted as her private secretary and she now began to think of Arthur taking on that role. Prince Arthur was ready to do this, if that was what the Queen really wanted. His readiness to oblige was helped by the increasing disillusion which he felt about his position and usefulness in India, but, on the other hand, he was reluctant to do anything which might be construed in India as amounting to his departing in a huff. Meanwhile, he carried on with his routine duties in command of the Meerut Division and continued to take every opportunity of learning what he could of India and its complex system of government. He had been working at Hindustani and, in September 1884, he sat and passed the examination for the lower standard in that language. The Queen soon began to relent about the need for him to come home to replace Prince Leopold at her side.[32]

The Queen's more accommodating attitude to Prince Arthur's career in India was, however, by no means entirely a help to his prospects there for she now embarked upon a vigorous campaign to obtain the Bombay command for him on terms which were ill-judged and unrealistic. She asked that he should be appointed for a term of eighteen months during four or five of which he would be on leave so that he might come back to England to see her. Such demands provided the Liberal ministers with simple arguments for dismissing them. The Secretary of State for War, Lord Hartington, told her that it would not be in the interests of H.R.H.'s future military career if he was given the Bombay command on conditions different from 'any other officer in Your Majesty's Service' and he said that the Secretary of State for India, Lord Kimberley, and the Commander-in-Chief, the Duke of Cambridge, both concurred in this view. A further complication was that neither Hartington nor Kimberley thought that the Duke of Connaught yet had enough experience to take on the Bombay command and Prince Arthur himself was distinctly under the impression that the Government meant to block his advance to that position.[33]

Prince Arthur, it is true, was very young to be a divisional commander let alone a Commander-in-Chief, but that this was necessarily a disadvantage to the Army was another question. The dismissive attitude of Hartington and Kimberley, made so easy by the Queen's naïvety, was based not so much on a military judgement as a political one; there were always plenty of people in and around Parliament who were ready to believe that any royal appointment was a 'job' and the ministers were clearly anxious to avoid any such inference. An alternative and militarily much more authoritative opinion of Prince Arthur was expressed by the Commander-in-Chief, India, Sir Donald Stewart, who, as he had direct responsibility for the Bengal Army, was his immediate superior. He was much struck by the sound and judicious opinions which Prince Arthur had expressed about the officers and regiments under his command and he gave him credit for being outspoken and fair in his estimates of character, the very point on which, Sir Donald Stewart thought, General Officers were so often at fault. He found that the Duke of Connaught had exercised his command without fuss or worry and that good sense characterised all his work. He was very modest and unassuming, but his work showed that he was made of the right stuff and Sir Donald Stewart hoped that he would soon get one of the chief commands in India.[34]

Certainly some of Prince Arthur's views were outspoken. For example, he reported, even to the Duke of Cambridge, that though the native cavalry regiments were magnificent material, they were still treated as though they were irregulars. Their British officers came straight from infantry regiments and knew nothing about cavalry work. Instead of teaching the native officers and setting them an example, they had to learn what they could from them. He said that at Agra he had found the 14th Sikhs to be a very fine regiment but their drill and outpost work was bad because, Prince Arthur discovered, their Colonel had drunk himself imbecile. Prince Arthur found this officer to be in such a shaky state that he had him sent home pending retirement. He was very well impressed by the 13th Hussars. They had first rate N.C.Os and men and, with a few exceptions, their officers were all that could be desired. The 8th Hussars, on the other hand, wanted putting together and Colonel Langtry was not the man to do it. He was a poor creature and, Prince Arthur thought, an awful snob. The 2nd Goorkhas marched wonderfully for such small men and Prince Arthur simply could not conceive of better light troops. As to the capacity of the Division as a whole, his chief anxiety was the lack of transport and he thought there should be a Railway Engineers Battalion, or at least three companies, for railway work on the northern frontier. This inadequacy, he added, was a general one throughout the armies in India.[35]

Such directly expressed and radical views may not have pleased the Duke of Cambridge but they did not alienate another, and a much more effective old soldier, Field-Marshal Lord Napier, the victor of a famous campaign in Abyssinia and also a former Commander-in-Chief, India. Writing to Major-General Dillon, who also had much experience of service in India, he raised a comparison between a 'young sympathising Prince full of zeal for the military service' and the 'stiff representatives of the old school who looked on India as a necessary bore, hated Indians and despised Indian officers.' He thought that Prince Arthur's appointment to the command of the Bombay Army would be especially welcome to the Native army and the people in general. He conceded that the Duke of

Connaught's promotion had been special, but he pointed out that he had worked with zeal and industry in every branch of the Army and that, though it had only been for a short time, he had been on active service in war. His 'discreet and prudent' character would be likely to prevent any unseemly outbursts of jealousy on the part of disappointed competitors. Bearing in mind the possibility that the Bombay Army might be involved in war with Russia, General Dillon added a note of his own to this expression of Lord Napier's views. He thought that, though he was only 34, the Duke of Connaught had received more careful military instruction than most, that he would be better than some who had commanded in war and as good as anyone else who might be selected for this command. He would also enjoy the confidence which would arise from his high position. The Government, however, was unmoved by such arguments and at the end of June 1884 the Queen had to telegraph to Prince Arthur that he could not have the Bombay command.[36]

General Dillon's reference to the possibility of the Bombay Army being involved in a war was inspired by the threat to the North-West Frontier created by supposed Russian designs on Afghanistan. In an attempt to defuse the growing tension, a boundary commission was set up but whether this could avert a military clash continued to be an open question. Prince Arthur thought that the Russians already controlled the key strategic points and, in so far as they did not, they would simply break any agreement which might be reached when it suited them to do so. He reckoned that the Russians were well aware of the weakness of the British and Native armies in India and he thought that they could be in Herat as soon as the British could reach Candahar. He believed that the solution lay in a defensive treaty with Afghanistan under which the British would gain the right to build a railway to Herat and to maintain an occupying force in that area. Russia could then be told that any threat by them to Herat would be taken as a *casus belli*. He was hoping that Lord Ripon would raise no objections to his making a visit to the North-West Frontier so that he could see the situation for himself. Meanwhile, he wrote privately to the Duke of Cambridge to say that at the Queen's wish he would be resigning his command of the Meerut Division with effect from 1st March 1885. He added, however, that he was sure that the Queen would allow him to prolong his tour in India if there was a military expedition into Afghanistan, for, in that event, he hoped to get a command in the force which was sent. He said that he had done his utmost to command the Meerut Division to the best of his ability and he

hoped that he would be able to hand it over to his successor in as efficient
a condition as the regulations at present permitted. He told the Duke of
Cambridge that he had hoped to command a large camp at Delhi in the
approaching cold weather season but that this would be impossible as the
Viceroy had withheld the necessary funds. Prince Arthur thought this was
a great mistake as the troops had so little experience of operating in large
formations.[37]

At last the Viceroy permitted Prince Arthur to make a visit to the
North-West Frontier but he insisted that it must be private. Despite this
there were crowds out in the streets of Rawalpindi when Prince Arthur
and the Duchess arrived there on 27th September 1884 and most of the
houses were illuminated. They stayed with the local commander, Sir
Michael Biddulph, a veteran of the Crimean War and of the march to
Candahar. He insisted on holding a big parade of his troops in Prince
Arthur's honour but, in deference to Lord Ripon's order that the visit
should be private, the Duchess, instead of Prince Arthur, took the salute.
Prince Arthur was immediately impressed by the appearance of the
Indians in this part of the country. They were taller and more manly than
he had become used to seeing; nearly all were Mohammedans who wore
beards and turbans. They struck him as the very picture of good material
for soldiers and their wild and daring appearance suggested that they
would be more pleasant to meet as friends than as enemies. In Peshawar
they were received by the Commissioner and Political Agent, Colonel
Waterfield. The house was surrounded by British and native infantry and
police and they noticed that Colonel Waterfield was never without a
revolver. Three of his predecessors as well as several of their officers had
been assassinated. They went out to see the Fort, but there was no gun
salute as this would, apparently, have been likely to bring down the mud
walls of the edifice. From it they had a fine view of another fort, which
stood at the mouth of the Khyber Pass. Peshawar was quite different from
anything Prince Arthur had seen in India. The houses were built of earth
coloured bricks and were adorned with handsomely carved woodwork.
The women were mostly covered from head to foot, but the men were
fine and fierce looking; most wore turbans and some had sheepskin coats.
They had a proud and independent look and they reminded Prince Arthur
of Scottish Highlanders. Most of them were armed. Many were refugees
from the recent Russian advances. After dinner Colonel Waterfield held
a reception for the leading Europeans and important local people
from Peshaware, Kabul and Candahar. The Duchess slipped away, but

Prince Arthur said a few words to each of them.[38]

Next morning, 1st October, they were up early and, at six, they set off in carriages with a strong escort and drove at high speed to Jumrood. Here they drove into the outer court of the Fort and mounted horses. Amongst those who accompanied them was Major Warburton, who was the Assistant Political Officer in special charge of the Khyber Pass. His father had been assassinated while he was Commissioner of Peshawar; his mother was an Afghan Princess. They set off up the Khyber Pass at a canter. The heights to either side were occupied by Afridis who, Prince Arthur thought, were devil-may-care men of cruel features but splendid physique. Though well known robbers and murderers, they were now in British pay and, under Major Warburton's command, were responsible for movements up and down the Khyber Pass. Entering the Khyber Pass with its stark lack of vegetation seemed to Prince Arthur like coming to the end of the world, but it was not as narrow as he had expected and he noted that there was scope for troops to spread and skirmish. Two Khyber Chiefs came out to meet him. They were mortal enemies, one having killed the other's brother and the other having destroyed the first's village. However, for the day, they seemed content to ride together and they both presented shields and daggers to Prince Arthur. Both affirmed their loyalty to the Queen Empress. When the Queen heard of this expedition, she felt envious of Arthur and more so of Louischen for having ridden into the Pass and seen those wild men. 'It is *just the* thing *I* sh*ld* like to have seen,' she wrote.[39]

The Khyber Pass was the highlight of the visit to the North-West Frontier, but, among the many new places and scenes which Prince Arthur saw, two were of particular interest. One was Attock at the junction of the Indus and Kabul rivers where Akbar had built a fort when this was, in effect, the entrance to India. Part of the building survived and it was still a defensive fort which opened fire to demonstrate the fact to Prince Arthur. With the Duchess, he walked over the new road and rail bridge, which was a grand piece of engineering. Another remarkable sight was Srinagar, to which they had a hard journey by land and river from Rawalpindi, sleeping on the way in primitive bungalows with mud floors and no windows. The town struck the Duchess as being an Indian Venice but Prince Arthur noted that the people were dirty and miserable. They were Mohammedan, but the Maharaja and all the authorities were Hindu and the people were oppressed and heavily taxed. Prince Arthur and the Duchess stayed in a grand but very uncomfortable palace. Dr Scott had to wash in a soup dish. On the whole, Prince Arthur was disappointed with Kashmir; it was burnt up and barren and full of squalor and filth.[40]

In November 1884 the Commander-in-Chief, India, came to Meerut to inspect Prince Arthur's Division. He was most favourably impressed and sent home an excellent report on the Divisional commander. He said that Prince Arthur knew everything that was going on in his command and did his work quietly and thoroughly. At dinner one night, he told Cecilia Downe that Prince Arthur was his best General and that he hoped he would be the next C-in-C, India. The Duchess seized the opportunity to interest the Chief in the Women's Hospital in Meerut, with which she was very dissatisfied. To her great delight, he gave orders that the points of which she had complained were to be remedied. In that hospital at least, soldiers' wives would in future be more comfortable. The Duchess thought that the previous neglect was in large measure caused by the fact that the officers' wives took so little interest in the welfare of the wives of their men. Cecilia Downe thought that life in India had greatly improved the Duchess. She had become much less shy and, she told her mother, her dinner parties now always did well.[41]

Prince Arthur was clearly very pleased to find that his efforts had made a good impression on Sir Donald Stewart and his hopes of getting things done improved with the departure of Lord Ripon and the arrival, as the new Viceroy, of Lord Dufferin. In January 1885, Prince Arthur went to Calcutta to welcome the latter. He found him much more *au fait* with the military situation in India than Ripon had been and he became more optimistic about getting the strategic railways built which he had been advocating for such a long time. On the other hand, he foresaw that the Viceroy would continue to be obstructed by his Council. Prince Arthur thought that many of its members were too old for their work and he thought a term of five years should be placed on their membership.[42]

The Queen took a tremendous interest in the news from India which she got from Prince Arthur, the Duchess and members of their entourage. She constantly sought to have Prince Arthur's views conveyed to the Government and she plied him with questions on a range of topics. One, which was always of the greatest interest to her, was Prince Arthur's household and servants. When he began to make plans for leaving India, which he expected to do in May 1885, she wondered if he would bring some of his Indian servants home with him. There were, however, many difficulties about this. The Duchess's Ayah, for example, had a husband and family and, as she was a Hindu, she would have lost caste by crossing the sea. Also the conditions under which servants worked in India were completely different from those prevailing in England. In India the servants slept in outhouses or in the open and there was no accommodation for them in the house. Mohammedan servants would gladly eat what was left over by their employers, but the Hindus each cooked their own food and their employers must not touch their cooking utensils or even cast their shadows on them. Prince Arthur had about a hundred servants, all of whom were natives, except for M. Guibert, the French cook, and Mr Hole, a Driver in the Royal Horse Artillery, who was in charge of the stables. He had two native bearers; one Amar Khan, who was really his valet, was a Mohammedan who spoke no English and with whom Prince Arthur conversed in Hindustani. The other, Chamga, was a Hindu who spoke English, though, in general, Prince Arthur noticed, the better servants did not speak English. Among the others were a *Khansakman*, or steward, eight *Khitmagars*, or table servants, and four Bearers for general charge of rooms. A native tailor sat cross legged on the floor outside one's room or on the veranda wearing a large calico cloak and brass spectacles. He would copy clothes, make cushions, hem towels and sew on buttons and he was always painstaking and quick. He would respond to Hindustani. In addition to all this, Prince Arthur had a guard by day and night made up of native troops, from which all guards in India were found, except regimental guards and those at hospitals.[43]

So, despite its size, scope and versatility, Prince Arthur's Indian domestic staff was unlikely to be exportable to England, however, much the Queen might wish for that. Before she would have had the opportunity of appreciating this however, doubt was cast upon whether Prince Arthur himself would be able to come home as planned. On 6th February 1885, The Queen wrote from Osborne to tell him of the 'dreadful misfortune-disgrace-shame' of the fall of Khartoum. The disaster would harm the British position in India where the Russians were waiting to pounce. Prince Arthur still hoped that Gordon might be alive. Though 'very mad,' he was a fine and plucky soldier. He thought that the British position in the Sudan should be reinforced by Indian, not British, troops. The British would suffer terribly at this season, but the Indians would be able to do long marches and would give a good account of the Arabs. Prince Arthur wished he could be in the Sudan serving with the Indians, many of whom were, he said, as good soldiers as anyone could wish. Tears came to his eyes as he watched the Duchess presenting new colours to the Connaught Rangers and thought of all the fellows in danger on the Nile.

Cecilia Downe was even more affected; was there ever such a fiasco as this, she asked her mother. She had been planning to come home with the Duke and Duchess via Constantinople, but now she wondered if by then England would be embroiled with the Turks as well as the Egyptians.[44]

At once there were rumours in India of a Russian advance to Herat and, perhaps potentially more dangerous than that, the native Indians showed signs of getting excited about affairs in Egypt and on the North-West Frontier. The Collector at Muttra, where Prince Arthur was staying, told him that his servants had turned rude and the Duchess heard that houses in Agra had been illuminated when the news of the fall of Khartoum arrived. People said that things had been like this on the eve of the Mutiny. The Viceroy thought that he might be driven to extremities by Russian moves towards Afghanistan. Much would turn on a meeting which he had arranged with the Amir of Afghanistan in Rawalpindi. A show of military strength was to be put on in the hope of impressing the Amir and, in aid of this, Prince Arthur was ordered to send a field battery, the 19th Bengal Lancers and the 4th Rifle Brigade. The C-in-C, India, summoned Prince Arthur to Rawalpindi and told him that if it came to war with Russia, he was to take command in the field of a Division of 10,000 men for service in Afghanistan.[45]

On 30th March 1885 Prince Arthur and the Duchess arrived in the Viceroy's camp at Rawalpindi. The camp was enormous and was said to be the biggest which had ever been assembled in India. There were 20,000 troops and seventy guns in it. Prince Arthur was with the Viceroy when the Amir arrived and he went with him to return the call. The Amir spoke in Persian and, though he could understand a good deal of this, Prince Arthur conversed with him through an interpreter. He noted that the Amir dressed *à la Russe* and that his troops wore knickerbockers and high boots. At a great parade which followed, the Duchess hoped that the Amir was more impressed than his studied look of boredom and indifference suggested; Cecilia Downe thought it a curious sight to see the Amir in his white uniform and astrakhan cap sitting between the Viceroy and the Duke of Connaught with the three Indian Commanders-in-Chief and their staffs. His own followers were of a most rugged type and were dressed in Cossack style. At a second great parade, in which all the 20,000 troops were on show, Prince Arthur thought that the Amir was impressed, though of course he did not allow his feeling to show. This was followed by a durbar held by the Viceroy in an enormous and gorgeous tent. The approach was lined with cavalry and the Viceroy's elephants with red and gold trappings were drawn up outside. The Viceroy sat on a throne set on a dais with the Amir on one side and Prince Arthur on the other. Before them was an audience of 8,000 people. Presents were brought in by splendidly dressed natives, who placed them in line down a centre carpet leading up to the dais. It was a dazzling scene, very eastern in style and, Prince Arthur thought, right out of the Arabian Nights. He thought the Viceroy had behaved with dignity and tact and looked the part of a Viceroy. The Amir also acted with much dignity and Prince Arthur thought that he was struck by the magnificence and solemnity of the ceremony. Twice he expressed his determination to be an ally of the British. When the Viceroy presented him with a General's sword, he said he hoped to strike down the enemies of Britain. He was then invested with the G.C.S.I., with which he seemed to be tremendously pleased. The Viceroy later wrote to the Queen that, being the nominee of the British, the Amir had feared that he would not receive the honours due to him as an independent ruler. Nothing had reassured him more on this point than the consideration shown to him by the Duke of Connaught. When he first arrived and found the Queen's son waiting to greet him, his gratification had been great.[46]

It soon began to seem that peace would be patched up with the Russians, though Prince Arthur feared that Gladstone was purchasing it by giving away the Amir's territory. The C-in-C, India, told him that the receding threat of war meant that there was now no objection to his leaving for England. Even if war did come, it would take six to eight weeks to assemble the Division which Prince Arthur was to command and much longer than that to concentrate it at the front. Indeed, it would be possible to run no more than four troop trains a month if congestion at the outlet of the pass was to be avoided. There would, therefore, he was told, be ample time for his return to India if he was required. Neither the Queen nor the Prince of Wales seemed to understand this and both objected, rather to Prince Arthur's annoyance, to his coming home at a time which they still regarded as one of crisis. At last, however, the Queen got the message and, on 14th May, she wired that Prince Arthur might return to England.[47]

On the morning of 23rd May Prince Arthur and the Duchess arrived at Grant Road station in Bombay. The train was ahead of time and the Governor of Bombay, Lord Reay, was late in coming to greet them, but it quickly became apparent that this was not a discourtesy. The Duchess was soon in deep conversation with Lady Reay about India, its people and especially its women and Lord Reay proved be a charming, clever and kind host. The Reays came with them on 26th May to Apollo Bunder, from where, watched by a huge crowd and to the accompaniment of the national anthem, they went out by launch to the P & O liner *Sutlej*. A salute was fired from the Fort and a member of the old Delhi royal family came on board to take leave. He wore a gorgeous dress and a gold crown. They sailed at 5.30 and, though they had only known the Reays for a few days, they felt they were parting from friends. When they got off the ship at Marseilles, they were amused by the extraordinary hats, bonnets and dresses worn by the ladies. How fashions had changed during the time they had been away in India! On the train journey across France, Prince Arthur could not take his eyes off the beautiful green vegetation which adorned the country. As they approached London in a special of the South Eastern Railway, they felt quite excited, like children coming home from school. The Prince and Princess of Wales and many other members of the Royal Family met them at Charing Cross whence they drove to Buckingham Palace. A considerable crowd cheered them on their way and it was a happy reunion, marred only by their bitter disappointment that their children were not there to greet them. Prince Arthur also reflected upon those many who might have come to welcome him home who had died while he was away and he reflected too upon what an interesting time they had spent in India, which he now wrote down as a thing of the past.[48]

CHAPTER 9

The Bombay Command
1885-1890

PRINCE ARTHUR'S return from India precipitated a constitutional contretemps. Gladstone's government had fallen and Salisbury had formed a new one. Lord Randolph Churchill became Secretary of State for India and the Queen supposed that he would not make the sort of difficulties about Prince Arthur's future which had been the stock in trade of Lord Kimberley. She, therefore, opened a campaign to secure Prince Arthur's appointment as C-in-C of the Bombay Army. Her hopes were soon trimmed; Lord Randolph said that the matter was not for him but must be decided by the Duke of Cambridge with the approval of the Secretary of State for War, who was now Mr W. H. Smith. So to speak, in the same breath, he submitted to her that Sir Frederick Roberts should succeed Sir Donald Stewart as C-in-C, India, and that his advice to this effect was approved by Smith and Salisbury. Obviously exasperated, the Queen told Salisbury to cypher the Viceroy of India to obtain his opinion as to the suitability of the Duke of Connaught for the Bombay command. Salisbury said that he did not have access to the India Office cypher and, therefore, could only wire through the India Office, in which case the content of his message would become known to Lord Randolph. He could write, but the letter would take three weeks to travel. Without more ado, the Queen then herself cyphered to the Viceroy, 'Do you consider Duke of Connaught would be well fitted for Command at Bombay.' She told him to take account of the views of Sir Donald Stewart and Sir Frederick Roberts before replying. If this was mentioned to Salisbury, it was not to Lord Randolph, who, when he heard of it, resigned on the ground that the Queen should not communicate with the Viceroy except through him. The crisis abated when it was pointed out that the Queen habitually communicated directly with the Viceroy and Lord Randolph seems to have pleaded in excuse that when he took offence he was suffering from congestion of the lungs. After taking 'calomel', he withdrew his resignation.[1]

The Viceroy duly replied through the Prime Minister that he entirely approved the appointment of Prince Arthur to the Bombay command. He thought it was a very good thing that one of Her Majesty's sons should be in India and that the Duchess exerted a very wholesome effect on Indian society. He said that Sir Frederick Roberts concurred as also did Sir Donald Stewart, who said that Prince Arthur had been among his best General Officers and one who possessed great tact in dealing with the native peoples. Even so, neither this apparent success nor numerous subsequent attempts which the Queen made in the next several months, availed her anything. The Government was simply not prepared to put the Duke of Connaught forward for this high command. There seems to have been no military objection, but the feeling in the Cabinet evidently was that Prince Arthur's appointment would provide the Radicals with ammunition in the forthcoming general election. There was also the argument that if the Duke of Edinburgh was appointed C-in-C of the Mediterranean Fleet, as later in the year he was, it would not do for the Duke of Connaught to have an Indian army as well. Such arguments made no headway with the Queen. Prince Arthur, who was only told a little of these transactions, was rather displeased with what he thought might be taken as something of an imputation upon himself by Lord Salisbury. Nonetheless, he told the Queen that she had better regard the matter as closed. This advice, however, also had no discernible effect upon her.[2]

Though he was disappointed at not being offered the Bombay command and embarrassed by the Queen's repeated endeavours to obtain it for him, Prince Arthur was, nevertheless, quite prepared to return to India for a second tour as a divisional commander. As though in compensation, Roberts had little difficulty in getting for him the command of the Rawalpindi Division, which was the largest in India. Prince Arthur had seen something of it during his visit to the North-West Frontier and the challenge of taking it over was enhanced by the continuing possibility of war with Russia in the approaches to the Indian Empire. Writing to the Duke of Cambridge on the eve of his return to India in September 1886, Prince Arthur said that he would seek to maintain his Division in a state of readiness to take the field. He thought war might come at any time now that Germany and Austria seemed to be playing Russia's game and Turkey was 'perfectly paralysed.' Leaving the children behind again was even worse than last time, for now there were three of them. The new baby had been born on St Patrick's day, 17th March, 1886. She was the Queen's twentieth grand-daughter; the grandmother wished she had been her twelfth grandson as she reckoned there were too many Princesses in the family. There was the usual argument about the names; the parents wished the child to be known as Patricia but the Queen wished for Victoria. They called her Patsy except when the Queen reminded them that she was Victoria Patricia.[3]

On 27th September 1886, Prince Arthur and the Duchess arrived in Bombay. On that day the *Times of India* printed an article which predicted that the Duke of Connaught would stay some time in India, that he would be appointed C-in-C of the Bombay Army and then of India and that, in the fullness of time, he would succeed the Duke of Cambridge as C-in-C of the Army. Prince Arthur stuck the article into his journal, but how he himself regarded the prospects, he did not record. During the few days which they spent in Bombay, he and the Duchess went to see Mr van Ruith's studio. Except for some clever sketches, Mr van Ruith did not have much to show, but Prince Arthur wrote to the Queen that she ought to see the exhibition of his work which was at the time showing in the Albert Hall. He said that she should buy some of his pictures and put it in the Court Circular that she had done so. He said that no one understood Indian life better than van Ruith. This was the second student of the Indian scene whom he had recommended to the Queen for, on his first Indian tour, he had suggested to her that she should choose a Kashmir landscape and a Delhi architectural scene by Olivier, who had been coaching the Duchess in sketching.[4]

Undoubtedly Prince Arthur and the Duchess would have enjoyed being reintroduced to India through the eyes of an artist whose work they admired. Equally, they must have been delighted to receive an invitation from Lord and Lady Reay, with whom they had so quickly made friends at their first meeting, to stay at Government House, or Ganesch Kind, in Poona. They left the handsome new station in Bombay for Poona on 28th September, travelling in the Governor's very comfortable carriage. At the last stop before Poona the gentlemen changed into uniform and the ladies into smart frocks and bonnets and in Poona they were received by Lord Reay, all the civil and military authorities and the leading natives, including the Maharaja of Jodhpur. Their route to Ganesch Kind was lined with troops and crowded with Europeans on horseback and in carriages, as well as by a great concourse of natives. Ganesch Kind proved to be a fine house with a tower and columns of Aberdeen granite and capacious dining and ball rooms. Roundabout, the vegetation was most brilliant and the city of Poona and its cantonments were almost lost in gardens; towers and churches were practically all that was visible of the buildings. Prince Arthur told the Queen that nothing could exceed the kindness of Lord and Lady Reay. He seemed to be doing well as Governor and was apparently much liked by Europeans and natives. Prince Arthur expressed the hope that the Queen's Golden Jubilee in 1887 would be the occasion of the G.C.S.I. for Lord Reay. Sir Charles Arbuthnot, the C-in-C of the Bombay Army, was in Poona and Prince Arthur took the opportunity of seeing him. The only disappointment was that Sir Frederick Roberts, the C-in-C, India, was not there but he had already written to Prince Arthur inviting him to correspond directly with him, which Prince Arthur had said he would not fail to do.[5]

While still filling in time before going to Rawalpindi to take command of the Division, Prince Arthur went to Simla to see the Viceroy. Lord Dufferin gave him and the Duchess a grand and very cordial reception. On the second night there, while they were dining, news arrived of the sudden death of the C-in-C of the Madras Army, Sir Herbert Macpherson. Immediately, there was speculation that Prince Arthur might be his successor and the Viceroy lost little time in recommending that this should be so. Prince Arthur himself now felt confident of his ability to fill the position, for, while he conceded that he was very young, he considered that he had a more varied military experience than many of the older officers; also, he was now, apart from General Dillon, the senior Major-General in India. Showing the cutting edge of ambition more than he usually did, Prince Arthur wrote to the Queen, took the matter up with Roberts, who told him that he was sure that he would get the command, and telegraphed to Sir Henry Ponsonby that the Madras command was the legitimate object of his ambition. Hearing no more of the matter, he then proceeded to Rawalpindi and, in the expectation of receiving another rebuff from the Government, took up his divisional command.[6]

The Rawalpindi Division amounted to 13,000 men and it included two intact brigades. Prince Arthur, who immediately and energetically set about getting to know his command, went round all the camps and hospitals and held a great parade within the first few days. He found that, in the immediate area, there were only two cases of enteric fever, though

19. *Prince Arthur (nearest the camera) on manoeuvres in India, c1888.*

20. *Coburg, 1894. Seated: Queen Victoria and the Empress Frederick. Standing, left to right: Prince Arthur, Prince Alfred, Duke of Coburg, Emperor William II, the Prince of Wales.*

21. On 21st May 1896 'Prince Arthur, dressed in the uniform of the Scots Guards and wearing the riband of the Russian Order of St Andrew, rode on horseback with many other royalties directly behind the Tsar, who, mounted on a white charger, made his state entry into Moscow.' (p. 202)

22. *Prince Arthur and Tsar Nicholas II at Balmoral, September 1896.*

there were many more in Sialkote, which was within the command. He found that his regiments were up to strength and looked well. He must have been pleased too by the spectacular reception which Rawalpindi afforded him. At the station there was a guard of honour of the Suffolk Regiment and the Municipal Council and all the leading natives were there for the presentation of an address. As his carriage drove off, a salute was fired and the route to his house was crowded with people. That evening, the cantonments were illuminated and all society waited to greet him and the Duchess at the Club. As had happened three years earlier when Prince Arthur arrived to take command of the Meerut Division, he was now again almost at once required to attend on the Viceroy for reasons of state with which ordinary Major-Generals would not have been concerned. This time the function was at Lahore, where the Viceroy had set up a great camp.[7]

The purpose of this display was to impress the Chiefs of northern India and to receive the members of the Boundary Commission, who had returned from their negotiations with the Russians in Afghanistan. Prince Arthur accompanied the Viceroy when he received the Maharaja of Kashmir, the Nawab of Bhawulpur and the Rajas of Kuppurthulla, Jhind, Nabha, Furreedkote, Chumba and Mundi and he went with him to return their calls in the camps which each had set up for the occasion. A salute was fired as each Chief arrived and it was repeated as he left. The same was done at each of the eight camps as the Viceroy and Prince Arthur arrived and left. As Kashmir was entitled to nineteen guns, Bhawulpur, seventeen and the Rajas eleven each, the cannonade went on for most of the day. Prince Arthur thought that the most picturesque of the Chiefs' camps was that of the Maharaja of Kashmir, which was equipped with perfectly lovely tents with embroidered carpets of red, brown and white stuffs, looking like shawls. Next morning, Prince Arthur and the Duchess received Sir West Ridgeway, the head of the Afghan Boundary Commission. He was very glad to be back in British territory. Later in the morning, Lord Dufferin came to tell Prince Arthur that he had been appointed C-in-C of the Bombay Army. This came as a complete surprise to Prince Arthur and he and the Duchess were delighted. Having resigned themselves to the probability of losing the Madras command, they had now attained the much superior Bombay Army.[8]

The Queen grieved at the longer separation which this appointment would mean because Arthur was so useful to her and such a comfort. Affie was away and, in any case, he 'never was of the same use' and she had never been intimate with him as she was with Arthur. Poor dear Leopold was in another and happier world. Arthur was to remember his mother's age and he was to come home on leave for the Jubilee in 1887. She wished Louischen joy 'of darling Arthur's getting up so high & obtaining *without any difficulty or any opposition* what last year was so unjustly & foolishly denied him.' She attributed this to the difference between Lord Randolph Churchill, who was now Chancellor of the Exchequer, and the excellent, amiable and loyal Lord Cross, who had become Secretary of State for India.[9]

On 9th December 1886, General Dillon arrived in Rawalpindi to take over the command of the Division from Prince Arthur, who, before leaving for Poona to assume command of the Bombay Army, reported to Roberts that the chief need of the Division at Rawalpindi was housing. The men were largely accommodated in tents, which were thoroughly uncomfortable and did not allow space for tables and kit boxes nor means of combatting white ants. A good many men were repaying their bounties and taking discharge and Prince Arthur hoped that Roberts would impress upon the Government the urgency of remedying the situation. He said he had written to the Quarter-Master-General about it and he hoped that the C-in-C would not mind his mentioning it directly to him as well. With the Duchess, Prince Arthur then set out on the journey of 1,761 miles to Poona, which meant spending five consecutive nights in the train. He was met on arrival by a guard of honour of the 3rd Bombay Infantry and a reception party of the HQ and divisional staffs. His command comprised 36,000 men and included nine regiments of cavalry and eighteen batteries of artillery. The area of responsibility covered the whole of the Bombay Presidency and extended westwards for about 1,500 miles to include Aden. All appointments, promotions and other arrangements in the Bombay Army were now entirely in his hands. He was promoted to the local rank of Lieutenant-General and he became a member of the Council of the Governor of Bombay. When the Queen heard all this, she hoped that Arthur would remain as dear and modest as ever and that he would be a firm but kind C-in-C and would be kind to the 'poor Natives.'[10]

It made Prince Arthur sad to find that for a third Christmas in succession he was separated from his children, especially as he thought Poona had about the healthiest climate in India. He thought little of the European society there; they seemed to be an uninteresting lot, but he took a different view of his visit to the Chief of Jath in Poona. To his great surprise, he was received by the Chief's wife, who escorted him upstairs and sat down on a sofa beside him. She wore a nose ring, which was studded with pearls, and she wore rings on her toes and ankles. She put scent on Prince Arthur's handkerchief and placed a garland round his neck. She proved to be an intelligent and well-mannered woman and it gave Prince Arthur great pleasure to talk to her. He had never before been received socially by a native lady.[11]

Prince Arthur tackled the serious business of his new command with his usual promptitude and vigour. He noted from the outset that Bombay itself was virtually defenceless and could, he told the Duke of Cambridge, easily be destroyed by an invading enemy. Early in January 1887, he left Poona on an extensive tour of inspection. Also, as usual, his military duties were constantly punctuated by functions and social activities which he undertook, not as the C-in-C of the Bombay Army, but as the son of the Queen Empress. Among the many Chiefs he met was the Gaekwar of Baroda, who appeared, stick in hand, dressed in white trousers, black jacket and small puggaree and a large diamond brooch. The Viceroy regarded him as the most important of the Indian Princes. He was very pleasant and spoke perfect English and, so liberal was his regime, that Prince Arthur was allowed to see his mother and his wife. The latter was much in awe of the former, who was said to have taken to drink. The Duchess, who had accompanied Prince Arthur on this tour, also went with him on his inspection at Aden. Here he found that the French were causing trouble by raising their flag in areas which were under British protection. His reception at Obok, which was in French territory on the coast of Africa opposite Aden, was, nevertheless, very courteous. The French marines and artillerymen who garrisoned the wretched little village, were slovenly and the officers, who entertained him to dinner, enjoyed themselves very much. Prince Arthur went on board a French troopship, which had come in from 'Tongarin'. She had accommodation for eight hundred men, but there were 1,400 on board, a hundred and thirty of whom had fever or dysentery and were unlikely to live to see France again. In the Aden Protectorate, he found the detachments of his army in very good order, but the main purpose of his visit produced a less satisfactory conclusion. New fortifications were being built, which Prince Arthur hoped would be among the most powerful in the world. Work on them was getting on well but, if they were to be made operational, the garrison would have to be reinforced and, to make this possible, new barracks would have to be built. Nothing had been settled about these last points and, before they could be put to the Government of India, Prince Arthur had to try to steer them through the Governor's Council in Bombay. Such matters usually moved slowly, if at all.[12]

From Aden, Prince Arthur sailed to Karachi. It struck him as a curious sort of place rather like the German coast with sand everywhere and driving winds. The English church had a striking clock which sounded like the one at Osborne and carried him back there. Karachi had now become an important commercial place, but Prince Arthur learnt that trade had lately fallen off badly, which he hoped was a temporary set back. The garrison consisted of a battalion of field artillery, two battalions of the South Yorkshires, the 26th Bombay Infantry and a torpedo detachment of the Bombay Sappers. The forts were being rearmed and a system of torpedo defence was being laid down. Prince Arthur attached much importance to this part of his command as he foresaw that Karachi might become a base for operations in Afghanistan. The largest troopships could come alongside and, from the wharfs, trains could take the troops and supplies to Quetta or Peshawar.[13]

The line to Quetta was the one which Prince Arthur now took; it involved three nights and two days in the train. He stopped at Hyderabad and Jacobabad to carry out inspections, on one of which he saw the 29th Bombay Infantry (Beluchis), the Duke of Connaught's Own. Coming up the Bolan Pass by the wonderful railway laid in the dry bed of a mountain torrent was a remarkable experience. The people looked as wild as the country in their picturesque embroidered jackets and sheepskin lined coats. Most were armed with long knives or swords. Many were refugees from Afghanistan. Quetta was a wretched little place consisting mostly of mud huts, but good roads were being built, trees planted and gardens started. Prince Arthur and the Duchess stayed with the Chief Political Officer, Sir Oliver St John, in one of only two brick built houses in the place. There were twelve degrees of frost on their first night. Prince Arthur inspected some three thousand troops on parade.[14]

In the further pursuit of the outlying stations of his command, Prince Arthur and the Duchess arrived on 19th March at Killa Abdulla. This lay in territory which, until recently, had been part of Afghanistan; it was now British. Thirty Afghan Chiefs, who professed loyalty to the Crown, came to meet the Empress's son. The Political Officer addressed them on his behalf in Persian and they then all rode into a camp which had been set up in a recently active fort. After dinner Pathans came and danced round a bonfire in a style which was reminiscent of the Scottish Highlands. Next morning the whole party, mounted on sixty horses, rode up the Kojak

Pass. It was very cold and their path was strewn with loose stone and scrub, beyond which there was no vegetation. Dead camels lay round about and they saw a dead donkey being eaten by a pariah dog. At the head of the Pass a panorama of Afghanistan opened before Prince Arthur's eyes and, eighty miles distant, the road to Candahar was clearly visible; they all gazed and no one said a word.[15]

The Duchess now returned to Quetta and Prince Arthur pushed on to Harnai, from where he rode out, covering twenty miles or so a day, until he had seen what he thought was an almost indescribable variety of scenery. He rode with an escort of the 3rd Bengal Cavalry, a few Frontier Police and some Afghan Levies, which were made up of wild looking men with flowing hair, beards and garments. At Loralai, where a new cantonment had been built, the head people came out to shake hands with Prince Arthur, but he knew well enough that the maintenance of law and order in these parts was extremely brittle. The Political Officer, Mr Bruce, who rode with him, had twenty-five years experience of these frontier tribesmen and he seemed able to exercise considerable influence over them. However, when there were raids or murders, which were regarded as ordinary occurrences, it was hardly ever possible to discover who had committed the crime and the only remedy was to impose a fine on the head man.[16]

Having so recently returned to India, Prince Arthur was not yet, of course, due for home leave. Nevertheless, the Queen, understandably, wished him to be present at the celebration of her Golden Jubilee, an event which, after all, is not common even in British history. The regulations, however, were such that Salisbury's government felt that the only way in which Prince Arthur might be enabled to come home was by the passage of specific legislation. On 18th April 1887 the *Duke of Connaught's Leave Bill*, price ½ d, was published. Dr Tanner, the Member for mid Cork, at once gave notice of opposition, as it was said he did to all government measures, and it was only on 12th May that the Government dared to face a debate on the second reading. It then claimed that a general repeal was needed, but that, in view of the pressure of business, they had decided upon a special measure for this individual case. Mr Dillwyn then moved the rejection, but his speech was somewhat inaudible and incoherent. So far as could be gathered he did not approve of those connected with the throne being treated in an exceptional manner. He disclaimed any disloyalty and said that the Duke of Connaught was a 'very estimable person' but that, if he had not been connected with the throne, he would not have been asked home. Sir John Swinburne then rose; he was armed with an alarmingly large sheaf of notes and a tumbler of water. He said that the Duke of Cambridge had never served in the lower ranks of the Army; he was called to order. He said that the Duke of Edinburgh held a high position in the Navy and he was called to order again. He then said that had it not been for the Duke of Edinburgh, Admiral Field might possibly hold a higher rank than he did. He was called to order for a third time and collapsed with his notes unread and the tumbler of water unconsumed. The second reading was carried by three hundred and eighteen votes to forty-five. On 24th May 1887, Prince Arthur and the Duchess sailed from Bombay in the nick of time to attend the Queen's Golden Jubilee in London. Amongst the delights of this for them was the reunion with their children which it made possible. Little Arthur was looking well and had improved in his walking and the way in which he held his left side; neither he nor Daisy were shy with their parents and sweet Patsy was simply delightful.[17]

There can be no doubt that Prince Arthur's presence in the procession to Westminster Abbey on 21st June 1887, when he rode ahead of the Queen's carriage with his two elder brothers, was a great comfort to her. Afterwards, when he returned once more to India, she wrote to her 'Most beloved & darling Arthur' that he had become dearer and dearer to her. He was 'so like dear Papa — so dear & good & *wise* [and] such a help to me!' Also, her interest in his Indian servants had resulted in her now having two such people herself. The elder one, who she said was called Mohomed Buxsch, spoke a little English, but the younger one knew not a word of it. So that she might say something to her two men, she asked Louischen to tell her the Hindustani for go away, milk, coffee, bread, come here, shoes, stockings, it is cold, it is hot, are you cold, are you warm, open the door, come in, a knife, a spoon, a fork, a cup, a plate, a cloak, a carriage, a child, a son, a daughter, no, yes, beef, mutton, chicken, potatoes and a glass. The name of the younger servant who spoke no English was Abdul Karim.[18]

The Duchess's leg, which had never got much better, had now got a lot worse and it was decided that she should undergo Dr Bracket's cure at Aix. Prince Arthur, having taken her there and got back to London, resolved that he would return alone to his duties in India and he felt sure that she would not wish him to shirk his duties, though he also felt she would know what it would cost him to be separated from her, whom he loved so much. Late at night, he wrote again from Buckingham Palace to say that their bedroom looked cold and gloomy and that he would feel sad all alone in the big bed. He said that he would sleep on her side. Writing to him, the Duchess thought that 'poor you' would have a dreary time of it going to India alone, but that when he got there he would have plenty to occupy his time. As for herself, she would have the children, but they, she said, 'are only very little to me my own darling compared to you.' She felt that her whole life was wrapped up in him and she said that her happiness 'depends on *you* & *only you*!' She feared that his Mama would be terribly cut up when he took his leave. She was indeed, and almost at once had occasion to miss him. At an audience she was giving at Osborne, her gentlemen seemed to lose their heads; Colonel Byng caught his spurs in the carpet and nearly tumbled into the fireplace. The Queen wished Prince Arthur had been there to give them all a good punch. Instead, he embarked at Brindisi and, on 22nd August, sailed for India.[19]

When he got back to India Prince Arthur was somewhat under the weather; he had constant headaches and diarrhoea and spent many sleepless nights. The one complaint prevented him from taking his 'effeavescing' draught to cure the other. Even so, he carried on with his office work and inspections, he dined frequently with the Reays and galloped round the race course at Poona. Some of his troubles were doubtless due to the glamour of his position as C-in-C of the Bombay Army being dimmed a bit by the difficulties and frustrations of the job, which arose from the clash between his own wish to bring about radical improvements and the lethargy of parsimonious higher authorities. In many matters of detail Prince Arthur achieved reforms. For example, he succeeded in persuading the Bombay Government to persuade the Secretary of State for War to arm the troops in Aden with lances instead of sabres. Similarly he persuaded the Bombay Government to persuade the Government of India to re-equip the 4th Bombay Rifles with long Snider breechloading rifles. But in larger matters he inevitably encountered much less success. Despite his direct line to Roberts, the C-in-C, India, his easy relationship with Dufferin, the Viceroy, and his quite close friendship with Reay, the Governor of Bombay, there almost always seemed to be reasons why his ideas should be rejected or shelved. Indeed, in later years, Lord Reay recollected that 'perfect harmony' had reigned between himself and the Duke of Connaught throughout their time together in Bombay. He attributed the fact that he had, nevertheless, always remained 'absolutely independent' to the earlier training he had got from his contacts with German and Dutch royalties. In other words, his claim was that he could charm the Duke of Connaught without conceding any viewpoint which he did not endorse.[20]

Part of the trouble arose from India seeming to be, in the minds of the authorities in London, a very long way away and the sort of dangers with which Prince Arthur was concerned, such as the threat to the North-West Frontier by Russia, seeming to the authorities in Calcutta, Simla and even Bombay, almost as far off. When the treacle was so thick and sticky, Prince Arthur found it hard to stir the porridge and the Duke of Cambridge, from whatever angle he viewed matters, was nowadays opposed to almost any form of change. The much more radical Wolseley, now the Adjutant-General to the Forces, who, in many respects, was so sympathetic to Prince Arthur's reforming ideas, did not believe that the Russians would risk a campaign in Afghanistan or that the British ought to.[21]

One of the first things which Prince Arthur discovered when he got back to Bombay in the middle of September 1887 was that the camps of exercise, which he had been planning for his army, had been curtailed by the Government on grounds of economy. From what the Queen told him of her letters from the Viceroy, he thought that Dufferin was complacent about the fortifications at Bombay and Karachi, where, apart from one battery in Bombay, not a single gun had yet been mounted. He also thought that the Viceroy was much too sanguine about the ability of the 1st Corps to take the field in the event of war. The truth, he told the Queen, was that, due to jealousies in Simla, the C-in-C of the Bombay Army was prevented from doing anything about these matters. Prince Arthur thought that his troops were much too widely dispersed, but, to concentrate them, he would need to build the requisite barracks and this he could not do as there was no money available. Economy was the order of the day since the depreciation of the rupee had set in. Its 'proper' value, Prince Arthur thought, was 2/- but, by January 1888, it was worth only 1/4½d. Prince Arthur had radical ideas for improving the status and usefulness of native Indian officers. They were treated by the British more as if they were N.C.Os than officers, which lowered their status in the eyes of their men and they travelled second class, which was derogatory to their position. He believed that the only way to improve their standard and efficiency was by providing them with a better education before they were commissioned and, for this purpose, he advocated the establishment of military colleges. Ideally, there should be one of these in each Presidency, but as that would be too expensive, he conceded that one would probably have to do. The students should be drawn from two classes, first, the sons of nobles and others of good position, who would pay fees and then receive direct commissions and, secondly, those recommended for promotion from the ranks, who would not pay fees. So that the successful candidates would feel like, and be regarded by their men as, real officers, they should be encouraged to associate with British officers. The difficulty was that the native officers would not like to eat their meals in British messes, but Prince Arthur thought that they should be honorary members of the messes with access to them whenever they wished. They should also be considered for some of the higher commands. Though Roberts seemed not to be against these ideas, the inference was that Prince Arthur was in rather too much of a hurry.[22]

Pouring out his woes to the Prince of Wales, Prince Arthur wrote in May 1888 that he spent most of his time in his office working up military and political questions. He said that he was engaged in a constant fight with the Governments of India and Bombay for money to meet the most essential military needs. Over-centralization of administration led to a great waste of time and money and resulted in the Bombay Army not being ready to take the field. He had a strong artillery force but it was armed with old muzzleloading guns and worn out carriages; there were not enough reserves of horses for a single battery. The garrison artillery in Bombay had hardly sufficient gunners to furnish one relief for the batteries and the positions in Aden and Karachi were about the same. The native cavalry, infantry and sappers were still armed with the old Sniders, most of which were worn out and could not be relied on at ranges of more than four hundred yards. Much had been done on the railways and fortifications, but the army itself was not properly organised or equipped and all the regiments were inadequately officered. The Bombay Army, he told the Queen, had hardly any transport, the medical service corps was wretched and there was no railway corps. He said he had made all this known to Roberts, but he seemed unable to get anything done about it.[23]

The sovereign military reform which Prince Arthur most eagerly and persistently sought was the abolition of the Presidential armies of Bombay, Bengal and Madras and their replacement by army corps. The commanders of these would be directly subordinate to the C-in-C, India, who would have a distinct staff drawn from all India. It would then be possible to introduce a common system of accounts, returns and regulations, which would not only be much more efficient but also more economical than the three separate systems operating in the three

Presidential armies. It would also then be reasonable to bring such aspects as transport, commissariat, medicine, accounts and building, which, in the Presidential system, were removed from the control of the Cs-in-C, and place them under the C-in-C, India. It seemed that there was considerable support in India for such ideas and Prince Arthur was led to believe that the new system would be introduced before the end of 1888 and, if not, by April 1889. He understood that the Government of India had been convinced. He stressed to the Queen that the need to increase the efficiency and economy of the military system in India made the introduction of the reform 'positively necessary.' The Duke of Cambridge, however, could not enter into such views. He had, he wrote to Prince Arthur, always been opposed to any 'organic' changes in the Indian Presidential armies. Prince Arthur believed that Uncle George did not understand the changes which had come about in India, especially in the light of new responsibilities in Burma and Afghanistan. Nor did he understand how limited was the scope of the existing Commanders-in-Chief of the Presidential armies. It was, therefore, a great disappointment to Prince Arthur when, on 20th August 1888, mail came in from England with the news that the army corps system would not be introduced that year. He was very sorry that the Duke of Cambridge took such a false view of the Presidential armies and he feared that he would now never have the chance of commanding one of the proposed army corps instead of remaining a nominal Commander-in-Chief with little or no authority.[24]

The Duke of Cambridge's opposition to the new scheme was implacable, but he had his reasons. The army corps system would result in the removal from the Presidential Councils of the existing Presidential Cs-in-C, it would mean that the pay of the Duke of Connaught would be less than it was at present and that the patronage which he and Sir Charles Arbuthnot exercised so well, would be removed and placed in the hands of the C-in-C, India, Sir Frederick Roberts, who was a terrible jobber. It would also mean that the organisation of the Army would come under discussion in Parliament, where the inclination was to make even more sweeping changes than had yet been proposed. These, perhaps, were not very large minded views. In the short term, however, they were much more powerful than those of the Duke of Connaught, whose vision of an Indian army capable of defending India and serving overseas in the cause of the Empire was not to be realised until Kitchener came upon the scene at the beginning of the next century.[25]

In another almost equally intractable matter, Prince Arthur had more success. At last, he overcame the Queen's rooted objection to his children going out to India and when the Duchess arrived in Bombay on 14th November 1887, she was accompanied by all three of them. Prince Arthur, who was waiting to go aboard her ship as soon as it was fast to a buoy, sent a few lines to her by the pilot, who was to bring it in to harbour. He expressed the happiness it would be to clasp her in his arms and to hug the children. He was soon dreading to think how he would miss them when they returned to England, which it was planned they would do in March 1888. From this fate, however, he received a partial reprieve when the Queen agreed that Patsy might remain in India as it was only children older than she was who were endangered by the Indian climate. Patsy began to speak a mixture of English, German and Hindustani and, though her father thought she was rather wilful, he was much too indulgent to be annoyed. She romped all day and he found her clever and amusing. It was such a nice age and he had not known Daisy or Arthur at that stage. Indeed, even at the same time, he did not know that Daisy was seriously ill in England. Patsy, for sure, was her father's favourite, which was, perhaps, fortunate as she alone of his children was to outlive him.[26]

More sunshine was brought into the Connaught household by the arrival to stay with them in December 1888 of the Duchess's sister, Ebi, and her husband, August of Oldenburg, and Count and Countess Hohenau, Fritz and Lottka. Prince Arthur could not remember if the Queen had met Fritz and his pretty wife Lottka but there is no doubt that he was delighted to do so. In the evenings August was full of teasing, Ebi played the piano and sang and the Duchess sang, but Lottka whistled charmingly. She and Ebi were always keen to have a cigarette, but the Duchess told them not to smoke in front of other ladies and so they had to wait until the other guests had gone. At the party on the evening of New Year's Day, Prince Arthur, wanting some fun with Lottka, climbed onto a chair to reach the mistletoe and jumped down and landed heavily on his knee, which he sprained so badly that Dr Keith had to apply foment-ations. By 4th January, when some other guests were there, the ladies sat after dinner and smoked with the gentlemen. Two nights later, Lottka drove out with Prince Arthur who, because of his knee was almost an invalid, and picked scented pink oleanders, roses, hibiscus and pome-granates. At dinner she wore the hibiscus and pomegranates on what the Duchess thought was a lovely grey dress. On another evening the A.D.Cs,

Captain Herbert and Captain Fergusson, fought blindfold with knotted handkerchiefs and Fergusson played the bagpipes; there was a great deal of laughter. A few days later they all went to the gymkhana at Kirki. Prince Arthur had to stay seated in his carriage but the others got out. They came across the Maharaja of Patiala, who kept walking up to Lottka and surveying her from top to toe with a monocle planted in one eye. Ebi and Lottka were curious to see Captain Fergusson in the kilt and Captain Herbert in the mess dress of the Central Indian Horse, so Prince Arthur asked them to dine thus. He himself put on white mess dress and Fritz Hohenau appeared in satin tights, which officers now wore in Berlin or Potsdam after hunting. Lottka came in a lovely green ball dress and the Duchess, who 'happened' to have a little new French dress, wore that. After dinner the A.D.Cs again fought blindfold with knotted hand-kerchiefs but Prince Arthur was afraid that the kilt might not be the most suitable dress for this so he stood behind Captain Fergusson and all went well. In April, Ebi and Lottka insisted on smoking after lunch in Government House at Malabar Point and they succeeded in getting the Duchess to do the same, a thing she had never before thought of doing.[27]

On 11th April 1889, Prince Arthur and the Duchess gave a farewell dinner at the Bombay Yacht Club to August and Ebi, the Hohenaus and Prince Hohenlohe, who had joined them more recently. It was very cheery, despite the impending separation, which the Duchess felt was a load on all their heads. They then saw them aboard their ship for Europe and looked forward to seeing them again in Germany in the following year. They returned to Government House silent in their thoughts of those dear ones who had made their Indian winter so bright, happy and cheery. At 11 that night they left Bombay for Poona in an ordinary and somewhat dilapidated train, on which the door of their carriage would not shut. It was not only Prince Arthur, but the Duchess too, who had been enchanted by the pretty and adventurous Lottka Hohenau, without whose presence life was so much more mundane. Queen Victoria hoped that the Hohenaus had enjoyed India and that they had appreciated the natives, but the last part of this wish was probably in vain; when Prince Arthur and the Duchess went to see the hospital for women in Udaipur, they did not take Ebi or Lottka with them. Both had expressed a strong dislike of going round hospitals and, though the Duchess thought Lottka would have come if pressed, she decided not to ask either of them. Indeed, in later years, Lottka proved to be a much less good friend than Prince Arthur and the Duchess had at first assumed. In this respect, she was very different from another lady whose friendship they were both to embrace under rather similar circumstances in years to come. This was Léonie Leslie.[28]

Meanwhile, a yet more illustrious visitor was about to arrive. This was Prince Albert Victor of Wales, Prince Arthur's nephew and, it seemed, the future Emperor of India. The Queen hoped that Eddy would take a great interest in everything but he was, she told Prince Arthur, a little apathetic. She was sure, however, that he would be kind and courteous to the natives. Prince Arthur already knew that Eddy was apathetic but he hoped that Sir Edward Bradford, who was coming in his suite, would keep him up to the mark. He too was sure that Eddy would be civil to the natives. He was glad of that, as he thought that the modern young officers, civil and military, were, almost all of them, devoid of manners and seemed unable to tell the difference between coolies and gentlemen. The Queen feared that too much was being crammed into the programme for Eddy's visit; as he was so slow and listless, it would tire him and make a jumble in his head. Yet she hoped that he might return from India developed and improved in mind, for this, she thought, was his only chance of winning the hand of her grand-daughter, Alicky of Hesse. Poor Eddy earnestly wished to marry her and she was 'in *every* way *fitted* for it, from g^t beauty, much strength of character & amiability.' Alas, though she liked him as a cousin, she felt she could not marry him. Though much distressed by this, the Queen could not help admiring Alicky's conscientiousness in not looking at the brilliant and in many ways enviable position, but acting in accordance with her feelings. As, however, she still had no attachments and was only seventeen, there remained a faint hope that she might take to Eddy when he returned from India. Fate, however, was to decree otherwise and when Alicky came to fall in love, it was not to be with the future King of England, but with the heir to the Russian Tsardom.[29]

Prince Arthur was in Bombay to meet Prince Albert Victor when he arrived there on his father's birthday, 9th November 1889. With Lord Reay, he then accompanied him on the train journey to Kirki, whence they drove to Ganesch Kind. While they were travelling, the Duchess was dressing in full fig, which, for this occasion, was her new smart German dress with sapphires and diamonds and a new tiara, which at first she found it difficult to fix. It took her half an hour to dress and she was then ready to drive off to Ganesch Kind with her lady-in-waiting, Mrs Hannay. On arrival, they were relieved to find that Lady Reay, Lady Hayter and

Mrs Lyttelton were also in evening dress. They assembled in the green drawing room where they were presently joined by Lord Reay. When the Bodyguard could be heard trotting up, Lord and Lady Reay, followed by the Duchess, went to the front porch to meet the carriage bringing Prince Albert Victor, Prince Arthur and Sir Edward Bradford. Greetings were exchanged and presentations made and then Lord Reay took Prince Albert Victor to his rooms, which were those usually occupied by the Connaughts. Prince Arthur and the Duchess followed and established themselves in Eddy's sitting room until dinner time. After dinner the Maharaja of Kolhapur and other Chiefs came. The visit had got off to quite a good start.[30]

Next day was Sunday so Prince Arthur took Eddy to the parade service at Kirki and in the evening they rowed on the river. They dined at Ganesch Kind, where there was a party of thirty or forty. On 11th November they had a pleasant informal lunch at Ganesch Kind and then Prince Albert Victor held a durbar for First Class Chiefs in the Ballroom. At 4.15 they all drove off in a procession of carriages to Parbutti. There, Prince Albert Victor and the Duchess got onto an elephant and started riding up to the Temple. The elephant was nervous and was then 'indisposed', which they were later told was not a pleasant sight from behind. The Mahout lost his head and the elephant slipped back onto stones which had been made slippery by his indisposition and he began to shake all over. The howdah swung in a horrible way and, had the elephant turned round, he would probably have bolted down the hill with results which might well have been fatal. The Duchess and Eddy were terrified and had a horrid feeling of insecurity and danger. All the gentlemen around them were alarmed, but at last the elephant regained something of its composure and Captain Herbert managed to get some steps up so that the Duchess and the Prince could escape. Both were badly shaken and it was some days until the Duchess felt right again. All the same they went on up to the Temple and came down after dark by the light of sulphur torches which made everyone cough. They then drove through the city of Poona, which was illuminated. The crowds gave Prince Albert Victor a very cordial reception, which the Duchess thought gratifying as Poona was a turbulent and discontented place.[31]

Prince Arthur held a parade of 7,000 of his troops in honour of Prince Albert Victor and this was watched by an enormous crowd. That evening the Reays gave a very grand ball, to which, despite her still shaken nerves, the Duchess managed to come. Next evening, 13th November, Prince

Arthur and the Duchess gave a dinner party for Prince Albert Victor, which was followed by a tattoo. This was a tremendous success. Carpeted tents had been put up in the grounds which were illuminated by 15,000 lamps. Among the six hundred guests, there were many natives and special enclosures were provided for N.C.Os and their wives from the local regiments. People said they had never seen such a lovely sight as the illuminations which were laid on and the newspapers gave much attention to the occasion. Prince Arthur told the Queen that he had found Eddy quicker and more punctual than, evidently, he had expected. On 14th November, Prince Albert Victor set off on his tour of India and Prince Arthur left to carry out an inspection in Aden.[32]

On 6th January 1890, Prince Arthur and the Duchess arrived in Calcutta. The Viceroy, who was now Lord Lansdowne, received them at the top of his staircase and Prince Albert Victor was also there. He had wished to meet his Uncle and Aunt at the station and was very indignant at not having been allowed to do so. After lunch, Prince Arthur and the Viceroy rode, and the Duchess and Lady Lansdowne drove, to the polo ground to watch Prince Albert Victor play. They managed to avoid meeting Lord Badstock, who preached very low church and boasted that he could convert all India in six months; the conceit of it, the Duchess thought. Dinners, balls and other entertainments for Prince Albert Victor followed. 8th January was his twenty sixth birthday; he was twenty minutes late in starting on a ride which his Uncle and Aunt had arranged for him at 8.0. In the evening Uncle and nephew dined at the Bengal Club. The Duchess heard that Arthur had made an excellent speech, but that Eddy had been frightfully nervous and had dropped his voice too much. A Press observer was more charitable and reported that his closing words had been greeted with prolonged outbursts of cheering.[33]

During these days in Calcutta Prince Arthur saw a good deal of his nephew as he and the Duchess were in and out of his rooms all the time. He found him much improved but, he told the Queen, his mind was not as active as his body and he was often slow at taking things in. He was really a mere boy and was happiest with people of his own age or younger. He was thoroughly good and natural and quite unspoilt, but he was absurdly young for his age and had very little *savoir faire*. They had been out snipe shooting, at which Eddy had done well, but the hard walking had tired him out. He feared that he had been extravagantly brought up and had extravagant ideas; the amount of clothes he had brought out to India was something enormous. Prince Arthur thought that all would come right in time and that it would be a mistake to try to force him on. The verdict on this judgement cannot be given by history for, within two years and a day, Prince Albert Victor lay dead and the direct line of succession to the throne passed to his younger brother, the future King George V.[34]

As Sir Frederick Roberts's time as C-in-C, India, drew to an end, the prospect arose that Prince Arthur might be offered the position. He, however, was beginning to think that he had been long enough in India and that, if he stayed longer he would lose touch with affairs at home. He also thought that the Duchess had been in India for as long as was good for her and that he would have to look after the education of his children. A feeling that India was, perhaps, a military backwater may have contributed to this attitude, but it failed to dampen the enthusiasm of many in India who encouraged him to change his mind. Among these was Roberts himself, who told the Duke of Cambridge that he hoped that his successor would be someone acquainted with India who understood the Indian army. He thought there were few of the requisite rank with this knowledge. 'Indeed,' he wrote, 'there is scarcely anyone but the Duke of Connaught,' who, he believed, would make an excellent C-in-C, India.' The Queen thought that Prince Arthur ought to take the appointment and, so that he could have a year at home, Roberts should stay on in India for an additional year. She told Prince Arthur that there were strong reasons behind her argument, especially as being C-in-C, India, would facilitate his eventual succession to Uncle George. The latter was now seventy and she thought might have to retire at any time; she would then expect Arthur to take over from him. Though still somewhat reluctant, Prince Arthur told the Queen that he would be willing to do this, provided Roberts was given an extension of a year, which he thought he was very anxious to have. There were, however, two hitches; all this seems to have been devised without Mr Stanhope, who was Secretary of State for War, having approved it and whether or not Roberts really did want to stay an extra year in India became doubtful. Prince Arthur's next military appointment, therefore, remained in the balance as he came towards the end of his term as C-in-C of the Bombay Army.[35]

In these last months Prince Arthur made several more extensive journeys, carrying out both his royal and his military duties as he went. Though society in such places as Poona might be dull or vulgar, these journeys served as a reminder of the extent to which India was both a small and a large world. In Rajkot, for example, Prince Arthur was received by the Acting Political Agent, Major Hunter, whom he had known as a boy during his time at Ranger's House and who had been a fellow cadet of his at Woolwich. A few days later he arrived with the Duchess in the approaches to Jamnagar, where he was met by His Highness the Jam Sahib of Noanuggur and his seven year old son. Prince Arthur and the Jam drove on in one carriage and the Duchess followed in another with the boy, who pointed out the sights to her. At his palace, the Jam received them in durbar, during which champagne and then a very horrid and fiery concoction called rose wine was offered. Apparently the Jam had been a drunkard until he promised his mother on her deathbed that he would only drink for one hour in each twenty four. After the durbar the Jam entertained Prince Arthur and the Duchess to dinner. At this the European guests sat along one side of a table and the Jam at a small one to himself. Before the meal began the Jam had his waistcoat removed by a servant, who pulled his arms out of it as though he were a baby. He was thus able to eat in his white Hindustani clothes. Between each course, he indulged in elaborate ablutions of the hands and between each dish or drink, his mouth was wiped by an attendant. At the end of the meal he had become very unsteady on his feet and he had great difficulty in placing garlands round the necks of his royal guests. When he conducted the Duchess to their carriage, she found it necessary to support him. In Wadwar, on the other hand, the Thakor sat at the same table with Prince Arthur and the Duchess when he gave them lunch and he ate the same food as they did. The different manners of the Hindu Princes were interesting to compare. So too were the different means of transport. On 18th December 1889, Prince Arthur rode from Palanpur to Deesa on a camel, which took three hours. In Deesa he stayed with Brigadier-General Beville, who commanded the district, and he inspected the Gloucester Regiment, a field battery, the 1st Bombay Lancers and the 20th Bombay Infantry. He then rode back to Palanpur, where he visited the Agricultural Show, called on the Sahib and dined at the Residency.[36]

These were only incidents in a huge programme of inspections taking in Karachi, Hyderabad, Jacobabad, Quetta, the Kojak Pass, which was now served by a new railway, Ferozepore and Nasiabad. On this basis, Prince Arthur produced his final report for Sir Frederick Roberts. On the whole, he was pleased with what he had seen, but he did find fault with some of the native infantry lines, which he thought were unhealthy, and he was critical of one of the native military hospitals. The main weakness of the Bombay Army, he thought, was the poor quality of its British officers.[37]

These observations referred to the Bombay Army from the regimental point of view. This was one in which Prince Arthur was deeply interested but it did not, of course, relate to the large issues of army reform and modernisation with which he was also so much concerned. From the regimental point of view, there was much for Prince Arthur to be pleased about in his command; from that of the larger issues, there was, however, very little. No more progress had been made towards the great step of converting the Presidential armies into army corps, even though this was a step which would have produced, not only much greater efficiency, but also a financial saving. What Prince Arthur regarded as greatly insufficient progress had been made with the other large measures he advocated and especially the provision of adequate guns and gunners at the reconstructed forts at Bombay, Karachi and Aden and the greater use of strategic railways to facilitate the deployment of troops on the North-West Frontier.

Much of the larger issue as Prince Arthur saw it was epitomised in an important memorandum written for him by Colonel W.Luckhardt, an expert in military transport. This tackled the question of what was needed in view of the Russian threat to the North-West Frontier through Afghanistan. Hitherto, Colonel Luckhardt stated, all military issues had been dominated by the matter of expense, which had been restricted to the narrowest possible limit. He thought that the fact that India, a subjugated country of such immense extent and heterogeneous population, had been successfully governed with so little display of military force spoke volumes for such a policy, but the Russian threat, he reckoned, had changed all that. When plans were made for the movement of an army onto the North-West Frontier, it had been found that the despatch of one army corps would depend upon the employment of 64,000 transport animals. As one army corps would not be the limit of what was needed, this meant, in effect, that it would be impossible to meet a Russian attack, for an army so encumbered by such a sluggish system of transport could neither advance nor retreat. Though he thought that the threat of a Russian attack was still one in the far future, he, nevertheless, believed that the steps to counter it must be taken in good time. The solution, Colonel Luckhardt recommended, lay in the abandonment of the pack system, which involved huge numbers of animals and men to manage them, and the development and use of strategic railways together with the adoption of the draught system, or hauling of materials in carts.[38]

The threat of Russian attack was the main incentive to the reform and reorganisation of the Indian armies and, to that extent, the realisation or otherwise of Prince Arthur's larger aims depended on the assessment made of Russian intentions. In London, the Director of Military Intelligence, Lieutenant-General Brackenbury, and the Military Secretary at the India Office, Major-General Newmarch, put their minds to this question. Their verdict was that, even in the event of war with Russia, it would be folly for the British to advance to Herat and equally so for the Russians to advance to Candahar. Under the existing arrangements, the Indian armies could put two army corps, amounting to nearly 64,000 men, into the field and this would be sufficient to meet any eventuality other than a full scale Russian invasion. The likelihood of an armed revolt in India was considered to be very remote and the development of railways and a telegraph system would enable troops to be concentrated quickly in vital areas if there was one. The view, in other words, was that existing military strength in India was adequate to the probable requirements and such a view favoured inertia and reaction, as represented by the attitude of the Duke of Cambridge, and handicapped the aim of reform and modernisation, as represented by the view of the Duke of Connaught. His suspicion that India was, at least for the time being, something of a military backwater, was therefore well founded.[39]

On 8th March 1890 the Royal Bombay Yacht Club gave a farewell dinner to Prince Arthur and the Duchess. The dinner was very well done, but the Commodore's speech was not a great success. It was given in a hesitant way and when everyone thought he had finished, he started on some poetry which, unfortunately, he could not remember. He was followed by Admiral Freemantle, who was fond of talking and of his own voice. Prince Arthur started with a reference to the influenza epidemic and apologised for the bad cold which he had got. He said that the C-in-C, Bombay, was in the leading strings of the Government of India. Only one Native regiment in his army had been equipped with modern rifles and the Bombay forts were armed with old fashioned muzzle-loaders. One 6″ breech-loader had been delivered by mistake and would be sent back immediately. The quiet gravity of this parenthesis, a press reporter wrote, was apparent to everyone at the dinner. Prince Arthur said that recent exercises had proved that the defences of Bombay were 'absolutely useless' against naval attack. He said that, though this opinion was not shared by others, he had a high opinion of the Bombay Army, which had done well in the fighting in Burma and the Sudan.[40]

On 13th March 1890, the eleventh anniversary of his wedding, Prince
Arthur handed over the command of the Bombay Army to General
Greaves and gave a farewell lunch for his staff. He then said goodbye to
his leading native servants and gave them presents. One of the men, Akbar
Khan, the *Khansama*, or cook, who had been with him throughout his time
in India, cried like a child. Prince Arthur and the Duchess then said
goodbye to their three children, who were going to stay with the Reays
until their departure for England a few days later, and then, at five in the
evening, they left for the Apollo Bunder. They were seen off by a guard of
honour of the 4th Bombay Rifles and by the servants, who came out to
make a last salaam. They drove in Lord Reay's barouche with four horses
and an escort of the Poona Horse. The houses on their route were decked
with flags and the balconies and streets were crowded with people.
Troops turned out and cheered lustily. At the Bunder, there was a guard
of honour of the Gloucester Regiment and they were received by Lord
Reay and members of the Bombay Council. A farewell address was
presented by the Municipality and there was much handshaking with
native Chiefs, foreign Consuls and numerous British and native officers.
Amidst tremendous cheering and under a royal salute, they made their
way in a launch to the P & O liner *Kaiser-i-Hind*, which, after some last
farewells and many tears, got under way.[41]

A few weeks before this departure, an article in the *Indian Spectator*
summed up Prince Arthur's services in India. He was the first in his
position to study Urdu sufficiently to be able to address his troops in that
dialect and, better than that, was his love of justice as between Europeans
and natives of all ranks, his personal regard for the Princes and Chiefs of
India and his work for the improvement of Indian education. The writer
of this tribute added that his unfailing courtesy and kindness had earned
him an unique popularity in India.[42]

CHAPTER 10

On Round the World 1890

THE VOYAGE HOME, upon which Prince Arthur started from Bombay on 13th March 1890, was not his usual one westwards via Aden and the Suez Canal. This time, he embarked upon the completion of an eastwards circumnavigation, which was to take him to Ceylon, Malaya, Hong Kong, China, Japan, across Canada from west to east and so home from Quebec to Liverpool. It was not a state tour, which would have been full of ceremonial functions, but neither was Prince Arthur travelling incognito. While, therefore, some official functions and exchanges of courtesies were required, there was also ample time for sight-seeing and the absorption of local atmospheres. Similarly, though this was not an official tour of military inspections, there were good opportunities for Prince Arthur to see some of the military points which specially interested him. For Prince Arthur it was almost a case of having his cake and eating it; few travellers would not have envied the wealth of experience which was now to fall within his ambit and seldom can a Prince have found the advantages, albeit temporarily, so far outweighing the penalties of royal rank.

The journey to the east began under idyllic circumstances. The *Kaiser-i-Hind* was comfortable and convenient and, as there were scarcely more than twelve other first class passengers, there was plenty of room. Travelling with them in their suite was Sir John McNeill, a proven and sage counsellor and one now in high spirits and full of fun who could be relied upon to keep the ball rolling at meals. Prince Arthur was on the bridge at 5.30 a.m. on 17th March to watch the entry to Colombo harbour. It was a delicious morning and the hills showed up clearly with Adam's Peak standing out splendidly. When they had been made fast, the Governor's A.D.C. came on board to arrange the formalities of the landing. He also brought the shocking news that Sir Howard Elphinstone had been washed overboard and drowned on his way to Tenerife on the night of 8th March. 'He was my friend & confidant,' Prince Arthur wrote in his Journal, '& occupied a position which no one else could ever fill.' Home would never be the same now that he who, as the Queen wrote, had been a father to Prince Arthur when he lost his own, was dead.[1]

The Governor of Ceylon came on board and conducted Prince Arthur and the Duchess ashore in his barge, which was done under a royal salute. Among those waiting at the landing place were Arabi Pasha and his son, Mohamed Fehmi, with two or three other Egyptian exiles. When Prince Arthur had last seen Arabi and his son, both had been his prisoners at the Citadel in Cairo in the early days after the Battle of Tel-el-Kebir. He now greeted them cordially and heard of their great wish to be allowed to return to Egypt in exchange for a promise to take no further part in public affairs, but, of the interview, Prince Arthur recorded no more than that Arabi, though looking well, had grown stouter and greyer. This unusual exchange being completed, Prince Arthur and the Duchess drove to the railway station along a route which was decorated with many novel and striking welcoming arches; they were much gratified by the warmth of the reception given to them by the crowds and they were impressed by the escort of the Governor's Bodyguard, who were Malays dressed in red puggarees, each with a red curtain falling behind, blue and red jackets, red knickerbockers and black patent leather boots. The journey by train to Kandy passed through what seemed to Prince Arthur to be like a gigantic park, than which he thought it would be difficult to see anything more beautiful. Every station was crowded with natives who had turned out to see them pass; everyone was very cheery and Prince Arthur particularly noticed that the women seemed to be treated with perfect equality and that they were of excellent physique, which was a great contrast to India. Presumably his eye was sharper than that of Mrs Cavaye, who was travelling in attendance on the Duchess. She wrote to the Queen that the people of Ceylon looked contented and prosperous, that there had been tremendous cheering, but that she found it hard to tell which were men and which women. They spent a night at Government House in Kandy and saw some of the famous and beautiful sights of the place, including the so-called Buddha's tooth and the Botanical Gardens, which contained bamboos of eighty feet in height. On returning to Colombo, Prince Arthur and the Duchess were entertained to a large official dinner, which proved to be rather a dull party, and they then attended a reception to which five hundred came. The *Bombay Gazette* reported that the Duchess looked remarkably well in a dark heliotrope dress of corded silk cut in a V shape, with a plain skirt and hardly any trimming. With her remarkably good carriage, she had looked exceedingly stately and dignified. The Duke was reported to have been in great form and very affable to all who were presented to him, laughing and chatting with each in turn for a few moments. From the reception, they drove through illuminated streets to re-embark in the *Kaiser-i-Hind*.[2]

On 22nd March the *Kaiser-i-Hind* entered the Straits of Malacca and Prince Arthur sighted the Golden Mountains rising to 7,500 feet in the distance. He also saw three Dutch gunboats, which he understood were attempting to prevent the import of arms from the Malay side to Sumatra, where he heard that the Dutch were so hated in their colony that they dare not venture out of their cantonments. Due to adverse currents, they came to Penang at dusk instead of, as planned, much earlier in the day, which caused disappointment to the crowds who had waited to see them and who had put up so many decorations which the royal visitors never saw. As their ship was carrying mail, they could not extend their visit. However, the Resident came on board and dined with them and they then went ashore and drove to a large square in the town. Here a great crowd was watching an open air play and Prince Arthur and the Duchess pushed their way in to see what was happening. It was an unfamiliar experience for them to be surrounded by a sea of Chinese faces with shaved heads and pigtails. Prince Arthur wrote to the Queen that the Resident had told him that Penang was the richest Colony in her dominions. The trade in opium, tin, silver and spices produced so much money that the authorities did not know what to do with it.[3]

As had been the cases at Colombo and Penang, the approaches to Singapore, which the *Kaiser-i-Hind* entered on 25th March, were full of shipping, the greater part of it British. The Governor of the Straits Settlements, Sir Clementi Smith, brought Prince Arthur and the Duchess ashore in a launch and they saw that Singapore was a pretty place wooded right down to the water's edge. It had a well-to-do look about it and reclamation works were producing a fine promenade, on one side of which was the sea, and, on the other, beautiful lawns and a cricket ground. Passing along roads lined with British and Sikh troops and Malay police, they came to Government House, which Prince Arthur thought was a very fine and cool building set in a lovely park. He was also much impressed by many other new buildings, including especially the English cathedral, built in the gothic style. The crowds who watched them were of many races, but the Chinese predominated. Prince Arthur set off by launch to inspect the forts, which had just been completed. He was impressed by their power and range but he was told that there were difficulties about keeping the magazines dry in the damp climate and he observed that the positions were undermanned. He thought it was urgently necessary that the manning deficiencies, not only in Singapore, but also in Colombo and Hong Kong, should be remedied, for these fortresses protected such important coaling stations for shipping. On one of the evenings during the visit there was a large reception after dinner in Government House. Prince Arthur and the Duchess stood in the centre of the landing with the Governor and Lady Smith to receive about four hundred guests. An astonishing proportion of them was European, but there were some Chinese. There were also a number of Malay chiefs, to each of whom Prince Arthur spoke through an interpreter. They had voluntarily placed themselves under British protection and it seemed that they were satisfied with their positions.[4]

On 29th March, Prince Arthur and the Duchess re-embarked and sailed for Hong Kong. Here, once again, they found the harbour full of shipping, but this time it was of all kinds, including eleven British, a Russian, a German and two French warships. The visitors were carried from the landing place to the Town Hall in sedan chairs by Chinamen dressed in red coats, loose white trousers and black and white boots. The streets were crammed with Chinese who stared hard, but gave vent to not a sound. Having received an address, they were carried by the same means to Government House, feeling by now slightly ludicrous; being in line they could not speak to one another while they continued to be relentlessly stared at in complete silence by the crowds.[5]

The military and naval commanders at Hong Kong laid on an exercise to test the defences at the Lye Moon entrance. Prince Arthur took up a central position to watch the proceedings. Suddenly, a new 'torpedo cruiser,' H.M.S. *Porpoise* appeared round the Point and opened fire on the fort while steaming rapidly across the Bay. She brought her heavy guns to bear and the fort was rather slow to reply. Immediately astern, covered by *Porpoise's* guns and steaming at full speed, came H.M.S *Leander*. She turned and made a dash for the entrance, bringing heavy fire to bear on the fort as she did so. While *Porpoise* continued to draw the fire from ashore, a third ship, H.M.S. *Severne*, also dashed for the entrance. The fighting tops of these two ships were fully manned and they poured fire into the fortress as they came through the entrance keeping up a much more rapid rate than they got back from land. As they passed under the fort, the ships were much exposed to fire by the Highlanders but the heavy breech-loading guns of the fort did not get off as many rounds as Prince Arthur had expected; they managed only five or six rounds each and the muzzle-loading guns fired only two or three rounds each. Prince Arthur reckoned that there would not have been many hits on the ships and he afterwards had a long discussion with General Edwards, the military commander, about what should be done to improve the position. There was one comfort; in war, they thought, torpedoes would have been fired from the shore at the ships. Why this was not included in the exercise was not explained.[6]

On another occasion, viewing things so to speak from the other end of the telescope, Prince Arthur crossed from Hong Kong to Kowloon in a first class torpedo boat, which took only six minutes to complete the journey. He thought the Kowloon docks were very fine; the newest was five hundred and thirty-one feet long and was one of the largest in the world. An even grander project than the construction of these magnificent docks was, however, an ambitious scheme of reclamation along the northern shore of Hong Kong Island which would yield an extra thirty-one acres of building land for the town of Victoria and provide a splendid esplanade seventy-five feet wide along the sea front. This would give on to an average sea depth of twenty feet at low tide, which would be a great improvement on the existing mud banks with their 'unwholesome exhalations.' These works were inaugurated by Prince Arthur on 2nd April and as soon as he had laid a memorial stone, junks appeared and began to dump stone along the outer edge of the barrier. To survey the whole scene, Prince Arthur and the Duchess then ascended the 1,300 feet to the Peak by the wonderful railway, which in places negotiated gradients of one in two. At the top they saw large hotels under construction, but it was rather bleak and they thought it would be very pleasant in the warm weather. In the evening they drove through densely crowded and illuminated streets to the Ko Shing Theatre in the centre of the Chinese town, where they were entertained to dinner by Dr Ho-Kay. The menu included birds' nest soup, stewed shell fish, cassia mushrooms, crab and shark fins, roast beef, roast chicken and ham, pigeons' eggs, boiled quail, fried marine delicacies, roast turkey and ham, fish gills, larded quails, sliced teal, Peking mushrooms, roast pheasant, winter mushrooms, roast fowl and ham, *Beche-de-mere*, sliced pigeon, snipe and macaroni. There were cold roast side dishes of suckling pig, duck, fowl and mutton and table dishes of cold sausage, prawns, preserved eggs and liver. The fruits were preserved apples, citrons, Tientsin pears, pomegranates, carambolas, greengages and pineapples. In addition, there was sweet lotus soup, almond custard and rice. To drink, there was champagne, claret, orange wine, rice wine, rose dhu, Optimus wine and pear wine. This was not quite to Prince Arthur's taste. The dishes all seemed to have been cooked in pork fat and he found them very nasty. During the meal, which lasted three hours, a play was acted, but the falsetto voices, on which the Chinese seemed to pride themselves, though remarkable, were rather trying and Prince Arthur and the Duchess could not understand the language. They had to take it on trust that the play was very good and, in parts, very improper. The music was extraordinary but there were some clever acrobatics. Prince Arthur thought the experience was worthwhile, but he was glad when it was over. After this Chinese introduction, he and the Duchess boarded a river steamer and were glad to get to bed in the sea cabin, which they shared.[7]

When they woke next morning they were well on the way up the Canton River. Batteries fired salutes as they passed and Prince Arthur was told that this was the highest form of Chinese salutation. The dirty water of the river was full of junks and rowing boats and they saw several Chinese gunboats at anchor but they had hardly any men on board. It was a dark, damp and chilly morning and, as they got to Canton, the rain came down. They dropped anchor off the European Settlement and were saluted by three gunboats, a British, a German and an American. The Captain of the British one came on board and accompanied them ashore. They walked down a broad road lined by Marines to the Consulate where they got into chairs and were carried into the city. Ahead of them went a small guard of Chinese soldiers in large straw hats and orange coats, with crimson sashes in which pistols were lodged. The rear was brought up by a Mandarin sent by the Viceroy of Canton. The streets were less than six feet broad and they were almost closed above by overlapping roofs. As they approached, people had to flatten themselves to the walls and tip up their broad hats to make a passage. Every house seemed to be a shop and the number of barbers was astounding. These were all full of men being shaved and having their pigtails retied. The food shops smelt horrid and the butchers appeared to take a pride in displaying meat in its most hideous forms. There were portions of rats, cats, dogs and so on, which made Prince Arthur feel sick. The fishmongers were no less disgusting and everything reeked of blood. Their cruelty was such that they carved up the fish alive. The teeming population presented a cruel and repulsive face and everyone seemed to be fat or lean; there was no mean. There were no sanitary arrangements and the smell was beyond description. The only relief was in a street of carpenters, who were making furniture and coffins. They went to the Temple of the Great Bell, which had been struck by a British shell in 1859 and they had lunch in the Yanum Palace, which was now in British hands. Afterwards they visited the Examination Hall, where, every three years in delapidated cells, 13,000 candidates for eighty-eight Government appointments were shut up for three days with only two pieces of furniture, a board on which to sleep and another on which to write. After another overnight sail, they got back to Hong Kong on the morning of 4th April. From there they sailed in the *Ancona* for Shanghai.[8]

Ancona, flying the royal standard, dropped anchor off Woosung and Commodore Yee, commanding a detached squadron of three Chinese men-of-war, came on board with the British Consul-General and the Manager of the Chinese customs. Prince Arthur heard that the Chinese warships had been built in Newcastle by Armstrong and he noted that Commodore Yee had served for two years as a Sub-Lieutenant under the Duke of Edinburgh in H.M.S. *Black Prince*. The forts fired a salute of twenty-one guns but Commodore Yee felt it necessary to apologise for the slow rate of fire. He said that this was the first time they had fired an English royal salute and the most they had done before was three guns. After more salutes, Prince Arthur and the Duchess proceeded by launch to a landing place in Shanghai where they were received by British, German and Chinese officials in the so-called British Settlement, which was, in fact, a compound of British, German and American. Everything looked brilliantly bright, there were welcoming arches of bamboo covered in moss and the houses were decked with flags and Chinese lanterns. After receiving an address and unveiling a statue of Sir Henry Parkes, who had been British Consul in Shanghai and then, in turn, British Minister in Japan and Peking, Prince Arthur and the Duchess went on a tour of the city, starting with the French Settlement, which remained distinct from the British, German and American, which functioned under a single Municipality. They then crossed a bridge and entered the Chinese city through a narrow gate in the wall. It was rather like Canton, but without the repulsive shops; it smelt sweeter and the inhabitants looked pleasanter. They visited the equivalent of the Chamber of Commerce where Chinese merchants met to settle business and impose punishments.

Apparently a favourite one was to make the miscreant pay for a theatrical performance. At a street corner they saw a man with his head through a board and chained round the neck to a gate. Though sentenced to ten days of this punishment for some social trouble with his brother, the man seemed very cheerful and he joked with all who passed by. They were entertained to dinner by two *Taotais*, or Deputy Governors. During the meal, there were performances by gorgeously dressed actors and wonderfully clever acrobats. *Taotai* Chang, proposed the Queen's health; Prince Arthur replied by proposing that of the Emperor of China. Prince Arthur found the food more palatable than that in Hong Kong but whether it was better or he was getting more used to it was not clear. After dinner, they were taken to a balcony to see the illuminations and then a very splendid procession of the fire brigades. Huge crowds were out to see these festivities. Prince Arthur and the Duchess sailed from Shanghai early in the morning having very much enjoyed their visit.[9]

The success of the visit to Shanghai, by no means entirely reconciled Prince Arthur and the Duchess to the Chinese. They continued to think of them as a cruel people who hated all foreigners. They believed that, for some temporary political reason, orders had been sent from Peking that they were to be treated in a most civil way. Now they were heading for Japan and, on 10th April, they came to the threshold of Nagasaki. A British and a Russian man-of-war saluted and the British Captain, followed by the Consul and the Japanese Governor, who appeared in European black clothes and tall hat, came on board. On either side of the almost landlocked harbour, the hills were covered with trees and the extremely tidy town had a pretty European appearance. They went ashore to see the temple of the god Sua, where they were received by three priests in white robes with their hair done in a sort of horn with an extraordianary cap on top. Each carried a pan and they made low bows, bringing their heels together in German fashion. Prince Arthur and the Duchess entertained the Governor, the British Consul and the naval Captain to dinner on board *Ancona* before sailing. They were enchanted by their first glimpse of Japan, which was so clean and so different from China. The only blemish was that the married women dyed their teeth black to make themselves unattractive to men.[10]

Sailing into the Inland Sea provided further delights and Prince Arthur thought that what he had been led to expect had not been exaggerated. Masses of fishing junks with large square white sails flitted across the water in every direction. Ashore, the light colours of the cultivated crops made a pleasing contrast with the darker green of fir trees and, though it was bitterly cold, the weather was fine. In the harbour of Kobe, Prince Arthur was saluted by nineteen Japanese warships as well as by a Russian and an American, the last two of which were both flagships. Vice-Admiral Baron Ionye, the commander of the Japanese squadron, the Russian, Vice-Admiral Nagornoff, and the American, Rear-Admiral Balknab, the British Consul and the Japanese Governor of the District of Hiojo came on board. Prince Arthur had to give up his idea of going straight to Kyoto as the Emperor, who wished to receive him in Tokyo, was there at the time. He decided, therefore, to go to Osaka instead. Meanwhile, he and the Duchess went ashore to dine with the British Consul. Among the other guests were the Governor of Nagasaki and his wife. The latter wore European clothes for the first time, which Prince Arthur regretted as the dress of bright blue satin was ugly. The dinner, which was done by a Japanese cook, was particularly good and it included a green tea ice, which was a novelty. Prince Arthur and the Duchess returned in the Governor's brougham, which was evidently made for small people, to sleep in the ship. Next day, they left by train for Osaka.[11]

The journey, which was of an hour, took them through carefully cultivated land all the way and they saw many neatly kept villages with wooden roofed temples. The locomotives, carriages and all the railway accessories were of British manufacture. As they came to Osaka, the second town of Japan, with a population of 500,000 and a garrison of 3,000, they were met by a sea of factory chimneys. The Governor received them and they drove in his carriage to the Hotel Osaka, which was built over a canal, as were many other buildings in the town. Osaka, the Birmingham of Japan, was also known as the Venice of Japan. The order of this visit for only a day was energetic sight-seeing, including the very striking fort, which was eight hundred years old and commanded the whole neighbouring countryside, and the new museum, which was showing a loan exhibition of gigantic gods, some good specimens of lacquer and wonderfully made artificial flowers. There were lots of people there and all semed to be interested and enjoying themselves. There were several delightful Japanese babies in quaint national dress; Prince Arthur thought they were most cheery and intelligent looking and none of them seemed to cry. On their way back to the station, they were given tea, which appeared to be kept in readiness in every house. They sailed that night from Kobe.[12]

When *Ancona* arrived at Yokahama on the morning of 15th April, it was drizzling and Prince Arthur thought the climate was quite European. He was saluted by two German, a Russian and a French man-of-war and the British Minister, Mr Fraser, the Secretary of the British Legation, the Master of Napier, the German Minister and the Captains of the warships came on board. Mr Fraser presented the Marquis Kido, Viscount Matzo Dida and Major Muraki, who had been attached to Prince Arthur by the Emperor. Prince Arthur and the Duchess went by train to Tokyo, where they stayed at the British Legation. It was a dark afternoon and everything looked rather dingy. The public buildings, most of which were on high ground, were fine and there were some new houses built in European style, but in the shopping streets most of the buildings were wooden and of only one story. The Emperor's Palace stood on the highest ground and at night it was lit up by electricity. In an interval of sightseeing on their second day in Tokyo, Prince Arthur and the Duchess met the Minister of Foreign Affairs, Viscount Aoki, and his wife at lunch. He had lived many years in Germany and had become a Lutheran. His wife was German. In everything except face and complexion, the Minister seemed to be thoroughly German. After this lunch Prince Arthur received the Diplo-ic Corps. The 'Corean' representatives were most striking; they wore extraordinary hats over a sort of wire frame and, though they had Chinese looking faces, they had full beards and they were dressed in long robes. Later, Prince Arthur and the Duchess visited a theatre where perform-ances lasted twelve hours and sometimes even two or three days. The pit was divided into squares in each of which seven or eight people squatted with little baskets of food and teapots from which they made a regular meal. They watched a famous actor who was fifty three, but, for this play, was dressed as a young girl. After dinner at the Legation, just as the ladies had gone into the drawing-room, there was an extraordinary creaking noise and the chandeliers began to swing. Mrs Napier was in a great fright; she seized the Duchess by the hand and rushed her off under the arch of a doorway. Mrs Napier had experienced several earthquakes. During the night there were two more shocks.[13]

On 17th April, Prince Arthur and the Duchess paid calls on members of the Imperial Family who were in Tokyo. First they went to see *S.A.I. Le Prince Takéhito, Capitaine de Frégate à la suite de l'état Major général de la Marine Impériale.* The Prince, who was in naval uniform, met them at the door and the Princess, who wore a plain black silk European dress with her hair done in what the Duchess thought was much the same style as her own, at the top of the stairs. Both spoke excellent English and they had recently been in Europe. They extended a very courteous reception to their visitors. The second visit was to *S.A.I. Le Prince Yoshihissa, Major général commandant de la 1re Brigade d'Infantrie de Ligne*. He had visited Germany in 1880 and spoke German quite well. The Princess knew no foreign tongue and conversed through an interpreter. She also was dressed in European fashion. Both the palaces were in European style, the first rather French and the second more German. The Emperor had ordained that European clothes should be worn at court, which Prince Arthur thought was a pity; the Japanese, who looked nice to his eye in their traditional dress, looked like monkeys when they aped European fashion.[14]

Having performed these courtesies, Prince Arthur and the Duchess left Tokyo to see something of the countryside. Basing themselves upon Niko, they sallied forth to see some famous temples which were set in magnificent woods of cryptomeria of up to two hundred feet in height. The Duchess thought that the temples were the finest thing they had ever seen after the Taj at Agra. The exquisite beauty of the carving, gilding and painting was of the most refined nature; they heard that the cost of four wooden pillars alone had been 80,000 dollars each. The wooden figures within were almost life-size and were in the sitting position. They were dressed in robes and their faces were painted so that in the dim light they looked almost like mummies. The priests wore paper respirators as they were not supposed to breath in the presence of these holy images. Prince Arthur and the Duchess were allowed to go right up to the figures, which was forbidden to ordinary visitors, and, indeed, very few people had ever seen them. Their origin was uncertain, but they seemed to be Shoguns; the inspiration was partly Shinto and partly Buddhist. The reverent behaviour of the priests gave the impression of a house of worship and the constant praying and chanting reminded Prince Arthur of Catholic churches.[15]

Another expedition took Prince Arthur and the Duchess to Kyoto, where they stayed for a few days at the end of April. Among the things they saw was the new Houganji temple there, which was being built to replace one which had been burnt down. Most of the wood for its construction had been brought from Korea and already five million dollars had been spent on it. They were shown coils of rope, which had been used in connection with driving the piles and extended to a length of one mile. The difficulty of obtaining material of sufficient strength had been overcome by women, who had cut off their hair and sent it to the priests. From this the coils had been woven. Bits of these had found their way to various places, including one which was in the British Museum and the Duchess stuck a small piece into their Journal. Despite the need there had been to postpone the original plan for visiting Kyoto because of the Emperor's presence, he, nonetheless, returned while Prince Arthur and the Duchess were still staying there. This, however, seems to have caused no awkwardness and the Emperor sent them a friendly message by the hand of one of his Chamberlains, Count Nagasaki. Also, when they left Kyoto, a cold supper was put on Prince Arthur's train by order of the Emperor.[16]

This journey brought them to Majanoshta where they celebrated Prince Arthur's fortieth birthday while staying at the Fujiama Hotel. From there they visited Hakone where the Japanese took health cures in the sulphur springs. In a nearby village they found a public bath fed by one of the hot springs and in this they watched men and women bathing together in nature's costume. Prince Arthur thought that the Japanese were such a wonderful happy little people that there was no shame or indecency about it. Walking up to one of the springs, Prince Arthur met some Europeans, one of whom had been a Judge at Shejianpur in northwest India and was an old acquaintance of his. They had a talk with him in the evening at their hotel. In incessant rain they returned to Tokyo on 3rd May.[17]

Marquis Kido, one of those attached to Prince Arthur by the Emperor, came to the British Legation on 5th May to take Prince Arthur and the Duchess out to dinner at the Maple Club. He was dressed in national costume. Prince Arthur and the gentlemen wore morning clothes and the Duchess and the ladies smart tea gowns and high silk dresses. On arriving at the Club they were received by the Committee, who were all connected with the Court, and by some of the Empress's ladies. Girls took their hats and coats and removed their boots. The Master of Napier and others who preceded them within went down on their knees and bowed their foreheads, which Prince Arthur thought had a very funny effect. The Chief host, Marquis Naheshima, took them upstairs and into a long room with sliding wall panels and no furniture. Down its centre there were two rows of tapers like high church candlesticks. Cushions were arranged round three sides and on these, with Prince Arthur and the Duchess in the centre, the company sat down. Twenty girls, one for each of the diners, then appeared with lacquer basins on lacquer stands and each diner was provided with chopsticks. Each girl presented her dish

23. *Prince Arthur and the Prince of Wales driving to the hackney stud
at Wolferton, Easter 1895.*

24. On 29th December 1902 Prince Arthur, and the Duchess 'ascended a magnificently caparisoned elephant and sat in a silver and gold howdah. While a white umbrella was held over the Duchess's head, they rode out through the lines of Princes . . .', and made their state entry into Delhi. (pp. 224–5)

25. *The party at Glenveagh Castle, Letterkenny, Ireland, 1902. Seated on the ground, left to right: Arthur Campbell, W. F. Lascelles, the Marquis of Hamilton, Arthur Pakenham. Behind, left to right: R. P. Butler, Henry G. O. Bridgeman, Lieutenant-Colonel John Leslie, the Duke of Connaught, Cornelia Adair, Léonie Leslie, the Duchess of Connaught, Lilian Pakenham, Princess Margaret of Connaught, the Marchioness of Hamilton.*

26. *The Esher Committee. Left to right: Admiral Sir John Fisher, Lord Esher, Sir George Clarke.*

kneeling and remained so until it was time to bring the next one. Hot saki was served in little china cups poured from small china bottles, each with maple leaves in it. There were soups, fish, some of it raw, minced meat, quails, vegetables, bamboo shoots, lily bulbs and very good cakes. Prince Arthur and the Duchess had asked that bread and champagne should also be served, but when it came to the point, Prince Arthur found that he preferred the saki. The hosts came in turn and drank the health of their guests. The procedure was that the beneficiary washed his cup and gave it to the one who was to drink his health; it was then filled by the girl. When it had been drunk, it was washed and the drinker returned it on the palm of his hand. The guests then drank the health of their hosts in similar style and in this way a good deal of saki was got through, but luckily, Prince Arthur thought, the cups were small. During the meal there was excellent and extremely graceful dancing by one, two or four girls at a time and after each dance one of the girls was called up to show her dress. These were made of magnificent material and richly embroidered. According to custom, Prince Arthur gave each of these girls a cup of saki. When the dinner was over, Prince Arthur's girl thought that, after all the saki which had been drunk, he would be in danger going down the steep and slippery black lacquer stairs and she insisted on leading him by the hand, but Prince Arthur found that the saki, which tasted like hot dry sherry, did not give him a headache, which, he thought, the same amount of wine would have done. The evening had been most enjoyable and full of novelties; when they got back to the Legation, the Duchess went straight to bed, but Prince Arthur took a light supper.[18]

Major Muraki, another of those whom the Emperor had attached to Prince Arthur, took him to see the Arsenal on the day following the Maple Club dinner. In the small arms factory, Prince Arthur was shown the new magazine rifle; it seemed to be of very strong construction and simple in its mechanism, it was handy to use with simple sights from point blank to four hundred metres and it had an extra range of up to 1,600 metres. 100,000 had been ordered, a thousand had been delivered and production was running at about sixty a day. Prince Arthur thought that it might well be superior to the British rifle. He learned that the Japanese infantry amounted to no more than 42,000 men and that there was only a small force of cavalry, which were more in the nature of mounted infantry. There were also some field and mountain batteries.[19]

On 7th May the Emperor returned to Tokyo in the afternoon. That evening Prince Arthur and the Duchess were to dine with him at the palace. They dressed in good time and started in a very smart state carriage with an escort of Lancers at 7.40. Prince Arthur wore full dress uniform with the riband and star of the Garter and the Duchess wore a low dress with tiara and orders. Marquis Kido accompanied them in their carriage. In the palace they were received by Household officials in gala uniform and these, accompanied by Prince Arthur's suite, preceded them along several long and handsome corridors before bringing them to a halt. A panel in the wall on their left then opened and, as Prince Arthur later recorded, 'we found ourselves in the presence of the Mikado.' He shook hands with them and greeted them very kindly and then gave his arm to the Duchess. The panel in the wall closed and a few steps took them to another room, at the door of which they found the Empress and some of her ladies. The Emperor wore a dark blue double breasted uniform with the riband and star of the Chrysanthemum and two or three other stars and medals. He struck Prince Arthur as being above the ordinary Japanese height; his features were dark, coarse and ugly and he wore a thin straggly beard and moustache. The Empress was smartly dressed in a pale green low cut dress trimmed with pearls with a tiara of magnificent diamonds, which came from Garrards. She wore the riband and star of the Imperial Crown and two or three smaller orders. She was very short, but had a pretty slim little figure and was, Prince Arthur thought, decidedly nice looking. He thought her expression showed firmness of character, but her chin was too straight and she kept her mouth slightly open. She was thirty-eight, but looked less and her manners were pleasing and dignified. They had already discovered that she was an enlightened and intelligent woman, active in the development of education for women and other trends in the modernisation of Japan. After some civil conversation through interpreters, the Princes and Princesses joined the party, court officials were presented to Prince Arthur and his suite and members of the British Legation to the Emperor. Dinner was announced and the Emperor again gave his arm to the Duchess and Prince Arthur his to the Empress. They passed along several corridors and into a handsome dining-room, lit, as all the palace was, by soft electric light. The ceiling of the room was divided into squares of gold and black lacquer with paintings of flowers and birds in brilliant but harmonious colours. The panelled walls were hung with silk curtains in subdued colours. The doors, as were the others in the Palace, were of magnificent lacquered wood with gilt fretwork plates and hinges; the floor was a beautiful French parquet. The table was laid in European style with gold ornaments and service and there were lovely flowers. They ate from gold plate until the dessert, which was taken from Minton china. The Emperor and Empress sat together at the centre of the table with the Duchess on his right and Prince Arthur on the Empress's left. A band played under a German bandmaster. The dinner lasted an hour and the conversation flowed throughout, but it was rather difficult as there was only one interpreter. Both Their Majesties questioned Prince Arthur and the Duchess about their travels in Japan and the Emperor spoke a good deal of horses and dogs. After dinner they walked arm in arm into a charmingly decorated drawing-room, which contained beautiful gold lacquered cabinets and *étagères*, on which lovely flowers and branches of flowering trees and bamboos were arranged in the most artistic Japanese style. Over coffee, the Emperor conversed with Prince Arthur and the Empress and Princess Kumatzu with the Duchess. Then, with many apologies for not having received them earlier and after directing Prince and Princess Kumatzu to show Prince Arthur and the Duchess the rest of the Palace, the Emperor and Empress withdrew. Sir John McNeill, who was at the dinner, wrote to the Queen that the scene of the Emperor and Empress of Japan conversing freely with the Duke and Duchess of Connaught was not one which could easily be forgotten.[20]

Next day, 8th May, Prince Arthur and the Duchess were seen off to Yokahama by Imperial court officials and members of the British and German Legations. There, to the accompaniment of God Save the Queen played by a Japanese band and the hoisting of the royal standard, they embarked in the Canadian Pacific Steamer *Abyssinia*. They left Japan with the greatest regret and, as Sir John McNeill put it, there was not one of their party who would not wish to visit it again. The Duchess thought that Japan was now not far behind European standards and she was impressed by the people, who were quick and clever and ready to learn and improve. The Emperor had given Prince Arthur the Order of the Chrysanthemum and that of the Imperial Crown to the Duchess, who thus became the only foreign lady, other than the Empress of Russia, to have that distinction. Prince Arthur was concerned that, though the Russians and the Germans had given the Emperor and Empress their highest orders, the British had not and he suggested to the Queen that she should send a gift to the Emperor and that Prince Kumatzu should be given the civil G.C.B.[21]

The compensation in leaving Japan was the return to Canada, where Prince Arthur was looking forward to seeing the places he had known twenty years ago. On 21st May, *Abyssinia* dropped anchor off Victoria. The Lieutenant-Governor of British Columbia, Mr Nelson, the Commanding Officer of the Canadian Militia, Colonel Prior, and Captain Hamilton, who commanded H.M.S. *Amphion*, came on board. On landing, Prince Arthur and the Duchess were received by the Mayor and Corporation of Victoria, there was a guard of honour of the Canadian Militia Artillery and an address was presented. In Victoria all the main buildings were covered with flags but the roads were bad and very dusty. It struck Prince Arthur as curious that there were so many Chinese about. Every laundry was Chinese and so were all the gardeners and servants. The electric tramway, a novelty to Prince Arthur, was most impressive. Mrs Nelson received him at Government House; he remembered her as a little girl in Ottawa twenty years earlier. After lunch, Prince Arthur opened a new hospital and visited the naval base at Esquimault where *Amphion* was being repaired in dry dock after having run on the rocks with the Governor-General on board.[22]

Prince Arthur's return caught the headlines in the Canadian press. 'Hail to the Duke,' one read, 'Connaught and his Princess in the Queen City.' The article declared that when the Duke had last been in Canada he had been a 'golden haired youth fresh from the Woolwich Academy and fired with military ardor.' He came this time as a warrior turned forty returned from India, 'his handsome face colored a nut brown by the fierce sun of the Orient.' Another paper reported the view that he would soon succeed the Duke of Cambridge as Commander-in-Chief of the British army and that he was said to be thoroughly versed in military tactics and was considered to be one of the cleverest members of the Royal Family. Another informed its readers that his face was set off by a handsome brown moustache.[23]

Meanwhile, Prince Arthur and the Duchess arrived in Vancouver. As they approached by sea through the rain, they beheld a densely wooded scene with rather weird houses rising in irregular fashion on the sloping ground. Everywhere there were burnt trees giving an initial effect which was dingy. The Mayor, Mr Oppenheimer, and the Corporation came on board and on the quayside there was an address. Prince Arthur and the Duchess then drove to the Canadian Pacific Railway Hotel, which was a fine building with a good staircase and large open corridors; it was very well furnished and lit by electricity. This, indeed, was symbolic of the amazing revolution which had taken place in her prospects since Prince Arthur had last been in Canada, for now the railway linked west and east. The opportunity of travelling the length of this line, which was one of the wonders of the world, had been among the principal attractions to

Prince Arthur of returning home, so to speak, through the looking-glass. Driving in Vancouver after lunch, Prince Arthur thought it was marvellous to see what had been done since the great fire of thirty-seven years ago, which had completely destroyed the city. The fine new houses were all of brick or stone, as wood was no longer allowed. He visited some of the saw mills; everything was used, including the saw dust, which became fuel for the furnaces, which produced the steam for the lifting machinery. The workmen were of many nationalities, which was another sign of Canadian development, and, in addition to French and British Canadians, there were Americans, Red Indians, Chinese, Japanese and Lascars. That night, Prince Arthur and the Duchess boarded a train before starting next morning on their epic journey by rail across Canada.[24]

The Canadian Pacific Railway had put a special train at their disposal. Prince Arthur and the Duchess were accommodated in a car which belonged to Sir George Stephen. Sir John McNeill and Dr Kilkelly were in another, which belonged to Mr van Horne, a director of the C.P.R. Thus, Prince Arthur and the Duchess, their staff and their servants, travelled in the utmost comfort, for in addition to sleeping places, saloons and ample passages, there were kitchens and dining rooms. Mr van Horne had also put on board his cook, Jimmy French, a negro, who cooked for them all throughout the journey. The train wound its way up a series of wonderfully engineered curves and was carried across tremendous ravines on high trestle bridges built of wood, which were rather alarming despite Prince Arthur's confidence that they had been most carefully built. It passed through artificial tunnels, also built of wood, which were to enable avalanches to pass over the line, and then it descended to Donald, the last station in British Columbia. From there, now headed by two engines, the train began the ascent of the Rockies amidst the most splendid scenery, the grandest of all of which was when the line passed close under Mount Stephen. Prince Arthur and the Duchess got out at Banff and spent the night in the very fine C.P.R. hotel, where Prince Arthur made a number of new acquaintances, among whom was a former Prime Minister of New Zealand.[25]

After Calgary, where he drove round the young town in a police brake, Prince Arthur was much struck by the sudden cessation of hills and the beginning of the rolling prairies. At Medicine Hat, he drove with the Duchess to a new hospital, where they saw some sad cases of frost bite. Regina, the Headquarters of the North-West Mounted Police, proved to be uninteresting, being no larger and much less pretty than Medicine Hat.

Shortly before Winnipeg they turned off the main line and travelled up a private one to Silver Heights, the home of Sir Donald Smith, who was Governor of the Hudson's Bay Company, where they spent the night. Sir Donald Smith, who was away, had left his agent to entertain the royal guests. At dinner they met Mr John Schultz, the Lieutenant-Governor of Manitoba, the Bishop of Rupertsland and the American Consul. Next morning, while the Duchess rested, Prince Arthur went into Winnipeg, where he was greeted by a very smart guard of honour of the Mounted Infantry School, who wore bandoliers, high gaiters and hunting spurs. Prince Arthur recognised one of the officers, who had formerly been a Sergeant in the 10th Hussars and who, he noticed, was wearing the Afghan and Egyptian medals as well as the Canadian medal for the North-Western Expedition of 1887. He thought the handsome town hall was a great credit to the city, but he also saw numerous half-built houses on which work had been stopped at the end of the boom two or three years ago. Nevertheless, Prince Arthur felt sure that Winnipeg would become a great city; when he had been last there it was a village of a few hundred inhabitants; now, he understood, it had a population of 25,000. When he had gone, the Lieutenant-Governor wrote to the Prime Minister, Sir John Macdonald, about the visit. He said that the Duchess had been too exhausted to appreciate the city, but that this had occasioned, not disappointment, but sympathy. Prince Arthur, he wrote, had done all the right things in the right places and everybody had been satisfied. The Duke and the Duchess had been charming and he thought it no wonder that the Royal Family was respected if Prince Arthur was a 'fair sample.' The Duchess, he added, was 'exceedingly nice.'[26]

At Fort William, Prince Arthur inspected what he was told were the largest grain elevators in Canada and then went on to Port Arthur, his own namesake, where he received an address on the steps of the hotel. The train now ran onto the Grand Trunk Line at North Bay and they travelled on to Toronto, passing through civilised country dotted with lakes, pretty villages and trees coming into leaf. Prince Arthur and the Duchess spent two nights at the Queen's Hotel and they had a tremendous reception from the people of the city, who turned out in force to see the functions, of which there were no less than fourteen. One of these was in the Pavilion, which was crammed with 4,000 people, who had come to witness Prince Arthur's reception of three addresses. He feared that the galleries might not be strong enough to bear their weight. Prince Arthur went to call on Mrs Kirkpatrick, whom he had known on his first visit as

Miss Macpherson. He remembered that she had been a very pretty girl, but he now found that she had lost her looks and was very large. The Lieutenant-Governor, who was in such poor health that he could scarcely stand, and the Premier of Ontario, Mr Oliver Mowat, paid a formal call on Prince Arthur at his hotel and there were grand dinners and receptions. In Toronto, Prince Arthur's working day had been from 10.30 in the morning until 11.30 at night; it had been worth it, for he got a magnificent reception wherever he appeared.[27]

At Niagara Falls, Prince Arthur took the Duchess to see the view of the cascade from the same nice rooms in the Clifton House Hotel, which he had occupied twenty years earlier. It was a lovely day and after lunch they drove to the American side and then travelled on the New York Central Railway to Buffalo. They drove through the newest part of the town, where Prince Arthur was struck by the nice gardens, which had no walls or railing round them, and the tree-lined thoroughfares. They watched people playing baseball and riding bicycles in the park and then, 'by a little management,' returned to Niagara before anyone had realised who they were. That night, they rejoined their train in Toronto and left for Montreal. A host of people were waiting on the platform to greet them, among whom were three of Canada's great magnates, Sir George Stephen, with whom they stayed, Sir Donald Smith and Mr van Horne. Addresses were read in English and French and Prince Arthur replied to them in both languages. Large crowds gave them a warm reception on their drive to Sir George Stephen's house. This proved to be charming. The ceilings and walls were covered in various Canadian woods, which were left in their natural colours. Prince Arthur saw many of the great improvements which had been made to the city since 1870 and he was specially struck by the handsome Windsor Hotel. He also saw some old haunts, including the Victoria rink, where he had so much enjoyed skating in the old days. He went to see Rose Mount, where he had lived. It now belonged to Mr Ogilvie, who owned most of the grain elevators in Canada and who had entirely rebuilt it, making, Prince Arthur thought, a great improvement. He drove with the Duchess to the Champ de Mars, where they were cheered by an immense crowd. Prince Arthur inspected the fire brigade and the cadet corps and they watched a game of lacrosse, which the Duchess enjoyed immensely. At dinners and receptions, on their many tours in and around the city and at the functions, Prince Arthur made many new acquaintances but he also met innumerable people whom he had known and now remembered from twenty years ago. At the Art

Gallery, for instance, he met his old friend, Mr Jacobi, who had been a sketching companion of Sir Howard Elphinstone's in the Rose Mount days. He was now President of the Royal Canadian Academy. Prince Arthur was especially pleased to be in Montreal again, where, as he wrote to the Queen, he found so many old friends and was shown such warm feeling. He said that nearly everyone recognised him when he walked in the streets.[28]

On 4th June, Prince Arthur and the Duchess went to Ottawa, where they were greeted by the Governor-General, Lord Stanley of Preston, and the Prime Minister, Sir John Macdonald. They drove with an escort of Princess Louise's Dragoon Guards through great crowds to the Parliament Building, where Prince Arthur received an address in the upper house. They lunched with the Prime Minister and Lady Macdonald and then drove to the Governor-General's residence, Rideau Hall. Ottawa had grown very much since Prince Arthur had last seen it and he thought the red brick houses which had sprung up were nice, but he felt that the city needed more trees and he found the mud on the streets dreadful. They left Ottawa by train at 4 p.m. and arrived back in Montreal at 7. In 1870 that journey had taken all day. Now they were back in time for a large dinner at Sir Donald Smith's, after which there was a reception for five hundred people. The journey to Quebec was broken for a few days at Causapscal, where a fishing party had been organised for Prince Arthur. No one, however, seemed to catch anything. In Quebec, they drove in the Governor-General's carriage to the Citadel while a salute was fired, but not as previously from the Citadel itself, for, in the previous year, the firing had caused a terrible fall of rock, which had killed more than a hundred people. Once again the streets were full of crowds and flags. Prince Arthur received an address in the chamber of the Legislative Council and, among the visits he made, was one to the Convent, where, in the absence of the Archbishop, he was received by the Vicar-General and then by the Lady Superior. Only members of the Royal Family and the Governor-General and his party were allowed to visit this convent. After dinner on the second night in Quebec the Governor-General gave a large reception in the Citadel, to which six or seven hundred people came. This was followed by impromptu dancing and supper. On 12th June, Prince Arthur and the Duchess embarked in the Allan Royal Mail Steamer *Sardinian* and sailed for Liverpool.[29]

Prince Arthur was tremendously impressed by the transcontinental railway, over so much of which he had travelled. He supposed that, running as it did from Vancouver to Halifax, it was the longest railway in the world which was operated under a single management. He thought it was of Imperial importance. He told the Queen that Canada had grown much more loyal than it had been in 1870 and that there was now no wish to separate from the mother country nor to be annexed by the United States. The Queen was delighted that he had been back to Canada; 'You are so *looked up to* & *beloved*,' she wrote. The *Sardinian* reached Liverpool at midnight on 21st June; Prince Arthur and the Duchess left immediately by special train for Windsor.[30]

CHAPTER 11

Home Commands 1890-1898

ON 22ND JUNE 1890, the Queen drove down from the Castle to the South Western Railway station at Windsor in an open landau with two outriders dressed in scarlet. On her arrival, she was met by the Prince of Wales and, among others already there, were the Princess of Wales, the Duke of Clarence and the Duke of Cambridge. When Prince Arthur's train was signalled, the Queen walked out onto the carpeted platform to await its arrival. It came in at about 1.45 p.m. and Her Majesty advanced and kissed the Duke and Duchess, who received the same affectionate welcome from the other members of the Royal Family, including their children, who, according to a reporter from the *Standard*, showed 'a natural eagerness to receive the caresses of their parents.' The Duke looked bronzed, but otherwise unchanged; the Duchess wore a grey felt hat, a brown grey jacket and a light grey costume. The Queen entered her carriage with the Duke and Duchess and their children and they drove off through Datchet Road and up Thames Street to the Castle.[1]

There was much to discuss, for the question now arose as to what the next step in Prince Arthur's military career was to be. Previous expectations had to be reconsidered because the tide of army reform was now running higher than at any time since Cardwell's measures of twenty years earlier. Indeed, the Hartington Commission had already reported in favour of the abolition of the post of Commander-in-Chief and the establishment in its place of a staff system. Though this proposal found no favour with Wolseley, the arch military reformer, it had much political appeal as a means of distancing the Crown from its direct control of the Army. This meant that, in addition to the usual difficulties attendant upon the appointment of royalties to any position, with which the Queen and Prince Arthur were already familiar, there was now the added one that any appointment offered to him would be subjected to a scrutiny as to whether it would increase or diminish the prospect of abolishing the

Commandership-in-Chief. Prince Arthur was already well used, in the matter of his appointments, to being batted about like a shuttlecock between the Cabinet, the House of Commons, the Press and the Queen, but it was now to be a much more intensive business. Instead of being in far off India, the issues were in London and they concerned a Prince, who, through the combination of his experience and achievements as well as his birth, had already risen to a position of appreciable national import-ance.[2]

Lord Wolseley, the Adjutant-General, and Sir Redvers Buller, the Quarter-Master-General, both wished for Prince Arthur's appointment to succeed Buller as Quarter-Master-General and the Duke of Cambridge duly made the necessary recommendation to the Secretary of State for War, Mr Stanhope. Stanhope at first demurred on the ground that this would be rather a come down for an officer who had already been Commander-in-Chief of the Bombay Army, but then fell back upon the more general and impregnable argument that it would be 'very un-desirable' that the Duke of Connaught should take up an appointment at the War Office at the present time. Instead, he suggested that he should be offered the Aldershot command. But this was not vacant and Prince Arthur told the Queen that it would be unfair to put pressure on Sir Evelyn Wood, who held the command, to make it so. The Queen was very much annoyed. She was 'surprised,' Ponsonby drafted, 'much surprised,' the Queen amended, to hear the suggestion, as Aldershot could only become vacant if Wood was offered the Commandership-in-Chief in India, which also was not vacant. The military authorities had suggested that the Duke of Connaught should be made Quarter-Master-General and this 'might,' Ponsonby wrote, 'sh^ld,' the Queen inserted, be adopted. Stanhope, armed with observations made in the Cabinet, put it to the Queen that if two of the three principal offices in the Army, that is those of the Commander-in-Chief, Adjutant-General and Quarter-Master-General, were occupied by members of the Royal Family, there would 'almost certainly' be considerable objection in the House of Commons. This, he said, would be unfortunate at the very time that the Government had persuaded Parliament to maintain the post of Com-mander-in-Chief. The Queen saw no reason to be afraid of the House of Commons and declined to admit that being royal should be a dis-qualification for appointment. That, she said, would be putting politics before professional qualifications. Stanhope felt that it would be un-seemly for him to enter into any argument with the Queen; he hoped that being royal would not disqualify the Duke of Connaught from holding high appointments in the public service and, indeed, that it would enable him to be considered for them at a somewhat earlier age than other officers. He suggested that he should be the Commander-in-Chief at Portsmouth, a position which could be made vacant by posting Sir Leicester Smyth, the existing occupant, to Gibraltar, which he was anxious to accept.[3]

The Queen, who was not always quick to see when she was losing an argument, would, perhaps, have made further objection had it not been for the advice she received from another member of the Cabinet for whom she had a much greater regard than she did for Stanhope. This was the Lord President of the Council, Lord Cranbrook. He told her that the Cabinet had been unanimous in the conclusion that the Duke of Connaught should not be the Quarter-Master-General, for that would have given the impression that he was being lined up to succeed the Duke of Cambridge as Commander-in-Chief. Such an impression would have aroused the susceptibilities of the House of Commons, which had just been persuaded to keep the post of Commander-in-Chief in being. The Opposition would then vote against the Government and the Unionists would probably follow Lord Hartington, who was pledged to vote for the abolition of the post, as many Tories would also do. Lord Cranbrook hoped that one day the Duke of Connaught would become the Commander-in-Chief; in the meantime, he thought it best that he should accept the Portsmouth command. This settled the matter. The Queen entirely accepted what Lord Cranbrook had said. He was, she felt, such a strong upholder of the throne and, as was so often the case, she was more influenced by who the advisor was than by what was the advice. She seems to have paid little attention to Wolseley's plea that she should drop a hint to the Duke of Cambridge to resign so that an immediate vacancy would arise, which might be filled by the Duke of Connaught, who would be the ideal instrument for the modernisation of the instruction, organisation and tactical efficiency of the Army. In contradistinction to that idea, the extent to which Prince Arthur's long grooming for the position of Commander-in-Chief was now militating against his advancement in the Army had become clear.[4]

Prince Arthur accepted the Portsmouth command, but he did so without enthusiasm and he was in no great hurry to take it up. Stanhope told him that it was undesirable to leave such an important fortress in the hands of subordinate officers but proceeded, in the same letter, to contradict that by suggesting that he should assume the command and then go on leave until January 1891. Prince Arthur acted in the sense of the second part of Stanhope's requirements and, having drawn attention to what he regarded as the undue weakness of the artillery element in his new command, he went off to attend the German manoeuvres. These centred on Breslau and Liegnitz and Prince Arthur was greatly impressed by the efficient state of the corps which were involved. He noted that the infantry got over the ground very rapidly and that there was much less rigidity in their marching than he had seen in earlier years. The Company commanders were given a large measure of independence of action, which he thought was something which should be adopted in the British army. He was amused to find that he was frequently mistaken for the German Emperor and was cheered all the way down the streets, but this did not seem to upset his nephew who made himself very agreeable to his uncle. The Duke of Cambridge, however, was rather alarmed by the prospect that Prince Arthur might come home with the idea of introducing German standards to the British army. One could not, he warned Prince Arthur, demand of a voluntary army what the Germans did of a conscript one.[5]

When he took up the reins at Portsmouth, Prince Arthur found that he had 10,943 troops and twenty-six guns under his command, but scarcely had he counted them than he met with a rebuff. He was anxious to test the efficiency of the force in the face of a surprise attack from seaward, which, of course, depended upon the Navy joining in the exercise. Though this, in Prince Arthur's opinion, could have been done without affecting the naval classes in Portsmouth, the Admiralty refused to cooperate and Prince Arthur had to tell Stanhope that, in those circumstances, there was no point in spending his small allowance on mobilising for a pointless exercise. Nevertheless, Prince Arthur was sufficiently absorbed in his duties at Portsmouth to say that he could not come up to London at the behest of the Prince of Wales, though the importance of the duties was probably less of a deterrent than the subject of the proposed interview. The Prince of Wales wished to speak to Prince Arthur about Sir William Gordon-Cumming, an officer in the Scots Guards, of which Prince Arthur was the Colonel. While a fellow guest with the Prince of Wales of Mr and Mrs Arthur Wilson at Tranby Croft, Gordon-Cumming had been accused of cheating in a game of baccarat. As a result of various indiscretions, a court case was impending in which the heir to the throne would be required to give evidence. Whatever it was that he wanted to say to Prince Arthur beforehand, Prince Arthur did not wish to hear. He was determined not to be used in such a way as to suggest to the world that Gordon-Cumming was being sacrificed to save the Prince of Wales from embarrassment. This attitude, prudent as it was, did not endear Prince Arthur to his brother and the relationship of the two Princes cannot have been improved by the Queen's reaction. She found it humiliating that the Prince of Wales should be dragged in the dirt, as she put it, to a Court of Justice for the second time. 'Oh if only *you* were the *eldest*,' she burst out to Prince Arthur.[6]

Prince Arthur's routine duties as General-Officer-Commanding, Southern District, which was the technical name of what was colloquially known as the Portsmouth command, were largely concerned with inspections of the troops at their various stations and the writing of reports on the regiments. These activities, together with his Indian experience, gave him valuable insights of which he made use in the evidence which he was required to submit to a Commission, under the chairmanship of Lord Wantage, which had been appointed to report on conditions of service in the Army. As to troops serving in India, the chief crime, Prince Arthur told the Commission, was drunkenness. Time bore heavily on the men in the hot weather when they had to be kept in barracks from 9.0 a.m. to 4.0 p.m. with little or nothing to do. He feared drunkenness was inevitable in India. The second great problem was the youthfulness of many in the drafts. Sickness in men under twenty was much greater than in the case of older and more seasoned troops. Prince Arthur recalled walking down a line of drafts at the Deolali depot in October 1889. Not one of the two hundred and fifty men had a vestige of hair on his face and Prince Arthur asked a good many of them if they were really twenty years of age; one said he 'might be about 19.' He later heard that about half of these men had died. Venereal disease, he told the Commission, was a great problem in India, as he had also found it was in the Portsmouth command. The older soldiers, however, tended to recover from it; the younger ones usually died. Prince Arthur conceded the difficulty of determining the true age of recruits, who often lied about it, and he reckoned that as many as half the men under his command at Portsmouth were, in truth, under twenty. Such men, he considered, were not fit to go on active service and they were not even strong enough to carry their marching kit.[7]

The system of serving seven years with the Colours and then five with the Reserve seemed to Prince Arthur to be too rigid and he advocated that men should be allowed to go to the Reserve after three years, as was already done in the Guards. He said that as many as half the soldiers in the Guards took this option, but he thought that this was primarily due to the exceptionally heavy incidence of the very unpopular sentry duty to which the Guards were exposed. Prince Arthur told the Commission that, in his opinion, much of this duty was pointless as, in the event of trouble, the sentry could only summon a policeman to deal with it. He said that on his return to Windsor at the end of his Indian service, he had persuaded the Queen to make drastic reductions in the number of sentries posted at Windsor Castle, but that this had met with strong opposition from the military authorities. He thought that one policeman, could effectively do the work of six sentries, and he hoped that further cuts would be made, including at Buckingham Palace. Sentry duty, he insisted, was detrimental to recruiting and also to the proper training of recruits as well as to their health.[8]

Prince Arthur was very doubtful as to the value of deferred pay for those going to the Reserve. He recognised that the intention was to provide these men with a spring board to civilian life, but the result was often that they spent the money on drink or other debaucheries. He also felt that it was essential that Reservists should receive training at regular intervals instead of on the existing haphazard or even non-existent basis. He believed that the incentives to men to stay with the Colours long enough to qualify as efficient N.C.Os were inadequate and he said that in the Portsmouth command the Sergeants and Corporals were too inexperienced to be effective. He said that the pay of Lance Corporals and Corporals was 'wretchedly low' and he wanted the rate to be increased by at least 6d, and preferably 1s, a day. He was much concerned about the status of soldiers in society and he told the Commission that he had heard of a man being refused permission to be married in uniform by the officiating clergyman, of a Staff Sergeant being resented in a bar by commercial travellers on board a steamer sailing between Holyhead and Kingstown and of a Corporal in the Life Guards being refused dinner with his wife by the White Hart at Windsor because he was in uniform. In the last case the slight was the greater as the Corporal had once been an officer in the German army. Finally, Prince Arthur took issue with the Adjutant-General, Sir Redvers Buller, who had said that no man should serve with the Colours beyond the age of twenty-seven, by which stage his best time for fighting had passed. Prince Arthur judged that a man often came to his prime at thirty-five to forty years of age.[9]

Prince Arthur's evidence had no dramatic effect on the findings of the Wantage Commission nor were the latter to be of any great importance in the history of the reform of the British army, but the points made by Prince Arthur are testimony to his interest in ordinary soldiers and the realism of his views about their conditions of service. Meanwhile, the military importance of the fortress at Portsmouth and of others in the Southern District was rapidly diminishing thanks to the improvement in Anglo-French relations, which, in turn, was caused by a growing appreciation in both those countries of an emerging threat from Germany. During his last visit to Germany for the manoeuvres in September 1890, Prince Arthur had stayed briefly at *Königliches Schloss* near Kiel with the Emperor's brother, Prince Henry, who was serving in the German navy, and he had then looked with interest at some of Germany's most modern warships. Now he was to see something of the French fleet, with which a conjunction might possibly be expected in the future.[10]

Through an evening haze on 20th August 1891, Prince Arthur watched from Southsea Castle as a French Squadron approached on a goodwill visit. The ships seemed to be cumbersome and they did not keep good station. They looked hideous to Prince Arthur's eye as they were painted all over in grey green. He accompanied the Queen when she received the French Admiral Gervais and his Captains. The Admiral struck Prince Arthur as being sound, tactful and firm and the Captains, most of whom came from the north of France, made themselves very pleasant; he did not like the junior officers so much. Lying off Southampton was the yacht *Aline* with Prince Henry of Prussia on board, remaining, as the Prince of Wales thought, unseen, but seeing everything.[11]

That night there was a dinner party for the French at Osborne House. Admiral Gervais sat beside the Queen and directly opposite Prince Arthur, who proposed the health of the French President and extended a welcome to the French Squadron. Afterwards there was a circulation in the drawing room, which Prince Arthur and his sister Beatrice had cleared out to make such a thing possible. Mama was in a very good humour and talked to everyone and Prince Arthur wrote to the Duchess that he had talked French until he was blue in the face. One of the Queen's entourage, General Biddulph, distinguished himself by addressing Lord Clanwilliam, the British naval Commander-in-Chief at Portsmouth, in French and asking him which was his ship, where he had got his medals and so on until Clanwilliam burst into laughter. On 21st August the Queen, accompanied by Prince Arthur and her grandson, Prince George, sailed down the line of the French ships in the royal yacht *Victoria and Albert* and anchored off the flagship, *Marengo*, so that Admiral Gervais could come aboard to take leave of her. For the next several days there was a succession of dinners and balls to entertain the French visitors, which culminated in an entertainment given by Prince Arthur at his residence, Government House, in Portsmouth. They sat down to dinner thirty-two, which was the most that the dining-room could accommodate. In the Duchess's absence undergoing another cure for her leg, Prince Arthur had blue silk on the table and along it there were alternate arrangements of red roses and white marguerites so that the French colours were reproduced. Admiral Gervais was suitably impressed and said he had never seen a table so arranged. It was a pleasant dinner and not at all stiff and the guests did full justice to what several of them declared was the best food they had eaten for a long time. The band of the Marines, stationed on the lawn near the dining-room windows, played splendidly and after dinner the party debouched into the garden, which was hung with chinese lanterns and adorned with two supper tents surmounted by flags. After the trumpeters had sounded *Retraite*, the *Marseillaise* was played and the escorts presented arms. Admiral Gervais exclaimed to Prince Arthur 'je suis profondement ému.'[12]

Accompanied by the Duke of Cambridge, who had come to stay with him for a field day, Prince Arthur paid a visit to the French Squadron. A considerable sea was running and they had some difficulty in getting aboard *Marengo* but, having done so, they were received with all honours and entertained to lunch on board. Admiral Gervais proposed the Queen's health as though, Prince Arthur thought, he was one of her subjects. Uncle George, who had grown very sleepy, decided to attempt no more but, when he had gone ashore, Prince Arthur boarded *Marceau*, which struck him as a very powerful ship with a formidable central battery of heavy guns mounted forward and aft. He discovered, however, that these took twice as long to load by comparison with what could be done in the newer British ships. He was sure that the Royal Navy's ships were smarter than the French and he felt that there was more energy aboard them too. Meanwhile, the Queen had left for Balmoral, taking with her the Connaught children. This was a sad blow to Prince Arthur, who missed them very much, especially as he was also deprived of the company of his wife.[13]

Prince Arthur and the Duchess hated the separations caused by her constant need to be abroad for cures. In August 1891, when she was at

Aix, Prince Arthur told her that their bedroom at Osborne seemed 'terribly deserted' and, in March 1892, he complained to her of how strange it was to be alone in their bedroom at Buckingham Palace. After a refreshing bath and an excellent dinner in Bourbon, where she had gone in June 1892 to try another variety of cure, the Duchess retired to a comfortable bed where she longed for Arthur to be with her. What was worse was that the regimes did no good; indeed, Dr Bracket's system of massage at Aix was presently pronounced to have done harm, but always, it seemed, something else might be successful. And so it went on and on with massages and douches for the terribly swollen leg, cigarette smoking for the seemingly related constipation and even the suggestion that the douches would also cure young Prince Arthur's so-called infantile paralysis. At last, in October 1894, the Duchess went to Dr Rheyer in Dresden. Prince Arthur's eldest sister, the Empress Frederick, was horrified; she thought that Dresden was a place of quack doctors and there was no doubt that Rheyer made a somewhat alarming start. He took the Duchess's pulse with an electric machine and then thumped her on the back with hammers while she remained quite dressed, complete even, with a hat. He kneaded her stomach, which, due to the constipation, was a painful business, and he told her to take an hour's ride every day and forbad her to visit art galleries where she would be standing about. Whether by accident or design, something in Rheyer's system, more probably the riding rather than the hammers, seems to have answered, for, at least for a time, the Duchess's leg was much less often mentioned as a cause of anxiety, or even of news. This was remarkable for it appears that Rheyer was a specialist of a rather different kind, having, it seemed, written a book on the treatment of diabetes by massage. He also found it within his scope to diagnose slight angina in Daisy, though he was able to assure the Duchess that this would not result in a skin disease.[14]

There was a general recognition that the Portsmouth command was an insufficient appointment for Prince Arthur and, in October 1891, the Government seemed willing to offer him that of Commander-in-Chief, India. He was, however, very unwilling to go as he was now hoping for a period in which he could see more of his children and, in addition to that, he was worried about the Duchess's health. In January 1892, the Duke of Clarence died and the Prince of Wales was left with a single male heir. The Queen, knowing that the Duke of Edinburgh was not very 'efficient' at public functions, began to feel that it would hardly do for Prince Arthur to go abroad again. Prince Arthur, in any case, suspected that the real motive of the Government was to get him out of the way, so that he would not be in waiting as a possible successor to the Duke of Cambridge when he gave up the Commandership-in-Chief. So the chance of getting the highest military position in India, for which he had strong qualifications and for which he had been canvassed before, passed; this time primarily because Prince Arthur did not want it. Obviously he would much have preferred to succeed Uncle George as Commander-in Chief at the Horse Guards.[15]

While the authorities discussed the possibilities of his becoming Governor and Commander-in-Chief at Malta or of his succeeding Sir Evelyn Wood in the Aldershot command, Prince Arthur continued to apply himself to the limited tasks of his Portsmouth appointment and also to the discharge of numerous public functions. These, for example, led him to inspections of the Dorset Militia at Weymouth and the artillery established near Ryde and to the observation of exercises in the Isle of Wight, on which he noticed the military importance of bicyclists. He also took the opportunity of calling on Lord Tennyson, whom he found sitting in his study smoking a clay pipe. Though the old man talked cheerfully, he was suffering from gout in the throat and Lady Tennyson lay on a sofa covered by two large plaids. He presided at a meeting of the Army Scripture Reading Society, which was addressed by Canon Wilberforce, who was not only interesting, but also most amusing, and attended numerous Yeomanry and regimental dinners. He was annoyed with the Queen for accusing him of not entertaining at Portsmouth. He told her that in the first fifteen months of his command there, he and, when she was there, the Duchess, had entertained over eight hundred people to dinner and more than 1,800 had attended their garden parties. If the Queen wished him to do more, she had better send someone else to Sigmaringen to attend the wedding of his niece, Missy, to the Crown Prince Ferdinand of Rumania. The Queen withdrew at once saying that she had not intended to suggest that he did not entertain; only that he should not give up doing so. She insisted that he should go to Sigmaringen.[16]

The Queen had done Prince Arthur an injustice, but he was, all the same, a good deal away from Portsmouth. In London, he now sat with Sir Evelyn Wood on the Selection Board under the chairmanship of Lord Wolseley. They were trying to introduce merit as an alternative to seniority in the choice of officers for promotion, but, according to Wolseley, they could not make much progress as long as the Duke of

Cambridge, 'our great Bumble Bee,' as he called him, held on to the Army. There were other duties, too, for Prince Arthur in London. He inspected the Chelsea Pensioners in June 1892; there were 1,300 on parade and Prince Arthur saw a wonderful show of medals. He lunched with Sir Patrick Grant, who was eighty-eight, but very cheery and full of anecdote. On the same visit to London, he lunched one day at Marlborough House with the Prince of Wales and Prince George, who, now that he was in the direct line of succession, had been created Duke of York. Afterwards, Prince Arthur and his brother, dressed in their peer's robes and wearing their collars of the Garter, proceeded to the House of Lords to introduce Georgy. Another eleven months passed before Prince Arthur made his maiden speech there; this was on 4th May 1893 and it was on the subject of the amalgamation of the Madras and Bombay Armies. Prince Arthur supported the measure, but he urged that the former Commanders-in-Chief, who would now become the equivalent of Corps commanders, should retain their seats on the Councils of the Governors. He had clearly not forgotten the political obstacles which had so often obstructed military improvements in India. He argued too in favour of a system by which all Indian troops would get the opportunity of service on the North-West Frontier, for, though some of them would find the cold conditions hard to bear, they needed the experience if they were to win any prestige. Among those who listened, Lord Reay thought the speech was admirable and devoid of all pose. Lord Ripon, who in years past had been much less friendly than Lord Reay, thought this the best first speech he had ever heard in the House of Lords. He thought the manner and voice were excellent, the statement lucid and the arguments clearly given. Prince Arthur found it most nervous work, but it is interesting to observe that the undoubted excellence and sincerity of his public speaking was later reflected by the same qualities in that of his nephew, whom he had introduced to the House of Lords. King George V's voice and style were strikingly similar to those of his Uncle.[17]

London, of course, also gave Prince Arthur opportunities for the social and cultural round which he enjoyed so much. Dining one night at the French Embassy, he was introduced to a charming American who came to the tail afterwards. Her name was Mrs Astor and though she was not the Nancy Astor of such great subsequent fame, she nonetheless made a great impression on Prince Arthur. Next day, and probably even better, he met Lady Listowel and one of her girls riding in Hyde Park. His old Indian friend, the Gaekwar of Baroda, called on him and he visited an Indian exhibition which was being shown at the Imperial Institute. He viewed the summer exhibition at the Royal Academy, where, however, he saw a lot of trash and found it trying looking at so many rows of pictures hung so close together. He found time to superintend improvements at Bagshot Park, which included the installation of electric light, and, in December 1892, he went to stay at Uppark. The Duchess could have accompanied him, but she had not been invited. Prince Arthur, therefore, wrote to her of the steep ascent to the house, during which the horses had to stop for breath. He arrived outside the front door in the dark and it was some time before the bell was answered, a delay to which Prince Arthur was evidently not accustomed. Eventually a footman came out with a lantern and he was let in. Among the other guests, he found a Mr Legg, who looked like the scoundrel in the *Prodigal Daughter*. The old lady, who owned the place, showed him to his room, which, like the rest of the house, was bitterly cold. He noticed that there were many lovely things in the way of china and plate and his hostess played for her guests on the piano after dinner. Next day there was a shoot, which would have been better, Prince Arthur thought, if the keepers had been sober.[18]

The German Emperor was a frequent visitor to England and especially to Cowes. The Prince of Wales did not especially welcome his presence and the Queen was going through a phase of dreading it. Prince Arthur, on the other hand, was much more at ease with his enigmatic nephew, whose damaged and immature character sometimes made him a difficult companion. He seemed quite content to act as a go-between and was often prepared to pour oil on the water when it threatened to become turbulent. He smoothed over an awkward situation when the Queen threatened to forbid William to attend the wedding of her grand-daughter, Marie Louise, to Prince Aribert of Anhalt in July 1891, and he was generally on hand to placate the Emperor whenever he failed to win at Cowes. Apart from the unsettling German habit of appearing in un-expected uniforms, he was often able to report that everything was going smoothly and to claim that the German dislike of losing races was not William's fault. Prince Arthur also played a leading part in entertaining the Emperor at the numerous and sumptuous dinners which were given for him. For example, on 4th August 1892, he, sitting on one side of William and the Prince of Wales on the other, gave a dinner on board *Victoria and Albert*, at which twenty-four were accommodated at a horseshoe table in the aft cabin. Afterwards the party was reinforced by William's suite, the embassy people and numerous other officers. The proceeding went on until past midnight, by which time the smoking and drinking had given Prince Arthur such a headache that all he could face the next day was paper work from his office and he gave up sailing.[19]

A quarter of a century later, when the Germans and the British were mowing each other down in France and Flanders and everything between William and his English relations had gone bad, Prince Arthur reflected upon the Kaiser's character. He thought that he had a great respect for his grandmother, Queen Victoria, and that he did listen to her advice, though he never did to that of his own mother. He was very jealous of the Prince of Wales and this feeling was fanned by toadies around him who urged him, whenever rapprochement was in the air, to seek to wring something out of his Uncle. The result, Prince Arthur thought, was Edward VII's increasing affection for, and the Kaiser's growing hatred of, France.[20]

Meanwhile, Prince Arthur declined the offer of the Malta command, hoping that, if he stayed at Portsmouth, he would eventually be selected to succeed Sir Evelyn Wood in the Aldershot command. The chances did not seem to be very good; the Secretary of State for War, Mr Stanhope, though he did recollect telling the Queen that the Duke of Connaught might go to Aldershot in due time, now brought forth the argument that this was undesirable as the appointment required 'certain special qualities.' Nevertheless, when pressed, Stanhope took the view that Prince Arthur was suitably qualified for Aldershot and that the only difficulty was that Sir Redvers Buller wanted him to come onto the staff at the Horse Guards. Such was the position when Salisbury's government fell and the Queen was compelled to send once more for Gladstone. Thinking that Mama would need cheering up, Prince Arthur hastened to Osborne where he heard that the Queen had vetoed the inclusion of Labouchere in the government on the ground that he was the editor of *Truth*. Gladstone said that he had not known this, but, when he found it to be true, he promised that he would not submit his name and when it came to the point neither Labouchere nor Dilke were brought into the government. Prince Arthur found that Mr Gladstone was tremendously '*Unterthänigst*' (humble servantish) to Mama and her family, but he walked with a stick, looked feeble and was very deaf.[21]

More to the point from the aspect of Prince Arthur's military career, was that Mr Campbell-Bannerman succeeded Stanhope as Secretary of State for War. The Queen had him up to Balmoral and was very pleased with him. She told Prince Arthur that he was quite different from Stanhope and was easy to speak to and reasonable. She now thought there would be no difficulty about the Aldershot command. One, however, did remain; Roberts wanted the job and the press championed his cause. Campbell-Bannerman began to fear that if Roberts was not given the command, the press would start an attack on the Duke of Connaught and he thought that it might perhaps be better for him to take the Malta command after all. The Queen was intensely annoyed and Ponsonby suggested that an appeal might be made to Roberts. Prince Arthur, however, dismissed that as being out of the question and decided that he would stay at Portsmouth. Campbell-Bannerman sought to resolve the problem by offering Roberts the combined command of Malta and Gibraltar and, when he refused that, taking the line that, as reasonable offers had been made to Roberts, there was no longer any objection to Prince Arthur being offered Aldershot. He accordingly was and, on 15th August 1893, he formally accepted it. He declared that he would do his utmost to promote the efficiency, drill and well-being of the troops in the command. He said that Sir Evelyn Wood had done an immense deal during his command, but he hoped that he might be found to be a not unworthy successor.[22]

Unfortunately the announcements of Prince Arthur's appointment in the popular press were printed without mention of the offers which had been made to Roberts, nor of the important position of Quarter-Master-General to which Wood was going. This enabled many papers to make adverse comment. The most striking headline concerning Roberts, his biographer thought, was 'Shunted for a Royal Duke.' The Broad Arrow and Naval and Military Gazette took the matter up in detail and with some sarcasm. Military education, it said, was looking up. Not long ago anything connected with teaching was regarded as low. Now the mantle of the chief military instructor in England was assumed by the son of our most gracious Queen. The Duke of Connaught, it claimed, had not shown that individuality of character which some of his brother Generals possessed in so marked a degree. Anxiety about the proximity of Bagshot Park was expressed and it was said that it seemed certain that the Duke would have frequent civil duties as well as his military ones. It was no light task to succeed Wood, who had kept training at concert pitch. Roberts was rather concerned and wrote to congratulate Prince Arthur on the appointment and to express his regret at what had been said in the papers. Prince Arthur replied that he had understood that Roberts would not have minded having the post himself if the authorities had considered that his high military position admitted of their offering him the command of a division. As to the newspapers, he told Roberts not to imagine that he took any notice of what he saw in them and he added that he had always been very proud to serve under him.[23]

There were some rumblings in the House of Commons, especially on the part of Mr Morton, who, according to the *Saturday Review*, suddenly became intensely military and expressed discontent with the position of the Duke of Connaught at the Battle of Tel-el-Kebir. Not all the press, however, was hostile to Prince Arthur and this paper remarked that there were at least two members of the House who had been present at the Battle, but they did not include Mr Morton, who was in a state of confusion between the actions at Tel-el-Kebir and Kassassin. Having neither brains nor merit, the *Saturday Review* said, Mr Morton had cried out against privilege. Mr Morton's ideas were then picked up in a letter published in the *Manchester Guardian,* which was signed anonymously by one who described himself as the paper's special correspondent at Tel-el-Kebir. He said that the House had been wrong to laugh Mr Morton down because the Duke of Connaught had been withdrawn at the last minute from the front line as a result of a telegram from a high quarter ordering that he was not to be exposed to danger. Mr Childers, who had been Secretary of State for War at the time, supposed that he might be thought to have been this high quarter and having no recollection of having given any such order, he had the record in the War Office checked. From there he was assured that he could safely deny the truth of the story. Wolseley was incensed by what he read in the *Manchester Guardian* and he wrote to Childers emphatically denying that he had any orders to deal with the Duke of Connaught differently from any of the other General Officers in command of brigades; nor, he said, had he done so. He said that he had no better Brigadier in his force than the Duke of Connaught and he concluded that the accusation made in the *Manchester Guardian* was as ungenerous as it was untrue. With Wolseley's encouragement, Childers had this and his own denial published in the *Manchester Guardian.*[24]

Prince Arthur had not stayed to observe the cooking up of these rather transparent myths. As he was not due to take up his new command at Aldershot until October, he was, in the meantime, able to accept an invitation from the Emperor to attend the Austrian manoeuvres. When he arrived at the railway station in Munich to join the *Orient Express* for Vienna, he heard that the train was forty minutes late, so he had a basin of soup and then drove about the town to pass the time. The train waited no more than five minutes at the platform so that there was only just time for Prince Arthur and Colonel Howard, who was accompanying him, to tumble their luggage and servants into it. Prince Arthur got half a carriage to himself, the servants got another half carriage and Colonel Howard travelled with other passengers. Prince Arthur found that he could walk from one end of the train to the other and that the corridors were filled by ladies of Jewish features from southern climes and their children and baggage. In the smoking compartment he came across an American, whose acquaintance he had made at the German manoeuvres in 1890, who spoke in great praise of William. As the *table d'hôte* was not until 6 p.m., he had some lunch with Colonel Howard at 2.30. When it appeared that the *Orient Express* was not picking up time, Prince Arthur told the station master at one of their stopping points to telegraph to the Emperor in Vienna that he would be arriving forty minutes late. Meanwhile, he enjoyed the journey for it was a glorious day to see the pretty wooded countryside. It proved to be difficult to get into full dress uniform in the small compartment, but, having done so, Prince Arthur had a very kind reception from the Emperor at the station in Vienna. In the Hofburg, he was given a bedroom hung with Gobelins tapestries, which was large enough for a ball. Though the bed was hard, he slept well and was up next morning at 7.45 to start on his calls.[25]

The manoeuvres were based on Günz, a pretty little town with low houses decorated in white or yellow wash. Prince Arthur, who had travelled there by train with the King of Saxony, was lodged in a private house owned by a local Hungarian magnate, who appeared in a gorgeous costume to receive him with an English speech. Several Hungarian magnates turned out to receive the Emperor and the Archdukes; the German Emperor arrived to a warm welcome. A local military school had been turned into a palace to accommodate the two Emperors and there Prince Arthur dined with them that night. As Franz Joseph could not stand draughts, the heat was terrible. Afterwards, Prince Arthur visited William in his rooms and he got to bed at 11, having been up that morning at 5.45. He had to be up the next morning at 5.30 for the commencement of the manoeuvres. On the whole, he thought there was not much to be learnt from them except to take note of the splendid marching of the infantry, which went wherever the cavalry did and covered the ground at five miles an hour, and the good equipment of the infantry and cavalry, whose riding was superior to the British. The artillery was well handled, but he doubted if the infantry had much dash and they certainly did not

fire as well as the British or the Germans. He also doubted if they would
be able to maintain their speed of marching under war conditions and he
was not impressed by the Company officers or the N.C.Os. Nevertheless,
the operations were a splendid and interesting sight and one did not often
see 140,000 men engaged at the same time. He thought the cavalry, who
were well mounted and rode beautifully, were, perhaps, the finest in the
world.[26]

Prince Arthur's first substantial undertaking in the Aldershot command was the conduct of the manoeuvres, which began at the end of July
and went on throughout most of August 1894. Even the arrival of the
German Emperor on another of his visits to the Queen was treated as a
secondary matter and Prince Arthur told her that there would only be a
few days on which he could come to help to entertain him. William did,
however, make a visit to see Prince Arthur at his post in Aldershot. On
17th August Prince Arthur was at his HQ Camp at Wishanger, a mile
beyond the Guards camp at Frensham and that of the Flying Column at
Stockbridge Pond. He rode through both camps and watched the placing
of outposts and, on the next day, he observed the action as a force heading
for Borden was engaged. On the third day of this phase, he rode into the
camp at Borden and found General Utterson's troops, which had got the
better of the Guards and the Flying Column, comfortably established
there. Further actions followed, some of which were seen by the French
military attaché who came out with Prince Arthur, who was putting him
up. On the evening of 21st August, Prince Arthur ordered a night attack
upon Utterson's position at Borden by the Guards. He joined the main
column of Grenadier and Scots Guards as they wended their way steadily
and silently along tortuous roads with high hedges until they debouched
onto open ground and came upon an enemy picket. As there was no patrol
out in front of it they were able to rush it; they then ran through high ferns
and gorse and stormed the camp at Borden, breaking into it in the middle
of the ground occupied by the cavalry and artillery. They were met with
no more than a volley from the few cavalry men who had turned out of
their tents and at that moment they were joined by the Coldstreams, who
had also broken in almost unopposed. Before any serious resistance could
be organised, the Guards had occupied half the camp and captured all the
enemy's guns and horses. Prince Arthur got back to his camp at 4.20 a.m.
and slept until 7.30, when he was up again to watch further operations
between Borden and Keepers Hill. After this the weather worsened to
such an extent that the Duchess thought that Prince Arthur would break

up his camp and come home. She was afraid that the poor men might not be able to get their clothes dry. But, of course, Prince Arthur did nothing of the kind and he was out as usual, though now clad in a waterproof and puttees.[27]

By the time Prince Arthur had held the Aldershot command for a little over a year, the *Broad Arrow and Naval and Military Gazette* revised the somewhat harsh judgement it had made of him at the outset. Though it said that the Duke of Connaught could not be said to be of exceptional ability, he had, it suggested, quietly assimilated Sir Evelyn Wood's reforms; if he lacked Wood's initiative, he did realise the value of the changes which had been made and was modest enough to continue with them. He was, the Journal said, devoid of jealousy, he was conscientious and would not sacrifice the public good to his own vanity; indeed, he had shown himself to be an excellent chief of the great training camp, which constituted the Aldershot command. He had worked quietly and well, while a small man would have striven for sensational innovation. He was straightforward, unselfish and honest and he was no favourer of flatterers and neither a jobber nor an intriguer. Wolseley was more forthright in his appreciation of Prince Arthur's qualities and he recognised that his brigade commander of the Egyptian campaign was now approaching the summit of the Army. He knew that 1895 was going to be an eventful year for those who were in this position and he speculated to his brother as to what would happen to himself, the Duke of Cambridge, Sir Redvers Buller and the Duke of Connaught in the course of the new year. The first moves were not long delayed; in May Wolseley learned that Roberts would succeed him as Commander-in-Chief in Ireland and he hoped that he would thereafter never hear of him again or of his 'dreadful little wife.' In June it became known that the Duke of Cambridge would be resigning and that new arrangements would be introduced at the War Office with effect from October. On 28th July Wolseley wrote assuring Prince Arthur that, if he was proposed as the next Commander-in-Chief, he, Wolseley, would withdraw any claim he might have. He wished to be the first to congratulate Prince Arthur if he was appointed to succeed to the position of head of the Army. He went on to say that, as Roberts had been provided for in the Irish command, the Government might feel disposed to offer him some employment. Idleness, he said, would kill him and he said he would like to be appointed either as British Ambassador in Berlin or as Viceroy of India. The occupants of both posts, he believed, had resigned. Asking Prince Arthur to help him to obtain one of these positions, he signed himself off as his most obedient servant and faithful comrade.[28]

Prince Arthur sent this letter on the Queen, who thought it was a very odd one. She did not think that Wolseley would do, either as Ambassador in Berlin or as Viceroy of India. Meanwhile, Wolseley was cast into despair by the rumour that Campbell-Bannerman was about to choose Sir Redvers Buller as C-in-C, but at the critical moment the Government fell, Salisbury came back into office and Lord Lansdowne became Secretary of State for War. Wolseley then thought that he would be the new Minister's choice. He would still honour his undertaking not to stand in the way of the Duke of Connaught, but he now thought it doubtful if the Government would tolerate another royal C-in-C for fear of having a second Duke of Cambridge on their hands. The Queen, seeing how things were shaping, though doing so rather late in the day, abandoned her view that Wolseley would not do for Berlin and suggested to Salisbury that he should go there. The Prime Minister agreed and the German Emperor was consulted. He welcomed the idea. Lansdowne, however, asked Wolseley whether, if he accepted the Berlin appointment, he would be prepared to forego the prospect of succeeding the Duke of Cambridge as Commander-in-Chief. This was tantamount to offering him a choice between the two appointments; Wolseley chose to be C-in-C. Salisbury told the Queen that Prince Arthur could have been selected if Wolseley had accepted Berlin, but that he could not be chosen over Wolseley's head, for that would have led to adverse comment. The Queen pointed out that Prince Arthur would not have been appointed over Wolseley's head as the latter had said that he would not stand if Prince Arthur was a candidate. But the die was cast and Prince Arthur's chance of being promoted to the position for which he had been groomed throughout almost all his life had gone. Though the Queen still hoped that there would be another chance, that was now very unlikely. What seemed, however, to be a cruel turn for Prince Arthur was later to come to light as a blessing in disguise, for the post, which did nothing to enhance the reputations of Wolseley or his successor, Roberts, might well have been the graveyard of Prince Arthur's. Above all, had he been Commander-in-Chief, he would not have been Governor-General of Canada. Difficult as that position was to be, that which awaited Wolseley as C-in-C under the new arrangements was impossible.[29]

Towards the end of August 1895, the Duchess's sister, Elizabeth, who had married the Grand Duke of Oldenburg, was taken ill and died. She had the same leg swelling from which the Duchess suffered, but Prince Arthur sought to assure the Queen that the cause of her death had nothing to do with this. As his season of manoeuvres had just come to an end, Prince Arthur went with the Duchess to attend the funeral. He told the Queen that he had been to a good many funerals in Germany, but had found this one the most touching. On the way home through France, Prince Arthur visited Vincennes, where he inspected the garrison, a new fort, the stables, the military hospital, the prison and the artillery museum. He also reviewed the 12th and 13th French artillery regiments. In Paris, Prince Arthur called on the President, who struck him as being a thorough man of the world and very pleasant to talk to. He heard that the Queen was counting on him to meet the King of Portugal and escort him to Balmoral for his visit to her. He said he would do this but that he would not have long to spare as he had a great deal of work to do at Aldershot. In truth, he regarded this as an awful and unexpected bore. Nor was the Queen very enthusiastic. She thought Carlos's visit was very inconvenient, but that it could not be helped.[30]

So, on 8th November 1895, Prince Arthur met his brother-in-law, Prince Henry of Battenberg, at King's Cross and travelled with him to Peterborough, where they got out and met King Carlos. They then went on with him to Aberdeen, which they reached at 7 the next morning. They went to the hotel for a wash and breakfast before going on at 8.50. As they started up Deeside it became dark and foggy. A guard of honour and the band of the 42nd met them at Ballater, whence they set out for Balmoral in a carriage and four to the accompaniment of sleet and snow. After lunch the next day the Queen gave Carlos the Garter and then drove with him and Prince Arthur to the gates of Birkhall, which Prince Arthur thought looked bleak and deserted; it was also very cold. That did not matter, as Mama and Carlos had both gone to sleep. Balmoral Castle, however, was well heated and Prince Arthur even found that his rooms were too hot.[31]

King Carlos's visit may have been inconvenient, but at least the man himself was inoffensive. The German Emperor, despite the trouble which had been taken to entertain him, was less rewarding. He punished the Duchess's brother, Prince Fritz Leopold, for making derogatory remarks about him, by placing him under arrest and he sent a congratulatory telegram to President Kruger, who was at daggers drawn with his Grandmother's government. Prince Arthur, who had no great opinion of Fritz Leopold, thought that, of the two, William had more of a 'tile loose.' The Queen was boiling with indignation. Another member of the European family, the Princess of Wales's nephew and the Queen's grandson-in-law, the newly acceded Tsar of all the Russias, Nicholas II, now needed attention. Prince Arthur and the Duchess were to attend his coronation in Moscow. The Queen, who normally liked things to be simple, was determined on this occasion that her daughter-in-law should not be lost without trace amidst the unparalleled splendour of the Russian court. She lent her a collection of her own jewels. The lucky recipient and Prince Arthur were slightly nonplussed; they wondered if they were expected to insure these valuables; if they were, cover to the value of £30,000 would be needed.[32]

At 1 p.m. on 18th May 1896 the royal yacht *Victoria and Albert* with the Duke and Duchess of Connaught on board came alongside the commercial quay at St Petersburg. That night they left by special train for Moscow, where they were lodged in the *Grande Dimitroska Maison Vostraikoff,* which belonged to a rich merchant and was situated near the Kremlin. They dined that night with the Tsar and Tsaritsa, Nicky and Alicky, at the Petrofski Palace. Prince Arthur thought that Alicky was looking particularly well and handsome and that being a little stouter suited her. She and Nicky were very nice and as simple as they had always been. After dinner, Prince Arthur and the Duchess drove the four miles back to the Kremlin and called on Affie and Marie, who were accommodated there. Nearly all the houses were covered with decorations and the streets were full of people and carriages, which made the atmosphere gay and festive.[33]

On 21st May, Prince Arthur, dressed in the uniform of the Scots Guards and wearing the riband of the Russian Order of St Andrew, rode on horseback with many other royalties directly behind the Tsar, who, mounted on a white charger, made his state entry into Moscow. In the crowds of onlookers on the pavements and in the windows along the route, every hat was removed and the people sent up a long low cheer which continued without intermission for three hours. The clash of this sound and the deep tolling bells gave Prince Arthur a fearful headache. The leaves on the trees were out and the sun shone producing a dazzling effect on the gilded domes of the churches. Flags hung from roof to street level and the route was lined by 47,000 troops, who in places stood eight deep. There was a tribune of representatives from various divisions of the Empire, including a row of curious looking Mongolians in 'dressing gowns' of every imaginable hue. Behind the mounted royalties came the carriage procession led by the Dowager Empress, the sister of the Princess of Wales. She sat alone in a gorgeous golden coach drawn by eight snow white horses and surmounted by a crown on its velvet covered roof to show that she had been crowned. She was dressed in a white and gold court dress and train and she was surrounded by grooms and Cossacks. Behind her came the new Empress in a similar carriage and then the Grand Duchesses in somewhat less grand coaches. Prince Arthur thought that the Tsar looked so dignified, but also very young and pale, almost sad, it seemed. Eventually the cavalcade came to the Kremlin, where a foot procession was formed to the Church of the Assumption. Here a short mass was sung by priests dressed in the most gorgeous robes.[34]

The Coronation took place on 26th May, or, by the Russian style, 14th May. Prince Arthur wrote to the Queen that he imagined that it was the most magnificent pageant one could ever see and he thought he had never witnessed anything finer than the gold cloth vestments of the Bishops and priests. He said there was a fine moment when Nicky read out the belief in a strong and impressive tone. As he and the Duchess walked across the courtyard from the Palace to the Cathedral, Prince Arthur again heard the long low sound of cheering, which was now accompanied by the strains of the Russian national anthem, the beating of drums and booming of canon as well as the pealing of deep toned bells. The Duchess wore a dress with a body and skirt of white satin studded with glittering steel and diamond *paillettes*. Her train was of gold brocade and she wore a necklace of diamonds and the Queen's large stars in the form of a tiara. Across her breast she wore the red and silver riband of the Order of St Catherine and its large diamond star. Alicky, the new Tsaritsa, looked perfectly lovely in a simple white satin gown and nothing on her head. Her grace and modesty were most striking. The Tsar was clothed in robes of gold embroidered with the Romanov double eagles in black and lined with ermine. His crown of diamonds and pearls was surmounted by rubies; it weighed seventeen pounds and his sceptre was topped with the Orloff diamond. The sun blazed on the jewels and the heat was scorching. The service lasted three and a half hours and at the end of it their new Russian Majesties looked terribly tired.[35]

There then followed three days of receptions, at which, on fourteen occasions, Prince Arthur appeared on the arm of seven different Princesses, a gala opera, embassy balls and then a great popular fête at which 700,000 people assembled to receive food and coronation mugs. The rush to get the first gifts turned into a stampede and a terrible number of people were squashed to death casting an awful gloom over the remainder of the ceremonies, which by this stage, seemingly, could not be counter-manded. Prince Arthur reckoned that the police were to blame for this horrible disaster, for they only arrived on the ground when it was too late to do anything. Dinners in the Kremlin were on an immense scale, but they were quickly and well served and at the last one, in the Kremlin's beautiful white St George's Hall, no fewer than 860 people sat down. There was a rather different atmosphere at Princess Yousoupoff's, where Prince Arthur and the Duchess dined before leaving Moscow. The house was quaint and pretty in the old Russian style with low rooms and Byzantine carved pillars and arches. The Princess, with £300,000 a year, was said to be the richest heiress in Russia. Mrs Egerton, who had come in waiting on the Duchess, was struck by the extremes of magnificent luxury and want of finish which she noticed in Russia. The dinner tables were bare, the staircases and offices were rough, the linen coarse and, except in the Kremlin, there were no salt spoons. Also, and in greater counterpoint to the glories of the Coronation, Prince Arthur and the Duchess visited a foundling hospital, where there were a thousand babies under a month old and nine hundred wet nurses. Most of all these babies were illegitimate and one ward was full of seven month infants in incubators. When he returned from Russia, Prince Arthur told the Queen that Nicky and Alicky had borne the fatigues well, but he thought Nicky was more tired than Alicky. This, as also the disaster at the popular fête, was a portent of things to come.[36]

In the summer of 1897 the Queen's Diamond Jubilee was celebrated and Prince Arthur was not only a prominent figure in the processions and parades, but he also had a substantial hand in organising them. On the great and memorable day itself, 22nd June, he commanded the troops which kept the streets as the Queen drove to St Paul's and a few days later he held a splendid parade at Aldershot. He had also shown a special interest in the many troops who had come from India and the Colonies to take part in the occasion and when he reviewed them at Chelsea Barracks beforehand, he noticed that the only ones who had any trouble in keeping step were the Chinese from Hong Kong. The Duke of Cambridge thought that these activities had brought Prince Arthur into favourable public prominence and he advised the Queen that this was the time to secure his appointment to the Horse Guards as Adjutant-General. Rumours of this idea leaked out and Prince Arthur was once more engulfed in the maelstrom of press controversy. An anonymous letter appeared in The

27. *Mr R. B. Haldane at Balmoral. This visit was in 1910.*

28. *Lord Knollys, King Edward VII's Private Secretary.*

29. *Prince Arthur in the uniform of the Grenadier Guards, 1905. Sargent.*

30. *Prince Arthur and King Edward VII, both in Field-Marshal's uniform.*

Times over the signature *Civis* claiming that the public would receive such an appointment with dismay if not resentment. *Civis* said that, though Prince Arthur was a keen soldier and an excellent officer 'within certain well defined limits,' he had not been a success at Aldershot. Another anonymous writer signing himself *General*, considered that the best candidate for the Adjutant-Generalship was Sir Evelyn Wood, but he repudiated *Civis's* suggestion that Prince Arthur had been a failure at Aldershot. 'Let a man's work be judged by the results,' he declared, and he asserted that Wood's excellent system at Aldershot had been fully maintained and, in many respects, improved under the Duke of Connaught. The Prince of Wales was much annoyed by the selection of Wood to be Adjutant-General in preference to his brother, but Prince Arthur seems himself to have made no reaction. He was in any case extremely busy organising more manoeuvres in the Aldershot command. On 10th August, for example, he rode between forty and fifty miles and that was on top of a heavy morning of office work.[37]

The culmination of Prince Arthur's tenure of the Aldershot command came with the manoeuvres of August and September 1898, which, for the British army, were on a large scale. They involved a battle between the Southern Army, commanded by Sir Redvers Buller, who had now been nominated to succeed to the Aldershot command in the following month, and a Northern Army, commanded by Prince Arthur. The latter assembled in camp at Homington whither it was transported by a succession of trains, most of which were late. The supervision of this operation kept Prince Arthur in the saddle from 5.30 a.m. until 7 p.m. The fog of war commenced on 1st September when Prince Arthur's army began to make contact with Buller's outposts; the battle between armies, each of about 25,000 men, had begun. Next day the fog lifted and the intentions of the two commanders became clear. Prince Arthur launched a bold attack in brigade strength on Buller's extreme left, but it was repulsed and one of his Highland regiments was put out of action for a time. Buller then made a strong attack on Prince Arthur's centre, but the positions there had been strongly entrenched and they held firm. An artillery action followed after which Prince Arthur counter-attacked with two brigades to restore his position. The roll of musketry, the grinding of machine guns and the roar of artillery competed to make the din of battle, until Wolseley, who was acting as the Director of the manoeuvres, sounded the cease fire and called a conference of the antagonists. He judged that Buller's attack had failed for the reason that his artillery preparation had been inadequate.

Prince Arthur was now ordered to keep contact with Buller's force, but, if he was attacked, he was to fall back on Salisbury. Buller was told to take the offensive and advance upon Salisbury. After four days of probing, Prince Arthur was ordered to take the offensive and try to force a passage of the Avon between Amesbury and Old Sarum. After pinning Buller's right, he crossed the Avon and drove back the enemy left on a front of three to four miles.[38]

Neither army had won a decisive victory, but the general impression seemed to be that, on the whole, Prince Arthur's had had the better of it. This caused some surprise, but Colonel Hale, the Military Correspondent of *The Times*, concluded that perhaps Buller, who was such a successful exponent of irregular warfare, was not so effective when handling large formations. Colonel Hale was also disappointed by the performance of Buller's staff, which, at the outset, he had expected would be better than Prince Arthur's. Wolseley took the neutral ground that the Duke of Connaught and Sir Redvers Buller had both commanded their army corps 'with great efficiency.' Considering the high reputation which Buller enjoyed, Prince Arthur had undoubtedly scored a success and one which was much greater than he had anticipated.[39]

It must have seemed to Prince Arthur to be more like a holiday than a war when, immediately after these taxing but rewarding experiences, he left to attend the French manoeuvres. On 13th September 1898, the second day of his visit, Prince Arthur was at the station at Moulins at 5.15 a.m. to meet M. Felix Faure, the President of the Republic. The authorities were so particular that, evidently to Prince Arthur's surprise, they made a chalk mark on the platform to show exactly where he was to stand as the train came in. The President proved to be most civil and, throughout the day of manoeuvres, he rode with Prince Arthur, lunched with him and in the evening met him again at a dinner given by General Négrier whom Prince Arthur very much liked. In the next few days, Prince Arthur, who had already received all the foreign officers, made friends with all the French, though he did not find the operations especially interesting or realistic. He had a narrow escape when his horse backed off the road into a deep ditch, fell on its head and rolled on Prince Arthur, hurting his knee; his good one. On the last day he was horrified to find that he had to address a hundred and fifty French officers in their language. That evening he left with the President in a special train for Paris where they arrived at midnight. During this journey and at the dinner, which they ate on the train at a small table *vis à vis*, they talked of every type of subject and the President frequently proposed the health of the absent Duchess.[40]

On 8th October there was a farewell parade for Prince Arthur at Aldershot. As large numbers of men had been detached to form drafts for India and the colonial stations and as many more were on leave, the number who turned out was under 10,000, but all Aldershot and the neighbourhood also turned out to watch the spectacle. When it was over, Prince Arthur addressed the General Staff and the Commanding Officers, shook hands with them all and then, for fear of breaking down, rode off fast to Government House from where, with the Duchess and the two Princesses, he drove home to Bagshot Park. The road all the way to their entrance gate was a sea of faces, the bands played and the people cheered. Louischen and the girls, Prince Arthur told the Queen, broke down completely and he said that he was not much better himself. Parting after five years of congenial endeavour, to which he had been so deeply committed, was hard and he found it very trying. When he got to Bagshot, he felt low and dazed for the rest of the day. In the evening he and Louischen went to dine with their neighbour, the Empress Eugénie.[40]

CHAPTER 12

The Coburg Succession, The Irish Command and The Queen's Death 1898-1904

TWO DAYS AFTER Christmas 1898 the Queen wrote to Prince Arthur that the accounts of Affie's boy were most grievous and that the terrible state of his health was causing serious anxiety. The trouble, she said, was due to the dissipated life he had led at Potsdam, where he should never have gone. The unfortunate boy was the Duke of Edinburgh's only son and, since his father had acceded as Duke of Coburg, he was the heir to that throne. Prince Arthur thought this provided a dreadful outlook for the future as indeed it did, especially from his own point of view, for, after Affie's boy, the next heir to the throne of Coburg was himself. Young Prince Alfred died on 6th February 1899 and, as his father's health was very precarious, urgent consultations began regarding the succession. Prince Arthur was relieved to hear that the Queen did not think that the situation need result in his being removed from the British army or his own country, but events were to show that this comfortable assumption did little justice to the feelings of the people and court of Coburg or the views of the German Emperor, whose vassal the Duke of Coburg was.[1]

The Queen next seemed to assume that Prince Arthur and his son would abdicate whereupon the heir would become Leopold's son, Charlie. He, however, was a minor and was still being educated at Eton. His widowed mother did not much fancy the idea of him being removed to Germany and of herself, as she expected, being brought into 'collision' with the German Emperor. The Queen thought such anxieties were unnecessary; Charlie could stay at Eton until he was sixteen or seventeen and he need not live entirely in Germany after that, though whether she meant this to apply to the time during which he was the heir or after he had become the reigning Duke was not made clear.[2]

This rather cavalier attitude on the part of the Queen, which suggested that she would decide who was to succeed to these German Duchies, did not go down well in their Diet; nor was it well received by the German Emperor. Though the population of the Duchies of Coburg and Gotha was only about a quarter of a million, it was not likely to accept the idea of the reigning Duke's palace being little more than a holiday home for whichever of the Queen of England's sons or grandsons she should allocate to it. And, of course, since the creation of the German Empire in 1871, these people also had an allegiance to the Emperor, who, though also a grandson of Queen Victoria, was distinctively German. An official of the Duchies, von Strenge, impressed upon Prince Arthur that, while the abdication by the Prince of Wales of their throne was understood, as they knew that he would become the King of England, abdication by the Duke of Connaught would be ill-received, as he was not due to become King of anywhere else. Prince Arthur took the point and allowed it to be announced that, by the death of Prince Alfred, he had become the heir to the throne of the Duchies.[3]

Even so, he still had not thought the matter out; still less had he faced the music. Probably he was encouraged in these evasions by his sister, the Empress Frederick. She wrote to the Queen, and the Queen sent on the letter to Prince Arthur, saying that Arthur and Louischen should visit Coburg and take their children with them. She thought they should say nothing about how they proposed to educate young Arthur, but they should make a detour to Berlin to see William and there they should ask for an honorary German commission for young Arthur. He would then not need to enter the German army but could continue at Eton, go to Sandhurst and enter what she described as 'our English service.' He could make the odd visit to Coburg and perhaps take a course at Heidelberg University. This, she thought, would appease opinion in the Duchies and young Arthur would continue to be an English Prince. She told Prince Arthur that he need not worry about what the Diet might think as they had no voice in the succession to the throne. Prince Arthur did not quite accept the last point; he thought that, in the modern age, it was advisable to show some consideration of the voice of the people, but otherwise he seems to have taken it that his sister's view was a satisfactory basis of action, especially as the Queen also took this view. If so, Coburg became quite an attractive proposition. Prince Arthur and the Duchess had long worried about the future of their son. Their daughters could marry almost anyone in Europe they wished from the unmarried Kings and Crown Princes down, but young Arthur would get no civil list and, being a Prince, might find that he was debarred from the conventional means of earning a living. Coburg would provide him with an income and part-time employment without, it seemed, prejudicing his position as a member of the British Royal Family.[4]

Perhaps there was something about Coburg, the Rosenau and the romance with which the Queen had invested his father's birthplace which blinded Prince Arthur to realities, or perhaps he did not see what came to him by inheritance from his father as anything of note by comparison with the position in the British Royal Family which he had inherited from his mother. However these possibilities may have been, Prince Arthur was surprised and annoyed when the German Emperor raised objections and said that the Duke of Coburg must be a German, not a British, Prince and that if young Arthur was to be the heir to Coburg and Gotha, he would have to complete his education in Germany and enter the German, not the British, army. There was also the awful thought of what Prince Arthur himself would be required to do. The matter needed discussion and Prince Arthur set off to Coburg to see his brother Affie, the reigning Duke. The German Emperor happened to be there and Prince Arthur took the opportunity of having a good talk with his nephew. He was pleased to find that he was not dictatorial and, on the contrary, was most kindly. Nevertheless, William was adamant that the heir to Coburg must settle in Germany and, indeed, be a German. Affie pointed out that he had not done this until his Uncle and predecessor had died and he had acceded, but William insisted that times had changed and that such a course would no longer be acceptable. He told Prince Arthur that if he would make up his mind to this, he would gladly appoint him to the command of a German army corps, or give him the inspection of one or more army corps. Prince Arthur felt that William did not have right on his side in insisting on this point, but he recognised that he did have the newspapers behind him and he did not take much longer to decide upon abdication for himself and his son.[5]

Thus, for the second time, Prince Arthur escaped the fate of becoming the Duke of Coburg. If at this moment, William had been more accommodating, or if German national susceptibilities had been less pronounced, he might not have done so, for the Queen was very determined that the beloved Prince Consort's country should not be left

"THE DUKE'S MOTTO."

"But in spite of all temptations to belong to other Nations,
He remains an Englishman." (Vide "Pinafore.")

The Coburg succession, Mr Punch's opinion.

to strangers. As it was, his good fortune and that of young Prince Arthur were to be the ill fortune of Leopold's son, Charles Edward, Duke of Albany, who succeeded to the title in 1900 when Affie died and thus found himself on the wrong side in the Great War of 1914-1918. It can, however, hardly be doubted that, cosmopolitan as he was, the very Englishness of Prince Arthur and his devotion to the British army, would, in any case, have saved him from becoming Duke of Coburg, once he realised that this would involve becoming a German.[6]

During much of the time that the Coburg succession hung in the balance Prince Arthur had been travelling. Using the hiatus which occurred between his laying down of the Aldershot command and the decision of the authorities as to what he was to do next, he visited Egypt and the Sudan, travelling this time with the Duchess and the two Princesses. They paused on the way in Rome, where they were received by the Pope and dined with the King and Queen. The Duchess had to give up a Court ball as she had not got a tiara or a ball dress with her, but, for the Pope, she was able to dress suitably in black with a mantilla, as also did Daisy. Patsy was in white with a white veil and Prince Arthur put on full dress uniform. Pope Leo XIII was clad in a scarlet cloak and he wore a beautiful cross of diamonds and pearls. For his age, Prince Arthur thought he was a wonderful looking man and he was struck by his bright and intelligent eyes. The audience lasted half an hour and the Pope, speaking in French, recalled having sat near the Queen at a dinner in Brussels many years earlier. He also talked of a levée at St James's Palace and he remembered Palmerston and Aberdeen. He expressed gratitude for the kindness shown to his spiritual subjects by the Queen and the Government throughout the British Empire.[7]

After calls at Naples, Cyprus and Cairo, Prince Arthur and his family cruised up the Nile to Wadi Halfa, where Mahmud, who had commanded the dervishes at the Battle of Atbara, and Mohamed Ezain, who had done the same at the Battle of Abu Hamid, were brought before Prince Arthur as prisoners. Both were cousins of the Khalifa who was still in the field. They then journeyed on towards Khartoum. On 18th February 1899, they entered the sixth cataract at Shabluka and passed the hill of Gabel Royan from where Colonel Gordon, the nephew of General Gordon, had first seen Khartoum when the Anglo-Egyptian troops advanced in August 1898. Here they were met by the Sirdar or Commander-in-Chief, Kitchener, who had the formidable task of pacifying this unruly part of the world. That evening at sunset they reached Omdurman. In Khartoum

Prince Arthur reviewed 9,000 men of all arms, including a Camel Corps, who were under Kitchener's command and he was shown the staircase on which Gordon had been killed. Prince Arthur and the Duchess rode over the battlefield of Omdurman, which was still littered with masses of bodies of men and horses, skulls and bones and *gibbas*, or dervishes' coats. The sight was sickening; so was the smell. On the way back from Khartoum, Prince Arthur and a small party left the direct route and rode more than a hundred miles across the desert to see the battlefield of Atbara. Here he again found the site littered with the bodies of dervishes, horses, camels and donkeys. Quantities of camping things, ammunition and food were also still lying about.[8]

Despite the victories at Atbara and Omdurman, Prince Arthur told the Queen, the country was by no means pacified, nor did he think it would be until the Khalifa was killed or captured. An attempt to corner him at Khordofar had failed and he was now strongly entrenched with 8,000 men. Of the 9,000 of Kitchener's men, whom Prince Arthur had seen, many were not yet fit to take the field as they were recruits who had been sent out to fill the places of 2,000 men who were sick and, in addition to that, Kitchener had to detach large bodies of men for garrison duty. The Khalifa's rule, he said, was based on slavery and fanaticism and the people, he thought, were fatalistic, cruel and conceited. Prince Arthur had engaged with the military problems of the Sudan, for which he would, in time, have responsibility himself.[9]

Meanwhile, his attention focussed on another area of the British Empire where war had followed the flag. Things were not going well in South Africa. The Battle of Farquhar's Farm near Ladysmith had been gallant but unsuccessful, Prince Arthur told the Queen. The British losses were unfortunate and would not have happened if the communications between the detached and main forces had been properly provided. Prince Arthur feared that Ladysmith would now be invested and that this would entirely upset Sir Redvers Buller's plan of campaign. Instead of advancing into the Orange Free State, he would have to relieve Lady-smith. This would retard matters and cost many lives. Sir George White should not have allowed himself to be shut up in Ladysmith; he should have retired to Colenso and he should not have divided his forces. Prince Arthur thought that he had underestimated the Boers.[10]

These reflections were intended to be more than merely the flourishes of arm chair strategy. Prince Arthur told the Queen that he considered that he had a claim to be appointed to the command of a corps in South

Africa. He told her that he was the only General Officer in the British army who shared with Buller the experience of having commanded a corps in manoeuvres and he could not believe that the Queen would wish her soldier son to stay at home unemployed when her army was engaged in a serious war. If she would give her approval, he was sure that Wolseley would offer him the appointment. If this was so, Prince Arthur was nonetheless somewhat over optimistic. Though he was Commander-in-Chief, what Wolseley wished did not necessarily happen. When Roberts was appointed to take over as C-in-C in South Africa, Wolseley was not only not consulted; he was, Prince Arthur understood, not even informed. Nor was the Queen at all inclined to give the approval for which Prince Arthur asked. Instead, and much to his dismay, she sought his appointment to succeed Roberts as Commander-in-Chief in Ireland. This proved to be agreeable to the Government and, though it was a very great disappointment to Prince Arthur to have to go to Ireland when he had hoped for a command in South Africa, he felt, in all the circumstances, bound to accept the appointment. He was sworn in at the Castle in Dublin on 10th January 1900.[11]

The duties of the C-in-C Ireland, provided no risings took place, were not very onerous. The Lord Lieutenant, Lord Cadogan, pointed out that most of them occurred in the first three months of the year and then in June, July and August. At other times, Roberts and his predecessors had often been absent in England and he clearly expected that Prince Arthur would operate on similar lines. There was the usual routine office work, and the rest of it consisted of inspections of troops and fortifications, into which Prince Arthur threw himself with his usual energy and thoroughness, the disposal of the forces throughout the country and, since the South African War had begun, the mobilisation of reinforcements to be sent out. Though Prince Arthur found Irish society a good deal changed from when he had been in the country twenty-two years ago, he did find a number of old friends still in the social circuit there. When he was in Cork inspecting the barracks, hospital, gymnasium and prison and also reviewing the 4th Battalion of the 60th, he found the Listowels waiting for him in the drawing-room of Government House there. The 'lovely Mary' sat next to him at lunch. He was entertained to bridge and rabbit shooting by Lord Kilmorey at Mourne Park in Kilkeel, County Down and, in November 1900, after inspecting the depot of the Royal Irish Fusiliers at Armagh, he went to stay with Lord Rossmore at Rossmore, County Monaghan. He found a large house party there, among whom were, Lord

Cowley, the Duke of Montrose and Mrs Jack Leslie. Prince Arthur was particularly pleased to meet Mrs Leslie again, for, as he wrote to the Duchess, who was again abroad taking another cure, she was such a nice, straight woman and clever.[12]

From this meeting with Léonie Leslie, who had previously been no more than an agreeable occasional acquaintance, there soon developed a deep friendship sealed by close and enduring mutual affection. It was an unusual relationship, if only because the Duchess joined in it to the full and came to be quite as enchanted by Léonie as was Prince Arthur. It began to grow at a period of particular emotional tension for Prince Arthur. After a time of rather better health, the Duchess was now back in the doldrums with her swollen leg and constant cures, during which she increasingly became depressed and complaining. At such times her mind seemed to travel in circles about trivialities and she was usually at loggerheads with Prince Arthur's staff, especially Egerton, the Comptroller, the maids or her companions or daughters. Not only, therefore, was Prince Arthur frequently and for long periods deprived of her company, which he found grievous, but also he was in constant anxiety as to her well-being. He himself was suffering the double disappointment of having been passed over for the Commandership-in-Chief, and, even more woundingly, for an active command in the South African War and his natural tendency to go from optimism to depression had been exacerbated by a bad bout influenza at the beginning of the year, which was followed by attacks of worse than usual asthma. Affie's death meant more to the Prince of Wales than it did to Prince Arthur, for the two elder boys had been much together as children, but it cast a gloom over the whole family and caused the Duchess to begin planning her own funeral. There was also another and overwhelmingly larger factor; the Queen's grip on life was beginning to relax. Her subjects at large found it hard to envisage the death of the Sovereign who seemed always to have been on the throne; how much harder it was for her children, who, comfortably or otherwise, had for so long been so closely subjected to her pervading tutelage, to accept the same inevitability.[13]

Such were the circumstances in which Prince Arthur's deep attachment to Léonie Leslie took root. That it proved to be so happy a relationship was due in essence to the strong physical attraction which had existed between Prince Arthur and the Duchess since 1878 and evidence of which we have from time to time noticed. As we shall see, this endured until death did them part in 1917. The friendship with

Léonie was not at the expense of the marriage with the Duchess, which, indeed, belied the Victorian image of husbands selfishly and hypocritically expecting a joyless submission from their wives and then, when their children had been born, seeking their pleasure with mistresses and prostitutes. Fortunately for our understanding, Prince Arthur and the Duchess left ample evidence of their strong and enduring physical love.

For the Queen's visit to Ireland in April 1900, which Prince Arthur planned with the greatest care, he had to provide for her to be carried up and down stairs at Viceregal Lodge and he had to modify the arrangements for her entry into Dublin to meet the limits upon the time which she could now face sitting in a carriage in public. Indeed, for the last five years, the Queen had been suffering from rheumatic stiffness of the joints, which progressively reduced her to the use of a wheelchair. From 1898, her eyesight began to fail, she had difficulty in reading and her writing became more and more illegible. It had never been easy to read, but now she began to apologise for it and to wonder what mistakes she had made. In November 1900 she came down from Balmoral to Windsor complaining of a loss of appetite and sleeplessness. On Sunday 11th November 1900, Prince Arthur, who had arrived early that morning in London, took the 10 a.m. train to Windsor where he arrived in time for church. Mama was not at all well and did not come wth him. She seemed to be low and depressed.[14]

Prince Arthur returned to Ireland, but towards Christmas he came to Osborne to help the Queen when she received Roberts on his return from South Africa. He found her 'very feeble & unable to do anything.' She did not appear at meals and went out of doors at odd times. He tried to stop his sisters, Beatrice and Lenchen, giving her reports on Vicky's health, which were now full of alarm. He found it difficult to make even a semblance of being cheerful and on Christmas day it was impossible to conceal from the Queen that her devoted friend, Lady Churchill, had died. Mama, however, took this news better than he had expected and three days later he was full of hope. The Queen had begun to scold the maids, to object to going to bed early and she complained when she was not woken from sleeping in her chair. Prince Arthur believed that she would soon be quite herself again. On 10th January 1901 he left Osborne for London and, a few days later, travelled to Berlin to attend the investiture of the Crown Prince with the Order of the Black Eagle.[15]

Prince Arthur soon realised that his thought that the Queen would get better was wishful and he hastened home, accompanied on the journey by his nephew, the German Emperor. After being joined by the Prince of Wales and the Duke of York, they arrived at Osborne House in the forenoon of 21st January 1901. The Queen's principal doctor, Sir James Reid, took each of them in turn into her room so that they could see her from the foot of the bed, but he did not think it right to rouse the Queen or that any of them should try to speak to her. She later rallied and had some last moments of lucidity, but, at 6.30 on the following evening she died. On 25th January, the King, the Kaiser, the Duke of Connaught and Prince Arthur of Connaught stood side by side at the Queen's bedside holding the straps which had been passed under her body, while three others held the opposite ends on the other side of the bed. By this means, and under Sir James Reid's supervision, they lifted the Queen into her coffin.[16]

On 9th February 1901 Prince Arthur returned to his duties in Dublin. He found the C-in-C's residence at the Royal Hospital painfully silent as the Duchess had remained in England. She went to stay at Windsor where she found the almost empty house horribly sad. She drove in one of Mama's carriages with Beatrice to the Mausoleum at Frogmore where they found Louise with the Clerk of Works, Mr Nutt. Mama's statue had been put in place but, though it looked very beautiful, it was not very like and made her look so tall. The three sisters were not bearing up well. Louise spent a whole afternoon pouring out her grievances about her marriage and her sisters to Louischen; it was awful. Lenchen was more stately and pompous and on her high horse than ever and Beatrice seemed to be preoccupied with some glass that she was expecting the Connaughts to give her. When he returned to London in March, Prince Arthur found the King silent and absent. He got cross very easily, his voice was hoarse and he constantly went to sleep. Everyone in the family seemed to be completely out of sorts and Prince Arthur found the playing of God Save the King a great trial. He was also very much upset at being turned out of his rooms in Buckingham Palace before Clarence House, which had been allocated to him on Affie's death, was ready for his occupation. He also felt cut off from sources of information which had been open to him when the Queen was alive. Though he was the King's only surviving brother, this was proving very different from being the Queen's favourite son.[17]

'Dear Mrs Leslie,' Prince Arthur wrote from the Royal Hospital in Dublin at the beginning of April, to preface the news that he had received a gushing letter from her mother-in-law, 'Lady Boo,' expressing pride and pleasure that he was coming to stay with the family at Glaslough. He told Mrs Leslie that he would arrive by train at 6.19 in the evening and that he would leave the following afternoon at 1.07. He said that the stuffs which she had sent to the Duchess were charming and he asked her to believe him always 'your sincere friend Arthur.' He added a postscript saying that he was looking forward to his visit more than he could express and that he sometimes felt unworthy of such friendship and affection 'from you dear Léonie.' He said that he looked up to her and felt such pride in her caring for him. In November, hearing that Jack and Léonie were coming to stay in a hotel in Dublin, Prince Arthur invited them to put up at the Royal Hospital instead. He looked forward to some good rubbers of bridge with them. The Duchess, who was in London, was pleased to hear that they were coming as she was sure their visit would cheer Prince Arthur up. They stayed two nights and Prince Arthur thought they had enjoyed their visit. Léonie had asked him to say how sorry she was that the Duchess was not there. He said that he could not remember if she liked Léonie, but he added, 'I do very much.'[18]

When she wrote to thank Prince Arthur for the stay in Dublin, Léonie evidently made him a formal offer of her friendship, to which he replied that she already had his, but that he was glad to accept hers which he so greatly valued. Friends in this world, he said, were rare and he had very few lady friends, but the one or two he did have were worth all his other acquaintances put together. He now hoped that he would hear from Léonie more often and that they would see more of each other. Once again, he added a postscript; 'Dont ever begin your letter H.R.H. again,' he said. Whereas Prince Arthur had always occupied the role of mentor to, and guardian of, Louischen, who looked up to him as such, he looked upon Léonie as his superior, whose advice he could rely upon, whose encouragement would help him to face disappointments and carry out his duties, and the thought of whom would lift his depressions. 'Dear Mrs Leslie,' as she still was at the beginning of 1902, had, however, caught the King's attention and something he said to his brother contained a nasty innuendo. Prince Arthur was not unduly disturbed. Those who lived in glass houses, he told Léonie, should not throw stones.[19]

Prince Arthur, who recognised that he must not annoy the King, was, of course, very ready to serve him and in May 1902 he undertook his first foreign mission of the new reign. This was to Madrid, where King Alfonso XIII was deemed, at sixteen, to be coming of age and upon whom King Edward VII now wished to confer the Order of the Garter. Prince Arthur was to represent him in both these regards. He sailed for Bilbao on board the royal yacht *Victoria and Albert* on 12th May 1902. He was accompanied by a specially appointed suite, which included the Duke of Wellington, whom Prince Arthur found was not all that dull after all. On the eve of his departure, he had written to Léonie of their 'real & pure love' and of how it helped him bear the many disappointments he had suffered and more of which he expected in the future. He told her, however, that he must always wear the mask and be on his guard for the world was always 'prying & putting the wrong construction on the best & purest of feelings.'[20]

As *Victoria and Albert* steamed south from Ireland at fourteen and a half knots on the first evening of the voyage, Prince Arthur played bridge and lost; the others held splendid cards. He was on the bridge at 7.15 the next morning which broke lovely and bright. At 8.20 they sighted the German fleet thirty-two miles south-west of the Scilly Isles. At 9.20 they began to pass through it. The German ships, nine in number, including four first class and three second class cruisers, were drawn up in two lines and all were manned and carried mast head flags. They looked very powerful and smart. They fired a salute and their bands played and crews cheered. It was a beautiful sight and Prince Arthur thought it was not often that one passed through a powerful fleet under way in mid ocean. He wished the Duchess had been there to see it.[21]

As the doyen of the numerous foreign Princes who had come from Russia, Austria, Germany, Italy, Sweden, Greece, Monaco and elsewhere to attend the ceremonies, Prince Arthur took the Queen Mother in to the grand dinners and receptions. He found this rather a nervous proceeding, but the Queen was charming and the King's aunt, the Infanta Eulalie, had been a friend of his since 1875. The King seemed to be very nice, simple and boyish. The Garter ceremony went off without a hitch and the Queen Mother thought that Prince Arthur must have bestowed the Order on many occasions because he did it all so well. In return, Prince Arthur received the coveted Order of the Golden Fleece. At a great military parade he was mounted on a large Irish hunter, which, though handsome, was not used to such occasions, or the bands which went with them, and was very fresh. Most of the other Princes were also mounted, but the Russians, Italians and Swedes preferred to look on from a stand with the Queen and the Princesses. Sometimes the receptions and balls in the evenings seemed to be crowded and hot, but at others things were very pleasant. One night at a ball in aid of the charitable schools of Madrid, which was held in the Mexican Embassy, Prince Arthur flirted dreadfully with a pretty Spanish woman, whose name he could not remember the next day, though he knew she was the wife of the Spanish Ambassador in St Petersburg. He danced with her a little and took her in to supper. She was most agreeable and he did not get home until 4 a.m., he wrote to Léonie, who was now his 'beloved black head.' Prince Arthur, who was clearly beginning to rely on Léonie for the advice and encouragement which he had been used to receiving from his mother, could fill in some details of his activities when writing to her which he would have left out of letters to the Queen in former years.[22]

The Duchess too was increasingly depending on Léonie for advice and friendship and, after a visit to her at Glaslough in September 1902, she expressed her admiration of the qualities of kindness, unselfishness, goodness and all the other excellencies which she saw in Léonie's character. She wrote of Léonie's power of self-denial, which made the foundation of all that was good and true and provided a lesson which the Duchess hoped to study herself. She told Léonie that the Duke was now full of good resolutions and, despite his severe neuralgia, was trying not to give way to depression and, indeed, to follow Léonie's doctrines. The Duchess thought there had been a crisis in his relationship with Léonie. The Duchess knew that Léonie had been near to folding up her tent and the Duke had confided to his wife how miserable he was and she thought this must have been caused by such a moment. The Duchess told Léonie that she was determined that the Duke and herself would continue to be her friends, though she conceded that it was difficult to know how to steer absolutely straight and for the right goal. She was sure Léonie would always help her. With the Duke, she said, she had 'but to touch the chord of honor & all is well & with it all I know I still count for something & am not put aside.' She realised that everyone had difficulties in life, but she said she would rather give up hers than lose the Duke. If anything was to go wrong, she doubted if Léonie would ever see or hear of her again and people would say, poor thing; she was silly and of no account. Feeling that she had now said everything and that it was perhaps easier to write than to speak, she sent Léonie her best love and signed herself 'Ever Y^r grateful & aff. L.'[23]

Prince Arthur told Léonie that he had taken her advice; he was trying to take no notice of neuralgia and doing his best to make Louischen happy. He asked Léonie to appreciate that he lacked her power of being cheerful and he told her that he thought Louischen understood their friendship and was herself very fond of Léonie. He soon began to fear, as a child might have done, that Léonie cared more for Louischen than for himself. Thus, it became apparent that Prince Arthur's relationship with Léonie depended upon a continuing bond of marriage and love with Louischen; rather than threaten the marriage, Léonie would fold up her tent; rather than risk his friendship with Léonie, Prince Arthur would do nothing to weaken his marriage. This was a very unusual form of love triangle, but that is the best way of describing it. The world, however, was liable to take a different view. Léonie's sister, Lady Randolph Churchill, was not famous for her high moral tone and, as we have noticed, the King had already made an innuendo. We have seen too that Prince Arthur was on guard against prying society, which he thought would put a wrong interpretation on things. The Duchess was disappointed to hear that Léonie would be cutting short her visit to Blenheim Palace, where she and Prince Arthur had expected she would be staying while they paid a visit to the Marlboroughs, but she quite understood that Léonie did not wish the vulgar world to pry into their friendship.[24]

Even so, there was not much consistency in this policy. Prince Arthur had been happy to join Léonie at the opera in Lady de Grey's box for a performance of *Tannhäuser*; the Duchess told Prince Henry of Prussia, the Emperor's brother, to look out for Léonie when she came to Kiel on board Mr Armour's yacht and Prince Arthur had capital runs in a motor to and from Maidenhead for a boating party with Mensdorff, the Austrian Ambassador in London, and Léonie. In any case, Léonie and her husband, Jack, were now about to spring into the limelight of a royal tour, for Prince Arthur and the Duchess decided to take them to India as lady-in-waiting and A.D.C. respectively. Prince Arthur had commanded the troops at the King's coronation in London and next he was to go out to represent the King-Emperor at his Coronation Durbar in Delhi.[25]

Meanwhile, he had escaped another duty; the King, who wanted Prince Arthur to have some time in which to resume his Irish duties, had excused his attendance on the Shah of Persia during the latter's state visit to England in August 1902; the duty fell upon young Prince Arthur. He duly went down to Dover to meet the Shah on 17th August 1902. The Shah, who spoke in bad and very indistinct French, was accompanied by a suite of no less than forty-eight. He was very nervous of trains and insisted on not exceeding twenty miles an hour in them. It thus took over three hours to travel from Dover to London. Young Prince Arthur then had the pleasure of several days in close company with His Imperial Majesty, who was not very talkative beyond the occasional ejaculation, for no apparent reasons, of *très magnifique* or *très bon*. No one in the suite said anything except the Grand Vizier, who constantly made jokes, the points of which, however, eluded young Prince Arthur. The only things which seemed to interest the Imperial visitor were the guns which he was shown at Woolwich. In the mess afterwards he enthusiastically drank his own health in barley water. One never knew what he would do next, young Arthur complained to his mother. The suite seemed to be extremely jealous of one another and there were several ugly rushes at railway stations when they vied for the best seats. Uncle Bertie was evidently grateful for his nephew's pains; he invited him to Balmoral for a September visit.[26]

On 29th November 1902, Prince Arthur and the Duchess, with Jack and Léonie Leslie in attendance, left for India. From Genoa they travelled in H.M.S *Renown*, a first class battleship of 14,000 tons, in which accommodation had been specially fitted for them. Prince Arthur and the Duchess had two nice large cabins opening into each other with a bathroom attached and they had a dining room and the Admiral's cabin, which opened onto the stern walk. There was a crew of 897 officers and men. They reached Port Said on 6th December, where they were welcomed by the Agent, Lord Cromer. From here they travelled to Cairo by special train, changing gauge at Ismailia and pausing on the way at Tel-el-Kebir. Prince Arthur looked at the graves there and found it sad reading the names of so many he had known. In Cairo they were met by the Khedive, Ministers and British officers and they then drove to the Abdin Palace, where they stayed. Cromer gave a big dinner party for them and next day Prince Arthur carried out military inspections and held an investiture, at which he was assisted by Colonel Jack Leslie.[27]

The Duchess, accompanied by Léonie, drove with an escort of Egyptian cavalry to the Khoubée Palace where they were met on the steps by four eunuchs. Inside, they were received by the Khedive Mère, who the Duchess knew from earlier visits. She was surrounded by harem attendants wearing brightly coloured silk dresses and turbans. The Khedive Mère introduced her daughter-in-law, the Khedive's wife, who looked almost as old as her mother-in-law. She was of no family and had been a 'Sicussian' slave. Both ladies wore Parisian looking dresses, the elder one of pale blue embroidered satin and the younger a white painted muslin with pearls and diamonds and huge solitaire diamonds worn as ear rings. *Shibouks* were brought in and the Duchess was offered one with a magnificent diamond and amber mouth piece. As none was offered to the other ladies, she felt rather shy about smoking on her own; so she asked Léonie to try one as a curiosity. The hostesses could not smoke as Ramadan fasts were in force and they could not eat, drink, smoke nor smell nor indulge any of the other senses between sunrise and sunset. That evening Prince Arthur's party left by special train for Luxor. At all the stations on the way, there were illuminations, crowds of people and bands and at one place a native school master, at the head of a hundred and fifty boys all dressed in khaki, called out three times 'Long Live Their Royal Highnesses the Duchess & the Duke of Connaught.' He was so serious and excited; 'it was very comical,' Prince Arthur recorded.[28]

The special train arrived at Luxor on the following morning and Prince Arthur met his old friend, Mustapha Aga, who was the British Consul, and M. Le Grand, who was in charge of the excavations at Karnac. With the Duchess and their party, he then embarked in one of the Khedive's yachts, *Feirouz*. The Khedive had provided other yachts for his brother, Prince Mohammed Ali, the Cromers and himself and at 9.45 this luxurious flotilla moved off on a cruise up the Nile. Prince Arthur was pleased to be going up the grand old river again and there was much interest on board in the river life of the Egyptians, the women filling their pitchers at the water's edge, the camels, donkeys and water buffalo, the curious mud villages, the graceful palm groves and the enormous sugar factories with their painfully European chimneys. At every village the inhabitants turned out and waved; there was a beautiful yellow, orange and pink sunset. When it got too cold to stay on deck, Prince Arthur, the Duchess and their companions withdrew to play bridge.[29]

At Assuan, Prince Arthur found the town much grown since he had last seen it four and a half years ago and two new large hotels had been built. The water level was also quite different. The Temple of Philae was no longer on a rocky island, but at the water's edge. Prince Arthur was told that it had been underpinned at a cost of £200,000. The remains of the coptic village near the temple had been cleared away, which he thought was a great improvement. On the way back to the yacht, there was a glimpse of the new barrage. Again, there was a lovely sunset and the royal party sat on the upper deck until it was time to dress for dinner. During dinner one of the Khedive's bands played near their yacht and afterwards the Leslies came with Prince Arthur and the Duchess for a sail in one of the ship's boats. It was quite charming and not too cold. The impression of the illuminations suggested Venice and Prince Arthur thought he had never seen anything more effective. Next day he and the Duchess went by

special train with the Khedive to the dam, where they were received with
God Save the King and a guard of honour. They went in trolleys along the
dam, which was composed of two thousand yards of fine granite wall. The
Duchess laid its last stone, the Khedive opened some sluice gates and
Prince Arthur operated the lock gates. He then returned with the
Duchess and their companions to the yacht by boat, but the Khedive went
to his by train as he had been told that it would be dangerous to go by
water. After dinner Sir Ernest Cassel came on board Prince Arthur's yacht
for coffee and cigarettes, bringing with him, amongst others, the five
Michael Hicks-Beaches, Mrs George Keppel and Léonie's nephew,
Winston Churchill. By the light of the illuminations, delicious reflections
appeared in the water.[30]

After the inaugural ceremony at the Assuan Dam, the Khedive's yachts
cruised back to Luxor and Prince Arthur and his party made visits to the
Temples of Edfu and Karnac and the Tombs of the Kings, to which Prince
Arthur, at his special request, was accompanied on the donkey ride by
Yussaff, who had been his donkey boy in 1873, 1882 and 1899. He was
now a dragoman at the hotel in Luxor. After a further short stay in Cairo,
Prince Arthur and the Duchess, the Leslies and their other companions
re-embarked in *Renown* at Suez and resumed their voyage to India.[31]

On 27th December 1902, *Renown* was escorted by six torpedo boats
into harbour at Bombay and that evening Prince Arthur and the Duchess
left by special train, travelling in the Governor of Bombay's carriage,
which they knew well. They arrived in Delhi on the morning of 29th
December and here they were met by the Viceroy, Lord Curzon, Lady
Curzon, the Grand Duke Ernest of Hesse, the Governor of Bombay and
Lady Northcote, the Governor of Madras and Lady Ampthill, the C-in-C,
India, Lord Kitchener, the General-Officers-Commanding the armies
and divisions, the Lieutenant-Governors and Chief Commissioners, the
members of the Council of India and those of the Presidential Councils,
the Nizam of Hyderabad and all the Princes of India, the Feudatory Chiefs
of Aden, the Khan of Khalor and the representative of the Amir of
Afghanistan. It was a most striking picture full of different dresses of
every hue and a wonderful show of jewelry. No end of people were
presented to Prince Arthur and he spoke to all the Chiefs. The Indian
Princes had parked their elephants outside the station and they now all
mounted these and formed a double row. Prince Arthur and the Duchess
then ascended a magnificently caparisoned elephant and sat in a silver and
gold howdah. While a white umbrella was held over the Duchess's head,

they rode out through the lines of Princes and formed a procession. They were preceded by a herald and twelve state trumpeters, six of whom were British and six Indian. Then came 'H' Battery of the Royal Horse Artillery, the 4th Dragoon Guards with their band and the Viceroy's Bodyguard, a hundred strong. Behind them came the Imperial Cadet Corps, which consisted mainly of ruling Chiefs or their sons; they were dressed in white, blue and gold. The procession was closed by the 11th Bengal Lancers. There were sixty-four elephants in the cavalcade, including that of the Viceroy, which walked immediately behind Prince Arthur's. Behind this, the Governors drove in their carriages and, in the rear of them, the Biluch Chiefs rode on horseback. The whole of the four mile route to the Delhi Fort was lined with troops and Prince Arthur particularly noticed the smartness of the Argyll and Sutherland Highlanders and Gordons, the 3rd Battalion of the Rifle Brigade, the 2/60th Rifles, the 15th Sikhs and the 2nd Gurkhas. As he passed through the Kashmir Gate and into the Fort, a salute of thirty-five guns was fired. From there he drove with the Duchess in a carriage to the Viceroy's Camp nearby.[32]

Lord Curzon had assembled a huge camp which accommodated no fewer than fifteen thousand people, including a hundred and fifty cooks. Seven tents had been provided for Prince Arthur and the Duchess and there was a vast reception tent in which Curzon could give lavish dinner parties. In addition to all this, Kitchener had a camp of his own nearby and there were many others besides. From this camp, on 1st January 1903, Prince Arthur and the Duchess drove to the Durbar with an escort of the 9th Lancers and the 19th Bengal Lancers. As they reached the arena, an artillery salute was fired, a guard of honour, found by the Gordon Highlanders, was drawn up and there was cheering and applause. Prince Arthur, representing the King-Emperor, took a seat with the Duchess on the dais. Lord and Lady Curzon, escorted by the Imperial Cadets, on black horses, and the Viceroy's Bodyguard, in scarlet and blue on bays, followed and also took their seats on the dais. The proclamation was read by a herald and cheers were given for the King-Emperor. Curzon then addressed the assemblage, after which the Indian Princes came forward to offer their congratulations to Prince Arthur and the Viceroy. That night, Curzon gave a state dinner in his camp and, in the course of proposing the King's health and that of Prince Arthur and the Duchess, made a long speech. Prince Arthur replied.[33]

It was curious that Curzon took the leading role, even at the Durbar itself, for this was the function at which Prince Arthur was the King-Emperor's representative and Curzon, by rights, should have deferred to him as such. Prince Arthur, however, before he left England, had told Curzon that he wished to meet the Viceroy's wishes in every way; Curzon had taken him at his word and clearly wished that the Viceroy should be at the centre of the picture throughout the proceedings. Such he certainly was, and the Duchess of Marlborough, who was in the Viceroy's camp, later remembered that Curzon never allowed Prince Arthur to forget who was Viceroy. Nevertheless, this was evidently not enough and his wife found it necessary, when the ceremonies were over, to boost his ego further by telling him that the Connaughts were no more than 'an extra gargoyle to a most intricate and wondrous building every stone of which had been carved and placed' by Curzon. Neither of the Connaughts, she assured him, had personalities. Prince Arthur, she conceded, had 'a most exquisite manner,' but the Duchess was only a 'German *Hausfrau*.' Prince Arthur offered no judgement of Curzon, but history subsequently did.[34]

After the Coronation Durbar, Prince Arthur and his party made an extensive tour visiting many of his old haunts and indulging in some of the same sport which he had enjoyed during the years of his military commands in India. He went up to the North-West Frontier and then came back to Rawalpindi, Meerut, where he found one of his former servants, and Agra, where he and the Duchess once more visited the Taj by moonlight. There was bison, boar and tiger shooting with the Maharaja of Gwalior, whose camp was lit by Chinese lanterns and Prince Arthur had a sleeping tent hung with coloured silks and another for bathing fitted with a marble bath. Before he left Bhurtpur, the Maharaja there came to take formal leave of him and impressed Prince Arthur by his calmness and self-possession; he was three years old. In the evening on 27th February 1903, Prince Arthur and the Duchess embarked again in H.M.S. *Renown*, which had been awaiting them at Bombay. Before going aboard, they sailed round the ship in their launch to see her illuminations. She was completely marked out in electric light with a large illuminated crown suspended between the two masts. They then entertained the Governor of Bombay and Lady Northcote to dinner on deck and next morning they sailed for England. During this visit to India, Prince Arthur had travelled from Bombay to Delhi, Peshawar, Dargai, Rawalpindi, Meerut, Shagpur, Gwalior, Agra, Bhurtpur, Jaipur, Bikanir and back to Bombay, covering a distance of 4,333 miles.[35]

Before he left, Prince Arthur wrote to Curzon thanking him generously for the arrangements which had been made for his visit and expressing the hope that it had done something to bring out the latent loyalty of Indians to the King-Emperor, which he said Curzon had done so much to foster. Earlier he had praised Curzon for his efforts to preserve the splendid antiquities of India. He wished that the Maharaja of Bikanir would take as much interest in the administration of his territory as the Maharaja of Gwalior did in his and he told the Viceroy that, of the Political Officers he had met, Major Stratton at Bhurtpur had impressed him the least. Curzon thought Stratton must have been peculiarly tactless and indiscreet to have attracted Prince Arthur's attention in this way, but he admitted that this officer had a bad manner and was dominating towards the Natives. Curzon's dismissive attitude to Prince Arthur was evident from his surprise that such a slow-witted man could have spotted a bad Political Officer and his assumption that this could have been caused only by some positively crass action by the officer. He had, of course, quite under-estimated Prince Arthur's shrewd and experienced eye. But Curzon was given to the underestimation of others, a fault which was soon, and then not for the last time, to cost him dear.[36]

On 11th March 1903, *Renown* reached Port Said. Mail was brought on board and among it was a letter informing Prince Arthur that he was to be offered the post of Adjutant-General of the Forces. *Renown* took on six hundred tons of coal and then sailed into the teeth of a strong and chilly wind. This was not unusual for the time of year in this part of the Mediterranean, but it was a portent of the political climate in London and the effect of it on the future of Prince Arthur's military career. The King had it in mind that Prince Arthur should hold the position of Adjutant-General for a year and then become Commander-in-Chief. One of the obstacles was that Roberts still had three years to run in the position, but perhaps he could be persuaded to give up two of those years to make way for the Duke of Connaught. It would be difficult for the King to broach this with Roberts, but perhaps the Queen could do so. Not surprisingly this rather curious plan, about which, it seems, Prince Arthur was not consulted, ran into a stiff adverse breeze. So far from wishing to pave the way to the Commandership-in-Chief for Prince Arthur, the Government wished to abolish the post altogether and there were few men in the country less likely to make a sacrifice for Prince Arthur's sake, or for anyone else's, than Lord Roberts.[37]

Meanwhile, on 27th March, *Renown* came into Portsmouth harbour and berthed alongside the North railway jetty just ahead of *Victoria and Albert*, which was preparing to embark the King. Prince Arthur and the Duchess travelled to London by special train and there they bad farewell to the Leslies and the rest of their staff before driving to their new home, Clarence House. 'So ended our delightful & interesting trip,' Prince Arthur recorded. It had certainly been a highlight of his life and in years to come he was often to reminisce with Léonie about the romance of their odyssey in H.M.S. *Renown*. If she had not appreciated it before, Léonie now certainly realised the glamour of a royal progress to the East and she admitted to Prince Arthur that she rather dreaded the return to the *vie de famille* in County Monaghan, she wished she need only see people she liked and she wondered when she would see her *Bon Ami* again. Prince Arthur too was depressed. How he missed the three soft little taps on his door, which had been Léonie's token of good night. Though he thought of her by day and dreamt of her by night, he promised that he seldom thought of things which she would not have wished him to do.[38]

Though it was now virtually settled that Prince Arthur would come to the War Office when he laid down his command in Ireland, there was much doubt as to the position which he would occupy. The King had hoped that, as Adjutant-General, he would be afforded direct access to the Secretary of State for War, but Mr St John Broderick, who was that Secretary of State, resisted the suggestion and complained that he had enough difficulty in dealing with the C-in-C without adding that which would be caused by the Adjutant-General. Indeed, and on the contrary, he was planning to prune the scope of the Adjutant-General by removing from his field the responsibility for military training. Prince Arthur told the King that he did not think he could accept appointment as Adjutant-General if training was to be removed from his control. Roberts, who may well have sensed the potential threat to his own position, advised Broderick that responsibility for training would overload the work of the Adjutant-General and so Broderick's argument became unassailable and Prince Arthur's avenue to that particular appointment was closed. Something else was in the wind and the advent of Mr Arnold-Forster to the War Office in place of Broderick portended a more radical bout of army reform. The Government decided to create the post of Inspector-General of the Forces and, at the end of February 1904, it was offered to Prince Arthur.[39]

CHAPTER 13

Inspector-General
of the Forces and
the Mediterranean Command
1904-1909

SOME TIME BEFORE he was offered the post of Inspector-General of the Forces, Prince Arthur had been astonished to hear from Léonie that Lord Esher had told her that he would soon be getting a big position in England. Prince Arthur told Léonie that Esher was very clever and that he liked him in a way but that he was not really to be trusted. He warned her that Esher would know that she was a friend of his and would therefore praise him to her. What Prince Arthur did not realise was the extent to which Esher not only knew, but himself decided, who was going to get the big military jobs, for Esher's was the hand which principally guided the so-called army reforms and the selection of the officers who were to occupy the principal positions in the reorganised superstructure which resulted from them. This was odd, for Esher had no military experience or knowledge and he held no military appointment; he was, in fact, an *éminence grise* who owed no responsibility for the significant powers which he wielded. He presented himself to the King as one who was deeply attached to the person of His Majesty and without ambitions of his own, but who could smooth the way for the prevalence of the Royal wishes with Ministers of the Crown. To the Ministers, he would show himself as fully aware that the wishes of the King were of no importance as against the will of the Minister in question, but he would also hint at the difficulties which the King could make unless he was humoured and that none was more expert in humouring the King than himself. It was primarily Esher who decided that there would be an Inspector-General of the Forces and it was principally he who secured the support of the King and the Ministers for the appointment to that post of the Duke of Connaught. Later, as we shall see, the same influence was exerted in the creation and filling of the post of Commander-in-Chief in the Mediterranean.[1]

Esher's business was the manipulation of Kings and Princes, Ministers and Generals and, through that, the exercise of power from behind the scenes. His concern with the Army was with its higher organisation and administration; the troops themselves were not his field. In that setting, the choice of Prince Arthur as Inspector-General was a conspicuously bad one. Before he left Ireland, Prince Arthur had made it abundantly clear that in his opinion the army reforms were starting at the wrong end of the matter. Reform, he had said, would be of little use if the problem of the quality of the fighting troops was not faced. The term 'fighting soldiers,' he had pointed out, was often used without any understanding of what it meant. The public and the legislators were liable to believe that if, say, 10,000 men were sent out, the fighting force would be increased by that amount. They did not realise that many of these would be utilised on garrison and regimental duties. Army reforms, he had asserted, were being directed at the superstructure without first ensuring that the foundation was secure. The foundation, he thought, should be the first object of reform. A small fighting army would be of more use than a large half trained one. Race horses ate hay, but what trainer, Prince Arthur had asked, would use them to cut and draw that hay. The Army was employing potential fighting men in capacities which unfitted them for fighting and he had pointed out that in the Irish command six hundred N.C.Os and men were employed on garrison duties. Much domestic and ancillary work could be done by reservists or civilians, so that a higher proportion of the troops would become fighting soldiers.[2]

These were not the sort of ideas which interested Lord Esher or his brain child, the newly created Army Council, into which the powers of the former Commander-in-Chief had been dissolved. Nor were they of much concern to the Secretary of State for War, Mr Arnold-Forster, whose real brief was less to improve the Army than to make it cheaper. From the outset, Prince Arthur's appearance on the scene as Inspector-General was likely to spell trouble.

The nature of that trouble, indeed, was inherent in the terms in which the duties of the Inspector-General were defined. The post was designed to provide the Secretary of State and the Army Council with eyes and ears and to report on the practical results of the Army Council's policies within the financial limits laid down by the Cabinet. The Inspector-

General, whose duties covered forces at home and abroad, was to form a judgement of the efficiency of the officers and men, the handling of troops, the standard and system of training, the suitability of equipment and 'all that affects the readiness of the Forces for war.' As Lord Salisbury noted at the time, there was a real need for such eyes and ears, for the members of the Army Council would be seated in their offices all day immersed in small departmental details and they would see little of what was going on in the real Army. Esher saw the Inspector-General as a protection to the Army Council against this isolation, but Salisbury, more shrewdly, foresaw that such 'protection' might also be a threat. The Inspector-General might say things which the Secretary of State and the Army Council did not wish to hear and, as Salisbury could also see, the Inspector-General, in the person of a Royal Duke with the ear of the Sovereign and now himself a Field-Marshal, for so he had been made in 1902, would be a formidable authority. In addition to that, the Inspector-General was also to be the President of the Selection Board, which would be responsible for the recommendation of promotions above the rank of Captain, except in the case of General Staff officers, and he would also be the Umpire-in-Chief at large manoeuvres. Virtually the only protection given to the Army Council against the Inspector-General was the injunction that the latter was to report facts without expressing an opinion of policies, a well-worn formula often employed before and since by administrative authorities to disarm unwelcome comments. Despite this limitation, however, Prince Arthur's appointment as Inspector-General was, as Esher had foreshadowed to Léonie Leslie, a big position.[3]

On 6th May 1904, Prince Arthur laid down the Irish command and entered upon the duties of the Inspector-General. While he did so, the Army Council fell to lengthy discussions of the details of his appointment; deciding, for example, that his wish to include the Yeomanry in his reports should not be allowed and considering the question of salutes and guards of honour which, on the one hand, should be accorded to themselves, and on the other, to him. They decided that they, corporately, would be given a salute of nineteen guns; the Secretary of State would get seventeen and the Inspector-General need not be mentioned. The King did not miss such points, but he was told that the Inspector-General would be better able to carry out his duties if he was not impeded by ceremony and that the Duke of Connaught, as a member of the Royal Family, would in any case receive a royal salute. They grappled with the question of what the Chief of the General Staff would do at manoeuvres if the Inspector-General was the Umpire-in-Chief. The Secretary of State for War, Mr Arnold-Forster, occupied himself with the production of a series of schemes to reform the Army, telling the Cabinet that he could knock £1,412,000 off the army estimates, and, when they thought that not enough, producing another plan, which he said would save £3,500,000. However, none of these in the end seemed to save anything at all and led only to Arnold-Forster complaining to the Prime Minister that he could not find out what was the purpose of the Army; a question which Mr Balfour clearly thought was very silly.[4]

The King, at the outset, had thought that Arnold-Forster would not be a success as a reforming Secretary of State for War and, after a year of his efforts, Prince Arthur may well have put his finger on the reasons. While both were staying at Balmoral in October 1904, Prince Arthur had a long talk with Arnold-Forster. The latter gave an impression of optimism about his latest army scheme and quoted many statistics to support it. Prince Arthur, however, was not convinced and thought that, though he was an earnest man, he was too cock-sure and very vain. Prince Arthur noticed that, as they sat near a fireplace, Arnold-Forster constantly regarded himself in a mirror. Neither the Secretary of State nor the Army Council were, in fact, making much of a fist of what was intended to be the dawn of a new age after the abolition of the Commandership-in-Chief.[5]

Prince Arthur's concern was now to tell them something about the needs of the foundation, by which he meant the troops, and to which he believed that reforming efforts should have been devoted in the first instance. He had been enjoined to submit a report annually to the Army Council and, in preparation for the first of these, he embarked upon a vigorous tour of inspections designed to keep his already enormous knowledge of the Army up to date and to enlarge it. On the night of 21st to 22nd July 1904, for example, he travelled from London to Edinburgh on the night train and went up in the lift from the station platform to the North British Station Hotel, where he was pleased to find that very comfortable rooms with two splendid bathrooms were awaiting him. After breakfast he drove out of Edinburgh in a motor and then, mounted on a 17th Lancers horse, he rode through several camps of troops engaged on manoeuvres. The terrain gave good opportunities for defence and attack and Prince Arthur was well impressed by the operations which he watched. He noted with interest that dogs were used to trace the whereabouts of 'wounded' men and he was impressed by an effective attack on a convoy, which was delivered by Volunteers. On another day he went to Leith whence he inspected coastal defences and a new battery in the course of construction. As he approached the Forth Bridge, batteries there opened fire on his ship with blanks. He steamed under the bridge to the site which the Admiralty had just bought for the establishment of a naval dockyard. He lunched at Queensferry under the bridge and then inspected two forts, their electric lights and large minefields. Britain was beginning to think of Germany and not France as the potential enemy. A few days later he was at Aldershot where he inspected three artillery battalions of 'Long Toms', three of howitzers and two of the Royal Horse Artillery.[6]

In September 1904 a more ambitious scheme than usual was undertaken. At 6a.m. on 5th Prince Arthur embarked at Spithead in H.M.S. *Good Hope* and then sailed in a fleet of sixteen vessels, ten of which were transports laden with troops, to effect a landing in the area of Clacton. Before it embarked, this invasion force had met with a set-back. There had been a stampede of horses belonging to the 8th Hussars at Southampton and many of them had been killed. The King's Dragoon Guards were summoned by telegram from Aldershot to replace them and, within fourteen hours, they were embarking. Prince Arthur thought this was good going, as the stampede had been on a Sunday, which was the worst day for getting anything done. Prince Arthur duly watched these replacement troops entering Colchester in the face of a defending force commanded by General Sir John French. Two months later Prince Arthur submitted to the Army Council his first annual report as Inspector-General.[7]

The report did not make comfortable reading. Prince Arthur said that all arms were wanting to various extents and he found that the Army was terribly over-regulated by voluminous instructions, which were loosely worded and often mutually conflicting. He regretted to have to report that the 'British Army at home is far from being ready and efficient for war.' Having read the report, Esher told Prince Arthur that nothing could have provided more justification for the efforts of his own committee to secure the appointment of an Inspector-General and he congratulated Prince Arthur on what he said would provide the Army Council with a careful examination of the facts. Neither the Secretary of State nor the Army Council, however, received the report in anything like that spirit. Arnold-Forster thought he had detected in some of Prince Arthur's remarks about the Army Service Corps matters of policy rather than mere fact and he asked that these should be omitted before the report was presented to Parliament. Moreover, he thought, after talking to him on 22nd December 1904, that Prince Arthur had agreed to such a course and he tried to get this confirmed by an exchange of letters between his Private Secretary, Colonel Shute, and Prince Arthur's Military Secretary, Colonel Congreve. When Congreve told Shute that Prince Arthur could not consider altering his report, which was for the Army Council to use as they wished, and that to alter it would be to stultify himself, Arnold-Forster resumed the matter by insinuating to Prince Arthur that the inclusion of remarks which he did not like would weaken the impact of the report and the future position of the Inspector-General. If Prince Arthur insisted on leaving the report as it was, he would regard the awkward parts as '*non avenue*.'[8]

Prince Arthur, who was now in Lisbon, assured Arnold-Forster that he knew he had no right, nor had he any intention, to criticise questions of policy in his official reports, but he could not see that he had done so; he had merely reported what he had seen and found in the course of his inspections and it was for the Army Council to decide what should be done in the light of what he had said. He told Arnold-Forster that it would be a great mistake if he was now to alter his report to suit the Secretary of State's views. His one object, he said, was the good and efficiency of the Army and he felt that he had to report openly and fearlessly on everything connected with it. This was bad news for Arnold-Forster and it was made worse when he heard that the King felt bound to mention that he thought that the Duke of Connaught had taken a proper view of his duties and that it would make the reports of the Inspector-General valueless, if he were to consent to make alterations or omissions because the authorities at the War Office did not like certain passages.[9]

Any hopes which may have been entertained by the King and Prince Arthur that this would dispose of the difficulties were soon dispelled for, in truth, the real objection to the Inspector-General's report was not the trivial matters which Arnold-Forster had mentioned, but the statement in the report that the Army was not efficient for war. Among the reasons which Prince Arthur had advanced in support of this contention was his view that there was a growing feeling of uncertainty as regards the future in all ranks of the Army. Regimental officers, in particular, were finding that the tests to which they were subjected had increased in severity and that their responsibilities were daily becoming greater; yet, when they had negotiated these issues, they found as their reward nothing but half-pay in the prime of life. This was because places could not be found for them at the Staff College, the certificate of which had now become the key to extra-regimental promotion. Prince Arthur had also noticed considerable unrest in the lower ranks of the Army caused by uncertainty about the changes which were in the air. Such views were far from gratifying to the Secretary of State and the Army Council, who were now supposed to be in charge of an improved and reformed army.[10]

Seeing that they could not prevail upon Prince Arthur to change his reports into the particular form of bromide which they desired, they turned to other means. First, they decided, with the concurrence of the Prime Minister, Mr Balfour, that the reports should not be presented to Parliament and therefore made available to the public, as had originally been intended, but that they should be restricted to the Army Council. Secondly, the Army Council set about trying to wear down Prince Arthur's arguments by challenging him to produce further evidence in support of them. The first step, despite Prince Arthur's protests, was effective; the second was not, for Prince Arthur now presented further evidence of the Army being inefficient for war, which made his charge much more damning than it had originally been. He pointed out, for example, that the Horse and Field Artillery were still without Quick Firing (QF) guns, the howitzers were without shrapnel and the striking force at Aldershot was equipped with two different types of gun, the parts of which were not interchangeable. A new rifle was being introduced to the Army, but its pattern had not yet been decided. The grouping of the Army into corps had been abolished, but the brigades and divisions, which formed the new scheme, had been left without commanders. There was a lack of telephones for field work and there was no proper organisation of searchlights. There was no training in field entrenchment, except at Aldershot. There was a shortage of junior officers and the army establishment did not provide for enough transport, signal and machine gun officers. Moreover, even before the Army Council had been able to digest these unwelcome additional observations, they received a report from their energetic and troublesome Inspector-General on the forces in Egypt and the Mediterranean area.[11]

Prince Arthur set forth on his journey to Egypt and the Sudan at the beginning of January 1905. The Duchess came with him and they took their daughters. Princess Margaret was within a few days of her twenty-third birthday and Princess Patricia was going to be nineteen in three months time. News of the grace and beauty of these girls had spread across Europe and they were the cynosure of many royal expectations, which their Uncle, the King, was hoping would be converted into useful alliances. He insisted that Prince Arthur should go ashore in Lisbon on the way out and, though Prince Arthur thought this a great bore on account of the extra expense in which it would involve him, he duly did so. King Carlos and his family gave them a very warm reception and in the evening took them to the opera where *Le Roi de Sahare* was given. Prince Arthur and the Duchess shared a box with the King and Queen and the Connaught Princesses were in the next one with the two young Portugese Princes. All the glasses in the house were fixed on the Princesses, for in Portugal one or the other of them was expected to be the next Queen.[12]

On 13th January 1905, H.M.S. *Essex* carrying Prince Arthur, the Duchess and the two Princesses, came into Cadiz. The crowds were awful and the authorities were nearly swept off the platform at the railway station. The same thing happened along the line to Seville. People pressed their noses against the windows of the royal carriage and shouts of *viva l'Inglaterra, viva Duque di Connaught* and *viva la futura Reina d'España* were everywhere to be heard. By the time they got to Malaga, the cry had become *viva la Reina d'España* and their visit to the cathedral was ruined by the mob which invaded it and prevented them from seeing anything. When they came out, they could scarcely get into their carriage, so dense were the crowds. The Duchess was angry and, according to Prince Arthur, visited it all on him. He was disgusted by the want of reverence which the crowds showed within the cathedral, but he reckoned this was a characteristic of Catholic countries. Patsy, who had always hated crowds, was furious and very shy; being stared at and shouted at made her dislike Spain. This was to prove unfortunate for the young King Alfonso XIII. Daisy, who was the immediate object of the shouting and staring, held her counsel, which was also unfortunate for King Alfonso. Prince Arthur was not sorry to get back on board *Essex* and he did not give much for the chances of the King of Spain.[13]

At Algiers and Tunis, where the French authorities were very nice and civil, life returned to normal and, for Prince Arthur, who had so often travelled that way before, it continued to be so on the journey from Alexandria to Khartoum. In the course of the tour and the military inspections which he carried out, Prince Arthur came to the conclusion that some five million people had lost their lives in the wars and persecutions which had lately taken place in the Sudan. Realising that the country was half the size of India and very thinly garrisoned he felt that it

31. *Prince Arthur, Rudyard Kipling and the latter's son, John Kipling, on board R.M.S. Armadale Castle bound for Cape Town, December 1905 or January 1906.*

Margaret 1907. *Gustaf Adolf.*

Vesterbotten –

Princess Margaret, Prince Gustaf Adolf and the
first-born : (Duke of Vesterbotton, called Edmund.)

32. *The Crown Prince and Princess of Sweden with their eldest son, Prince Arthur's first
grandchild, the Duke of Vesterbotton, 1907.*

33. *Prince Arthur (centre) greeting King Edward VII on his arrival in Malta,*
21st April 1909.

34. *Prince Arthur taking leave of King Edward VII (nearest the camera) and his party on*
board the royal yacht at Malta, 25th April 1909.

35. *Prince Arthur on safari in Kenya, 1910.*

was dangerous to have only five companies of British infantry in Khartoum. He was also worried by the huge distances which separated the English civil officials, who were scattered throughout the country, each with districts the size of Great Britain. Such were some of the considerations which convinced Prince Arthur that he must write a strong report to the Army Council.[14]

Meanwhile, pausing at Luxor on their homeward journey, Prince Arthur and his family found that Prince Gustaf Adolf, the eldest son of the Crown Prince of Sweden, was also there. He looked like his father, but Prince Arthur thought he was not quite so ugly. When they went to Cairo, the Swedish Prince came with them. Prince Arthur saw that Patsy took no notice of him, but he walked about with Daisy all the time and went out riding with both girls. Daisy was suddenly brighter and in better looks; Prince Arthur thought that she and Gustaf had taken 'quite a liking to each other.' Indeed, on 23rd February 1905, Prince Gustaf wrote to the Duchess from the old Shepheard's Hotel asking if she, the Duke and the Princesses would honour him by attending a small dance which Mrs Slade was organising for him at the Zirch Palace Pavilion. He said there would be about seventy guests, but, he added, all depended on the Duchess, as he would not have the party unless she had occasion to be present at it. In the event, the party was scarcely necessary, for on the day following his letter to the Duchess and three days before the dance, the Swedish Prince and Princess Margaret were among Lord Cromer's guests at a dinner at the Agency. After the meal they found their way to the conservatory and there, without further ado, Prince Gustaf proposed and was accepted.[15]

Though the young lovers had known each other for only a few days and none of the groundwork, such as that which used to be supplied by Queen Victoria, the Crown Princess of Prussia and Sir Howard Elphinstone, had, in this case, been done, the pace of Daisy's romance was, perhaps, hardly greater than that of her parents twenty-seven years before. Though Portuguese and Spanish advances may have helped to concentrate Daisy's mind, she had certainly fallen completely in love with Gustaf, or 'Gusty' as they were soon to call him, and he with her. Prince Arthur was delighted and the Duchess was very happy and somewhat excited. Though Gustaf, who was ten months younger than his wife to be, was short-sighted and condemned to wear spectacles, he was tall, dark, well-informed, fond of music and said to be an excellent shot and a good dancer. Prince Arthur judged him to be honest and straightforward, intelligent and unassuming and he found that he improved on acquaintance. Daisy was in tremendous spirits and good looks. She and Gustaf were subsequently married in St George's Chapel, Windsor, on 15th June 1905.[16]

Patsy, alas, was not in such high spirits; she was in floods of tears, complained that she would miss her sister and declared that she would not marry the King of Spain. This was rather awkward because the Connaughts had planned to come home via a second visit to Spain, where King Alfonso was still full of hope. Prince Arthur, who would have liked to go by another route, consulted his brother, who, in turn, consulted the British Ambassador in Madrid, Sir Arthur Nicolson. Nicolson explained that King Alfonso and the Queen Mother would be very disappointed if the visit was cancelled and it would be embarrassing for them too because the King had told the German Emperor that he could not come to meet him at Viso as he would be entertaining the Connaughts. Prince Arthur would have to make the visit, but, in the new circumstances, it would be best if he made it alone.[17]

Before leaving Cairo to undertake this rather awkward mission, Prince Arthur wrote his report to the Army Council on the local military situation. He explained that the cost of the British army of occupation in Egypt had increased from L87,000 to L100,000 and that, as Egypt was now so prosperous, the British Treasury had thought that the increase should be borne by the Egyptian government. Lord Cromer had thought not and so the army of occupation had been reduced instead. Prince Arthur thought this was a grave error. If the question was viewed as purely Egyptian, then, no doubt, Cromer's attitude was correct, but Egypt, Prince Arthur asserted, had much more than a local significance; it also had a major Imperial importance which was due to its proximity to the Sudan and to the fact that it was a key link in the line of communications with India. As to the Sudan, Prince Arthur thought that the position was imperfectly understood by the Army Council. He wished them to realise that, though the country had previously been remote in the sense that it took about six days to move a battalion from Alexandria to Khartoum, the completion of Port Sudan thirty miles to the north of Soakin would bring Khartoum to within sixteen hours of the sea. Within two years a railway would cover this route and it would then probably be cheaper to reinforce by that way than by the Nile. The Sudan, in addition, offered an excellent training ground for the army and a climate which made it ideal for the acclimatisation of troops on their way to India. Cromer, he said, had to think in terms of the interests of the Egyptian government; the Army

Council should view the question from those of the defence of India.[18]

The Army Council met on 26th May 1905 to consider what should be done with this last report from the Inspector-General. To assist their deliberations they had before them the views of the Director of Military Operations and the Chief of the General Staff. The former stated that he agreed generally with what Prince Arthur had said, but he doubted if there was any chance of altering the existing arrangements. The Chief of the General Staff stated that the greater part of the report dealt with matters of policy and that therefore, 'with all deference to His Royal Highness,' he had travelled 'outside his legitimate functions in making the proposals.' Thus, the Army Council was able to resolve that Prince Arthur's report should be ignored.[19]

Prince Arthur soldiered on. After a further series of inspections, including in the Scilly Isles, Guernsey, Alderney and Portland, he produced the Inspector-General's second annual report. In this he conceded that some efforts had been made to remedy defects, but he said that many of the things mentioned in his first report were still in an unsatisfactory state and he mentioned several new issues of neglect. For example, he had found that the meat tins issued to the cavalry were too heavy, their field glasses were of poor quality, there were defects in their rifles and the standard of their barracks was poor. He observed that the rearmament of the artillery and the field army was seriously behind schedule as a result of late delivery by the manufacturers. Prince Arthur also incorporated a number of radical and positive suggestions into his report. He suggested that all soldiers should be trained in the use of rifles at short range, he recommended that balloons and kites, connected to the ground by telephone cable, should be introduced as a new form of observation post and he wanted the lessons of the Russo-Japanese war, especially in so far as the employment of applied science was concerned, to be studied and then implemented. Though he believed that the treatment of military prisoners had improved, he thought that their conditions in India were still degrading. He complained that little progress had been made towards the creation of the promised general staff and he was sorry that nothing had been done to establish a military historical section of it. The Army Council was largely unmoved and it ducked most of this barrage with verdicts such as that it had the matter suggested under consideration, or that it was outside its scope, or that not much could be expected from a voluntary army.[20]

Balfour's Conservative government was progressively losing its grip,

Arnold-Forster's series of abortive schemes for the reform of the Army had nearly run their course and new men of the Liberal Party were already negotiating their future portfolios. At the centre of this flurry of political expectation, there lay entrenched a triumvirate consisting of Mr Asquith, Mr Haldane and Sir Edward Grey. While the Army Council, on behalf of Balfour's government, was fending off Prince Arthur's suggestions, the King was talking to these Liberals about the next government. Haldane was at Balmoral in October 1905 and, though he had been invited to talk to the King about the Imperial Institute, he took the opportunity to disclose the triumvirate's plans to him and his Private Secretary, Lord Knollys. The King was attentive and appeared sympathetic to the idea that their nominal leader, Sir Henry Campbell-Bannerman, should be persuaded to withdraw from the contest for the premiership and retire to the House of Lords, thus paving the way to Downing Street for Asquith. Esher was also at Balmoral and Haldane noticed that he was much consulted, so he had a long talk with him too. The plan did not, at least as far as Campbell-Bannerman was concerned, come to fruition, but the episode provides an important clue to the next and curious development of Prince Arthur's career. This is to be seen in the King's easy relationship with Haldane, with whom, though he was still in opposition, he was quite willing to discuss the formation of a new government. Secondly, it is clear that Knollys was equally sympathetic and accessible to Haldane. Thirdly, Esher was evidently much in the confidence of both the King and Knollys and was anxious to be on the same footing with Haldane.[21]

Esher had a long interview with Prince Arthur on the morning of 13th December 1905 and he afterwards wrote to Knollys to describe what had passed. Ostensibly he had come to discuss the role of the Militia and he reported to Knollys that Prince Arthur's view was the same as that of other distinguished soldiers, that is, that the Militia could not be put into the field. Really, however, he had come to sound Prince Arthur on another proposition. This was the creation of a new command in the Mediterranean theatre, a supreme command apparently, which might also have some civil responsibilities attached to it. Esher wanted to know if Prince Arthur would accept such a post. Prince Arthur was not enthusiastic. He had no wish for civil responsibility and, if he did accept the command, he hoped that the military responsibilities would be clearly defined. Esher told Knollys that if Prince Arthur did unfortunately refuse this offer, Sir N. Nicholson, the Chief of the General Staff, or Sir J. French would jump at it. He evidently also put it to Prince Arthur that after one more year in the post of Inspector-General there would be no possibility of his being extended in that position. In other words, Esher offered Prince Arthur the alternatives of accepting the Mediterranean command, or of being unemployed.[22]

Arnold-Forster once complained, though only to his journal, that, when the Army Council was brought into being, Esher had 'apprised' officers of their various appointments without consulting him. It is most unlikely that, in approaching Prince Arthur about the Mediterranean command, Esher was taking a similar liberty with the new Secretary of State for War, for he and Haldane were hand in glove. Haldane had become Secretary of State for War in succession to Arnold-Forster when, after all, Campbell-Bannerman became Prime Minister following Balfour's resignation on 4th December 1905. The creation of the Mediterranean command was a matter of policy settled between Esher and Haldane from the outset of the new government's administration and, though they had put little or no thought into defining the purposes of the command, they were resolved that Prince Arthur should be persuaded, or, if necessary, coerced, into accepting it. Moreover, through Knollys, they had the King's ear, even for the vaguest of their arguments. The reasons which lay behind this curious situation are best left to emerge as the narrative develops and for the present it suffices to note that the object was to remove Prince Arthur from the centre of the Army at home, where, whether the Army Council found it agreeable or not, he exercised real influence, and to place him in a position abroad, where, beyond a somewhat glittering title, there was little substance.[23]

For the immediate future, the threat of unemployment was, however, the least of Prince Arthur's anxieties. His continuing duties as Inspector-General now demanded a visit to South Africa to report on the military situation there. Taking the Duchess and Patsy with him, he set sail in R.M.S. *Armadale Castle* from Southampton on 23rd December 1905. There were some interesting fellow passengers on board, but the only two of whom Princess Louise would have heard, Prince Arthur wrote to her, were Brigadier-General Baden-Powell and Mr Rudyard Kipling, the son of their friend of Indian days, Lockwood Kipling, who had been the inspiration of the billiard room at Bagshot Park. They arrived at Cape Town on 9th January 1906 and Prince Arthur immediately set to work on his military inspections and the civil functions, which, as usual, accompanied them.[24]

His initial impressions led him to warn the King that it would take ten

years for the effects of the war to wear off and that, in the meantime, he
saw the seeds of many troubles. The Dutch, he said, still cherished their
'insane' idea of a South African republic under their control; British rule
was much too liberal and progressive for their taste. They disliked the
South African *nouveau riche* and stuck to their narrow and old fashioned
ideas. The Germans in South-West Africa were intriguing and were
enlisting Boers, ostensibly as transport drivers, but, in reality, as armed
soldiers. The British had only 19,000 troops in the whole area, which
Prince Arthur regarded as a dangerously small number. The only hope of
averting trouble would be by nipping it in the bud and he felt there was a
need to raise and train mobile columns, which would be constantly alert
and ready to move. After travelling extensively throughout the country by
train and visiting many of the battlefields of the war, often in company
with the Boer commanders who had taken part in them, Prince Arthur
and his party left Durban, which he thought was the finest city he had
seen in South Africa, in the German steamer, *Prinz Regent*.[25]

The homeward voyage followed Africa's eastern littoral by way of
Lorenço Marques, Beira, Mozambique, Dar-es-Salaam, Zanzibar, Mom-
basa and Aden, where they visited the Prince and Princess of Wales, who
were returning from India on board H.M.S. *Renown*. Prince Arthur's
nephew inveighed against Curzon. Some of his stories of how the Viceroy
was treating Kitchener, the C-in-C in India, seemed almost incredible and
Prince Arthur thought that Curzon had perhaps gone off his head. They
passed the Suez Canal and berthed at Marseilles on 4th April. Here they
went on board *Victoria and Albert* to see the King and then left for Paris and
home. On their coastal voyage, they had made a number of inland
expeditions, including one to Nairobi, so that, in addition to what he had
seen in South Africa, Prince Arthur had greatly extended his first hand
knowledge of colonial Africa. When he got home, however, and as his
fifty-sixth birthday approached, he felt that he now had no prospects and
ought to be put aside. In real terms such an idea was, however, probably
more in Esher's than his own mind. Prince Arthur, after all, was merely
and momentarily giving way to one of his depressions, whereas Esher was
pursuing a relentless, if devious, policy.[26]

As Prince Arthur knew in his heart, there were usually compensations
for the hardships and anxieties which from time to time came his way.
One such was now at hand; he and the Duchess, taking Patsy with them,
set out for Stockholm to attend the christening of their first grandchild.
They sailed in the *Enchantress* at the beginning of June 1906 and passed

through the *Kaiser Wilhelm* canal at Kiel in seven and a half hours, which Prince Arthur found only 'fairly interesting.' As they reached the lock at the end of the canal, they met the German battleship *Wörth*, which was entering from the other end. Her guard presented arms and the crew gave the official cheer, which *Enchantress* answered with three cheers. Count Moltke, the Admiral commanding at Kiel, came off to pay his respects and, as *Enchantress* cleared the canal and entered Kiel harbour, the whole German fleet saluted. This produced a splendid effect in the darkness of the evening. Prince Arthur had finished reading *The Siege of Port Arthur*, which Léonie had given him, and he now turned to Fortescue's 'three volume' *History of the British Army,* which somebody had been misguided enough to tell him was very good. After the christening, the baby Prince Edmund was placed in Charles XII's cot, the Order of Seraphim was laid on him and the King of Sweden gave the toast to his great-grandson's health. Alas, this baby was not to live to succeed to the throne of his long-lived progenitors. After the ceremonies Prince Arthur went to see the Swedish army on manoeuvres. The operations seemed to be very realistic and the troops were well commanded, but he thought they made too much noise and that their ordnance was over-exposed. He regretted that he could not converse with the Swedish officers, as he knew no Swedish and they knew no English, French or German.[27]

Haldane and Esher were now conferring with each other as to how and when they should put their proposal for the Mediterranean command to the King. From their point of view, the time was ripe, because the King was wondering what should be done with Prince Arthur when his appointment as Inspector-General expired. Prince Arthur had told him that he would be content to retire and lead a quiet life in his own house, but the King seemed to think that this would never do and he thought it undesirable that his brother should stay at home and become a leader of society. Prince Arthur, who did not see himself as a leader of society, thought this was absurd, but he felt that the King was jealous of him for some reason which he did not understand. Prince Arthur, evidently, had not recognised the depth of feeling which must have been engendered in the King by their mother's pronounced and, not infrequently, proclaimed preference for Prince Arthur above himself; yet the King must surely have sensed, even if he was not actually told, how much she wished that the positions of the two boys could have been exchanged. For whatever reason, there is no doubt that the King did not want Prince Arthur constantly around the throne. When, therefore, Haldane came to see him in Marienbad at the end of August 1906, the King was very ready, more ready than Haldane had expected, to deal with what he and Esher had christened 'the Duke of Connaught question.' Indeed, it was the King who broached the subject of the Mediterranean command to Haldane.[28]

Esher had already primed the King on the subject, telling him that an officer of high authority, sound judgement and especially high rank, should be placed in command in the Mediterranean. He suggested that 'perhaps Your Majesty would consider the advisability of calling Mr Haldane's attention, on Your Majesty's initiative,' to the advantage of such a plan. If the officer selected was the Duke of Connaught, this would add 'éclat and prestige' to the appointment. It would also, which Esher did not explain, remove Prince Arthur, a highly popular figure in the Army, who now enjoyed immeasurable prestige in it and who had proved to be embarrassingly outspoken, from the centre to the perimeter of affairs. Prince Arthur's appointment to the Mediterranean command would suit the King, it would suit Haldane and Esher and it would suit the War Office and the Army Council.[29]

While the King, Haldane and Esher were engaged in these manoeuvres, Prince Arthur was out on military ones in the south of England collecting information for his next report as Inspector-General. Writing to the Duchess from the White Hart Hotel in Lewes on 28th August 1906, he said that he was flourishing though tired, after being out in the field for eleven hours. Nor was he expecting to see much of his bed that night, as more operations were to take place after dark. Among those watching them were the military attachés of Austria and the United States. A few days later he was in Breslau, having travelled from Berlin with Winston Churchill, for the commencement of the German manoeuvres. These began with the arrival on horseback of the Emperor, dressed in a white cuirassier uniform and bearing his baton as a Field-Marshal. That night Prince Arthur dined with the Emperor, who was in very good form and told stories which made him roar with laughter. Afterwards there was a *cercle* at which the Emperor concentrated his attention on Lord Lonsdale, who was got up in some form of fancy mediaeval uniform. It made Prince Arthur angry to see an Englishman appearing as such a guy in front of foreigners. The proceedings next day started with a parade of 40,000 men. William made Prince Arthur a Field-Marshal in the German army and they then all set off for Liegnitz, where the operations were to take place. Being well mounted, Prince Arthur succeeded in seeing a lot of what went on and he was impressed by a great improvement in German tactics, which he had thought was overdue because of the much increased range and accuracy of modern guns. He was often in company with Winston Churchill, to whom, he noticed, great civility was shown by the Germans.[30]

The King was suddenly very gracious to Prince Arthur. He was restored to his old rooms in Balmoral to the right of the entrance, with their light-coloured birch wood furniture, for the first time since 1900, when he had stayed with the Queen during her last time there. He found the King in splendid good humour. It seems that they did not discuss the Mediterranean command, but that was to come later. Meanwhile, Prince Arthur issued his third report as Inspector-General. He said that the change of government heralded yet another change of policy for the Army, but, he added, the nature of that policy had not yet been disclosed. The Army, he said, longed for some continuity in policy and the constant changes tended to sap its discipline and to undermine its confidence in those who governed its destiny. The claim that the new policies would enable a stronger and more efficient army to be put into the field seemed to relate to a strength of 150,000 men. As this was none too large a force to meet the possible requirements, Prince Arthur felt it was all the more important that it should be a force of the highest quality. For that reason, he noted with concern that, of these 150,000 men, 30,000 would have been trained only on a Militia basis. The success of the scheme, he thought, would depend upon a means being found of welding the Volunteers, Yeomanry and Militia into a unified force of even quality. He welcomed the progress which had been made in the development of a general staff, but he thought too much emphasis was being placed on its peacetime workings and not enough on how it would function in war. The German example, he suggested, had been too slavishly followed. If the requirement was for home defence only, the system might work, but Prince Arthur expected that in war, British operations would be expeditionary; wherever German operations had been expeditionary, he said, their staff work had been wanting.[31]

These ideas were highly germane to the plans for the future of the Army with which Haldane was grappling, but the Secretary of State for War, in so far as Prince Arthur was concerned, had, as a more immediate priority, the settlement of the plan for the Mediterranean command and the King was now ready to lend the necessary support for it. On 8th November 1906, Knollys told Haldane that the King would, at the proper moment, press the Duke of Connaught to accept the command and, on

13th November, when they were both at Windsor, Haldane took the opportunity to 'burst rather a bomb' by offering it to Prince Arthur. Prince Arthur told Léonie that he did not much fancy the idea of being abroad for ten months in the year for four years, but in addition to that, he had many reservations about the proposed command and he avoided any definite commitment to Haldane on the subject. The 'proper moment' had now come and, when he left Windsor on 15th November, Prince Arthur was chased by a letter from the King urging him to accept the appointment. The King asked him to 'put private feelings & your own comfort on one side by accepting this new & important post,' which had his 'entire approval.' He said that he was convinced that Prince Arthur would fill it with the greatest credit and 'Believe me,' he signed himself, 'Your very affectionate Brother Edward R & I.' Prince Arthur still hesitated and the King wrote again. He now said that he would 'deeply regret & be much disappointed' if Prince Arthur did not accept. Refusal, he said, would be a bad example to the Army and he feared that it would also close the door on any future military employment for Prince Arthur, besides giving the impression that he preferred the life of amusement, which could be found in London, to continuing the important duties of his profession.[32]

The King's expressions left Prince Arthur with very limited options. He could not turn down the appointment, as he would have liked to do; he could only seek clarification of the duties which he would be expected to undertake. Very little progress, however, had been made in this direction when his existing duties as Inspector-General, which still had over a year to run, required him to embark upon another extensive overseas tour. Once more taking the Duchess and Patsy with him, Prince Arthur travelled to Egypt, Ceylon, Singapore, Hong Kong, Canton, Penang, Rangoon, Mandalay, Calcutta and then home by Colombo, Kandy, Diyatalawa, Cairo, Port Said, Marseilles and Paris. What he saw at most of these places, Prince Arthur had seen before on his tour in 1890 and, in several cases, many times since as well.[33]

He concentrated now on noticing the changes which had taken place, carrying out his usual military inspections and also some civil functions. He was more impressed than ever by the importance of Hong Kong and its harbour, which he supposed must be the finest and largest in the world. He told the King that its strategic significance was now enormous due to the advance of Japan, the occupation of the Philippines by the United States and the near prospect of the opening of the Panama Canal. As a fortress, he thought it was of supreme importance to the Empire, especially as a naval base. He was dismayed to find that this prize was defended by no more than four very weak companies of the Third Middlesex Regiment. He suggested to the King that there should be at least a strong battalion of a thousand British infantry stationed in Hong Kong. In Singapore, he told the King that he had inspected every military unit individually as well as their barracks, hospitals and the forts. He reported that Singapore would be very difficult to defend as all the best places for guns were on the wrong side of the harbour. He thought the Sultan of Johore's troops, which he inspected on the Racecourse, looked awfully well, but he was most unimpressed by the Volunteers. Burma was new ground for Prince Arthur and he was intensely interested in what he saw in Rangoon and Mandalay. At the latter place he presented new colours to the 93rd Burmah Regiment and addressed them in Hindustani. He visited the place where King Theebaw had had seventy of his relations murdered and also the house where he and his Queens had given themselves up to General Prendergast in 1885. He received some of the ladies of the old royal family, who had survived those turbulent times, and then set off with the Duchess and Patsy by river into Upper Burma.[34]

In Calcutta, Kitchener appeared to have grown much stouter and was looking puffy, but Prince Arthur was very pleased by what he had achieved for the Native troops, whose conditions had been greatly improved and by his reorganisation of the Indian army on modern lines. He also thought that Minto was doing well as Viceroy and that he and Kitchener worked well and easily together now that the cumbersome intervention of the military members of the Viceroy's Council between them had been abolished. Indeed, much of what Prince Arthur had hoped for while he had held commands in India, had now been achieved. As always, however, the Amir of Afghanistan was the subject of much speculative discussion. The bright colours of the costumes in Kandy and the beautiful things of Ceylon proved to be in delightful contrast to the dirty white of the Bengalis. Prince Arthur sat on a chair of state, which had belonged to the Kings of Kandy, and received the Chiefs, who were dignified men with long beards and beautiful clothes. In Colombo, Prince Arthur inspected the 75th Carnatic Infantry and the Ceylon Light Infantry. He motored round the forts and watched heavy guns being fired as well as bursts by Maxim machine guns. He received a Japanese Admiral, who had arrived there flying his flag in the battleship *Tsukubi*. In Egypt, he carried out many inspections of the troops under the command

of General Bullock and went into the desert to observe a field day near
Abassiéh. Cromer was already too ill to see him.[35]

During his travels, Prince Arthur reflected upon the prospects of the
Mediterranean command, for, while he was abroad, Haldane had announced publicly that it would be created, though he did not mention any
names. Prince Arthur had come to the conclusion that the only purpose
would be to garrison Malta, Gibraltar, Cairo and Alexandria. If, however,
the troops in the Mediterranean area were to become an effective fighting
force, they would have to be trained and organised. This would cost
money, which Prince Arthur did not think the Government would be
prepared to spend. The C-in-C, he therefore thought, would be no more
than a post office and, perhaps, an inspector of garrisons. Such thoughts,
however, he confided, for the time being, to no higher an authority than
Léonie and when he saw Haldane soon after his return from abroad, he
found it difficult to make any of his points, as it was hard to get in a word
edgeways, so full of talk, mostly about other military matters, was
Haldane. Though it had been settled between the Colonial and War
Offices that the title of the post would be Field-Marshal Commanding-in-
Chief, British troops, and High Commissioner in the Mediterranean, very
little specific as to what this meant had been said to Prince Arthur when,
undoubtedly against his own better judgement but in deference to the
King's wishes, he formally accepted the appointment on 27th June
1907.[36]

A War Office memorandum, which went through several drafts
between June and September, had little to say about what the new
Commander-in-Chief's functions would be, though it dwelt at length on
matters which would not be embraced by them. The Governors of Malta
and Gibraltar would continue substantially as before, the Agent and
Consul-General in Egypt and the Sirdar there would carry on, also as
before. Local military questions in Gibraltar, Malta, Egypt, the Sudan,
Cyprus and Crete would continue to be handled by the Governors of
Malta and Gibraltar and the General-Officer-Commanding in Egypt. It
was said that matters of strategy, defence and training would be dealt with
by the new C-in-C in communication, on the one hand, with the
subordinate commanders and, on the other, with the War Office. What
was meant by questions of strategy and defence was not defined. There
was also reference to the fact that the C-in-C, when he was present,
would represent the King throughout the command and it was stated that
he would be appointed High Commissioner by the Foreign Office, though

this would be only a formality. In other words, Prince Arthur's expectation that this new command would be one without real substance was amply borne out by the instructions which now appeared.[37]

Neither Prince Arthur's expectation nor the War Office revelation were matters only of secret knowledge. The Military Correspondent of *The Times* had somehow informed himself fully and, for the most part, accurately on the subject. In a prominently placed article, which appeared on 12th August, he said that the Duke of Connaught's departure from the United Kingdom would be regretted on several counts. His well known fairness and impartiality on the Selection Board had contributed to the prestige of that body and, as Inspector-General, he had been able to keep in touch with officers and men serving at home and in the Colonies and thus to maintain his 'unequalled acquaintance' with the Army. No successor would be able quite to replace him. His 'indefatigable energy' would now be restricted to the 'comparatively unimportant' area of the Mediterranean garrisons. Having noted that the existing authorities in the Mediterranean and Egypt were to continue as before, the Military Correspondent of *The Times* observed that it was easier to explain what the new C-in-C was not going to do than to say what duties he would perform. He dismissed the suggestion that the Duke of Connaught would be consulted on strategic questions by pointing out that it would take anything up to two or three weeks for him to convey his opinions to London from wherever he might be in the Mediterranean area and that this would be 'inconvenient' in peace time and 'dangerous' in the event of war. The article also, though more gingerly, explored the motives which had led the Government to make this appointment. It said that the Duke of Connaught had not invariably been well treated during his term as Inspector-General. He had not been kept sufficiently in touch with proceedings in the War Office and his reports, 'reputed to be of much value,' had never seen the light. A former Minister, by whom, of course, Arnold-Forster was meant, had even gone so far as to suggest that the Duke of Connaught should change one of his reports.[38]

Whether or not the King read this article in *The Times*, he would certainly have heard the gist of its arguments from Prince Arthur himself. Nevertheless, at the beginning of September, he approved the terms of the War Office memorandum setting out the duties of the new post. This substantially destroyed any remaining chance Prince Arthur had of negotiating revisions and it was now left only for the Colonial Office and the War Office to conclude their agonised argument about which should

pay for the upkeep of the Palaces which Prince Arthur would inhabit and
the furniture which would be needed for them, as well as for the War
Office and the Admiralty to do the same with their similar contest about
the payment for the coal which would be burnt driving Prince Arthur
about on board ship in the Mediterranean. It was settled that Prince
Arthur would take up the Mediterranean command on 1st January 1908.[39]

On the way to this assignment, Prince Arthur and the Duchess, who
were accompanied by young Prince Arthur and Léonie Leslie, spent New
Year's Eve in Paris, where they stayed at the Ritz Hotel. In the evening
they went to the play and saw *L'Affaire des Poissons* after which, Prince
Arthur, the Duchess, Léonie and the Duchess's new lady-in-waiting,
Evie Pelly, driving in one carriage together, set off for supper at the Café
Durand in the Place Madeleine. On the way, it struck midnight and they
all sang *Auld Lang Syne* in their carriage. Next day, young Prince Arthur
and Léonie went home and Prince Arthur and the Duchess left for
Marseilles. There, on 2nd January 1908, they embarked for Malta in the
Royal Naval cruiser, *Aboukir*, which had been allocated for the use of the
Field-Marshal Commanding-in-Chief and High Commissioner in the
Mediterranean.[40]

Hardly had Prince Arthur set foot on the island than his worst fears
about the appointment began to be realised. The Governor of Malta,
General Grant, was clearly very displeased to have a figure on his doorstep
who was senior to himself and he was reluctant for Prince Arthur to see
anything of the Army, except through himself. His humour was not
improved by expulsion from the palaces of Valletta and San Antonio,
which were now required by the C-in-C. Prince Arthur felt that if he
issued an order of almost any kind, General Grant would be up in arms.
Within a few more days he concluded that there was little useful for him
to do; he was getting fat and he felt older. A small island was an awful
place for gossip. There seemed to be no reason why he should not pay a
short visit to the King of Italy and so, on 3rd February 1908, he and the
Duchess sailed for Naples. The King and Queen met them at the railway
station in Rome and in the next few days Prince Arthur was given an
insight into the Italian army which greatly interested and impressed him.
He saw a new flying machine, which they were testing, and he was struck
by how hard-working and intelligent the officers were. Even so he was not
in good form. One night when he was dining with the King and Queen,
Lady Egerton, the wife of the British Ambassador in Rome with whom the
Connaughts were staying, thought he was looking seedy. He seemed to be

very deaf and she heard that he constantly suffered from neuralgia in Malta. She was well placed to make these observations for she had been seated next to Prince Arthur. She thought he would much have preferred the company of a very good-looking Italian lady, who was in waiting. Another reason for his poor humour was that he had been given a tremendous wigging by his brother for going to see the King of Italy on the day after the assassination of the King and Crown Prince of Portugal. King Edward VII had some thoroughly Victorian traits.[41]

Despite these tribulations, Prince Arthur did try to throw himself into such duties as he had with his customary energy and the trip to Italy was no more than a minor diversion from a tour of inspection in Egypt and the Sudan which took him from Alexandria to Khartoum and back. In Cairo he had long discussions of the military position with the General-Officer-Commanding and the Agent. In addition to that, he received all the local commanding officers. As he had thought before, Prince Arthur still thought that the situation of the Sudan was very insecure. There were only six thousand British and fifteen thousand Egyptian troops there and he felt that the whole area might easily be set ablaze. His own luck still seemed to be out. Having taken the Agent's wife, Lady Gorst, in to dinner in Cairo, he was just turning to speak to his other neighbour, Lady Edward Cecil, when a waiter trying to serve her, struck him a heavy blow on the head with a large silver salver. It knocked him quite silly and gave him a headache which lasted several days. As usual, however, Prince Arthur enjoyed being in the Sudan; he liked the people there; they looked him straight in the face and he found them manly. On the way back to Cairo he visited the Tombs of the Kings where he found Lord Carnarvon working on his excavations. So far, he had found nothing of note.[42]

In Gibraltar, Prince Arthur watched the 9.2″ guns being fired at night for the first time in an exercise designed to test the shore defence against naval attack. The whole rock shook and he was impressed by the efficiency with which the searchlights found their targets. He also watched field firing of Maxim machine guns and he saw a newly introduced American rifle, which he thought was a very handy weapon. While he was in Gibraltar, Prince Arthur heard of the death of Sir Henry Campbell-Bannerman, that the King had sent for Asquith and that Lloyd George would be the Chancellor of the Exchequer, which latter, he thought, rather surprisingly perhaps, would be a good appointment. With his characteristic generosity and lack of vindictive feeling, he regretted the expected departure of Haldane from the War Office and he only hoped that Margot, now that her husband was Prime Minister, would do nothing foolish.[43]

At the end of April 1908, there were three days of military and naval manoeuvres in the Mediterranean command. A complete infantry brigade was embarked in H.M.S. *Aboukir* and three other warships in the Grand Harbour of Malta and then, escorted by six naval vessels, they sailed in convoy to Melheiha Bay on the north-east corner of the island, where, in the dead of night and without any lights, the troops were disembarked and waded ashore over a distance of a mile onto an open beach. During the landing the men were covered by four torpedo boats. Prince Arthur went ashore with the assault force and marched with it to occupy the high ground above the Bay, which was defended by two companies of the 60th Rifles and a section of cyclists. These operations concluded the active military season of the command and Prince Arthur prepared to come home on leave, though, much to his surprise, the King expressed displeasure at this prospect. Before leaving Malta, however, Prince Arthur despatched his first report to the Army Council on the opening phase of the Mediterranean command.[44]

In this report Prince Arthur said that he conceived it to have been the Government's intention when it created the command that there should be a co-ordination of the subordinate commands under one executive head. He reckoned that this could not be effectively achieved, if only because the postal services between the components of the command, Malta, Gibraltar, Crete and Egypt, were intermittent and irregular. This meant that, if vexatious delays in communicating with the War Office were to be avoided, he, as C-in-C, had to allow wide discretion to the subordinate commanders as to their doing so directly without consulting, let alone being directed by, him. He also pointed out that, under the new arrangements, there was a Field-Marshal Commanding-in-Chief, a General-Officer-Commanding-in-Chief, Gibraltar, a Lieutenant-General-Officer-Commanding-in-Chief, Malta, a General-Officer-Commanding, Egypt, and another in Cyprus and that all these officers had under their several commands no more than eighteen thousand British soldiers. The length and detail of the comments which followed on all the elements of the command over which Prince Arthur theoretically presided, showed that he had considered virtually every aspect from the strategic purpose to the health and accommodation of the troops, but there was nothing in the report which in any way diminished the force of its opening passages, which were to the clear effect that there was no room in the Mediterranean for a supreme commander with such a brief as he had been given.[45]

Nor, despite minor modifications in his directive, did anything happen in the following year to lead Prince Arthur to modify this verdict. His presence in the Mediterranean made Malta more the centre of the world than it would otherwise have been, for, in addition to visits from the King and the German Emperor, a stream of other notables came to see him there. But this was of no strategic consequence and, by the end of 1908, Prince Arthur had concluded that his only achievements in the Mediterranean were that he had infused rather more energy and discipline into the troops, that he had somewhat raised the standards of training and that he had encouraged the Army and the Navy to pull more closely together. These were not negligible improvements, but they were certainly not an adequate result from the creation of such a high sounding appointment. Prince Arthur believed that, as Field-Marshal Commanding-in-Chief, he was no more than a fifth wheel in the coach. As he believed, too, that his appointment was not only useless, but also, because of confusion in the chain of command, that it might be positively dangerous in time of war, he now saw it as his duty, as well as his wish, to resign. From his point of view the only remaining important question was how this might most conveniently be done without upsetting the King and Government and, if possible, destroying his own military career.[46]

At first it seemed that the King at least would be sympathetic. When he came to Malta in April 1909, Prince Arthur told him of the difficulties which bedevilled his command and showed him a draft of a letter which, in due course, he proposed to send to the Army Council. The King seemed to concur in Prince Arthur's point of view and said that he had always thought the command could not be made to work, but that he had been persuaded against his better judgement. He added that he thought that the authorities had not liked Prince Arthur's reports as Inspector-General and had been anxious to get him out of the country. If that is really what the King had thought, it is curious that he had acquiesced; at any rate, Prince Arthur clearly thought it was. The King, however, was soon to return to the camp of acquiescence.[47]

At the beginning of June 1909, when he was on leave in London, Prince Arthur sent the letter, which he had discussed in draft with the King, to the Army Council. In it he stated unequivocally that the Mediterranean command had proved to be a failure. The three components of it were distinct and unconnected in their systems of military defence and the attempt to combine them was undesirable. The geographical distances between them and the poor communications which existed also made their co-ordination impossible. The size of the forces in the area did not justify the superimposition of a C-in-C over the local commanders. Prince Arthur reminded the Army Council of the doubts which he had had from the outset, but he said he had decided to suppress them in the cause of taking up the responsibilities for which the Government had nominated him. In the light of the experience he had now gained of the real possibilities, however, and because it seemed to him that the multiplication of command involved might have dangerous consequences, he felt he could now no longer accept responsibility for arrangements of which he did not approve.[48]

The Army Council seemed unable to think of any substantial arguments in favour of a continuation of the command, but they told Prince Arthur that his occupation of it enabled him to be on leave in England during the summer and that this, in turn, made it possible for him to preside over the Selection Board. If he gave up the Mediterranean command he would become inactive and, as such, would be ineligible to sit on the Board. The threat was not veiled at all. Haldane, who was, after all, still at the War Office, took a rather different line. He saw the King and told him that the Mediterranean command must continue and that the Duke of Connaught must remain in it. The King arranged for him to meet Prince Arthur at Windsor and there Haldane gained, or thought he had gained, the impression that Prince Arthur had not yet decided to resign the Mediterranean command and he subsequently wrote to him that the Government could not consider its abolition so soon after it had been created. He also warned Prince Arthur that if he did resign, he could not continue as President of the Selection Board. Though the draft which Haldane made of this letter showed that he had encountered much difficulty in deciding exactly how to word it, there was no doubt that the final version contained the same threat made by the Army Council, to wit, that resignation of the Mediterranean command would mean the ending of Prince Arthur's active military career.[49]

Such an outcome was probably the severest penalty which the Government could inflict on Prince Arthur and he did not at once accept it as inevitable. He told Haldane that he could not understand how their short conversation at Windsor could have been construed as Haldane had done, for he had said nothing to suggest that he had changed his mind about the Mediterranean command. He thought that the Army Council really agreed with his view and he wondered why the Government could not now say that, in the light of experience, they had decided to scrap the command. If they did so, he did not believe there would be any criticism; certainly, he said, there would be none from the Army or the Navy. He appealed to Haldane to show him sympathy and support in acting on a decision which he believed was in the best interests of the Army, to whose service he had devoted his life. At this of all moments, Prince Arthur found himself sitting between Haldane and Esher at a dinner in the Ritz Hotel in London. Esher tried to draw him but Prince Arthur managed to prevent him raising the question of the Mediterranean command. He had less success with Haldane, who began on the question of the letter which Prince Arthur had just written to him. Prince Arthur got the impression that Haldane did not understand the position, but that, having got himself committed, he could not now admit that an expensive mistake had been made. He, therefore, came away without much hope that the Government would see his point of view and he thought he was, as a result, in for a serious row with the King. All the same, he felt that he ought not to give in.[50]

As to Haldane, Prince Arthur read the situation correctly. So far from sympathising with Prince Arthur, Haldane wrote, after the dinner at the Ritz, that the Mediterranean command must stand, on the ground of high strategy and its importance in the developing concept of the defence of the Empire. He even claimed that its importance was greater than the Government had originally envisaged. He said again that Prince Arthur could not remain on the Selection Board if he resigned the command. Prince Arthur replied that the consideration of the Selection Board could not be used to induce him to change his mind about the Mediterranean command. And so the die was cast; or almost so. As to the King, however, Prince Arthur's expectation also proved to be correct, for it seems that Knollys and Haldane had seen to it that there was no reversion on his part to the views he had expressed to Prince Arthur while on his visit to Malta. Indeed, the King was shown Haldane's slightly absurd letter about the Mediterranean command before it was sent to Prince Arthur and he approved it.[51]

On 8th July 1909 the King saw Prince Arthur and told him to go and talk to Knollys about the Mediterranean command. Knollys, displaying a condescension, which is a characteristic of courtiers of the lower quality, and advancing rapidly into territory of which he had little or no understanding, told Prince Arthur that a public servant should not resign for the reasons which he had given if the Government thought that would be detrimental, and that, if he did so, he would suffer from a personal point of view. Prince Arthur, needless to say, was not diverted by such talk. He told Knollys that if the King ordered him to do so, he would remain in the command; if he did not, he would not. Thus, Prince Arthur retained his integrity and regained the initiative, for the King was not prepared to issue any such order. On 22nd July Prince Arthur sent in a formal letter to the Army Council resigning the Mediterranean command. Their acceptance of it, Prince Arthur was told at once, meant that he could not remain on the Selection Board. Prince Arthur's active career in the Army, which had extended for a period of forty-two years, was over.[52]

CHAPTER 14

In the Shade 1909-1911

THE TRIUMVIRATE OF ESHER, Haldane and Knollys, by making the issue of the Mediterranean command seem to be one of major strategic importance, had engineered the termination of Prince Arthur's active career in the Army and, surprisingly, they had done this with the concurrence of the King. Indeed, without that concurrence, as the subsequent history of this vexed question indicates, their plan would probably have come to nought. Having thus disposed of Prince Arthur, they then sought to apply the same dose of immunisation to the next most prestigious active soldier in the Army, Lord Kitchener, whose term as C-in-C, India, was now coming to an end. There would be no need for us to consider this development were it not for the revelation which it affords of the extreme brittleness of the connection between the expressed views of the triumvirate about the Mediterranean command and any strategic or military realities. As this revelation is the ultimate justification of Prince Arthur's decision to resign the Mediterranean command, we must notice, if only briefly, what happened.

Even before Prince Arthur had submitted his formal resignation, Haldane wrote to Kitchener offering him the command and telling him that the King and the Prime Minister had approved the suggestion. When Kitchener expressed his doubts, the King, as he had done in Prince Arthur's case, intervened directly. He cabled to Kitchener, who was in Simla, pressing him to accept Haldane's offer, which, he said, was strongly supported by himself and his Ministers. He added that he took a personal interest in the outcome and that he attached great importance to Kitchener's acceptance. This produced the same result as it had done with Prince Arthur; it left Kitchener with very little option and, despite his continued scepticism as to the utility of the command, he accepted it, though only for a short term and on condition that the powers given to him were radically revised by comparison with what had been entrusted to Prince Arthur. No one, however, seemed to feel that there was any urgency about the command being taken up and it still had not been when Kitchener came to see the King on 28th April 1910, nearly ten months after Haldane had originally offered the command to him. Kitchener came away from his audience saying that the King had absolved him from his promise to accept the command and eight days after that, before much more could be said, the King died. Shortly thereafter the Mediterranean command was scrapped.[1]

Years later, after Kitchener had been drowned, his Military Secretary of Indian days, the officer who subsequently became Field-Marshal Lord Birdwood, recalled how surprised they had been when Haldane and the King pressed Kitchener to take over the Mediterranean command from the Duke of Connaught. They assumed that the ploy was to keep Kitchener out of the country, but, in view of the King's direct intervention, they felt it was impossible to refuse. The plot, indeed, had unfolded in almost precisely the same way as it had done for Prince Arthur, and, no doubt, with the same motives in mind. There was a reflection, too, of what the King had said to Prince Arthur on the royal yacht in Malta in April 1909, though, in Kitchener's case, he seems to have gone farther and advised against the command on the ground that it was a 'damn rotten one.'[2]

Whether Birdwood's recollection of what Kitchener had said the King had said was exactly accurate or not, the fact remained that the Mediterranean command, that 'astute invention' as it was dubbed in the *Morning Post*, was a sham, devised, not as a means of achieving strategic advantages or military reforms, but as one of marooning, in turn, the two most prestigious active soldiers in the British army, who were not required on board by Esher, Haldane and Knollys and by the King himself. Thus, the ground was cleared for Esher's object of dissolving the Army's voice into the advice of a dependent Council to secure the 'absolute military autocracy' of the Secretary of State for War. The result was to cast Prince Arthur and Kitchener into the shade but, through the ironies of such situations, it was also to lead both in the direction of higher places and greater achievements than either of them, as Field-Marshals, could have aspired to reach had they remained active in the Army.[3]

We can now return to the closing months of the reign of King Edward VII, whose first proposal for the solution of the Connaught question was that his brother should go to Ireland as Lord-Lieutenant. When, however, Asquith demurred, because he could not think what to do with the

THE SHAM COMMAND.

LORD ESHER (to Mr. Haldane) : "Kitchener is taking the same line as the Duke of Connaught. You will have to fall back on one of the red-tape men after all."

["*Express*" *cartoons—sixty in booklet form—at all bookstalls, and from the "Daily Express," 23, St. Bride-street, E.C. Sixpence.*]

The Daily Express's *view of the Mediterranean command. Left to right: Prince Arthur, Kitchener, Esher, Haldane.*

incumbent, Lord Aberdeen, the King took up a much more interesting suggestion. In January 1910 he met at dinner Sir Thomas Shaughnessy, an American by birth, but now a towering Canadian figure. Shaughnessy remarked to the King that he hoped a worthy successor would be found for Lord Grey as Governor-General of Canada; the King answered that there would be no disappointment as the choice would probably fall upon a member of the Royal Family. Shaughnessy, of course, drew the inference that this would be the Duke of Connaught and that, indeed, is what the King was planning. In the meantime he saw no objection to Prince Arthur going abroad on a safari expedition in East Africa.[4]

On 13th February 1910, Prince Arthur and the Duchess, accompanied by Arthur II, as his mother called him, and Patsy, together with a lady-in-waiting, Evie Pelly, an A.D.C., Captain Bulkeley, and a doctor, Captain Brackenridge, left Nairobi by train for Naivasha, where they went into camp at the beginning of the safari. It was no mean thing; there was a huge Indian Cawnpur tent, which served as the mess, and there was a row of eight green tents, each furnished with a bed, mosquito net, table, mirror, chair and, behind a partition, a large canvas bath and tripod washstand. These were allocated to the seven in Prince Arthur's party and the eighth was for Captain Riddell, who was the organiser of the safari. Numerous carriers brought the baggage in and while, this was being sorted, Patsy began to sketch and the Duchess rode out on a pony with Evie, Bulkeley and Riddell. They dressed for dinner and all were in bed by 9.0. in readiness for an early start the next morning. The first day of operations yielded a shot at a Grant gazelle for the Duchess, which she missed; Prince Arthur shot a kongoni, or Coke's Hartebeeste, and Arthur II a hare. Patsy sketched.[5]

On 16th February the camp at Naivasha was struck and the safari moved off under Captain Riddell's command. Prince Arthur's standard was carried at the head of the column and then came a drummer, who was followed by two headmen, seven Somali gun-bearers, three hundred and eight porters, fifty-six porter *totos*, or boys, fifteen askaris, or military police, ten personal boys, who acted both as valets and maids, four cooks, eleven syces, or grooms, seven mule boys, two Masai and two Kikuyu runners, eleven ponies and thirteen mules. The royal party, accompanied by Mr Perceval, the white hunter, boarded a train, which had been specially stopped, and travelled to Gilgil, where the second camp was established. That night fires sprang up all round them, lit, it was supposed, by Natives. Beating them out produced what Prince Arthur described as a veritable Valhalla. Thereafter, until 22nd April, when their thirty-eighth and final camp was struck and they returned to Nairobi, there were many adventures and several new experiences, including, for the Duchess, the cutting of Prince Arthur's hair and the trimming of the beard which he had grown. There were also one or two anxieties. Patsy suddenly developed a temperature of 101.2°, but the doctor gave her a massive dose of castor oil which put her right. Arthur II came back to camp one day, shaking and shouting, his eyes staring out of his head and his nose bleeding. It seemed there had been a terrible accident, but all that had happened was that he had shot a rhino. Prince Arthur, who found these animals virtually bullet proof, came across a game trap and was very glad he had not fallen into it; the Duchess's pony slipped while crossing a stream and gave her a good ducking and, at another stage, her leg reverted to its nasty old tricks.[6]

Around N'gare N'dare Prince Arthur was particularly struck by the size of the country and the vast possibilities which it contained. The soil was excellent, the climate fine and he began to think that money and water could achieve almost anything. He was impressed too by the native population at Miru Bama. Though the Government regarded these people as dangerous, Prince Arthur found them to be most friendly. There were, he reckoned, some 280,000 Miru people and he thought they were a fine race. The men wore khaki coloured togas, festooned on one shoulder and they carried spears or long staffs and, in some cases, swords. The women were nude to the waist, below which they wore tanned leather aprons, some with patches of beads sewn on and their arms were adorned with brass hoops. They had good figures and carried themselves well, but alas, Prince Arthur wrote to Léonie they were beasts of burden for the men and were used to carrying up to a hundred and eighty pounds each. They too were interested in their visitors, for hardly any European women had been seen before in this part of the world. The men, dancing stark naked, put on a wonderful display, which included great leaps into the air performed with remarkable precision. On 7th April, at the twenty-eighth camp near the Rupengazi river, Prince Arthur despatched a runner to Nairobi bearing a telegram to the King saying that he had received a letter from the Prime Minister offering him the appointment of Governor-General of Canada and that he had accepted.[7]

On 5th May 1910, Prince Arthur's party reached Suez on their homeward voyage. The other passengers had to walk past a doctor or lady doctor to see if they had the plague, but Captain Brackenridge gave the royal party a clean bill of health and they were excused this indignity. Mail was brought on board and among it was a letter for Prince Arthur from Princess Louise; it told him that Bertie had not recovered well from the influenza he had caught in Biarritz and Paris. On 6th May they reached Port Said and, as they did so, Prince Arthur was thrown into a great state of alarm by the Captain of their ship coming up to him and offering condolences on the death of the King. Bulkeley was sent ashore to make enquiries and he presently returned with the news that the King had indeed died. The Duchess was caught at a disadvantage; for the first time in her life, she thought, she had left home without taking mourning clothes with her. Prince Arthur decided that they would now go home with all speed.[8]

The new King and Queen were at the station to meet them when they arrived in London on 13th May. They drove straight to Buckingham

Palace where there was a painful meeting with Queen Alexandra. The late King's coffin had been kept open so that Prince Arthur could see him for the last time; he looked calm and natural. Prince Arthur then went with the new King to Marlborough House, where they sat talking until nearly midnight. There was much to settle, including the question of who should now go to South Africa to inaugurate the first Union Parliament. Edward VII had intended his son to go as Prince of Wales, but George V now felt that his son could not take his place as he was in the midst of his studies at the Royal Naval College. The mantle duly fell upon Prince Arthur's shoulders. Undoubtedly, from the first, there was a relationship of the closest cordiality and mutual trust between the new Sovereign and his uncle. The fading from the King's favour of both Esher and Knollys removed what might have been an obstacle to this happy situation.

Though his bad knee restricted his activities somewhat, Prince Arthur thoroughly enjoyed his first visit of the new reign to Balmoral. He was given his usual rooms near the entrance hall, except that he had to give up the dressing room, which had been allocated to Sir George Reid, the Australian High Commissioner, who was too fat to get up stairs. He felt that the King and Queen could not have been kinder to him and he was clearly flattered when he learned that they intended to come specially to London to see him off when he left for South Africa.[10]

As part of his preparation for this mission, Prince Arthur got Rudyard Kipling to set down notes on some of the leading personalities with whom he was likely to have dealings. For the most part they were not very encouraging. Abe Bailey was described as a multi-millionaire and an unscrupulous financier, Burton, who had a seat in the Union Parliament, was said to be a bitter-tongued anti-British politician without many manners and very much on the make. De Villiers was old, but, though disguised as an impartial judge, he was an astute politician who did not commit himself beyond generalisations. Patrick Duncan was a member of Milner's *Kindergarten*. He was a Balliol man, who had once been an optimist and a great believer in the virtues of the South African Union. Kipling thought that he was now probably more enlightened. Kipling suggested that the Transvaal Dutch were uneasy about the Prime Minister, Botha, whose liberalism, advocacy of conciliation, encouragement of immigration and opposition to racialism, did not suit their book at all.[11]

On the voyage out to Cape Town, Prince Arthur learned by heart the speech he was to deliver from the throne, but before he came to that point

THE MALTESE WALL-FLOWER.

H.R.H. the Duke of Connaught (*aside to* Lord Kitchener). "GOT MY HANDS PRETTY FULL. YOU'RE STANDING OUT, I SEE."

Lord Kitchener. "YES, SIR. I MIGHT HAVE HAD YOUR LATE PARTNER, MISS MEDITERRANEA, BUT—WELL, YOU KNOW WHAT *SHE'S* LIKE."

Mr Punch's view of the Mediterranean command and the Governor-Generalship of South Africa and Canada as seen by Prince Arthur (left) and Kitchener.

of his mission, there were functions galore, which followed one another
so quickly that the Duchess even failed for a few days to keep a journal
and Prince Arthur thought that, by comparison, the Delhi Durbar had
been child's play. The birthday of the Union of South Africa's Parliament
was 4th November 1910. The weather was splendid and everything
looked its best. From an early hour, large crowds gathered on the royal
route from Government House to the Parliament building along which
Prince Arthur and the Duchess drove at the end of a procession of
carriages. The Duchess wore a pretty black dress, a large hat and pearl
ornaments, the white ribbon of the Order of Victoria and Albert and
miniature orders on her shoulder. Prince Arthur wore his full dress Field-
Marshal's uniform with jack-boots and white breeches, the collar of the
Garter and the riband of the Order of St Michael and St George. In the
Parliament building they processed to the throne on which Prince Arthur
took his seat. The Duchess and Patsy sat on his left and Lord Gladstone,
the Governor-General of South Africa, on his right. The national anthem
was played, salutes were fired from the Fort and by H.M.S. *Defence*,
which had escorted Prince Arthur on the last stage of his voyage. Prayers
were read by the Archbishop of Cape Town and then by the Moderator of
the Dutch Church, after which Prince Arthur declared Parliament open.
In the afternoon he attended a magnificent pageant, on land which had
been reclaimed from the sea, in which the history of South Africa was
enacted by 6,200 performers. That night there was a grand dinner and, on
the next day, Prince Arthur laid the foundation stone of the University of
Cape Town.[12]

Prince Arthur saw his mission as being one of conciliation and he knew
that he must make no distinction in race or feeling and that he must not
spare himself in his efforts to promote harmony. He formed a strong
friendship with the Prime Minister, Botha, whose tact and good sense
would, he believed, moderate the burning question of language. At least,
he hoped, no one would be forced to learn the other's language. He
believed too that Botha would seek to relieve the lot of the native
populations and that the Indian question could be settled on lines which
were acceptable to the Imperial government. Subsequent history was to
show that in all these expressions Prince Arthur veered heavily on the side
of over-optimism, but there is no doubt that he exerted every possible
influence he possessed and a huge physical effort as well to improve the
prospects of the new Union of South Africa. The Governor-General
thought that the tour had worked wonders and he told Prince Arthur that

it had been a brilliant success. Botha telegraphed to the same effect. Prince Arthur himself believed that his mission had done good, but when he got back to Durban to embark for home after a vast train journey through much of the Union and Rhodesia, he felt that the strain had been too hard and too continuous and that he could not have stood another week of it.[13]

To the accompaniment of tremendous cheering, the national anthem and masses of tug and pleasure boats crowded with people, the royal party sailed from Durban in *Balmoral Castle* on 3rd December 1910. Prince Arthur found it nice to have a quiet dinner, the first he had enjoyed for six weeks. He was not, however, inactive for long and a few days later he transferred to the escort vessel, H.M.S. *Defence*. She was of sixteen thousand tons and could do twenty-four knots. She carried a crew of eight hundred and conditions below were cramped and very hot; the temperature in the stoke hole was 160° and the stokers were 'rather suffering.' Prince Arthur and the Duchess went ashore in Freetown, where the streets were lined with enormous crowds of negroes cheering, clapping, shouting, grinning and laughing. The women jumped and waved their arms in delight, joyously showing rows of splendid white teeth, and the trees were full of men and boys. When they got back on board their ship, the Duchess recorded that the day had been the 'most quaint, picturesque & amusing of the whole trip.'[14]

When he arrived home a few days after Christmas, Prince Arthur went to stay with the King at Sandringham. He was put up in the only spare room in York Cottage, which was awfully small, but the King continued to live there, so as not to disturb his mother in the big house. Prince Arthur found that the King was planning to go to India for his Coronation Durbar and that he was being advised that while he was abroad, his uncle should be at home. This raised the question of what was to happen about Canada, which Prince Arthur certainly did not want to give up. He felt that he was still young enough to be of service to his country and he did not think it was sufficient for him to do nothing beyond a few functions at home with the occasional mission to a European sovereign thrown in. He wished to occupy a public position in which he could do good for the Crown and Empire. The Duchess and all his friends thought that he ought to go to Canada and that is what he now wished to do, even if he did have to come home temporarily while the King was in India.[15]

The King, who, from the outset, showed marked signs of being his own man, was not much impressed by alarmist ideas of what might happen if he and the Duke of Connaught were out of the country at the same time and, when Prince Arthur came to Windsor in January 1911, it was soon settled with Asquith that he should go to Canada in the late summer or early autumn. The Canadian Government welcomed the proposal and Prince Arthur's appointment as Governor-General was quickly formalised. The only objector seemed to be Queen Mary, who wrote to her Aunt Augusta that as Uncle Arthur had to go to Canada, 'poor George really has no one to help him.' Even so, the Queen recognised that the matter had been pressed and Canada would be delighted.[16]

Certainly, if the Canadian Prime Minister was a guide to Canadian opinion, that was so. As the oldest servant of the Crown in Canada, Sir Wilfrid Laurier wrote to Prince Arthur that he wished to be the first of His Majesty's Canadian subjects to convey the gratification they felt at the appointment and he placed his 'poor services' at Prince Arthur's command, not only in his official capacity, but in any respect which might be thought useful. All the same, there were many people in Britain who thought it was a mistake for Prince Arthur to go to Canada. The King was at the very outset of his reign and it could scarcely have begun at a more difficult time. There was an acute crisis in the matter of home rule for Ireland and an equally serious one in connection with the powers of the House of Lords. International relations, though apparently less immediately threatening than these constitutional issues, were in many respects unpromising and dangerous. It is hardly surprising that the King complained that his position in these opening months of his reign was a purgatory. Some, including his Aunt, Princess Louise, thought that he was not managing very well and, though Prince Arthur did not share that opinion, he distrusted Esher, who was still about the Court, and he thought that Knollys, whom the King had inherited as the principal private secretary, and whom he knew was a bosom friend of Esher's, was old and tired and not a good advisor. In all the circumstances, Prince Arthur thought it would be a mistake for the King to go to India and he hoped that Kitchener would have used the opportunity provided by a visit to Balmoral in September 1911 to persuade him to give up the idea.[17]

When, however, Prince Arthur arrived at Balmoral at the end of September, he found that the King, having been urged by the Government to stick to the plans, had no intention of giving up his Indian visit and that he also turned down a suggestion from the Secretary of State for the Colonies that Prince Arthur's departure for Canada should be delayed until the new government there had settled in. Sir Wilfrid Laurier's

Liberal government had been defeated in the general election and a Conservative administration was being formed under the premiership of Mr Robert Borden. Prince Arthur was greatly impressed by the sense of what the King said to him about the decisions which had been made and his mind was relieved of the anxieties he had felt about the possible ill effects of his departure for Canada and of the King going to India.[18]

For the past several months Prince Arthur had been briefing himself about Canadian affairs and, since his appointment as Governor-General had been decided upon, he had been in regular correspondence with the reigning Governor-General, Lord Grey, and, in addition to that, he already had a considerable first-hand knowledge of the country. In the Colonial Office, however, there was some feeling that these qualifications might not be sufficient and that words of wisdom and instruction should be added by the Secretary of State, Mr Harcourt. The civil servants involved found the problem rather daunting. They had difficulty in deciding whether or not it was customary to issue instructions to Governors-General designate, but, having in the end decided that it was, they wondered how the situation would be affected by the fact that, in this case, the man in question was a royal Duke. Such a personage after all had never before been a Governor-General and in the Colonial Office matters which were without precedent were rather unwelcome. They were not even sure of the correct manner in which to address Prince Arthur in a letter. Nor did Mr Harcourt's magisterial ruling that 'I mean to treat the Duke of Connaught exactly as I do any other Governor' help very much, because he had little or no idea how he did treat other Governors. At last it was decided to lay down for Prince Arthur's benefit the Colonial Office's view of some of the subtleties inherent in the Governor-General's position, lying as it did between the interests of the Empire in general and of Canada in particular. He was to assent to or reserve Canadian Acts of Parliament. If he reserved them, the Acts became subject to the King's pleasure, which meant, in effect, the view of the Imperial government, or, in other words, that of the British Government. The issues which might call for reservation were international treaties, merchant shipping, discrimination against Asiatics and appeals from the Canadian Supreme Court to the Privy Council. It was recognised in the Colonial Office that reservation was undesirable and that a better solution was to head off undesirable bills in advance.[19]

As we shall see in due course, these instructions had little or no bearing upon Prince Arthur's conduct as Governor-General of Canada; in many respects they were obsolete before they were issued and in others they became irrelevant as the course of Canadian affairs developed. They did, however, underline the extent to which there was a certain delicacy in the position of a Governor-General, especially, perhaps, a royal one, and how nationalist feeling in a self-governing dominion might be affronted by his very existence. Nevertheless, the Imperial ideal, enshrined in the concept of a British Empire composed of increasing numbers of self-governing dominions linked together by a common allegiance to the Crown, but otherwise virtually free agents, was in great esteem, indeed, probably at its zenith, and nowhere more so than in Canada.

Being a member of the Royal Family gave Prince Arthur an immense and unique advantage as a Governor-General who might identify the Crown with the government of Canada and engender in the people a sense of personal allegiance to it. His tact, charm, great conviction and fluency in public speaking and his high standing as a soldier and public servant added an extra dimension to his royal rank, which was also unique. Lord Grey fully recognised the great potential which these aspects provided for the prospects of his successor, but, as Lord Grey also recognised, those very qualities also offered hazards. Some Canadians feared that a royal Governor-General would bring a stiff etiquette to Canada, which might be all very well in London, but would hardly do in Ottawa and that there would be altogether too much pomp and ceremony. As in all the Dominions, there was the ever present suspicion of being patronised by the British. In Canada in 1911 these were big questions, for, as yet, it was 'undiscovered by the rest of the world and unknown to itself' and the people were 'neither American nor English, nor even sure what they wanted to be.' Over this 'unborn mightiness' there stood a great question mark.[20]

Correspondingly, as the interlude of shade between the end of Prince Arthur's long military career and his term of office as Governor-General of Canada came to an end, a question mark stood against what was to be the most important element of his place in history. His objects at least were plain enough; he hoped, he wrote in a farewell letter to the King, that his time in Canada might be a success and that he would be able to do all he wished to promote the best interests and prosperity of the great Dominion and also of the Empire.[21]

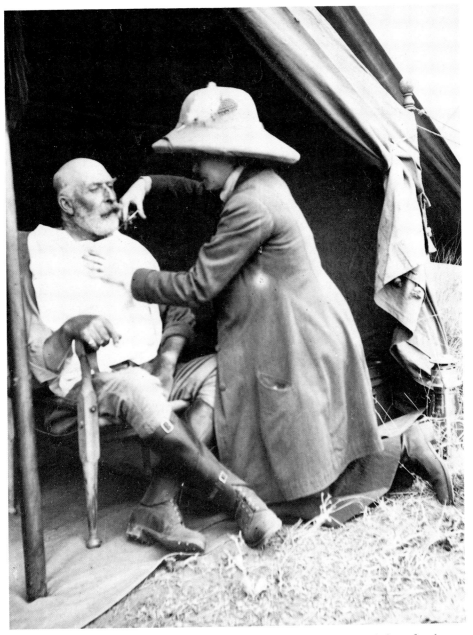

36. '... there were many adventures and several new experiences, including, for the Duchess, the cutting of Prince Arthur's hair and the trimming of the beard which he had grown.' (p. 260)

37. *The funeral of King Edward VII, 20th May 1910. The new King George V rides slightly ahead of, on his left, Prince Arthur and, on his right, mounted on a white horse, the German Emperor William II.*

38. *Prince Arthur and, to his left, the Duchess and Princess Patricia, at the opening of the first Union Parliament of South Africa, 4th November 1910.*

39. *The Duke and Duchess of Connaught returning from South Africa on board H.M.S. Balmoral Castle, December 1910.*

CHAPTER 15

First in the Land
of the Premier Dominion
1911-1913

AT NOON ON 13th October 1911, Prince Arthur was sworn in as Governor-General of Canada. The ceremony, which he told the King was simple and dignified, took place in the Senate chamber at Quebec, which was handsomely decorated for the occasion and crammed with representative Canadians, including the whole Ministries of the Dominion and the Province as well as legal, military and religious leaders. The Dominion Prime Minister, Mr Robert Borden, and his Cabinet then entertained the new Governor-General and the Duchess to lunch at the Chateau Frontenac, where they sat down about a hundred. Prince Arthur found it very strange walking in to this entertainment ahead of the Duchess; etiquette demanded that he should do so, for he was now the first in the land of the premier Dominion.[1]

This event brought Prince Arthur to the summit of his career, for none of his previous appointments nor any of his subsequent functions were of such high importance as the five years in which he was to serve Canada as the first royal Governor-General of any Dominion within the British Empire. Indeed, much of history's verdict upon his public service at large must turn upon how his Governor-Generalship of Canada is judged. The trial was not an easy one; Prince Arthur's royal birth heightened the intensity of the spotlight which played upon the Crown in Canada. While it increased public interest in, and popular enthusiasm for, the person of the Governor-General in a country where loyalty to the Crown was most pronounced, it also sharpened the suspicions of those who resented the British Imperial influence or had large ideas of their own destinies.

Canada too, in 1911, stood at many thresholds. Her relationship with the United States was yet to be settled on amicable lines, her coast to coast transcontinental railway system was introducing new political, economic and cultural possibilities, she was beset with the old friction between French and English and Catholic and Protestant elements and the newer one of immigration from China, Japan and India as well as many European countries, and she was in an accelerating phase in the development of her self-governing status. In addition to these matters, which had been occupying Prince Arthur's mind for the past several months, there was another, which had come very suddenly and, to his predecessor, Lord Grey, surprisingly. This was the defeat of Sir Wilfrid Laurier's Liberal Government in the general election which had taken place shortly before Prince Arthur's departure from England. The new Conservative Government under Borden had scarcely any ministerial experience whatever.

Even before he was sworn in as Governor-General, Prince Arthur was involved in a seemingly unimportant incident which was, nevertheless, later used to fuel a myth about his conduct as Governor-General. Normally, but not invariably, the outgoing Governor-General left the country before the incoming one arrived and this Lord Grey had intended to do. Because of the change of Government, however, he had postponed his departure and when the *Empress of Ireland*, with Prince Arthur on board, tied up in Quebec after dark on the evening of 12th October, he was still there. Naturally, in these circumstances, he came on board to welcome his successor and old friend of boyhood days. Lady Grey came too and the Duchess was also there as they sat talking in Prince Arthur's cabin. Prince Arthur then escorted the Greys back to their yacht, which the next day was to take them to their ship for the voyage back to England. What was discussed is a matter of supposition, but Dr Haycock, the biographer of Colonel Sam Hughes, whom Borden had just appointed Minister of Militia and Defence, has convinced himself that one of the topics was Sam Hughes and that Grey had 'no doubt' expressed 'substantial reservations about Sam Hughes as Minister of Militia.' Dr Haycock also invests the meeting with an air of conspiracy by saying that Grey came aboard the *Empress of Ireland* 'secretly.' Dr Haycock is satisfied that whatever else may have taken place between 'the two aristocrats,' Connaught was 'not long' in portraying Hughes as an impossible fellow. He says that Hughes claimed that Connaught had snubbed him on the first of his days as the Governor-General and he asserts that their relationship had got off to a bad start. Clearly, Dr Haycock thinks that Prince Arthur was severely prejudiced against Sam Hughes even before he had met him and that his attitude to him went downhill from there on. Developing his views on these foundations, Dr Haycock describes Prince Arthur as 'overbearing and arrogant' and says that he ran his office as Governor-General as though it was one of his previous military commands and that he meddled in governmental and military affairs.[2]

These conclusions and the array of other charges which Dr Haycock levies against Prince Arthur, whom he repeatedly peppers with pejorative adjectives, leave the impression that the contest between the Governor-General and the Minister of Militia was between, on the one hand, an apoplectic old royal Field-Marshal whose uniform collar was too tight and whose vision was restricted to that of a stuffed-shirt English aristocrat, and on the other, a good, bluff, self-made Canadian whose worst fault was impulsiveness.

As the Canadian chapters of this volume proceed, the reader will be able to judge the rights and wrongs, as also the causes, of what did develop into a very serious dispute between Prince Arthur and Colonel Sam Hughes, but there are compelling reasons why these judgements of Dr Haycock's should be weighed at the outset. Though Dr Haycock has not seen the papers of Prince Arthur, nor, more surprisingly, those of Colonel Sam Hughes, he is an eminent Canadian historian and his book was produced under the most distinguished auspices. As such, it seems to set in concrete some myths about Prince Arthur's conduct as Governor-General which had previously circulated in more or less unsubstantiated form and which had originated in two passages in Borden's memoirs, which were published in 1938. These inferred that Prince Arthur understood neither the constitutional limits of his position as Governor-General nor that his title of Commander-in-Chief had no substance.[3]

Let us therefore pause for a moment to consider Dr Haycock's description of Prince Arthur's initial attitudes in the first days of his Governor-Generalship. There is no ground for supposing that he had any notion of conspiracy in meeting Grey on the evening of 12th October. Had he done so, he would not have escorted him back to his yacht which, of course, drew attention to the visit. If Grey did speak to Prince Arthur about Sam Hughes, neither he nor the Duchess thought what he had said was important enough to mention in their descriptions of the meeting. More to the point, if Grey did seek to prejudice Prince Arthur against Sam Hughes, he certainly did not succeed. Writing to Léonie on 24th October, Prince Arthur told her that he had entertained Colonel Sam Hughes and his wife and Mr Hazen, who was the Minister of Marine, to lunch. He said that he liked both Ministers, whom he described as strong Imperialists and keen on the improvement of their two Services. Three days later he wrote to the King that he had now met most of the Ministers, among whom we know Sam Hughes was included, and that he was very favourably impressed by them; he thought they all had a strong sense of duty and devotion to Canada, that they were Imperialists and thoroughly honest. In looking for the reasons which led Prince Arthur to form his later opinion of Hughes, we shall find an explanation which is quite different from that postulated by Dr Haycock and we must look, too, for the real grounds of the complaints made by Borden in his memoirs.[4]

Meanwhile, in Quebec on the evening of 13th October, Prince Arthur and the Duchess dined with the the Lieutenant-Governor of the Province of Quebec and Madame Longelier at Spencer Wood, where the conversation was all in French, and then attended a reception in the Parliament Building at which they shook hands with more than eight hundred people, most of whom were French.   It was past midnight when they boarded their special train, headed by two engines and more than five hundred feet in length, and left for Ottawa. In the Dominion capital, they drove through gaily decorated streets crowded with enthusiastic people to Parliament Square. Here, in front of 40,000 people, Prince Arthur received and replied to addresses from the Municipality and then one each from the four societies of English, Scots, Irish and French. They then drove across the Rideau River to Government House, or Rideau Hall, which was to be their principal residence for the next five years. As they approached, the Duchess almost thought that a mistake had been made and that they were coming to a gymnasium flanked by a riding school. The house was painted slate grey and the poor little porch a nondescript shade of dirty brown. Inside, however, the rooms were much more welcoming and the sunny day gave them a cheerful impression. They both felt determined to make themselves at home and to like the place, Prince Arthur wrote to the King.[5]

'I am a sort of constitutional sovereign which means a Post Office,' Prince Arthur wrote to Léonie. He read several Canadian newspapers every day and was also working at the history of the Dominion. He wondered if Léonie realised that Canada was larger than the United States, which he thought made the glib talk there of annexation rather absurd. He had established himself in an office near the Prime Minister's in the Parliament Building and he was giving a series of lunch parties at

Rideau Hall to each of which he invited a few Ministers so that he could get to know them better. He also planned to start giving large dinner parties so that he could show kindness and hospitality to as many as possible. As ever, Prince Arthur found Canadians easy to get on with and he made a great point of talking to all the ladies after his dinner parties, as the Duchess did to all the men. He told Léonie that they were trying to avoid all stiffness and he mentioned that he had met Miss Gordon, who had taught him to skate in 1869 and 1870 and who had then been very good-looking, but was now rather large.[6]

Prince Arthur's pronounced sociability, always an asset in a Prince, was a particular advantage in a Governor-General and meeting as many people as possible by entertaining and travelling was high in the priorities of this one. Prince Arthur also immediately immersed himself in what his Ministers advised him, or, in some cases, he himself saw, were the main issues now confronting Canada. One of the most obvious was the naval question. The German threat had raised in the minds of many Canadians the need for their Dominion to keep the command of the sea British. Though the issue had not been a dominant one in the recent general election, there was, nonetheless, a sharp division between the parties as to how best this could be achieved and, in some French Canadian circles, the view that it should not be attempted at all. Laurier's policy, on which a start had been made, was to found a distinctively Canadian Navy. This had the advantage of appeasing independently minded Canadian opinion and the disadvantage that it would be many years before anything emerged to influence the balance of sea power between the British Empire and Germany. The *Montreal Daily Star* branded the plan as a 'theoretical error, a political blunder and a financial folly.' Instead, it suggested, Canada should make a contribution to the cost of expanding the British fleet and this, Prince Arthur wrote to the King, was the policy which he thought the new Conservative government would adopt, but he also thought that, before a subsidy was voted, it might be necessary to put it before the country in another general election.[7]

Public health was not an issue about which Ministers were talking, but it did attract Prince Arthur's concern. In their early days in Canada the Duchess visited several hospitals, most of which seemed to her to be inadequate. At one, for example, she was horrified to find that medical and surgical cases were intermingled, including even one of enteric. The building, which was only thirteen years old, seemed to be insanitary and it was hot and stuffy. The small kitchens on each floor were poky and dirty.

Health, Prince Arthur wrote to Princess Louise, was the most important and least controversial matter in Canada. The insanitary state of the towns, the ravages of enteric and small pox and the rate of infant mortality were, he thought, 'frightful', and he resolved to try to bring home to the country the need for improvements. There was much preventable disease in Canada, he wrote to John Burns, the President of the Local Government Board in Asquith's Cabinet, and he hoped to wake up the Canadian authorities to this. The difficulty, he said, was that housing and sanitation were in the hands of the Provincial and Municipal authorities, which ran on political lines.[8]

Running things on political lines or, in other words, by a system of patronage doled out by Ministers and their supporters in Parliament, was the dominant method of administration and procurement in Canada, as it had been in Britain in the eighteenth century. Prince Arthur was amazed by the amount of time Ministers and M.Ps spent in receiving deputations seeking employment in the public service and he noted that in the first three months of the new government's existence, the Member for Ottawa alone had handled some 2,500 applications. It was a system which shocked Prince Arthur, who came to believe that it was one of the greatest evils in the Dominion and certainly the greatest bar to efficiency in the public service. Its baneful influence, he believed, was the rock on which so many Dominion governments had come to grief, but he hoped, naïvely as it turned out, that the new Government would be strong enough to overcome this corruption. Here was one of the grounds on which he was later to pitch into the methods of the Minister of Militia, Colonel Sam Hughes.[9]

Even more politically sensitive than patronage was the issue of mixed Catholic and Protestant marriages, which had come to something of a head when a Catholic husband in Ontario, who was said to have tired of his Protestant wife, was told by his priest that he could dispense with her. This caused much ill-feeling, not only in Ontario, but throughout the West and Prince Arthur, who persistently preached peace between Catholic and Protestant, feared that it might lead to acrimony in the House of Commons. As the Archbishopric of Toronto was vacant, Prince Arthur set about trying to secure the appointment of a liberal-minded successor, who would be prepared to evade the Papal decree known as *ne tenere* by which the errant Ontario husband had been able to escape. He promised Borden, who was also becoming worried, that he would write to the Duke of Norfolk, who might be able to influence the Pope, Pius X.

He also discussed the matter with Sir Charles Fitzpatrick, the Chief Justice of Canada, who was himself a Catholic and was daily becoming a closer and closer friend of Prince Arthur's. He consulted Laurier, who supported the view that Catholic priests should not intervene in family affairs in a sense which was against the law of the land, and in the end he secured a satisfactory letter from the Duke of Norfolk, which seemed to indicate that the Pope would not drive matters to extremes. On the morning of 16th November 1911, though he had a very important and taxing afternoon ahead of him, Prince Arthur received the newly appointed Catholic Bishop of Regina, who was introduced to him by the Archbishop of Quebec. He found him to be a young looking, bright and pleasing man, who seemed to be broad-minded and sympathetic. Prince Arthur thought it unlikely that he would tread on the toes of those of other religions.[10]

Prince Arthur began his important afternoon by putting on the full dress uniform of a Field-Marshal with jack-boots and white breeches. He donned the star of the Order of the Garter and the riband of that of St Michael and St George. The Duchess dressed in the gown she had worn at the coronation of King Edward VII. Captain Worthington, the doctor, sprayed Prince Arthur's throat as a guard against hoarseness and the royal couple then drove, in a closed carriage, as it was a cold day, to the Parliament Building, where they were received with a salute of twenty-one guns and a guard of honour. The Prime Minister was among those who waited at the door to greet them and there was a large crowd of onlookers, all of whom, Prince Arthur noticed, took off their hats. They proceeded to the Speaker's private room and then, Prince Arthur walking on the right and holding the Duchess's right hand, they processed through the corridors and into the Senate Chamber. The Duchess's train was borne by two pages in scarlet with white waistcoats and silk stockings. The Chamber was crowded with ladies in full evening dress and men in uniform. Prince Arthur mounted a dais and sat on the throne under a canopy with the Duchess on his left. He put on his hat and told the company to be seated. Black Rod then summoned the Commons and when they arrived the Speaker of the Senate read the manifesto of the Governor-General in English and French in which it was declared that the Governor-General would respect the rights of the Commons. The Military Secretary, Colonel Lowther, handed Prince Arthur the text of the speech from the throne, which he had rehearsed several times with the Duchess beforehand. He first read the speech in English which took five and a half minutes and then he repeated it in French which took two minutes longer. Each time he mentioned the House of Commons he took off his hat and at the end he thought he had got through it well, the Duchess thought 'extremely well.' He was told later that his words were heard all over the Chamber and the Speaker said that it was the first time he had been able to hear a speech from the throne. Having thus opened the new Parliament, Prince Arthur rose, took off his hat and made three bows to the front, to the right and to the left and then, with the Duchess, processed out and drove back to Rideau Hall to the accompaniment of cheering. The only hitch was that the carriage was late in drawing up at the door for the return journey, which the Duchess found rather awkward in her evening dress, as there was a piercing wind.[11]

There were one or two more hitches at the state dinner which Prince Arthur gave in the ballroom at Rideau Hall that night. Several of the guests arrived late and one was so drunk that he had to be smuggled into a corner. Even so, Prince Arthur received each of the one hundred and three guests as they arrived and then entered the ballroom last with the two principal guests, the Lieutenant-Governors of Ontario and Quebec, who then sat on either side of him. They proved to be old and dull. Colonel Lowther sat opposite flanked by the Lieutenant-Governor of Prince Edward Island and the Papal Nuncio. After dinner Prince Arthur received the wives and daughters of those who had dined and the Duchess received all the men. They then walked through the rooms talking to as many of their guests as possible. This perambulation was followed by supper, to which Prince Arthur took in Mrs Borden. This entertainment was more thorough and painstaking than tradition demanded, for it seemed that, in past years, the Governor-General, having once received the guests, paid little or no further attention to them. Prince Arthur's new procedure seemed, however, to be much appreciated. When at last all the civilities had been extended, Prince Arthur and the Duchess slipped away into his study, which was the only room which had not been thrown open to the guests, and refreshed themselves with barley water and cigarettes.[12]

Next day Prince Arthur attended a lunch given by Colonel Sam Hughes for Militia officers. When he arrived with his host in the guest room of the restaurant of the House of Commons, he found a party of about a hundred already in their places. Most of the Ministers were there and Prince Arthur was given a seat between Colonel Hughes and Sir Wilfrid Laurier. Many of the guests wore rough shooting coats, which gave the entertainment the look of a farmers' dinner. Prince Arthur, Hughes, Borden and Laurier all made speeches and Prince Arthur, who was very pleased by the ovation which he received at the end of his, was much impressed by the fact that there had never before been such an assemblage of Militia officers. There was, however, something about Colonel Hughes's behaviour which disquieted him and the occasion marked the beginning of a change in his attitude to the Minister of Militia. He wrote to Léonie that he was 'rather a bounder & very mad.' He added that he was the only Minister who might not be a success.[13]

Before coming out to Canada Prince Arthur had intended to start his Governor-Generalship with an extensive tour of the Dominion and, in particular, he had wished to visit the West at an early stage. Grey had counselled against this and warned Prince Arthur that the older Provinces would feel aggrieved, as would an old established dame 'if she were to see Your Royal Highness pass her by, and take in to dinner the youngest beauty of the party.' The parable was so apposite that Prince Arthur seems to have been unable to resist its conclusion and his first sortie as Governor-General took him only as far as Toronto, Hamilton and Kingston. As he approached Toronto by train on 27th November 1911, he noticed signs of prosperity everywhere and he admired the orchards and the wood and brick houses. He went with the Duchess to stay at Government House with the Lieutenant-Governor and Mrs Gibson, who gave a tremendous dinner in their honour on the first night. After the ladies had left, amongst whom Prince Arthur had recognised many he had known and some he had danced with in 1869 and 1870, several of the men came in turn to sit beside him for a talk. In the streets of Toronto, Prince Arthur noticed that there was an enormous preponderance of girls who sang the national anthem and *The Maple Leaf Forever*. In the course of functions he carried out in the city, he came across Mr George Fleming, who was the son of a Page who had been in Queen Victoria's service at the time of her accession and had been a play fellow of Prince Arthur's elder brothers. He also met Mr and Mrs Grant; he was the brother of the head stalker at Balmoral and the son of the preceding one. Mr Grant was now the head of a large Canadian firm. Prince Arthur thought it was wonderful how successful people could be in Canada. He received an honorary degree from the University of Toronto, which he understood to be the largest in the Empire. He felt very nervous at having to speak before such an audience as the University provided, but he seems to have been more at ease when he addressed the Press Association of Toronto. He gave them some advice about trying to be less picturesque and more grammatical, which was received with much good-humoured laughter. When he sat down there was frantic applause and the members stood on their chairs and waved their napkins. Three thousand people came to a ball given in honour of Prince Arthur and the Duchess by the Toronto Yacht Club in the Armoury and Drill Hall and Prince Arthur was able to talk to endless people, including several Americans from Buffalo and other towns in the United States. He saw many ladies in pretty dresses and he noted that the members wore a kind of naval coat with white facings. The Militia officers were in full dress uniform and men of the Canadian Dragoons in brass helmets and plumes were posted about. Prince Arthur and the Duchess also visited what she first described as the 'poorest' part of Toronto and then corrected to the workman's quarter, as it seemed that there were really very few poor people in Canada.[14]

In Hamilton a great mass of school children, formed up and dressed to represent a vast Union Jack, had turned out to welcome the royal visitors. They made such a noise that the address and Prince Arthur's reply to it could scarcely be heard. A rather dreadful lunch followed at the Royal Hotel where the Mayor of Hamilton was the host. He seemed to be very muddled and was not sure which room was to be used. As he was a teetotaller, only water was offered and, as Prince Arthur and the Duchess had been advised that the water was not safe, they left it alone. They sat twenty minutes at the table before any food appeared, which was time enough for them to discover that the Mayor and Mayoress were very uninteresting and stiff. When the food did come, there was not much of it and it was very nasty. At least a quarter of an hour elapsed between the end of one course and the beginning of another and the meal lasted nearly two hours. Nor was this the end of the ordeal, for that night the Mayor entertained them to a large dinner in the same hotel. Two hundred guests were presented and they then filed to their places, but the Mayor seemed unable to decide where Prince Arthur and the Duchess were to sit. It cannot have been with much regret that they left for Kingston, where Prince Arthur was greatly impressed by the military cadets, who did a three year course under British instructors. These cadets, Prince Arthur told the King, were fine, healthy young men, but he thought their accommodation was inadequate and this was a matter which he intended to take up.[15]

Despite Patsy having come out to join her parents in Canada and put a little gaiety into their lives, Prince Arthur began to feel depressed as

Christmas approached. The Duchess had been unwell and cross throughout their short visit to Montreal and Prince Arthur was beginning to find it tedious being able to see people only *en cérémonie* and never to see anyone privately. He was out of sorts and had a cough, which he thought might develop into bronchitis. Ottawa suddenly seemed to be a detestable place and he could but try to look forward to the new year with hope. But all this was only what he wrote to Léonie. To Mr Harcourt, the Secretary of State for the Colonies, he sent, as a despatch, a copy of a speech which Borden had just made in New York and which Prince Arthur thought would soothe the irritation felt in the United States at the emphatic way in which Canada, by a verdict at the polls, had rejected the Laurier plan for trade reciprocity with America. To the King he wrote to thank him for all the kindness and affection which he had shown to him in the old year. At Christmas time, though he had not done it for twenty-six years, Prince Arthur took up skating again and soon got used to it. The Duchess, however, had a nasty fall and bruised her forehead, which was a nuisance just before a dinner party.[16]

Prince Arthur was now thinking of paying a private visit to New York. He consulted the British Ambassador in Washington, Mr Bryce, whom he had recently entertained in Ottawa, as to the niceties. Mr Bryce thought that President Taft, who, he said, was neither suspicious nor punctilious, would take no offence at the visit being purely private, though he did say that, in that case, it was possible that the press would take it amiss. To this, Mr Bryce rather unhelpfully added that, on the other hand, they might not. Prince Arthur was not much impressed. He emphasised to Mr Bryce that he would come, not as the Governor-General of Canada, but as a private guest of the Whitelaw Reids, who had invited him in the previous summer. Even so, he thought it would be courteous if he paid a call on the President. He told the Ambassador that when he was serving with his Regiment in Montreal during his first visit to Canada, he had paid a private visit to New York, but that he had gone down to Washington, stayed at the British Embassy, paid a call on President Grant and dined one night at the White House. The hint was obvious, but Mr Bryce did not take it. He said that he would be delighted to entertain Prince Arthur at the British Embassy if he came to Washington, but he persisted in the advice that it was not necessary to do so. Thereafter, matters quickly got out of hand. Whitelaw Reid, who happened to be in Washington, invited Bryce to a dinner, which he said he was giving for the Duke of Connaught in New York and he told him that he had also invited a number of officials of the American Government. Mr Bryce had to tell him that such a dinner for a guest who was on a private visit would cause misunderstanding and he now lost no time in suggesting to Prince Arthur that he should call on the President in Washington. He urged that this was so important that Prince Arthur should, if necessary, delay his return to Canada. By the time these thoughts had occurred to Mr Bryce, Prince Arthur had already left Ottawa.[17]

On the evening of 21st January 1912, one of the Governor-General's carriages was attached to the train for New York from Ottawa. As this was an expensive process, no more were attached and Patsy and the rest had to fit into the ordinary bits of the train, but, despite the luxury of their conveyance, Prince Arthur and the Duchess had a very bumpy ride; the track was in poor condition. They arrived in New York at 7 next morning. To avoid 'snapshotters' and reporters, they went up to their motors in a luggage lift, a manoeuvre which Prince Arthur described as a 'flank march.' It succeeded quite well; Kitty Mott, who had been travelling on the same train, was photographed and described in the press as the Duchess of Connaught. The real Duchess and Prince Arthur duly arrived with Patsy at the Whitelaw Reids' house and here Prince Arthur was handed Bryce's letter about the need to call on the President. He at once saw that he would have to do so, but also that he could not delay his return to Canada at the cost of engagements he had already made there. He therefore decided to travel down to Washington overnight, call on the President and then dine at the British Embassy before returning to New York over the next night, and then leave for Ottawa on the day following, as had already been arranged.[18]

Annoying as all this was for Prince Arthur, it was not a surprise to him. He knew that all the world in New York knew about his so-called private visit and, even before leaving Ottawa, he had declined two hundred private and official invitations from Americans. Bryce had misjudged the interest which the American press would take in Prince Arthur, he had misjudged the standing of the Governor-General of Canada, he had misjudged the feelings of President Taft and he had overlooked the jealousy which existed between New York and Washington. Prince Arthur, however, scarcely complained, though he did tell the King that he thought Bryce might have got things straight a bit sooner.[19]

The Whitelaw Reids' house at 451 Madison Avenue proved to be charming and it was full of beautiful things and pictures. Prince Arthur set off to call on Mr Dex, the Governor of New York, and he then took a walk in Central Park. He found New York difficult to recognise from what he remembered of it on his last visit forty-two years ago. The streets were now wider, the traffic was well managed and the place had a more cosmopolitan air about it. After lunch he took the Duchess to see the Metropolitan Museum, where they were taken round by former Ambassador Cloat. Prince Arthur was struck by some lovely Chinese ceramics which had been lent by Mr Pierpont Morgan. There was a dinner party at the Whitelaw Reids that night to which seventy people came. Among them were General Grant, the son of the former President, and Mr and Mrs Carnegie, the former of whom thought that Prince Arthur was Mr Lawrence. Afterwards, music was provided by Madame Alma Gluck and Clements from Paris. Next morning Prince Arthur and the Duchess went by lift up the forty-four stories of the Metropolitan Insurance building and viewed New York from the vantage point of six hundred and fifty feet above it. They thought it marvellous and the people in the streets looked like ants. This was one of the tallest buildings in New York. Pierpont Morgan's son showed them round his father's library, which contained untold treasures, manuscripts and pictures. Now, however, they were pursued by snapshotters wherever they went. Colonel Roosevelt came to lunch and in the afternoon they visited the Cathedral, Columbia University and Grant's tomb. At dinner that night, the jewels of the ladies were quite astounding.[20]

On their third day, they motored down Broadway to Wall Street, where they were met by the President of the Stock Exchange. As they entered the building there were cheers and business came to a standstill. A large crowd had gathered outside to watch their departure and a snapshotter leapt on top of a hearse, which contained a coffin, to get a picture of them. They lunched with Mrs Cornelius Vanderbilt Junior, who was known in Europe as the Kingfisher, and afterwards they visited Mills Hotel, which was a tenement house similar to Rowton House in London. They dined with the Ogden Mills in a marble and gilt palace where the tables groaned under the weight of gold plate and money shrieked at one. Prince Arthur was delighted to meet an old acquaintance, Mrs Royal Carroll. Though she now looked old and thin and was a little deaf, she was simple, intelligent and such a lady. There was dancing after dinner at which the *Turkey Trot* and the *Bunny Hug* were done. It all filled the Duchess with disgust at the worldliness of the owners, but everyone was most civil and anxious to be hospitable. That night Prince Arthur left for Washington.[21]

In Washington, President Taft sent a motor to the British Embassy to pick Prince Arthur up and he was driven to the White House with an escort of a squadron of cavalry, which, Bryce reported to the Foreign Secretary, Sir Edward Grey, was a troop more than had been accorded to Prince Henry of Prussia. People on the pavements gave him an extremely cordial reception by cheering and waving their handkerchiefs. President Taft struck Prince Arthur as having an open and cheery expression and he found him easy to talk to. Mrs Taft was ladylike and well dressed, but she had had some kind of stroke and could only repeat what Prince Arthur said to her. While Miss Taft poured tea, he was introduced to all the Ministers and their wives. Shortly after Prince Arthur had got back to the British Embassy, President Taft returned his call there and they had a further twenty minutes of conversation. The President launched on one of his favourite topics, which, most fortunately, was the success of the British Empire in solving the problems of Colonial government. His interest in this evidently arose from his experience in the Philippines. Mr Bryce entertained Prince Arthur to dinner at the Embassy. All the foreign ambassadors in Washington were there and so were the judges of the Supreme Court, Senators, members of the Foreign Relations Committee and the leading officers of the civil and military services. The American Secretary of State proposed the King and then the Governor-General of Canada and Prince Arthur, according to Bryce, in the most felicitous terms, proposed the President. After dinner there was a reception at which Prince Arthur talked to no end of people of the Corps Diplomatique, the Senate, the Government and their wives. On the way to the railway station, he called at the Press Club where he received a warm welcome from two hundred journalists. He left Washington at half-past midnight and arrived in New York at 7.15 the next morning.[22]

While Prince Arthur was away, the Duchess lunched with Mrs Vanderbilt, the mother of them all, in another marble and gilt palace which was overpowering in every way. The ballroom alone had cost £80,000 to build and decorate. When he got back, Prince Arthur and the Duchess lunched in yet another such palace with Mr and Mrs Sloane; she was a Vanderbilt. There were eight footmen in livery and on the table were white orchids, lilac and violets. Flowers were another of the marvels of New York and they represented mints of money. They dined with the Whitelaw Reids and then left for Ottawa. It seemed astounding how hospitable and easy to get on with everyone had been, but the Duchess felt she had seen too much gold and marble and all that the mighty dollar could produce. It seemed a pity that they always saw the same rich people and not the 'more interesting ones,' she thought.[23]

In Ottawa Prince Arthur had now established a routine of work. In addition to his functions and entertaining, he went to his office four days a week to deal with the 'post office' side of his appointment and also to hear the views of the legislators of the Dominion. On his office days he received individually six or seven Senators or Members of Parliament. Each sat with him for about ten minutes as they had done with his predecessor, Lord Grey. In Grey's time, however, a little pressure had been applied, but Prince Arthur let it be known that these visits were entirely informal and voluntary. As to entertainments, Prince Arthur had now added spectacular skating parties, such as the one he and the Duchess gave on the evening of 4th March 1912. It was a beautiful night under a bright moon and the air was quite still. The grounds of Rideau Hall were illuminated by the light of Chinese lanterns and three huge bonfires. On the rink the skaters went round in single, double and triple lines bearing Chinese lanterns held aloft on the end of long sticks; it was a Canadian version of the European court balls and nearly a thousand people came to it, including the Bordens and Hazens. Supper was taken in the curling rink and log house and the guests did not begin to leave until past eleven o'clock. The opinion seemed to be that it was a better party than ever. Prince Arthur was not at the top of his physical form, as he was suffering from sciatica, but he and the Duchess were in enhanced spirits because Léonie and Colonel Leslie had come to stay. Indeed, the sciatica was a thinly disguised blessing for, while the others went out on the town, Prince Arthur lay down and Léonie stayed at home to keep him company. The Duchess found it a 'great joy' to see Léonie again and when she had gone, Prince Arthur wrote to her that it was delightful for him to look back on her visit; it had been so good of her to sit by his bedside when he was the poorest of companions and the others were out at the opera. If Colonel Leslie had any thoughts, no one seems to have recorded them.[24]

In continuing, as ever, to see the relationship between Prince Arthur and Léonie as a great asset, not only to him but also to herself, the Duchess showed mature and good judgement; in other matters she sometimes showed a naïvety which was surprising and even dangerous. One such arose from the arrival in Ottawa of a West Indian delegation, which had come to discuss trade. Prince Arthur made every effort to ensure that the delegates met the Canadian Ministers, former Ministers, Members of Parliament, bankers and men of business. Among those whom the Duchess met under these auspices were Sir Donald Mann and Sir William Mackenzie, who, in conjunction, were developing the Canadian Northern Railway. Sir Donald Mann evidently saw his chance at once. Why, he asked the Duchess, were the Governor-General and herself so much easier to get on with than any of their predecessors, which was a question to which the Duchess did not object at all. She told him that they had thought of buying some land for their son in Canada and Sir Donald at once offered to arrange this for them. The Duchess said she had very little money for the project, but he said this was of little consequence and he began to suggest that she should buy some land near Montreal which would shortly be opened up. At this stage it was time for supper to which Prince Arthur took Mrs Borden in and the Prime Minister turned up to do the same honour for the Duchess. Sir Donald, however, had established his impression. The Duchess heard that, having begun life as a blacksmith, he and Sir William Mackenzie were now about the richest men in Canada and a few days later she heard from Prince Arthur's Comptroller, Captain Bulkeley, that Sir Donald had bought some land for her on his Canadian Northern line and that, as the interest would cover the outlay, there was no need for her to send any money. She might expect to receive £4,000 in a year or so if she allowed the money to roll up. It sounded to the Duchess like a fairy tale and it still did so even after Bulkeley had told her that no one was to know about this except himself and a Colonel Davidson, who did the purchasing for Mann and Mackenzie. Perhaps the Duchess, in keeping this from Prince Arthur, meant one day to give him a pleasant surprise; it would not have been like her to conceal it from him for any other reason. News of further similar purchases arrived after another short interval and soon Sir Donald was smoking his cigar in the Duchess's room, telling her of his railway and how he had started life, not it now seemed as an blacksmith, but as a lad driving a tram at the age of eight or ten. He talked to her on all sorts of topics and it was all most interesting. He told her, and she recorded in her Journal, the amount of money which she might expect to make from his transactions on her behalf in a year or so, but how much this was cannot be told for the Duchess later made a thorough job of erasing the figures she had written.[25]

These were heady days for the Duchess and they were not made less so by Herr von Warlich, who was staying at Rideau Hall. He was a classical concert singer with a bass voice and he was also full of philosophical talk. His singing in the evenings for the Connaughts and their guests was, the

Duchess thought, a 'wonderful treat' and his talk was 'delicious.' Sir Donald Mann backed some horses for her and sent her the takings of £82. Sir William Mackenzie told her that Sir Donald did all this because he had taken such a fancy to her. Apart from the 'winnings' on the race course, however, nothing materialised from all these promises and others made by Sir William Mackenzie, nor was the exact purpose of trying to buy the Duchess of Connaught apparent. If Prince Arthur had known what was going on, he would, no doubt, have had to bring the Duchess down with rather a bump and he might have been excused for thinking that his Equerry and Comptroller, Captain Bulkeley, should have known better than to be a party to such an absurd and potentially damaging series of transactions.[26]

Sir Donald Mann's Northern Railway was not among the great entrepreneurial triumphs which at this time were changing the face and the future of Canada, but such triumphs did account for the growing sense of Canadian identity and self-assertion, which increasingly characterised the political atmosphere of the Dominion. A symptom of this was the feeling that Canada should have some say in Imperial strategy if she was to contribute to the cost of the British, or Imperial, Navy. Prince Arthur warned the King that this raised a very important Imperial question and that the feeling about it in Canada was so strong that it would be difficult to ignore. A different sign of the same thing was a short parliamentary bill transferring the Department of External Affairs from a Secretary of State to the Prime Minister, removing its office from a small flat over a barber's shop three-quarters of a mile from the centre of Ottawa, and bringing it under the same roof as that of the Prime Minister and the Governor-General. Canada was taking a step forward in the management of her own, foreign policy. Prince Arthur welcomed the decision and thought it would improve the cohesion and expedition of the running of Canadian external affairs. In London the Foreign Office was much less pleased and saw in the development a threat to its own sovereignty in such matters. Fortunately, however, the Colonial Office felt that the matter was an awkward one and was therefore best left aside.[27]

A larger sense in which Prince Arthur displayed his profoundly Canadian feeling was his ready acceptance of the fundamental changes which were taking place and, in addition to his constant efforts to soothe bitterness between French and British Canadians and Catholics and Protestants, his wish to use his Governor-Generalship as a symbol of new

Dominion integration from East to West, or more precisely, as he saw it, from West to East. Indeed, Prince Arthur told the King, Ottawa was not the ideal capital of the Dominion; it was not central enough and eastern bias stimulated the feeling of people in the West that they did not belong to Canada. Unity was Prince Arthur's ideal and he hoped that the tour of Canada which he was now about to begin and which would take him back to the West, where he had not been since 1890, would do a great deal of good. He wished to be seen by the people as a person, and not only as a name, and he wanted to learn at first hand about the whole country and its inhabitants.[28]

With such thoughts and ambitions in mind, Prince Arthur and the Duchess set forth in May 1912, intending first to visit Winnipeg, then to tour the Maritime Provinces and finally, as Grey had advised, to go west. They had, however, not got farther than Quebec when the Duchess was suddenly seized by an alarming illness. The symptoms seemed to be of appendicitis or peritonitis and they caused Prince Arthur and the doctors serious anxiety. The Duchess was removed into the Victoria hospital in Montreal but no operation was carried out, seemingly because the doctors were unable to determine what was the cause of the trouble. The Duchess shortly began to make a surprisingly good recovery and Prince Arthur decided to resume his tour, taking Patsy with him to stand in for her mother. He also took great trouble to avoid causing inconvenience to Borden, who wished to see him before going to London for talks about the contribution to the cost of the Navy. Borden offered to come to Montreal, but Prince Arthur told him that he would come to Ottawa and see him there. Relations between the Governor-General and the Prime Minister were excellent; Prince Arthur had told the King that Borden was able and broad-minded and, for a Canadian, wonderfully well up in world politics. He said that he was scrupulously honest, not at all stiff and full of humour. The seeds of a doubt were, however, already growing in Prince Arthur's mind. Borden's one fault, he now concluded, was that he was 'rather wanting in backbone.' Evidently matters had come up between them about which Prince Arthur thought that Borden had followed a less than courageous line.[29]

Borden displayed an affectionately respectful attitude to Prince Arthur; he consulted him regularly and, when they were geographically separated, wrote frequent and informative letters about his doings, almost as a son might do to his father. On 13th July 1912, for example, Borden wrote to Prince Arthur from the Savoy Hotel in London saying that he had received an exceptionally warm welcome in England. He said that his speech at a gathering of the Royal Caledonian Irish had been well received, that he had attended a meeting of the Defence Committee of the Cabinet at which Sir Edward Grey and Mr Churchill had made illuminating statements. He had been commanded to luncheon at Buckingham Palace and he was going to Arundel for the weekend. He was to go to a state ball and would be sworn in as a Privy Councillor. He was going to Hatfield, but his visit to Bowood had been cancelled as he was going to Paris instead. He had been entertained by the National Liberal Club and the Carlton Club. He had had the pleasure of meeting Prince Arthur of Connaught and his aunt, Princess Christian. He felt sure that his mission would achieve satisfactory arrangements about the naval contribution and Canadian representation in the strategic counsels of the Empire.[30]

Prince Arthur replied congratulating Borden on the excellent speeches he had made and expressing his pleasure at the good reception he had had in England. He said that this reflected the warm feeling there was for Canada in England and he thought that the visit would increase that. He was particularly glad that Borden and the three colleagues with him had all been invited to attend the Defence Committee and he hoped that this insight into affairs at home would be a help to the Prime Minister when he got back to Canada. He trusted that the mission would be a success and that this would redound to Borden's credit in Canada. He feared that Borden was being overwhelmed with hospitality, which, however well meant, was terribly fatiguing, but he was glad that he had been entertained by the Liberal and the Conservative clubs, which he thought showed that the parties were putting Empire before politics. He told Borden that the reception he had just had in Winnipeg was the best he had yet received in Canada.[31]

The people of Winnipeg had turned out en masse to welcome Prince Arthur and on the evening of his arrival, there were more than a hundred thousand of them out on the streets, which were beautifully illuminated and decorated; there was hardly a house which did not fly the union jack or the Canadian flag and, above the warmth of the greeting, Prince Arthur did not hear a discordant note. The experienced eye of one who was with him, reckoned that Prince Arthur's welcome was the biggest ever seen in Canada; it was one roar of cheers all the way and the King did not get a better reception in London. During his stay of eight days, Prince Arthur gave four dinner parties and a garden party and he told the King that all the people he met were pleasant and interesting. They seemed to him to be devoted to their city and Province, and also to the Dominion and Empire, and it struck him that the people of the West combined for the general good much more readily than did those in the East. Though the population now included Americans, Russian Jews, Lithuanians and Italians they seemed able to sink their political and religious differences. Even the Mayors he met in the Western cities, he told Princess Louise, were intelligent and hardworking gentlemen, quite unlike the violent and ill-educated politicians who ruled the cities in the East.[32]

Moncton, which Prince Arthur thought a rather second-rate place, and Summerside, on Prince Edward Island, offered a complete contrast. The countryside around the latter seemed to the Duchess, who was now well enough to accompany Prince Arthur on a drive with the Mayor, to be rather dull and they both slept a good deal during the expedition. Perhaps it was as well that only a few people turned out to see them. In Charlottetown, Prince Arthur found that the Lieutenant-Governor was not on speaking terms with the Provincial Premier but in the pretty little hilly town of Pictou, where the houses were dotted about among the trees, the faces of all the people were smiling. On 1st August 1912, Prince Arthur visited New Glasgow and Truro and in both places he was received with great enthusiasm. He went to see the steel works a mile from New Glasgow, which had been no more than a forge thirty years earlier, but which now had up-to-date machinery and employed 3,000 men turning out fishplates and 'nails' for the railways. A start was being made on the production of steel railway cars. It belonged to Mr Plummer, known as the Steel King of Canada, whose company also owned the coal mines and smelting works in Sydney, which Prince Arthur visited a few days later. 6,000 men were employed there. Cruising in St Ann's Bay, the royal yacht, *Earl Grey*, was surrounded by boat-loads of people cheering and firing salutes with rifles. Here Prince Arthur met Mr Bell, the American telephone man, and his dumb wife, whom he led about by the hand; they lived in quite a castle on the Lake.[33]

On 13th August *Earl Grey* arrived at Halifax in a fog and tied up under the Naval College. Prince Arthur received the military and naval authorities on board and was handed a letter from the King, which told him that young Arthur was to go to Tokyo for the funeral of the Emperor of Japan. It seemed to Prince Arthur to be rather a long way to go for a funeral, but as he would be coming back by St.Petersburg, it might give him an opportunity of seeing his young lady again; young Prince Arthur was hoping to marry one of the Tsar's daughters. His father had come to Halifax to take part in the celebration of the one hundred and fiftieth anniversary of the British grant to Nova Scotia of a self-governing Parliament, which was the first such grant to any British Colony. Prince Arthur gave an address and then ascended a tower which had been put up to mark the occasion. As the place had been discovered by a Bristol man, the English representative was the Lord Mayor of Bristol, but he was immensely fat and kept dropping off to sleep during the ceremony and, when it came to the tower, nearly died of apoplexy. At the delightful little town of Windsor, Prince Arthur received an honorary degree from King's College, which, he was told, was the oldest university in Canada, having been granted its charter by George III in 1805.[34]

From Wolfville Prince Arthur and the Duchess had a delightful drive through really lovely country with wooded hills and large valleys covered with meadows, apple orchards and well built houses to Grand Pré, Borden's birthplace. They stopped at Kent House where Prince Arthur's grandfather, the Duke of Kent, had stayed and which was now a boarding house occupied mostly by Americans. They had a great reception at Kentville, where they rejoined their train, and another in Middleton. They drove out to Annapolis Royal, named after Queen Anne, which was the scene of the first French landing in 1604 and then, having got back into their train, they skirted the beautiful Annapolis Royal basin with its endless pretty creeks until they came to the lovely little watering place of Digby, where once more they were met by an enormous crowd. Here they re-embarked in the *Earl Grey* and sailed for Saint John. Prince Arthur was very sorry to leave Nova Scotia.[35]

Having visited Saint John and arrived in St Andrews, Prince Arthur wrote to the King that, apart from Fredericton, which he was going to visit next, he had now completed his tour of the Maritime Provinces. Everywhere, he said, he had been to see what was of historical or commercial interest and he had made the acquaintance of vast numbers of people. He told the King there was room for many more inhabitants, but he thought the Provinces had not taken sufficient steps to attract immigrants. Great mineral wealth was available and there was fine alluvial soil. More could be done with coastal fishing and better communications between the sea ports were needed. Steel production was becoming very important and fifteen million barrels of apples had been exported to England from Annapolis Royal in 1911. He mentioned to the King that he had heard that Winston Churchill and Asquith were planning to visit

Canada. He thought this would be inadvisable as it would be taken as undue pressure on the Dominion to make a naval contribution, a subject on which Churchill was not showing much sensitivity in his dealings with Borden.[36]

The next stage of the tour was to take Prince Arthur to the extreme west. With the Duchess, he started from Toronto on 28th August 1912 in a magnificent C.P.R. train. Three newspaper correspondents travelled with them, one, Mr Hamilton Fife, had been sent by Lord Northcliffe to represent *The Times* and the *Daily Mail*. The other two were from the Eastern and Western Canadian press. Travelling by way of Sault Ste. Marie, they reached Prince Arthur's namesake, Port Arthur, two days later. The cheering was very enthusiastic and the developments which had taken place were most impressive. The population was now about 15,000 and shipbuilding was getting under way. Already three large ships had been built and the harbour works were being extended. As they journeyed on to Saskatoon and Prince Albert there were crowds of people waiting to see them at all the intermediate stations. Prince Arthur made a point of talking to as many of these as possible. He found that several were Germans or Swedes and he had a long talk with a young Yankee from Boston, who was a nice and intelligent fellow. In Edmonton, he opened the new Legislative Building. The weather here was wet and, as only the main streets were paved, there was a foot and a half of black clay mud in the lesser ones. Despite torrents of rain in Calgary, great crowds of smiling people were out to welcome Prince Arthur. When he had last been there in 1890, the population had been no more than a few hundred; now it was one of the largest cities in Canada. After passing some of the dramatic scenery of the Rocky Mountains, the royal train reached Banff on 9th September. The Duchess thought the scenery here must be the most beautiful in the world and this, and the profusion of wild flowers, prevented her and Prince Arthur from doing much good at the game of golf. The C.P.R. Hotel, in which they stayed, was comfortable and nicely and quietly furnished. Each bedroom had its own bathroom and the water was deliciously soft. The nearby Bow River provided a delightful run in a motor boat. The bright yellow of the poplar trees, the red of the scrub and the weirdly shaped reflections of the hills were most striking. Prince Arthur took the opportunity, which these few days of rest offered, to get some riding. The country around was a Dominion Park of some 5,760 square miles in extent. Shooting was prohibited in it, but Prince Arthur enjoyed seeing some yaks, which had been presented by the Indian

Government, buffaloes, moose and other such animals. In the evenings at the hotel Miss Gladys Clarke played the violin. After leaving the Royal Academy of Music, she had spent two years in Russia and now wanted to go to New York, which Prince Arthur thought might already be overstocked with artists; he also complained to Léonie that Miss Clarke did not bow gracefully while playing and that she swung her figure about.[37]

On 18th September 1912 Prince Arthur and the Duchess arrived in Vancouver. Immense crowds of all nationalities, including Japanese, Chinese and Germans, turned out to welcome them and three thousand children greeted them in song. They went to stay in the C.P.R. hotel and Prince Arthur called on Sir Charles Tupper, a former Prime Minister, who was now ninety-one; he had known him in 1869 and '70. Great and good building was going on and Vancouver now reminded Prince Arthur of Hong Kong and Messina. Everywhere there were cheering people and waving flags, as he went about to open the new bridge over the harbour and name it Connaught, to lunch with the Canadian Club, give new colours to the 72nd Seaforth Highlanders of Canada and to visit North Vancouver, which was only two years old. He presented certificates at the Royal Academy of Music and called on the half-breed poetess, Miss Pauline Johnson, who was in hospital suffering from cancer. Her father and grandfather had been Mohawk Chiefs and had assisted at the making of Prince Arthur into a Chief of the Six Nation Indians at Brantford, Ontario in 1869. On the chair provided for Prince Arthur, she had put the same red cloth on which he had sat at that ceremony. With the Duchess, he held a reception in their hotel at which 1,100 people passed in forty-seven minutes. Prince Arthur came away giddy with everything which had whirled past him and the Duchess thought that Colonel Lowther had read out the names too quickly. Prince Arthur made an excursion to New Westminster and visited the saw mills, where English, French, Sikh and Japanese labour was employed. He laid the foundation stone of a new High School and presented prizes at a Roman Catholic school for girls at which, however, most of the pupils proved to be Protestants.[38]

At the end of their stay in Vancouver, Prince Arthur and the Duchess embarked in the C.P.R. steamship *Princess Alice*. They sailed all day amongst the islands north of Vancouver on 23rd September and the next day came to Prince Rupert, a curious looking place on a rocky shore. Though the streets were not yet paved, indeed, they had scarcely been levelled, they were met by the Mayor and an enormous crowd of people.

The town was only two years old and much of it was still tree stumps and rock, but it was expected that it would soon be a flourishing place as it was the terminus of the Grand Trunk Pacific Railway. They travelled a hundred miles up the new Pacific railway and back again, a journey which took three hours each way. Most of the line had been cut out of the rock at enormous cost. It was planned to run 1,100 miles when it was completed in 1913. Dead salmon, which had been left high and dry after spawning, were to be seen everywhere and the enormous spruce trees were impressive.[39]

From Prince Rupert, they sailed down the Pearse Canal, round Pearse Island and into the Portland Canal and came to Port Simpson, a largely native place, where they made an unscheduled landing. Even so the inhabitants had spotted the ship and they turned out in force. Sailing on they came to Nanaimo on Vancouver Island, which already had a population of 12,000 and had been developed into a port for the lumber trade as well as for minerals and coal. Such developments seem to have underlined in Prince Arthur's mind the extent to which Vancouver Island was still undeveloped and even unexplored. At Victoria on its southern tip, he was greeted by fine weather and another splendid reception from the people, among whom he saw there were many Chinese and Germans. With the Provincial Premier, Sir R. McBride, he walked through a dense crowd to the new and handsome Government Building where he received an address. Prince Arthur was especially pleased by the enthusiasm of his reception, as there had recently been coal strikes, which, he thought, had been caused by American agitators. He and the Duchess stayed with the Lieutenant-Governor and Mrs Paterson, who were so inert that they seemed to the Duchess to have been carved from wood. By contrast, Sir R. McBride was full of vitality, such an enthusiast, humorous and the perfect master of the situation. He never stopped talking and was always entertaining, amusing and interesting.[40]

Prince Arthur went off to inspect the naval base at Esquimault. He went aboard the Canadian Navy's *Rainbow* and a British vessel. *Rainbow* seemed to be very much undermanned and the recruits on board were young and small. Prince Arthur reckoned that the difficulty was due to the high wages labourers could earn, which had now risen to as much as fifteen shillings a day. The Navy, evidently, could not compete. Before sailing from Victoria, Prince Arthur and the Duchess gave a dance for young people on board the *Princess Alice*. The girls, Prince Arthur wrote to Léonie were pretty well dressed but he thought the fashionable panniers, cut like a bathing dress, which they wore, were designed to reduce a stout figure and kill a good one. After a second visit to New Westminster, where Prince Arthur opened a fisheries exhibition, he and the Duchess motored through fruit growing country by way of Vernon to Okanagan and so on to Arrowhead. On these stages, they were accompanied by Mr Burrell, the Dominion Minister of Agriculture, whose constituency this was. Prince Arthur was on very easy terms with him and there was much chaffing. After visits to Nelson and the little fruit ranch of Balfour, Mr Burrell took his leave and Prince Arthur and the Duchess rejoined their train. Starting from Kootenay, they travelled all day on 8th October, climbing the Rockies and reaching the Crowsnest Pass. They were now in Alberta and it was much colder; they found snow on the line at Fort MacLeod where Prince Arthur did not much look forward to his functions as he had a cold and cough. All the same he went to see a ninety year old Rifleman who had served in the Indian Mutiny and in New Zealand. The man had set his heart on meeting Prince Arthur. Mr Sifton, the Premier of Alberta, came with them over this stretch of the journey, which led on to Medicine Hat and Moose Jaw. This last was a rising Prairie town of 20,000 inhabitants. They used natural gas for heat and light. In Regina there were few apparent signs of the cyclone which had hit the place in the previous June and killed forty people. According to a lady who sat next to Prince Arthur at dinner, it had left only one house in two standing. Here Prince Arthur opened the new Parliament Building and he noticed that the people were better dressed and more correct in their manners than any he had seen in Canada. He was very surprised by the warmth of the reception and the send-off which Regina gave him. He thought it extraordinary that such a cosmopolitan place should do this; for example in a crowd of 2,000 school children he had seen, he was told that twenty nationalities were represented.[41]

Crossing from Saskatchewan into Manitoba, Prince Arthur and the Duchess passed through Brandon and came to Portage la Prairie. From here Prince Arthur motored a hundred miles with Mr Graham of the Indian Government Department to visit Indian reserves. When he got to Poplar Point on the evening of 16th October, he considered that his tour was over and he went for a few days of duck shooting on Lake Manitoba. This was rather marred by gales; there were few ducks about and those there were came at an awful speed. Prince Arthur still had a cold and sore throat, but he seems, all the same, to have enjoyed himself. At least for the moment, he was not *en cérémonie*.[42]

On the last leg of the journey from Toronto to Ottawa, there was a banquet in the general dining car of the royal train. Prince Arthur thanked the household and staff for all they had done on the tour and he gave their healths. Surprisingly no one replied. Perhaps this was due to the heat in the car being indescribable. When they arrived in Ottawa, the warmth of their reception was unmistakable. Though it was after half past ten at night, large crowds had gathered and they cheered while a band played *Home Sweet Home*. The Bordens and many of the Ministers and their wives were on the platform. The Duchess thought there was genuine pleasure at their return and she was pleased to have come home to Government House and got through the tremendous journey so well.[43]

Since leaving Toronto on 24th August, Prince Arthur's tour had carried him from coast to coast and he now felt, he told the King, that he had a real knowledge of the Dominion. Every town he had seen was growing and especially was this so in Vancouver, Victoria, Edmonton, Saskatoon, Lethbridge, Brandon, Medicine Hat and Regina. All the larger towns he had visited had been lavishly decorated and illuminated. At all the small towns and railway stations there had been great displays of bunting and flags. He told the King that he had replied to two hundred addresses and had made several hundred speeches. The people he had met seemed to be optimistic and full of confidence for the future. Everywhere there was a strong Canadian sentiment and there was no talk of the West separating from the East. Prince Arthur was also optimistic; he said that in two years he expected Canada to be as well off as America. He was less sanguine about Europe and he feared that the Balkans would be causing the King much anxiety.[44]

These anxieties about the possibility of war in Europe lay behind the Borden Government's wish to contribute to the cost of the expansion and modernisation of the British navy. They also wished, provided Parliament could be persuaded to vote the subsidy, now set at $34,000,000, which they understood to be the cost of three battlecruisers or battleships of the most modern type, to use their contribution to develop the influence of Canada in the counsels of the British Empire. In addition to that, Prince Arthur put it to the Colonial Secretary that the Canadian compensation should be that some of the ship building effort should be diversified into Canada. It was also understood that the ships paid for by Canada would be maintained by Britain, but that in the fullness of time, when the British had been able to replace them, they would pass under Canadian control. If the Canadian Parliament voted the subsidy, there would be obvious advantages for Britain and the Empire, but there would also be much potential gain for Canada. That at any rate was how Prince Arthur saw it and on this point Borden saw entirely eye to eye with him, though both knew that the Liberal majority in the Senate might be an insuperable obstacle.[45]

Canadian military affairs were much less reassuring to Prince Arthur's judgement. He presently came to the conclusion not only that the Militia was lamentably inefficient, badly officered, badly trained and devoid of discipline, but that the Minister, Colonel Sam Hughes, though zealous, was militarily ignorant, conceited and very mad. That Prince Arthur should now have reached this last conclusion was hardly surprising in the light of the grievances which Sam Hughes raised against the British authorities on account of their failure to recognise his services in the South African War and reward them in the manner which he himself thought fit, namely by the award of the V.C. and Bar. Colonel Hughes raised this issue with Prince Arthur in conversation and then followed up with a memorandum which Dr Haycock describes as 'wearisome'. It was a rather curious document because, though it appeared to be written by a third party, its was certified as true by Hughes and seemed, in fact, to be his own work. It stated that Hughes had always taken the ground that he was first a British subject and that Canadian citizenship ranked second to that. This consideration was held for some reason to entitle Hughes to contribute a Canadian regiment to the field in the South African War. When it was decided to send Canadian troops to South Africa, it was also apparently proposed that they should be commanded by Sam Hughes. This, however, was vetoed by the Canadian General-Officer-Commanding, General Hutton, who was a British officer. He was said to have decided that Hughes should be second in command and then declined to confirm that. Hughes, nevertheless, went and, having got there and become an intelligence officer, he outrode the force and captured Upington. Subsequently he directed the British forces in many actions and, though the positions were always in favour of the Boers, victory always fell to Hughes. In May 1900, General Warren assured him that he would recommend him for the Victoria Cross and, after further successes, Warren assured him that he would recommend him for a second Victoria Cross. Having achieved such feats of arms, or, at any rate, subsequently imagined them, Hughes heard that the end of the war was at hand and so he decided to go home. When he learnt this, General Warren sobbed like a child and implored him to stay, but Hughes took command of the steamship *Gascon* and, with upwards of eight hundred British soldiers on board, sailed for England. When he got there he was told that he had been dismissed the service.[46]

The two salient features of this fantasy are that Hughes had convinced himself that, with practically no previous experience of soldiering and none of seafaring, he was fully competent to command in the field and to take command of a troopship on a voyage from South Africa to England. More astonishing still was his conviction that somehow or other he had proved brilliantly successful in both roles. Secondly, it was clear that he believed that he merited the highest form of recognition for having said that this was so. In his reply to the memorandum, Prince Arthur, however, commented on neither of these points. He merely told Colonel Hughes that he had read the memorandum with care and that he had studied some of the other papers bearing on the case. Amongst the latter, he had come across a letter from Hughes written in 1903 in which he had said that he wished to bury the hatchet. Prince Arthur now advised him that this was the right course and that it would be unwise to reopen the case. This answer did not please Sam Hughes at all. He told Prince Arthur that he had only offered to forget the past when the then Governor-General, Lord Minto, had pleaded with him to do so and had promised him that full justice would be done. This, Sam Hughes observed to Prince Arthur, meant full recognition of his South African services, his many mentions in despatches, the war gratuity and the honours which had been given to other Canadians. Though Hughes had now scaled down his demand from two Victoria Crosses to several mentions in despatches, it was obvious that Prince Arthur's attempt to put some oil on the water had been ineffective. All he felt he could now do was to hand over the correspondence to Borden with the suggestion that it might not be very agreeable for him and his colleagues in the Government if the events of thirteen years ago, in which Colonel Hughes had figured rather prominently, were now to be recalled to the public mind. This seems to have concluded the matter, but, as Dr Haycock observes, the episode may well have induced in Sam Hughes resentful feelings against Prince Arthur. It certainly also, though Dr Haycock does not mention it, undermined Prince Arthur's confidence, not only in Sam Hughes's suitability for Ministerial office, but also in his sanity. Here were the seeds of many troubles to come, even before their importance was immeasurably increased by the outbreak of war and the committal to battle of tens of thousands of Canadian troops.[47]

During this affair of Sam Hughes's service in South Africa, Prince Arthur had to contend with another and a grave anxiety. On 5th January 1913 he and the Duchess entertained to dinner, among others, Sir Wilfrid Laurier and Mr Mackenzie King. Afterwards Grace Smith, a charming little pianist from Toronto, played. The Duchess was in good form, but she spent a bad night and soon was suffering terrible pain and sickness. On 8th January she was removed into the Victoria hospital in Montreal. Prince Arthur felt worn out and upset. He thought it was impossible for the wife of the Governor-General not to exert herself, and, though he still hoped to finish the term of two years for which he had been appointed, he told the King that he did not believe that he would be able to extend it. He would have to bring the Duchess back to England for medical treatment and it seemed likely that she would have to undergo a very serious operation. His one wish, he wrote to his Comptroller, Colonel Malcolm Murray, was 'to do what is right, both as regards my duty as Governor Genl: & also as a husband.'[48]

Prince Arthur advised the King that his successor should not be a politician, nor one who would try to force his views on Canada. He said that Grey had meant things for the best but had been impulsive and too forward with his own views. In her present state of development, Canada, he thought, needed most careful handling. Borden was not looking forward to a successor and when he heard of the possibilities, he urged Prince Arthur not to resign, but to continue as Governor-General, even if he had to leave Canada for a time. Borden said that the country would understand if he had to take the Duchess home and when, indeed, he did so, Borden's Cabinet undertook to pay his travelling expenses to England and back, an offer which Prince Arthur most gratefully accepted as a mark of their appreciation of his services to Canada. These services were highly rated by the Chief Justice of Canada, Sir Charles Fitzpatrick, who wrote to the British Ambassador in Washington that the Connaughts had done remarkably well and that Prince Arthur would be very difficult to replace as Governor-General. For his own part, Prince Arthur told Grey that he felt very sorry to have to leave Canada, to which he was so much attached. He said that he had met with nothing but kindness from one end of the Dominion to the other. Though politics often played an ugly role, there was a fine spirit of optimism in Canada.[49]

There were inevitably a few discordant notes and one, in particular, hurt Prince Arthur' feelings. The *Montreal Herald*, enlarging on the Duchess's ill-health, asserted that the Connaughts had not found life in

Canada as entertaining as they were accustomed to in England or on the Continent. Prince Arthur, of course, made no public response, but to Léonie he castigated this sentence as a lie and thought it like the world to pretend that he was using the Duchess's illness as an excuse for giving up the Governor-Generalship. The *Montreal Daily Star* was much kinder and more characteristic of the general reaction. It said that, through his visits to so many parts of the country, the Duke of Connaught had augmented the Canadian perception of royalty and made it both more impressive and more human. He had combined dignity with democratic feeling. This son of a Queen, brother of a King and uncle of another was without ostentation and showed a simple sincerity. People would no longer think of the Royal House as something detached from human joy and sorrow or as mediaeval. The Catholics too responded to the sympathetic friendliness which Prince Arthur had shown them; the Roman Catholic Archbishop Grunthier offered prayers for the Duchess in Ottawa and this, according to Sir Charles Fitzpatrick, was the first time a heretic had been prayed for there; no prayers had been said when Edward VII was ill.[50]

On 22nd March 1913, Prince Arthur and the Duchess were seen off from Ottawa by the Bordens, Fitzpatricks, several of the Ministers, members of the opposition, Senators, M.Ps and the military and naval authorities. Large crowds cheered them as they set off to embark in the *Empress of Britain* for their voyage to England and the hope of successful treatment for the Duchess. Most of those who had said farewell to Prince Arthur genuinely hoped that he would soon return to resume his office in Canada and he certainly wished to do so himself. Meanwhile, though removed from the Canadian scene, Prince Arthur continued to be the first in the land of the Premier Dominion and, as events were presently to show, he still had many years of service to do in Canada under conditions which were yet more difficult than those he had so far experienced.[51]

CHAPTER 16

Canada, the Empire and the War 1913-1914

IN LONDON, the doctors did not take long to make up their minds and a drastic operation was carried out on the Duchess by Mr Arbuthnot Lane. She bore it wonderfully well and the doctors gave Prince Arthur the hope that, though her recovery would be slow, it would in the end be complete. It seemed that nothing malignant had been found and that the cause of the trouble had been the appendix. Prince Arthur was at once emboldened to tell Borden that he hoped to extend his term of duty as Governor-General by a year. Meanwhile, he hoped that his absence from Canada was not putting the Government to inconvenience. For his own part, through his correspondence with Borden, he kept closely in touch with Canadian affairs and did his best to explain them in London, where they were not always readily understood. He also seized the opportunity to renew his acquaintance with some of the problems which in earlier years had been among his main preoccupations. He listened to part of the debate on the Army Bill in the House of Lords and thought that Haldane's speech was inconclusive and not quite truthful. His immediate anxieties, however, were directed much more towards the Canadian army than the British and his doubts about the truthfulness of Haldane were as nothing in comparison with those which he entertained about the wisdom of Sam Hughes. Indeed, he had scarcely reached London when he heard that the latter had forced the resignation of the Chief of Staff, General Mackenzie.[1]

Prince Arthur told Borden that this was most regrettable; he thought that Hughes had gone beyond his proper position as Minister of Militia and Defence and he feared that, if he continued in this vein, it would be difficult to get a British officer to serve in Canada as her military Chief of

Staff. Behind these overt expressions, lay Prince Arthur's still covert fear that Canada's military forces were drifting under the system of political patronage which he so much deplored and that the last vestiges of military professionalism were being eliminated. Borden, however, affected to think that the affair was little more than a storm in a teacup. Mackenzie had complained that the Minister had assumed the role of a Commander-in-Chief as well as that of a Minister and was taking both military and civil decisions without reference, on the one hand, to himself as Chief of Staff and, on the other, to the Militia Council. He said that Hughes was now packing the military appointments and the membership of the Militia Council with his own nominees, who were often quite unqualified for their posts. On the other side of the argument, Hughes claimed that Mackenzie had adopted a frigid and superior demeanour, that he had declined to co-operate with the Minister in the execution of his plans and that he had asserted that the Minister had no authority to make military decisions. Borden concluded that it was a matter of six of one and half-a-dozen of the other and he extricated himself from the situation by making no complaint to Hughes while, albeit secretly, giving Mackenzie an excellent reference for the zeal with which he had discharged his duties in Canada. This was a little more writing on the wall about the relationship which was developing between the Governor-General, the Prime Minister and the Minister of Militia. Any strain which it might have put on the very cordial and relaxed terms which had grown up between Prince Arthur and Borden was, however, still conspicuous by its absence.[2]

Not only did Borden take great pains to keep Prince Arthur informed of the issues which were before him, especially the problems which had arisen in the execution of his plans for a naval contribution, which now seemed likely to be blocked by the Senate unless a political compromise could be reached, but he also took the time and trouble to add touches of humour. He related, for example, how he and Bryce, clad in Prince Albert coats and high hats, had crept along a path overlooking the river in Rockcliffe Park; Bryce had explained a point about the Panama Canal as he climbed over the trunk of a fallen tree and Borden had discoursed on the Canadian attitude to the Anglo-Japanese treaty while clinging to the edge of a precipice. He also showed constant solicitude for the Duchess, who had suffered a grave relapse, undergone a second operation and then begun a slow but encouraging recovery. When this became pronounced, Prince Arthur decided to accept the invitation to extend his term of office until October 1914 and he told Borden that he hoped to return to Canada

40. *The Duke and Duchess of Connaught (seated) with left to right: Princess Patricia, young Prince Arthur, Princess Margaret and the Crown Prince of Sweden, dressed for the coronation of King George V, 22nd June 1911.*

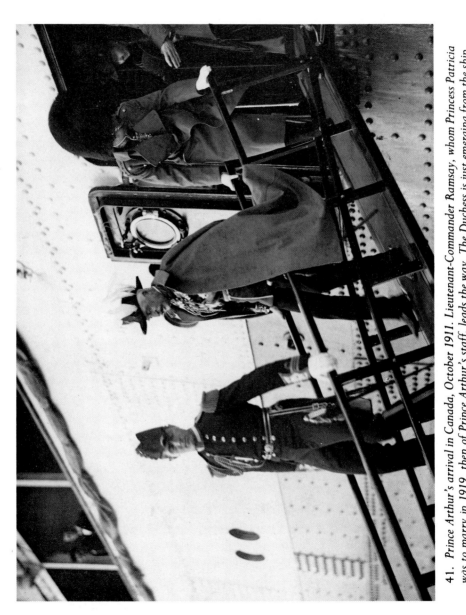

41. *Prince Arthur's arrival in Canada, October 1911. Lieutenant-Commander Ramsay, whom Princess Patricia was to marry in 1919, then of Prince Arthur's staff, leads the way. The Duchess is just emerging from the ship.*

42. 'At noon on 13th October 1911, Prince Arthur was sworn in as Governor-General of Canada. The ceremony, which he told the King was simple and dignified, took place in the Senate chamber at Quebec, which was handsomely decorated for the occasion and crammed with representative Canadians . . .' (p. 269)

43. The Duke and Duchess of Connaught driving away from the swearing-in ceremony, Quebec, 13th October 1911.

44. Mr Robert Borden and his Cabinet after being sworn in by Lord Grey at Rideau Hall, 10th October 1911. Left to right: Sam Hughes, R. Rogers, J. D. Reid, C. J. Doherty, W. J. Roche, George E. Foster, J. D. Hazen, R. L. Borden, L. P. Pelletier, T. W. Crothers, A. E. Kemp, George H. Perley, Senator J. A. Lougheed, Frank Cochrane, Bruno Nantel, F. D. Monk, W. T. White.

45. Sir Robert Borden.

46. Prince Arthur, Borden (nearest the camera) and Sam Hughes (on Prince Arthur's left) inspecting new Canadian contingents, Ottawa.

in August 1913. Borden cabled to him that this news had been received by himself and his colleagues with the greatest pleasure and that it would be hailed by the people of Canada.[3]

Borden's proposed deal with the Liberals in the Senate collapsed and his naval bill was lost. This caused much disappointment in London, to which Prince Arthur responded by speaking out boldly on behalf of Canada at a Dominion Day dinner. He assured Borden that he understood his difficulties and regretted the Little Canada policy of Laurier. All the same, as the Anglo-German naval race approached its climax, he also dropped the hint to Borden that Canada had not done very well in comparison with other Dominions. He expressed his pleasure that Borden had seen fit to send Mr Hazen, the Minister of Marine, to Vancouver to welcome the arrival there of H.M.S. *New Zealand*, a splendid battleship, which New Zealand had given to the King to defend the Empire.[4]

The need for naval expansion and modernisation was brought somewhat starkly home to Prince Arthur. In the hope of helping the Duchess's recovery, the King had put one of the royal yachts, *Alexandra*, at their disposal for a cruise to Stockholm, so that they could visit their daughter, Daisy. *Alexandra* sailed from Cowes towards the end of August 1913 in dark wet weather and they had a rough crossing of the North Sea. As they entered the Kiel Canal it was still raining. When they debouched into the harbour at Kiel, they found that the whole German High Seas Fleet 'happened' to be there assembled in four lines, the inner two of which consisted of battleships and the outer of cruisers. The German ships hoisted white ensigns at their mains and saluted Prince Arthur's standard. The sides were manned and, as *Alexandra* passed, the German sailors cheered and the guards saluted. Prince Adalbert, one of the Kaiser's sons, came on board to welcome his Great-Uncle. He was accompanied by the commander of the fleet, Vice-Admiral Ingenohl, who, only a year later, was to lead it into action against Jellicoe in the opening phases of the First World War. Prince Arthur wrote to the King that the German ships were very smart and powerful-looking and that the fleet was anchored in very exact lines. Alas, Aunt was far from well. She was depressed and Prince Arthur found her difficult to manage. He told the King that there was no chance of her being well enough to come up to Balmoral and that he had given up all hope of her being able to accompany him back to Canada. This was a great blow to them both and Prince Arthur now wished that he did not have to go himself. All the same he was determined to do so, though not as soon as he had earlier intended.[5]

Things, however, turned out much better than expected and when he got back to Bagshot Park from staying with the King at Balmoral, Prince Arthur found the Duchess in greatly improved form. She was in excellent spirits, was walking strongly and had lost the look of an invalid. Another cause for thanksgiving was that young Arthur and his new wife Alix, the daughter of the Princess Royal, who had been married in the Chapel Royal, St James's Palace on 15th October 1913, seemed to be quite happy and she had lost her shy manner and become a changed person. Though Prince Arthur had not been successful with the stags at Balmoral, his spirits had been uplifted by a short stay at Glaslough with the Leslies. Writing to thank Léonie and her husband for their hospitality, he said that he had been through a great deal of anxiety and that the visit had done him as much good morally as physically. He had been pleased to see Léonie's son Jacky getting on with his father and he had thought that he now looked 'tidy' and 'quite human.' He hoped that another son, Lionel, might be persuaded to apply himself to his work, but he rather doubted it, as he was at Eton. Prince Arthur had also very much enjoyed attending the military manoeuvres, for which he stayed, with the King, as a guest of Lord Spencer at Althorp. It seems that it was a long time since a reigning sovereign had been there and Spencer had had fifteen bathrooms put in for the occasion. Prince Arthur took the opportunity to talk to several of the Canadian officers who were observing the operations and he had a meeting with Colonel Sam Hughes, who was also in the field.[6]

On 17th October 1913, instead of taking leave of one another as they had feared they would have to do, Prince Arthur and the Duchess were established together on board the *Empress of Britain*. Unfortunately she had just been repainted and the smell gave Prince Arthur a headache. The Duchess was no more than a little tired and, as Prince Arthur wrote a letter of farewell to Léonie at six that evening, she was already resting in bed clad in a very smart pair of new pyjamas. They were in company with ninety first class passengers and there were another nine hundred travelling steerage. With the crew, there were 1,600 souls on board bound for Quebec, which they reached at midnight on 24th October. As the voyage had neared its end, Prince Arthur had sent a marconigram ahead inviting Borden to accompany him on the royal train from Quebec to Ottawa and it was thus that the two men were able to have a long talk. Borden assured Prince Arthur that he intended to persevere with his naval policy of making a contribution of $35,000,000 for the construction of three capital ships for the British fleet, but he does not seem to have explained how this was to be done in face of the Senate's opposition. He also gave Prince Arthur the impression that he planned to unburden the Cabinet of Colonel Sam Hughes's membership, but he must have given an uncertain impression of how and when, because Prince Arthur, in reporting the conversation to the King, said that he expected that the Prime Minister would probably change his mind on this last point.[7]

Meanwhile, Colonel Hughes had scored a considerable success. Sir Ian Hamilton, the Inspector-General of Overseas Forces, issued a report on the military institutions of Canada which was broadly favourable to Hughes's administration. In 1910, Sir John French had found that a considerable time would be needed before the Canadian Militia could be actively put into the field. In 1913, Hamilton reported that since that time great improvements had been made. Organisation was much more thorough, training had been levelled up in some respects and the education of the higher ranks had been improved. Though the criterion was still the defence of Canada as opposed to the despatch of an expeditionary force, these and other such comments were grist for the mill of Sam Hughes. He and Hamilton, indeed, seemed to have got on extremely well while travelling some 13,957 miles together during the inspection of one hundred and twelve units of cavalry, infantry and artillery. When the report arrived in London, Harcourt suspected that Hughes had edited out any parts of it which did not suit him, but it seems unlikely that Hamilton had put him to any such trouble; nor was it necessary for the Colonial Office and War Office officials to devote so much energy to the question of when and how much of the report should be published; though the document had been marked secret, its contents were immediately released to the Canadian press. Hamilton had forborne to comment on the organisation of the Militia Headquarters in Ottawa and Sam Hughes had not only scored high marks, he had done so publicly. If Borden weighed the alternative views of the Minister of Militia which were offered by the Governor-General and the Inspector-General of Overseas Forces, he may, perhaps, have felt that those of the latter excused him from the unpleasantness which acceptance of the former's would have involved. Anyhow, he was run down and unwell and he went off to recuperate in Hot Springs, where Prince Arthur advised him to stay as long as possible so that he might return to Canada strong and fit to face all the bother and worry which were inseparable from his position as Prime Minister.[8]

Much of this bother and worry, in Prince Arthur's view, was caused by Sam Hughes. There was now open talk of his vagaries and extravagances at the Militia Department and Prince Arthur heard that many people thought that he would be unable to retain his position as Minister. Prince Arthur told the King that he longed to see him go, but he conceded that he had very little authority in the matter. Nevertheless, he took it up with Borden as soon as the latter returned from his holiday in the United States. He complained that Hughes had made a wild speech in Vancouver, which had harmed the position of the Government, especially in an election at South Bruce. He had made himself look ridiculous by taking with him to the English manoeuvres no fewer than two hundred officers in attendance on himself and nineteen ladies. Thirdly, he had made a speech in Halifax in which he had referred to the Canadian Permanent Force, or regular army, as bar room loafers. From a military point of view, the Militia Department was now no less than an autocracy, since the Minister would not listen to any advice from professional officers. Perhaps, Prince Arthur thought, most of these vanities and eccentricities, would, if regarded singly, not be of great moment, but, taken together, he told Borden, their cumulative effect was likely to be very serious. Prince Arthur said that he found it distasteful to write in this vein, but he felt that he would have been wanting in his duty as Governor-General were he not to draw the Prime Minister's attention to questions which were being generally discussed in the country.[9]

Dr Haycock tells us that these observations alienated Borden, who had, he says, had enough of the Duke's 'interference in Canadian politics.' In fact, however, Borden undertook to Prince Arthur that he would take up the matters complained of with Hughes at an early date and that he would already have done so had not Hughes been away in Western Ontario. He added, as Dr Haycock reports, that while there had been strong criticisms of the matters alluded to in the newspapers, there had also in 'important quarters' been 'warm commendation' of the Minister's administration in 'certain other respects.' The trouble which Sam Hughes had taken to secure Sir Ian Hamilton's approbation was paying a good dividend for the Minister of the Militia. How profitable this would be for Canada, time would tell. Prince Arthur was not optimistic, but he told the King that Hughes did have his good side.[10]

Concerned as he was about the political situation in general and Sam Hughes in particular, Prince Arthur had many other occupations at this time. Colonel Sherwood, the Inspector-General of the Dominion Police, brought Mrs Alice Stebbins Wells to see him. She was the pioneer American policewoman and she was in Canada to lecture on social questions. She appeared in a sort of brown waisted jacket and skirt and wore the standard American silver-plate police badge. Her work was concerned mostly with women and principally with the prevention of immorality and the white slave traffic, which, Prince Arthur was told, was very bad in America and in Canada too. Prince Arthur found Mrs Stebbins Wells was an intelligent and interesting woman and he thought that a woman's police force would soon be started in Canada. Another social problem came to his attention through his visit to the City Mission in Montreal. This was run, largely at his own expense, by a Baptist Minister and its efforts were directed principally towards the foreign population in the city, which numbered some 160,000 people. Many of the Russian Jews in this element were living in squalor and Prince Arthur saw some of these in a wretched little room which was crowded to suffocation. His arrival at the City Mission was greeted by an address which was read by an Assyrian. A Bulgarian doctor then presented some flowers to him and, after he had replied, the inmates sang the national anthem. Prince Arthur regretted that there was no corresponding organisation in Quebec, but he heard that the Catholic Church was opposed to this form of charity. He was also shocked to hear that the Catholic Archbishop had told his flock to boycott *Madame Butterfly*, which the impresario, Max Rabinoff, had put on in Montreal and which Prince Arthur had thought was uncommonly good. The reason was that Rabinoff was a Jew. Prince Arthur thought it 'too childish.'[11]

Catholic attitudes to the Jews, however, were not the only, nor were they the worst, of the symptoms of racial tension in Canada. The flow of Japanese and Chinese immigrants to British Columbia had been successfully regulated, but the influx of Indians was more or less out of hand. British Columbia did not wish to be inundated with Asiatic labour and a nasty feeling towards the Sikhs was growing up in the white population. Prince Arthur told the King that he was urging the Government to adopt a tactful attitude; both the Sikhs and the whites, after all, were the King's subjects, but he recognised that the problem was most delicate and that there was a great deal of friction between the Dominion and Provincial Governments over the issue. Among other anxieties which weighed Prince Arthur down in the closing days of 1913, were two unfortunate legacies which the Government had inherited from their Liberal predecessors. These were the Grand Trunk Pacific Railway, which had been built at vast expense and now seemed to be of doubtful utility, and the Canadian Northern Railway, which was quite unnecessary, or so it seemed to Prince Arthur. Borden's Government, he told the King, now had no alternative other than to dole out huge sums to both. It was as well for Prince Arthur's peace of mind that he did not know of the transactions which the Duchess had had with Sir Donald Mann and Sir William Mackenzie, for it is very unlikely that both were not substantial gainers from the Government's plight. Borden now stood less well in the Governor-General's eye than he had done at first. Though Prince Arthur still thought him able and upright, he felt that his policies were not constructive and that he lacked Laurier's vigour. In retailing these problems to the King, Prince Arthur realised that his nephew had himself been beset with problems and especially the Irish one. He hoped that 1914 would turn out to be a less anxious year for the King and for himself.[12]

In Canada, Prince Arthur thought, the word 'war' was little more than an expression and he was, therefore, agreeably surprised when Borden, at the outset of 1914, convened a conference of Deputy Ministers to consider defence questions. This may not have sounded a very exciting development, but Prince Arthur looked on it as a most important one. Planning for war by the Departments of Militia and Marine had been vitiated by jealousies between the two sets of officials; Borden's conference would be a step towards overcoming this difficulty and a move in the direction of increased efficiency. The preparation of a war book, in which the duties of the officials in the two departments would be defined, marked a distinct advance and, Prince Arthur thought, would do much to avoid confusion in any future period of emergency. It would also bring it home to those concerned that war was a possiblity.[13]

In other respects Prince Arthur was much less well pleased and he had come to some conclusions about the Militia which differed severely from those reached in Sir Ian Hamilton's report. Prince Arthur, more immune to the charm of Colonel Sam Hughes than Hamilton had been, observed that the force's peace establishment was set at 75,000, but that it was understrength by 21,000. Moreover, the position was much worse than that, for many Militiamen had received no training at all in 1913. As the war establishment of the Militia was 157,000, it would, in effect, in the event of war, be necessary to find more than a hundred thousand recruits. Though some progress had been made with the development of defences at Halifax, both Esquimault and Quebec were virtually defenceless. In addition to all this, there had been a reduction in the stock of small arms ammunition, since large numbers of rounds had been condemned after an inspection at Quebec. When this news reached the Colonial Office in London there was much fuss about how Canada could be urged to prepare for war when she was a self-governing Dominion and had not asked for advice. The Secretary of State, Mr Harcourt, supercilious as ever, took a less ponderous view; he minuted that 'Colonel Hughes will declare war when he wishes.' Such attitudes were not much use to Prince Arthur. Nor was he impressed when he heard that Colonel Hughes was proposing to bring over to Canada the Queen's brother, Prince Alexander of Teck, who was a junior squadron leader in the 2nd Life Guards, to command a cavalry brigade at the annual training camp. How absurd, Prince Arthur thought, and 'too snobbish.'[14]

Such thoughts of war were far in the background when ex-President Taft arrived at Rideau Hall to spend the night with the Connaughts on 30th January 1914. Prince Arthur had a long talk with him and found him cheery and easy to get on with, but, though his conversation was full of humour, he was rather inclined to embark on long-winded stories. Prince Arthur gave a dinner in his honour, which included the Bordens, Laurier and the Fitzpatricks. The Duchess went to bed when the ladies withdrew, but Taft kept the others laughing until the party broke up at about eleven. Next day Prince Arthur took his guest to a lunch at which he met most of the Canadian Cabinet and many of the opposition. Speeches by Taft and Prince Arthur were warmly received; Canadian-American relations were steadily improving. Taft came back to Rideau Hall for tea and Captain Graham of Prince Arthur's staff, who was a dab hand on the piano, provided music for dancing. Though Taft had lost some weight, he was still a very big man, but Prince Arthur thought that he danced uncommonly well and moved like a feather in the arms of another of his guests, Irene Gibson. The former American President seemed very readily to recognise the role of the Canadian Governor-General and the style which Prince Arthur brought to the office. In writing to thank him and the Duchess for his stay under their 'hospitable roof,' he said that he would not soon forget the honour and pleasure of dining at Government House seated between the Duchess and Princess Patricia and meeting 'doughty political antagonists in amity under your kindly peace compelling influence.'[15]

Borden was a thoroughly political animal, but he evidently also sensed something of Taft's view of Prince Arthur as Governor-General. The extension of his original term of office would expire in October 1914, and, though it was still only February, Borden began to take soundings as to the possibility of Prince Arthur being persuaded to stay on for a fourth year. The Military Secretary, Colonel Farquhar, did not give him much encouragement, but Borden was not to be put off and, at the end of March, he urged on Harcourt the desirability of the Duke of Connaught's term being extended again. He said that he and his colleagues in the Cabinet were strongly of this opinion. Canada, he wrote, was composed of at least five main centres of population, which were divided by distance, supposed or real divergence of interest and sometimes by racial or religious prejudice. A million of the people had been citizens of the Dominion for less than three years. The Duke of Connaught had spared neither time nor effort in visiting every part of the country and in becoming acquainted with every community and he had secured a firm hold on the affections of the people. The Duchess's illness had touched their sympathy and they admired her pluck and devotion in returning to Canada when she was scarcely convalescent. Prince Arthur, who had been undecided in such situations before, was undecided again. He had been suffering from a cold and he never found the winter climate in Ottawa at all agreeable. He had, indeed, mentioned to the King that if there should be a vacancy in the Governor-Generalship of South Africa, he would like to fill it; the country had such a glorious climate. A more immediate reason for his wishing to come home at the end of his third year was his anxiety about the Ulster crisis and the extent to which it had embroiled the Crown. He had been a great deal worried by the more or less hostile references to the King's actions which had recently been proclaimed by the political opponents of Asquith's Government, and its Irish policy, and he evidently asked himself if he ought not to be near his nephew to lend him support. Even so, he indicated that if the King thought it was essential for him to stay in Canada, he would do so and he added that he would be influenced by Canadian opinion.[16]

In a curiously inadvertent manner the King made up Prince Arthur's mind for him. There had for some time been a rumour that the next Governor-General of Canada was to be Prince Alexander of Teck, to whom Sam Hughes had already paid court. As Prince Alexander was still only a Major, his principal qualification seemed to be that he was the Queen's brother. In Prince Arthur's view, this was not enough; notwithstanding that Prince Alexander was forty, he thought the man was too young and too pompous to fill the post. Before he had closed his letter to Léonie giving expression to this opinion, however, Prince Arthur heard that the King had fixed on Prince Alexander. It seemed to him to be an extraordinary decision, which flattered neither Canada nor himself. If it was so, it is, perhaps, explicable in the light of the terrible anxieties which beset the King at this time, when he was confronted with the imminent possibility of civil war in Ireland and a mutiny in the Army. Prince Arthur, therefore, or so it seemed, would come home in October 1914.[17]

The situation which now arose had the curious effect of allowing Prince Arthur, so to speak, to read his obituary while he was still alive. On 9th May, the Duchess recorded in her Journal, an M.P. got up in the House and strongly objected to Prince Alexander's appointment as Governor-General designate. Canada, he said, did not want a Prince as Governor-General and especially a German one. This seems to have been Mr H. R. Emmerson, who had been Minister of Railways in Laurier's Government and whose views were the subject of an article by Mr E. W. Thompson. Thompson wrote that in so far as Emmerson's opinion might be taken to mean that the Duke of Connaught's term should have been extended, it was a wish which might reasonably be applauded. Canada, he declared, never had a Governor-General more precisely suited to Viceroyalty than the Duke of Connaught. He had not meddled in politics, but he had quietly promoted all manner of good works and no foolish ones. He had ever spoken with the 'exquisite, modest, almost self-effacing tact for which he was long famous among the quiet wise of Great Britain.' He had been 'cordial with all manner of people without ever appearing to tout for popularity.' Emmerson retorted that he was against Canada being governed by royalty, which he thought was bad for a young nation. The Duke of Connaught, he conceded, was a splendid man, but royalty raised social barriers. Thompson rejected this as utterly wrong. Royalty, he said, discouraged the superior class of enriched traders, money mongers and politicians, whereas aristocrats as Governors-General blended with the moneyed. Lord Grey had been the pet of profiteers; there was no danger to democracy from the superior person or family represented by royalty. Public opinion is a difficult commodity to measure, but these expressions of it may well have portrayed its Canadian spectrum in 1914.[18]

In the brilliance of lovely Canadian summer weather, Prince Arthur embarked on what he planned as his farewell tour of the Dominion. He travelled with the Duchess to Peterborough, Port Hope and Cobourg and then to Belleville, Kingston, Brockville, Cornwall and Quebec. Here they took up residence in the Citadel for a time and were met by somewhat less enthusiasm than generally greeted them in Canada. For a ball they gave on 15th June, six hundred invitations were sent out, five hundred and eighty acceptances were received, but only two hundred and seventy people turned up. There were also other things of which Prince Arthur disapproved in Quebec. He visited the so-called Detention House where immigrants arriving in Quebec were incarcerated for pecuniary reasons. He saw two hundred such people, who were English, Italian, Russian, Polish and Gallician, living in shameful conditions. They had been required by the authorities to show that they had $5 and they had not been able to do so. Prince Arthur thought that the Dominion Government was to blame for this iniquitous situation and he intended to rub that in pretty hard.[19]

On the other side of the country an even more threatening crisis was developing. On 6th June 1914, Gurdit Singh telegraphed to the King from the Japanese liner, *Komagata Maru*, which was lying off Vancouver, that he and his fellow Indian passengers had been denied any provisions for four days and that they were now starving captives. The King was shocked and he caused the Colonial Office to be told that this raised a very serious issue 'if we are still to consider ourselves all members of one Empire.' The Colonial Office observed that the starving of the Hindus might be caused, not by the denial of provisions, but by a hunger strike. The King was told that a telegram had been sent to the Governor-General asking for a statement from the Canadian Ministers. Prince Arthur replied that force would not be used unless the Captain of the ship asked for protection or if there was an unlawful landing of the Hindus. He added that the situation was difficult because of the excited state of public opinion in Vancouver. Opinion on board the *Komagata Maru* was also inflamed. The authorities decided that there should be an official enquiry on the ship, but when Mr W. C. Hopkinson of the Immigration Branch of the Department of the Interior went on board, Gurdit Singh and all the Hindus to a man declared that they would not take part in it. Hopkinson recognised that the situation was very delicate and, as he reckoned that the passengers had been without food for two days, he said that provisions to last for about thirty-six hours would be put on board, on the understanding that the ship would later be provisioned for a voyage to Hong Kong and that the cost would subsequently be recovered by the Canadian Government from the parties involved. He had had twenty-five years experience of these people in India and he was convinced that the position had become extremely serious. It had indeed, for it soon emerged that the Hindus were buying revolvers in Victoria and trying to do the same in Vancouver. Matters thereafter moved swiftly to a climax. The Japanese owners of the *Komagata Maru* instructed the Captain, Yammamoto, to sail, but when he set about doing so, his Indian passengers seized control and prevented him from getting up steam. He then appealed to the Canadian authorities for protection and at midnight on 18th July a tug with police and officials, to the number of some two hundred, went out to the ship with thirty days of provisions for it. They were met by a fusillade of coal and bricks and as the tug rode about ten feet below the deck of the liner, it was forced to withdraw with several wounded policemen on board.[20]

The Viceroy of India now telegraphed to the India Office in London that rumours that the Canadian Government was about to use force against the would-be immigrants was likely to have a bad effect in India. The Viceroy's intelligence was correct. Borden told Prince Arthur on 21st July that he had telegraphed to Mr Hazen to place H.M.C.S *Rainbow* at the disposal of the immigration authorities. It was then discovered, however, that the complement of *Rainbow*, as Prince Arthur had noticed long since, was inadequate and steps had to be taken to put Militiamen on board to act in the role of Marines. It seemed that the next move would be an armed boarding party or even something more violent than that, but, whether because of such a threat or for some other reason, the Hindus suddenly came to terms with the Canadians and it was agreed that the *Komagata Maru* would be provisioned and that she would then sail. Prince Arthur believed that this settlement was due to the tact of the Minister of Agriculture, Mr Burrell, who had arrived in Vancouver on 21st July. He was also impressed by the firmness with which Borden had acted and his determination to settle the matter with the least possible embarrassment to the Indian and Imperial Governments. He emphasised to the Colonial Office, however, that they needed to bear in mind that feelings in British Columbia about Indian immigrants were very bitter. In the early hours of 23rd July 1914, the *Komagata Maru* sailed from Vancouver and transferred the problem she posed from Canada to other parts of the world.[21]

The saga of the *Komagata Maru* was one, often anticipated before and repeated since, of people in depressed areas of the world taking to boats in the hope of reaching more prosperous ones, only to be turned away. In this case, the interest of the Empire, exemplified by the King-Emperor himself, tended to weigh on the side of the Hindus, but the Canadian national interest found its expression in the mobilisation of H.M.C.S.

Rainbow. Prince Arthur, who so often was confronted with the clash between imperial and national concerns, ruled in this case for the national one. Perhaps he had little constitutional alternative, but his instinct about this issue was on that side too. He availed himself of the opportunity which the *Komagata Maru* provided to impress upon Borden the importance of having some naval force available on the Pacific coast and he thought that the Prime Minister now appreciated this. Prince Arthur had long believed that Borden's wish to contribute to the cost of the Imperial navy was not inconsistent with Laurier's to lay the foundations of a national navy for Canada.[22]

During most of these difficult days of the sojourn of the *Komagata Maru* off Vancouver, Prince Arthur was away from Ottawa on the continuation of his farewell tour which took him to Sherbrooke, Lennoxville, Magog, Perkins Landing, Mansville and then to Petawawa for the military manoeuvres. To these last, Borden also came and in his memoirs it was subsequently noted that the Duke seemed pleased and Colonel Hughes was in his element. The Duchess, however, recorded at the time that Prince Arthur had returned from the experience 'really disgusted' with Sam Hughes. After this he planned to pay a visit to Newfoundland and then to tour the West, returning to Ottawa on 7th September. In a brief interval before embarking on these journeys he heard that Archduke Franz Ferdinand had been assassinated in Sarajevo on 28th June 1914. 'How shocking,' he wrote to his sister Louise, 'poor old Emperor there is apparently no end to his sorrows and troubles.'[23]

Prince Arthur sailed for Newfoundland in H.M.S. *Essex*, which had been detached from Admiral Craddock's Squadron. She was soon amidst huge icebergs. The first one Prince Arthur saw was fifty feet high and, when another came in range, *Essex* fired two broadsides of lyddite shell from her six inch guns. She was surrounded by broken ice, but the main bulk of the iceberg remained. At one stage, Prince Arthur could see twenty-two icebergs, one of which was computed by *Essex*'s range-finder to be four hundred feet high. Scarcely less novel was the visit to Newfoundland, which Prince Arthur found extremely interesting. He was especially impressed by some fine fishermen with light-red hair whom he met on board their motor vessel. On 23rd July, accompanied by the Duchess, he started for the West, but on 1st August, when they were at Banff, he decided that the international situation had become so grave that he must return at once to Ottawa. Sixty-eight hours later, after a hot and dusty journey during which he stopped nowhere for more than ten minutes, Prince Arthur arrived back in the capital. Writing to tell the King of this change of plan, he said that he had completed the journey at an average speed of forty-five miles an hour, but before he got further with his account, he was interrupted by the news that war had been declared. However powerful the Navy might be, he continued, the British military forces were so weak that they could do little to help the Belgians and French against overwhelming masses of Germans. He felt awfully anxious and wished he could be with the Army, but he knew that his duty was in Canada and that he must help in organising a Canadian force which would eventually go to the front. He had, in fact, decided at once, that he could not now go home. To Léonie he wrote that this was the greatest crisis since the Napoleonic wars and he cursed the fate which now separated him from the Army.[24]

The response of Borden's Government to this challenge was robust. There never was any question but that Canada would play a full part in the war and in a series of Cabinet meetings, at which Prince Arthur was invited to preside, it was decided that an expeditionary force of 25,000 men would be raised for service at the front. Sam Hughes sprang into the most vigorous and effective action. To accommodate these men, he ordered the building of a camp at Valcartier near Quebec. Four hundred workmen completed the job in thirty days and Sam Hughes came in for some well-earned plaudits. Even the Governor-General, Dr Haycock tells us, was 'grudgingly forced' to admit that it was a splendid performance. In truth, however, Prince Arthur was not at all grudging. Writing to Princess Louise on 9th August, he said that he was very pleased with Borden and the Government, which he thought was working admirably. He said that everything was gone into carefully, but that there was no delay in giving effect to the Cabinet's decisions. He said he was in constant touch with the Ministers of Militia and Marine and that both of them were doing much better than he would have thought possible. He told her that the camp was being built at Valcartier and that men were flocking to join up. He said that he and Colonel Sam Hughes were working very well together and he hoped that the division they were raising would be a credit to Canada.[25]

From the first, Prince Arthur was determined that these Canadian recruits should not be sent to the front until they had been given the best possible training and were imbued with a proper spirit of military discipline. In both cases his criteria were the standards of the regular army. He was all too well aware of the capacities of the German army against which these men would be pitted and it was on this principle that relations between Prince Arthur and Sam Hughes began to break down again. The Minister of Militia, Prince Arthur told Kitchener, was loyal and well-meaning, but he was also an ignorant and conceited demagogue, who was always surrounded by the press and toadies who enabled him to believe that he was the heaven-born commander of the age. He laughed at regular soldiers and spurned all discipline. Indeed, his opinion was so high of himself and so low of professional soldiers, that he believed himself to be perfectly competent to command the Canadian Division at the front, where he seemed to think it would be going almost at once. Prince Arthur told Kitchener that he had had some difficulty in convincing the Government that their Minister of Militia was unfitted for this role, but in the end Borden devised the formula that Hughes could not be spared from his post in Canada.[26]

This rising tension between Prince Arthur and Sam Hughes did not alienate the Governor-General from Borden and the rest of the Cabinet, though Dr Haycock claims that it did. Through a series of odd misunderstandings, the King seemed to be under the impression that Prince Arthur was coming home and he was proceeding with arrangements for Prince Alexander to take over the Governor-Generalship. When at last the situation became clear to the King, Borden was able to rise in the House on 20th August to state that in the urgent conditions confronting Canada and the rest of the Empire, the Government considered it 'highly important' that His Royal Highness Field-Marshal, the Duke of Connaught, should continue to give Canada the benefit of his services as Governor-General. 'His knowledge of conditions in Canada,' the Prime Minister continued, 'and his wide experience in public and military affairs, render his services especially valuable at this juncture.' Borden then announced that, at the request of the Canadian Government and with the approval of the King and the Imperial Government, the Duke of Connaught would continue as Governor-General while the war lasted. Borden had assured Prince Arthur that even the ablest successor could not have picked up the threads of the Governor-Generalship from him at this time. These were hardly the words of alienation.[27]

So, at this point, we must return to Prince Arthur's interpretation of his constitutional position and the view of it which Borden took, which was alluded to at the beginning of Chapter 15, for it is from the criticism made in the Borden Memoirs that much of the misunderstanding arises. In the Memoirs it is stated that in the early days of the War, the Duke of

Connaught failed to realise that his status and powers as Commander-in-Chief were purely nominal and it is said that, on 26th August 1914, Borden explained to the Duke's Military Secretary, Colonel Farquhar, that Prince Arthur's impression in this respect was 'wholly false.' In Canadian historiography and biography, this phrase has been quoted and requoted, expanded and developed over and over again; its damaging nuance has achieved the status of received knowledge. Yet there is no evidence that Prince Arthur was in any doubt as to the nominal position which he occupied as Commander-in-Chief, nor that he suffered from any delusions about his functions as Governor-General, which he himself described as being largely those of a Post Office. Questioning, probing, encouraging, advising and warning are, of course, proper functions for a constitutional sovereign, and so they were for Prince Arthur as Governor-General of Canada, even though such activities were at times very irritating for the Prime Minister and other Ministers. Apart from such irritations, however, there seems to be no primary evidence that Borden entertained serious doubts about Prince Arthur's ability to interpret his constitutional position in a reasonable manner. We have seen that he was keen that Prince Arthur should remain in Canada, when the prospects were that he might return home, and we should now notice that on the very day on which he was supposed to have read Colonel Farquhar the riot act, that is 26th August 1914, he actually instructed Colonel Hughes that communications between himself and the War Office in London should be shown to the Governor-General and that, on important matters, the Governor-General should be consulted. Thus, when recollection would have it that Borden was telling Farquhar to tell Prince Arthur not to interfere in military matters, he was, in truth, telling Sam Hughes to consult Prince Arthur about them.[28]

The first effective Canadian fighting formation of the war which had just broken out was intimately connected with Prince Arthur, for it was named after his daughter, having been given the title of Princess Patricia's Canadian Light Infantry. Immediately on the outbreak of war, the Regiment had been raised and half its costs paid for by Mr Gault, a rich citizen of Montreal, who had served in the South African War and who now became the second in command. It was commanded by Prince Arthur's Military Secretary, Colonel Farquhar, and its Adjutant was his senior A.D.C., Captain Buller. Eighty per cent of the men had already seen war service, but it also contained some new recruits, including a number of cowboys, who had joined in a body from Moose Jaw, and an excellent pipe and drum band, which had also joined as a body from Alberta. After reviewing the Regiment, Prince Arthur wrote to Lord Roberts that it consisted of men of fine physique who were seasoned troops. It would be ready to sail for England before the end of August and after three weeks at Aldershot it would be ready to go anywhere. Prince Arthur felt confident that it would be a credit to Canada, an expectation which was more than fulfilled, for, though Princess Pat's did not sail as soon as Prince Arthur had expected, in consequence of shipping difficulties, they were to be the first Canadian formation to take the field in the Great War and, having covered themselves with glory, they then endured to become a prime symbol of Canada's greatest military virtue.[29]

Princess Pat's were a thousand strong and nearly all seasoned men, but the problem of raising the main expeditionary force of twenty-five thousand or more men was naturally a much greater one. The principles in Prince Arthur eyes were, however, the same; the men must be experienced and, if they were not, they must be trained to the highest possible standard. Though much impressed by the speed with which things had been put together at Valcartier, he became increasingly anxious about what was going on there. The men were very good, being physically fit, intensely patriotic and full of enthusiasm, but most of the officers were ignorant of military duties, in which they had received no instruction. Sam Hughes seemed to change the brigades and their commanders and staffs every day and he was showing much favouritism in his selections. Nevertheless, Prince Arthur thought that Hughes deserved credit for the driving power and indefatigable energy with which he had got the force together. His complaint was that the Minister interfered in everything regardless of whether or not he knew anything about it. Prince Arthur feared that there would be difficulties in disembarking the force when it reached England because Sam Hughes had overturned the arrangements of the Quarter-Master-General and taken charge himself of the embarkation of the 31,000 men and 8,000 horses. He was also showing what Prince Arthur thought were alarming symptoms of instability. In the heady atmosphere of the outbreak of war, he seemed to have run riot and become quite mad with conceit. He insulted everybody right and left, but he commanded many votes and press correspondents were always buzzing round him. Prince Arthur thought that Borden and the Cabinet were afraid of him.[30]

To these fears others were now added. Prince Arthur was very anxious about the way in which contractors for the supply of war materials were selected and his information was that a nice adjustment of patronage was a bigger factor than the instant production of the goods and, which was of even more immediate concern, he heard ugly rumours about the Ross rifle, with which the entire Canadian expeditionary force was equipped and which Sam Hughes had long proclaimed was the best in the world. In short, Prince Arthur now saw in Sam Hughes signs of incipient madness and he was beginning to wonder if he was not also corrupt. As the man in question was the Minister responsible for the raising, equipment and command of the troops which Canada was about to send to the front, Prince Arthur, however constitutional was his position as Governor-General or nominal that of Commander-in Chief, could scarcely turn a blind eye. Nor was he by any means alone in these fears and suspicions. Mr White, the Minister of Finance, told the Duchess that he had spoken at least twenty times to Borden about Hughes, but that he thought nothing would move the Prime Minister short of the whole Cabinet resigning. In the end, however, he believed that Hughes would commit some act of supreme folly which would of itself convict him of insanity. Meanwhile, the inference was, the Canadian army would have to soldier on. Sir Charles Fitzpatrick, who thought it was a great blessing for Canada that she had Prince Arthur as Governor-General at this time, was critical of him, all the same, for not, as he saw it, taking a stronger line about Hughes.[31]

Prince Arthur's suspicions that Sam Hughes might be not only unbalanced, but also corrupt, were reinforced by the emergence from the shadows of Colonel J. Wesley Allison. On 1st November 1914, Sir Cecil Spring-Rice, who had succeeded Bryce as British Ambassador in Washington, telegraphed to Prince Arthur that persons who claimed to be agents of the British Government were offering contracts in the United States for the supply of war materials at exorbitant prices. Among the names which he mentioned was that of Allison. He wanted to know if these were indeed agents officially appointed by the Canadian Government to place these orders on behalf of the British Government. Prince Arthur realised at once that a scandal was blowing up and he knew that Sam Hughes was mixed up in it, but, of course, he passed the question to Borden. Borden, presumably after consulting Hughes, who, Dr Haycock tells us, denied that he had appointed Allison or anyone else, stated that the Canadian Government had not appointed any official agents and that this applied, in particular, to the persons named in Spring-Rice's telegram, including, of course, Allison. Meanwhile, in London Harcourt was investigating the ugly rumours about Allison which were coming into circulation. The Contracts Branch of the War Office averred that they knew nothing of Allison except that they had been warned against him by Mr George Perley, the Canadian Acting High Commissioner in London. No sooner had this reassuring letter been despatched than it was discovered that, in fact, Colonel Allison had called on the Director of Contracts at the War Office on 24th October. Saying that he had an introduction from Colonel Sam Hughes, of which, however, he did not produce documentary evidence, he offered large quantities of stores of all kinds. The unfortunate official who now had to correct his first letter and admit these facts could not understand how they had arisen. Visitors to the Director of Contracts always had to come through his office, but this one had not. Realising now that Colonel Allison had no official standing and was 'entirely rascally', the Colonial Office alerted the Foreign Office, so that the allied governments could be warned against him, which was a point which Borden had also made.[32]

The warning against Allison which it was proposed the allied governments should now be given, was not before time; Mr Perley had in his possession a dossier on the case which showed that Allison had been reaping huge profits at the expense of the British and allied governments, but he had also obtained documents which made nonsense of the statement that Allison had no official Canadian standing. They showed that he had, in fact, been formally appointed and introduced at the highest levels by Colonel Sam Hughes. For example, there was a telegram sent in September 1914 by Hughes to Kitchener, the British Secretary of State for War. In this the Minister of Militia referred to the purchase of war materials in Canada and the United States for the British and French Governments. As far as future orders were concerned, he nominated General James A. Drain, Colonel J. Wesley Allison and Colonel William McBain as 'associates with me to do all purchasing committed to my care.' He added that 'these gentlemen have great experience and are thoroughly reliable.' Kitchener replied on 22nd September accepting the nominations. Mr Perley had also got a message sent by Ena Macadam, the typist to Sam Hughes, which was sent to the Russian and French ambassadors in Washington, saying that the Minister of Militia and Defence, the Honourable Sam Hughes, had 'officially instructed' Colonel Allison to aid the allies in the purchase of their requirements. When Mr Perley showed these documents to Harcourt's Private Secretary, Mr J.C.C.

Davidson, the poor man could hardly believe his eyes and he obviously at first doubted if the telegrams between Sam Hughes and Lord Kitchener were genuine. Kitchener's Private Secretary, Mr Herbert Creedy, had to tell him that they were. Further enquiries also showed that the French and Russian ambassadors had received Ena Macadam's telegram.[33]

Borden was rather concerned when he heard all these things, but he decided to do nothing about it and Perley, therefore, had no alternative other than to tell Harcourt that the Canadian Government had not appointed Allison or anyone else to be official agents in the purchase of supplies for the allies. All three, of course, knew that this was untrue, but Harcourt wondered what Prince Arthur thought and he telegraphed to ask. Prince Arthur replied that the Canadian Government had not authorised any agent to make purchases for the British or allied governments in the United States. At the outset, he had suspected that Sam Hughes was involved in the scandal, but how much he knew of the precise evidence which had now come to light is not clear; however, whatever he knew or did not know, he could not, in an official despatch, have sent a reply which differed from that which had already been given by the Prime Minister. Dr Haycock is, therefore, rather ungenerous in saying that 'Borden and Connaught, through ignorance or political fears' denied the existence of the Allison group. Borden, we know, was not ignorant of the facts and whether Connaught was or not, he could not have officially contradicted Borden. Had he done so, there would, indeed, have been grounds for accusing him of being an unconstitutional Governor-General.[34]

We shall meet Colonel Allison again, but in the meanwhile it is sufficient to note that, despite the evidence which was now in Borden's hands, the Minister of Militia took no harm at all. He was in London where praise was being heaped on him and he rejoiced in the rank of Major-General, which promotion Borden had insisted that Prince Arthur should approve. Among those who lionised him were Lord Roberts, who wrote to Prince Arthur that he had seen him several times and had him to dinner at Englemere. He told Prince Arthur he was on capital terms with him and the little South African incident seemed to be forgotten. He said that Hughes was in some respects a wonderful man and that one could not help being impressed by his driving power. This was much what Prince Arthur had himself thought at first.[35]

While Sam Hughes was in England seeing the Canadian Division, which had now arrived there, Borden was once again recuperating at Hot

Springs in the United States, where Prince Arthur wrote to him to enquire
how he was. Perhaps without all his customary tact, he said that in the
absence of the Prime Minister and the Minister of Militia, everything was
running smoothly in Ottawa. Mr Hazen was acting for Sam Hughes and
there was no friction. He hoped that General Hughes would not upset all
this when he returned, but he said that several people thought that was
what he would do. He felt sure Borden would not approve of that and he
continued by remarking that he had no personal interest and that his sole
concern was for the smooth and efficient working of the military machine
during the crisis. Borden, as he so often did, made a sympathetic reply. It
would be his endeavour, he said, to see that the harmonious state of
affairs in the Militia Department was maintained. The particular reason
for which Prince Arthur was so anxious was his hope that the raising and
training of the Canadian Second Division would be more efficiently
carried out than had been the case with the First. He wished to see less
fanfare in the press and more solid hard work.[36]

The state of the First Division in England provided a good deal of
justification for these views. The King went to see it on Salisbury Plain.
He told Prince Arthur that they were certainly a splendid body of men,
but the discipline was not of the best and there was too much drinking.
Some of the officers were not much good. Nevertheless, he was sure that
after adequate training, they would give a good account of themselves.
Borden took a yet harsher view. He was disturbed by reports of
indiscipline, drunkeness, absence without leave and one case of rape. He
hoped that the English commander, General Alderson, would impose
strict discipline, or the whole force and the Dominion would be
discredited. Perhaps neither the King nor Borden made sufficient
allowance for the very poor conditions under which the Canadians were
living on Salisbury Plain, even if this was only a soft prelude to what
awaited them in France and Flanders.[37]

The awful losses which the British army had already suffered in
attempting to stem the German advance were brought home to Prince
Arthur by a series of letters from his son, who was serving on French's
staff, and more tragically by the death in action within the first few weeks
of his nephew, Prince Maurice of Battenberg, Tommy Bulkeley, who had
been on his staff as A.D.C., Equerry and Comptroller for seven years, and
Léonie's son Norman. The rest of Prince Arthur's staff had followed
Bulkeley in the direction of active service, including Colonel Farquhar,
commanding Princess Pat's, and Captain Buller, their Adjutant. The King

thought that Prince Arthur had made a mistake in allowing all these to go, as it left him without effective people to interpose between himself and Ministers when contentious issues arose. The stop-gap replacements, Major Stanton as Military Secretary, and others who had been wounded or were unfit, were not everybody's idea of the most accomplished staff officers for the Governor-General. Mr Sladen, now acting as Comptroller, though experienced in Canadian affairs, had been no more than the head clerk in the Governor-General's secretariat and, according to the Duchess, could only judge matters in Ottawa through the eyes of his friends in the Rideau Club, in Montreal through those of a single friend, Mr Joseph, and in Toronto, not at all. If this was so, it was unfortunate. Very contentious issues were to arise or to increase in the near future.[38]

CHAPTER 17

O Canada 1915-1916

As THE HARSH EVENTS of 1915 began to unfold, Prince Arthur was approaching his sixty-fifth birthday. There was little sign of any diminution of his energetic nature nor of the physical endurance with which his strong constitution had endowed him. Unlike his elder brothers, he had not grown too fat, as Edward VII had done, nor was he excessively addicted to alcohol, as the Duke of Edinburgh had been. All the same, some signs of age were beginning to assert themselves and these, coupled with Canadian winter weather and the severe tensions of Canadian politics, militated against his usual form. He had always suffered from asthma and hay fever, but now, more often than before, he seemed to be burdened with a heavy cold or a bad throat. Indeed, at the turn of the year he had such a bad one that the Duchess became anxious. Armed with some nitrate of silver, supplied by Dr Gibson, she painted his throat, as she had often done before. This time, however, the treatment resulted in a sudden and awful fit of suffocation, which seriously alarmed the Duchess and later led Prince Arthur to say that he had thought that the end had come. His normally optimistic outlook upon life had always been punctuated by moments of pessimism, but now he seemed to swing a little more violently and more often between the two extremes. At times he felt that he was really doing good in Canada, but, at others, that he had no effective influence as Governor-General and might as well go home. He was also growing somewhat deaf. A nice little American lady who recited had come to stay in April 1914 and after dinner she had entertained the company. The Duchess found her very clever and amusing, but Prince Arthur had not been able to hear much of what she had said. This was Miss Ruth Draper. Then, in February 1916, the Prime Minister of Australia, Mr Hughes, visited Canada and at a dinner in his honour Prince Arthur made what the Duchess described as a charming speech to which, she said, Mr Hughes made a very clever little reply.

Borden recorded that neither could hear what the other said as both were deaf. In addition, Prince Arthur was often anxious about the Duchess. Though she seemed to have recovered from her very serious illness, her health was precarious and she was often in very bad form and difficult to manage. Lastly, things did not run so smoothly for Prince Arthur now that his staff was reduced and those he had were no more than substitutes for better ones who had gone to the front.[1]

Sam Hughes, the Minister of Militia and Defence, recently promoted to the rank of Major-General and, by further curious twists of influence, about to be knighted and then made a Lieutenant-General, was a little over three years younger than Prince Arthur. Despite the very bad feeling which had now grown up between him and the Governor-General, and many of his colleagues in the Cabinet, and despite the suspicions which had arisen, even in the mind of the Prime Minister, about his connections with the already infamous Colonel Allison, Sam Hughes was going from strength to strength and seemed still to be a star in the ascendant. Prince Arthur and many others believed that he had some hold over Borden, which ensured his position; the King heard that he was supposed to control the whole of the Orange vote in Canada and that, if he wished, he could turn Borden out of office. Given to the use of violently abusive language, he was also a teetotaller, who was inclined to burst into tears at critical moments. Under pressure, Borden thought that he reacted with 'wonderful energy,' but lost control of his two worst enemies: 'his tongue and his pen.' Though the only member of the Cabinet with any military experience, or even knowledge, Sam Hughes's service as a soldier had been distinctly amateurish and highly eccentric. Any damage to his self-confidence which this might have caused was, however, more than compensated by his firm belief that amateur part-time soldiers were superior to professional ones and that Canadians could always out-perform the British. His virtues, among which were his tremendous energy and driving power, and yet more so his defects, combined to place and keep him at the centre of attention and, of all the Canadian Ministers, his profile was far the highest. The patronage which he disposed as Minister of Militia provided him with an army of retainers to whom he doled out war contracts or Colonelcies in the Militia, or both, and he had a special understanding with Max Aitken, whose murky eminence had made him a formidable centre of political power and intrigue in London.[2]

Sir Robert Borden, who had been made a Knight Grand Cross of the Order of St Michael and St George in 1914, was four years younger than

Prince Arthur. He had steered a path round the political minefields, which lay in wait for any Prime Minister of Canada, with consummate skill and he had carried the Dominion into the war with courage and conviction. Intensely loyal to the Crown and deeply respectful to Prince Arthur, he also had a clear and independent view of Canada's war aim; the achievement of a significant place in the counsels, not only of the Empire, but also of the world at large. In dealing with the ins and outs of politics, the products of the Canadian system of patronage and, in particular, the dangerous vagaries of Sam Hughes, Prince Arthur thought he detected in Borden the signs of serious, he presently thought criminal, weakness and, indeed, Borden often did say one thing to one man and quite another to another. It seems evident, too, that he found confrontation with Sam Hughes painful and usually impossible, but whether the cause was some hold which Hughes had over him, or the different strengths of personality in the two men, is impossible to say. One searches Robert Craig Brown's scholarly biography of Borden in vain for a convincing answer to this conundrum and the suggestion which has sometimes been made, that the connection was no more than gratitude for a seat made available by Hughes in an election of past times, seems scarcely an adequate explanation. Fortunately, it is not the task of Prince Arthur's biographer to determine the underlying cause of this curious relationship; it suffices for his purposes to recognise, as we shall see in succeeding pages of this chapter, that Borden was powerfully reluctant to discipline Hughes even at his most outrageous, even when he had insisted on equipping Canada's troops with boots which disintegrated in the mud, earning for Sam Hughes the soubriquet of 'Sham Shoes', trenching shovels, patented by his Secretary, which buckled in their hands and, worst of all by far, rifles with a propensity to jam, which had become notorious. Borden undoubtedly was tired and he was often unwell too. At lunch in June 1915, the Duchess found him looking dazed as if drugged, he spoke very little and looked a bad reddish colour in the face; when he returned from visiting the troops in France in September 1915, she found what he had to say interesting, but she noted that he recited it like a schoolboy, or a parrot, without any personality.[3]

Such were some of the traits of the three men most intimately concerned at the top level with the raising, training, equipment, command and administration of Canada's expeditionary force. The relationship between them and the manner of their responses to the exacting challenges of 1915 and 1916 are a major component in the understanding of this period of Canadian history; any true judgement of Prince Arthur's Governor-Generalship depends primarily on the same issues, for, compared to them, the problems of the years since 1911 were simple.

1915 was to bring the awful realisation that there was no short cut on either side to a quick military victory. Neither the German tactical surprise of introducing gas to the battlefield, nor the allied attempted *coup de main* at the Dardanelles, succeeded in dissolving the stalemate of trench warfare, which had set in at all too dreadful a cost in life and suffering. The early weeks of the year also brought Canada's men onto the battlefield, first Princess Patricia's Canadian Light Infantry and then, in February, the First Canadian Division. From then on, it was apparent that, if the war was to be ended by military means, vast armies on an unprecedented scale would be needed. The raising of these would make huge inroads upon the peace time economies of the nations involved, for the armies would swallow not only millions of men, but also mountains of ammunition and equipment to sustain them. The Canadian Government had to decide how many men could be sent to the front without crippling the home economy and leaving the Canadian border and coasts defenceless. It had to decide who was to command these men at the front and how they were to be equipped, in the light of the fact that they would be a component of the much larger British Expeditionary Force, and, in addition to that, it was asked by the British Government to undertake the manufacture of armaments in Canada and the purchase of them from the United States for the British forces.[4]

Three principal specific issues, as far as the Canadian Government was concerned, emerged from these various problems and these were, first, the size and command of the Canadian Expeditionary Force, secondly, the effectiveness of the Ross rifle with which the Canadian army was equipped, and thirdly, the organisation of purchases of arms on behalf of the British Government, or, to be more precise, the conduct of the so-called Shell Committee. As these matters produced sharp divergences of opinion between the Governor-General, the Minister of Militia and the Prime Minister, it is necessary to examine them in some detail and to form views of whose judgements were sound or unsound, or, at any rate, sounder or less sound. The fact that most good intentions were to sink alongside the bad ones in the morass of France and Flanders does not excuse those who took reckless decisions, or ones which were based on self-aggrandisement, corruption or weakness.

In entering upon this phase of Prince Arthur's life, it must be remembered that, though the issues which have just been outlined were the principal preoccupations of his mind, they were by no means the only ones, nor did they even occupy the greatest part of his time. The duties of the Governor-General, both routine and exceptional, such as have been described in the preceding two chapters, were remorseless. For example, the new year of 1915 began for Prince Arthur with his usual levée. Nine hundred men passed and when the last had done so, there was no need for the A.D.C. to invite them to partake of the champagne cup; they made a rush for it. In April, while he was staying in Montreal, Prince Arthur visited the Vickers Maxim works there and saw ten submarines under construction. These were the first men-of-war ever to be built in Canada. During the same visit, he inspected a hospital which had been established in the grounds of McGill University, visited the Medical School, where the hall was filled with undergraduates in uniform, and held a parade on Fletcher's Field. In September, Prince Arthur travelled four thousand miles carrying out military inspections in Manitoba, Alberta, British Columbia and Saskatchewan. At the beginning of 1916, as we have already noticed, he entertained Mr W. M. Hughes, the Labour Prime Minister of Australia. He found him a very simple man, but he thought him able and evidently a leader of men. He asked him if the Australians were discouraged by the dreadful experience of Gallipoli, but Mr Hughes told him they were not and only wished to fight somewhere else. Prince Arthur wished that Canada had a Prime Minister of the same class.[5]

However he might compare the Prime Ministers of Australia and Canada, Prince Arthur had no fear that the Canadian troops would fall short of the Australians in martial spirit and, indeed, at the end of April 1915 in their first major action on the Western Front, Prince Arthur heard from the King that the Canadian Division had saved the situation around Ypres when their flank had been exposed. Alas, this had cost them between six and seven thousand casualties, a loss rate which Prince Arthur thought was not only terrible, but probably higher than was necessary. In fact, in their first battle, the Canadians had lost a third of their infantry. By June, Princess Patricia's Canadian Light Infantry had been practically wiped out and the King told Prince Arthur that only a hundred and fifty of its men were left.[6]

These sombre events weighed heavily upon Prince Arthur's mind and, as he went round inspecting the splendid young men who were coming forward to join, not the Second, nor the Third, Canadian Divisions, but the Fourth, he began to ask himself if Canada should not draw a line of limitation upon the numbers of men she would send to the front. At the beginning of June 1915, he had thought that it would be possible to weld two divisions into a Canadian Corps and he had hoped that sufficient reinforcements could be found to keep it up to strength. Within a few weeks, however, he began to feel that this would be too much. It would drain Canada of her fortress and frontier troops, and might expose Halifax and Quebec to the danger of attack from armed German ships, and it would leave thousands of miles of frontier open to the risk of raids by German-Americans, who, he believed, numbered some ten million. It was also to be remembered that Canada now had a large element of alien population, which might not be reliable in times of trouble. Finally, there was the effect on wheat production, which had to be reckoned, if able-bodied men were withdrawn on such a scale. For these reasons, Prince Arthur wrote to Kitchener, it was doubtful if Canada could, or should, maintain an army corps at the front, as Sam Hughes wished to do, possibly, Prince Arthur thought, with a view to commanding it himself. Despite these considerations, the two Canadian divisions were duly formed into an army corps and in September 1915 this stood ready for action on the Western Front. The first round of the argument about the size of the Canadian Expeditionary Force ended decisively in favour of Sam Hughes.[7]

This, however, was only a beginning. By the end of October, when Sam Hughes was making himself quite agreeable, he, nonetheless, appeared to Prince Arthur to be madder than ever. He now talked of enlisting 400,000 men, whom he said he could recruit in a day. Prince Arthur was quite unconvinced, but Borden was more easily taken in and, on the last day of 1915, the Prime Minister suddenly announced that the establishment of the Canadian army would be expanded from 250,000 to 500,000 men. Prince Arthur was surprised and wondered why he had not been informed before such an announcement was made public. He doubted that Canada could raise such a number of men. Borden's plea that illness had prevented him from mentioning the plan to Prince Arthur was rather thin, as it had not prevented him mentioning a number of other and less contentious matters. He conceded, however, that he shared Prince Arthur's doubts as to the possibility of raising 500,000 men, but he maintained that more would be achieved with this target than without it. That, all the same, was not Prince Arthur's point; he thought the target was destructive of Canada's true interests. As he put it to the King in

January 1916, the Dominion had, up to then, raised 212,000 men; the total population of the country was only eight million and, of these, two million were French Canadians, many of whom would not volunteer. He talked the matter over with Sam Hughes and suggested to him that the proposed increase should be scaled down from an extra 250,000 to 100,000. Hughes laughed at him and said he could get a million men if he wanted. So far, Prince Arthur noted, he had got 25,000. Prince Arthur was convinced that it would be impossible to raise 500,000 under a voluntary system and it was perfectly clear that he thought it would be against Canada's interest to raise so large an army by any means. By the middle of May 1916, 170,000 Canadian troops had been sent for service overseas and a further 140,000 were under training in Canada. Sam Hughes, and apparently Borden too, thought this was not nearly enough.[8]

Some of Prince Arthur's reasoning in this argument about the size of the Canadian military contribution was unsound and some of the anxieties which he voiced about sending such large Canadian forces overseas were not justified by events. Canada successfully sustained larger forces at the front than he had thought advisable, there was no invasion of Canada by German-Americans and neither Quebec nor Halifax was attacked by German warships. Nevertheless, Prince Arthur did receive repeated warnings from British intelligence sources in the United States that an invasion might be attempted and for considerable periods the British Ambassador in Washington, Sir Cecil Spring-Rice, was apprehensive that the pro-German element there might gain control of the country. Though Prince Arthur regarded such reports as exaggerated, or the product of undue pessimism, he could scarcely ignore them altogether for, in either of the two events, Canada's position would have been perilous. Nor can the verdict of history unquestioningly come down against Prince Arthur's view that Canada would have been wiser to send somewhat smaller forces to France. However such questions may be judged, the boasts of Sam Hughes about the number of volunteers he could spirit up were, in truth, little more than eyewash, but they do seem seriously to have misled Borden.[9]

The question of who should command the Canadian troops proved to be a yet more divisive issue than how many of them there should be. At the outset, Canada seemed not to have a General of sufficient experience to command a division at the front and the First Division was committed to an Englishman, Major-General Alderson. As the Second Division came towards the point of sailing for Europe, Prince Arthur thought that he had found a Canadian suitable to lead it; this was Major-General Lessard, and he tried to persuade Borden that this officer was the best Canadian available for the job. He feared, however, that his advocacy would damn the man in Sam Hughes's eyes and, from that point of view, Lessard also suffered the disadvantage of being a regular soldier and a French Canadian. Hughes, whether he ever considered Lessard or not, was committed to another candidate, Major-General Steele. Steele, Prince Arthur thought, was not a bad man, but he was older than himself and was, in fact, sixty-six. He had some military experience, but had been a policeman most of his life and Prince Arthur believed that, though he had now given up, he had been a hard drinker. He seemed to be a heavy and slow man, who looked even older than he was. Such considerations carried no weight with Borden, who was guided entirely by Sam Hughes. Steele would therefore come over to England in command of the Second Division. Prince Arthur had to be content with assuming that Kitchener would find a younger and more experienced officer to take over from him before the men went to France. Sam Hughes was displeased when he heard that this was what Kitchener intended to do. He told the British Secretary of State for War that Steele, and he now added his own brother, Colonel John Hughes, were as well qualified to command a division at the front as any officer in the British army. He said he had fifty better than Baden-Powell, who he heard had been suggested. Kitchener stood his ground and laid it down that Steele might come in command of the Second Division only on the understanding that he would be replaced before it went into action. Sam Hughes accepted this with an ill-grace, but countered almost at once with a campaign for the dismissal of General Alderson from the command of the First Division on the grounds that he had mishandled the actions around Ypres in April. He claimed to know precisely where the faults had been and he told Kitchener that half-a-dozen hidden machine guns would have saved the Canadian Division.[10]

Prince Arthur was incensed by this attack on Alderson, which he thought was based on what Hughes had been told by subalterns, and he observed to Borden that it was dangerous to place too much reliance on the impressions of officers in the firing line, as their view was circumscribed by the immediate surroundings of their own part in the action, and they could have little opportunity of knowing what was going on to the right, to the left, or behind them. But, though he supported Alderson in the face of what he considered were ill-informed attacks, Prince Arthur was entirely sympathetic to the idea that, wherever possible, Canadian troops should be commanded by Canadians supported, again as far as possible, by Canadian staff officers. The difficulty was that divisional commanders needed to have sound military backgrounds and staff officers were specialists, who needed to have been trained for their work. Sam Hughes completely rejected these views. The essential qualification for the commanders, in his opinion, was that they should be Canadians and, in addition to that, Canadians of his own choice. As to staff officers, he thought that the Canadians, who had fought so well at St Julien and Festubert, needed no staff college theorists to direct them. If the feelings of returned Canadian soldiers were known, he reckoned that another Boston tea party might be looked for.[11]

In these and other disputes about the command and direction of the Canadian troops, Prince Arthur's principles were clear enough. The prime consideration was that the chosen men should be the best available professionally competent officers and that, only when that criterion had been met, could Canadians be considered. Sam Hughes saw the issue approximately from the opposite point of view, but he also had other and much more complicated motives. His wish to see Alderson removed from the command of the First Canadian Division was not based wholly upon his view of the manner in which he had handled the actions in April, nor upon the fact that he was an English professional soldier. There was also the consideration that General Alderson, like the Canadian troops under his command, had lost confidence in the Ross rifle.

On 19th June 1915, the Commander-in-Chief of the British Expeditionary Force in France, Sir John French, wrote to the War Office that he had heard rumours of a 'growing want of confidence' by the Canadian Division in their rifles. The men had been taking every opportunity of exchanging their Ross rifles for Lee Enfields, especially when they came upon casualties in the field. French had instituted an enquiry which revealed that 3,000 men, or more than a third of the Division, had done this. The committee of enquiry also reported that the Ross could not be relied on to work smoothly and efficiently with any ammunition other than that made in Canada, of which none was available in France. As a result, the Commander-in-Chief ordered that the Canadian Division was to be re-equipped with Lee Enfield rifles before it was again sent into action. When he heard of Sam Hughes's attack upon his competence, General Alderson concluded that one of the reasons was that Hughes thought that he had been responsible for exposing the Ross rifle. In fact, he said, he had issued an order that the men of the Canadian Division

CH. 17 O CANADA 1915-1916

were not to throw away their rifles and pick up other ones, but in issuing it, he said that he had remembered that he had eyelids as well as eyes. On 16th July, Sam Hughes telegraphed to the Ross factory in Quebec that they were to try enlarging the chamber of the rifle by two thousandths of an inch at the neck increasing to four thousandths at the base.[12]

Meanwhile, to the surprise of General Steele, who was still in command of the Second Division at Shorncliffe, a Colonel Harkom turned up there, having apparently been appointed by Sam Hughes to look into the trouble in the Ross chamber and fix it. Sir Charles Ross, the designer and manufacturer of the rifle, thought that this sort of tinkering would not improve its performance and might well make it worse. He pointedly added that the correction of the rifles should be undertaken 'free from intrigue' and that Canadian troops at the front were entitled to serviceable arms. Such expressions, however, were easier to state than to realise. Prince Arthur, who thought that the Ross was a good match rifle but unsuitable for soldiers, was trying to persuade the Canadian Government to order firing tests under service conditions so that the performance of the Ross could be compared with that of the Lee Enfield. His proposal was being strangled by what he described as the muted members of the Militia Council, who, he said, were in abject fear of Sam Hughes; he went so far as to tell the King that Hughes had a financial interest in the Ross.[13]

Sir Max Aitken now appeared on the scene. He had been appointed to take charge of the records of the Canadian Expeditionary Force and, perhaps in this capacity, or perhaps in one of the many and obscure unofficial ones which he also exercised, he had gone to France, where he heard that the Commanding Officer of a detachment of the Canadian Second Division had been sent to the First Division for training. This officer had filed a written report complaining of the Ross rifle, which Aitken heard would be sent by the staff of the First Division to General Headquarters. Aitken immediately cabled this information to Sam Hughes, adding that he thought there would be some delay and that there would, therefore, be time for Hughes to send some instructions. Aitken warned him that the matter needed careful handling and he returned to London, whence he evidently believed his messages would be more secure. Sam Hughes cabled back to Aitken, 'Better remove the officer making this report,' and he said he would not tolerate intrigue on the part of ignorance. The fellow, whoever he might be, knew nothing of rifles and he wanted to know what his name was. Aitken replied that the situation regarding the Ross rifle was serious, but that it was in hand for the time being. He suggested that he and Sam Hughes should at once institute a secret code for communicating with each other. This was in October 1915.[14]

Also in October, it later transpired, a firing test was carried out in France. Aitken was present and he was accompanied by Colonel Carson, who was some sort of representative of Sam Hughes in London, though no one seemed to know exactly what sort. Aitken then reported that the Ross was a satisfactory service rifle provided the right ammunition was used. It is difficult to see what qualification Aitken had for making such a judgement, beyond that Sam Hughes had made him a Colonel, but it is easy to see the object he had in mind. To his eye, as to Sam Hughes's, the Ross rifle was a political, not a military, issue. To Prince Arthur's eye, Sam Hughes and his henchman, Max Aitken, were 'outsider bounders.'[15]

General Alderson, who had organised these tests, later wrote to the Canadian Chief of Staff, General Gwatkin, about them. He said that the Lee Enfield had fired from a hundred to a hundred and fifty rounds as quickly as possible with all three marks of ammunition, while the Ross had jammed from the twenty-fifth to the thirtieth round. In addition, the hands of the men who had fired the Ross were cut and bleeding from knocking back the bolt of the rifle. He said that none of those who had been present at the test could have failed to notice these important points. Aitken and Carson, all the same, had not mentioned them in the report which they had both signed. He said he did not mind who saw these comments of his, as he considered he would not be fit for his position if he passed anything which endangered the lives of the Canadian soldiers under his command, or the success of their arms. Given this mandate, Gwatkin showed Alderson's letter to Sam Hughes himself. Probably by the same route, Aitken also saw it.[16]

Aitken's response was prompt and robust. He told Alderson that he did not understand the controversy, but that it had seemed to him that the Ross had stood up at the test very well and that no complaint could be made of jamming. Even with what he described as bad ammunition, the Ross had held out for forty rounds, which he thought was sufficient for military purposes. He added that he did not understand the mechanisms of either the Ross or the Lee Enfield. Sam Hughes was under no such inhibition. He wrote to Alderson that there were very few officers, Canadian or British, who knew much about any rifle, especially a new one

47. *Princess Patricia and Lieutenant-Colonel A. H. Gault, who was chiefly instrumental in raising Princess Patricia's Canadian Light Infantry and who served at the front as second in command of the Regiment.*

48. *Prince Arthur on a military inspection at Rockcliffe, Ontario, 1915.*

49. *Sir Sam Hughes arriving in France, August 1916.*

50. *Sir Sam Hughes inspecting Canadian troops in France, August 1916.*

51. *Sir Sam Hughes demonstrating martial skills in France, August 1916.*

52. *Prince Arthur with (behind him) young Prince Arthur and (on the extreme left) Sir Malcolm Murray, speaking to American troops at a training school behind the British front, 1917 or 1918.*

53. *'At Messines, however, where the fighting had died down only a fortnight before, the going was difficult because of the trenches, gun emplacements, masses of wire and huge craters.' (p. 357) Left to right: Young Prince Arthur, General Plumer, Prince Arthur, June 1917.*

54. *Prince Arthur examining an experimental trench mortar, September 1917.*

like the Ross. Every battalion in the British army had been more or less cut to pieces thanks to the jamming of the Lee Enfield and Alderson, he thought, ought to have known that. He felt that Alderson was strangely familiar with the suggestions about the Ross, which had been concocted to prejudice Canadian soldiers against it. He did not feel, however, that it was worth taking up these points with people who knew nothing about rifles; no one other than a novice would have advanced them in the first place. Anyway, the chamber of the Ross had now been enlarged.[17]

So the life of the Ross rifle in the Canadian army was further prolonged but, by May 1916, Aitken began to see the writing on the wall. He cabled to Sam Hughes on the 10th that a formidable attack on the Ross rifle was developing and he wanted Hughes's authority to communicate directly with Borden on the subject. It seems that Hughes did not reply and Aitken telegraphed again on the 12th, entering this time into greater detail. He said that the commander of the Canadian Corps, General Alderson, had asserted that a number of battalion commanders in the Third Canadian Division had made strong representations to their commander about the Ross rifle. The divisional commander had felt bound to report the situation to Alderson, who had then called for reports from all the brigade, battalion and company commanders. These had been forwarded to the Commander-in-Chief, Sir Douglas Haig. The First Division was out of it, as this had been re-equipped with the Lee Enfield, but the reports from the Second Division, Aitken told Hughes, were disquieting. The divisional commander and all the Brigadiers had expressed confidence in the Ross but, of the battalion commanders, five were in favour of it and five were not. One did not seem to know. Of the company commanders, twenty-two were in favour and twenty-one against while four were vague. Aitken had not yet heard what the opinions from the Third Division were, but he knew enough to see that the situation was serious. He said that Haig would consult him before coming to any decision and he wanted to know what line he was to take. He asked Hughes to show his cable to Borden.[18]

Sam Hughes did reply this time. He told Aitken that he was to stand firm on the Ross rifle. He was to organise tests at the front which were to be seen by as many soldiers as possible. He discounted the importance of Alderson's views, on the ground that his influence was diminishing and he could now do no more than inspect and report. Borden was more cautious; he telegraphed directly to Aitken saying that he and Sam Hughes were content to leave the decision as to the future of the Ross rifle to Sir Douglas Haig, but either he did not trouble Hughes with the knowledge of this, or Hughes forgot it, for, two days later, Hughes cabled to Aitken that he was to secure the immediate promotion to the rank of Major of one of the officers he had nominated to carry out the tests of the Ross rifle, which he had ordered. On 23rd May, Hughes followed this up with another cable to Aitken telling him to leave no stone unturned to crush out the intrigue against Canadian rifles.[19]

Aitken, who was beginning to pay rather less attention to Sam Hughes, whom, indeed, he would presently ditch, had now heard something about how the Ross rifle was regarded in the Canadian Third Division. Carson, who nowadays was a Major-General, passed on to him a letter he had received from Major-General M.S.Mercer, the Third Division's commander. Mercer said that it was becoming increasingly difficult to prevent the men from getting rid of their Ross rifles in exchange for Lee Enfields. Officers and men were sending in reports of the Ross having jammed seriously during recent enemy attacks. Battalion, company and platoon commanders reported 'overwhelmingly' against the Ross. It had jammed to such an extent that the offensive and defensive power of the men had been weakened. The lives of Canadian soldiers and the integrity of their section of the front were at stake and Mercer said that to withhold the issue of the Lee Enfield, and to compel the men to continue with the Ross, would be 'criminal in the extreme.' He concluded by stating that every effort had been made to get the best out of the Ross rifle and the Division had had the best ammunition in the field, but, in spite of this, the rifle had failed.[20]

On 28th May 1916 Sir Douglas Haig reported to the War Office that the Ross rifle was less trustworthy than the Lee Enfield and that the majority of the troops which were equipped with the Ross had lost confidence in it. He said there had been a high percentage of jams in the Canadian Third Division during an enemy attack on 1st May. He recommended that the Canadian Second and Third Divisions should forthwith be re-armed with the Lee Enfield. He sent a second report to the same effect on 21st June and at last, on 3rd July 1916, the Ross rifle, Sam Hughes and Max Aitken met their Waterloo. The Army Council approved the proposal that the Canadian Second and Third Divisions should be re-equipped with Lee Enfield rifles. As the decision to re-equip the First Division was taken on 12th June 1915, in the light of the grave doubts as to the efficiency of the Ross in the field, it is reasonable to say that Sam Hughes's uncompromising and threatening defence and advocacy of it prolonged the life of this defective weapon in Canadian hands on the Western Front by more than a year.[21]

The evidence against the Ross rifle, which had been piling up since as long ago as 1901, had now become overpowering and, even after full allowance for the hopes which are so often raised in such cases by promised improvements in the next mark, and with full regard for the natural Canadian aspiration to produce her own rifles, Sam Hughes's conduct in the matter can hardly be described as other than criminal in the extreme. Prince Arthur's condemnation of him on the grounds that he had a financial interest in the Ross may or may not have been justified. Dr Haycock tells us that the truth about this has never been established. But, whatever may be the ultimate answer to that question, there can no longer be any doubt that Sam Hughes amply merited Prince Arthur's description of him as a 'hopelessly inefficient' Minister, who did nothing except what benefited himself, his party or his patronage.[22]

The fact that Sam Hughes's obdurate defence of the Ross rifle was at the direct expense of the Canadian soldiers on the Western Front, of whom he claimed to be the champion, distinguishes the issue as perhaps the most disgraceful aspect of his curious conduct as Minister of Militia. It was, however, only one more of the grounds on which Prince Arthur became preoccupied with the need to get the man dismissed. This brings us to the third of the principal issues which dominated the final phase of Prince Arthur's Governor-Generalship of Canada; namely, the procurement of arms by the Canadian Government for Britain, a matter which was centred on the so-called Shell Committee and which involved the operations of Colonel J. Wesley Allison, whom we have already met.

Lloyd George, who was the British Minister of Munitions from June 1915 until July 1916, touched on the matter in his Memoirs in the briefest of terms. He referred to Sam Hughes as a man of 'infectious enthusiasm and energy' and related that at the outbreak of war, in response to an appeal from Britain, he formed a Shell Committee to organise munitions production in Canada. Lloyd George said that the Committee made a 'fine start' with this work, but presently the requirements exceeded its scope, and at the end of 1915 it was superseded by the Imperial Munitions Board, under the chairmanship of Sir Joseph Flavelle. More than twenty years after the event, Lloyd George was, as he had been at the time, unwilling for any stones to be turned over from underneath which something real about the Shell Committee and its connected activities might have crawled out. Prince Arthur's biographer is compelled to be less squeamish, for, unless at least some of the salient elements of the matter are understood, Prince Arthur's attitude to Sam Hughes cannot be.[23]

By the end of January 1915, Colonel Allison had emerged from the shadows and now loomed over the Canadian High Commission in London, and the Colonial Office there, as a serious threat to the future of the Canadian Government and possibly even to the capacity of the allies to obtain armaments from American sources. It seemed that Allison, working through a syndicate, had secured huge contracts from the Russian and Italian Governments involving, in the Italian case, half a million rifles and, in the Russian, two million shells. The syndicate appeared to be cornering supplies of vital war materials, so that it could then sell them to the highest bidder. In the Colonial Office, the feeling was that the sooner this was stopped the better, but it was strong meat for the refined tastes of Harcourt and Davidson, respectively the Secretary of State and his Private Secretary. Perhaps, the latter suggested to the former, Kitchener and the War Office could smash the Allison syndicate, but if they did, they might turn important American financial interests against the allies. And, of course, there was the difficulty that the Canadian Minister of Militia had given Allison official backing, so that nothing much could be done until Borden had been fully informed.[24]

The extent of Sam Hughes's complicity in these dealings of Allison's was a matter of hearsay and not of tangible evidence, but the rumours were sufficient to suggest to Prince Arthur's Military Secretary, Colonel Stanton, that his downfall was 'practically certain.' Why the Prime Minister was hanging on to him so long, no one seemed to know. Stanton's theory was that Borden must have owed Hughes a debt of gratitude for something in the past and the Duchess was driven to the more dramatic and less likely explanation that there might have been 'some private affairs' between Lady Borden and Sam Hughes. Stanton's view that Sam Hughes's downfall was imminent was, however, naïve in the extreme. Publicly, he continued to deny that there was any official connection between himself and Colonel Allison. On 14th April 1915, Harcourt cabled to Prince Arthur asking if the Canadian Government, in view of 'certain disclosures,' would object to a disclaimer of Allison and some of his associates being issued. Prince Arthur replied on the same day, 'My Ministers inform me that the persons mentioned have no connection whatever with the Canadian Government' and that there would, therefore, be no objection to a disclaimer. Prince Arthur, of course, suspected that this was not true and Borden knew for certain that it was not. So did Harcourt. No wonder Prince Arthur was disappointed with the session, which ended on 15th April when he prorogued Parliament. The debates had been full of party recrimination and there had been a disgraceful show up of the way contracts were given out and accepted by the Militia Department. Patronage and graft, Prince Arthur wrote to his sister, dragged people down in Canada, especially General Sam Hughes. He told the King that he found himself in a very difficult position; he saw it as his duty to get rid of Hughes, but Borden was sticking to him through thick and thin and, if he demanded Hughes's dismissal, he thought Borden would resign. The King was slightly alarmed; he sympathised with his Uncle in his difficulties with Sam Hughes and the weakness of Borden, but he said it would never do to kick Hughes out and bring about the resignation of the Prime Minister.[25]

After another six months of turning the blind eye or hoping for the best, Borden, prompted by articles in the press, and notably the *Toronto Globe*, began to show signs of serious anxiety and started to make his own enquiries into the activities of Sam Hughes's Shell Committee. These showed that, not only had the Shell Committee been placing contracts through Allison, but that they had been instructed to do so by Sam Hughes. Colonel D.Carnegie, a member of the Shell Committee and its ordnance advisor, told Borden that Allison had been a friend of Hughes's for many years. He said that the Minister of Militia had always spoken highly of him and, in the light of that, the Shell Committee had taken it that Allison was an honourable man. He conceded that they had heard ugly rumours about Allison, but he said they saw no reason to believe them. As to the prices they had been paying for fuses, the Shell Committee had been guided in large measure by Allison. Borden kept his counsel for the time being, but in London, Lloyd George's Ministry of Munitions had also become dissatisfied with the Shell Committee and, after enquiries had been made on their behalf by Mr Thomas and Mr Hichens, they abandoned it as their agency for purchases in Canada and the United States. In its place, as Lloyd George recalled in his Memoirs, they established the Imperial Munitions Board.[26]

Mr J.W.Flavelle, a wealthy Canadian business man, was engaged on a round of golf on 23rd November 1915 when a message was brought to him saying that the Governor-General wished to see him. He took it that he would be invited to help with one of Prince Arthur's charities. He was greatly surprised when, instead of that, the Governor-General invited him to become chairman of the newly formed Imperial Munitions Board. He had long wondered why Sam Hughes and all his iniquities had been left so long in power and it is evident that he had no idea that Prince Arthur had for months been attempting to get rid of him. In accepting the appointment, he had no inkling, as Prince Arthur had not either when he offered it, that this was the catalyst which initiated the decline and fall of Sam Hughes. One of the latter's principal sources of power and patronage had effectively been wrenched from his control; it passed to the capable, upright and, as far as Sam Hughes was concerned, hostile, direction of Flavelle.[27]

Sam Hughes greeted the new regime with a strong challenge, in which he laid down the law to Flavelle on the issues of munitions manufacture and procurement and protested vigorously about the abandonment by Flavelle of a contract he had placed through Allison with the R. B. Phillips Manufacturing Company of Boston for the production of fuses in Canada. This, he told Borden, would mean that the British Government would be throwing away $670,000. Flavelle was unmoved. Though he tried to humour Hughes, who had been given an honorary position in the new Board as President, he declined to be influenced in favour of what he well knew were Allison's dirty deals. Nor did he have any confidence in Hughes's own ideas. Indeed, Flavelle thought that Hughes was either a child, a fool, or a corrupt man, who was in the hands of a corrupt gang on the one hand and powerful greedy men on the other. When he saw that Flavelle was not to be persuaded, Sam Hughes characteristically began to threaten him, by insinuating that he had an interest in the companies to which he was giving contracts and also that he was an incompetent novice in the field. He protested that Allison was the friend of every honest man and that his enemies were all dishonest grafters. These threats had no more effect on Flavelle than the earlier cajolery had done. Sam Hughes's record in the production of war materials was not, after all, very impressive. By the end of 1914, his Shell Committee had placed orders for 2,050,000 shells and 1,900,000 cartridge cases, which were farmed out to seventy-two shell, and sixty-seven component, companies. By May 1915, only two per cent of the orders had been delivered on time. Huge sums of money were changing hands but much smaller quantities of actual materials were coming forth.[28]

On 11th February 1916, Borden cabled to Perley in London that Laurier had given notice of his intention to call, in the House of Commons, for an enquiry into the purchase of shells and other munitions by the Shell Committee and into all the contracts and orders which had been placed by the Committee. Borden told Perley that he intended to oppose the motion, on the ground that the issue was a matter for the British, not the Canadian, House of Commons. He asked Perley to sound the British Minister of Munitions, Lloyd George, 'quietly and confidentially.' Lloyd George was not quite happy about the proposal. He thought that the responsibility for the Shell Committee was partly British and partly Canadian. He, therefore, preferred that Borden should take the line that he could not properly order an enquiry without the consent of the British Government and that, when he had sought it, he had been told that the British Government felt that this was not the proper time for such an enquiry. Pressure of work meant that the time to have it would be after the war was over. Laurier moved his resolution for an investigation on 7th March. Borden pointed out the inexpediency of having it in wartime and said that, if there was to be an enquiry, it was a matter for the British Parliament. He pointed out that the Shell Committee had spent only British money. He promised Laurier that, if the British Government did initiate an enquiry, the Canadian Government would co-operate. He added that if there was any charge against the Canadian Government or any member of it, an immediate investigation would be granted without question.[29]

Mr G. W. Kyte seized the opportunity which this last offer of Borden's had provided and, on 29th March, he startled the House with a series of allegations. Among them were that Sam Hughes's friend, Allison, had formed an association with B. F. Yoakum of New York and Eugene Lignanti, the leader of the orchestra in the Ritz Carlton Hotel of Montreal. They had secured huge contracts from the Shell Committee. The rake-off was to be shared as between Allison and Lignanti in the proportion of $600,000 and $266,000. Of the five million fuses contracted, however, none were delivered for nearly a year and only 445,000 were ever delivered. When Mr Kyte sat down, the corridor talk in Parliament among the Conservative Members against Allison's connection with Sam Hughes was raised to 'boiling point.' It seemed that Borden would now have to face an enquiry, which would reveal the misdeeds of the Minister of Militia, or face a revolt in the Conservative party. Borden appointed a Royal Commission to carry out an enquiry. Prince Arthur, who had heard that Allison was accused of having made $2,000,000 out of fuse contracts, thought that the Government might be forced to resign, or at least go to the country. He regretted this, as he thought that a change of government in a time of crisis would not be in Canada's interests. The whole thing, he wrote to Sir Cecil Spring-Rice, was most disagreeable and the worst of it was that it was Borden's fault. He said that he had been warning him against Sam Hughes for eighteen months and, more recently, against Allison as well. Members of his Cabinet had done the same, but it had all been to no avail.[30]

News of the appointment of the Royal Commission reached Sam Hughes in London as he was about to sit down to dinner with Bonar Law. Harcourt was there and he thought that Hughes, who was as white as a sheet, looked an utterly broken man, as indeed Harcourt thought he was likely to be, if the Commission carried out its enquiries effectively. Sam Hughes, however, had no need to appear so disconcerted. The Commission was unable to carry out a conclusive enquiry thanks to Lloyd George's decision that the British Ministry of Munitions could release information about the prices paid for fuses only if it was kept confidential. As the Commission had decided that it would receive only evidence which could be put on the record, Mr Lloyd George regretted that he could not give them the information. This and the somewhat restricted terms of reference which the Commission had, effectively crippled the scope and authority of the report, which was issued on 20th July 1916. It was, nonetheless, a lengthy and, in some respects, a detailed, document, in which several of the key contracts were discussed. Allison was found to have been guilty of profiteering and of misleading Sam Hughes into thinking that his efforts were guided entirely by his friendship for the Minister and without remuneration for himself. Sam Hughes's name occurred again and again in the tangled story of the contracts, but, though the report left the impression that his actions had been rather curious, it was nowhere suggested that they were anything more than that. His only offence, it seemed, was that he had been taken in by Allison. All the world knew that Allison was a crook; Prince Arthur knew it, so did Borden, Perley, Davidson, Harcourt, most of the Canadian Cabinet, many M.Ps and several newspapers. Sam Hughes, the Royal Commission on the Shell Committee found, did not. The Government need not fall; Sam Hughes could resume office as Minister of Militia and Defence, from which he had been suspended during the enquiry. One of Prince Arthur's anxieties; namely, that the scandal would lead to the fall of the Government, was relieved; but another, his wish to see Canada released from the baneful and, as he saw it dangerous, influence of Sam Hughes was apparently utterly frustrated.[31]

Such then were the three principal issues, the size and command of the Canadian Expeditionary Force, the efficiency or otherwise of the Ross rifle and the conduct of the Shell Committee, which dominated the final period of Prince Arthur's Governor-Generalship of Canada and such were the parts played in them by, on the one hand, Prince Arthur and, on the other, Sam Hughes. There is no need to seek further for the reasons which led Prince Arthur to disapprove of the Minister of Militia and to seek his dismissal from office. Hughes's inflated idea of his own genius and infallibility, which was shown by his belief that he could attract now 400,000 Canadian volunteers for the army and then a million, that he could produce vast quantities of armaments simply by placing contracts, that he could loosen the deadlock on the Western Front by issuing running shoes to Canadian troops or placing half-a-dozen machine guns here or there and that he himself was competent to command major formations in this great war, made him a dangerous candidate for any ministerial post and most of all for the one which was responsible for Canada's army in the greatest of all wars. Had the Governor-General let all this pass without comment, he would have been derilect in his duty. The question remains, however, as to whether, having made his observations to the Prime Minister, he should have let the matters rest and turned his attention to other things. The King from time to time indicated to him that perhaps this might be the better course. 'I beg of you,' he wrote, for example, in October 1915 regarding that 'dreadful man,' Hughes, 'to exercise patience & do your utmost to endure him in spite of what he may do.' Half of Prince Arthur's inclination led him to follow this advice, but the other half made it impossible for him to do so and, as he repeatedly told the King, he found himself in a very difficult position; one which was not made easier by the view of the Chief Justice of Canada, Sir Charles Fitzpatrick, that he did not speak strongly enough to the Ministers.[32]

The extent of Prince Arthur's difficulty is more readily understood if, in addition to the three major issues which we have already considered, three more are also taken into account for, though these were much lesser matters, they were ones in which Prince Arthur was more directly and personally involved and on which he was, in some respects, on less sure ground. They were the recruitment of Americans while the United States was still a neutral country, the granting of honours to Canadians and some remarks which the Minister of Militia made about the Governor-General in the Militia Council.

From early in the war Sam Hughes had planned to recruit Americans into the Canadian army, but this raised delicate issues which affected not only Canadian relations with the United States, but also British and Imperial interests. Borden, who had heard that the King and the British Government were keen to enlist Americans, was apprehensive that this might endanger the good relations which had been established with the United States. Prince Arthur, who always kept in close touch with the British Ambassador in Washington and who, like Borden, was well aware of the importance of American opinion to the allied cause, shared these doubts, though he later had to admit that it was difficult to prevent Americans from joining. He had, however, or thought he had, succeeded in preventing them from using American insignia, to which the American Government so strongly objected. Recruitment went ahead and by May 1916 the American Battalion, the 97th, was ready to sail from Canada for Europe. Borden agreed, at the wish of the British Government, that Prince Arthur should cancel their sailing orders pending consideration of the issues by the British Foreign Office. Thus, before any hard words had been exchanged, the matter had become muddled and a policy, which the Prime Minister seemingly opposed, had, nonetheless, been carried out. Henceforth matters became much more muddled.[33]

Within a few more weeks, Prince Arthur was credibly informed that no less than five American battalions were being formed in Canada and he received a protest from the United States about the use of the American flag in Canada for recruiting purposes. Feeling that the attitude of the British Government and the complaints of the American were being ignored, Prince Arthur forwarded the American protest to Borden and accompanied it with some observations of his own, which included a warning against the dangers of German-Americans enlisting and then deserting to the Germans with secret military information in their possession. Clearly, Prince Arthur was incensed, for he felt that the assurances about the recruitment of Americans, which he had given to London and Washington, with the concurrence of the Canadian Government, had been dishonoured behind his back. Either for this reason, or perhaps, as Borden is said to have thought, because of bad advice from Stanton, Prince Arthur went beyond his usual tone of advice and warning. He added that if no action was taken in the light of what he had now passed on, he would feel bound to alert the British Government to the possibility of friction with the United States and the danger which that would pose to the British Empire. Borden replied that the Canadian

Government had not been a party to the British assurance that American citizens would not be recruited. He said that he had always sought to work in harmony with the British Government, but they had no right to control the Canadian Government. Prince Arthur could make any representations he liked to the Home Government, provided that they took account of Canada's status as a self-governing Dominion.[34]

Though this reply of Borden's did not face the questions which Prince Arthur had raised, it was laced with sensitive issues of Canadian nationhood. Prince Arthur, however, felt so strongly on the matter, that he noticed the first point virtually to the exclusion of the second. He continued to insist on the dangers of recruiting German-Americans and on the need to take notice of the protests of the American Government about the misuse of their flag. In addition to the consideration which he thought should be afforded to the American and British points of view, he now added that there were also his own 'personal objections as Governor-General and a Field-Marshal in His Majesty's Forces.' This was rather a gift to a politician as skilled as Borden, who also had a legal training. He hoped that he and his colleagues would not be found wanting in 'respect or indeed in admiration for the wide military experience of Your Royal Highness and the high position which you hold as a Field-Marshal in His Majesty's Forces,' but, he said, it appeared to him and to them that the matters under consideration did not call so much for the exercise of military skill or the application of military experience as the consideration of international law and the exercise of common sense. Nevertheless, Borden now conceded Prince Arthur's main point by enclosing a copy of a letter he had written to Mr F. F. McCurdy, who had recently been appointed to the newly created office of Parliamentary Secretary to the Department of Militia and Defence. In this, Borden said that H.R.H. the Governor-General had recently seen an American recruiting office advertised as such in Calgary and that at Moose Jaw he had seen an officer in uniform wearing the emblem 'American Legion' on his cap and that H.R.H. had handed Borden a metal badge of the 97th which bore the same legend. Borden told McCurdy that he had been assured by the Adjutant-General that such things were explicitly forbidden and that, if the existing instructions were now found to be insufficient, new ones should be issued at once of such a character that there could be no possibility of mistaking or evading them. This quite satisfied Prince Arthur, for it made good the pledges which he had given to London and Washington and it forced Borden to insist on the policy which he had theoretically adhered to throughout. In standing on his rank as a Field-Marshal, however, he had committed something of a *bêtise* for though it did not justify the exaggerated suggestion that he failed to understand that his position as Commander-in-Chief was nominal, it did provide some room for sneers. It is beyond doubt that Prince Arthur's extreme irritation at these American irregularities was exacerbated by his conviction that they were being encouraged by Sam Hughes without the authority of the Government.[35]

In the years with which we are concerned, inclusion in the British New Year's Honours List, or that for the King's Birthday, was eagerly sought in Canada and, as elsewhere, was often the subject of somewhat unsavoury manoeuvring, either on the part of the aspirant, or on that of the Minister putting forward the recommendation, who wished to repay a debt, which, alas, was by no means always one of honour. Prince Arthur had a rather idealistic attitude to such matters and believed that honours should be the reward for honourable service. He understood, however, that, as Governor-General of Canada, he was bound to forward such names as the Prime Minister might require. He knew, therefore, that he would have to sign some pieces of unpleasant paper. If that had been the end of it, the matter would scarcely be worth a mention in this volume. This, however, was unfortunately not so and, in two cases, Prince Arthur was subjected to extreme provocation by underhand procedures and, in the second, was also subsequently held up by a celebrated historian, Mr A. J. P. Taylor, as having himself been 'not over scrupulous when his personal feelings were involved.' The subjects of these two cases were Sam Hughes and his London ally and fellow-Canadian, Max Aitken. The recommending Minister, who also had Canadian origins, was Bonar Law, who had joined Asquith's coalition government, which was formed on 26th May 1915, as Secretary of State for the Colonies.[36]

Bonar Law, his biographer tells us, was not, as was sometimes supposed, a man of great wealth. On entering the Government, his income was about £10,000 a year and before that it had averaged a little under £6,000. Whether for this or for other reasons, he lived virtually in Max Aitken's pocket and seemed always to consult him before making any political decision and to take him with him when going anywhere of political significance. Within days of his appointment to the Colonial Office, he recommended Aitken to the Governor-General of Canada for the K.C.M.G. Prince Arthur, who believed that Aitken was very little esteemed in Canada, where it was thought that he had made money by shady means, replied that he had no objection to Bonar Law's proposal, provided it was clear that Aitken was not recommended on the Governor-General's list. Bonar Law then offered Aitken a baronetcy on the British Prime Minister's list, but Aitken, recognising that this would look too much as though the honour was given 'on account of personal friendship,' declined it. Bonar Law learnt to be more wily and within a few weeks he was in action again.[37]

This time the recipient was to be Sam Hughes, who was in London explaining to the authorities how to win the war and being temporarily reconciled with General Alderson. Bonar Law, or more probably Max Aitken, decided that he was to be made a Knight Commander of the Bath. Bonar Law planned this time to tie Prince Arthur's hands by securing Borden's support and Kitchener's before approaching Prince Arthur. The second step, which was also taken before Prince Arthur was approached, was to tell Sam Hughes, which Aitken did on 18th August 1915. In these circumstances, Prince Arthur felt unable to turn down the request, but he telegraphed to the King saying that he disapproved of it. He said that many of Sam Hughes's appointments had been made on political grounds without military justification and that there were ugly rumours connecting his name with undesirable persons. He thought the honour should be postponed until these matters had been cleared up. He hoped there would be no obstacle to Hughes being knighted after the war. The King entirely agreed. He had heard bad accounts of the Ross rifle and thought it a pity that its production was being continued. He was told, however, that this depended on Hughes's decision and that it affected his pocket. If he was to have the honour, it should be given after the war. On 24th August, Bonar Law saw the King and told him he must bestow the honour that afternoon, as Sam Hughes was sailing for Canada the next day. He also wrote to Prince Arthur thanking him for having put forward the recommendation. The King telegraphed to Prince Arthur that he had conferred the K.C.B. civil on Sam Hughes and said that he much regretted the circumstances which had compelled him to act contrary to Prince Arthur's views. Sir Sam Hughes wrote to Bonar Law to thank him for the honour and to say that he would pay a formal call upon him which, as he was a Major-General, would necessitate his being accompanied by a staff officer. The latter, he said, would be 'Colonel Sir Max Aitken.' If, as the King put it, people had known what he knew, what would they have said? Prince Arthur was left with the duty of handing Sir Sam, when he got back to Canada, his patent as a K.C.B., when he found him madder than ever.

This was the occasion when the Minister of Militia told the Governor-General that he could raise 400,000 volunteers in a day.[38]

In May 1916 Bonar Law returned to the charge on behalf of Aitken. He telegraphed to Borden that he had written suggesting a baronetcy, but that the matter must be decided at once. Borden replied that he had had the letter and that he agreed that Aitken deserved recognition; that he personally approved of the proposal but that, before anything further was done, the Governor-General must be consulted. Bonar Law asked Borden whether he could not consult the Governor-General himself, because, if Bonar Law did, and exception was taken, it would be difficult to get it done 'in the other way.' Thus, it was clear that Bonar Law wanted Borden to put the matter to Prince Arthur, because, if he did so, it would be constitutionally impossible for the recommendation to be turned down. The 'other way,' by which he meant his own recommendation through the British Prime Minister to the King, would land him with the same disadvantage that had spoilt his endeavour last time, namely, that it would be obvious that he was giving Aitken an honour to pay a personal debt. Mr A. J. P. Taylor states in his biography of Aitken that Borden 'duly recommended Aitken to the duke of Connaught,' but this is precisely what, in truth, he did not do. In fact, Borden wrote to Prince Arthur saying that the Colonial Secretary had enquired if there would be any objection to including a baronetcy for Aitken in the Canadian honours list. He said that Bonar Law thought that Aitken's services to Canada in connection with the war merited the honour and that, if the name was put forward in the English list, it would be regarded as being as a result of personal friendship. Borden enclosed the correspondence that had passed between himself and Bonar Law, which, of course, did show that Borden agreed with the proposal, but he, nevertheless, did not make a recommendation to Prince Arthur. On the contrary, he wrote that he 'had the honour to leave the matter for the determination of Your Royal Highness' and, going further than that, he added that, if Prince Arthur was to agree with the proposal, he presumed that he would communicate directly with the Colonial Secretary. In other words, Borden had distanced himself from the recommendation, but he had done so in such a way as to give as little offence as possible to Bonar Law and Aitken. This gave Prince Arthur a sufficient mandate to exclude Aitken from the Canadian list and it is, therefore, quite understandable that he was astonished to read in the papers a few weeks later that Aitken had been created a baronet in the Birthday Honours on the British Prime Minister's list.[39]

Mr A. J. P. Taylor states, in his biography of Aitken, that the Duke of Connaught forwarded the recommendation, which we have just seen was never positively submitted to him by Borden, to the King, accompanied by a private letter in which he 'alleged' that Borden 'regretted an honour being conferred on a man with a Canadian reputation such as the particular individual possessed.' Taylor goes on to say that it was most unlikely that Borden had said this, as he had been promoting Aitken's various appointments and Taylor, therefore, concludes that the Duke of Connaught was 'not over scrupulous when his personal feelings were involved,' or, in other words, that he lied to the King about the attitude of his Prime Minister. In support of this extreme charge, Mr Taylor quotes a document, which was subsequently deposited in the Record Office of the House of Lords and which Prince Arthur's biographer has also read. It proves to be an unsigned and undated minute addressed to Sir George Fiddes, the Permanent Under Secretary of State at the Colonial Office. Its subject matter suggests that it was written in January 1917 and it is most probable that its author was Davidson, Private Secretary to Bonar Law, who by that time was Chancellor of the Exchequer. The author of the minute stated that Borden had told the Duke of Devonshire, who had succeeded Prince Arthur as Governor-General of Canada, that he was withdrawing a proposed honour, while at the same time telegraphing to London behind the Duke's back that he would resign if it was withdrawn. This, the writer of the minute said, was 'on all fours' with Borden's double-faced action in the case of an earlier baronetcy given to a 'certain individual,' who, we can safely assume, was Aitken. In that case, the writer of the minute stated, Borden had told Bonar Law, through Perley, how much the granting of this baronetcy would be appreciated in Canada and at the same time had told the Duke of Connaught how much he 'regretted an honour being conferred on a man with a Canadian reputation such as the particular individual possessed.' Here then are the exact words which Mr Taylor says the Duke of Connaught used in a private letter to the King. They are, in fact, the words written by an unknown author, who was probably Davidson but certainly not Prince Arthur, and they are not an extract from a private letter to the King, but are contained in a civil service minute to Sir George Fiddes. How could Mr A. J. P. Taylor be so careless, or disingenuous?[40]

Fortunately, we have no need to ponder that question further, for we have seen enough to be sure that there is no foundation whatsoever for Mr Taylor's serious and, no doubt widely read, charge against Prince Arthur's integrity; we have also delved enough into the granting of honours to Canadians to see the extent of the provocation which, in some unfortunate cases, it exerted upon Prince Arthur.

In the last of the three lesser issues which we are considering, Prince Arthur was the most personally and directly involved of all. This was the situation which arose after Sam Hughes had made some derogatory remarks about the Governor-General to the Militia Council. Before leaving for his third wartime visit to London in March 1916, Hughes came to take leave of Prince Arthur. They seem not to have got on very well; at any rate, Prince Arthur told the King that Hughes had been pretty rude. Recruiting was not going well and Prince Arthur thought that too many new battalions were being formed, with the consequence that drafts could not be found for existing ones. Perhaps the Governor-General and the Minister exchanged words about this, but, if not, there were by now plenty of other subjects upon which they could easily disagree, such as the Ross rifle. Hughes left the audience in a bad temper and went to a meeting of the Militia Council. Almost at once a report reached Prince Arthur that Sam Hughes had abused him to the Council. By this time Hughes had left for London, so Prince Arthur sent for the deputy Minister, who confirmed the rumour. Prince Arthur then sent for Borden and told him that he must be given a written apology, failing which Hughes must be dismissed, failing both of which, he would resign his office as Governor-General. Borden questioned the deputy Minister and all the members of the Militia Council, who seemed to bear out what Prince Arthur had complained of, though two of them thought the matter was of little importance. Borden, however, owned to Prince Arthur that Hughes's behaviour had been 'highly improper and unconstitutional,' but he said that Hughes was annoyed with Prince Arthur for not putting the confidence in him which he did in the other Ministers. Prince Arthur replied that he was sorry to say that this was the case and he gave Borden a number of reasons for that. Borden affected to be surprised, but Prince Arthur decided that he must stick to his guns. He felt that, on the one hand, he was dealing with a very weak man, Borden, and, on the other, a conceited lunatic, Hughes.[41]

Borden now had no alternative other than to telegraph to Hughes in London and ask him for an explanation. Hughes replied 'Not a word of truth see Macdonald.' Borden cabled that he had seen Macdonald, who was the Quarter-Master-General, and all the other members of the Militia Council and that it was evident to him that Hughes had said a great deal more than he realised. He cabled a third time to ask Hughes when he proposed to return to Canada and put it to Prince Arthur that the matter should be shelved until he did. Prince Arthur agreed to this. Having returned to Canada, Hughes produced a memorandum which he gave to Borden. In this he denied that he had said anything disrespectful about H.R.H., though he had read the riot act to his Military Secretary, Colonel Stanton, about the Ross rifle, but even this, he said, had been in a 'semi-jocular way.' All he had said to the Militia Council was that no member of it had the right to discuss anything with H.R.H, without his permission. He concluded by saying that he was sorry that H.R.H. thought that intemperate language had been used. Armed with this, Borden now began to put a different construction on what he already knew had happened. He told Prince Arthur that of the six people present at the Militia Council, three absolutely supported Hughes's denial that intemperate language had been used, one substantially supported it and a fifth did not entirely support the account which had been given to Prince Arthur by a 'somewhat excitable gentleman.' Prince Arthur pointed out that this was not consistent with what Borden had discovered at the time of the alleged remarks, and reported to him then, but Borden was becoming harder and harder to pin down. So far as he could remember, what he had reported in the first place had been based on what he had been told by those present at the meeting. Though Prince Arthur knew that Hughes, and now Borden too, were not speaking the truth, he thought it best to settle the matter and he, therefore, told Borden that he would accept Hughes's memorandum, but he insisted upon Borden reading it to the Militia Council, and he also observed to the Prime Minister that it was constitutionally quite proper for him to obtain information from government officials, as any comments which he had to make, he put confidentially to Borden. This, he pointed out, was not only his prerogative, but his duty as Governor-General. He said that he mentioned this only as it was alluded to in Hughes's memorandum.[42]

Prince Arthur made an issue of this case with the obvious intent of disciplining the unmanageable Sam Hughes or, better still, serving the public interest by securing his dismissal. He was clearly disappointed by the outcome, which, so far as he was able to see, showed Borden to be as weak or even weaker than ever, and Sam Hughes correspondingly able to lie his way out of anything. The irony is that, though it was not apparent to Prince Arthur, Borden was seeking the means of ridding the Government of Sam Hughes and, in his initial reaction to the affair of the remarks in the Militia Council, there was even a hint that he might have thought of using it for that purpose. In the event, however, he found another means. Sam Hughes, having been let off by the Royal Commission on the Shell Committee, returned to London. There, without the sanction of the Canadian Government, he set up a sub-committee of the Militia Council, through which he hoped to preserve his personal influence in the control of the Canadian overseas forces. Borden complained to him of his 'strong tendency' to assume powers which he did not possess and which could only be exercised by the Governor-General in Council. He told Hughes that the difficulties he had made had consumed much of his time and energy, which, as Prime Minister, should have been devoted to more important work. He said that he had often cautioned Hughes, but without effect. The unauthorised appointment of a Sub-Militia Council was the last straw; he demanded Sam Hughes's resignation. When he received it, Sir George Foster, the Minister of Trade and Commerce, 'saw no tears, heard no regrets;' the nightmare was over. There was a yet greater irony in this, for these events took place in November 1916. In October, Prince Arthur had laid down the office of Governor-General and had returned to England.[43]

Dr Haycock asserts that Borden had got the Governor-General recalled, or, in other words, sacked, but this is no more than another gratuitous calumny. Prince Arthur had written to Lord Stamfordham, the King's Private Secretary, on 2nd March 1916 and had reminded him that he would have completed five years as Governor-General in the following October. He said that he hoped that he might then be allowed to come home. The King agreed that it would be unreasonable to expect him to serve beyond that time and undertook to begin the search for a suitable successor. Two months later, on 20th May, he cabled to Prince Arthur that he might now tell Borden that he would be leaving in October. Thus, Prince Arthur's departure from Canada was the result of his resignation with the permission of the King. His advancing years and the hard Canadian winters together with the precarious state of the Duchess's health were factors in the decision, but much the most important was Sam Hughes. 'Much as I like & take a deep interest in the country,' Prince Arthur wrote to the King, 'I shant be sorry to go on account of the impossibility I find in getting on with Sam Hughes whose behaviour continues to be of the worst. He has push and energy, but he is wanting in any honesty or decency & will stick at nothing to reach his own ends.' Flavelle made the same points with greater severity. He judged that Sam

Hughes was mentally unbalanced and showed the low cunning and cleverness which was often associated with the insane; he had great energy, loved the spectacular and commanded wide attention. But Flavelle went further; he had decided that the 'crooked men' with whom Hughes surrounded himself were there 'through design' and that Hughes had been sharing in their profits; he was inclined to think that Hughes 'is without moral appreciation of his conduct, and is not fully responsible.'[44]

There could scarcely have been a more succinct explanation of why Prince Arthur found it impossible to tolerate Sam Hughes; nor could Sam Hughes have given more convincing evidence of the correctness of Flavelle's judgement than by his reaction to Borden's enforcement of his resignation. He wrote to Aitken saying that he had been knifed while sawing wood, but that he controlled the situation. He could allow Borden and Laurier to fight it out in a general election, or he could raise a third party and hold the balance, or he could fall in behind Borden and see him through. Or Borden could be sent to the Supreme Court and Hughes, with the support of the Conservative party and of the English speaking Liberals, could form a coalition government, or fight a general election. Of the various courses he had outlined, the one he favoured was that which would make him Prime Minister, but to achieve that he needed a friendly press. Aitken and Rothermere could buy up the necessary country papers, from which they would make a fortune and bring him to power. He addressed his letter to Lady Aitken and told Aitken to reply to his Secretary using some other name. Whether Aitken replied or not hardly matters, for Sam Hughes was no longer important to him.[45]

The surviving mystery is why Borden hung on to Sam Hughes for so long. Neither his biographer, Robert Craig Brown, nor Hughes's, Dr Haycock, offer any convincing explanation. Prince Arthur thought it was due to weakness and some old debt of gratitude. Flavelle thought the same, but here too he was more explicit. He thought that Borden was not only reluctant to remove one who had been a friend, but that he disliked anything disagreeable and shrank from it to such an extent that he lived in a 'perpetual atmosphere of the disagreeable rather than deal decisively with the troublesome factor.'[46]

It was sad that Prince Arthur should have left Canada with a feeling of failure caused by the continued occupancy of the Ministry of Militia and Defence by Sam Hughes; for, though he had failed in this respect, he had succeeded in much else, which, in the long perspective, was more important. Most who met him testified to his courtesy and tact and, through his endless tours and excellent speeches, as well as his friendly manners and dignified bearing, he won the good will of the Canadian people to a remarkable extent and perhaps contributed more than any other Governor-General to the promotion of Canadian feeling above that of Provincial loyalty. In the same sense he advanced the cause of Canada through his tireless advocacy of reconciliation between Protestant and Catholic and English and French speaking Canadians. In the Great War he strove his utmost to secure the proper training and equipment of the Canadian volunteers, who went forth in the Canadian Expeditionary Force, and he grieved deeply for the terrible losses which they sustained.[47]

When Prince Arthur and the Duchess left Ottawa for the last time on 11th October 1916, there were many tears among the huge crowd which thronged the Grand Trunk Railway station and the approaches to it. They sang the national anthem and then *O Canada*, *The Maple Leaf Forever* and *Auld Lang Syne*. The people reached up to shake hands with Prince Arthur and the Duchess when they came onto the observation balcony of their train and the Bordens stood pressed against it so as to be the last to say farewell. As the train steamed away, the Prime Minister called for three cheers, which rang throughout the whole station. As we shall see, Prince Arthur stored up no ill feelings about Borden; Sam Hughes, he seems never to have mentioned again. Laurier wrote that he had hoped that Prince Arthur would remain as Governor-General for the rest of the war. No Canadian, he said, would forget his service to Canada.[48]

CHAPTER 18

A New Way of Life
1916-1930

WHEN HE RETURNED to England from Canada, Prince Arthur was sixty-six years of age. Though he was more prone to bronchitis and other respiratory complaints than he had previously been, it did not occur to him that his activities and services would now be scaled down, through the removal of the regular demands which had been exerted upon him in the past forty-nine years by the various military appointments he had held and, latterly, by the Governor-Generalship of Canada. There was talk of reviving the post of Inspector-General of Overseas Forces and asking the holder of it to watch over the Dominion and Empire troops, while in their final phases of training in England before going to the front, and Prince Arthur hoped that he would be selected for this role. Though a question mark had been suspended over the Duchess's health for many years, she had lately seemed to be better and she now intended to play her part in support of the war effort against her former homeland to the best of her ability and especially in alleviating the hardships which Canadian prisoners of war were suffering in Germany. Events, however, were to frustrate both these aims and, in doing so, were, in fact, to usher in for Prince Arthur a radically new way of life.[1]

Writing as President of the Canadian Red Cross Society in January 1917, the Duchess took up with the Director of Prisoners of War, General Belfield, the inadequacy, as she saw it, of the issues of clothing to which prisoners of war in Germany were entitled. She pointed out that many of the deficiencies could be remedied by the Red Cross, but that under new regulations they were prohibited from doing so. These restrictions were caused by the requirements of the Contraband Committee and by the feeling in the War Office that an improvement in provision for prisoners of war would relieve the Germans of the pressure upon them to take these steps themselves, and that it would also tend to make the prisoners more fit for heavy labour on German projects and would thus, in effect, amount to assistance to the German war effort. The Duchess was not impressed by this mixture of motives, but within a few days of telling General Belfield so, she went down with what seemed to be a slight attack of bronchitis. By 6th March, when she had been in bed at Clarence House for seventeen days, she was diagnosed as having bronchitis, 'flu and measles. Sir Edward Worthington, who had been Prince Arthur's and the Duchess's doctor in Canada, and Sir James Kingston Fowler, whom Prince Arthur described as a throat specialist, were looking after her and Sir Bertrand Dawson, the King's doctor, had been sent for. Late on the night of 13th March, the thirty-seventh anniversary of their wedding, Prince Arthur began to give up hope, but, though he recognised that Louischen was in God's hands, he still prayed that she might live. She died on the following day.[2]

Their daughter Daisy, the Crown Princess of Sweden, realised how 'absolutely lost & perfectly miserable' her father would now be, for she felt that her parents had been 'all sufficient for each other.' Indeed, as it had begun, the marriage had always remained a love match. Prince Arthur felt that the parting would have been unbearable had he not believed that there would, in the future, be a reunion. A few days after the funeral he went down to Bagshot resolved to sleep in his marriage bedroom, but he found the house sad and lonely, the rooms cold and forlorn and in the middle of the night he woke to find Louischen's dog curled up at the foot of the bed. He had never before lived at Bagshot alone. On Good Friday he took Dorothy Yorke, one of the Duchess's ladies-in-waiting, with him to Bagshot Church for part of the three-hour service. The King and Queen were coming over to Bagshot for tea and Léonie Leslie was expected shortly. Despite the comfort and sympathy with which he was fortunate enough to be surrounded, life could never again be the same for Prince Arthur and, to his intimates, he conceded, throughout the rest of his long life, that it never was.[3]

The Crown Princess was, however, not quite right in suggesting that Prince Arthur and the Duchess were 'all sufficient for each other,' for though, in almost every respect, he was for her, she was not entirely so for him. As one who felt that the advice and guidance which men had to offer was insufficient, Prince Arthur leant heavily on that provided by women and, for all her qualities which appealed so deeply to him, Louischen never stood to him, in the role of advisor; she, on the contrary, depended on him as a daughter on a father. Her views on life and affairs were too much coloured by sudden and temporary enthusiasms for the often rather absurd views of women around her, and occasionally of men, who appealed to her for reasons other than their real wisdom. Nor, being so self-deprecating, was she sufficiently immune to the snares of flattery, as her contacts with some of the Canadian railway magnates had demonstrated. There had, therefore, always been room in Prince Arthur's life for other women whose *savoir faire* impressed him. As he was also a lifelong admirer of feminine beauty, and as it was so common for Princes to have mistresses in addition to a wife, there had been an inherent threat to the stability and happiness of his marriage.

That this threat never materialised was in large measure thanks to the Duchess herself and especially to the love and affection which she extended to Léonie Leslie upon whom, in the years following Queen Victoria's death, Prince Arthur had come more and more to depend, as the repository of his confidences and the regulator of his anxieties, depressions and confusions. But Léonie was also American and untarnished by the staleness of British etiquette; she was gifted and amusing and she was married to a husband who could scarcely be described, even charitably, as more than rather ordinary. Her strong appeal to Prince Arthur was based upon more than her level-headed and sympathetic interest in the problems and hopes which confronted him and many were the wives who would have distrusted her. But not so the Duchess, who positively welcomed Prince Arthur's affection for and trust in Léonie, feelings which she also shared to the full. It was the Duchess who made the relationship between Prince Arthur and Léonie into a triangle of intimate friendship embracing all three of them and the trust which each had in the others made anything which would have damaged the marriage unthinkable. Nor did Léonie's husband seem to find anything to complain of.

In the loss of his wife, Prince Arthur recognised that he must bow to God's will and he also thought that in the midst of a terrible war he ought to bury his private feelings. He would try, he wrote to the British Ambassador in Washington, to resume his 'multifarious duties' as soon as possible and in that way to distract himself from his sorrow. He was already much more personally aware of what the war meant than had been possible by thinking about it from the other side of the Atlantic. On returning from Canada he had scarcely touched England before going out to the Western Front to see the conditions for himself. On 31st October 1916, he had gone up to the front 'somewhere in France' and heard German shells flying over his head and bursting behind him. He was amazed by the destruction he saw; whole villages had disappeared altogether; it rained without ceasing and the mud was indescribable. One had to wade through it, he wrote. He went into a captured German dugout which was like the catacombs outside Rome. He toured the front extensively throughout November, visited several of the Army commanders in their Headquarters, Haig, the Commander-in-Chief, in his and the King and Queen of the Belgians, bravely holding on to the tiny part of the Kingdom at La Panne, which had not been overrun by the Germans. He went to see the French Commander-in-Chief, Joffre, at Chantilly and several of the French Army commanders at their various posts, including Verdun, which was still under German artillery bombardment. He called on President Poincaré in Paris, made a second visit to the Somme battlefield and went to see the Headquarters of the Royal Flying Corps.[5]

Prince Arthur hoped that what he had learnt in France would be helpful to him if he was appointed Inspector-General of Overseas Forces, which it seemed he shortly would be. When the proposal was put to the Dominion Governments in January 1917, it seemed that the matter would quickly be concluded. The Canadian Minister of Militia and Defence, Mr A.E.Kemp, who had taken over from Sam Hughes, welcomed the idea. He proposed to write to London saying that the Duke of Connaught had taken the keenest interest in the Canadian Expeditionary Force while he was Governor-General and that Canadians would be particularly gratified if he now became Inspector-General of Overseas Forces. Borden, however, would not have this and he told Kemp to drop his draft; he would take the matter into his own hands. Evidently he was much less afraid of Kemp than he had been of Hughes, but it is clear that he was also afraid of the Duke of Connaught. He asked the Governor-General to cable to London that while the appointment of the Duke of Connaught was 'desirable and appropriate,' the scope of the duties should be limited in accordance with the views of Sir George Perley, the Canadian High Commissioner in London. He then cabled to Perley advising him that his view would be that the Duke of Connaught's duties should be 'strictly limited,' in view of the fact that he was inclined to interfere in petty matters of administration and to occupy the time of Ministers with 'trifling details of comparatively small moment.'[6]

It was clear that Borden had heard enough from the Duke of

Connaught as Governor-General about such 'trifling matters' as the jamming of Canadian rifles, the disintegration of the soldiers' boots and the lack of discipline in their transit camps, to feel that he did not want to hear any more from him as Inspector-General. It was also clear that, in putting himself forward for the post, Prince Arthur had not been seeking an honorary position, but one through which he could make an actual and useful contribution. Thus, when, at the beginning of March, the Secretary of State for War offered him the appointment on terms which would have given him no effective functions, he declined it. So, on 27th March 1917, the Colonial Office told the Canadian High Commission that, in consequence of unforeseen difficulties, it had been decided to abandon the idea of having an Inspector-General of Overseas Forces. Thus, thirteen days after the Duchess's death, Prince Arthur's chance of receiving a professional appointment was lost. It proved to be his last chance and henceforth, though he was yet to carry out many functions and missions, some of which were to be of major importance, he was, for the first time in his adult life, a Prince without a professional appointment, or the imminent prospect of one. His long period of continuous public service as a soldier and administrator, which distinguishes him from all his contemporaries and successors in the British Royal Family, had come to an end.[7]

But, official appointment or otherwise, Prince Arthur took very literally the technicality that Field-Marshals did not retire and during the rest of the Great War he travelled extensively and energetically, to many of the various fighting fronts, to see as many of the British, Empire and allied troops as he could. On 25th June 1917 he returned to the Western Front, hoping to find signs of an impending end of the stalemate in the trenches. He went to the top of Vimy Ridge, which the Canadians had captured, and, standing there with Major-General D. Watson, the commander of the Canadian Fourth Division, looked towards Lens, which he expected would soon be taken. In the two and a half months since the epic Canadian action which had carried them to the top of this tactically important feature, Prince Arthur saw that the grass had grown over the scars of battle sufficiently to conceal the old German trenches and the shell holes. At Messines, however, where the fighting had died down only a fortnight before, the going was difficult because of the trenches, gun emplacements, masses of wire and huge craters, one of which, Prince Arthur noted, was a hundred and ten feet across and sixty feet deep. He found it incredible that such strongly held positions could have been wrenched from the Germans. On the Somme and the Ancre he found fifteen miles of complete devastation, which had reduced the countryside to a wilderness covered with unexploded shells, unburied bodies, masses of equipment and many British graves. All this area had been in German hands, when he had come out in November 1916. After sleeping three nights in Cassel and two at Bavincourt, he went on to the Italian front.[8]

Prince Arthur was again in France from 15th to 22nd October 1917. This time he worked up to the front through several of the behind-the-lines support organisations, such as the Royal Flying Corps engine repair shop near Rouen, hospitals, veterinary hospitals and ordnance workshops. At the front he concerned himself especially with the Canadians. Near Poperinge he met General Currie, who commanded the Canadian Corps, in a hut covered by sandbags as a protection against the constant German bombardment. He was greatly impressed by the three brigades of Canadians whom he saw there and he recognised them as fully seasoned troops of the finest appearance. The numerous aeroplanes overhead all seemed to be British and Prince Arthur began to feel that the days of the Bosche were numbered, though he feared that their actual downfall might yet be some way off. He was told that an attack on Paschendale would start any day and that this was the key to the whole position, as that ridge commanded the going all the way to Roulers. He noted, however, that the ground was lamentably wet. Even so he found Haig in a very optimistic frame of mind, for he thought that the Germans might go pop in January; Prince Arthur could not help doubting it.[9]

In January 1918 he set off to visit more distant fields of battle and areas of strategic or diplomatic importance in the Near and Middle East, where the allies were seeking to drive Germany's Turkish ally from her suzerainty over the Arabs and to engage the Austro-German southern front. He was very unwell, had been suffering from paroxysms of coughing and was inseparable from his handkerchief. On the way out, he happened to come across Sir Bertrand Dawson in Paris, who urged him to work up more gradually than usual to his normal scale of activity. Prince Arthur, who always found it hard to disobey doctors, therefore, paused a day or so in Monte Carlo, where he found there were more waiters than people at dinner, before travelling to Taranto, where he embarked for Egypt. Though the Riviera was very empty, he had found it heavenly to be there and obviously he felt that the change of air had done him good. From Cairo, he travelled the route he knew so well to Khartoum, where he found a splendid new bridge across the Blue Nile, which brought the train into the middle of the city. It was hard to take much interest in all the sights of the journey, which was dreadfully sad without the Duchess, who had so often accompanied him that way. He was, however, greatly interested in the talks he had with the Governor-General, Sir Lee Stack. Turkish prestige in the whole area was declining precipitately, especially since they had been expelled from Mecca by Arab troops operating under the King of Hedjaz. Prince Arthur hoped that the vacuum would be filled by an understanding between the British and the Arabs, whose armies were already being supported by the Royal Flying Corps and the loan of British officers to advise them. Returning to Egypt, he found the country in a very prosperous condition and the atmosphere in Cairo made it hard to believe that there was a war on. There were, however, fifteen thousand officers and men in hospital there and in Alexandria, Port Said and Suez. Prince Arthur busied himself in going round many of these; there was comparatively little sickness and nearly all the inmates had been wounded in the fighting in Mesopotamia, Palestine, Salonika and elsewhere in the Near and Middle East.[10]

On 13th March 1918, Prince Arthur arrived at Allenby's Headquarters at Beit-Mabala in Palestine. It was very cold after the warmth of Egypt and the Sudan, but he was greatly impressed by the splendid quality of Allenby's troops, most of whom seemed to be Territorials, and he found it very interesting to see the scenes of recent fighting nearby and at Gaza. He went on to Jerusalem, where he stayed in the Kaiserin Augusta Hospice on the Mount of Olives. This had been built by the reigning German Emperor, partly as a sanatorium for Germans with weak lungs and partly as a hotel. Prince Arthur occupied rooms which William had provided for himself as Grand Master of the German Order of St John. Prince Arthur enjoyed the irony that he was the Grand Master of the English Order of St John and he hoped that his nephew would come to hear of his stay. While he found the rooms very cold, Prince Arthur conceded that the building was a splendid one, though it had some touches which were all too characteristic of the German Emperor. In the large and very handsome chapel, the domed roof accommodated a mosaic which represented the Almighty in the centre with William and Dona in close attendance. Facing the main entrance of the building, there were life-size statues of William and Dona, the former clad in the chain mail of a crusader and grasping a double edged sword. Palestine, Prince Arthur told the King, was unlike any other country in the world. The various factions there were liable to make political issues from any event and he took care to restrict his activities to British and military functions, which he hoped could be done without controversy. He thought that England did not realise what Allenby's troops were going through; the conditions for campaigning were most unfavourable and there was great difficulty in bringing up supplies.[11]

Prince Arthur was next directed to Athens, in response to strong appeals from Lord Granville, the British Minister there. A rather awkward situation had arisen; a pro-allied government under Venizelos had been installed and the pro-German King Constantine had chosen to abdicate for himself and his eldest son. This made his second son, Alexander, King of the Hellenes. He had fallen in love with a commoner, which was not considered convenient in Greece. The British Minister was hoping the young lady, Madememoiselle Aspasia Manos, would be patient. He thought she ought to go to the front in the ambulance service and thus make herself better known and more popular. She seemed willing to do this, but insisted that she would marry the King first. The objection to this was that she would not be allowed to go to the front if she was the King's wife. Lord Granville believed that Prince Arthur would be able to influence the King in the right directions. Clearly, he did not want the pro-allied government to be embarrassed by the abdication of the King, whom they had virtually placed on the throne.[12]

From the outset this was a sensitive mission and it also proved to be rather dangerous. On the voyage from Port Said to the Piraeus and as she neared Crete, Prince Arthur's ship, H.M.S. *Liverpool*, narrowly undershot a German torpedo, which crossed her course from starboard to port just ahead. A few hours later there was a heavy thud as the ship fouled some underwater object, which the Captain thought was a submarine. The impact damaged one of *Liverpool*'s screws and for the rest of the voyage there was severe vibration. In Athens the situation proved to be even more difficult than Lord Granville had explained. The impression seemed to be that Prince Arthur had come to arrange the marriage of the King, either to his own daughter, Princess Patricia, or, from the Greek point of view, even better, to the King of England's daughter, Princess Mary. Prince Arthur was sure that King George would not give his daughter to so uncertain a country as Greece and he thought that Patsy, who in any case would not consider such an idea, was too old for young King Alexander and, of course, there was also the problem of Mademoiselle Manos. Prince Arthur's reaction to the further rumour that he had come to arrange for the accession to the Greek throne of his own son seems not to be recorded.[13]

Lord Granville wrote to King George of his gratitude to Prince Arthur for his readiness to do 'anything, however tiresome, which Lord Granville ventured to suggest,' and he thought the visit had made a most favourable impression on the young King, society and the public in general. He reckoned that it would make his own task easier than it had been before. Prince Arthur, however, had not seen things quite in that light. He told the King that wherever he appeared in public in Athens, he had received a tremendous ovation; he hoped it was a sign of enthusiasm for his host, King Alexander, but he obviously feared that it probably was not. Though he thought the young King was a nice boy, he found that he was thoroughly ignorant of anything connected with his role as a constitutional sovereign and he was afraid that he hated being King, hated the government with which he had to deal and missed the liberty he had had when his father was King and his elder brother heir to the throne. He was now lonely, for all his former friends of his own age had been banished, as they were supporters of his father. Prince Arthur felt that he was still devoted to his father and he believed that he was probably really pro-German himself. If he was not allowed to marry Mademoiselle Manos, he would most probably abdicate. Prince Arthur had interviewed the young lady and had thought her very nice, simple and well educated, though, at least according to Lord Granville, he had been disappointed by her looks. Even so, he thought her nice looking and he hoped that the marriage might be allowed to come off. The difficulty was that her family was considered to be undesirable and the idea of the marriage was much disliked in Greece. It was an awful impasse and Prince Arthur was sorry for the poor King.[14]

It seems that Prince Arthur's somewhat Ruritanian mission more or less succeeded. King Alexander refrained from marrying Mademoiselle Manos until 14th November 1919 and the event then passed off without causing a revolution. His wife, however, was not accorded the title of Queen of the Hellenes and, on 25th October 1920, at the sadly early age of twenty-seven, the King died, seemingly from the effects of a monkey bite. Greece had, however, remained on the allied side until the end of the war.

During the weeks in which Prince Arthur was in the Middle East and Greece, the decisive phase of the war at last arrived. The stalemate in the trenches on the Western Front was broken and a war of movement began.

Ironically, in view of the outcome, this was initiated by a series of German offensives, the first of which was launched on 21st March 1918, and a break-through, which seemed to threaten the collapse of the whole allied line. For the first time since the beginning of the trench war, the attack had prevailed over the defence and it seemed that it might have done so decisively. On his way home across France, Prince Arthur came to grips with the gravity of the crisis. He was told that a hundred and sixteen German divisions had been thrown against fifty-seven British and, though the line seemed to be stabilising by the middle of April, Prince Arthur was desperately anxious lest sheer exhaustion might yet open further flood gates to another German advance. And he, who had always sought to avoid the exposure of soldiers to hazard too young, was deeply disturbed to find that many of the British troops facing this German onslaught were under nineteen years of age and had never seen a shot fired before. He thought it was an unfair ordeal for them and he blamed Lloyd George for having failed to reinforce this beleaguered force with greater strength. Politics, he considered, had been regarded as more important than the safety of the British troops. He saw Haig at Montreuil a few days after the latter had issued his subsequently famous 'backs to the wall' order of the day. He found him naturally anxious, but still hopeful. At the end of May, Prince Arthur continued to be extremely anxious, but he was now back in Clarence House in London and had no access to inside information of the kind which he had when he was in France.[15]

We need not dwell upon the course of events which transformed the German successes of March, April and May into the rout of their armies by the allies in August, September and October and how what was at the time the most terrible of all wars in history came to an end with the Armistice of 11th November 1918. We need only observe that Prince Arthur followed every development as closely as he could, while enjoying the relief of being able to express his hopes and fears to his confidante, Léonie Leslie. He had half expected that the long separations, which duties had imposed upon him and Léonie might have led them to drift apart, but this did not happen and, at the height of the crisis on the Western Front in April, he was deeply touched to get a letter from her confiding how she thought their friendship of the last eighteen years had helped them through many trials and sorrows. Her son, Norman, had been killed in action and she had had many other anxieties and troubles to bear. Prince Arthur replied by assuring her of how true and deep was his affection for her, his 'dearest of friends.'[16]

Lady Cynthia Asquith has recorded sitting next to Prince Arthur at a luncheon in Downing Street at the end of 1916. She wrote in her diary that he was charming and she thought him 'the only gentleman royalty, with manner and presence.' Apparently he boasted of his daughter-in-law's prowess as a nurse and said that she had herself amputated a finger, which Lady Cynthia thought a 'shocking bit of royal licence.' Lady Cynthia was a colourful raconteur, but her meaning is clear enough and it also incidentally offers an insight into Prince Arthur's easy relationship with women and his ready acceptance of them as people in their own right. Some of this liberalism was fostered by Léonie and it is interesting to note that it was in a letter to her, in the last weeks of the war, that he expressed his sympathy with striking women bus and tram drivers in London. Though he thought it outrageous that they had gone on strike with hardly a day's warning, he also thought it wrong that the employers should have thought that they could get women to do men's work at a lower rate of pay. Employers, he thought, should recognise that they could not continue to treat women as they had done in the past. For one whose instinct was increasingly conservative, who had deplored the suffragette movement and feared the influence of Bolsheviks behind strikes, this was a remarkable, but nonetheless, for Prince Arthur, a not uncharacteristic, point of view.[17]

His fear of the Bolshevik influence was characteristic of the times, but he and the rest of the Royal Family had reason for a more personal identification with the horrors of Leninism than had the great majority of the British people. In the concluding stages of the war, the three great Empires, the Russian, German and Austro-Hungarian, crashed; the Russian and German onto the path of violence and totalitarian dictatorship and the Austrian into the dust. The German Emperor, Prince Arthur's nephew, and the Austrian, the successor of his great friend Franz Joseph, who had died in 1916, were consigned to exile; but the Tsar Nicholas II was shot in cold blood in the dead of night by the Bolsheviks, with his wife, who was Prince Arthur's niece, his children and his remaining servants. As Daisy wrote from Sweden, one had read of the death of Louis XVI and shuddered, but now it seemed 'too awful to have actually known and liked another monarch to whom these dreadful things have happened.' At that time the Crown Princess of Sweden did not know of the deaths of her first cousin, the Tsaritsa Alexandra, the children and the servants, but this awful truth soon became apparent to Prince Arthur. The King heard, through the Intelligence Department on the Murman coast, from the British Consul, who had lived next door to Ipatiev's House in Ekaterinburg, that when the Tsar and Tsarevitch were killed there, the Tsaritsa and the four girls were also shot. At first Prince Arthur tried to believe that there might be an element of doubt, but what the King told him soon convinced him that it was all too true. He remembered what a charming girl his niece had been before her marriage to the Tsar and what a sad and anxious life she had had since. It is not to be wondered at that Prince Arthur found the King depressed and gloomy and that neither of them was able to see the good in the Bolshevik revolution, which was apparent to so many others, albeit, as time was to show, with shorter sight than that of the King or Prince Arthur.[18]

At the end of 1918 Princess Patricia became engaged to a naval officer, Captain Alexander Ramsay, who was the third son of the thirteenth Earl of Dalhousie. He had distinguished himself in the Gallipoli campaign, but she had fallen in love with him before that, while he was on Prince Arthur's staff in Canada. Princess Patricia, who might, if she had wished, have been the Queen of Spain, or Portugal or sundry other countries, or have become a Russian Grand-Duchess, was now permitted to give up her royal title and, when she was married on 27th February 1919, she became simply Lady Patricia Ramsay, as if she was the daughter of an ordinary Duke. Though this made no difference to the regard in which she was held both within and without the Royal Family, her marriage did make another fundamental change in Prince Arthur's life. He was deeply devoted to her. Queen Victoria, it will be remembered, had prevented his other two children from being with him for much of their babyhoods, because she would not allow them to go to India. In Patsy's case she had relented, or been overruled, and the bond between father and daughter had grown in more natural circumstances than had been the case with the other children. And, as Patsy did not marry until she was almost thirty-three, she stayed 'at home' longer than the other two. As Captain Ramsay was a sailor, Patsy continued to be more with her father than would probably otherwise have been the case, but, of course, much less than before her marriage. Prince Arthur missed her tremendously and began to feel more and more that he was left alone.

This feeling, together with the belief that the climate there would benefit his bronchitis, drew Prince Arthur to the French Riviera. Here, at the right time of year, there was a lively, if slightly raffish, society of American expatriates, Russian emigrés and British such as Mrs Arthur Wilson of Tranby Croft fame, who did not quite flourish in England.

55. *Prince Arthur arriving in India, 1921.*

56. *Prince Arthur with Lord Willingdon at the Indian officers' garden party in Delhi, 1921.*

57. *The family party at Bagshot Park, August 1935. Left to right: (top of the steps) Princess Arthur of Connaught, Alastair, Earl of Macduff, Prince Arthur of Connaught. Seated: Crown Prince Frederick of Denmark, Lady Patricia Ramsay, Princess Helena Victoria, Crown Princess Ingrid of Denmark, Prince Arthur and (standing on his left) Léonie Leslie.*

58. *Prince Arthur watching troops crossing the Hog's Back, Surrey, during Army manoeuvres in which 20,000 troops took part, 18th August 1931.*

59. *Farewell. Prince Arthur taking the salute at Sandhurst, September 1937.*

There was golf to play and tennis to watch, there were charming motor drives, lovely sea and landscape views and there were delightful villas with enchanting gardens. Though many of these were still closed in consequence of the war, some, including Mrs Arthur Wilson's, were occupied, when Prince Arthur went to stay at the *Hôtel des Réserves* in Beaulieu in March 1919. Mrs Wilson's villa, he wrote to the King, was beautifully situated, had a lovely garden and was very comfortable inside. It was not long before Prince Arthur was negotiating to buy a villa of his own. Meanwhile, he dined and lunched with Adèle Essex, the American widow of the Earl of Essex, in her villa, *Loo Mas*, and at Mrs Arthur Wilson's, *Maryland*, where her daughter, Muriel, was in residence with her husband. In both houses roulette was the order of the day and was played until nearly midnight. During these, or some such junkets, Prince Arthur came across two fascinating American women, Gladys Deacon and Rhoda Doubleday, to both of whom he quite lost his heart.[19]

Gladys Deacon made the first moves to strike up a friendship with Prince Arthur and some thought that she perhaps aimed to marry him. Her biographer, Hugo Vickers, tells us, however, that this was not so, for she had long been bound by the rather strange ambition of taking the place of her old friend, Consuelo Vanderbilt, as Duchess of Marlborough and this, indeed, she was duly to do. Friendship with the Duke of Connaught, she seems to have thought, would be a leg up in that direction. If so, this was neither a pure nor a good basis of friendship, but Gladys was a celebrated beauty, had the reputation of being a cultivated Bohemian and, though, in fact, she was thirty-eight, she seemed still to be in the flush of youth. Whatever bad Prince Arthur may have heard of her, he chose not to believe and her instant appeal nearly swept him off his feet. For the next year he constantly sought her out, urging her to drop all formality in addressing him, to entertain him alone, so that other guests would not impede their conversation, and pouring out to her his views on the world at large. A few weeks were sufficient to make him feel that she had added new enjoyment and interest to his lonely life.[20]

When Prince Arthur got back to Bagshot he found himself wondering what Gladys was doing, while he should have been joining in prayers and listening to the sermon in church. When she missed replying to two of his letters in succession, he wondered if he had been chucked and when she seemingly accused him of looking down on artists, singers and actors, he defended himself by denying that he did so, if they were accomplished and also nice. As to intellectuals, he told her that he knew some who were nice and some who were not. He felt bound to defend Englishmen against what was evidently her charge that they were snobs. Regardless of their breeding, he thought snobs were the most objectionable people and he denied that he stood up for all aristocrats; there were some he thought odious. He put his faith, he said, in the common sense of ordinary English people. Obviously his young friend made him think and take into account some ideas which had not, perhaps, meant much to him before. Obviously too, Gladys dealt with him on terms which ordinary English people did not. That, undoubtedly, was among her great attractions for him.[21]

The refreshment of this friendship was, alas, to be short lived and it was to end on a strangely bitter note. In a little over a year after it had begun and out of the blue, so far as Prince Arthur was concerned, Gladys wrote him a severely astringent signing-off letter. Prince Arthur was deeply hurt, but he conceded that he was to blame for what had happened, as he had, apparently, asked her about some rumours concerning her life, which he now thought he saw he should not have done. He hoped that they could part on forgiving terms, but this, it seems, was not within Gladys's compass.[22]

The other friendship, struck up contemporaneously with the encounter with Gladys Deacon, proved to be of considerably longer endurance. Rhoda Doubleday and her husband, Felix, seemed to arrive on the Riviera from nowhere, but they had the entrée at Mrs Arthur Wilson's, which, by the end of his stay on the Riviera, Prince Arthur had come to regard as his second home. Here he met these further American recruits to the Beaulieu scene. Felix, perhaps, did not make a great impression on Prince Arthur; he was a minor part-time diplomat and businessman. Rhoda, however, was much more striking and, having apparently made her début in New York in the season of 1913 to 1914, she can by now have scarcely been more than twenty-four years old. In no time at all Prince Arthur was lunching out with the Doubledays in Monte Carlo and golfing with them and, on his return journey home, he was already looking forward to seeing Rhoda in London. The reunion was not long delayed and in May 1919 the Doubledays arrived at the Lansdowne Hotel in Curzon Street. Invitations from Prince Arthur rapidly followed one after another. Would she like to motor down to Kew Gardens with him? It would take about twenty minutes to get there and the gardens would look lovely at this time of year. His messenger would wait for a reply, as he had tried four times unsuccessfully to get through on the telephone. Yes, her husband would

be very welcome to come to Bagshot to see the azaleas, but if that meant
throwing over his tennis elsewhere, Prince Arthur would be quite content
if he did not bother. He was sorry that the photograph of herself, which
she had sent him, was not more like; the original, he assured her, was
much more attractive. Her maid's train to Bagshot, he wrote in the
middle of June, was the 4.20 from Waterloo travelling via Ascot. He
would call for Rhoda in his motor at her hotel at 3.45 and would take her
and Felix down to Bagshot Park. After their stay, he was delighted to hear
that they had enjoyed it; he only regretted that he had been so much of an
invalid. Despite all their bluff and bluster, Prince Arthur told Rhoda, he
reckoned that the Germans would sign the peace treaty at Versailles.
Rhoda responded with charming attentiveness; she would like to come to
Bagshot to say goodbye to Prince Arthur before she left the country.
Prince Arthur was pleased; she could come to tea or lunch, whichever she
preferred, and his motor would call at the Lansdowne Hotel and take her
to and fro.[23]

As the Doubledays voyaged back to their home at Effendi Hill, Oyster
Bay, on Long Island, Prince Arthur, accompanied by both his daughters,
attended the King's Garden Party at Buckingham Palace on 11th July
1919. The weather was lovely and it was almost too hot, but it was rather a
sad occasion for Prince Arthur because, after going with him to dine at
the American Embassy to meet General Pershing, Patsy was leaving for
Paris to join her husband, who was now the naval attaché there and Daisy
was returning to Sweden. He would therefore, he wrote to Rhoda, be left
alone. For forty-three years he had not lived alone and he was not looking
forward to it. He found solace in gardening at Bagshot, where he was busy
trimming his yew hedges, and he was looking forward to going to
Balmoral to stay with the King and Queen in September. He thought it
was nice of Rhoda not to have forgotten him.[24]

The bond of friendship seemed now to be well established and a regular
flow of correspondence ensued for the next nine years in which 'dear Mrs
Doubleday' was in turn promoted to 'dear Mrs Doublejoy' and eventually
'dearest Rhoda.' This was punctuated from time to time by meetings on
the Riviera, in Paris, London or Bagshot, whenever Rhoda touched those
points in the course of her almost continuous, and sometimes quite
adventurous, globe trotting. Felix gradually faded from the picture and in
1924 the Doubledays were divorced. Prince Arthur counselled Rhoda not
to be in too much of a hurry to be married again and to be careful not to
fall into the trap of accepting someone for whom she might then find she

did not care. There were, he thought, endless men who would want to marry her, but there were not many Rhodas. These romantic expectations did not, however, materialise and, instead of finding a soul mate, Rhoda was, in 1935, to sue an elderly millionaire for breach of promise and to engage in a slander action against another, who had allegedly told her that only a chorus girl would act as she was doing. Then in December 1936, in the midst of the abdication crisis, Rhoda wrote Prince Arthur what he thought was the maddest of letters, which she asked him to pass on to the King, suggesting that Edward VIII, whom she had always loved, might as well marry her as Mrs Simpson. Had Prince Arthur foreseen these developments during the years between 1919 and 1928, when his friendship with Rhoda flourished, he might, perhaps, have thought that he was skating on rather thin ice. As it was, she brought a breath of youthful fresh air into his life without a hint of scandal; for it was only after his death that Mrs Doubleday ventured to publish her claim that he had proposed marriage to her. Perhaps she had forgotten Prince Arthur's clear message to her early in their friendship that marriage was not in his mind. After telling her that he had seen reports in the press that he was engaged to Lady Essex and of another rumour that he was going to marry Gladys Deacon, he added that he supposed the next thing he would hear was that 'I am going to *marry you*'. Perhaps she had also forgotten that after her divorce Prince Arthur's advice to her was that she should be in no hurry to marry again. These were scarcely the arguments of a suitor.[25]

Meanwhile, another terrible blow fell upon Prince Arthur. Towards the end of April 1920, he went to Windsor Castle. He found the King looking greyer and balder, but, as ever, he and the Queen were most kind to their Uncle. The Winston Churchills were there; she was in very good looks, but he was getting fat and looked extraordinarily old for his age. There was to be a family dinner in honour of Prince Arthur's seventieth birthday, but alas, he wrote to Léonie on 25th April, none of his children would be at it. On the eve of this celebration, Prince Arthur wrote to Léonie again thanking for her good wishes for 1st May. He supposed that he ought to feel very patriarchal on reaching the age of seventy, but he owned that he did not do so at all and that, were it not for his stupid throat and the cold weather, he would have been awfully fit. Daisy, who had had ear trouble earlier in the year, had seemed to be quite well again at the beginning of February, when she told her father that she was expecting her sixth child in June; but she had then got chicken pox and some trouble in her cheek bone. She went north for a change of air and caught a severe chill, but, on 30th April, Prince Arthur did not realise that she was anything more than poorly again. She died on the next day, so that ever afterwards Prince Arthur's birthday was a sad anniversary for him. She was only thirty-eight.[26]

Since the war, the Prince of Wales, already recognised as among the most romantic Princes of modern times, had been engaged in a series of overseas tours. Though there were occasional hitches, the enthusiasm evoked had been quite without precedent. It was, however, one thing for him to travel in America or Canada or other such relatively friendly countries, and quite another to visit India, for India was now in a growing state of turmoil and uncertainty, in the wake of the openly declared demand for independence sponsored by Gandhi. Yet it was India which beckoned, for constitutional reforms, designed by the British to carry her a step in the direction of responsible government within the Empire, were now to be inaugurated and it was intended that the Prince of Wales should carry this out. But when, in the summer of 1920, planning for his tour began, it was found that the unfortunate Prince was in a state of near collapse resulting from the nervous exhaustion of his over-energetic life. He could not go. So, while the Prince of Wales was put out to grass in the hunting-field with the Pytchley, Prince Arthur was invited to take his place in the Indian arena.[27]

Prince Arthur was somewhat taken aback by the invitation, which the King extended to him on board the Royal Yacht in Cowes Roads, but, after consulting his doctor as to his fitness, he agreed to undertake the mission. It was not an enviable one. The Viceroy, Lord Chelmsford, wrote to the King that there was the risk of an untoward incident, as no one could guard entirely against political extremists. He said that the presence of the Prince of Wales would have added an *éclat* to the opening of the new Legislative Assemblies, which no substitute could provide, though he said he was not unmindful of gratitude to the Duke of Connaught for taking his place. This was not very encouraging, but at least it was better than the view expressed by Lord Sydenham, who believed that the royal visit to India would only associate the Crown with a political fiasco. He thought there should be a public announcement to the effect that Prince Arthur's visit had been cancelled because of the continued activities of the agitators. For some reason, he expected that this would have a good effect on moderate opinion in India. Prince Arthur took a less sophisticated view. He expected to find things in India better than they were made out to be and he thought that the agitator Gandhi had shot his bolt. He intended to do all he could to pour oil on troubled waters and to urge upon Indians the need for charity, unity and concord, as the prerequisites of advance and self-government.[28]

On the voyage to India in H.M.S. *Malaya*, which began a few days before Christmas 1920, Prince Arthur was laid up in his cabin with bronchitis for several days and as the ship approached Madras, where the mission was to begin, it was caught in a cyclone, the hatches had to be battened down and the battleship's speed reduced to twelve knots. The weather in Madras was similarly awful and many of the planned ceremonies had to be abandoned. Prince Arthur, however, successfully initiated the first step in his mission by inaugurating the Legislative Council of Madras. Despite the efforts of agitators to have the visit boycotted, he considered that there was a very good reception in the streets, which were crowded and gaily decorated. Even so, it was not pleasant being 'agitated against,' though he was determined not to mind, however unpleasant it might be. In Calcutta, where he arrived on 27th January 1921, he opened the Bengali Legislative Council; Gandhi's agitators were very noisy. Gandhi himself had come to Calcutta some days ahead of Prince Arthur and a number of strikes ensued. Organised efforts were also made to prevent people from assembling in the streets to see Prince Arthur. However, at least in the opinion of the Governor, Lord Ronaldshay, the only effective strike was on the tramways, which were out of action throughout the visit, and there were considerable crowds and a hearty welcome. In Delhi, where Prince Arthur arrived on 8th February, the ceremonies were on a very grand scale. He first opened the Chamber of Princes in the Fort and then the highlight of the mission was reached, when he inaugurated the first Legislative House of all India in the old Council Chamber. In his speech he delivered an impassioned appeal for reconciliation.[29]

This speech had, in the main, been drafted by Sir Harcourt Butler, the Governor of the United Provinces, with whom Prince Arthur had stayed in Agra immediately before going to Viceregal Lodge in Delhi. But there had been some embarrassment about the wording of it, because Prince Arthur was incensed by what he believed were the unnecessary humiliations inflicted by British officers on Punjabis, who had been involved in disturbances in Amritsar, and he inserted some passages of his own, in which he declared that no one could deplore those events more than he himself did. He said that he had felt bitterness and estrangement around him, since he had landed in Madras, between those who should have been friends. On what he felt must be his last visit to India and as an old friend of the country, he appealed to everyone, British and Indian, to bury the mistakes and misunderstandings of the past and to work together for the realisation of the hopes which arose from the inauguration of the new constitution. Perhaps these words had no abiding effect, but at least, in the opinion of Sir John Maffey, the Chief Commissioner of the North-West Frontier Province, they were largely responsible for the magnificent reception which Prince Arthur received when he arrived in Bombay to carry out the last act of his mission, which was the inauguration of the Bombay Legislative Chamber.[30]

The enthusiasm of huge crowds in Bombay compensated Prince Arthur for the dust, flies and heat of the sixty hours in the train which it took to get there and he obviously enjoyed some of the anciliary functions, which included an evening party at Government House for two thousand guests, half of whom were Natives. As always, Prince Arthur noted the costumes and especially how the brightly coloured dresses of the Indian ladies added to the scene. Before re-embarking in H.M.S. *Malaya* for his homeward voyage, on 28th February 1921, he reported to the King upon the completion of his mission. He said that all the Legislative bodies, which he had inaugurated at Madras, Calcutta, Delhi and Bombay, had already begun work and that, so far, thorny questions had been discussed with forbearance. He hoped that these assemblies would gradually become useful and that they would represent the will of the people. Nevertheless, he warned the King that Gandhi was now looked upon as a saint and that he had the backing of clever propaganda exponents and an unscrupulous press.[31]

Though Prince Arthur was to continue for many years to carry out numerous royal functions, often as the direct representative of the King, this Indian mission was the last great sustained undertaking in his illustrious career of service to the Crown. Though he certainly spoke for, and personified, the best elements of British rule in India, his journey proved to be only of limited historical importance. The people of the sub-continent were irrevocably launched upon the course of independence and the determination that they would, sooner or later, even, as it proved, at a vast cost in human life, confront their own problems in their own ways. Some of the best elements of the British system were to survive by adoption, but the regime itself was to go and, in that sense, Prince Arthur's appeal fell on deaf ears. Biographically, however, the mission was most significant; it showed how Prince Arthur, bowed down by two terrible losses, constantly troubled by bronchitis and now seventy years of age, was anxious to serve his sovereign and nephew, King George V, as, in his younger years, he had served his mother, Queen Victoria. His reaction to the Indian challenge also revealed his fundamentally optimistic outlook upon life and the resilience both of his character and his physique. Indeed, as he sailed homewards, he wrote to Princess Louise that he was always able to work harder in a warm than a cold climate and that he felt a different person from what he had been when he set out. Young Prince Arthur, who was now Governor-General of South Africa, was relieved that his father was none the worse for his exertions.[32]

Prince Arthur's voyage from India ended at Villefranche and, on 20th March 1921, he moved into the villa Les Bruyères at St Jean Cap Ferrat, near Beaulieu, which he had bought from the French Government, who had confiscated it from its former owner, a German lady doctor. It was, as Prince Arthur described it to his sister, a nice little villa standing well above the sea, but very fairly protected against the wind and with a lovely view. It caught the sun nearly all day and, with some extra ground, which he had also been able to buy, he felt that a very nice and interesting garden could be made. The villa also had the advantage of being close to Lady Essex's and she was now helping Prince Arthur to fit it up. He was pleased with the chintzes which she and Léonie Leslie had chosen for him, but he was sorry that Rhoda Doubleday was cruising on a slow Dutch steamer and so, for the time being, could not come to see his new acquisition.[33]

Prince Arthur now had such an ample supply of American lady friends, and a Canadian, Ethel McGibbon, whom he and the Duchess had befriended in Montreal, that Léonie was prompted, most uncharacteristically, to show a touch of jealousy or, perhaps, caution. She had evidently dropped the hint that she felt that Prince Arthur now had so many friends that the room for her was diminishing. He firmly dismissed any such idea. His feelings for Léonie, he told her, were those of the most intense affection, the deepest sympathy and the greatest respect. In other words, he saw no clash between his uniquely special relationship with Léonie and his more flirtatious ones with such as Rhoda Doubleday and Gladys Deacon, or even his more loving one with Ethel McGibbon, whom, had she been free, he would, perhaps, as he admitted to Léonie, have wished to marry. As he had conceded to Léonie, Prince Arthur knew that he had many faults and that among them was his tendency to keep falling in love. Probably Léonie, inadvertently, was herself partly to blame for this. Her absolute discretion, which was most marked in contrast to that of her rather rackety sister, Lady Randolph Churchill, her patience and tact and her wisdom and reliability may have so far enhanced Prince Arthur's instinctive liking for American women, as to tempt him to trust them all. When Americans were unaffected and not too rich, they were charming, he remarked to Rhoda, and nicer than anyone else.[34]

The garden at *Les Bruyères* was such a success that Prince Arthur was quite reluctant to leave it in April 1923, when he returned to London for the marriage of the Duke of York to Lady Elizabeth Bowes-Lyon. He had not previously met the bride, though Rhoda had pointed her out to him, at a dance which she had given in London, before the engagement was announced. Like many others, however, Prince Arthur took to her very quickly and he thought Bertie was very lucky to have married so charming a girl. Prince Arthur noticed that she was so nice with the King and Queen and he saw that she was possessed of tact as well as great charm and he also thought her very clever. After the wedding in Westminster Abbey, on 26th April, upon which the sun shone, there was a lunch in Buckingham Palace, which was served at small round tables. Prince Arthur sat with the King and Queen and the newly married pair sat between the Empress Marie of Russia and her sister, Queen Alexandra. The latter was now stone deaf. It was a happy and auspicious occasion and, as history was to determine, yet more auspicious than could be realised on the day.[35]

During these years Prince Arthur settled down to a routine of living on the Riviera from November to April and at Clarence House and Bagshot Park during the rest of the year. In August he was usually the King's guest on board his racing yacht *Britannia* at Cowes and he was generally invited to Balmoral in September. In London, he often breakfasted with the King and he continued to visit him frequently at Windsor. When they were apart, they corresponded regularly, so that Prince Arthur was well-informed about affairs at home and abroad. He was, however, rather surprised by the King's reaction to the formation of the first Labour Government in 1923. Prince Arthur was alarmed by the prospect, which he thought would be disastrous for the country. The King, on the other hand, proved to be well satisfied with the Government and Prince Arthur heard that he got on well with the Labour Prime Minister, Ramsay Macdonald.[36]

This political development was, of course, a reflection of the considerable social and industrial changes which were taking place in the country and, when he returned from France in May 1926, Prince Arthur was brought face to face with one of the symptoms; the general strike. Arriving at Dover on Saturday 8th May, Prince Arthur found that the piers were lined by Cambridge undergraduates, who received him with cheers. They were doing the work of porters, and very quickly they did it too, and he thought they were a splendid body of young men. He then drove to London by a route specially chosen by the police, which took him through Canterbury, Sevenoaks, Chiselhurst, Bromley, Sydenham and Vauxhall to Clarence House; a journey which took two hours. On Sunday morning he breakfasted with the King at Buckingham Palace and that afternoon he met most of the rest of the Royal Family at a private view at the Royal Academy. He did not think it was a very good exhibition, but the streets of London seemed to be fairly normal except for the number of cars flying about packed with people, the quantities of bicycles and the number of people on foot. There were numerous special constables on duty, both mounted and otherwise, and everyone seemed to be buckling to and helping everyone else. People appeared to be in a good humour. Prince Arthur, who had read a report in a French newspaper of two policemen being killed at Hyde Park Corner, believed that, in fact, no one had been killed. He was told that troops were posted at the docks and other possible trouble spots, but that they were being kept in the background and would be used only in the absolutely last resort.[37]

Prince Arthur's sense that the general strike had failed to engage sympathy on a national scale was more or less correct, but it is ironic that it was less the strikers, whom he so often castigated as agents of Bolshevism, who posed the threat to British liberties, than the Cambridge undergraduates, from whom, in the years now following, the Bolsheviks succeeded in recruiting a series of dangerous traitors.

Meanwhile, one of the duties which especially engaged Prince Arthur's interest and attention was the scheme to erect a war memorial to the Guards Division facing Whitehall. He presided at the committee charged with the planning of the monument and its unveiling, which he hoped would be done by the King. But the King, perhaps remembering that in 1882 Prince Arthur had commanded the Brigade of Guards in action, decided that it would be more appropriate for his Uncle, who was the senior Colonel of the Brigade, to do this ceremony. Prince Arthur felt that the design of the monument was nothing wonderful as a work of art, but he thought that its details were interesting and particularly the inscription, which had been written by Rudyard Kipling. On 16th October 1926, he unveiled the monument in the presence of a large crowd, who were enabled to hear his speech through loudspeakers. Prince Arthur found it a very touching and imposing sight, especially as some sixteen thousand serving and ex-service Guardsmen marched past him after the ceremony.[38]

The inauguration of this tribute to the men of the Guards Division, who had sacrificed their lives in the war, was certainly one of the functions to which Prince Arthur attached the greatest importance, but, though most of them were on a lesser scale, he continued to carry out such duties, though much less frequently than in the past. Despite being more or less incognito when on the Riviera, he also did some functions there, including an annual appearance at the war memorial in Beaulieu on Armistice Day. Nor, when he called on the King of Afghanistan in January 1928, while he was visiting Nice, did he do so on purely social grounds. Prince Arthur, speaking in French, communicated through an interpreter with the King, whom he found as easy to get on with as was possible in such circumstances. He thought the King was distinctly intelligent and he was pleased to find that he knew something of his own career, especially in India. Their conversation, which never flagged, lasted half an hour and afterwards the King sent his Foreign Minister round with a box of Afghan coins and a silver branched candlestick with a lapislazuli base as presents for Prince Arthur. All this he duly reported to his own King.[39]

There is no doubt that King George was much attached to his Uncle, that he appreciated the supporting role played by him, and enjoyed his company. When Prince Arthur left for the Riviera in October 1928, the King thought it a pity that he had to go, though he supposed that the doctors were right to insist on it. One of the reasons for his regret was that two of his sons, the Prince of Wales and the recently created Duke of Gloucester, were in East Africa on safari and another, Prince George, was in Bermuda. Perhaps Prince Arthur's departure left the King feeling slightly exposed, or perhaps he had a premonition of the grave illness which, a few weeks later, nearly carried him off. Prince Arthur, too, was not keen to go. The six months which his doctors liked him to spend on the Riviera were a good deal longer than the season there and, out of season, life was liable to be very quiet. Already Prince Arthur was looking for ways of satisfying the doctors without necessarily spending so much time at *Les Bruyères*. In August 1928, he tried the appropriately named Princes Hotel in Hove for the second time. He was pleased to find that not one in a thousand of the people recognised him, for he seems to have been rather apprehensive as to their behaviour. As it was, the holidaymakers did not interfere with him and he never saw a drunkard or rowdily behaved person anywhere. He found that his nasal catarrh and cough were much better.[40]

The Riviera too had now lost some of its attractions. Adèle Essex had died in July 1922. Half the pleasure of *Les Bruyères*, Prince Arthur wrote to Léonie, had been having her at *Loo Mas* as a next door neighbour. Then, in June 1929, Ethel McGibbon, who had settled in a flat in Monte Carlo, also died and Prince Arthur lost another beloved friend. He still derived great pleasure from his Mediterranean garden and, in October 1929, he continued to branch out by starting a wild garden on some new ground across the road from *Les Bruyères*. All the same, he was beginning to lose his zest for the adventure and the health-giving value of living in the South of France.[41]

In other ways too, Prince Arthur was coming to the end of things. On 1st May 1929, he entered his eightieth year. Fifteen days later, he was mounted to review the Grenadier Guards on the twenty-fifth anniversary of his appointment as their Colonel. Though he did not notice him doing so, a press photographer took a picture as he rode onto the Horseguards parade ground, which Prince Arthur later adopted as his Christmas card for 1930. He told the King that it would probably be his last equestrian portrait. Though he was at the time at *Les Bruyères*, he was finding it hard to shake off his bronchitis and Miss Charlotte Hoskins, who was now his constant companion as nurse, secretary and hostess, and his doctors, took the view that riding was now too much of a risk. Prince Arthur was grateful to have been spared so long, but he told the King at the end of 1929 that he wished he was younger, so that he could be of more use to him.[42]

A new generation of Princes were now putting their shoulders to the wheel and there was discussion as to the positions in which they might be most useful. Colonel Clive Wigram, the King's Assistant Private Secretary, told Queen Mary that in his opinion the finest example of a Royal Prince, whom all might follow, was the Duke of Connaught. He gave her a note of the appointments he had held and the periods in which he had occupied them. She was rather surprised that he had begun to hold highly responsible positions at such an early age, having been, she noticed, Commander-in-Chief of the Bombay Army at the age of thirty-six. Wigram's observation was an appropriate epitaph, not on Prince Arthur's life, for he yet had another decade to live, but upon the first eighty years of it.[43]

CHAPTER 19

Finale 1931-1942

ADVANCING YEARS and declining physical strength had remarkably little effect upon Prince Arthur's character and attitudes. Signs of intolerance occasionally appeared; for example, he thought the design of the proposed statue of Haig in Whitehall was hideous and he could not bear to see an equestrian officer hatless. He found it tiresome and disagreeable that the King of Sweden smoked during the meal when he came to lunch with him at *Les Bruyères* in March 1932 and, as for De Valera, he wished someone would shoot him. It has to be admitted, however, that such views have not only been echoed, but, in some cases, substantially reinforced, by subsequent generations. In other ways Prince Arthur continued to be open-minded; more so, perhaps, than octogenarians tend to be. While he approved of the efforts which Alfonso XIII was making to stabilise the political situation in Spain at the beginning of 1931, he hoped that he would realise that the day of absolute monarchy had passed and that a more liberal regime was needed. He believed that Charlie Chaplin fully deserved the fame which he had achieved and he regretted that Austria had been ruined by the Versailles treaty.[1]

Prince Arthur's delight in children and young people was also undiminished. His five Swedish grandchildren, and especially Princess Ingrid, who was later to be the Queen of Denmark, were often with him at Bagshot Park or *Les Bruyères,* whence, for example, he wrote to the King in April 1933 that Ingrid was such a dear and cheery girl, who enjoyed everything so much. He always retained a most intimate relationship with their father, Prince Gustaf, who, after Prince Arthur's day, came to the Swedish throne and was one of the most distinguished and well-loved sovereigns of recent times. Prince Arthur's grandson, Alastair, the issue of his son's marriage to Edward VII's grand-daughter, was rather a problem. Prince Arthur tried to think that he was a nice, sensible boy, not wanting in brains, but at times he could not help noticing that he was careless and unpunctual and that he did not concentrate on his work. Alas, despite his grandfather's belief in his very nice disposition, Alastair's life neither turned out well nor lasted long. When Prince Arthur died he succeeded as the second Duke of Connaught, but, a little over a year later, he died at the age of twenty-eight. Prince Arthur's last grandchild was to provide a much happier story. He was Patsy's son, Alexander Ramsay, always known in the family as Sandy. He was often with his grandfather, when his father was abroad on naval duties, and Prince Arthur, who constantly regretted his departures when he returned to school, was much attached to him. It is through Captain Alexander Ramsay of Mar that Prince Arthur's British line has continued to descend. His Swedish line is principally represented by his great-grandson, King Carl XVI Gustaf of Sweden and his great-grand-daughter, Queen Margrethe II of Denmark.[2]

Though Prince Arthur did not live to see these Swedish and Danish great-grandchildren, he did see six great-great-nieces and nephews in the British Royal family, the children of his great-niece, Princess Mary, the Princess Royal, Prince Albert, Duke of York and Prince George, Duke of Kent. At a luncheon in honour of Queen Mary's birthday in 1928, one of them, Princess Elizabeth of York, then just over two years of age, delighted him as she ran about beating time with both hands to the music of the band and then going up to shake hands with the bandmaster. He also lived long enough to know that, *Deus volens*, this little Princess would succeed her father as Queen Elizabeth II.[3]

Almost to the end of his days, Prince Arthur kept up closely with the affairs of the three great concerns of his public life: the Army, India and Canada. Though in April 1936 he was praying for 'real peace & Christian unity,' he was not an optimist about the international outlook. While he was inclined to believe that a German ascendancy might be better than a communist one, he reckoned that Mussolini was mad to attack Abyssinia against the will of the League of Nations and that Hitler's Germany stood against all modern civilised ideas. Ever since the end of the war, he had deplored the progressively severe cuts which had been made in Britain's military strength and he feared that the day would come when the Army would have to take the field again at a disadvantage. India, he thought, presented Britain with the most difficult problem she had ever had to decide. It was impossible to ignore the aspirations which were now coming to life in that part of the British Empire, but he condemned the simplistic solutions, which were all too often propounded on the basis of slender evidence, such as George Lansbury's recommendation, made after a short visit to India, that the British should clear out, so that the Indians could be united and happy. Prince Arthur supposed that by 'Indians' Lansbury must have meant Hindus. Canadian affairs were always among the closest of Prince Arthur's interests and he remained in correspondence with Sir Robert Borden about them until the end of the latter's life in 1937.[4]

This correspondence with Borden, which was marked throughout by the greatest courtesy and warmth on both sides, is interesting, not only to the extent that it shows the pleasure it gave Prince Arthur to receive news of Canadian matters from so acute an observer of them as the former Prime Minister, but also the revelation it offers of the virtually complete lack of vindictiveness in Prince Arthur's nature. He might well have resented the weakness and deviousness, the latter, no doubt, proceeding from the former, which, as personified in Borden, had so often obstructed the effectiveness of Prince Arthur's Governor-Generalship and, as he saw it, the welfare of Canada. He seems, however, not to have done so at all. 'It is so kind & thoughtful of you both remembering me at this happy season of the year,' he wrote to Borden in December 1932. He said how interested he had been in Borden's account of 'all that has happened in the Dominion during this trying year' and he rejoiced to hear that Borden thought that Canada had passed through her worst days. For his own part, he was not sure; he felt that so much depended on what the United States would do and how the questions of disarmament and war debts were resolved. Three years later he told Borden that he always looked forward to hearing '*your* opinion on the state of affairs in Canada, & the progress *you* consider they are making.' He said that he naturally read all the Canadian news in the papers, but that Borden's views were much more valuable to him.[5]

The terms of this mature friendship are further indicated by the charming mixture of formality and informality which characterised Borden's letters. 'On the eve of the Christmas season,' he wrote to Prince Arthur in December 1924, 'my wife and I have the honour to convey to your Royal Highness with an humble duty, the Season's Greetings and every Good wish for the approaching New Year.' He then went on to say that he and his wife had thought of visiting Italy, France and England, but had decided to postpone the trip and now would probably go to Bermuda or Augusta or West Palm Beach instead. He concluded his letter with the news that the Western farmers were recovering their confidence, but that

Eastern Canada was still losing population to the United States, where high wages were a great attraction to mechanics and labourers. And we shall see in the concluding pages of this chapter how much more Borden appreciated Prince Arthur's true qualities than his and Sam Hughes's biographers have suggested, or than Borden himself inferred in the published version of his memoirs.[6]

In 1934, when the time came at which Prince Arthur would normally have left for *Les Bruyères*, he decided to remain in England and, instead of seeking the Mediterranean air, he retired to Sidmouth, where he had taken a house. In addition to the expense of France, where Prince Arthur reckoned a pound was worth only twelve shillings, he now found the journeys to and from the Riviera long and fatiguing. Then, in April 1935, by which time he had moved to the Branksome Tower Hotel in Bournemouth, Prince Arthur decided that he would drive in a motor to St Paul's for King George V's Silver Jubilee Service. This, he told the King, was a disappointment as he had ridden at the two previous Jubilees in 1887 and 1897 and, at the latter, had commanded all the troops as well. Even so, he was enjoying walking miles on the sands at Bournemouth; he had not before realised that they were so fine and that the neighbouring countryside was so charming.[7]

The Silver Jubilee proved to be the swan song of the King's reign. On 24th October 1935, Prince Arthur went to see him and found that he was coughing and 'awfully absent.' He died on 20th January 1936. Prince Arthur had sat beside his wireless at the Pulteney Hotel in Bath listening to the quarter-hourly bulletins in the last night of his beloved nephew's life and he then wrote to Queen Mary of the years of incessant worry during which she had been the King's devoted wife. He expressed to her the gratitude he felt for all the kindness she and he had shown to him in their twenty-five years as King and Queen and he felt sure that George had known how fond of him he was. He realised what a difficult time this would be for David, but he hoped that Edward VIII would follow in George V's footsteps and that he would 'never forget what this country stands for.' He hoped that the new King would not 'ride roughshod over the tradition of centuries,' and that he would remember that the 'unity & friendship of all classes is what we must always keep before us.' The King and Royal Family must be kept as the centre of the family life of the Nation; he knew that this had been George's idea and he said that it was certainly his.[8]

Edward VIII, as history has amply recorded, had a somewhat different idea and it was not long before what Prince Arthur had evidently half suspected was more than half confirmed. The King followed in his father's footsteps by emigrating to Balmoral in September, but the party he entertained there did not fall into the same tread. Princess Louise noticed some unacceptable names amongst the guests and Prince Arthur told her that he too was very distressed. 'What a pity,' he wrote to her, and he wondered what the Scots thought of it. As always, less inclined than his sister to correct people, he told her, however, that he never referred to 'the *subject*;' it was none of his business and the King was over forty years old. Even so, he got an awful shock when he opened his newspapers on 3rd December 1936; he had had no idea that things had come to such a pass. At once he got in touch with Queen Mary, who was in the greatest state of grief because David had told her that he was determined to marry Mrs S and that, as he was at loggerheads with his Government over the matter, he had decided to abdicate. Queen Mary sent young Prince Arthur down to Bath to explain matters to his father; whereupon it began to appear that there might be no abdication after all. Prince Arthur was filled with apprehension, as he knew that David was 'terribly headstrong' and could not be 'made to *see* that *he as Sovereign*' was no longer a private person, but a public one. He earnestly hoped that matters would be settled 'for the good of all the King's subjects & not only as *he wishes*.'[9]

After the abdication, though he deplored what he had done, Prince Arthur felt deeply for the departing King, who, he recalled, had always been 'so dear and considerate to him,' especially after he had come to the throne. He thought the country was lucky to have such a nice and devoted couple to succeed and he was very surprised that Léonie seemed to think that the new King would not be popular. The fact that he had a speech impediment, he told her, was not a reason for disliking him. He might not be as brilliant as his elder brother, but he had plenty of sound common sense. He reminded her that he had taken part in the Battle of Jutland and that his visits to Australia and New Zealand after the war had been a great success. He felt that everyone ought to be loyal and helpful to him and his only reservation was that he had not the strongest of health. For his own part, he wrote to his great-nephew assuring him of his loyalty and affection and praying that his and Elizabeth's happiness in the future, as Sovereigns, would be as great as it had been in the past, as Duke and Duchess of York. King George VI responded warmly and Prince Arthur was touched and pleased to hear that he was looked upon as a friend and counsellor. He was doubly flattered by being invited to become the King's Senior Personal A.D.C. and by the King's wish that this should be the first appointment of the new reign. In his letter of acceptance, he observed that he had thus been spared to serve five sovereigns as Personal A.D.C. For her part, Princess Louise passed on to Prince Arthur the solution to the riddle 'What are Mrs S's hats like?' which was, 'all brim without any crown.'[10]

At the beginning of 1938, Prince Arthur found himself unable to write more than one or two letters a day. The rest were done for him by his Comptroller or Miss Charlotte Hoskins, who increasingly decided upon his activities, as she was, in Prince Arthur's phrase, now held responsible by his doctor for his health. Though Miss Hoskins ruled that it was too cold for Prince Arthur to go to lunch with the King and Queen in Buckingham Palace on 14th February, her regime was by no means an unduly restrictive one. On that day, for example, the Duke and Duchess of Gloucester came to Clarence House to see Prince Arthur, the King and Queen came to tea and on the day before Prince Arthur and Miss Hoskins had driven down to Bagshot to see some new apple trees which he had just bought. On 17th February, Colonel and Mrs Browning, she was the daughter of Gerald du Maurier, came to lunch and, a few days later, the Duke of Kent came to tea and then the Queen of Jugoslavia and the Crown Princess of Sweden, Prince Gustaf's second wife, came to lunch. On 4th April, Prince Arthur wrote in his own hand to Princess Louise, telling her that the King and Queen had come to tea at Bagshot. Though not looking as well as when he had last seen him, Bertie was in great spirits. Young Prince Arthur was less satisfactory. He had been to Bagshot the day before on his return from a cure in Switzerland. He was very cheery, but Prince Arthur thought him thin and he heard that he was having digestive troubles.[11]

Prince Arthur was very pleased indeed when Anthony Eden resigned as Foreign Secretary in February 1938; he had always thought him a 'very dangerous & conceited man.' He was also pleased when first Queen Mary and then the King wished to have photographic copies of the portrait of himself which de László had painted in 1937. It was done for the Royal Society of Arts, of which Prince Arthur was the President, and showed him in Garter robes. It was a particularly historic work for, as Prince Arthur told the King, he had given only four hours of sittings and the picture proved to be the last that de László painted; he died soon after he had finished it. The ordinary round at Bagshot, though enlivened by these little highlights and the constant stream of interesting visitors, now seemed to Prince Arthur to be a very quiet one, but he found that he liked it and that it agreed with him. His garden remained an endless source of enjoyment, hope and, at times, despair. A late frost in May 1938 wrought awful damage and Prince Arthur was full of anxiety that the garden would not look well when it was opened to the public a few days later. Most of the large trees, however, were in foliage, there were some early azaleas and a few rhodos were coming out. Much more grievous woes were now, unfortunately, only shortly ahead.[12]

Sir Malcolm Murray, who had been Prince Arthur's Comptroller for thirty-two years, had lately been in poor form, but, when lunching at Bagshot Park on 2nd August 1938, Prince Arthur had thought he was in better spirits. Two hours later, he was drowned in Virginia Water. Apparently he had gone out alone in a canoe, which seems to have capsized. The lake was dragged, but, by the next day, the body still had not been found. It was, as Prince Arthur put it, a ghastly tragedy, and a strange coincidence, when it is remembered what had happened to Sir Howard Elphinstone. Worse was now to follow.[13]

On 2nd September Prince Arthur went to see his son, who lay dying at his home in Belgrave Square. He found him sleeping soundly with a happy expression on his face. He sat beside his bed for ten minutes, but his son did not wake. He was glad, for he had dreaded his doing so and then not recognising his father. He thanked God that he seemed to be in no pain, but he grieved that he was still so young. He had always, Prince Arthur told the King, been an affectionate son. He died on 12th September at the age of fifty-five. The flood of kind messages from all over the world seemed to be a help to Prince Arthur, and when his doctor came to see him two days later, he found his heart in perfect condition. Miss Hoskins kept him as quiet as possible and encouraged him to continue to do the things he enjoyed, such as walking in the sunshine round his garden and farm. Patsy was with him, one of his Swedish grandsons, Prince Bertil, and Sandy were on the way. When they had gone, Princess Ingrid was coming. She thought she could be of greater help at this later stage.[14]

Within a few more days, Prince Arthur could think of nothing but the very serious state of foreign affairs. He admired Chamberlain's courage in steadily following what he saw as the only chance of saving the country from the horrors of war and he thought that, at least for the time being, war would be averted. He found it hard to believe that Hitler would plunge Europe into war without thinking twice. War was, for the time being, averted and when Prince Arthur entered his ninetieth year on 1st May 1939, the country was still at peace, if only just. Miss Hoskins, and the others of the household, gave him trees and plants for the garden and he took much pleasure in choosing the places in which they were to be planted. On 3rd December, exactly two months after Britain had for the second time gone to war with Germany, Princess Louise died. She was ninety-one and had been in bed for two years and, much to Prince Arthur's relief, had not known that war had broken out. He thanked God that she was now in safe-keeping, but, he was nonetheless grieved, for they had been devoted to one another ever since they were children and he now could not express how he felt at being parted from her. Of his eight brothers and sisters, only Princess Beatrice was now left and he had never been as close to her as he was to Princess Louise.[15]

Though he was now physically perilously frail, Prince Arthur's spirit still burned strongly. In 1940, Vincent Massey, the Canadian High Commissoner in London, and his wife, Alice, were invited to lunch at Bagshot Park. Despite his years, they found Prince Arthur 'in pretty full possession of his faculties' and 'as always, a charming host.' He told them some of his recollections of life at Osborne when he was a boy and that he retained vivid memories of his father, the Prince Consort, which impressed Massey as a most striking link with the past. And so it continued until the late summer of 1941 when at last Prince Arthur began to take more and more to his room and to be content to sit and do nothing, which had never before been something he could tolerate. As Queen Mary acknowledged, this was not surprising at nearly ninety-two, but it saddened her to realise that 'one who played such a pleasant & nice part in our lives, & was always the same kind Uncle,' was at the gate of departure.[16]

On 12th January 1942, the King's Librarian, Sir Owen Morshead, visited Bagshot Park to discuss with Lady Patricia Ramsay the possibility of a biography of Prince Arthur being written. Prince Arthur did not appear and Lady Patricia explained that he had now quite lost his memory, though, when the spirit moved him, he was still to be found from time to time sitting in one of the downstairs rooms. He was suffering from no ailment other than old age and Lady Patricia thought that he might live for as much as another year or as little as a day. In the event four days remained. Prince Arthur died on 16th January 1942. His death was 'utterly peaceful & without suffering;' only in the last three months had he given up taking an interest in the news.[17]

Sir Owen Morshead had thought of Roger Fulford or Osbert Lancaster as suitable candidates to write the biography, though presumably he realised what very different books these two would have produced. On further investigation at Bagshot Park and Clarence House, however, he came to the conclusion that there would be little material for such a work; he could find only one letter from His present Majesty, one from the Duke of Windsor and none from King George V or Queen Mary. He came on no more than a few scraps of diary, which he found to be of no interest, and Queen Victoria he did not mention at all. He concluded that Prince Arthur must have destroyed a great deal and the idea of a biography withered. Nor was it revived when a fortnight later Morshead discovered a large number of letters from Queen Victoria at Bagshot, for he then decided that these were almost the only letters which Prince Arthur had kept and they, he told Queen Mary, were 'naturally concerned with matters of no great moment.' Subsequent discoveries of larger amounts of primary material left Morshead unmoved and so, through this extra-ordinary aberration on the part of the King's Librarian, who somehow managed to overlook the greatest volume of documentation concerning any British Prince of any age, an authoritative biography of Prince Arthur was not put in hand. The inconsequential account of his life written by Sir George Aston and Mr Evelyn Graham, which had been published in 1929, was thus left in possession of the field. This work, based upon hearsay and the newspapers, was described by Prince Arthur himself as 'rather a weak production but harmless & evidently well intentioned,' and by Sir Malcolm Murray, who was said to have authorised it, but, in fact, had not, as 'dreadful trash.' It has, nevertheless, until now remained alone among the multiplying shelves of royal biography, as the only substantial attempt to describe Prince Arthur's life and achievements.[18]

This has been an extraordinary lacuna, but it must be remembered that Prince Arthur died ten years and more after he had ceased to play a prominent public role and that his death occurred at a dire stage of the war when German and Japanese arms seemed to be on the verge of total victory and those of Britain, the United States and Russia in disarray almost everywhere. Even the date of Prince Arthur's funeral, which otherwise would have been a great state occasion, was kept as a military secret to avoid the danger of offering the Germans an attractive target of concentrated notables. The result was that the most distinguished of modern British Princes faded, rather than passed, from sight and when he departed there was hardly the incentive or even the time to notice it.[19]

There was one important consequence of the otherwise unimportant biography of 1929, though even this seems not to have been much noticed. Mr George W. Brown, the editor of *The Canadian Historical Review*, invited Sir Robert Borden to review it. Borden wrote that the biography gave unnecessary stress to ceremonial aspects and that it failed to provide an insight into Prince Arthur's habits of thought, his estimates of changes and developments and his conception of the imperial and constitutional advances through which he had lived and with which he had been connected. Borden wondered what impressions Prince Arthur had brought back from his missions to South Africa and India, what he had thought of the German manoeuvres, which he had so often attended before the Great War, and he thought there should have been a more clear cut description of his role as Governor-General of Canada. Thus, when free from the political constraints of the Premiership and the threatening dominance of Sam Hughes, Borden revealed his recognition of Prince Arthur's real importance and gave the lie to the inferences which he himself had made to the contrary, when, for example, it was proposed in 1916 that Prince Arthur should be made Inspector-General of Overseas Forces.[20]

It is to be hoped that at least some of the points raised by Sir Robert Borden in his review have now been dealt with, but there do remain two important questions bearing on Prince Arthur's career which have yet to be fully explained. Why did Haldane, Esher, Knollys and even King Edward VII make so big an issue of the Mediterranean command, which had such a deleterious effect upon Prince Arthur's position, and why did Borden, having tolerated, one might say risked, Sam Hughes throughout Prince Arthur's Governor-Generalship, dismiss him almost at the moment of the latter's departure? The biographers of Haldane, Esher, Edward VII, Borden and Sam Hughes offer no clues to the solutions. An answer to the first question has been suggested in Chapter 13 of this book and, as to the second question, there is a hint in the Duchess of Connaught's Journal. On 11th October 1916, their penultimate night in Canada, she described a dinner party which she and Prince Arthur gave in Montreal. Among their guests were Lord and Lady Shaughnessy. Lord Shaughnessy, she recorded, was very interesting on politics. He said that he would now tell Borden that he and 'his people' would withdraw from the Conservative party if Sam Hughes was not dismissed. He said that he had decided to delay doing this until after Prince Arthur had left Canada as, otherwise, he had thought there would be a danger of the Royal

Governor-General being dragged into a political controversy. Lord Shaughnessy, alas, though a huge figure in Canadian history, has yet, apparently, to find a biographer.[21]

Despite the ups and downs of his relationship with Prince Arthur, it may, perhaps, be appropriate that the last words of this biography should be Sir Robert Borden's. He wrote in his review of 1929 that the 'outstanding characteristic of the Duke of Connaught throughout his long life has been his intense and unfailing devotion to duty and to the ideal of service. In this he gives an inspiring example and for this he will ever be remembered.'[22]

Appendix

Prince Arthur's principal military appointments

1867	Entered the Royal Military Academy as a Cadet.
1868	Commissioned as Lieutenant, Royal Engineers.
1869	Transferred to Royal Artillery.
1874	Promoted Captain and transferred to 7th Hussars.
1875	Promoted Major.
1876	Promoted Lieutenant-Colonel and placed in command 1st Battalion, Rifle Brigade.
1880	Promoted Brevet Colonel and Major-General.
1880-83	In command Infrantry Brigade, Aldershot.
1882	In command Guards Brigade, Egyptian Expeditionary Force.
1883-85	In command Meerut Division, India.
1885-86	In command, Rawalpindi Division, India.
1886-90	Commander-in-Chief, Bombay Army.
1888	Promoted Lieutenant-General.
1890-93	Commander-in Chief, Portsmouth.
1893	Promoted General.
1893-98	In command Aldershot Division.
1900-04	Commander-in-Chief, Ireland.
1902	Promoted Field-Marshal.
1904-07	Inspector-General of the Forces.
1908-09	Commander-in-Chief and High Commissioner in the Mediterranean.

Prince Arthur was Colonel-in-Chief of the Rifle Brigade, 6th Inniskilling Dragoons, Highland Light Infantry, Royal Dublin Fusiliers, Royal Army Service Corps, Royal Army Medical Corps, 6th Duke of Connaught's Own Lancers (Wason's Horse), 3rd/7th Rajput Regiment, 10th Baluch Regiment, 47th Sikhs (Duke of Connaught's Own), 1st British Columbia Regiment, Royal Indian Army Service Corps, Ceylon Army Service Corps, Royal Canadian Regiment, 3rd Victorian Rifles of Canada, Royal Winnipeg Rifles, Durban Light Infantry (11th), New Zealand Rifle Brigade and the Kaffrarian Rifles. He was Colonel of the Grenadier and Scots Guards and Senior Colonel in the Brigade of Guards. He was an Honorary Colonel of the Hampshire and Isle of Wight Artillery Militia, 3rd and 4th Battalions of the Highland Light Infantry, 3rd Battalion of the Queen's Own Royal West Kent Regiment, Royal Field Artillery (T.A.), Royal East Kent Mounted Rifles, 18th London Regiment (London Irish Rifles), 6th Duke of Connaught's Own Rifles of Canada, 3rd Regiment Victoria Rifles of Canada, Duke of Connaught's Own Sligo Artillery Militia, 6th Battalion of the Hampshire Regiment and the Transvaal Cycle and Motor Corps. He was also an Honorary Colonel of Prussian, Austrian, Russian and Spanish regiments and he was a Field-Marshal in the Prussian and a General in the Swedish army. He was a Captain in the Royal Naval Reserve. Prince Arthur was a Personal Aide-de-Camps to Queen Victoria, King Edward VII, King George V, King Edward VIII and King George VI.

Sources: *Burke's Guide to the Royal Family*, 1973; R.G. Harris: *Journal of the Society for Army Historical Research*, Spring 1986; Sir George Aston: *His Royal Highness the Duke of Connaught and Strathearn*, 1929.

Note on Sources

The greatest part of the evidence upon which this biography is based consists of original and largely unpublished correspondence, memoranda and journals. The three most important repositaries of this material are the Royal Archives at Windsor Castle (RA), the Public Record Office at Kew (PRO) and the Public, sometimes referred to as the National, Archives of Canada at Ottawa (PAC). The rest of the material is distributed over a number of Libraries and Archives in England and Scotland and I have made use of some private collections. Not much of importance about Prince Arthur is to be found in published sources, but there are some exceptions to this generalisation, especially as regards his term of office as Governor-General of Canada. Other published works have been useful in establishing the relevant historical background to the stage on which Prince Arthur appeared.

UNPUBLISHED SOURCES

THE ROYAL ARCHIVES contain some fifteen thousand items concerning Prince Arthur, which range individually in scope from single telegrams to long runs of journals. The most important collections are the papers of:

1. **Prince Arthur** (RA Add A15), of which there are more than 9,000 items. These include the large volume of his correspondence with Queen Victoria and the Duchess of Connaught, the letters he received from King George V, Queen Mary and other members of the Royal Family, his journals, those of the Duchess and others which they wrote jointly and a great amount of other correspondence with or about Prince Arthur.

2. **Sir Howard Elphinstone** (RA Add A25), which consist chiefly of his correspondence with Queen Victoria, and his journals.

3. **King George V** (RA Geo V AA41-2), which form the section containing the letters written to the King by Prince Arthur.

4. **Queen Mary** (RA Geo V CC45), which similarly contain the letters written to the Queen by Prince Arthur.

5. **Princess Louise** (RA Add A17), which include Prince Arthur's letters written to her over nearly the whole period of their lives.

6. **Léonie Leslie** (RA Geo V BB16 and Acc 1253), which are Prince Arthur's letters to her written from 1900 to 1938. These papers have not yet been arranged but they are located under the supposed, though not invariably the actual, year of their origin.

7. **Rhoda Doubleday** (RA Add A15/A), which are Prince Arthur's letters written to her from 1919 to 1928. These are a recent accession and they have not yet been arranged. They are categorised under their years of origin.

In addition to the yields of these seven collections, there is further substantial evidence elsewhere in the Royal Archives, including Prince Arthur's correspondence with King Edward VII and the Duke of Cambridge and letters about Prince Arthur written by Queen Victoria's Private Secretary, Sir Henry Ponsonby, and Prince Arthur's Comptroller, Sir Alfred Egerton, to their wives.

THE PUBLIC RECORD OFFICE contains several classes of relevant papers. These are:

1. **Cabinet (CAB)** in which the most important items are minutes of the Committee of Imperial Defence 1902-12 (CAB 2), Committee of Imperial Defence Memoranda 1903-11 (CAB 4), Cabinet Memoranda 1891-1907, which include the Arnold-Forster reforms, (CAB 37) and copies of Cabinet letters in the Royal Archives, especially letters from the Prime Minister to the King, 1902-9 (CAB 41).

2. **Colonial Office (CO)** which covers Hong Kong at the time of Prince Arthur's visit in 1890 (CO 129), and Malta while he was C-in-C in the Mediterranean during the period 1907-9 (CO 158). There is a large and important volume of material consisting of the Secretary of State's correspondence while Prince Arthur was Governor-General of Canada (CO 42/949-999). There is more material of the same nature, but which was given secret classification at the time (CO 537).

3. **War Office (WO)** which contains material concerning Indian military matters during Prince Arthur's service as a Divisional and Army Commander and material generated by the Wantage Commission in 1892. (WO 33). The same class contains the Army Council minutes while Prince Arthur was Inspector-General and then C-in-C in the Mediterranean and his reports as I-G and C-in-C (WO 163). There are some less important papers relating to the time in which Prince Arthur was C-in-C, Ireland (WO 35). Interesting maps and diagrams of the Battle of Tel-el-Kebir and of India are also in this class (WO 78).

4. **Foreign Office (FO)** which includes the papers of Sir Evelyn Baring, later Lord Cromer, which throw light on Egyptian affairs from the time of the Battle of Tel-el-Kebir to 1902 (FO 633), and those of Sir Cecil Spring-Rice during his embassy to the United States while Prince Arthur was Governor-General of Canada. (FO 800).

5. **Private (PRO)**. There are three important collections of private papers in this class: KITCHENER (PRO 30/57), CHILDERS (PRO 30/61) and MIDDLE-TON, formerly Broderick, (PRO 30/67).

THE PUBLIC ARCHIVES OF CANADA contain a great wealth of evidence bearing upon Prince Arthur's Governor-Generalship. The most important collections are the papers of:

1. **The Governor-General** (RG7) which are indexed under subject headings and deal with a very wide range of Canadian affairs.

2. **Sir Wilfrid Laurier** (MG 26G).

3. **Sir Robert Borden** (MG 26H) which include his private war file.

4. **W.L. Mackenzie King** (MG 26J).

5. **Lord Grey of Howick** (MG 11 B2). These are a selection of papers obtained in 1955 by the Canadian Dominion Archivist from the Archive of the University of Durham (see below). Where the greater part of a file concerned Canada, the original documents were taken. Where the greater part of the file did not concern Canada, photocopies were taken and the originals left in Durham. The resulting Canadian collection is aranged and listed; the material in Durham has yet to be arranged.

6. **Ivor J.C. Herbert** (MG29 E61).

7. **W.G. Gwatkin** (MG 51 F1).

8. **Sir George Perley** (MG27 II D12).

9. **Sir Charles Ross** (MG30 A95).

10. **Sir John MacDonald** (MG 26A).

Access to this Canadian material was obtained through an examination of photocopies and microfilm of the finding aids and then the provision of photocopies of the selected documents.

MISCELLANEOUS COLLECTIONS of the papers of:

1. **Lord Wolseley**, Hove Central Library.

2. **Lord Roberts**, National Army Museum.

3. **H.O. Arnold-Forster**, Wiltshire Record Office.

4. **Lord Grey of Howick**, Durham University Archive.

5. **Lord Haldane**, National Library of Scotland.

6. **Lord Minto**, National Library of Scotland.

7. **Lord Rosebery**, National Library of Scotland.

8. **Sir Cecil Spring-Rice**, Churchill Archives Centre, Churchill College Cambridge.

9. **Lockwood Kipling**, University of Sussex Library.

10. **Lord Reay**, School of Oriental and African Studies, London University.

11. **H.C.E. Childers**, Royal Commonwealth Society Library.

12. **The Duchess of Sutherland**, Staffordshire Record Office.

13. **Colonel D'Arcy Burnell**, Craven-Smith-Milnes Mss, Nottinghamshire Record Office.

14. **Lord Beaverbrook**, House of Lords Record Office.

15. **Andrew Bonar Law**, House of Lords Record Office.

16. **J.C.C. Davidson**, later Lord Davidson, House of Lords Record Office.

17. **Lloyd George**, House of Lords Record Office.

18. **Sir John French**, later Lord Ypres, Imperial War Museum.

19. **Sir Henry Wilson**, Imperial War Museum.

20 **Sir Herbert Belfield**, Imperial War Museum.

21. **Major E.G. Thompson**, Imperial War Museum.

22. **Lord Gladstone**, British Library.

23. **Lord Ripon**, British Library

24. **Sir Henry Campbell-Bannerman**, British Library.

25. **John Burns**, British Library.

26. **Lord Hardinge of Penshurst**, Cambridge University Library.

27. **Edward Stanhope**, West Kent Archives Office.

28. **Lord Curzon**, India Office Library and Records.

29. **Sir Spencer Harcourt Butler**, India Office Library and Records.

30. **Asquith**, Bodleian Library.

31. **Lord Bryce**, Bodleian Library.

32. **Lewis Harcourt**, later Lord Harcourt, Bodleian Library.

33. **Lord Selborne**, Bodleian Library.

PRIVATE COLLECTIONS

1. **Cecilia Lady Downe**, Lord Downe.

2. **Gladys Deacon**, Hugo Vickers.

PUBLISHED SOURCES

OFFICIAL PUBLICATIONS

Report of the Royal Commission on Shell Contracts. Ottawa, 1916.

Proceedings of the Wantage Commission, 23rd July 1891, C.68521.

Report of the War Office Reconstruction Committee, section VIII, 1904, Cd. 2002.

Report by the Inspector-General of the Overseas Forces on the Military Institutions of Canada, 1913. (Secret.)

Brief Account of the Visit of Their Royal Highnesses the Duke and Duchess of Connaught to Hong Kong in April 1890. Hong Kong Government Printers, 1890

SIX PUBLISHED WORKS WHICH RAISE SUBSTANTIAL ISSUES CONCERNING PRINCE ARTHUR AND WHICH ARE DISCUSSED IN THIS BIOGRAPHY

Ronald G. Haycock: *SAM HUGHES THE PUBLIC CAREER OF A CONTRO-VERSIAL CANADIAN 1885-1916.* Canadian War Museum Historical Publication No. 21, Wilfrid Laurier University Press in collaboration with the Canadian War Museum, the Canadian Museum of Civilisation, National Museums of Canada, 1986. Cited as Haycock.

Henry Borden (editor): *ROBERT LAIRD BORDEN: HIS MEMOIRS.* 2 vols, Macmillan of Canada, 1938. Cited as Borden Memoirs.

Robert Craig Brown: *ROBERT LAIRD BORDEN A BIOGRAPHY.* 2 vols, Macmillan of Canada, vol 1, 1975, vol 2, 1980. Cited as Craig Brown

Michael Bliss: *A CANADIAN MILLIONAIRE THE LIFE AND BUSINESS TIMES OF SIR JOSEPH FLAVELLE Bart 1858-1939.* Macmillan of Canada, 1978. Cited as Bliss.

A.J.P. Taylor: *BEAVERBROOK.* Hamish Hamilton 1972. Cited as Taylor.

Robert Blake: *THE UNKNOWN PRIME MINISTER THE LIFE AND TIMES OF ANDREW BONAR LAW 1858-1923.* Eyre and Spottiswoode, 1955. Cited as Blake.

OTHER PUBLISHED WORKS TO WHICH REFERENCE HAS BEEN MADE

Jagow: *LETTERS OF THE PRINCE CONSORT.* John Murray, 1938.

Milicent Garret Fawcett: *LIFE OF HER MAJESTY QUEEN VICTORIA.* W.H. Allen, 1937.

M.H. McClintock: *THE QUEEN THANKS SIR HOWARD THE LIFE OF MAJOR-GENERAL SIR HOWARD ELPHINSTONE, V.C., K.C.B., C.M.G. BY HIS DAUGH-TER, MARY HOWARD McCLINTOCK.* John Murray, 1945.

Elizabeth Longford: *VICTORIA R.I.* Weidenfeld and Nicolson, 1971 (second impression).

Roger Fulford (editor): *DEAREST CHILD, LETTERS BETWEEN QUEEN VICTORIA AND THE PRINCESS ROYAL 1858-1861*, Evans 1964. (Five further volumes, the last edited by Agatha Ramm and published by Alan Sutton, cover the correspondence to 1901.)

Alan Palmer: *THE KAISER WAR LORD OF THE SECOND REICH*. Weidenfeld and Nicolson, 1978.

Shane Leslie: *THE END OF A CHAPTER*. Constable, 1916.

C.E. Smith (editor): *JOURNALS AND CORRESPONDENCE OF LADY EASTLAKE*. Vol 2, 1895.

Sir Joseph Pope: *MEMOIRS OF SIR JOHN MACDONALD*. Vol 2, Arnold, 1894.

Georgina Battiscombe: *QUEEN ALEXANDRA*, Constable 1969.

Sidney Lee: *QUEEN VICTORIA A BIOGRAPHY*. Smith Elder, 1903.

J.F. Maurice: *MILITARY HISTORY OF THE CAMPAIGN OF 1882 IN EGYPT*. Reprinted by Eyre and Spttiswoode, 1973. Originally officially published in 1887.

Joseph H. Lehmann: *ALL SIR GARNET A LIFE OF FIELD-MARSHAL LORD WOLSELEY*. Cape, 1964.

Willoughby Verner: *THE MILITARY LIFE OF H.R.H. GEORGE, DUKE OF CAMBRIDGE*. 2 vols. Murray 1905.

Giles St. Aubyn: *THE ROYAL GEORGE 1819-1904 THE LIFE OF H.R.H. PRINCE GEORGE DUKE OF CAMBRIDGE*. Constable, 1963.

W.S. Hamer: *THE BRITISH ARMY CIVIL-MILITARY RELATIONS 1885-1905*. Clarendon Press, 1970.

George Earle Buckle (editor): *THE LETTERS OF QUEEN VICTORIA*. Third series, vol 1. Murray 1930.

Sir Michael Havers, Edward Grayson and Peter Shankland: *THE ROYAL BACCARAT SCANDAL*. Kimber, 1977.

David James: *LORD ROBERTS*. Hollis and Carter, 1954.

Michaela Reid: *ASK SIR JAMES*. Hodder and Stoughton, 1987.

Consuelo Vanderbilt Balsan: *THE GLITTER AND THE GOLD*. Heinemann, 1953.

Nigel Nicolson: *MARY CURZON*. Weidenfeld and Nicolson, 1977.

Hugh MacLennan: *BAROMETER RISING*. Harrap, 1942.

C.R.M.F. Cruttwell: *A HISTORY OF THE GREAT WAR 1914-1918*. Second edition, Clarendon Press, 1936.

David Lloyd George: *WAR MEMOIRS*. New edition, Odhams Press, 1938.

Robert Craig Brown and Ramsay Cook: *CANADA 1896-1921 A NATION TRANSFORMED*. McClelland and Stewart, 1974.

John Lewis (contributor): *CANADA IN THE GREAT WORLD WAR*. 6 vols, Toronto 1917-21.

Lady Cynthia Asquith: *DIARIES 1915-1918*. Hutchinson, 1968.

Hugo Vickers: *GLADYS, DUCHESS OF MARLBOROUGH*. Weidenfeld and Nicolson, 1979.

Rhoda van Bibber Tanner Doubleday: *ATLANTIC BETWEEN*. Doubleday, 1947.

Sir George Aston and Evelyn Graham: *HIS ROYAL HIGHNESS THE DUKE OF CONNAUGHT AND STRATHEARN A LIFE AND INTIMATE STUDY*. Harrap, 1929.

Anita Leslie: *EDWARDIANS IN LOVE*. Hutchinson, 1972.

PUBLISHED WORKS SUPPLYING SIGNIFICANT BACKGROUND MATERIAL

Sir George Arthur: *LIFE OF LORD KITCHENER*, 3 vols. Macmillan, 1920.

John Cowan: *CANADA'S GOVERNORS-GENERAL 1867-1952*. York Publishing Company, 1952.

R.M. Dawson: *THE GOVERNMENT OF CANADA*. Toronto, 1948.

R.C.K. Ensor: *ENGLAND 1870-1914*. Clarendon Press, 1936.

Nancy Gelber: *CANADA IN LONDON AN UNOFFICIAL GLIMPSE OF CANADA'S SIXTEEN HIGH COMMISSIONERS 1880-1980*.

R.H. Hubbard: *RIDEAU HALL*. McGill, 1977.

Sir Sidney Lee: *KING EDWARD VII A BIOGRAPHY*, 2 vols. Macmillan, 1925-1927.

Frank Mackinnon: *THE CROWN IN CANADA*. Calgary, 1977.

Philip Magnus: *KITCHENER, PORTRAIT OF AN IMPERIALIST*. John Murray, 1958.

Sir F Maurice and Sir George Arthur: *THE LIFE OF LORD WOLSELEY*. Heinemann, 1924.

D. Morton: *A MILITARY HISTORY OF CANADA*. Edmonton, 1985.

W.L. Morton: *THE SHIELD OF ACHILLES: ASPECTS OF CANADA IN THE VICTORIAN AGE*. McClelland Stewart, 1968.

Richard A. Preston: *CANADA AND IMPERIAL DEFENCE A STUDY OF THE ORIGINS OF THE BRITISH COMMONWEALTH'S DEFENSE ORGANISATION 1867-1919*. Duke, 1967.

Robert Rhodes James: *MEMOIRS OF A CONSERVATIVE JCC DAVIDSON MEMOIRS AND PAPERS 1910-1937*. Weidenfeld and Nicolson, 1969.

O.D. Skelton: *LIFE AND LETTERS OF SIR WILFRID LAURIER*. Toronto, 1922.

Peter Fraser: *LORD ESHER, A POLITICAL BIOGRAPHY*. Hart-Davis, McGibbon, 1973.

James Lees-Milne: *THE ENIGMATIC EDWARDIAN, THE LIFE OF REGINALD 2nd VISCOUNT ESHER*. Sidgwick & Jackson, 1986.

John Gooch: *THE PLANS OF WAR THE GENERAL STAFF AND BRITISH MILITARY STRATEGY c. 1900-1916*. Routledge & Kegan Paul, 1974.

Dudley Sommer: *HALDANE OF CLOAN HIS LIFE AND TIMES 1856-1928*. Allen and Unwin, 1960.

W. Stewart Wallace: *MEMOIRS OF THE Rt Hon SIR GEORGE FOSTER*. Toronto, 1933.

Cecil Woodham-Smith: *QUEEN VICTORIA HER LIFE AND TIMES 1819-1861*. Hamish Hamilton, 1972.

ARTICLES

Sir Robert Borden: *HIS ROYAL HIGHNESS THE DUKE OF CONNAUGHT AND STRATHEARN*. By Aston. *The Canadian Historical Review*, 1930, pp 264-6.

William Lewis Edmonds: *OUR GOVERNORS-GENERAL SINCE CONFEDERA-TION*. *The Canadian Magazine*, vol XLIX 1917.

James A. Gibson: *THE GOVERNORS-GENERAL OF CANADA 1838-1976*. Lecture given for the Foundation for Canadian Studies in the U.K. 1976.

Colonel Sam H.S. Hughes: *SIR SAM HUGHES AND THE PROBLEM OF IMPERIALISM*. Canadian Historical Association Report, June 1950.

Carman Miller: *SIR FREDERICK WILLIAM BORDEN AND MILITARY REFORM 1896-1911*. *The Canadian Historical Review*, 1969, pp 269-84.

Colonel Edward Owen: *TEL-EL-KEBIR AND THE DUKE OF CONNAUGHT*. *Army Quarterly and Defence Journal*, vol 114, no 1.

Donald M.A.R. Vince: *THE ACTING OVERSEAS SUB-MILITIA COUNCIL AND THE RESIGNATION OF SIR SAM HUGHES*. *The Canadian Historical Review*, vol XXXI, 1950.

Bradley King: *AMERICANS IN THE ROYAL FLYING CORPS: RECRUITMENT AND THE BRITISH GOVERNMENT*, *Imperial War Museum Review, No 6, November 1991*.

REFERENCE WORKS

Publications such as *Almanach de Gotha, Burke's Guide to the Royal Family, Who Was Who, Canadian Encyclopaedia* and *Canadian Annual Revue* are useful, but the entries for Prince Arthur are generally disappointing; see, for example, the surprisingly superficial and careless entries in the *Dictionary of National Biography* and *The Royal Encyclopedia*. Genealogically, Christopher Lake's *European Rulers 1060-1981* (Lairg Limited Editions) is most useful.

Source Abbreviations

Bodl. Bodleian Library.
Br Lib. British Library.
CASR. Churchill Archive, Churchill College Cambridge, Spring-Rice Papers
CID. Committee of Imperial Defence.
Cr Pss. Crown Princess.
D. Duke.
Dss. Duchess.
Dss of C. Duchess of Connaught.
Durham. Durham University Archive.
EVII. King Edward VII.
Empss. Empress.
GV. King George V.
GVI. King George VI.
GD. Gladys Deacon.
HE. Sir Howard Elphinstone.
HLRO. House of Lords Record Office.
   BBK Beaverbrook.
   BL Bonar Law.
Hove. Hove Central Library.
IOLR. India Office Library and Record Office.
IWM. Imperial War Museum.
KAO. (West) Kent Archives Office.
LL. Léonie Leslie.
LM. Princess Louise Margaret of Prussia, later Duchess of Connaught.
NAM. National Army Museum.
NAO. Nottingham Archives Office.
NLS. National Library of Scotland.
PAC. Public Archives of Canada.
PoW. Prince of Wales.
Pr. Prince.
Pr A. Prince Arthur.
Pr A of C. Prince Arthur of Connaught.
PRO. Public Record Office.
   CO Colonial Office Papers.

WO War Office Papers.
FO Foreign Office Papers.
CAB Cabinet Papers.
Pss. Princess.
QM. Queen Mary.
QV. Queen Victoria.
RD. Rhoda Doubleday.
RA. Royal Archives.
  Add Additional Victorian Manuscripts.
  Geo V George V Manuscripts.
  Geo VI George VI Manusripts.
R Comm Soc. Royal Commonwealth Society Library.
SOAS. School of Oriental and African Studies.
WRO. Wiltshire Record Office.

Source References

CHAPTER 1

1. Medical Bulletin, 1 May 1850, RA Add A15/1; Extract from QV Journal, 1 May 1850, RA Add A15/2; Pr Consort to his mother, 1 May 1850, Jagow, *Letters of the Prince Consort*, John Murray 1938, p. 158

2. Extract from QV Journal, 22 June 1850, RA Add A15/3.

3. Fawcett, *Life of Her Majesty Queen Victoria*, W.H. Allen 1897, pp 127-8.

4. Pr A to QV, undated, RA Add A15/5.

5. Pr Consort to Pr A, 18 September 1856, RA Add A15/22; Pr A to Cr Pss Prussia, 23 December 1855, RA Add A15/5633A; Miss Somerset to Lady-in-Waiting, 9 January 1855, RA Add A15/8.

6. Extract from QV Journal, 18 May 1855, RA Add A15/9.

7. McClintock, *The Queen Thanks Sir Howard*, John Murray 1945, pp 22-3; Jones to Cowell, (two letters) 3 September 1857, RA Add A15/31 and 32; Pr Consort to Cowell, 8 September 1857, RA Add A15/33.

8. Cowell to Pr Consort, 13 September; HE to Cowell, 13 September; Extract of Cowell to HE sent to Pr Consort, 15 September; HE to Cowell, 16 September; Phipps to HE, 1 October 1857, RA Add A15/35,37,38,40 and 41.

9. Mme Rollande to QV, 3 September 1856, RA Add A15/15; Longford, *Victoria RI* Weidenfeld and Nicolson 1964, p 257; QV to Pr A, 11 September 1856, RA Add A15/20, QV to Cr Pss Prussia, 5 March 1858, Fulford, *Dearest Child*, Evans 1964, p 70.

10. Memorandum by QV, 7 October 1858, RA Add A15/54.

11. HE Journal 23 October 1858, RA Add A25/819.

12. QV to HE, 18 February; 9 March; 10 March; 14 March; 4 April; undated; 19 April; 21 April; 30 April; 3 May; 5 May; 20 May; 31 May; undated; undated; 10 June; 19 June; undated; 12 September; 18 October; 20 October; and 11 December 1859, RA Add A25/1 to 22, (typed copies.)

13. HE Journal, 10 September and 26 November 1859, RA Add A25/819.

14. HE Journal, 11 January 1860, RA Add A25/819.

15. HE Journal, ?19 January; and 16 March 1860, RA Add A25/819; HE to Pr Consort, 3 October 1860, RA Add A15/82.

16. HE to Pr Consort, 8 October 1860, RA Add A15/83.

17. Memorandum by HE, 20 November 1860, RA Add A15/85.

18. QV to Pr Consort, 3 July 1861, RA Add A15/96.

19. HE to QV, 15 October 1861, RA Add A15/107; Pr A to QV and Pr Consort, 19 October 1861, RA Add A15/111; Pr A to QV, 20 October 1861, RA Add A15/112; QV to Pr A, 17 October 1861, RA Add A15/110.

CHAPTER 2

1. QV to HE, 11 April 1862, RA Add A25/71; Pr A to QV, 30 March 1862, RA Add A15/156; QV to HE, 1 April 1862, RA Add A25/66; HE to QV, 2 April 1862, RA Add A15/160.

2. HE to QV, 16 May 1862, RA Add A15/180; *Western Morning News*, 19 May 1862, RA Add A15/185; ditto, ? May 1862, RA Add A/15/182.

3. HE to QV, 2 October 1862, RA Add A15/191; QV to HE, 10 September 1862, RA Add A25/82; QV to HE, 5 October 1862, RA Add A25/86; QV to HE and HE to QV, 8 October 1862, RA Add A25/88 and RA Add A15/192.

4. HE to QV, 1 November 1862, RA Add A15/194; Pr A to QV, 5 November 1862, RA Add A15/197.

5. HE to QV, 6 November 1862, RA Add A15/199; QV to HE, 14 November 1862, RA Add A25/92; QV to HE, 23 November 1862, RA Add A25/94.

6. QV to HE, 30 January 1863, RA Add A25/100; HE to QV 2 February 1863,RA Add A15/248; HE to QV, 5 February 1863, RA Add A15/250.

7. cp Palmer: *The Kaiser*, Weidenfeld and Nicolson 1978,p.7 and Leslie: *The End of a Chapter*, Constable 1916, p.79.

8. Unidentified press cutting, RA Add A15/296; HE to QV, 5 June 1863, RA Add A15/299; HE to QV, 8 June 1863, RA Add A15/300.

9. HE to QV, 1-2 August 1863, RA Add A15/339; Pr A to QV, 2 August 1863, RA Add A15/340; Pr A to QV, 29 July 1863, RA Add A15/337; HE to QV, 21-22 July 1863, RA Add A15/325; Pr A to Pss Louise, 29 July 1863, RA Add A17/70.

10. HE to QV, 19 August 1863, RA Add A15/352; Pr A to QV, 23 August 1863, RA Add A15/355; HE to QV, 31 August 1863, RA Add A15/362; QV to HE, 6 January 1864, RA Add A25/112; HE to QV, 8 January 1864, RA Add A15/409.

11. Memorandum by HE, 5 December 1861, (shown to QV 11 April 1862), RA Add A15/8805; HE to QV, 19 January 1864, RA Add A15/413; QV to HE, 23 January 1864, RA Add A25/114.

12. QV to HE, 16 April 1864, RA Add A25/117.

13. HE to QV, 26 June 1864, RA Add A15/494; HE to QV, 27-28 June 1864, RA Add A15/495; HE to QV, 29-30 June 1864, RA Add A15/496; Pr A to QV, 3 July 1864, RA Add A15/498.

14. HE to QV, 5 July 1864, RA Add A15/499; HE to QV, 7 July 1864, RA Add A15/500; HE to QV, 10 and 12 July 1864, RA Add A15/504; QV to HE, 11 July 1864, RA Add A25/124; HE to Sir Charles Phipps, 13 July 1864, RA Add A15/505; QV to HE, 16 July 1864, RA Add A25/125; HE to QV, 19 July 1864, RA Add A15/513.

15. Pr A to QV, 1 August 1864, RA Add A15/529; Lt Gen Sir William Knollys to QV, 5 August 1864, RA Add A15/533; QV to HE, 4 August 1864, RA Add A25/129; Col

Seymour to QV, 11 August 1864, RA Add A15/540; HE to QV, 11 August 1864, RA Add A15/541.

16. Ed C.E.Smith, *Journals and Correspondence of Lady Eastlake,* 1895, Vol 2, pp 183-4.

17. QV to HE, 10 October 1864, RA Add A25/137; QV to HE (? dictated), 16 January 1865, RA Add A25/144; QV to HE, 4 February 1865, RA Add A25/145; HE to QV, 6 February 1865, RA Add A15/633.

18. HE to QV, 3 March 1865, RA Add A15/645; Cowley to Dean of Windsor, 3 March 1865, RA Add A15/648.

19. HE to QV, 6 March 1865, RA Add A15/650; HE to QV, 9 March 1865, RA Add A15/651; Craven to Cowell, 15 March 1865, RA Add A15/652; HE to QV 14-17 March 1865, RA Add A15/656; Wood to Lord Russell, 20 March 1865, RA Add A15/661; Lord Russell to QV, 1 April 1865, RA Add A15/665.

20. Storkes to Phipps, 19 March 1865, RA Add A15/660; HE to QV, 21 March 1865, RA Add A15/662; Pr A to QV, 14 April 1865, RA Add A15/668; HE Journal 19-27 April 1865, RA Add A15/677; ditto, 22 March-17 April 1865 (copy), RA Add A15/8449; ditto, 10-11 May 1865, RA Add A15/685; HE to QV 14 May 1865, RA Add A15/690; HE to QV, 20 May 1865, RA Add A15/693; HE to QV, 22 May 1865, RA Add A15/694.

21. Lt Francis Bacon to Rev John Bacon, 3 May 1865 (copy), RA Add A15/689; Pr A to QV, 28th April 1865, RA Add A15/673; QV to HE, 23rd August 1865, RA Add A25/160.

22. HE to QV, 25 July 1865, RA Add A15/722; QV to HE, 26 July 1865, RA Add A25/158; QV to HE, 29 July 1865, RA Add A25/159; Phipps to QV, 29 July 1865, RA Add A15/726; Pr A to QV, 30 July 1865, RA Ad A15/731; HE to QV, 2 August 1865, RA Add A15/734; Phipps to QV, 1 August 1865, RA Add A15/732; HE to QV, 1 August 1865, RA Add A15/733; Phipps to QV, 2 August 1865, RA Add A15/735.

23. QV to HE, 21 October 1865, RA Add A25/164; HE to QV, 24 October 1865, RA Add A15/770; HE to QV, 28 October 1865, RA Add A15/772; HE to QV, 31 October 1865, RA Add A15/773; HE to QV, 20 February 1866, RA Add A15/818; HE to QV 8 March 1866, RA Add A15/826; HE to QV, 25 March 1866, RA Add A15/836; King William of Prussia to Pr A, 21 April 1866, RA Add A15/846; QV to Pr A, 22 April 1866, RA Add A15/847.

24. General Grey to QV, undated, RA Add A15/977; QV to HE, 12 July 1866, RA Add A25/180.

CHAPTER 3

1. HE to QV, 5 January 1867, RA Add A15/996; QV to HE, 4 January 1867, RA Add A25/193; QV to HE, 8 January 1867, RA Add A25/194; HE to QV, 11 January 1867, RA Add A15/1009; HE to QV, 13 January 1867, RA Add A15/1015.

2. HE to QV, 12 February 1867, RA Add A15/1039; HE to QV, 14 February 1867, RA Add A15/1040; Report on Pr A, encl. with 17 February 1867, RA Add A15/1043; Pr A to QV, 17 February 1867, RA Add A15/1042; HE to QV, 19 February 1867, RA Add A15/1044.

3. HE to QV, 2 May 1867, RA Add A15/1073; HE to QV, 4 May 1867, RA Add A15/1074; HE to QV, 18 May 1867, RA Add A15/1080; HE to QV, 8 June 1867, RA Add

A15/1084; HE to QV, 13 June 1867, RA Add A15/1086; Pr A to QV, 16 June 1867, RA Add A15/1088.

4. QV to HE, 21 February 1867, RA Add A25/200; QV to HE, 23 June 1868, RA Add A25/229.

5. HE to QV, 27 June 1867, RA Add A15/1092; HE to QV, 30 June-1 July 1867, RA Add A15/1094; Pr A to QV, 1 July 1867, RA Add A15/1095.

6. Pr A to QV, 6 October 1867, RA Add A15/1117; HE to QV, 10 October 1867, RA Add A15/1120; HE to QV, 9 October 1867, RA Add A15/1119; HE to QV, 12 October 1867, RA Add A15/1122; HE to QV, 14 October 1867, RA Add A15/1124.

7. HE to QV, 27 November 1867, RA Add A15/1166; HE to QV, 29 November 1867, RA Add A15/1167; QV to HE, 6 December 1867, RA Add A25/210.

8. HE to QV, 10 January 1868, RA Add A15/1183; Pr A to QV, 9 January 1868, RA Add A15/1182; HE to QV, 6 January 1868, RA Add A15/1180; HE to QV, 17 February 1868, RA Add A15/1195; HE to QV, 22 February 1868, RA Add A15/1198; HE to QV, 5 March 1868, RA Add A15/1205.

9. Note on Pr A's course, encl. with 29 February 1868, RA Add A15/1203; HE to QV, 11th May 1868, RA Add A15/1224; HE to QV, 14 May 1868, RA Add A15/1225; HE to QV, 17 June 1868, RA Add A15/1230; HE to QV, 23 June 1868, RA Add A15/1238; HE to QV, 30 June 1868, RA Add A15/1239.

10. HE to QV, 18 July 1868, RA Add A15/1250.

11. HE to QV, 4 August 1868, RA Add A15/1263; *Notes and Reminiscences* dictated by Pr A from November 1926, RA Add A15/8870.

12. HE to QV, 6 August 1868, RA Add A15/1266 and e.g. Memorandum c January 1868 by HE, RA Add A15/8643; *Middlesborough and Stockton Gazette*, 14 August 1868, RA Add A15/1277; HE to QV, 11 August 1868, RA Add A15/1272; HE to QV, 13 August 1868, RA Add A15/1273.

13. HE to QV, 5 November 1868, RA Add A15/1301; HE to QV, 19 November 1868, RA Add A15/1306; HE to QV, 3 December 1868, RA Add A15/1310; HE to QV, 16 November 1868, RA Add A15/1304; QV to Pr A, 9 February 1869, RA Add A15/1339; HE to QV, 10 February 1869, RA Add A15/1340 and 1341.

14. General Grey to QV, 2 April 1869, RA Add A15/1374; Bruce to QV, 7 April 1869, RA Add A15/1380; QV to HE, 2 April 1869, RA Add A25/250.

15. HE to QV, 5 April 1869, RA Add A15/1378; Pr A to QV, 5 April 1869, RA Add A15/1379; HE to QV, 13 April 1869, RA Add A15/1390.

16. HE to QV, 15 April 1869, RA Add A15/1395; Sir Charles Napier to Bruce, 20 April 1869, RA Add A15/1403; HE to QV, 28 April 1869, RA Add A15/1415; HE to QV, 29th April 1869, RA Add A15/1417.

17. HE to QV, 1 May 1869, RA Add A15/1420; HE to QV, 2 May 1869, RA Add A15/1423; *Mona Herald and Fargher's Isle of Man Advertiser*, 5 May 1869, RA Add A15/1428.

18. D of Cambridge to QV, 1 August 1869, RA Add A15/1472; HE to QV, 1 August 1869, RA Add A15/1470.

19. Young to Granville, 14 July 1869 (copy), RA Add A15/1459; Thornton to Clarendon, 10 July 1869 (copy), RA Add A15/1463; Granville to QV, ?29 July 1869, RA Add A15/1458; Gladstone to QV, 29 July 1869, RA Add A15/1460; Clarendon to QV, 29-31 July 1869, RA Add A15/1461 and 1462; HE to QV, 30 July 1869, RA Add A15/1464.

20. Gladstone to QV, 31 July 1869, RA Add A15/1466; HE to QV, 31 July 1869, RA Add A15/1465; QV to Gladstone, 1 August 1869 (copy), RA Add A15/1468.

21. QV to HE, 11 August 1869, RA Add A25/263; HE to QV, 11 August 1869, RA Add A15/1475.

22. HE to QV, 22 August 1869, RA Add A15/1478; Pr A to Pss Louise, 26 August 1869, RA Add A17/311; HE Journal, 23-27 August 1869, RA Add A15/1479; Press cuttings, 24 August-2 September 1869, RA Add A15/1484-8; HE Journal 9-15 September 1869, RA Add A15/1493; ditto, 18-23 September 1869, RA Add A15/1496; ditto, 23-27 September 1869, RA Add A15/1502; ditto, 27 September-4 October 1869, RA Add A15/1507; HE to QV, 22 October 1869, RA Add A15/1516; HE to QV, 17 September 1869, RA Add A15/1491; Journal, 9-15 September *op cit*; Report by HE, ? 17 September 1869, RA Add A15/1492.

23. Pr A to QV, 26 August 1869, RA Add A15/1482; Pr A to QV, 8 September 1869, RA Add A15/1489; Pr A to QV, 16 September 1869, RA Add A15/1490; Pr A to QV, 26 September 1869, RA Add A15/1500; Pr A to QV, 17 October 1869, RA Add A15/1515; Pr A to QV, 23 October 1869, RA Add A15/1518; Pr A to QV, 3 October 1869, RA Add A15/1505.

24. *New York Herald*, report from Quebec, 18 September 1869, RA Add A15/1497-9; QV to HE, 29 September 1869, RA Add A25/269; QV to HE, 6 October 1869, RA Add A25/271; HE Journal, 27 September-4 October 1869, RA Add A15/1507.

25. HE to QV, 24 January 1870, RA Add A15/1557; Press cutting encl. with 29 January 1870, RA Add A15/1563; Pr A to QV, 24 January 1870, RA Add A15/1558.

26. Despatch, Thornton to Clarendon, 1st February 1870 (copy), RA Add A15/1566; HE to QV, 29 January 1870, RA Add A15/1562; HE to QV, 24 January 1870, RA Add A15/1557; Pr A to QV, 30 January 1870, RA Add A15/1564; Pr A to Princess Louise, 31 January 1870, RA Add A17/345; *Notes and Reminiscences*, RA Add A15/8870.

27. Thornton to Clarendon, 7 February 1870 (extract), RA Add A15/1570; HE to QV, 6-7 February 1870, RA Add A15/1571; Gladstone to QV, 25 February 1870, RA Add A15/1583.

28. Dadean to ?Pr A, 9 February 1870 (extract), RA Add A15/1574; General Sherman to Pr A, 10 February 1870, RA Add A15/1575; HE to QV, 11 February 1870, RA Add A15/1576.

29. HE to QV, 17 February 1870, RA Add A15/1580; Pr A to QV, 27 February 1870, RA Add A15/1584; HE to QV, 24 February 1870, RA Add A15/1582; HE to QV, 4 March 1870, RA Add A15/1586; Pr A to Princess Louise, 12 June 1870, RA Add A17/372.

30. QV to HE, 17 March 1870, RA Add A25/280; QV to HE, 24 February 1870, RA Add A25/279.

31. Pr A to QV, 15 May 1870, RA Add A15/1618; Pr A to QV, 29 May 1870, RA Add A15/1622; *Notes and Reminiscences*, RA Add A15/8870; Pr A to Macdonald, 3 July 1870, PAC Macdonald MG26A/253500-253504 (with minor alterations this letter is printed in

Pope, *Memoirs of Sir John Macdonald*, Arnold, London 1894, Vol II p.78); HE to QV, 7 July 1870, RA Add A15/1652; Granville to QV, 25 June 1870, RA Add A15/1651; Despatch, Young to Granville, 8 July 1870 (copy),RA Add A15/1653.

32. QV to Pr A, 15 July 1870, RA Add A15/1655.

CHAPTER 4

1. QV to HE, 4 August 1870, RA Add A25/289; ditto, 6 November 1870, RA Add A25/292; ditto, 25 July 1870, RA Add A25/288; Pr A to QV, 27 July 1870, RA Add A15/1656.

2. QV to HE, RA Add A25 *passim*, and specifically, 17 September 1872, RA Add A25/246; QV to HE, 13 January 1872, RA Add A25/325; QV to HE, 8 June 1872, RA Add A25/340; QV to Pr A, 28 June 1872, RA Add A15/1927; ditto, 25 February 1873, RA Add A15/1985.

3. e.g. QV to HE, 28-29 August 1874, RA Add A25/426; QV to HE, 7 August 1873, RA Add A25/373; Ponsonby to Lady Ponsonby, 12 July 1873, RA Add A36/582.

4. HE to QV, 14 July 1871, RA Add A15/1786; QV to HE, 17 July 1871, RA Add A25/317; HE to QV, 18 July 1871, RA Add A15/1788.

5. QV to HE, 13 January 1872, RA Add A25/325.

6. HE to QV, 18 January 1872, RA Add A15/1849; ditto, 19-20 January 1872, RA Add A15/1851; ditto, 21 January 1872, RA Add A15/1852; Pr A to QV, 2 February 1872, RA Add A15/1861; HE to QV, 23 January 1872, RA Add A15/1856.

7. QV to HE, 20 January 1872, RA Add A25/326; HE to QV, 24 January 1872, RA Add A15/1857; QV to HE, 29 January 1872, RA Add A25/328; HE to QV, 15 February 1872, RA Add A15/1873; ditto, 2 February 1872, RA Add A15/1862.

8. QV to HE, 24 February 1872, RA Add A25/330; QV to Queen of Denmark, 18 March 1872 (copy), RA Add A15/1881.

9. Queen of Denmark to QV, 21 June 1872 (copy), RA Add A15/1922; QV to Queen of Denmark, 16 July 1872 (copy), RA Add A15/1933; Empss Augusta to QV, 6 July 1872 (copy), RA Add A15/1929; QV to HE, ?22 July 1872, RA Add A25/344; HE to QV, 24 July 1872, RA Add A15/1937.

10. Pr A to QV, 20 January 1873, RA Add A15/1970; HE to QV, 24 January 1873, RA Add A15/1972; Pr A to QV, 27 January 1873, RA Add A15/1973.

11. QV to HE, 31 January 1873, RA Add A25/352; HE to QV, 13 February 1873, RA Add A15/1981; ditto, 7 February 1873, RA Add A15/1979; Ponsonby to Lady Ponsonby, 16 April 1873, RA Add A36/534.

12. HE to QV, 27 April 1873, RA Add A15/2008; QV to Pr A, 29 April 1873, RA Add A15/2009; QV to HE, 1 May 1873, RA Add A25/359; Pr A to QV, 7 May 1873, RA Add A15/2013; ditto, 1 May 1873, RA Add A15/2011; Queen of Denmark to QV, 19 May 1873, RA Add A15/2029.

13. QV to HE, 22 May 1873, RA Add A25/363; ditto, 24 June 1873, RA Add A25/369; Pr A to QV, 20 July 1873, RA Add A15/2051.

14. Telegrams, QV to HE, 18 July and HE to QV, 20 July 1873, RA Add A15/2053.

15. Pr A to QV, 29 July 1873, RA Add A15/2055; HE to QV, 29 July 1873, RA Add A15/2056; ditto, 1 August 1873, RA Add A15/2057; QV to Queen of Denmark, 13 August 1873 (extract), RA Add A15/2006; Queen of Denmark to QV, 27 August 1873, RA Add A15/2071; QV to HE, 19 December 1873, RA Add A25/393; Georgina Battiscombe, *Queen Alexandra*, Constable 1969, p 101.

16. e.g. HE to QV, 21 January 1874, RA Add A15/2135; ditto, 10 January 1874, RA Add A15/2125; ditto, 20 November 1874, RA Add A15/2248.

17. Telegram, Sydney to Ponsonby, 31 July 1871, RA Add A15/1802; Lee, *Queen Victoria*, Smith Elder 1903, p 412; QV to Gladstone, 6 April 1871 (copy), RA Add A15/1706; Gladstone to QV, 14 April 1871, RA Add A15/1718; QV to Pr A, 25 July 1871, RA Add A15/1797; QV to HE, 23 July 1871 (copy), RA Add A15/1794.

18. HE to QV, 14 February 1871, RA Add A15/1697; QV to HE, 16 February 1871, RA Add A25/298; Disraeli to QV, 14 March 1874, RA Add A15/2154; Ulster to Ponsonby, 21 March 1874, RA Add A15/2158; Note by Garter, 22 March 1874, RA Add A15/2157; Cairns to QV, 9 April 1874, RA Add A15/2166 and 2167; Ponsonby to QV, 10 April 1874, RA Add A15/2168; QV to Pr A, 18 May 1874, RA Add A15/2181.

19. HE to QV, 7 August 1875, RA Add A15/2318; ditto, 13 June 1876, RA Add A15/2474; QV to HE, 26-27 January 1876, RA Add A25/471; HE to QV, 29 January 1876, RA Add A15/2404.

20. HE to QV, 12 April 1875, RA Add A15/2290.

21. Telegram, Pr A to QV, 9 January 1875, RA Add A15/2259; Pr A to QV, 31 January 1875, RA Add A15/2270; ditto, 7 February 1875, RA Add A15/2273.

22. HE to QV, 17 February 1875, RA Add A15/2275; ditto, 25 February 1875, RA Add A15/2277; Pr A to QV, 5 March 1875, RA Add A15/2281; HE to QV, 14 March 1875, RA Add A15/2282.

23. HE to QV, 28 March 1875, RA Add A15/2285; ditto, 12 April 1875, RA Add A15/2290; QV to HE, 20 April 1875, RA Add A25/443; Empss Augusta to QV, 14 August 1875, RA Add A15/2324; Queen of Belgians to QV, 11 August 1875, RA Add A15/2321; QV to Empss Augusta, 19 July 1875, RA Add A15/2308; QV to HE, 20 July 1875, RA Add A25/449.

24. Pr A to QV, 28 August 1875, RA Add A15/2336; HE to QV, 29 August 1875, RA Add A15/2337; QV to HE, 9 September 1875, RA Add A25/459; Telegram, Empss Augusta to QV, 1 September 1875, RA Add A15/2341; Pr A to QV, 8 September 1875, RA Add A15/2348; QV to HE, 9 September 1875 *op cit*.

25. Pr A to QV, 22 September 1875, RA Add A15/2354; HE to QV, 22 September 1875, RA Add A15/2356; Pr Leopold to QV, 4-6 March 1876 (extract), RA Add A15/2425; HE to QV, 24 September 1875, RA Add A15/2357; Pr A to QV, 25 September 1875, RA Add A15/2358.

26. HE to QV, 2 May 1876, RA Add A15/2447; QV to HE, 3 May 1876, RA Add A25/485; Pr A to QV, 5 May 1876, RA Add A15/2449; HE to QV, 4 May 1876, RA Add A15/2448; Queen of Hanover to QV, 28 May 1876, RA Add A15/2458.

27. QV to HE, 30 May 1876, RA Add A25/491; QV to Queen of Hanover, 1 June 1876 (extract), RA Add A15/2463; Queen of Hanover to QV, 3 June 1876, RA Add A15/2469; HE to QV, 2 June 1876, RA Add A15/2464; Pss Helena to QV, 3 June 1876, RA Add

A15/2465; HE to QV, 3 June 1876, RA Add A15/2466; QV to HE, 5 June 1876, RA Add A25/493; HE to QV, 6 June 1876, RA Add A15/2471; Pr A to QV, 15 June 1876, RA Add A15/2476; Ponsonby to Lady Ponsonby, 19 June 1876, RA Add A36/1074; Pss Helena to QV, 19 June 1876, RA Add A15/2477.

28. King of Hanover to Pr A, 26 January 1877 (copy), RA Add A15/2569; King of Hanover to QV, 3 February 1877 (copy), RA Add A15/2585; Pss Mary of Hanover to King of Hanover, 27 March 1877   (translation), RA Add A15/2647; QV to HE, 6 April 1877, RA Add A25/518; Dss of Teck to Pss Helena, 8 April 1877, RA Add A15/2650; Pr A to QV, 8 April 1877, RA Add A15/2648; QV to HE, 10 April 1877, RA Add A25/519; Pr A to LM, 9 July 1878, RA Add A15/6744.

CHAPTER 5

1. Pr A to QV, 17 September 1871, RA Add A15/1817; HE to QV, 29 October 1871, RA Add A15/1826; HE to QV, 24 July 1872, RA Add A15/1937; Comment on report by Brigade Major, 2 September 1872, RA Add A15/1945; Ponsonby to QV, 11 April 1874, RA Add A15/2170; HE to QV, 18-19 October 1875, RA Add A15/2362; ditto, 5 October 1876, RA Add A15/2515.

2. Ponsonby to Lady Ponsonby, 10 April 1874, RA Add A36/729; Parke to HE, 24 August 1872, RA Add A15/1947; Ponsonby to Lady Ponsonby, 22 September 1877, RA Ponsonby; QV to HE, 15 April 1872, RA Add A25/335; Confidential report by McMahon, 11 September 1874 (extract), RA Add A15/2279; HE to QV, 22 October 1875, RA Add A15/2364.

3. QV to HE, 18 April 1877, RA Add A25/521; HE to QV, 19 April 1877, RA Add A15/2659; Pr A to QV, 21 April 1877, RA Add A15/2662.

4. Pr A to QV, 11 February 1877, RA Add A15/2602; e.g. Pr A to LM, 29th October 1878, RA Add A15/6836.

5. QV to HE, 24 July 1877, RA Add A25/523; HE to QV, 26 July 1877, RA Add A15/2684; Pr A to QV, 14 February 1878, RA Add A15/2717.

6. Pr A to QV, 18 February 1878, RA Add A15/2718; Pr A to LM, 22 February 1878, RA Add A15/6703; ditto, 24 February 1879, RA Add A15/6937; HE to QV, 3 March 1878, RA Add A15/2725.

7. QV to Lady Odo Russell, 27 February 1878 (copy), RA Add A15/2721; QV to Empss Augusta, 3 March 1878 (copy), RA Add A15/2723.

8. QV to Cr Pss of Prussia, 12 March 1878 (copy), RA Add A15/2737; QV to Empss Augusta, 13 March 1878 (copy), RA Add A15/2738; Pr A to LM, 21 September 1878, RA Add A15/6793; ditto, 22, 22-23 and 25 February 1879, RA Add A15/6935, 6936 and 6938; ditto, 20 September 1878, 29 January 1879, RA Add A15/6792, 6909 and 6910; QV to HE, 23 May 1878 (copy), RA Add A25/533.

9. Pr Frederick Charles to QV, 30 December 1878, RA Add A15/2949; Pr Frederick Charles to LM, 21 April 1878, RA Add A15/6711. Pr A to LM, 27-28 December 1878, RA Add A15/6882.

10. Pr A to QV, 6 July 1878, RA Add A15/2894; Pr A to LM, 12 July 1878, RA Add A15/6747; LM to QV, 16 May 1878, RA Add A15/2830 and 2831; ditto, 20 May 1878, RA

Add A15/6720; QV to LM, 23 May 1878, RA Add A15/6722; Pr A to LM, 27 July 1878, RA Add A15/6762.

11. Pr A to LM, 15 July 1878; 17 February 1879; 19 May; 1 June; 27 June; 13 July; 2 November; 23 October; 16 November; 18 November 1878, RA Add A15/6750; 6930; 6719; 6725; 6729; 6748; 6840; 6830; 6856; 6858.

12. Pr A to LM, 3 November 1878; 31 January 1879, RA Add A15/6841; 6913; QV to HE, 2 September 1878, RA Add A25/538; Pr A to QV, 5 December; 9th December 1878, RA Add A15/2938; 2940; Pr A to LM, 29 July; 3rd August; 7 August; 12 August 1878, RA Add A15/6765; 6770; 6774; 6780.

13. Pr A to LM, 20 July; ditto, 27 July; 18 September; 30 September; 28 October; 29 October; 29 September 1878, RA Add A15/6754; 6755; 6762; 6790; 6805; 6835; 6836; 6804.

14. Pr A to LM, 2 January 1879; 5 November 1878, RA Add A15/6897; 6844; QV to HE, 3 January 1879, RA Add A25/543; Pr A to LM, 5 January 1879, RA Add A15/6901; Pr A to QV, 23 January 1879, RA Add A15/2969.

15. Pr A to LM, 6 November 1878, RA Add A15/6845; Surgeon-Major Ramsay to Sir William Jenner, 27 June 1878, RA Add A15/2674; Pr A to LM, 13 October 1878,RA Add A15/6819.

16. Pr A to LM, 12 February; 18 February; 19 February 1879; 24 October; 27 October 1878, RA Add A15/6925; 6931; 6932; 6831; 6834; Pr A to QV, 28 November 1878, RA Add A15/2937; Pr A to LM, 1 February 1879, RA Add A15/6914.

17. Pr A to QV, 3 March 1879, RA Add A15/2995; HE to QV, 6 March 1879, RA Add A15/2996; Pr A to LM, 6 March 1879, RA Add A15/6952; Lady Odo Russell to QV, 1 March 1879, RA Add A15/2991; Pr A to LM, 7 March 1879, RA Add A15/6953.

18. *Illustrated London News*, 15 March 1879; Order of Ceremonial etc. RA unref.; German news cutting, 19 February 1879, RA Add A15/2978.

19. QV to Pr A and Dss of C, 13 March 1879, RA Add A15/3008.

CHAPTER 6

1. Pr A to QV, 16 March 1879, RA Add A15/3043; Dss of C to QV, 17 March 1879, RA Add A15/3054; Dss of C Journal, 26 March-29 May 1879, RA Add A15/8445.

2. Dss of C Journal, 26 March-29 May 1879, RA Add A15/8445; Pr A to QV, 26 April 1879, RA Add A15/3085; HE to QV, 1 May 1879, RA Add A15/3087; Pr A to QV, 7 May 1879, RA Add A15/3089; HE to QV, 12 May 1879, RA Add A15/3091; Pr A to QV, 18 May 1879, RA Add A15/3094.

3. QV to HE, 13 December 1879, RA Add A25/550; Dss of C to QV, 30 December 1879, RA Add A15/3277.

4. Pr A to QV, 20 October 1879, RA Add A15/3259; *London Gazette*, 29 May 1880, RA Add A15/3328; Pr A to QV, 6 September 1880, RA Add A15/3366.

5. HE to QV, 12 September 1880, RA Add A15/3367; Pr A to QV, 18 September 1880, RA Add A15/3369; ditto, 14 September 1880, RA Add A15/3368; HE to QV, 23 September 1880, RA Add A15/3370.

6. HE to QV, 14 October 1880, RA Add A15/3378; Pr A to QV, 17 October 1880, RA Add A15/3379; Pr A to Dss of C, 17 April 1881, RA Add A15/6957.

7. QV to HE, 18 March 1880, RA Add A25/551; Cr Pss Prussia to Pr A and Dss of C, 11 July 1881, RA Add A15/3436; Pr A to QV, 29 March 1880, RA Add A15/3302; Cr Pss Prussia to Dss of C, 22 November 1880, RA Add A15/3386; Pr A to QV, 6 June 1880, RA Add A15/3338; ditto, 13 June 1880, RA Add A15/3340; ditto, 7 December 1880, RA Add A15/3389; Beaconsfield to Dss of C, 27 February 1880, RA Add A15/3293; Pr A to QV, 14 March 1880, RA Add A15/3297; Pr Frederick Charles to Dss of C, 2 December 1880, RA Add A15/3388; ditto, 30 June 1878, RA Add A15/6731.

8. QV to Pr A, 1 January 1882, RA Add A15/3473; ditto, to Dss of C, 4 January 1882, RA Add A15/3475; Telegrams, Pr A and Playfair to QV, 15 January 1882, RA Add A15/3479; QV to Pr A 15 January 1882, RA Add A15/3478.

9. Harcourt to QV, 15 January 1882, RA Add A15/3480; Lady Adela Larking to QV, 16th January 1882, RA Add A15/3486; Playfair to QV, 15 January 1882 (copy), RA Add A15/3481; Pr A to QV, 16 January 1882, RA Add A15/3484; QV to Pr A, 17 January 1882, RA Add A15/3489.

10. Telegram, Pr A to QV, 19 January 1882, RA Add A15/3492; Pr A to QV, 19 January 1882, RA Add A15/3493; Cr Pss Prussia to Pr A, 19 January 1882, RA Add A15/3494; Court Circular, 21 January 1882, RA Add A15/3491; QV to Pr A, 21 January 1882, RA Add A15/3496; ditto, 26 January 1882, RA Add A15/3501; Dss of C to QV, 28 January 1882, RA Add A15/3504; Lady Adela Larking to QV, 31 January 1882, RA Add A15/3507; Telegram, Pr A to QV, 1 February 1882, RA Add A15/3508; Pr A to QV, 1 February 1882, RA Add A15/3510.

11. QV to Pr A, 1 February 1882, RA Add A15/3509; Telegram, Playfair to QV, 3 February 1882, RA Add A15/3514; Pr A to QV, 3 February 1882, RA Add A15/3515; QV to Pr A, 4 February 1882, RA Add A15/3517; HE to QV, 4 February 1882, RA Add A15/3520; QV to Pr A, 6 February 1882, RA Add A15/3526.

12. Jenner to QV, 5 February 1882, RA Add A15/3522; Pr A to QV, 5 February 1882, RA Add A15/3524; QV to Pr A, 6 February 1882, RA Add A15/3526; ditto, 12 February 1882, RA Add A15/3536.

13. HE to QV, 5 February 1882, RA Add A15/3523; *Morning Post*, 4 March 1882, RA Add A15/3544; *British Medical Journal*, 18 March 1882, RA Add A15/3553.

14. Dss of C Journal, 1 January-31 December 1882, RA Add A15/8445; Pr A to QV, 25 March 1882, RA Add A15/3559; Mrs Egerton to QV, 31 March 1882, RA Add A15/3564; Dss of C to QV, 6 June 1882, RA Add A15/3577; ditto, 10 June 1882, RA Add A15/3578.

15. Dss of C to QV, 13 June 1882, RA Add A15/3581; Pr A to Dss of C, 14 June 1882, RA Add A15/6963; ditto, 16 June 1882, RA Add A15/6965; ditto, 21 June 1882, RA Add A15/6966.

16. Pr A to Dss of C, 21 June 1882, RA Add A15/6966; Lawrenson to D of Edinburgh, 27 June 1882, RA Add A15/3589; ditto, 2 July 1882, RA Add A15/3595; Granville to Ponsonby, 4 July 1882, RA Add A15/3598; Telegram, Pr A to QV, 5 July 1882, RA Add A15/3599; Pr A to QV, 29 June 1882, RA Add A15/3594; QV to Pr A, 5 July 1882, RA Add A15/3600; ditto, 9 July 1882, RA Add A15/3603; Dss of C to QV, 15 July 1882, RA Add A15/3608.

17. Jenner to QV, 12 July 1882, RA Add A15/3607; QV to Pr A, 21 July 1882, RA Add A15/3609; Pr A to QV, 21 July 1882, RA Z 176/1.

18. Pr A to Colonel D'Arcy Burnell, commanding 7th Hussars, 20 February 1881, NAO Craven-Smith-Milnes Papers, DDCW 7/29.

19. QV to Pr A 29 July 1882, RA Add A15/3626; Telegram, Pr A to QV, 30 July 1882, RA Add A15/3631; HE to QV, 30 July 1882, RA Add A15/3634; Pr A to Dss of C, 30 July 1882, RA Add A15/6977.

CHAPTER 7

1. Pr A to Dss of C, 31 July 1882, RA Add A15/6978; Pr A to QV, 7 August 1882, RA Z176/4; Pr A to Dss of C, 4-6 Aug 1882, RA Add A15/6980; Journal, 3 August 1882, RA Z175; Pr A to QV, 31 July 1882, RA Z176/2.

2. Pr A to Dss of C, 1-4 Aug 1882, RA Add A15/6979; Journal, 31 July 1882, RA Z175; ditto, 7 August 1882; ditto, 3 August 1882; Pr A to Dss of C, 4-6 August 1882, RA Add A15/6980; QV to Pr A, 3 August 1882, RA Add A15/3639; Maurice, *The Campaign of 1882 in Egypt,* 1887, reprinted Eyr and Spottiswoode 1973, p. 20; Pr A to QV, 7 Aug 1882, RA Z176/4; Pr A to PoW, 10 August 1882, RA T8/66.

3. Journal, 4-6 August 1882, RA Z175; ditto, 7 August 1882.

4. Pr A to Dss of C, 8-11 Aug 1882, RA A15/6986.

5. Journal, 10 August 1882, RA Z175; QV to McNeill, 12 August 1882, RA Add A15/3649.

6. Pr A to Dss of C, 13 August 1882, RA Add A15/6989; McNeill to QV, 14 August 1882, RA Z176/7; Journal, 13 August 1882, RA Z175.

7. McNeill to QV, 14 August 1882, RA Z176/7.

8. Pr A to Dss of C, 16-17 August 1882, RA Add A15/6990; Lehmann, *All Sir Garnet,* Cape 1964, p 306.

9. Pr A to QV, 19 August 1882, RA Z176/10.

10. Pr A to Dss of C, 20-21 August 1882, RA Add A15/6992.

11. Journal 21 August 1882, RA Z175; Pr A to Dss of C, 20-21 August 1882, RA Add A15/6992.

12. Pr A to Dss of C, 22-23 August 1882, RA Add A15/6995.

13. Pr A to Dss of C, 26-29 August 1882, RA Add A15/6997.

14. Ditto.

15. Ditto.

16. Journal, 30 August 1882, RA Z175; Wolseley to QV, RA O.15/130.

17. Pr A to Dss of C, 6-8 September 1882, RA Add A15/7007.

18. Pr A to Dss of C, 11-12 September 1882, RA Add A15/7009

19. McNeill to QV, 14 September 1882, RA Z176/22.

20. Pr A to Dss of C, 16 September 1882, RA Add A15/7015.

21. Pr A to Dss of C, 16 September 1882, RA Add A15/7015; McNeill to QV, 14 September 1882, RA Z176/22.

22. Pr A to Dss of C, 16 September 1882, RA Add A15/7015.

23. Wolseley to QV, 13 September 1882, RA Add A15/3690; QV to Pr A, 14 September 1882, RA Ad A15/3704; D of Albany to Pr A, 14 September 1882, RA Add A15/3705; Wolseley to QV, 14 September 1882, RA O.16/25.

24. Wolseley to D of Cambridge, 16 September 1882, Willoughby Verner, *The Military Life of the Duke of Cambridge*, Vol 2, John Murray 1905, pp 248-50, (extract at RA Add A15/3724); Extract from Lord Coke's letter of c. 16 September 1882, RA Add A15/3732; McNeill to Ponsonby, 17 September 1882, RA Add A15/3733.

25. Pr A to Dss of C, 16 September 1882, RA Add A15/7015; Maurice, *The Campaign of 1882 in Egypt*, pp 100-1, Pr A to Dss of C, 18 September 1882, RA Add A15/7025; Pr A to QV, 17 September 1882, RA Z176/25.

26. Pr A to Dss of C, 18 September 1882, RA Add A15/7025; McNeill to QV, 16 September 1882, RA Z176/24; Pr A to PoW, 2 October 1882, RA T8/91.

27. QV to McNeill, 21 September 1882, RA Add A15/3745; Scott to QV, 22 September 1882, RA Add A15/3746; QV to Pr A, 23 September 1882, RA Add A15/3747.

28. Pr A to QV, 20 September 1882, RA Z176/27; Pr A to QV, 26 September 1882, RA Z176/30.

29. Pr A to QV, 4 October 1882, RA Z176/36.

30. Pr A to Dss of C, 24 September 1882, RA Add A15/7029; Childers to Ponsonby, 20 October 1882, RA O.17/89; Pr A to QV, 12 November 1882, RA Z176/53; QV to German Emperor, 18 November 1882, (copy/draft), RA Z176/55.

31. Pr A to Dss of C, 19-20 October 1882, RA Add A15/7053; HE to QV, 6 November 1882, RA Add A15/3825; D of Albany to QV, 6 November 1882, RA Add A15/3824; QV to Pr A, 4 November 1882, RA Add A15/3820; QV to Dss of C, 4 November 1882, RA Add A15/3819; Pr A to QV, 6 November 1882, RA Z176/51; Scott to QV, 17 October 1882, RA Add A15/3795; QV to Pr A, 2 November 1882, RA Add A15/3815.

32. QV to Pr A, 18 November 1882, RA Add A15/3843; St Aubyn, *The Royal George*, Constable 1963, p 216; Pr A to QV, 19 November 1882, RA Add A15/3846; Pr A to QV, 25-29 November 1882, RA Add A15/3850.

33. QV to Pr A, 1 December 1882, RA Add A15/3854; Pr A to QV, 3 December 1882, RA Add A15/3855.

CHAPTER 8

1. Pr A to Dss of C, 30 September-1 October 1882, RA Add A15/7036.

2. QV to Pr A, 18 December 1882, RA Add A15/3867; Press release, 13 January 1883, RA Add A15/3888; Memorandum by QV, 13 January 1883, RA Add A15/3890.

3. Telegram, Lady Adela Larking to QV, 13 January 1883, RA Add A15/3887; Dss of C Diary, 13 January 1883, RA Add A15/8445; Pr A to QV, 13 January 1883, RA Add A15/3889; QV to Pr A, 1 February 1883, RA Add A15/3942; QV to Pr A, 16 January 1883, RA Add A15/3918; Pr A to QV, 17 January 1883, RA Add A15/3920.

4. Pr A to QV, 18 February 1883, RA Add A15/3966; Pr A to QV, 22 February 1883, RA Add A15/3972; Telegram, Sussex to QV, 21 February 1883, RA add A15/3969.

5. Pr A to QV, 23 March 1883, RA Add A15/3985; QV to Pr A, 26 March 1883, RA Add A15/3986; QV to Pr A, 30 March 1883, RA Add A15/3987; QV to Pr A, 4 June 1883, RA Add A15/4007; Pr A to QV, 9 June 1883, RA Add A15/4009; *London Gazette* cutting, 15 August 1883, RA Add A15/4050.

6. *Daily Telegraph* cutting, 15 August 1883, RA Add A15/4050; HE to QV, 18 June 1883, RA Add A15/4013; Kimberley to Ponsonby, 7 August 1883, RA Add A15/4042; Ponsonby to Kimberley, 10 August 1883, RA Add A15/4043; Ripon to QV, 24 September 1883, RA Add A15/4072.

7. Pr A to QV, 27 September 1883, RA Add A15/4073.

8. QV to HE, 3 August 1883 (copy), RA Add A25/597; HE to QV, 5 August 1883, RA Add A15/4040; QV to HE, 15 June 1883, RA Add A25/596; HE to QV, 18 June 1883, RA Add A15/4013.

9. QV to Pr A, 27 October 1883, RA Add A15/4085; Dss of C to QV, 28 October 1883, RA Add A15/4088; Pr A to QV, 29 October 1883, RA Add A15/4089; QV to Pr A, 1 November 1883, RA Add A15/4091; Seven telegrams to QV, 2 November 1883, RA Add A15/4092; HE to QV, 3 November 1883, RA Add A15/4095; *Standard* cutting, 3 November 1883, RA Add A15/4096; Press cuttings, 3 November 1883, RA Add A15/4101.

10. Lady Downe to Lady Sefton, 2 November 1883, Downe; Pss Helena to QV, 3 November 1883, RA Add A15/4094; PoW to QV, 4 November 1883, RA Add A15/4099.

11. Journal, 2-3 November 1883, RA Add A15/8445; Lady Downe to Lady Sefton (3) November 1883, Downe; Journal, 8 November 1883, RA Add A15/8445.

12. Journal, 9 and 15 November 1883, RA Add A15/8445.

13. Journal, 21 November 1883, RA Add A15/8445; Pr A to QV, 20-23 November 1883, RA Z177/6; Lady Downe to Lady Sefton, 23 November 1883, Downe.

14. Journal, 24-26 November 1883, RA Add A15/8445; Pr A to QV, 27 November 1883, RA Z177/7.

15. Pr A to D of Cambridge, 30 November 1883, RA Add A15/4122; Journal, 28 November 1883, RA Add A15/8445.

16. Lady Downe to Lady Sefton, 2 December 1883, Downe: Pr A to QV, 3 December 1883, RA Z177/8; Journal, 3 December 1883, RA Add A15/8445.

17. Journal, 4 December 1883, RA Add A15/8445; Dss of C to QV, 16 December 1883, RA Z177/11.

18. Journal, 4 December 1883, RA Add A15/8445; Pr A to QV, 9 December 1883, RA Z177/10; Journal, 6 December 1883, RA Add A15/8445.

19. Dss of C to QV, 16 December 1883, RA Z177/11; Journal, 12 December 1883, RA Add A15/8445.

20. Journal, 13 December 1883, RA Add A15/8445; ditto, 15 December 1883; Pr A to QV, 24 December 1883, RA Z177/14; Pr A to HE, 7 January 1884, RA Add A25/602.

21. Journal, 11th January 1884, RA Add A15/8445; Pr A to D of Cambridge, 11 January

1884, RA Add A15/4160; Brigade Order, (9) January 1884, RA Add A15/4155; Pr A to QV, 12 January 1884, RA Z177/18.

22. Pr A to QV, 27 January 1884, RA Z177/23; Pr A to QV, 3 February 1884, RA Z177/26.

23. D of Cambridge to Pr A, 22 February 1884, RA Add A15/4191.

24. Lady Downe to QV, 5 February 1884, RA Add A15/4176; Journal, 7 February 1884, RA Add A15/8445; Dss of C to QV, 11 February 1884, RA Z177/28; Pr A to QV, 10-11 February 1884, RA Z177/27; Journal, 8 February 1884, RA Add A15/8445.

25. Journal 11-12 February 1884, RA Add A15/8445.

26. Journal, 13 February 1884, RA Add A15/8445; ditto 17th February 1884.

27. Journal, 23 February 1884, RA Add A15/8445; Pr A to QV, 25 February 1884, RA Z177/31.

28. Pr A to QV, 9 March 1884, RA Z177/36; Journal, 4-5 March 1884, RA Add A15/8445; Pr A to HE, 9 March 1884, RA Add A25/606.

29. Journal, 8-9 March 1884, RA Add A15/8445.

30. Journal, 10-11 March 1884, RA Add A15/8445.

31. Pr A to QV, 14 April 1884, RA Z178/6.

32. QV to Pr A, 30 April 1884, RA Add A15/4234; Pr A to HE, 11 May 1884, RA Add A25/614; Pr A to QV, 6 June 1884, RA Z178/21; Journal, 1 September 1884, RA Add A15/8445; QV to Pr A, 5 June 1884, RA Add A15/4255.

33. Hartington to QV, 14 June 1884 (copy), RA Add A15/4260; Pr A to HE, 12 June 1884, RA Add A25/618.

34. Stewart to D of Cambridge, 1 August 1884 (copy), RA Add A15/4295.

35. Pr A to D of Cambridge, 8 June 1884, RA Add A15/4257.

36. Napier to Dillon, 20 June 1884 (extract), RA Add A15/4271; HE to Ponsonby, 27 June 1884, RA Add A15/4275.

37. Pr A to QV, 21 June 1884, RA Z178/25; Pr A to QV, 11 July 1884, RA Z179/2; Pr A to D of Cambridge, 25 July 1884, RA Add A15/4289.

38. Journal, 27-29 September 1884, RA Add A15/8445; Dss of C to QV, 29 September 1884, RA Z179/20; Pr A to QV, 29 September 1884, RA Z179/21; Journal, 30 September 1884, RA Add A15/8445.

39. Pr A to QV, 4 October 1884, RA Z179/22; QV to Pr A, 30 October 1884, RA Add A15/4335.

40. Journal, 2 October 1884, RA Add A15/8445; Dss of C to QV, 10 October 1884, RA Z179/23: Pr A to QV, 10 October 1884, RA Z179/24; Pr A to QV, 24 October 1884, RA Z179/27.

41. Stewart to D of Cambridge, 18 November 1884 (extract), RA Add A15/4363; Lady Downe to QV, 17 November 1884, RA Add A15/4343; Dss of C to QV, 18 November 1884, RA Z179/32; Lady Downe to Lady Sefton, 6 January 1885, Downe.

42. Pr A to QV, 19 January 1885, RA Z180/4; Pr A to QV, 25 January 1885, RA Z180/5.

43. QV to Pr A, 23 January 1885, RA Add A15/4392; Dss of C to QV, 15 February 1885, RA Z180/11; Pr A to QV, 13 May 1884, RA Z178/13; Pr A to QV, 29 December 1884, RA Z179/44; FitzGerald to QV, 25 December 1883, RA Add A15/4147; Dss of C to QV, 12 January 1884, RA Z177/19.

44. QV to Pr A, 6 February 1885, RA Add A15/4406; Pr A to QV, 10 February 1885, RA Z180/9; Lady Downe to Lady Sefton, 9 February 1885, Downe.

45. Pr A to QV, 24 February 1885, RA Z180/13; Dss of C to QV, 24 February 1885, RA Z180/14; Dufferin to Pr A, 2 March 1885, RA Add A15/4418; Pr A to QV, 3 March 1885, RA Z180/15; Pr A to QV, 25 March 1885, RA Z180/21.

46. Telegram, Dufferin to QV, 31 March 1885, RA Add A15/4439; Pr A to QV, 10 March 1885, RA Z180/16; Dss of C to Lady Elphinstone, 4 April 1885, RA Add A25/662; Dss of C to QV, 6 April 1885, RA Z180/24; Lady Downe to QV, 6 April 1885, RA Add A15/4447; Pr A to QV, 14 April 1885, RA Z180/26; Dufferin to QV, 27 April 1885, RA N42/82.

47. Pr A to QV, 8 May 1885, RA Z180/30; Pr A to QV, 20 April 1885, RA Z180/28; QV to Pr A, 24 April 1885, RA Add A15/4462; PoW to Pr A, 22 April 1885, RA Add A15/4460; Telegram, QV to Pr A, 14 May 1885, RA Add A15/4483.

48. Journal, 23 and 26 May and 13-14 June 1885, RA Add A15/8445.

CHAPTER 9

1. Ponsonby to D of Cambridge, 19 July 1885, RA Add A15/4512; Lord R. Churchill to QV, 20 July 1885 (copy), RA Add A15/4513; Salisbury to QV, 31 July 1885, RA Add A15/4515; Telegram, QV to Dufferin, 31 July 1885, RA Add A15/4514; Memorandum by Ponsonby, 16 August 1885, RA Add A15/4526.

2. Cypher, Dufferin to Salisbury, 8 August 1885 (received), RA Add A15/4523; Ponsonby to QV, 15 August 1885, RA Add A15/4529; ditto, 11 October 1885, RA Add A15/4547; Pr A to QV, 3 September 1885, RA Add A15/4537.

3. Telegram, Roberts to Ponsonby, 20 October 1885, RA Add A15/4558; Pr A to D of Cambridge, 7 September 1886, RA Add A15/4673; QV to HE, 18 March 1886, RA Add A25/733.

4. Journal, 27 September 1886, RA Add A15/8445; Pr A to QV, 30 September 1886, RA Z181/7; ditto, 24 November 1884, RA Z179/35.

5. Journal, 28 September 1886, RA Add A/8445; Pr A to QV, 30 September 1886, RA Z181/7; Journal, 29 September 1886, RA Add A15/8445; Pr A to Roberts, 29 September 1886, NAM 7101-23-20/7.

6. Journal, 12-13 October 1886, RA Add A15/8445; ditto, 26 October 1886, RA Add A15/8445; Cypher, Pr A to Ponsonby, 22 October 1886, RA Add A15/4686; Pr A to QV, 1 November 1886, RA Z181/15.

7. Pr A to QV, 1 November 1886, RA Z181/15; Journal, 2 November 1886, RA Add A15/8445.

8. Journal, 2 November 1886, RA Add A15/8445; Titles and Salutes of Native Chiefs, India Office, 1875, IOLR X1062(a); Journal, 3 November 1886, RA Add A15/8445.

9. QV to Pr A, 4 November 1886, RA Add A15/4705; QV to Dss of C, 4 November 1886, RA Add A15/4706.

10. Pr A to Roberts, 9 December 1886, NAM 7101-23-20/8; Journal, 14 December 1886, RA Add A15/8445; Pr A to QV, 16 December 1886, RA Z181/25; Journal, 22 November 1886, RA Add A15/8445; QV to Pr A, 7 January 1887, RA Add A15/4751.

11. Pr A to QV, 30 December 1886, RA Z181/28; Pr A to QV, 6 January 1887, RA Z182/1.

12. Pr A to D of Cambridge, 21 December 1886, RA Add E1/11671; Journal, 12 January 1887, RA Add A15/8445; ditto, 1 February 1887; Pr A to QV, 4 February 1887, RA Z182/8; Journal 2 February 1887, RA Add A15/8445; Pr A to QV, 28 February 1887, RA Z182/15; ditto, 4 March 1887, RA Add Z182/17; Mrs Hannay to QV, 3 March 1887, RA Add A15/4795; Pr A to QV, 28 February 1887, RA Z182/15.

13. Pr A to QV, 13 March 1887, RA Z182/19.

14. Pr A to QV, 18 March 1887, RA Z182/21; Dss of C to QV, 18 March 1887, RA Z182/22.

15. Dss of C to QV, 25 March 1887, RA Z182/24; Dr Keith to Dr Reid, 26 March 1887, RA Add A15/4811; Mrs Hannay to QV, 26 March 1887, RA Add A15/4812.

16. Pr A to QV, 24 March 1887, RA Z182/23.

17. Bill: Duke of Connaught's Leave, 18 April 1887, RA Add A15/4828; W.H. Smith to QV, 20 April 1887 (copy), RA Add A15/4830; Telegrams, Lord Lewisham to Ponsonby, 12 May 1887, RA Add A15/4853 and 4854; Daily Telegraph, 25 May 1887, RA Add A15/4870; Pr A to QV,, 12 June 1887, RA Z182/38.

18. QV to Pr A, 15 August 1887, RA Add A15/4899; QV to Dss of C, 26 June 1887, RA Add A15/4874.

19. HE to QV, 4 August 1887, RA Add A15/4889; Pr A to Dss of C, 7 August 1887, RA Add A15/7090; ditto, 7 August 1887, RA Add A15/7091; Dss of C to Pr A, 14 August 1887, RA Add A15/7099; QV to Pr A, 19 August 1887, RA Add A15/4910; Pr A to Dss of C, 22 August 1887, RA Add A15/7100.

20. Pr A to Dss of C, 13-22 September 1887, RA Add A15/7107; Notes of Measures in the Military, Marine and Ecclesiastical Departments of the Bombay Government, 1885-1890, SOAS, Reay Papers, Mss 254560, Box 2; Reay to 'Sir William', 17 December 1890 (copy or draft), SOAS, Reay Papers, Mss 254560, Box 1.

21. Wolseley to Ponsonby, 12 November 1888, RA Add A15/5199; Memorandum by C.H. Brownlow on report of the Indian Mobilisation Committee, 1 February 1889, PRO WO33/49/A153.

22. Pr A to Dss of C, 13-22 September 1887, RA Add A15/7107; Pr A to QV, 6 October 1887, RA Z183/16; Pr A to Ponsonby, 11 January 1888, RA Add A12/1527; Pr A to Lorne, 5 January 1888, RA Add A17/796; Pr A to Roberts, 26 February 1888, NAM 7101-23-20/19.

23. Pr A to PoW, 18 May 1888 (extract), RA T9/108; Pr A to QV, 21 May 1888, RA Z184/34.

24. Pr A to Roberts, 1 June 1888, NAM 7101-23-20/26; Pr A to HE, 9 June 1888, RA Add A25/760; Pr A to QV, 16 July 1888, RA Z185/4; D of Cambridge to Pr A, 15 June

1888 (copy), RA Add E1/12215; Journal, 20 August 1888, RA Add A15/8445; Pr A to Ponsonby, 24 October 1888 (copy), RA Add A15/5181.

25. Ponsonby to QV, 31 October 1888, RA Add A15/5183.

26. Pr A to Dss of C, 13 November 1887, RA Add A15/7114; Pr A to QV, 19 January 1888, RA Z184/4; QV to Pr A, 9 March 1888, RA Add A15/5054; Pr A to QV, 28 March 1888, RA Z184/22; ditto, 10 May 1888, RA Z184/32; Telegrams, Dr Laking to Dr Reid, 23-24 April 1888, RA Add A15/5087-5089.

27. Journal, 22-23 December 1888, RA Add A15/8445; Pr A to QV, 27 December 1888, RA Z185/36; Journal, 25-28 December 1888, RA Add A15/8445; ditto, 1 January 1889; ditto, 4 January 1889; ditto, 6 January 1889; ditto, 9 January 1889; ditto, 17 January 1889; ditto, 1 February 1889; ditto, 8 April 1889.

28. Journal, 11-12 April 1889, RA Add A15/8445; QV to Dss of C, 25 January 1889, RA Add A15/5246; Journal, 5 April 1889, RA Add A15/8445.

29. QV to Pr A, 19 September 1889, RA Add A15/5359; Pr A to QV, 10 October 1889, RA Z187/20; QV to Pr A, 24 October 1889, RA Add A15/5371; ditto, 31 October 1889, RA Add A15/5373.

30. Journal, 9 November 1889, RA Add A15/8445.

31. Journal, 10-11 November 1889, RA Add A15/8445; Pr A to QV, 20 November 1889, RA Z187/26.

32. Pr A to QV, 20 November 1889, RA Z187/26; Journal, 13-14 November 1889, RA Add A15/8445.

33. Journal, 6 Jan 1890, RA Add A15/8445; ditto, 8 January 1890.

34. Pr A to QV, 13 January 1890, RA Z188/3.

35. McNeill to QV, 12 February 1889, RA add A15/5256; Pr A to HE, 19 September 1889, RA Add A25/799; Roberts to D of Cambridge, ?22 September 1889 (extract), RA Add A15/5361; QV to Pr A, 14 November 1889, RA Add A15/5377; Cypher, Pr A to QV, 6 December 1889, RA Add A15/5383; Memorandum by Ponsonby, 16 December 1889, RA Add A15/5388; Pr A to QV, 7 January 1890, RA Z188/2.

36. Journal, 7-8 December 1889, RA Add A15/8445, Pr A to QV, 10 December 1889, RA Z187/30; Journal, 11 December 1889, RA Add A15/8445; Pr A to QV, 14 December 1889, RA Z187/31; Dss of C to QV, 18 December 1889, RA Z187/32; Journal, 17 December 1889, RA Add A15/8445; Pr A to QV, 26 December 1889, RA Z187/33.

37. Pr A to Dss of C, 1 February 1890, RA Add A15/7137; Pr A to Roberts, 8 February 1890, NAM 7101-23-20/55.

38. Memorandum, Luckhardt to Pr A, c.1889, SOAS, Reay Papers, Mss 254560, Box 2.

39. Memorandum by Brackenbury and Newmarch, 19 August 1889, PRO WO33/49/A174.

40. Journal, 8 March 1890, RA Add A15/8445; Bombay Gazette, 10 March 1889, RA Add A15/5431.

41. Journal, 13 March 1890, RA Add A15/8445.

42. Press cutting in Journal, 15 February 1890, RA Add A15/8445.

CHAPTER 10

1. Journal, 14 and 17 March 1890, RA Add A15/8445; Pr A to QV, 18 March 1890, RA Z188/19; QV to Pr A, 14 March 1890, RA Add A15/5440.

2. Journal, 17 March 1890, RA Add A15/8445; Pr A to QV, 18 March 1890, RA Z188/19; Mrs Cavaye to QV, 23 March 1890, RA Add A15/5484; Journal, 18 March 1890 RA Add A15/8445; *Bombay Gazette*, 29 March 1890, RA Add A15/5495.

3. Journal, 22 March 1890, RA Add A15/8445; Pr A to QV, 24 March 1890, RA Z188/20; Journal, 23 March 1890, RA Add A15/8445.

4. Pr A to QV, 29 March 1890, RA Z188/21; Journal, 25 March 1890, RA Add A15/8445.

5. Journal, 31 March 1890, RA Add A15/8445.

6. Journal, 1 April 1890, RA Add A15/8445.

7. Journal, 2 April 1890, RA Add A15/8445; *Brief Account of the Visit of Their Royal Highnesses The Duke and Duchess of Connaught to Hong Kong,* Hong Kong Government Printers, 1890.

8. Journal, 3-4 April 1890, RA Add A15/8445; Pr A to QV, 11 April 1890, RA Z188/23.

9. Journal, 8 April 1890, RA Add A15/8445.

10. Dss of C to QV, 11 April 1890, RA Z188/24; Journal, 10 April 1890, RA Add A15/8445.

11. Journal, 12-13 April 1890, RA Add A15/8445.

12. Journal, 13 April 1890, RA Add A15/8445.

13. Journal, 15-17 April 1890, RA Add A15/8445.

14. Journal, 17 April 1890, RA Add A15/8445; Pr A to QV, 22 April 1890, RA Z188/25.

15. Journal, 18 and 20 April 1890, RA Add A15/8445.

16. Journal, 29-30 April 1890, RA Add A15/8445;

17. Journal, 1-3 May 1890, RA Add A15/8445.

18. Journal, 5 May 1890, RA Add A15/8445.

19. Journal, 6 May 1890, RA Add A15/8445; Pr A to QV, 17 May 1890, RA Z188/29.

20. Journal, 7 May 1890, RA Z188/27; McNeill to QV, 16 May 1890, RA Add A15/5558.

21. Journal, 8 May 1890, RA Add A15/8445; McNeill to QV, 16 May 1890, RA Add A15/5558; Dss of C to QV, 14 May 1890, RA Z188/28; Pr A to QV, 17 May 1890 RA Z188/29.

22. Dss of C to QV, 14 May 1890, RA Z188/28; Journal, 21 May 1890, RA Add A15/8445.

23. Cuttings stuck in Journal, 21 May 1890, RA Add A15/8445.

24. Journal, 22 May 1890, RA Add A15/8445.

25. Journal, 22 and 24 May 1890, RA Add A15/8445; Pr A to QV, 3 June 1890, RA Z188/30.

26. Journal, 25-27 May 1890, RA Add A15/8445; McNeill to QV, 3 June 1890, RA Add A15/5576; Schultz to Macdonald, 28 May 1890, PAC, Macdonald Papers, MG26A/120249-50.

27. Journal, 28-29 May 1890, RA Add A15/8445; McNeill to QV, 3 June 1890, RA Add A15/5576.

28. Journal, 31 May 1890, RA Add A15/8445; McNeill to QV, 3 June 1890, RA Add A15/5576; Journal, 1-3 June 1890, RA Add A15/8445; Pr A to QV, 3 June 1890, RA Z188/30.

29. Journal, 4 and 6-12 June 1890, RA Add A15/8445.

30. Pr A to QV, 3 June 1890, RA Z188/30; QV to Pr A, 19 June 1890, RA Add A15/5583; Telegram, Pr A to QV, 22 June 1890, RA Add A15/5584A.

CHAPTER 11

1. *Standard*, 23 June 1890, RA Add A15/5585.

2. Hamer, *The British Army*, Clarendon Press 1970, p 28.

3. Ponsonby to QV, 3 July 1890, RA Add A15/5585A; ditto, 5 July 1890, RA Add A15/5585C; Stanhope to QV, 24 July 1890, RA Add A15/5594; Pr A to QV, 20 July 1890, RA Add A15/5589; QV to Salisbury, 20 July 1890 (draft by Ponsonby amended by QV), RA Add A15/5588; Stanhope to QV, 29 July 1890, RA Add A15/5597; Ponsonby to Stanhope, 31 July 1890 (draft approved by QV), RA Add A15/5599 and 5598; Stanhope to QV, 1 August 1890, RA Add A15/5600.

4. Ponsonby to QV, 1 August 1890, RA Add A15/5601; QV to Ponsonby, 1 August 1890, RA Add A15/5602; Wolseley to Ponsonby, 7 August 1890, *Letters of Queen Victoria*, 3rd Series, pp 627-9.

5. Ponsonby to QV, 2 August 1890, RA Add A15/5603; Stanhope to Pr A, 15 August 1890 (copy), KAO U1590/0253; Pr A to Stanhope, 18 August 1890, ditto; ditto, 1 September 1890, ditto; *The Times*, 26 August 1890; Pr A to QV, 16 September 1890, RA Add A15/5620; D of Cambridge to Pr A, 6 November 1890, RA Add A15/5657.

6. Return of Troops, Southern District, 19 February 1891, RA Add A15/5678; Pr A to Stanhope, 17, 25 and 29 April 1891, KAO U1590/0253; Knollys to Ponsonby, 15 February 1891, RA Y182/11; Pr A to Ponsonby, 22 February 1891, RA Y182/22; For the Gordon-Cumming issue, see Havers, Grayson and Shankland, *The Royal Baccarat Scandal*, Kimber 1977; QV to Pr A, 8 June 1891, RA Add A15/5709.

7. Wantage Commission, Duke of Connaught examined 23 July 1891, paras 9378-9423, C. 68521, PRO ZHC1/5397.

8. Wantage Commission, C.68521, paras 9444-68.

9. Wantage Commission, C.68521, paras 9469-9525 and 9639-40.

10. Report of the Wantage Commission, February 1892, C. 6582, PRO ZHC1/5397; Pr A to QV, 2 October 1890, RA Add A15/5635.

11. Pr A to Dss of C, 20 August 1891, RA Add A15/7203; ditto, 21 August 1891, RA Add A15/7205; ditto, 14 August 1891, RA Add A15/7191.

12. Pr A to Dss of C, 21 August 1891, RA Add A15/7205; ditto, 22 August, 1891, RA Add

A15/7207; ditto, 23 August 1891, RA Add A15/7209; ditto, 25 August 1891, RA Add A15/7212.

13. Pr A to Dss of C, 26 August 1891, RA Add A15/7214; ditto, 25 August 1891, RA Add A15/7212.

14. Pr A to Dss of C, 2 August 1891, RA Add A15/7163; ditto, 9 March 1892, RA Add A15/7233; Dss of C to Pr A, 3 June 1892, RA Add A15/7238; Pr A to QV, 17 April 1892, RA Add A15/5782; Dss of C to Pr A, 24 June 1892, RA Add A15/7279; Empss Frederick to Pr A, 31 October 1894, RA Add A15/5970; Dss of C to Pr A, 1 November 1894, RA Add A15/7481; ditto, 5 November 1894, RA Add A15/7491; ditto, 9 November 1894, RA Add A15/7498.

15. Pr A to QV, 12 October 1891, RA Add A15/5728; QV to Ponsonby, 5 February 1892, RA W73/93; Ponsonby to QV, 13 December 1891, RA Add A15/5741A; Memorandum by Ponsonby, 25 February 1892, RA Add A15/5769; Pr A to D of Cambridge, 14 June 1892, RA Add A15/5803.

16. Pr A to Dss of C, 17 June 1892, RA Add A15/7264; Pr A to QV, 1 June 1892, RA Add A15/5798; Pr A to Dss of C, 4 June 1892, RA Add A15/7239; ditto, 8 June 1892, RA Add A15/7247; ditto, 3 June 1892, RA Add A15/7237; Pr A to QV, 2 November 1892, RA Add A15/5831A; QV to Pr A, 4 November 1892, RA Add A15/5832.

17. Wolseley to Sir G Wolseley, 15 June 1893, Hove W/W4/35; Pr A to Dss of C, 19 June 1892, RA Add A15/7266; ditto, 17 June 1892, RA Add A15/7264; Notices and Orders of the Day (House of Lords), 4 May 1893, RA Add A15/5856; *Morning Post*, 5 May 1893, RA Add A15/5858A; Reay to Pr A, 4 May 1893, RA Add A15/5857; Lady Reay to Dss of C, 4 May 1893, RA Add A15/5858; Ripon to QV, 5 May 1893, RA Add A15/5859; Pr A to Lorne, 6 May 1893, RA Add A17/1743.

18. Pr A to Dss of C, 14 June 1892, RA Add A15/7259; ditto, 15 June 1892, RA Add A15/7260; ditto, 29 May 1893, RA Add A15/7385; ditto, 5 December 1892, RA Add A15/7369; ditto, 7 December 1892, RA Add A15/7370.

19. QV to Pr A, 8 June 1891, RA Add A15/5709; William II to Pr A, 11 March 1891, RA Add A15/5680; QV to Pr A, 15 March 1891, RA Add A15/5682; Pr A to Dss of C, 1 August 1892, RA Add A15/7295; ditto, 2 August 1892, RA Add A15/7298; ditto, 3 August 1892, RA Add A15/7303; ditto, 1 August 1892, RA Add A15/7296; ditto, 5 August 1892, RA Add A15/7309; ditto, 5 August 1892, RA Add A15/7310.

20. Pr A to Stamfordham, 2 March 1916, RA Geo V O 991A/1.

21. Pr A to D of Cambridge, 26 July 1892, RA Add A15/5819; Stanhope to QV, 30 July 1892, RA Add A15/5820; Ponsonby to QV, 7 August 1892, RA Add A15/5825; Pr A to Dss of C, 12 August 1892, RA Add A15/7331; ditto, 13 August 1892, RA Add A15/7333; ditto, 16 August (1892), RA Add A15/7339.

22. QV to Pr A, 29-30 October 1892, RA Add A15/5830; Pr A to Dss of C, 1 June 1893, RA Add A15/7389; Ponsonby to QV, 20 June 1893, RA Add A15/5869; Pr A to QV, 22 June 1893, RA Add A15/5871; ditto, 26 June 1893, RA Add A15/5872; D of Cambridge to QV, 27 July 1893, RA Add A15/5881; Pr A to D of Cambridge, 15 August 1893, RA Add A15/5885.

23. James, *The Life of Lord Roberts*, Hollis and Carter 1954, p 240; *The Broad Arrow: The Naval and Military Gazette*, 19 August 1893, RA Add A15/5887; Pr A to Roberts, 30 August 1893, NAM 7101-23-20/61.

24. *Saturday Review*, 16 September 1893, RA Add A15/5895; *Manchester Guardian*, 26 September 1893; see Owen, *Tel-el-Kebir and the Duke of Connaught, Army Quarterly and Defence Journal*, vol 14, No 1, January 1984; Childers to Thompson, 2 October 1893, R Comm Soc Childers 5/206; Thompson to Childers, ditto, 5/207; Wolseley to Childers, 11 October 1893, ditto 5/211.

25. Pr A to Dss of C, 16 September 1893, RA Add A15/7440.

26. Pr A to Dss of C, 18 September 1893, RA Add A15/7445; ditto, 19 September 1893, RA Add A15/7447; Pr A to QV, 24 September 1893, RA Add A15/5901A.

27. Pr A to QV, 29 July 1894, RA Add A15/5946; ditto, 15 August 1894, RA Add A15/5948; Pr A to Dss of C, 17 August 1894, RA Add A15/7466; ditto, 18 August 1894, RA Add A15/7467; ditto, 21 August 1894, RA Add A15/7473; ditto, 22 August 1894, RA Add A15/7475; Dss of C to Pr A, 23 August 1894, RA Add A15/7477.

28. *The Broad Arrow: The Naval and Military Gazette*, 17 November 1894, RA Add A15/7518; Wolseley to Sir G Wolseley, 3 February 1895, Hove W/W4/46; ditto, 22 May 1895, Hove W/W4/58; Pr A to QV, 21 June 1895, RA Add A15/5999; Wolseley to Pr A, 28 July 1895, RA Add A15/6005.

29. Bigge to Pr A, 2 August 1895, RA Add A15/6004; Wolseley to Sir G Wolseley, 8 August 1895, Hove W/W4/61; Bigge to Pr A, 12 August 1895, RA Add A15/6007.

30. Pss Frederick Charles of Hesse to QV, 31 August 1895, RA Add A15/6016; Pr A to QV, 1 September 1895, RA Add A15/6017; ditto, 6-7 September 1895, RA Add A15/6021; *Morning Post,* 21 October 1895; Pr A to QV, 20 October 1895, RA Add A15/6036; Pr A to Egerton, 21 October 1895, RA Add C22/16; QV to Pr A, 24 October 1895, RA Add A15/6037.

31. Pr A to Dss of C, 9 November 1895, RA Add A15/7588; ditto, 10 November 1895, RA Add A15/7589.

32. Pr A to QV, 3 January 1896, RA Add A15/6053; QV to Pr A, 6 January 1896, RA Add A15/6055; Dss of C to Egerton, 7 May 1896, RA Add C22/23.

33. Pr A to QV, 18 May 1896, RA Add A15/6092; ditto, 20 May 1896, RA Add A15/6094; Dss of C to QV, 20 May 1896, RA Add A15/6095.

34. Pr A to QV, 23-24 May 1896, RA Add A15/6097; Mrs Egerton to QV, 22 May 1896, RA Add A15/6096.

35. Pr A to QV, 28 May 1896, RA Add A15/6100; Mrs Egerton to QV, 28 May 1896, RA Add A15/6101.

36. Pr A to QV, 30 May 1896, RA Add A15/6103; ditto, 4 June 1896, RA Add A15/6107; Mrs Egerton to QV, 8 June 1896, RA Add A15/6109; Pr A to QV, 16 June 1896, RA Add A15/6113.

37. D of Cambridge to QV, 4 July 1897, RA Add A15/6165; cuttings from *The Times, Morning Post*, and *Daily Chronicle*, July 1897, RA W73/149; Knollys to Bigge, 26 July 1897, RA W73/177; Pr A to QV, 20 July 1897, RA Add A15/6166; Pr A to Dss of C, 11 August 1897, RA Add A15/7605.

38. Pr A to Dss of C, 26 August 1898, RA Add A15/7638; Bigge to QV, 1 September 1898, RA Add A15/6215; Eustace to Davidson, 5 September 1898, RA Add A15/6219; ditto, 6 September 1898, RA Add A15/6220; ditto, 7 September 1898, RA Add A15/6221.

39. Eustace to Davidson, 7 September 1898, RA Add A15/6221; Wolseley to QV, 8 September 1898, RA Add A15/6222.

40. Pr A to Dss of C, 13 September 1898, RA Add A15/7649; ditto, 16 September 1898, RA Add A15/7655; Pr A to QV, 9 October 1898, RA Add A15/6232.

CHAPTER 12

1. QV to Pr A, 27 October 1898, RA Add A15/6249; Pr A to QV, 28 January 1899, RA Add A15/6255; ditto, 22 February 1899, RA Add A15/6280.

2. Collins to QV, 23 March 1899, RA Add A35/444; QV to Collins, 25 March 1899, RA Add A35/445.

3. Pr A to Bigge, 10 April 1899, RA Add A35/462; von Strenge to D of Coburg, 28 March 1899, RA Add A35/446; Stephen to QV, 8 April 1899, RA Add A35/455.

4. Empss Frederick to QV, 9 April 1899 (copy), RA Add A35/458; Pr A to QV, 10 April 1899, RA Add A35/461; QV to PoW, 10 April 1899, RA Add A35/457.

5. Pr A to Bigge, 10 April 1899, RA Add A35/462; Pr A to QV, 22 April 1899, RA Add A35/484; Pr A to D of Coburg, c 8 May 1899 (copy), RA Add A35/497.

6. Memorandum by QV, undated, c April 1899, RA Add A35/490.

7. Pr A to QV, 28 January 1899, RA Add A15/6255.

8. Pr A to QV, 5 February 1899, RA Add A15/6260; Journal, 10 February 1899, RA Add A15/8445; ditto, 14 February 1899, ditto; ditto, 18-20 February 1899, ditto; Pr A to QV, 26 February 1899, RA Add A15/6288.

9. Pr A to QV, 26 February 1899, RA Add A15/6288.

10. Pr A to QV, 5 November 1899, RA Add A15/6346.

11. Pr A to QV, 13 November 1899, RA Add A15/6347; Pr A to Davidson, 19 December 1899, RA W73/192; Lansdowne to QV, 25 December 1899, RA W73/210A; Pr A to QV, 22 December 1899, RA W73/209; Pr A to Egerton, 28 December 1899, RA Add C22/56; Cadogan to QV, 10 January 1900, RA Add A15/6356.

12. Cadogan to QV, 10 January 1900, RA Add A15/6357; Pr A to QV, 10 January 1900, RA Add A15/6358; ditto, 9 February 1900, RA Add A15/6366; Pr A to Dss of C, (28 March) 1900, RA Add A15/7663; ditto, 26-27 October 1900, RA Add A15/7705; ditto, 6-7 November 1900, RA Add A15/7731.

13. e.g. Pr A to QV, 22 July 1900, RA Add A15/6405 and Dss of C to Pr A, 25 October 1900, RA Add A15/7702; Dss of C to QV, 12 February 1900, RA Add A15/6367; Dss of C to Pr A, 25 June 1900, RA Add A15/7668; ditto, 19 March 1901, RA Add A15/7759; Pr A to Dss of C, (2 August 1900), RA Add A15/7676; Dss of C to Pr A, 1 August 1900, RA Add A15/7675.

14. Pr A to QV, 12 March 1900, RA Add A15/6376; QV to Pr A, 13 March 1900, RA Add A15/6377; Lee, *Queen Victoria*, Smith, Elder 1903, p 536; QV to Pr A, 27 December 1898, RA Add A15/6249 and QV to Dss of C, 15 April 1899, RA Add A15/6315; QV to Pr A, 8 November 1900, RA Add A15/6428; Pr A to Dss of C, 11 November 1900, RA Add A15/7740.

15. Pr A to Pss Louise, 23 December 1900, RA Add A17/970; Pss Beatrice to Pss Louise, 25 December 1900, RA Add A17/971; Pr A to Pss Louise, 27 December 1900,

RA Add A17/978; Pr A to Roberts, 10 January 1901, NAM 7101-23-20/74; Pr A to Dss of C, 18 January 1901, RA Add A15/7743 and 7744.

16. Reid, *Ask Sir James*, Hodder & Stoughton 1978, pp 209-12; ditto, p 216.

17. Pr A to Dss of C, 9 February 1901, RA Add A15/7746; Dss of C to Pr A, 9 February 1901, RA Add A15/7745; ditto, 10 February 1901, RA Add A15/7748; Pr A to Dss of C, 17 March 1901, RA Add A15/7755; Pr A to Roberts, 22 April 1901, NAM 7101-23-20/77; Pr A to Pss Louise, 28 April 1901, RA Add A17/992.

18. Pr A to LL, (4 April 1901), RA Geo V BB16/1908; Pr A to Dss of C, 30 November 1901, RA Add A15/7825; Dss of C to Pr A, 2 December 1901, RA Add A15/7828; Pr A to Dss of C, 2 December 1901, RA Add A15/7829.

19. Pr A to LL, (5 December 1901), RA Geo V BB16/Acc 1253; ditto, 25 February 1902, RA Geo V BB16/1902.

20. Pr A to Pss Louise, 12 December 1901, RA Add A17/1006; Dss of C to Pr A, 12 May 1902, RA Add A15/7835; Pr A to Dss of C, (13-14 May 1902), RA Add A15/7836; Pr A to LL, (11 May 1902), RA Geo V BB16/1903.

21. Pr A to Dss of C, (13-14 May 1902), RA Add A15/7836.

22. Pr A to LL, (16 May 1902), RA Geo V BB16/1908; ditto, (17 May 1902), ditto; Pr A to Dss of C, (18 May 1902) RA Add A15/7841; Dss of C to Pr A, 17 May 1902, RA Add A15/7840; Pr A to Dss of C, 19-20 May 1902, RA Add A15/7843; Pr A to LL, (21 May 1902), RA Geo V BB/Acc 1253.

23. Dss of C to LL, 7 September 1902, RA Geo V BB16/ Acc 1253; ditto, 10 September 1902, ditto.

24. Pr A to LL, c 6 September 1902, RA Geo V BB16/1902; ditto, c 7 September 1902, RA Geo V BB16/1903; Dss of C to LL, 26 September 1902, RA Geo V BB16/Acc 1253.

25. Pr A to Dss of C, 22 July 1902, RA Add A15/7854; Dss of C to LL, 10 May 1902, RA Geo V BB16/Acc 1253; Pr A to Dss of C, 26 July 1902, RA Add A15/7862; Pr A to Curzon, 16 November 1902, IORL Mss Eur F111/234/26-29; Pr A to Dss of C, 31 July 1902, RA Add A15/7873.

26. E VII to Pr A, 27 July 1902, RA Add A15/6436; Pr A of C to Dss of C, 18 August 1902, RA Add A15/7879; ditto, 23 August 1902, RA Add A15/7880.

27. Journal, 29-30 November 1902, RA Add A15/8445; ditto, 6-7 December 1902, ditto;

28. Journal, 7 December 1902, RA Add A15/8445.

29. Journal, 8 December 1902, RA Add A15/8445.

30. Journal, 9-10 December 1902, RA Add A15/8445.

31. Journal, 11-14 and 16 December 1902, RA Add A15/8445.

32. Journal, 27 and 29 December 1902, RA Add A15/8445.

33. Journal, 29 December 1902-1 January 1903, RA Add A15/8445.

34. Pr A to Curzon, 18 September 1902, IORL Mss Eur F111/234/11-15; Consuelo Vanderbilt Balsan, *The Glitter and the Gold*, Heinemann 1953, p 139; Nicolson, *Mary Curzon,* Weidenfeld & Nicolson 1977, p 167.

35. Journal, 12 January-28 February 1903, RA Add A15/8445; Lt Col A Weston Jarvis

(of Pr A's suite), *With the Duke and Duchess of Connaught in Egypt and India 1902-1903* (typescript), 30 October 1903, p 183, RA Add A15/8454.

36. Pr A to Curzon, 27 February 1903, IORL Mss Eur F111/234/40-41; ditto, 19 February 1903, ditto 43-47; Curzon to Pr A, 5 March 1903, RA Add A15/6440.

37. Journal, 11 March 1903, RA Add A15/8445; Kelly-Kenny to Knollys, 3 March 1903, RA W24/77.

38. Journal, 27 March 1903, RA Add A15/8445; LL to Pr A, undated, RA Geo V BB16/1903; Pr A to LL, undated, RA Geo V BB16.

39. Broderick to Knollys, 2 March (1903), RA W24/76A; Knollys to Broderick, 29 March 1903, PRO 30/67/18/953; Broderick to Knollys, 30 March 1903, ditto 955-6; Balfour to E VII, ? February 1904, PRO CAB41/29/5.

CHAPTER 13

1. Pr A to LL, 22 October 1903, RA Geo V BB16/1903; Evidence of Esher's technique is to be found in his correspondence with Knollys, Arnold-Forster and Haldane.

2. Pr A to Adjutant-General, 3 November 1903, RA Add A15/6442.

3. Report of War Office Re-Constitution Committee (Esher Report), 11 January-9 March 1904, Cd 1932, 1968-1, 2002; Note by Salisbury, 9 March 1904, PRO CAB 37/69/40.

4. Irish Command Order 106, 6 May 1904, PRO WO 35/59; Inspector-General's submissions to Army Council, 30 May-5 August 1904, PRO WO 163/9/232-40; Army Council 15th Mtg, 5 May 1904, PRO WO 163/9/26-9; ditto, 19th Mtg, paper and minutes, ditto/213; ditto, 22nd Mtg, paper and minutes, ditto/39 and 225; Proposals for reorganization of the Army by Arnold-Forster, 7 June 1904, PRO CAB 37/70/55; Balfour to E VII, 15 June 1904, PRO CAB 41/29/20; Revised proposals by Arnold-Forster, 2 July 1904, PRO CAB 37/71/92; Correspondence between Arnold-Forster and Balfour, 13 January-27 February 1905, PRO CAB 37/74/10.

5. Balfour to Selborne, 23 September 1903, Bodl. Mss Selborne 1/26-7; Pr A to LL, 3 October 1904, RA Geo V BB16/1904.

6. Pr A to Dss of C, 22 July 1904, RA Add A15/7968; ditto, 24 July 1904, RA Add A15/7973; ditto, 25 July 1904, RA Add A15/7975.

7. Pr A to LL, 6 September 1904, RA Geo V BB16/1904; Pr A to Dss of C, 8 September 1904, RA Add A15/8002.

8. Annual Report of Inspector-General, 1 November 1904, PRO WO 163/10/299-333; Esher to Pr A, 6 December 1904, RA Add A15/6448; Shute to Congreve, 23 December 1904, WRO A-F 1390/129/9; Congreve to Shute, 26 December 1904, ditto; Congreve to Shute, 2 January 1905, RA W26/V/12; Arnold-Forster to Pr A, 6 January 1905 (copy), WRO A-F 1390/129/9.

9. Pr A to Arnold-Forster, 10 January 1905, WRO A-F 1390/129/9; Knollys to Arnold-Forster, 15 January 1905, WRO A-F 1390/129/15.

10. Annual Report of Inspector-General, 1 November 1904, PRO WO 163/10/299-333.

11. C.I.D. 66th Mtg, 15 March 1905, PRO CAB 2/1; Army Council 53rd Mtg, 5 May 1905, PRO WO 163/10/30; Pr A to Army Council, 23 May 1905, ditto/361-2.

12. Pr A to LL, 2 January (1905), RA Geo V BB16/1904; ditto, 8-9 January (1905), ditto; Gosselin to E VII, 14 January 1905, RA W43/37.

13. Pr A to LL, 14-15 January 1905, RA Geo V BB16/1905; ditto, 17 January 1905, ditto; ditto, 19-20 January 1905, ditto.

14. Pr A to LL, 24-26 January 1905, RA Geo V BB16/1905; ditto, 2-3 February 1905, ditto; ditto, 5-6 February 1905, ditto; ditto, 9-10 February 1905, ditto.

15. Pr A to LL, 12-13 February 1905, RA Geo V BB16/1905; ditto, 20-22 February 1905, ditto; Pr Gustav to Dss of C, 23 February (1905), RA Add A15/6449; Pr A to LL, 25 February 1905, RA Geo V BB16/1905.

16. Pr A to LL, 25 February 1905, RA Geo V BB16/1905.

17. Pr A to LL, 25 February 1905, RA Geo V BB16/1905; Nicolson to Knollys, 11 March 1905, RA W45/128.

18. Report of Inspector-General, 27 February 1905, PRO WO 163/10/287-92.

19. Army Council 56th Mtg paper and minutes, 26 May 1905, PRO WO 163/10/286-7.

20. Annual Report of Inspector-General, 1 October 1905, PRO WO 163/11/155-216.

21. Haldane to Asquith, 6 October 1905 (copy), NLS Haldane Mss 5906/218-20; Haldane to Knollys, 12 September 1905 (copy), ditto/189-92; Knollys to Haldane, 16 September 1905, ditto/193-4.

22. Esher to Knollys, 13 December 1905, RA W40/75A.

23. Arnold-Forster Journal, 12 February 1904, WRO A-F 1390/129/27.

24. Journal, 23 December 1905, RA Add A15/8445; Pr A to Pss Louise, 26 December 1905, RA Add A17/1034; Journal, 9 January 1906, RA Add A15/8445.

25. Pr A to E VII, 14 January 1906 (copy), RA W40/9; Pr A to LL, 25 February-2 March 1906, RA Geo V BB16/1906.

26. Journal, 27 February-4 April 1906, RA Add A15/8445; Pr A to LL, 25-29 March 1906, RA Geo V BB16/1906; ditto, ? April 1906 (incomplete), RA Geo V BB16/Acc 1253.

27. Pr A to LL, 13-14 June 1906, RA Geo V BB16/1907; ditto, 15 June 1906, RA Geo V BB16/1906; ditto, 19-20 June 1906, ditto.

28. Haldane to Esher, 22 August 1906 (copy), NLS Haldane Mss 5907/81; ditto, 24 August 1906 (copy), ditto/82; Pr A to LL, ? July/August 1906 (incomplete), RA Geo V BB16/1908; Haldane to Esher, 29 August 1906 (copy), NLS Haldane Mss 5907/88.

29. Esher to E VII, 23 August 1906, RA W40/49.

30. Pr A to Dss of C, 28 August 1906, RA Add A15/8124; Pr A to LL, 7 September 1906, RA Geo V BB16/1906; Pr A to Dss of C, 9 September 1906, RA Add A15/8130; ditto, 10 September 1906, RA Add A15/8133; Pr A to LL, 11 September 1906, RA Geo V BB16/1906.

31. Pr A to Dss of C, 29 September 1906, RA Add A15/8151; Annual Report of Inspector-General, 1 October 1906, PRO WO 163/12/177/1-74.

32. Knollys to Haldane, 8 November 1906, NLS Haldane Mss 5907/114-15; Pr A to LL, 14 November 1906, RA Geo V BB16/1906; E VII to Pr A, 15 November 1906, RA Add A15/6467; ditto, 16 November 1906, RA Add A15/6470.

33. Memorandum of points for Esher, ? January 1907, RA Add A15/6474; Journal, 10 January-16 April 1907, RA Add A15/8445.

34. Pr A to E VII, 13 February 1907, RA W72/4; ditto, 19 February 1907, RA W72/5; Journal, 22-26 and 28 January 1907, RA Add A15/8445; Pr A to LL, 25 February-4 March 1907, RA Geo V BB16/1907.

35. Pr A to E VII, 11 March 1907, RA W72/7; Journal, 1-4 April 1907, RA Add A15/8445.

36. Pr A to LL, 8-12 March 1907, RA Geo V BB16/1907; ditto, 5-8 April 1907, ditto; ditto, 24 April 1907, ditto; Secretary, War Office to US of S, Colonial Office, 16 April 1907, PRO CO 158/357; Pr A to Haldane, 27 June 1907, NLS Haldane Mss 5907/169.

37. War Office memoranda, 26 July, 6 August and 15 September 1907, RA Add A15/6480, 6485 and 6495.

38. *The Times*, 12 August 1907.

39. Foreign Office to Colonial Office, 4 September 1907, PRO CO 158/356/31729; e.g. Colonial Office minutes, 31 January 1907, PRO CO 158/357 and Fisher (Admiralty) to Pr A, 10 August 1907, RA Add A15/6490; Knollys to Haldane, 21 August 1907, NLS Haldane Mss 5907/183; correspondence between War Office and Colonial Office, 18 and 28 December 1907, PRO CO 158/357; Pr A to Haldane, 10 October 1907, NLS Haldane Mss 5907/232-3.

40. Journal, 31 December 1907-2 January 1908, RA Add A15/8445.

41. Pr A to LL, 7-8 January 1908, RA Geo V BB16/1908; ditto 16-18 January 1908, ditto; ditto, 28-29 January 1908, ditto; ditto 5 February 1908, ditto; ditto, 6 February 1908, ditto; Lady Egerton to Sir A Egerton, 8 February 1908, RA Add C22/267.

42. Pr A to LL, 14-16 February 1908, RA Geo V BB16/1908; ditto, 24 February 1908, ditto; ditto, 2-5 March 1908, ditto.

43. Pr A to LL, 6-7 April 1908, RA Geo V BB16/1908; ditto, 9 April 1908, ditto.

44. Pr A to E VII, 2 May 1908, RA X3/36A; Pr A to Pss Louise, 8 May 1908, RA Add A17/1050.

45. Report of the Field-Marshal Commanding-in-Chief in the Mediterranean, 2 May 1908, PRO WO 163/13/App II.

46. Pr A to LL, 17-19 December 1908, RA Geo V BB16/1908.

47. Pr A to LL, ?22-23 April 1909 (PS only), RA Geo V BB16/1908; ditto, 22-23 April 1909, RA Geo V BB16/1909.

48. Pr A to Army Council, 4 June 1909 (copy), RA W28/97.

49. Ward to Pr A, 24 June 1909, RA W31/2; Haldane to Esher, 12 June 1909 (copy), NLS Haldane Mss 5908/114; Haldane to Pr A, 24 June 1909 (copy), ditto 6109/89-90; ditto (draft), ditto 5908/119-21.

50. Pr A to Haldane, 25 June 1909 (copy), NLS Haldane Mss 6109/91-2; Pr A to LL, 26 June 1909, RA Geo V BB16/1909.

51. Haldane to Pr A, 28 June 1909 (copy), NLS Haldane Mss 6109/93-4; Knollys to Haldane, 28 June 1909, ditto 5908/124-5.

52. Knollys to Haldane, 8 July 1909, NLS Haldane Mss 5908/134-5; Pr A to Army Council, 22 July 1909 (copy), ditto 6109/98; Ward to Pr A, 23 July 1909 (copy), ditto/99.

CHAPTER 14

1. Haldane to Kitchener, 8 July 1909, NLS Haldane Mss 5908/131-3; Lee, *Edward VII*, vol 2, Macmillan 1927, p 497; Knollys to Haldane, 26 July 1909, NLS Haldane Mss 5908/149-50; E VII to Kitchener, 25 July 1909, PRO Kitchener 30/57/38/SS19; Kitchener to Haldane, August 1909 (draft), ditto/SS9b.

2. Birdwood to Arthur, 25 August 1916, PRO Kitchener 30/57/91/GA2/10.

3. H.F. Prevost Battersby in the *Morning Post*, 23 August 1909.

4. Asquith to Haldane, 6 October 1909, NLS Haldane Mss 5908/178-9; Shaughnessy to Grey, PAC Grey of Howick MG27/II/B2/vol 30/8/18; Pr A to LL, 27 October 1909, RA Geo V BB16/1909.

5. Journal, 21 January and 13-14 February 1910, RA Add A15/8445.

6. Journal, 16 February 1910, RA Add A15/8445; Pr A to LL, 17-21 February 1910, RA Geo V BB16/1910; ditto, 13-22 April 1910, ditto; Journal, 4-6 March 1910, RA Add A15/8445; Pr A to LL, 4-12 March 1910, RA Geo V BB16/1910; Journal, 12 and 16 March 1910, RA Add A15/8445.

7. Pr A to LL, 4-12 March 1910, RA Geo V BB16/1910; Journal, 27 March 1910, RA Add A15/8445; Pr A to LL, 19-28 March 1910, RA Geo V BB16/1910; Journal, 7 April 1910, RA Add A15/8445; Asquith to Pr A, 5 March 1910, RA Add A15/8988; Pr A to Asquith, 23 April 1910, Bodl. Asquith Mss Vol 12/134-5.

8. Journal, 5-6 May 1910, RA Add A15/8445.

9. Pr A to LL, (14 May 1910), RA Geo V BB16/1910; Bigge to Burnham, 18 May 1910 (copy), RA Geo V O. 63/2.

10. Pr A to Dss of C, 28 September 1910, RA Add A15/8440; ditto, 27 September 1910, RA Add A15/8439; Pr A to LL, 27 September 1910, RA Geo V BB16/1910; ditto, 28 September 1910, ditto; Pr A to Dss of C, 29 September 1910, RA Add A15/8441.

11. Memorandum by Kipling, ? October 1910, RA Add A15/6504A.

12. Pr a to LL, 17-18 October 1910, RA Geo V BB16/1910; Journal, 7 November 1910, RA Add A15/8445; Pr A to LL, 7 November 1910, RA Geo V BB16/1910; ditto, 3-7 November 1910, ditto.

13. Pr A to LL, 7 November 1910, RA Geo V BB16/1910; Pr A to Curzon, 31 December 1910, IORL Mss Eur F 112/583; Hopwood to Bigge, 2 December 1910, RA Geo V O. 63/51; Gladstone to Pr A, 28 November 1910, Br Lib Add Mss Gladstone 45985(6)/145-6; Pr A to LL, 3 December 1910, RA Geo V BB16/1910.

14. Pr A to LL, 4-5 December 1910, RA Geo V BB16/1910; ditto, 6-27 December 1910, ditto; Journal, 15 December 1910, RA Add A15/8445.

15. Pr A to LL, 30-31 December 1910, RA Geo V BB16/1910; ditto, 20 January 1911, RA Geo V BB16/1911.

16. Pr A to LL, 24-25 January 1911, RA Geo V BB16/1911; Grey to Harcourt, 27 January 1911, Bodl. Mss Harcourt dep 483/156; QM to Grand Dss of Mecklenburg-Strelitz, 4 February 1911, RA Geo V CC25/88.

17. Laurier to Pr A, 15 March 1911, RA Add A15/9005; Pr A to LL, 10 August 1911, RA Geo V BB16/1911; ditto, 13 August 1911, ditto; Pr A to Kitchener, 14 September 1911, PRO Kitchener 30/57/104/PA5/13.

18. Pr A to LL, 25-26 September 1911, RA Geo V BB16/1911.

19. Colonial Office minutes, 20-27 September 1911, PRO CO/42/956/2546/254; exchange of minutes between Lucas and Harcourt, 30 September 1911, ditto/264; US of S, Colonial Office to Pr A, 3 October 1911 (draft), ditto/265-8.

20. Grey to Pr A, 26 January 1911 (copy), PAC Grey of Howick MG27/II/B2/vol 30/8/18; ditto, 2 February 1911 (copy), ditto; Grey to Bryce, 30 January 1911, Bodl. Mss Bryce 31/66-73; Hugh MacLennan, *Barometer Rising*, Harrap 1942.

21. Pr A to GV, 5 October 1911, RA Geo V AA41/1.

CHAPTER 15

1. Pr A to GV, 17 October 1911, RA Geo V AA41/3; Pr A to LL, 14-15 October 1911, RA Geo V BB16/1911.

2. Pr A to LL, 7-12 October 1911, RA Geo V BB16/1911; LM Journal, 12 October 1911, RA Add A15/8445; Haycock, p 154.

3. Borden Memoirs Vol 2, pp 601-4, vol 1, p 461.

4. Pr A to LL, 24-26 October 1911, RA Geo V BB16/1911; Pr A to GV, 27 October 1911, RA Geo V AA41/4.

5. Pr A to GV, 17 October 1911, RA Geo V AA41/3; LM Journal, 14 October 1911, RA Add A15/8445.

6. Pr A to LL, 3-6 November 1911, RA Geo V BB16/1911; ditto, 24-26 October 1911, RA Geo V BB16/1911; ditto, 7-9 November 1911, RA Geo V BB16/1911.

7. Pr A to GV, 2 November 1911, RA Geo V AA41/5; *Montreal Daily Star*, 20 October 1911 and Pr A to Harcourt, 24 October 1911, PRO CO42/949/35713.

8. LM Journal, 3 November 1911, RA Add A15/8445; Pr A to Pss Louise, 8 November 1911, RA Add A17/1095; Pr A to Burns, 6 December 1911, Br Lib Add Mss Burns A46281(6) 97-8.

9. Pr A to Pss Louise, 8 November 1911, RA Add A17/1095; Pr A to Harcourt, 27 December 1911, PRO CO42/949/720.

10. Pr A to LL, 14-16 November 1911, RA Geo V BB16/1911; ditto, 13-15 January 1912, RA Geo V BB16/1912; ditto, 10-12 April 1912, RA Geo V BB16/1912; ditto, 17-20 November 1911, RA Geo V BB16/1911.

11. Pr A to LL, 17-20 November 1911, RA Geo V BB16/1911; LM Journal, 16 November 1911, RA Add A15/8445.

12. Pr A to LL, 17-20 November 1911, RA Geo V BB16/1911; LM Journal, 16 November 1911, RA Add A15/8445.

13. Pr A to LL, 17-20 November 1911, RA Geo V BB16/1911.

14. Pr A to Grey, 27 February 1911, PAC Grey of Howick MG27/II/B2/Vol 30/8/18; Grey to Pr A, 21 March 1911 (copy), PAC Grey of Howick MG27/II/B2/Vol 30/8/18; Pr A to LL, 27-30 November 1911, RA Geo V BB16/1911; LM Journal, 30 November 1911, RA Add A15/8445; Pr A to LL, 1-4 December 1911, RA Geo V BB16/1911.

15. Pr A to LL, 1-4 December 1911, RA Geo V BB16/1911; LM Journal, 1 December 1911, RA Add A15/8445; Pr A to GV, 3 December 1911, RA Geo V AA41/7.

16. Pr A to LL, 8-11 December and 15-18 December 1911, RA Geo V BB16/1911; Pr A to Harcourt, 19 December 1911, PRO CO42/949/19; Pr A to GV, 27 December 1911, RA Geo V AA41/8; Pr A to LL, 29 December 1911-2 January 1912, RA Geo V BB16/1911.

17. Bryce to Pr A, 29 December 1911 (draft), Bodl. Bryce Mss Vol 32/280; Pr A to Bryce, 10 January 1912, Bodl. Bryce Mss Vol 33/15-16; Bryce to Pr A, 21 January 1912 (draft) Bodl. Bryce Mss Vol 33/50-1.

18. Pr A to LL, 22-23 January 1912, RA Geo V BB16/1912; Pr A to Bryce, 22 January 1912, Bodl. Bryce Mss Vol 33/52-3.

19. Pr A to Pss Louise, 21 January 1912, RA Add A17/1096; Pr A to GV, 7 February 1912, RA Geo V AA41/11.

20. LM Journal 22 January 1912, RA Add A15/8445; Pr A to LL, 22-23 January 1912, RA Geo V BB16/1912; LM Journal, 23 January 1912, RA Add A15/8445.

21. LM Journal, 24 January 1912, RA Add A15/8445; Pr A to LL, 28 January 1912, RA Geo V BB16/1912.

22. Pr A to LL, 28 January 1912, RA Geo V BB16/1912; Bryce to Sir Edward Grey, 26 January 1912 (copy), PRO CO42/962/554.

23. LM Journal, 25-26 January 1912, RA Add A15/8445.

24. Pr A to Pss Louise, 20 February 1912, RA Add A17/1098; LM Journal, 4 March 1912, RA Add A15/8445; LM Journal, 24 February and 27 February-4 March 1912, RA Add A15/8445; Pr A to LL, 15-17 March 1912, RA Geo V BB16/1912.

25. LM Journal, 2, 3, 5, 9 and 13-14 April 1912, RA Add A15/8445.

26. LM Journal, 15, 16, 22 February, 10, 13, 14 and 15 April, 26-28 May and 20 September 1912 (to the last of which the Duchess added a note in August 1914),RA Add A15/8445.

27. Pr A to GV, 5 May 1912, RA Geo V AA41/16; Pr A to Harcourt, 25 March 1912, PRO CO/42/958/10429; Foreign Office to Colonial Office, 16 April 1912, Colonial Office Minute, 18(?) April and draft Colonial Office letter, 26 April 1912, PRO CO42/963/236/4, 963/231 and 960/237-8.

28. Pr A to GV, 29 April 1912, RA Geo V AA41/15; Pr A to Pss Louise, 16 May and ditto, 23 August 1912, RA Add A17/1107 and 1114.

29. Pr A to GV, 10 June 1912, RA Geo V AA41/18; Borden to Pr A, 4 and 7 June 1912 (copies), PAC Borden MG26H/4/307 and 316-316A; Pr A to Borden, 7 June 1912, PAC Borden MG26H/4/314-5; Pr A to GV, 5 May 1912, RA Geo V AA41/16; ditto, 5 July 1912, RA Geo V AA41/19.

30. Borden to Pr A, 13 July 1912 (copy), PAC Borden MG26H/125/67283; See also ditto, 30 July 1912, PAC Borden MG26H/125/67292.

31. Pr A to Borden, 28 July 1912, PAC Borden MG26H/125/67290-1.

32. Pr A to GV, 22 July 1912, RA Geo V AA41/20; Sladen to Grey, 22 July 1912, Grey Durham; Pr A to Pss Louise, 23 July 1912, RA Add A17/1113.

33. LM Journal, 27-31 July 1912, RA Add A15/8445; Pr A to LL, 2-5 August 1912, RA Geo V BB16/1915; ditto, 6-7 August 1912, RA Geo V BB16/1912; ditto, 8-10 August 1912, RA Geo V BB16/1912.

34. Pr A to LL, 11-15 August 1912, RA Geo V BB16/1912; ditto, 22-24 August 1912, RA Geo V BB16/1912; LM Journal, 14 August 1912, RA Add A15/8445; Pr A to LL, 16-19 August 1912, RA Geo V BB16/1912.

35. Pr A to LL, 16-19 August 1912, RA Geo V BB16/1912.

36. Pr A to GV, 21 August 1912, RA Geo V AA41/21; Correspondence between Churchill and Borden, 26-29 August 1912 (copies), Bodl. Mss Harcourt dep. 443/27-37.

37. LM Journal, 28, 30 and 29 August 1912, RA Add A15/8445; Pr A to LL, 28 August-1 September 1912, RA Geo V BB16/1912; ditto, 2-6 September 1912, RA Geo V BB16/1912; LM Journal, 3, 5, 9 and 10 September 1912, RA Add A15/8445; Pr A to LL, 11-13 and 14-19 September 1912, RA Geo V BB16/1912.

38. LM Journal, 18 September 1912, RA Add A15/8445; Pr A to LL, 14-19 and 19-20 September 1912, RA Geo V BB16/1912; LM Journal, 19 September 1912, RA Add A15/8445.

39. Pr A to LL, 22-24 September 1912, RA Geo V BB16/1912; LM Journal, 24 September 1912, RA Add A15/8445.

40. LM Journal, 25 September 1912, RA Add A15/8445; Pr A to LL, 25-27 and 28-29 September 1912, RA Geo V BB16/1912; LM Journal, 27 and 29 September 1912, RA Add A15/8445.

41. Pr A to LL, 29 September-2 October and 3-5 October 1912, RA Geo V BB16/1912; LM Journal, 3-9 October 1912, RA Add A15/8445; Pr A to LL, 6-10, 10-14 and 14-17 October 1912, RA Geo V BB16/1912.

42. Pr A to LL, 14-17 and 18-21 October 1912, RA Geo V BB16/1912.

43. LM Journal, 20-21 October 1912, RA Add A15/8445.

44. Pr A to GV, 25 October 1912, RA Geo V AA41/23.

45. Pr A to Pss Louise, RA Add A17/1117; Pr A to Harcourt, 11 December 1912 (draft), PAC Borden MG26H/23/8108 and 8110; Pr A to Harcourt, 11 November 1912, Bodl. Mss Harcourt dep. 462/113-14.

46. Pr A to LL, 21-24 Decembrer 1912, RA Geo V BB16/1912; Haycock, p 154; Hughes to Pr A, 20 December 1912 with Memorandum (copies), PAC Borden MG26H/147/78476-78483.

47. Pr A to Hughes, 29 January 1913 (copy), PAC Borden MG26H/147/78474; Hughes to Pr A, 4 February 1913 (copy), PAC Borden MG26H/147/78473; Pr A to Borden, 17 February 1913 (copy), PAC Borden MG26H/147/78472; Haycock, p 155.

48. LM Journal, 3 January 1913, RA Add A15/8445; Pr A to LL, 4-6 January 1913, RA Geo V BB16/1913; LM Journal, 5 and 8 January 1913, RA Add A15/8445; Pr A to LL, 8-10 January 1913, RA Geo V BB16/1913; Pr A to GV, 10 January 1913, RA Geo V

AA41/27; Pr A to LL, 11-13 January 1913, RA Geo V BB16/1913; Pr A to Murray, 23 January 1913, RA Add A15/9010.

49. Pr A to GV, 24 January 1913, RA Geo V AA41/29; Pr A to Borden, 13 February 1913, PAC Borden MG26H/9-10/2284-6; Pr A to LL, 25-29 January 1913, RA Geo V BB16/1913; Fitzpatrick to Bryce, 11 January 1913, Bodl. Bryce Mss Vol 33/17; Pr A to Grey, 10 February 1913, PAC Grey of Howick MG27/II/B2/Vol 30/8/18.

50. Pr A to LL, 30-31 January 1913, RA Geo V BB16/1913; ditto, ? February 1913, RA Geo V BB16/1917; *Montreal Daily Star*, 31 January 1913, PRO CO42/968/5735/240-1; LM Journal, 14 January 1913, RA Add A15/8445.

51. Pr A to LL, 23-29 March 1913, RA Geo V BB16/1913.

CHAPTER 16

1. Pr A to Borden, 16 April 1913, PAC Borden MG26H/9-10/2322-9; Pr A to LL, 23 April 1913, RA Geo V BB16/1913.

2. Pr A to Borden, 8 May 1913, PAC Borden MG26H/9/2021-8; Mackenzie to Borden, 25 April 1913 (copy), PRO CO537/498/44607/13-16; Memorandum by Hughes, undated, ditto/3-12A; Borden to Pr A, 1 May 1913 (copy), PAC Borden MG26H/6 Pt 2/780-3D; Seely to Harcourt, 23 January 1914, Bodl. Mss Harcourt dep 476/124-5.

3. Borden to Pr A, 27 April 1913 (copy), PAC Borden MG26H/9-10/2334-6; ditto, 10 June 1913 (copy), PAC Borden MG26H/9/2031-4; Pr A to LL, 23 April 1913, RA Geo V BB16/1913; GV to Pss Louise, 4 May 1913, RA Add A17/1138; Pr A to Harcourt, 27 June 1913, PRO CO42/977/21903/308; Pr A to Borden, 28 May 1913, PAC Borden MG26H/148/79228; Borden to Pr A, 28 June 1913, PAC Borden MG26H/4/385.

4. Pr A to Borden, 9 July 1913, PAC Borden MG26H/9/2038-45C.

5. Pr A to GV, 20 August 1913, RA Geo V AA41/33.

6. Pr A to LL, 5 October 1913, RA Geo V BB16/1913; Pr A to GV, 5 October 1913, RA Geo V AA41/35; Pr A to LL, 14 September 1913, RA Geo V BB16/1913; ditto, 23 September 1913, RA Geo V BB16/1913; ditto, 27 September 1913, RA Geo V BB16/1913.

7. Pr A to LL, 17 October 1913, RA Geo V BB16/1913; Pr A to GV, 26 October 1913, RA Geo V AA41/36; Farquhar to Borden, 24 October 1913, PAC Borden MH26H/9-10/2180-1.

8. *Report by the Inspector-General of the Overseas Forces on the Military Institutions of Canada*, 1913, PRO CO42/976/32733/128-143; Colonial Office minutes, 28-30 October 1913, PRO CO42/970/37088/549; ditto, 19 September-17 November 1913, PRO CO42/976/32733/119-27; Pr A to LL, 30-31 October 1913, RA Geo V BB16/1913; Pr A to Borden, 20 November 1913, PAC Borden MG26H/9/2071-4.

9. Pr A to GV, 29 November 1913, RA Geo V AA41/37; Pr A to Borden, 3 December 1913, PAC Borden MG26H/147/78504-7.

10. Haycock, p 172; Borden to Pr A, 8 December 1913 (copy), PAC Borden MG26H/147/78508; Pr A to GV, 17 December 1913, RA Geo V AA41/38.

11. Pr A to LL, 22-24 November 1913, RA Geo V BB16/1913; ditto, 7-8 December 1913, RA Geo V BB16/1913.

12. Pr A to GV, 17 December 1913, RA Geo V AA41/38.

13. Pr A to Harcourt, 15 January 1914, PRO CO42/978/3846/88-9.

14. Pr A to Harcourt, 19 February 1914, and Colonial Office minutes, 10 and 11 March 1914, PRO CO42/978/7784/363-4 and 361-2.; Pr A to LL, 21-23 February 1914, RA Geo V BB16/1914.

15. Pr A to LL, 30 January-1 February (1914), RA Geo V BB16/1914; Taft to Pr A, 2 February 1914, RA Add A15/6505.

16. Farquhar to Borden, 28 February 1914, PAC Borden MG26H/9/2098-9; Borden to Harcourt, 28 March 1914, Bodl. Mss Harcourt dep 476/159-60; Farquhar to Butler, 29 March 1914, Bodl. Mss Harcourt dep 476/154-5.

17. Pr A to LL, 11-13 April 1914, RA Geo V BB16/1914.

18. LM Journal, 9 May 1914, RA Add A15/8445; Article by E.W. Thompson, 12 May 1914, PRO CO42/979/21110/275.

19. Pr A to LL, 1-2 June 1914, RA Geo V BB16/1914; LM Journal, 2-4 June 1914, RA Add A15/8445; ditto, 15 June 1914, RA Add A15/8445; Pr A to LL, 7-9 June 1914, RA Geo V BB16/1914.

20. Gurdit Singh to GV, 6 June 1914, PRO CO42/986/20850/117; Stamfordham to Butler, 6 June 1914, PRO CO42/986/20850/116; Butler to Stamfordham, 8 June 1914, PRO CO42/986/20850/115; Pr A to Harcourt, 25 June 1914 (received), PRO CO42/979/23160/465; Hopkinson to Cory, 10 July 1914 (copy), PRO CO42/980/28329/253-5; ditto, 16 July 1914 (copy), PRO CO42/980/29647/303-4; Stevens to Borden, 18 July 1914, PRO CO42/980/28333/238; Hopkinson to Wallinger, 20 July 1914 (copy), PRO CO42/980/29650/316-19.

21. Hardinge to Crewe, 20 July 1914, PRO CO42/980/26198/139; Borden to Pr A, 21 July 1914 (copy), PRO CO42/980/28333/219-20; Burrell to Borden, 21 July 1914, PRO CO42/980/28333/215; Stevens to Borden, 21 July 1914, PRO CO42/980/28333/218; Pr A to Harcourt, 22 July 1914, PRO CO42/980/28333/209; ditto, 23 July 1914, PRO CO42/980/27030/248.

22. Pr A to Harcourt, 22 July 1914, PRO CO42/980/28333/209; e.g. Pr A to Harcourt, 20 January 1913, PRO CO42/968/3440/96.

23. Pr A to LL, 18-22 June 1914, RA Geo V BB16/1914; Borden Memoirs, vol 1 pp 448-9; LM Journal 25 June 1914, RA Add A15/8445; Pr A to Pss Louise, 29 June 1914, RA Add A17/1202.

24. Pr A to LL, 8-11 July 1914. RA Geo V BB16/1914; LM Journal, 23 July-1 August 1914, RA Add A15/8445; Pr A to LL, 31 July-6 August 1914, RA Geo V BB16/1914; Pr A to GV, 5 August 1914, RA Geo V AA41/48; Pr A to LL, 7 August 1914, RA Geo V BB16/1914.

25. Pr A to LL, 31 July-6 August 1914, RA Geo V BB16/1914; Haycock, p 182; Pr A to Pss Louise, 9 August 1914, RA Add A17/1204.

26. Pr A to Kitchener, 19 August 1914, PRO Kitchener 30/57/56/WG32.

27. GV to Pr A, 18 August 1914, RA Geo V L662/17; ditto, 19 August 1914, RA Geo V L662/20; House of Commons, 20 August 1914, PRO CO42/980/32873/453; Pr A to Harcourt, 28 August 1914, Bodl. Mss Harcourt dep 476/166-7.

28. Borden Memoirs, vol 1, p 461; Borden to Hughes 26 August 1914 (copy), PAC Borden MG26H/46/21194.

29. Pr A to Roberts, 26 August 1914, NAM 7101-23-20/102.

30. Pr A to Kitchener, 12 September 1914, PRO Kitchener 30/57/56/WG34; ditto, 28 September 1914, PRO Kitchener 30/57/56/WG36; Pr A to Harcourt, 5 October 1914, Bodl. Mss Harcourt dep 476/175-9; Pr A to GV, 6 October 1914, RA Geo V AA41/52.

31. Gwatkin to Campbell, 28 September 1914, PAC Gwatkin MG30E/51/F1; Pr A to LL, 13-15 October 1914, RA Geo V BB16/1914; LM Journal, 15 October 1914, RA Add A15/8445.

32. Spring-Rice to Pr A, 1 November 1914, PAC Borden War File Vol 290 MG26H 1(e)/167471; Pr A to LL, 3-6 November 1914, RA Geo V BB16/1914; Haycock, p 229; Borden to Perley, 7 November 1914, PAC Borden War File Vol 292 MG26H 1(e)/169974; Lloyd to Davidson, 26 October 1914, PRO CO537/1117/19587; Davidson to Harcourt, 27 October 1914, ditto; Lloyd to Davidson, 28 October 1914, ditto; Davidson to Selby, 5 November 1914, ditto.

33. Memorandum by Davidson, 6 November 1914 and copies of eight documents from the Perley dossier, PRO CO537/1117/19587; Davidson to Creedy, 6 November 1914, ditto; Creedy to Davidson, 6 November 1914, ditto; Spring-Rice to Nicolson, 8 November 1914, ditto.

34. Davidson to Creedy, 10 November 1914, PRO CO537/1117/19587; Perley to Borden, 12 November 1914, PAC Borden War File Vol 292 MG26H 1(e)/169968; Harcourt to Pr A, 13 November 1914, PAC Borden War File Vol 287 MG26H 1(e)/161405; Pr A to Harcourt, 14 November 1914, PRO CO537/1117/19587; Haycock, p 229.

35. Pr A to LL, 24-25 October 1914, RA Geo V BB16/1914; Roberts to Pr A, 28 (October) 1914, RA Add A15/6524.

36. Pr A to Borden, 1 November 1914, PAC Borden MG26H/2113-6; Borden to Pr A, 5 November 1914 (copy), PAC Borden MG26H/2117-18; Pr A to Pss Louise, 15 October 1914, RA Add A17/1209.

37. GV to Pr A, 9 November 1914, RA Add A15/6530; Borden to Perley, PAC Borden War File Vol 292 MG26H 1(e)/169932.

38. e.g. Pr A to LL, 18-19 November 1914, RA Geo V BB16/1914; ditto, 24-25 October 1914, ditto; GV to Pr A, 25 October 1914, RA Add A15/6528; Pr A to GV, 30 November 1914, RA Geo V AA42/3; LM Journal, 4 October 1914, RA Add A15/8445.

CHAPTER 17

1. LM Journal, 3 January 1915, RA Add A15/8445; Pr A to LL, 25-28 September 1914, RA Geo V BB16/1914; ditto, 11-13 April 1914, ditto; LM Journal, 10 April 1914, RA Add A15/8445; ditto, 19 February 1916, ditto; Borden Memoirs, vol 2, p 573; e.g. Pr A to LL, 16-19 January 1915, RA Geo V BB16/1915.

2. GV to Pr A, 8 September 1915, RA Add A15/6579; Craig Brown, vol 2, p 14.

3. LM Journal, 12 April 1915, RA Add A15/8445; Bliss, p 244; LM Journal, 27 June 1915, RA Add A15/8445; ditto, 5 September 1915, ditto.

4. French to Pr A, 3 March 1915 (copy), RA Add A15/6540.

5. LM Journal, 1 January 1915, RA Add A15/8445; ditto, 19 and 21 April 1915, ditto; Pr A to LL, 22-25 April 1915, RA Geo V BB16/1915; Pr A to GV, 26 September 1915, RA Geo V AA42/25; Pr A to LL, 21 February 1916, RA Geo V BB16/1916.

6. GV to Pr A, 4 May 1915, RA Add A15/6550; Pr A to Pss Louise, 3 May 1915, RA Add A17/1230; Cruttwell, *A History of the Great War*, (2nd Edition), Clarendon Press 1936, p 157; GV to Pr A, 27 June 1915, RA Add A15/6553.

7. Pr A to GV, 3 May 1915, RA Geo V AA42/14; Pr A to Pss Louise, 5 June 1915, RA Add A17/1233; Pr A to Kitchener, 1 July 1915, PRO Kitchener 30/57/56/WG46; GV to Pr A, 21 September 1915, RA Add A15/6580.

8. Pr A to LL, 28-29 October 1915, RA Geo V BB16/1915; Borden to Perley, 31 December 1915, PAC Borden War File Vol 292A MG26H 1(e)/171170; Stanton to Blount, 31 December 1915, PAC Borden MG26H/206/115299-300 (printed in Borden Memoirs, vol 1, pp 528-9); Blount to Stanton, 31 December 1915, PAC Borden MG26H/206/115298; Borden to Pr A, 31 December 1915, PRO CO42/993/4081/16-18; Blount to Stanton, 1 January 1916 (copy), PAC Borden MG26H/206/115301 (printed in Borden Memoirs, Vol 1 pp 529-30); Pr A to GV, 4 January 1916, RA Geo V AA42/32; Pr A to Stamfordham, 2 March 1916, RA Geo V 0. 991A/1; Pr A to Grey, 17 March 1916, Grey Durham; Speech from the throne (by Fitzpatrick) 18 May 1916, PRO CO42/993/26719/346-7.

9. e.g. Pr A to Spring-Rice, 16 January 1915, CASR 1/25/9; Pr A to LL, 26 February-3 March 1915, RA Geo V BB16/1915; ditto, 10-12 June 1915, ditto; Spring-Rice to Pr A, 1 July 1915, RA Add A15/6554.

10. Pr A to LL, 19-22 March 1915, RA Geo V BB16/1915; Hughes to Kitchener, 20 March 1915 (copy), PRO Kitchener 30/57/56/WG3; Pr A to GV, 25 March 1915, RA Geo V AA42/11; Hughes to Kitchener, 29 March 1915, PRO Kitchener 30/57/56/WG5; Kitchener to Hughes, 1 April 1915, ditto WG6; Hughes to Kitchener, 7 April 1915, ditto WG7; ditto, 28 May 1915, ditto WG25, enclosing Hughes to Borden, 28 May 1915 (copy), ditto WG26.

11. Pr A to Borden, 31 May 1915, PAC Borden MG26H/151/80777; Pr A to Kitchener, 31 May 1915, PRO Kitchener 30/57/56/WG42; Pr A to Pr Adolphus of Teck, 6 February 1916, RA Geo V CC50/1194; Hughes to Aitken, 30 November 1915, HLRO BBK C/50.

12. French to War Office, 19 June 1915 (copy), PAC Borden War File Vol 289 MG26H 1(e)/164860-2; Alderson to Lambton, 26 June 1915, enclosing memorandum of same date, PRO Kitchener 30/57/56/WG27 and 28; Hughes to Craig, 16 July 1915, PAC Borden MG26H/19-20/5624.

13. Carson to Steele, 31 July 1915, PAC Borden MG26H/19-20/5629; Ross to Byrne, 15 August 1915 (copy), PAC Borden MG26H/19-20/5747; Pr A to GV, 1 August 1915, RA Geo V AA42/21.

14. Harcourt to Pr A, 26 February 1915 (copy), PAC Borden War File Vol 288 MG26H 1(e)/162044; Aitken to Hughes, 4 October 1915, HLRO BBK E1/24/1; Hughes to Aitken, 5 October 1915, ditto E1/24/2; Aitken to Hughes, 6 October 1915, ditto E1/24/2A.

15. Pr A to Bonar Law, 22 January 1916, PAC Borden War File Vol 288A MG26H 1(e)/163893; Perley to Borden, 24 January 1916 (copy), PAC Perley MG27/IID/12/4/ 107; Gwatkin to Stanton, 13 August 1915, PAC RG7/G21/Vol 436/2024; Pr A to LL, 25 January 1916, RA Geo V BB16/1916.

16. Alderson to Gwatkin, 6 February 1916 (copy), HLRO BBK E1/24/4.

17. Aitken to Alderson, 11 February 1916 (copy), HLRO BBK E1/24/7; Hughes to Alderson, 7 March 1916 (copy), ditto E1/24/9.

18. Aitken to Hughes, 10 May 1916, HLRO BBK E1/24/12; ditto, 12 May 1916, ditto E1/24/14.

19. Hughes to Aitken, 15 May 1916, HLRO BBK E1/24/17; Borden to Aitken, 16 May 1916, ditto E1/24/19; Hughes to Aitken, 18 May 1916, ditto E1/24; ditto, 23 May 1916, ditto E1/24/26.

20. Carson to Aitken, 13 May 1916, HLRO BBK/E1/24/16, enclosing Mercer to Carson, 10 May 1916 (copy), ditto E1/24/15.

21. Haig to War Office, 28 May 1916 (copy), PAC Borden War File Vol 289 MG26H 1(e)/164863; ditto, 21 June 1916, ditto MG26H 1(e)/164866; Cubitt to Perley, 3 July 1916, ditto MG26H 1(e)/164867-8.

22. Memorandum of evidence, 13 August 1901, PAC Borden MG26H/18/5571; Haycock, p 120; Pr A to GV, 18 April 1915, RA Geo V AA42/12.

23. Lloyd George *War Memoirs* (new edition), Odhams Press 1938, vol 2, p 2009.

24. Davidson to Harcourt, 2 January 1915, PRO CO537/1117/19587; ditto, 28 January 1915, enclosing a memorandum of same date and reference, ditto.

25. Stanton to Davidson, 11 April 1915, PRO CO537/1118/19587; LM Journal, 12 April 1915, RA Add A15/8445; Harcourt to Pr A, 14 April 1915, PAC Borden War File Vol 288 MG26H 1(e)/162682; Pr A to Harcourt, 14 April 1915, ditto 162680; Pr A to Pss Louise, 15 April 1915, RA Add A17/1228; Pr A to GV, 18 April 1915, RA Geo V AA42/12; GV to Pr A, 4 May 1915, RA Add A15/6550.

26. Bertram to Borden, 22 November 1915, PAC Borden MG26H/51/23922-3; Carnegie to Borden, 22 November 1915 (two letters) ditto MG26H/90/47195-7 and 23924-31; Borden's dossier of correspondence, 1-22 November 1915, ditto MG26H/90/ 47034-197.

27. Bliss, p 255.

28. Hughes to Flavelle, 8 December 1915 (copy), HLRO BBK E1/7; Hughes to Borden, 8 December 1915 (copy), ditto; Bliss, p 268; Hughes to Flavelle, 13 December 1915 (copy), HLRO BBK E1/7; Bliss, pp 240 and 245.

29. Borden to Perley, 11 February 1916, PAC Borden War File Vol 292A MG26H 1(e)/171066; Perley to Borden, 14 February 1916, ditto MG26H 1(e)/171057; Borden to Perley, 7 March 1916, ditto MG26H 1(e)/170949.

30. *Ottawa Evening Journal*, 29 March 1916, PRO CO537/1118/19587; Stanton to Davidson, 30 March 1916, ditto; Pr A to Spring-Rice, 8 April 1916, CASR 1/25/19-20.

31. Harcourt to Pr A, 13 April 1916 (copy), Bodl. Mss Harcourt dep 462/389-90; Phipps to Perley, 14 June 1916 (copy), PAC Borden MG26H/90/47349-51; *Report of the*

Royal Commission on Shell Contracts, 20 July 1916, HLRO BBK E1/6/64.

32. Hughes to Aitken, 15 July 1916, HLRO E1/6/7; GV to Pr A, 17 October 1915, RA Add A15/6581; LM Journal, 15 October 1914, RA Add A15/8445.

33. Harcourt to Pr A, 6 October 1914, PAC Borden War File Vol 287 MG26H 1(e)/161516-7; Borden to Perley, 28 November 1914, ditto, Vol 292 MG26H 1(e)/169912; Pr A to Spring-Rice, 9 May 1916, CASR 1/25/24-5; Bonar Law to Pr A, 19 May 1916, PAC Borden War File Vol 289 MG26H 1(e)/165252; Pr A to Bonar Law, 19 May 1916, ditto MG26H 1(e)/165251.

34. Pr A to Borden, 25 June 1916 (copy), PAC Borden MG26H/70/36230-1 (extract printed in Borden Memoirs, vol 2, pp 601-2); Borden to Pr A, 12 July 1916 (copy), ditto MG26H/70/36232-8 (extract printed in Borden Memoirs, vol 2 p 602).

35. Pr A to Borden, 2 August 1916 (copy), PAC Borden MG26H/70/36239-42; Borden to Pr A, 4 August 1916 (copy), ditto MG26H/70/36243-6 (extract printed in Borden Memoirs, vol 2, p 603); Borden to McCurdy, 3 August 1916 (copy), ditto MG26H/70/36247; Pr A to Borden, 5 August 1916 (copy), ditto MG26H/70/36254.

36. Taylor, p 98; Blake, p 256.

37. Blake, p 37; Bonar Law to Pr A, 31 May 1915 (draft cyphered and sent), HLRO Davidson 14; Pr A to GV, 8 June 1916, RA Geo V AA42/41; Pr A to Bonar Law, 31 May 1915, HLRO Davidson 14; Bonar Law to Borden, 5 June 1915 (copy), HLRO BL 50/2/2; Aitken to Bonar Law, 2 June 1915, Blake, p 256.

38. Note on the War Situation by Hughes, 15 August 1915, HLRO, Lloyd George D/23/1/4; Alderson to Pr A, 17 August 1915, RA Add A15/6564; Brade to Kitchener, 16 August 1915, PRO Kitchener 30/57/56/WG21; Hughes to Bonar Law, 18 August 1915, HLRO BL 51/2/16; Pr A to GV, 18 August 1915, RA Add A15/6566; GV to Pr A, 21 August 1915, RA Add A15/6570; Bonar Law to Pr A, 24 August 1915, RA Add A15/6576; GV to Pr A, 24 August 1915, RA Add A15/6577; Hughes to Bonar Law, 24 August 1915, HLRO BL 51/2/21; Pr A to LL, 28-29 October 1915, RA Geo V BB16/1915; Aitken's baronetcy was in the British Prime Minister's list, *The Times*, 3 June 1916.

39. Bonar Law to Borden, 16 May 1916, HLRO Davidson 31; Borden to Bonar Law, 16 May 1916, ditto; Bonar Law to Borden, 17 May 1916, ditto; Taylor, p 98; Borden to Pr A, 17 May 1916 (copy), PAC Borden MG26H/8/1222; Pr A to GV, 8 June 1916, RA Geo V AA42/41; *The Times*, 3 June 1916.

40. Taylor, p 98; ?Davidson to Fiddes, c January 1917, HLRO BL 84/6/40.

41. Pr A to GV, 13 March 1916, RA Geo V AA42/36; ditto, 7 April 1916, ditto/37; Pr A to LL, 13 and 15 March 1916, RA Geo V BB16/1916; Memorandum of Pr A's interview with Borden, 24 March 1916, PAC RG7 G21 Vol 142/265A; Pr A to LL, 18 March 1916, RA Geo V BB16/1916.

42. Memorandum of Pr A's interview with Borden, 24 March 1916, PAC RG7 G21 Vol 142/265A; Memorandum by Hughes, 21 April 1916, PAC RG G21 Vol 142/265A; Borden to Pr A, 21 April 1916, ditto; Pr A to Borden, 22 April 1916, PAC Borden MG26H/31/12835; Borden to Pr A, 22 April 1916 (copy), ditto/12834; Pr A to LL, 24-27 April 1916, RA Geo V BB16/1916; Pr A to Borden, 25 April 1916, PAC Borden MG26H/31/12836-7.

43. Borden to Hughes, 9 November 1916 (copy), PAC Borden MG26H/69/35884; Craig Brown and Ramsay Cook, *Canada 1896-1921 A Nation Transformed*, McClelland & Stewart 1974, p 217.

44. Haycock, p 295; Pr A to Stamfordham, 2 March 1916, RA Geo V O. 991A/1; GV to Pr A, 19 March 1916, RA Add A15/6591; ditto, 20 May 1916, RA Geo V L520/20; Pr A to GV, 26 June 1916, RA Geo V AA42/42; Bliss, pp 273-4.

45. Hughes to Aitken, 8 December 1916, HLRO BBK E1/6/65.

46. Haycock; Craig Brown; Bliss, p 274.

47. See John Lewis in *Canada in the Great World War*, Toronto 1917-21, vol 2, pp 47-8.

48. LM Journal, 11 October 1916, RA Add A15/8445; Laurier to Pr A, 23 June 1916, RA Add A15/6597.

CHAPTER 18

1. e.g. S of S Colonies to G-G Canada, 28 January 1917, PAC Perley MG27/II/D12/248; Pr A to LL, 27 January 1917, RA Geo V BB16/1917; Dss of C to Belfield, 16 January 1917, IWM Belfield.

2. Dss of C to Belfield, 16 January 1917, IWM Belfield; Belfield to Dss of C, February 1917 (draft), ditto; Dss of C to Belfield, 7 February 1917, ditto; Pr A to LL, 17 February 1917, RA Geo V BB16/1917; Pr A to Pss Louise, 6 March 1917, RA Add A17/1270; ditto, (13 March 1917), RA Add A17/1273.

3. Cr Pss Sweden to Lady Egerton, 2 April 1917, RA Add C22/196; ditto to Pss Louise, 16 April 1917, RA Add A17/1275; Pr A to Lady Minto, 28 March 1917, NLS Minto Mss 12449; Pr A to LL, 6 April 1917, RA Geo V BB16/1917.

4. Pr A to Spring-Rice, 1 April 1917, CASR 1/25/30.

5. Pr A to LL, 1 November 1916, RA Geo V BB16/1916; Memorandum by Stanton, October-November 1916, RA Add A15/6614.

6. Memorandum by Stamfordham, 11 November 1916, RA Geo V F1045/1; Deputy Minister of Militia to US of S External Affairs, 30 January 1917 (draft), PAC Borden MG26H/85/43375; G-G Canada to S of S Colonies, 3 February 1917, PAC Perley MG27/II/D12/248 and draft by Borden, 1 February 1917, PAC Borden MG26H/85/43376; Borden to Perley, 2 February 1917, PAC Perley MG27/II/D12/248.

7. Memorandum by Stamfordham, 11 November 1916, RA Geo V F1045/1; Lowther to Perley, 10 February 1917, PAC Perley MG27/II/D12/248; Pr A to Derby, ? 6 March 1917 (copy), RA Add A15/9016; Derby to Pr A, 7 March 1917, RA Add A15/9017; Batterbee to Perley, 27 March 1917, MG27/11/012/248.

8. Programme, 25-30 June 1917, IWM Thompson 69/73/2; Pr A to GV 1 July 1917, RA Geo V AA42/51; Pr A to LL, 1 July 1917, RA Geo V BB16/1917.

9. Programme, 15-22 October 1917, IWM Thompson 69/73/2; Pr A to LL, 24-25 October 1917, RA Geo V BB16/1917.

10. Pr A to GV, 12 January 1918, RA Geo V AA42/59; Pr A to Pss Louise, 24 January 1918, RA Add A17/1284; Pr A to LL, 10 February 1918, RA Geo V BB16/1918; ditto, 6 March 1918, RA Geo V BB16/1908 (sic).

11. Pr A to Pss Louise, 16 March 1918, RA Add A17/1287; Wingate to Stamfordham, 25 March 1918, RA Geo V P739/50; Pr A to GV, 20 March 1918, RA Geo V AA42/63.

12. Granville to GV, 9 March 1918, RA Geo V P1204/10.

13. Pr A to LL, 4 April 1918, RA Geo V BB16/1918; Pr A to GV, 4 April 1918, RA Geo V AA42/64.

14. Granville to GV, 5 April 1918, RA Geo V P1204/14; Pr A to GV, 4 April 1918, RA Geo V AA42/64.

15. Pr A to LL, 15 April 1918, RA Geo V BB16/1918; ditto, 18 April 1918, ditto; Pr A to Pss Louise, 31 May 1918, RA Add A17/1291.

16. Pr A to LL, 19 April 1918, RA Geo V BB16/1918.

17. Cynthia Asquith, *Diaries 1915-18*, Hutchinson, p 244; Pr A to LL, ? August or September 1918, RA Geo V BB16/1910.

18. Cr Pss Sweden to Lady Egerton, 28 July 1918, RA Add C22/210; Pr A to LL, 6 and 25 September 1918 RA Geo V BB16/1918.

19. Pr A to GV, 24 March 1919, RA Geo V AA42/76; Pr A to LL, 30 March (1919), RA Geo V BB16/1919.

20. Vickers, *Gladys Duchess of Marlborough,* Weidenfeld and Nicolson, pp 163, 169-70, 171, 164-5.

21. Pr A to GD, 29 May 1919, Vickers/Deacon; ditto, 18 December 1919, ditto.

22. Pr A to GD, 17 April 1920, Vickers/Deacon; Vickers, p 170.

23. Pr A to LL, 7 April 1919, RA Geo V BB16/1919; *New York Times*, 8 February 1935; Pr A to RD, 12 April 1919, RA Add A15/A; ditto,(28 May 1919), ditto; ditto, 30 May 1919, ditto; ditto, 24 June 1919, ditto; ditto 28 June 1919, ditto.

24. Pr A to RD, 12 July 1919, RA Add A15/A; ditto, 15 August 1919, ditto.

25. Pr A to RD, 12 November 1924, RA Add A15/A; ditto, 20 November 1925, ditto; *New York Times*, 8 February and 27 March 1935; Pr A to LL, 8 December 1936, RA Geo V BB16/1936; Rhoda van Bibber Tanner Doubleday, *Atlantic Between,* Doubleday 1947; Pr A to RD, 8 October 1920 and 2 November 1925, RA Add A15/A.

26. Pr A to LL, 25 April 1920, RA Geo V BB16/1920; ditto, 30 April 1920, ditto; Cr Pss Sweden to Pss Louise, 26 January 1920, RA Add A17/1309; Pr A to LL, 3 February 1920, RA Geo V BB16/1920.

27. Telegram to Chelmsford, (16 July 1920), IORL Mss Eur F136/34/148 and Wigram to Willcocks, 10 November 1920, RA Geo V Q2522/7/241; Cromer to Meston, 4 August 1920, IORL Mss Eur F136/34/153-4.

28. Pr A to LL, 1 August (1920), RA Geo V BB16/1920; Pr A to GV, 6 August 1920, RA Geo V AA42/85; Chelmsford to GV, 7 September 1920, RA Geo V P522/117; Sydenham to Stamfordham, 12 November 1920, RA Geo V N1612/9; Pr A to Pss Louise, 4 January 1921, RA Add A17/1322.

29. Pr A to GV, 6 January 1921, RA Geo V AA42/89; ditto, 13 January 1921, RA Geo V

AA42/90; Pr A to RD, 13 January 1921, RA Add A15/A; Pr A to GV, 2 February 1921, RA Geo V AA42/91; Ronaldshay to GV, 9 February 1921, RA Geo V P1154/25; Pr A to LL, 7-10 February 1921, RA Geo V BB16/1921.

30. Press cutting annotated by Butler, 10 February 1921, IORL Mss Eur F116/79/5; Maffey to Butler, 9 March 1921, ditto 78/2; Pr A to Pss Louise, 10 February 1921, RA Add A17/1328.

31. Pr A to Pss Louise, 23 February 1921, RA Add A17/1329; Pr A to GV, 24 February 1921, RA Geo V AA42/93.

32. Pr A to Pss Louise, 2-10 May 1921, RA Add A17/1330; Pr A of C to Pss Louise, 6 April 1921, RA Add A17/1333.

33. Pr A to RD, 8 April 1921, RA Add A15/A; Pr A to Pss Louise, 26 November 1920, RA Add A17/1314; Pr A to LL, 19 March 1921, RA Geo V BB16/1921.

34. Pr A to LL, 31 January- 1 February 1921, RA Geo V BB16/1921; ditto, 9 January 1920, ditto/1920; Pr A to RD, 20 December 1921, RA Add A15/A.

35. Pr A to Pss Louise, 18 April 1923, RA Add A17/1363; Pr A to RD, 1 February 1923, RA Add A15/A; Pr A to LL, 26 April 1923, RA Geo V BB16/1923.

36. Pr A to GV, 18 December 1923, RA Geo V AA42/117; Pr A to LL, 13 February 1924, RA Geo V BB16/1924.

37. Pr A to RD, 10 May 1926, RA Add A15/A.

38. Pr A to GV, 19 March 1926, RA Geo V AA42/131; Pr A to LL, 22 September 1926, RA Geo V BB16/1926; Pr A to RD, 23 October 1926, RA Add A15/A.

39. e.g. Pr A to LL, 15 November 1927, RA Geo V BB16/1927; Pr A to GV, 25 January 1928, RA Geo V AA42/144.

40. GV to Pss Louise, 30 October 1928, RA Add A17/1471; Pr A to Pss Louise, 7 August 1928, RA Add A17/1469.

41. Pr A to LL, 29 July 1922, RA Geo V BB16/1922; Pr A to Lady Minto, 11 June 1929, NLS Minto Mss 12450; Pr A to Pss Louise, 31 October 1929, RA Add A17/1481.

42. Pr A to GV, 25 March 1929, RA Geo V AA42/154; Pr A to LL, 17 December 1930, RA Geo V BB16/1930; Pr A to Pss Louise, 7 June 1930, RA Add A17/1493; Pr A to GV, 27 December 1929, RA Geo V AA42/160.

43. Wigram to Stamfordham, 30 December 1930, RA Geo V L2314/16.

CHAPTER 19

1. Pr A to LL, 23 January 1931, RA Geo V BB16/1931; Pr A to Pss Louise, 15 March 1932, RA Add A17/1526; Pr A to GV, 22 April 1934, RA Geo V AA42/190; Pr A to LL, 23 February 1931, RA Geo V BB16/1931; Pr A to Pss Louise, 19 February 1934, RA Add A17/1551.

2. Pr A to GV, 10 April 1933, RA Geo V AA42/184; Pr A to Pss Louise, 25 December 1933, RA Add A17/1547; e.g. ditto, ? September 1932, RA Add A17/1531.

3. Pr A to Pss Louise, 27 May 1928, RA Add A17/1468.

4. Pr A to Pss Louise, 9 April 1936, RA Add A17/1601; Pr A to LL, 13 August 1936, RA Geo V BB/1936; Pr A to GV, 19 September 1935, RA Geo V AA42/204; ditto, 7 February 1924, RA Geo V AA42/118; Pr A to Pss Louise, 21 January 1931, RA Add A17/1506; Pr A to LL, 7 January 1932, RA Geo V BB16/1932.

5. Pr A to Borden, 2 December 1932, PAC Borden MG26H/271/152355-6A; ditto, 11 December 1935, ditto/152368-8A.

6. Borden to Pr A, 10 December 1924 (copy), PAC Borden MG26H/271/52298.

7. Pr A to GV, 20 September 1934, RA Geo V AA42/192; ditto, 15 April 1935, RA Geo V AA42/201.

8. Pr A to LL, 23-24 October 1935, RA Geo V BB16/1935; Pr A to QM, 21 January 1936, RA Geo V CC45/995.

9. Pr A to Pss Louise, 29 September (1936), RA Add A17/1615; Pr A to LL, 4 December 1936, RA Geo V BB16/1936.

10. Pr A to Pss Louise, 14 December 1936, RA Add A17/1623; Pr A to LL, 11 December 1936, RA Geo V BB16/1936; Pr A to GVI, December 1936, RA Geo VI 342/1/16/05; ditto, 21 December 1936, RA Geo VI 342/1/16/06; Pr A to Pss Louise, 17 March 1937, RA Add A17/1635.

11. Pr A to Pss Louise, 31 January 1938, RA Add A17/1652; Miss Hoskins to Pss Louise, 14 February 1938, RA Add A17/1656; ditto, 17 February 1938, ditto/1657; Pr A to Pss Louise, 4 April 1938, ditto/1667.

12. Miss Hoskins to Pss Louise, 22 February 1938, RA Add A17/1658; Pr A to Pss Louise, 9 October 1937, ditto/1642; Pr A to QM, 29 December 1937, RA Geo V CC45/1124 and Pr A to GVI, 2 January 1938, RA Geo VI 342/1/16/13; Pr A to Pss Louise, 12 May 1938, RA Add A17/1677.

13. Pr a to LL, 3 August 1938, RA Geo V BB16/1938.

14. Pr A to GVI, 3 September 1938 RA Geo VI 342/1/16/20; Miss Hoskins to Pss Louise, 14 September 1938, RA Add A17/1686.

15. Pr A to LL, 26 September 1938, RA Geo V BB16/1938; Miss Hoskins to Pss Louise, 2 May 1939, RA Add A17/1695; Pr A to QM, 5 December 1939 (dictated), RA Geo V CC45/1211.

16. Massey to Mackenzie King, 19 January 1942, PAC Mackenzie King MG26/J1/329/280655-7; QM to Lord Athlone, 26 September 1941, RA Geo V CC53/931.

17. Morshead to QM, 19 January 1942, RA Geo V CC48/1001; Lady Patricia Ramsay to QM, 19 January 1942, RA Geo V CC45/1313A; Lord Athlone to Mackenzie King, 16 January 1942, PAC Mackenzie King MG26/J1/321/272052.

18. Morshead to QM, 19 January 1942, RA Geo V CC48/1001; ditto, 17 February 1942, ditto/1013; ditto, 4 March 1942, ditto/1017; ditto, 1 April 1942, ditto 1022; ditto, 13 April 1942, ditto 1028; Pr A to LL, 1 December 1929, RA Geo V BB16/1929; Murray to Borden, 27 June 1930, PAC Borden MG26H/271/152334 and accompanying memorandum by Murray, ditto/152335.

19. Redfern to Mackenzie King, 19 January 1942, PAC Mackenzie King MG26/J1/321/272057-8.

20. Brown to Borden, 1 May 1929, PAC Borden MG26H/271/152327; *The Canadian Historical Review,* September 1930, pp 264-6.

21. Dss of C Journal, 11 October 1916, RA Add A15/8445.

22. Borden's Review, September 1930.

Index